The Kurdish National Movement

Contemporary Issues in the Middle East

The
Kurdish National
Movement

Its Origins and Development

Wadie Jwaideh

With a Foreword by Martin van Bruinessen

SYRACUSE UNIVERSITY PRESS

First Edition 2006
06   07   08   09   10   11   6   5   4   3   2   1

Mohamad El-Hindi Books on Arab Culture and Islamic Civilization are
published with the assistance of a grant from the M.E.H. Foundation.

Permission to reprint textual material from the following sources is
gratefully acknowledged: Oxford University Press for excerpts from *Iraq
1900 to 1950* (London: Oxford Univ. Press, 1953) by Stephen Longrigg
and from *Loyalties: Mesopotamia* Vol. 2 *1917–1920* (London: Oxford
Univ. Press, 1936) by A. T. Wilson; the Middle East Institute for an article
by Archie Roosevelt appearing in the *Middle East Journal,* "The Kurdish
Republic of Mahabad" 1, no. 3 (July 1947), 2247–69.

The paper used in this publication meets the minimum requirements of
American National Standard of Information Sciences—Permanence of
Paper of Printed Library Materials, ANSI Z39.48–1984©™

Library of Congress Cataloging-in-Publication Data
Jwaideh, Wadie.
The Kurdish national movement : its origins and development / Wadie
Jwaideh ; with a foreword by Martin van Bruinessen.
p. cm.—(Contemporary issues in the Middle East)
Includes bibliographical references and index.
ISBN 0–8156–3093–X (pbk. : alk. paper)
1. Kurds—History—Autonomy and independence movements.
2. Kurdistan—History—Autonomy and independence movements.
I. Title. II. Series.
DS59.K86J87 2006
320.5409566'7—dc22   2006001871

Manufactured in the United States of America

✸ Contents

✸ *Illustrations*

Before his death in 2001, **Dr. Wadie Elias Jwaideh** served on the faculty of Indiana University for more than twenty-five years, receiving the Herman Lieber Memorial Award for Distinguished Teaching in 1972 and retiring in 1987 as chairman of its Department of Near Eastern Languages and Literatures, which he established, and professor of history. Even after his retirement, he continued teaching, serving as adjunct professor of history at the University of California at San Diego until 1990. Professor Jwaideh was educated in Iraq and the United States. His Ph.D. dissertation, the basis for this book, earned him recognition as one of the world's leading experts on the Kurds by the early 1960s. His broad knowledge of Middle Eastern history and culture prompted invitations to meet with President Jimmy Carter during the Iran hostage crisis and to participate in the inauguration ceremonies of several new universities in the Arab world, including the University of Kuwait and the University of the United Arab Emirates. His publications include articles in scholarly journals and in the *Encyclopaedia Britannica* and an annotated translation of the six introductory chapters of Yaqut's famous *Mu'jam al-Buldan.*

✸ *Foreword*

Where should one locate the beginnings of Kurdish nationalism as a modern mass movement, with well-organized political parties, explicit programs, and the mobilization of mass support transcending narrow tribal or regional boundaries? A number of dates and major events may be indicated, but there is considerable justification for considering the year 1961 the major breaking point. This was the year when the Kurdish guerrilla war against Iraq's central government began, which would result in the Iraqi Kurds gaining—on paper, at least—significant cultural rights, regional autonomy, and a share in the central government. The highly visible movement in Iraqi Kurdistan of the 1960s not only strengthened the awareness of common Kurdish identity among the Kurds of Iraq, but also galvanized the Kurds in neighboring countries.

In Turkey, moreover, 1961 saw the establishment of the first legal socialist party, the Workers' Party of Turkey (WPT), which for the first time publicly placed the Kurdish question on the political agenda and within which a left-inspired Kurdish discourse developed to which all later Kurdish parties and organizations in Turkey were to remain indebted. Unlike earlier Kurdish uprisings, the political and military movement led by Mulla Mustafa Barzani in Iraq and the Kurdish left of Turkey were sustained movements that did not dissipate after the first reverses, but kept growing and broadening their constituencies. There is a clear continuity from the 1960s to the present day.

So if 1961 is such an important breaking point, what could be the relevance of a study of Kurdish nationalism that was completed two years earlier? Wadie Jwaideh's history of the emergence and development of the Kurdish nationalist movement, which is finally being published now, was originally written as a Ph.D. dissertation and submitted to Syracuse University in early 1960. Most of the research for the thesis had been carried out in the mid-1950s, although Jwaideh makes some important observations on developments in Iraq in the wake of the 1958 coup that set the stage for large-scale Kurdish mobilization and the outbreak of guerrilla war.

The thesis was never published during Jwaideh's lifetime, owing at least in part to his own perfectionism and to the sheer size of the work. Its fame spread by word of mouth, however, and many later scholars, including myself, have recognized its importance not only as a study of the earlier phases of Kurdish nationalism, but also as a framework for understanding later developments. It has acquired a reputation as a classic in the field of Kurdish studies that no one seriously interested in the subject can afford to leave unread.

In 1999, a Turkish translation appeared, making it available for the first time to a large number of Kurdish readers (*Kürt Milliyetçili in Tarihi: Kökeni ve Geli imi* [Istanbul: leti im Yayınları]). Its contemporary significance was at once recognized by the Turkish public prosecutor, who had it banned and all copies confiscated, although many other and more overtly political books on the Kurds were left untouched. (The ban was later repealed, however, and the book was reissued.)

One thing that may have bothered the Turkish prosecutor and that may have contributed to the attention that the book drew from a relatively large and educated readership in Turkey was that Jwaideh showed convincingly how strong and how deep the historical roots of contemporary Kurdish movements were and how old their grievances and demands. The various Kurdish uprisings of the nineteenth and early twentieth centuries were not simply isolated incidents caused by economic decline or political dissatisfaction.

In his conclusion, Jwaideh cautions the reader that, whatever the economic and social causes of discontent, "it must be kept in mind that nationalism, which lies at the root of the Kurdish question, is largely political and psychological in nature." The nationalist ferment that had come to the surface in Iraq following the military takeover of 1958 had to be taken seriously precisely because it was rooted in a historical process of considerable depth, of which its actors were very much aware. Although Jwaideh's study ends in 1959, the developments of the following decade appear almost inevitable to the careful reader.

Jwaideh's study stands at a turning point not just chronologically; it also represents a transition in scholarship on the Kurds not unlike that from colonial to postcolonial scholarship in other parts of the world. While in England for his research in the mid-1950s, Jwaideh met the grand old men of the earlier phase of Kurdish studies, Vladimir Minorsky and Cecil J. Edmonds. Both had been trained as Orientalists and had become acquainted with the Kurds when serving their governments—imperial Russia in the case of Minorsky, the British administration of Iraq in that of Edmonds. Both had become great friends of the Kurds (though not necessarily of Kurdish nationalists; Shaykh Mahmud of Sulaymaniya had been one of Edmonds's headaches), and both published extensively and sympathetically on them.

Minorsky's long and erudite articles on Kurdistan and Kurds in the first edition of the *Encyclopaedia of Islam* (E. J. Brill, 1913–36) constitute the most competent summary of Orientalist knowledge of their subject. Edmonds laid down his observations and experiences as a political officer in Iraqi Kurdistan between 1920 and 1925 in his *Kurds, Turks, and Arabs* (Oxford University Press, 1957), which provides painstakingly detailed notes on social and political conditions, personalities, and local practices in the districts where he served. Both authors showed a special interest in the various heterodox religious communities they had encountered while serving in Kurdistan, notably the Ahli

Haqq and the Yazidis, perhaps at the expense of mainstream Islam and of the major po-litical issues faced by the Kurds as a people.

Wadie Jwaideh's relationship with the Kurds was a different one, and so was his ap-proach to his subject. He was born in Basra in southern Iraq to an Arabic-speaking Christian family and later moved to Baghdad, where he studied at the university and ob-tained his licentiate in law in 1942. During the war years that followed, he served in the Ministry of the Interior as inspector of supply for the northern provinces. It was in this position that he traveled extensively in Iraqi Kurdistan and came to know numerous Kurdish personalities. The direct acquaintance with the land and its people must have been of great use in his later historical research, and the shrewd insight into Kurdish society and politics that is apparent throughout this book no doubt owes much to this experience.

Jwaideh identified himself strongly as an Iraqi Arab but was also aware of belonging to a religious minority. This may have contributed to his appreciation of the Kurds' po-sition as a minority in the states in which they live and of their relations with their vari-ous neighbors. Whereas earlier authors writing on Kurdish nationalism tended to analyze it from the viewpoint of the administration or the dominant groups in the state, Jwaideh made a deliberate effort to present the Kurdish viewpoint. His is one of the more sympathetic studies of the subject and one of the most judicious in its under-standing of what moves the Kurds. It was the first serious study that focused on Kurdish nationalism as a movement in its own right and not just as a reaction to the process of modernization and administrative reform.

As Jwaideh saw the situation, it is the tragedy of the Kurds and of the people among whom they live that they awakened to a sense of nationalism rather belatedly. Turks, Persians, and Arabs had preceded them, and the regimes of the states that incorporated parts of Kurdistan after World War I had embarked on programs of nation building. The Kurds had become citizens, though never fully equal, of Turkey, Iran, Iraq, and Syria, and any effort on their part to establish a nation-state of their own would neces-sarily bring them up against more numerous Turks, Persians, and Arabs and against the armies of modernizing states. This status gave rise to frustration and anger at perceived injustice and inequality, causing Kurdish nationalism to become, at the time of Jwaideh's writing, "increasingly radical and uncompromising." Torn between dreams and pragmatism, Kurdish politicians have had to navigate a course between the struggle for full independence and accommodation with central governments.

The radicalization that Jwaideh refers to was very noticeable in Iraq after the 1958 coup, and ordinary Kurdish people's demands were probably more radical than those then voiced by their political leaders. Even though the odds were against them, many or-dinary Kurds increasingly just wanted to be in control of their own destiny. Jwaideh, more candidly than most Kurdish politicians, describes the odds and the ambitions: "Separated by impassable mountain barriers, divided by linguistic and sectarian differ-ences, rent by narrow tribal loyalties, and split up by international frontiers, they yearn to be what other more fortunate peoples are—a nation-state."

The developments of the past forty-five years have borne out Jwaideh's assessments. Mass literacy and mass education, increased mobility, and the communications revolution have drawn ever larger numbers of Kurds to the nationalist movement. Kurdish nationalism has become a force with which the governments of the region have to reckon not only on the domestic front, but also increasingly in the international arena. The tribal, linguistic, and religious divisions among Kurds to which Jwaideh refers have not been overcome, however; some have even spawned distinct identity movements within the larger Kurdish movement, such as those of the Yazidis, the Alevis, or the Zaza speakers, among whom some leaders have even claimed the status of being a separate nation.

Among the Iraqi Kurds, regional identities have remained strong, and the major political parties have distinct regional bases. To a lesser extent, this was also true of Iranian Kurdistan during the brief period that overt party activity was possible there. Urbanization and the settlement of nomadic tribes have resulted in a certain degree of detribalization, but tribalism was boosted by the government policies, most systematic in Iraq and Turkey, of recruiting tribal militias to fight against the Kurdish nationalist movement.

The borders between the Iranian, Iraqi, Turkish, and Syrian parts of Kurdistan have if anything become more significant, even though crossing them may have become easier. In each of these countries, the Kurds have engaged with the state and with other political forces. Distinct political cultures and socioeconomic and cultural policies have given the Kurdish movement a distinct character in each of them.

Writing on Turkey, Jwaideh notes positive developments in that in the 1950s the government appeared to be making a serious effort at rural development, also in the Kurdish region. However, he comments, "the issue that has always constituted the Kurds' major grievance in Turkey remained unresolved, for the Turkish government still refused to recognize the Kurds as a separate nationality or to allow them freedom to pursue their own cultural activities." The demands of the Kurdish movement that emerged in the 1960s, within as well as outside the WPT, were basically of two kinds: economic development and recognition of the Kurds as a distinct people with claims to cultural rights.

Repression led to radicalization of the movement, and in the 1970s self-determination and decolonization became the rallying slogans of most Kurdish associations. The most radical of Turkey's Kurdish parties, the Kurdish Workers Party (PKK), initially strove for a united independent Kurdistan, but once it had embarked on the guerrilla struggle in 1984, it focused exclusively on Turkey (although its activists operated from Syria, Iraq, and Iran). Eager to negotiate with the Turkish government, the PKK leadership gave up its more far-fetched demands and from the early 1990s onward began speaking of solutions within the existing framework of Turkey. Since the arrest of its leader Öcalan in 1998, the PKK has scaled down its demands even further and has been concentrating on cultural rights and political liberalization. It has become one of the strongest advocates of Turkey's accession to the European Union, perceiving that the incorporation of the Turkish nation-state in a strong supranational body is the best guarantee for Kurdish cultural rights and for its prospects of devolution and a degree of self-rule.

In Syria, the Kurds are much fewer in number than in the other three countries, constituting around 10 percent of the population (as against almost 20 percent in Turkey and in Iran, which have much larger populations, and a slightly higher percentage in Iraq), and their struggle has been for basic human rights rather than for autonomy. One major issue has been the denial of citizenship to hundreds of thousands of Kurds whose ancestors came from what is now Turkey and who are still treated as "aliens." Otherwise, the Syrian Kurds have seen their role often as one of supporting the struggles in Iraq and Turkey.

Although the Iranian Kurds are numerous, it has always been most difficult to find reliable information on what went on among them, and they have been seriously understudied compared to the Iraqi and Turkish Kurds. Readers can usefully supplement Jwaideh's chapters on Iran with a study of the political economy of the region, including some notes on political developments of the 1950s, by the well-known intellectual and politician Abdul Rahman Ghassemlou (*Kurdistan and the Kurds* [Prague: Czechoslovak Academy of Sciences, 1965]), and with William Eagleton's study of the Mahabad Republic (*The Kurdish Republic of 1946* [Oxford University Press, 1963]). During the 1960s and 1970s, politically active Iranian Kurds provided various forms of support to their Iraqi brethren, although the latter's increasing dependence on the Iranian government also caused dismay, especially after Iraqi Kurds assisted in the suppression of a minor uprising by young dissident Iranian Kurds in 1968. Relations between the Barzanis and most Iranian Kurds have remained tense ever since.

During the Iranian Revolution of 1978–79, there emerged a surprisingly broad-based movement for Kurdish regional autonomy, and for several years large parts of Iranian Kurdistan were de facto autonomous, as the Kurdistan Democratic Party and a number of smaller parties and movements took over local administration. By 1983, however, the Islamic Republic had succeeded (with some help from the Barzanis again) in reasserting complete control over the territory and expelling the last groups of Kurdish nationalist politicians and guerrillas to Iraqi Kurdistan. Since then Kurdish nationalist activism in Iran has necessarily been covert, but Kurdish cultural activities have flourished. Overt political involvement has overwhelmingly taken place within the larger opposition movement for democratization of Iran and been less focused on specific Kurdish demands.

The most spectacular developments have taken place in Iraqi Kurdistan. The agreement on autonomy reached in 1970 was not the end of the Kurdish struggle, but ushered in new problems, such as mass deportations from oil-rich Kirkuk and other regions the government wished to keep outside the autonomous region. Barzani Kurds received American and Israeli support as Iraq drew closer to the Soviet Union, turning Kurdistan briefly into one of the "hot" battlefields of the Cold War—until Iran and Iraq reached a settlement (1975) and the Kurds were no longer needed as proxies.

In the Iran-Iraq War (1980–88), the Iraqi Kurdish parties cooperated to some degree with Iran and brought large areas under its control, for which they suffered terrible retaliation from the Iraqi government. Toward the end of the war, a series of attacks with chemical arms sowed death and terror; thousands of villages were destroyed and their inhabitants taken away; more than one hundred thousand men of all ages disappeared, most or all probably ending up in mass graves in the southern desert. This genocide received some international attention only after Saddam Hussein had lost his position as the West's favorite ally against resurgent Islam.

In the wake of the U.S.-led war to expel Hussein from occupied Kuwait in 1991, the Kurds, like the Shi'ites in southern Iraq, massively rose up in rebellion. Unlike the latter, the Kurds were saved from harsh retaliation by an international intervention; a safe haven was created in the northernmost part of the country. Since then, a part of Iraqi Kurdistan has been a de facto independent self-governing entity, economically better off than the rest of Iraq. Cultural politics have created entirely new facts on the ground: education at all levels is in Kurdish. The Iraqi Kurdish leaders have gained an unprecedented degree of international recognition, making them major players in all efforts to build a new Iraq. With more than a decade of experience in administering their own region and with a large and well-trained military force, they are in a stronger position than ever before to take upon themselves an important role in Iraq and in the wider region.

Wadie Jwaideh's words on the importance of understanding the Kurds, made in the context of the situation following the 1958 coup in Iraq, apply equally well to the present situation: "Their behavior is one of the important factors in the future stability and security not only of the Kurdish-inhabited countries, but of the entire Middle East. Thus, it is important to know the Kurds and to understand their aims, their political orientation, and the course they are likely to pursue."

In attempting to make sense of the mess that is Iraq after the U.S.-led invasion beginning in 2003, much can be learned by looking at the two earlier periods of dramatic upheaval: the British occupation in and after World War I, which led to the creation of the Kingdom of Iraq, and the revolutionary years following the military coup that overthrew the pro-British monarchy. Major problems remained unresolved, both in the creation of the Kingdom of Iraq and in the establishment of the republic. Questions concerning the relation of the Kurds with this self-defined Arab state, their cultural and national rights, and the nature of their representation were central to these unresolved problems. Jwaideh's sensitive treatment of these issues gives his study great contemporary relevance.

Martin van Bruinessen
Utrecht, December 2004

 *Preface*

The Kurds, a gifted and vigorous people, have played an important role in Middle Eastern history. They have produced men of outstanding qualities as soldiers, statesmen, administrators, and scholars, and have enriched the life and culture of the Islamic countries of the Middle East. Next to the Arabs, the Turks, and the Persians, they constitute the most numerous ethnic group in western Asia. A bellicose and still largely untamed people, they have often been compared to the seventeenth-century clans of Scotland. Despite their pride of race as individuals, they have until comparatively recent times been content as a people to play a subsidiary role among their more numerous and better organized neighbors.

As a nation, the Kurds have been to the Arabs, the Turks, and the Persians what the Scots have been to the English. Although they have contributed such great soldiers and statesmen as Sala al-Din (Saladin), who ruled a great Islamic empire; Mulla Idris Bidlisi, who was one of the chief advisors to Sultan Selim the Grim; and Karim Khan Zend, who ruled Persia for twenty years, they have never established a great empire of their own. The empire of the Medes, one of the reputed ancestors of the Kurdish people, was the only great national state that may be said to have been established by the Kurds.

The Kurds awakened to a sense of nationhood rather belatedly, and in this lies their tragedy and that of the people among whom they live. They seek to wrest what they regard as their divided homeland from the Turks, the Arabs, and the Persians—a difficult and dangerous undertaking. The Kurdish environment, which has molded the Kurds' character as individuals, has also shaped their destiny as a people. Separated by impassable mountain barriers, divided by linguistic and sectarian differences, rent by narrow tribal loyalties, and split up by international frontiers, they yearn to be what other more fortunate peoples are—a nation-state.

Today the Kurds occupy an extremely important region in the heart of the Middle East. They constitute the most important single national minority in that area, forming a substantial proportion of the populations of Turkey, Iran, Iraq, and Syria. Despite the failure of numerous Kurdish rebellions in Turkey, Iran, and Iraq, Kurdish nationalism continues to be a source of deep concern to the governments of these countries. Aroused by the success of surrounding nationalisms—Turkish, Persian, and Arab—and goaded into desperation by its own failures, Kurdish nationalism has become increasingly radical and uncompromising. For these reasons, the Kurds have come to play an increasingly significant role in Middle Eastern affairs. Their behavior is one of the important factors in the future stability and security not only of the Kurdish-inhabited countries, but of the entire Middle East. Thus, it is important to know the Kurds and to understand their aims, their political orientation, and the course they are likely to pursue.

The purpose of this study was to answer the following questions:

1. Is there a Kurdish nationality with a highly developed national consciousness and distinctive characteristics shared by the members of this nationality?

2. If so, is the Kurds' national consciousness, combined with their determination to maintain their national identity and their desire for political self-government, strong enough to say that there is a Kurdish national movement?

3. Assuming that the two preceding questions can be answered affirmatively, what is the relation of this national movement to international politics in the Middle East?

By answering these questions, this Kurdish history should prove useful as a case study to those who are interested in nationalism as a modern mass movement.

I have attempted to connect the Kurdish problem with the past policies of both the Kurdish-inhabited states and the great world powers in an effort to demonstrate that no great power interested in the Middle East can afford to ignore the Kurdish problem or to avoid the formulation of a Kurdish policy as a part of an overall Middle Eastern policy.

I also intended in this study to fill a void in literature pertaining to the Kurds by presenting as complete a picture of the Kurdish problem as possible. Former studies of this subject have provided many valuable insights into various aspects of the problem, but no previous attempt has been made to deal with the whole issue, including its historical development, in a detailed manner.

My interest in the Kurds dates from 1943 and 1944, when I served as inspector of supply for the five northern provinces of Iraq. These five of Iraq's fourteen provinces include all of the Kurdish regions of that country. My duties required extensive travel throughout Kurdistan and brought me into contact with Kurds from all walks of life, including government officials, tribal chieftains, and religious leaders.

I gathered much of the material on which this study is based in England and France. There I was able to use the facilities of the Public Records Office, the Colonial Office, the British Museum, the Royal Institute of International Affairs, and the School of Oriental and African Studies of London University; the Bodleian Library, the Ashmolen Museum Faculty Library, and the library of St. Antony's College at Oxford University; and the Bibliotheque Nationale and the École des Langues Orientales in Paris. I obtained additional information at the Library of Congress, the Houghton Library at Harvard University, the New York Public Library, and the libraries of the Middle East Institute and the School of Advanced International Studies of Johns Hopkins University in Washington, D.C.

I wish to acknowledge my special debt of gratitude to a number of distinguished scholars in the field of Kurdish studies, especially Cecil J. Edmonds, lecturer in Kurdish at the School of Oriental and African Studies at London University and former adviser to the Iraq Ministry of Interior, and Vladimir Minorsky, professor emeritus at London University. Both gave generously of their valuable time for discussion on many points of Kurdish studies and made available to me materials not readily obtainable elsewhere. Similar assistance was given to me by Kamuran Bedir Khan, professor of Kurdish at the École des Langues Orientales in Paris, who, besides being a noted Kurdish scholar, is one of the foremost leaders of the Kurdish nationalist movement.

I also wish to express my indebtedness to Sir Hamilton Gibb, formerly University and Jewett Professor of Arabic at Harvard University and Laudian Professor of Arabic at Oxford University, who kindly arranged for me to do research at the Bodleian Library and the Ashmolean Museum Faculty Library; and to Albert Hourani of St. Antony's College, Oxford University, who arranged for me to use the facilities of the Royal Institute of International Affairs and the library of St. Antony's College. My thanks are also due to Rose Elphinston, widow of the late Colonel W. G. Elphinston, for making available to me some of her husband's unpublished papers, and to Colonel Cayley Bell, former British political officer in northern Syria and southern Turkey, for the information he gave to me.

Finally, I wish to express my appreciation to the Ford Foundation and to the International Affairs Center and the Graduate School of Indiana University for financial assistance that enabled me to complete the research upon which this work is based.

✳ *Acknowledgments*

As the widow of Wadie Jwaideh, I want to thank several individuals who have helped bring about the publication of my late husband's dissertation on Kurdish nationalism. Wadie always expected that this work, which so engrossed him and on which he labored for so many years, would be published during his lifetime. However, after he accepted a faculty position at Indiana University, he became so deeply engaged in establishing and developing the university's Near Eastern studies program and so devoted to his graduate students and their research that he somehow never completed the project of turning his dissertation into a book.

In his preface, my husband thanked several scholars in the United States and Europe who had contributed in various ways to his research. Now I wish to acknowledge a few other persons who have assisted in the process of getting the work published in English so long after it was originally written.

First, I want to thank Wadie's sister, Professor Albertine Jwaideh of the University of Toronto and her husband, Professor James Cox of York University, for reviewing the manuscript and providing valuable assistance with the spelling and diacritics of Arabic words and names. Also of help in this regard was Kadhim Shaaban of Bloomington, Indiana, who was a lecturer at Purdue University and a dear friend of Wadie. I also want to express my gratitude to Professor Amir Hassanpour of the University of Toronto, who was extremely generous with his time whenever I consulted him about the meaning and spelling of Kurdish names and terms. Our daughter, Dara (of Davis, California), read the manuscript many times and made a number of valuable suggestions.

Susan Meseilas, photographer and author of *Kurdistan in the Shadow of History,* and her assistant, Meryl Levin, were very helpful with regard to the illustrations. Susan's generosity in granting us permission to use a number of her photographs greatly facilitated the task of finding suitable images. I am also indebted to Dr. Burhan Elturan of Indiana University for permission to use several photographs he had taken of Kurdish landscapes and dwellings. The map of Kurdistan that appears at the beginning of the book was expertly prepared by cartographer Michael Hollingsworth of Indiana University.

For their conscientious production of a digital version of the manuscript, I wish to thank three competent young women in Bloomington, Indiana—Sandy Vincent for patiently supervising the conversion of the manuscript into digital form; Valerie Nikirk for carefully keyboarding a manuscript containing many unfamiliar words in Arabic, Kurdish, Persian, and Turkish; and Elizabeth Miller Maidi for meticulously proofreading both the manuscript and the page proofs. I also wish to acknowledge the help, many years ago, of my loving and devoted mother, Almeda Reid, who spent countless days and nights sitting at her dining room table where—with Wadie's guidance—she typed the entire 900-page dissertation in five copies, using a manual typewriter and carbon paper.

I want to express my gratitude to Mr. Ahmad El-Hindi, who was a friend of my husband since their student days at Syracuse University, and his wife Betty for their encouragement and their financial contribution toward the book's publication. Finally, thanks are due to the competent staff members of the Syracuse University Press who have devoted their efforts unsparingly to bring this book to completion, especially Annie Barva, who as copyeditor worked conscientiously in its editing.

In addition to those who helped in the publication process, I want to thank Professor Martin Van Bruinessen of the University of Utrecht, for kindly agreeing to write the foreword. Professor Van Bruinessen, who is one of the world's foremost authorities on Kurdistan, discovered my husband's dissertation many years ago, played a role in getting it published in Turkish, and has strongly encouraged its publication in English.

On my husband's behalf, I would like to dedicate this book to our beloved children and grandchildren: our daughter Dara Narmeen Jwaideh Pleasants, our late daughter Layl Diane Jwaideh Khan, and our three grandsons—Alexander Jwaideh-Khan, Devon Jwaideh Pleasants, and Derek Jwaideh Pleasants—who were a source of great joy and contentment to my husband in his later years.

Bloomington, Indiana   Alice Reid Jwaideh
March 2006

The Kurdish National Movement

Kurdistan.

1

Geographical, Historical, and Cultural Background

Geography

Boundaries

A vast, crescent-shaped area in the heart of the Middle East, Kurdistan encompasses most of eastern Turkey, northeastern Iraq, a considerable part of northwestern Iran, parts of north and northeastern Syria, and some territory on the southern and southeastern fringes of Armenia.[1] The hollow or inner rim of the crescent faces southwest, with one end resting on the western slopes of Kurd Dagh (mountain) near the Gulf of Alexandretta and the other on Manisht Kuh at the northwestern end of the Luristan Mountains.

Briefly stated, the boundaries of Kurdistan may be traced as follows.[2] Beginning from the Kurd Dagh, the boundary curves in a northeasterly direction along the eastern edges of the Ammanus and the anti-Taurus mountain ranges, passing close to Marash and thence to Malatya, and along the western bank of the Euphrates. It continues to the north and then swings sharply to the east, along the great loop formed by the Kara Su (western Euphrates) embracing the Dersim highlands. From here, it extends along the upper reaches of the Kara Su (river), passing in the vicinity of Erzerum. At this point, it sweeps toward the north-northeast to include parts of the Kars province in Turkey and crosses the Turco-Soviet frontier, passing along Mount Alagouze in Armenia. It then swerves sharply to the south of Erivan to include Nakhchivan in Armenia, from which point it stretches to the south, passing east of Koi and running along the western shores of Lake Urmiya, to include Salamas, Urmiya, and Ushnu. South of this lake it veers slightly to the east, passing beyond Miyanduab and thence to Bijar. It continues southward to Kangavar, cutting across the upper reaches of the Qizil Uzun River. From here, it swings to the southwest in a wide arc to include Kirmanshah, ending at Manisht Kuh on the northern borders of Luristan.

From this point, the boundary moves along the inner rim of the crescent in a northwesterly direction, passing near the Iraqi-Persian frontier at Khanaqin to include the plains of Zohab and Mahidasht. It then crosses the Diyala River near Qizil Ribat and moves in a north-northwesterly direction, passing close to Kifri and Kirkuk and crossing along the Lesser Zab at Altun Kupri. From here, it swerves toward the west to include the Qara Choq Mountain and the Arbil Plain, crossing the Greater Zab at Eski Kelek and moving along the southern edge of Jabal Maqlub to Dohuk and thence to Simayl. It then crosses the Tigris and moves southward and then northward, passing close to Faish Khabur to include the Sinjar Mountain. It then moves westward, passing through the northern part of the upper Jazira. From there, it skirts the southern slopes of the Tur 'Abdin and the Karaja Dagh and moves close to the Turco-Syrian frontier in a westerly direction, passing near Mardin, Viranshahar, Urfa, and Kilis, ending at Kurd Dagh.

Physical Geography

Fisher has pointed out that there is little physical unity in eastern Turkey.[3] This statement may be equally applied to the whole of Kurdistan. Numerous mountain ranges that change their strike suddenly as in central Kurdistan, large river basins such as those of the Tigris and the Euphrates, walled-in plains as in the Mush and Khinis areas, downthrown basins (ova) as in Urmiya and Koi, and vast outpourings of recent lava such as those that have covered most of the high Armenian plateau may be cited as evidence of the great diversity and lack of physical unity that characterize Kurdistan.

Topography. Three main mountain chains may be said to constitute Kurdistan: the Armenian or Eastern Taurus, the Inner Taurus,[4] and the Zagros. The southwest-northeast strike of the Central Taurus or anti-Taurus changes into a generally east-west strike in both the Eastern or Armenian Taurus and the Inner Taurus. These two mountain chains at first march parallel to each other, the distance between them gradually increasing. The Inner Taurus extends in an arclike manner north of Lake Van and continues for the rest of its length in a northeasterly direction, whereas the Armenian Taurus, which veers slightly to the south of that lake, extends in a southeasterly direction.

In the Kurdish-inhabited mountains of Dersim, the Inner Taurus begins with the massive Muzur Dagh and its eastern continuation, the Mirjan Dagh, which lie in an east-west direction.[5] Along a line running to the northeast of this area lie the Bingol Dagh (Mountain of a Thousand Lakes), the Tandurek Dagh, and Ararat, while slightly to the southeast of this area lie the Nimrud Dagh, the Sipan Dagh, and the Ala Dagh. All of these mountains are volcanic.[6]

The Eastern or Armenian Taurus, which begins with the mountains of Malatiya and al-'Aziz, continues south of Lake Van in the lofty Agherov Dagh, the Arnost Meleto, and the Bashit Dagh. To the south of this area lies the Norduz basin, which is a collection of high upland pastures (*yaylas*). It is in this region that the hitherto regular strike of these mountains shows signs of a sudden change. A remarkable feature in this area is the immense wall of rock known as Dahazir or Deria-i-zir, which stretches in a southwesterly direction, attaining an elevation of about 10,500 feet.[7] Beyond this point, to the southeast, begins the Hakari mountain area, a tangled mass of towering mountains and deep gorges and canyons, which culminates in Jilo and Sat Daghs, both more than 14,000 feet high. It is here that the Eastern Taurus veers suddenly toward the south and merges into the Zagros mountain system, beginning with the Bashi-Ruan range, a mass of black basaltic rocks reaching more than 11,000 feet in the Gumriaz Gavadan peak.[8]

According to Fisher, land forms at the northwestern part of the Zagros adjacent to the Anatolia "have been developed primarily as the result of differential tectonic move-

1. The Kurdish Frontier Mountains, Iraq. From E. B. Soane, *To Mesopotamia and Kurdistan in Disguise.* Courtesy of John Murray, London.

ments along well-marked faults."[9] He points out that horst blocks and downthrown basins are characteristic of this area, although in many cases their outlines have been modified by intense erosion.[10] In the central Zagros, the situation is different. Folding rather than faulting is the pattern. Numerous deep gorges, known locally as *tangs,* cut across these mountains, as a result of which drainage follows an intricate pattern.[11]

Hydrology. The main stream of the Tigris rises south of Lake Golcuk at a place called Devehbouyunou (Camel Pass), not far from Arghana, because of which it is sometimes called Arghana Su. About twenty miles below its source, it is joined by the Sebbeneh (Debbeneh) Su. These two streams form the river Tigris. It will thus be seen that the headwaters of the Tigris drain the southern slopes of the Eastern or Armenian Taurus. According to Cuinet, the Tigris is joined by more than thirty-four affluents between this point and its confluence with the Bohtan Su near Til. The most important of these affluents, most of which join it on the left bank, are the Batman Chai, the Chaklati Su, and the Gharzan Su. These affluents drain the Sasun and the Dorosh highlands, also a part of the Eastern Taurus. Some of the affluents it receives on the right bank in this area drain the Karaja Dagh and the Tur 'Abdin Mountains. It is in its passage through these mountains that the Tigris meanders through a series of deep gorges. The Bohtan Su, sometimes known as the Eastern Tigris, rises in the Farashin upland, which lies within the Norduz basin, one of the main watersheds in western Asia. This river drains the Norduz basin and the high mountains south of Lake Van known as the Arnost range, from which it receives the Muks (Moxoene) and Shattakh streams, the Bidlis Chai, and the Kezer Su.

After receiving the Bohtan Su, the Tigris flows past the Jazirat ibn 'Umar and emerges into the north Mesopotamian plain, flowing through a wide trough. Close to

Faish Khabur, it receives the Khabur River, which, along with its tributary the Hazil, drains the Norduz basin.

Thirty-five miles south of Mosul the Tigris is joined by the Greater Zab. This river rises in the low Chokh Mountains along the Turco-Persian frontier to the northeast of Bashkala. The Greater Zab, together with its numerous affluents, drains the Hakari mountains, which are the southeastern part of the Eastern Taurus, through its tributaries the Kochannes, the Julamerk, the Rubari Shin, and the Rukuchuk; it drains the Norduz basin through the Lawin and the western slopes of the Zagros through the Rubari Rawanduz.

About thirty miles south of its confluence with the Greater Zab, the Tigris receives the Lesser Zab, which drains the Iranian plateau and the Zagros mountains. Eighty miles to the south of this point it receives the waters of the 'Adaim River, which drains the western foothills of the Zagros in the Iraqi province of Kirkuk. The Diyala, known in its upper reaches as the Sirwan, joins the Tigris ten miles south of Baghdad.[12] The Lesser Zab and the Diyala rivers drain the Iranian plateau and the Zagros mountains.

The Euphrates is formed from the confluence of two large rivers, the Kara Su (western Euphrates) and the Murad Su (eastern Euphrates). The Kara Su rises in the Dumlu Dagh north of Erzerum at an altitude of 8,625 feet. It flows west-southwest toward Erzinjan. Between its source and the latter town, it is joined by a number of affluents, the most important of which are the Ovajik Su, the Mirjan Su, and the Chandukhu Su on the right bank, and the Tuzla Su on the left. Beyond Erzinjan, the Kara Su flows in a southwesterly direction through a rocky gorge to Kemakh, at which point it receives the Kumu Su. From this point until it joins the Murad Su, its gorge is renowned for its wild beauty.

The Murad Su rises on the northern side of Ala Dagh southwest of Diadin, at an altitude of 11,500 feet. It flows westward toward the Arishkerd plain, where it is joined by the Sharian Su. After running through the mountains, it is joined by the Patrotz on the left and by the Khanis Su on the right. From here, it takes a southwesterly direction, passing first through the plain of Bulamik and then through the plain of Mush, where it is joined by the Little Kara Su. Below Mush, the valley of the Murad Su becomes very narrow, and the Murad Su takes a west-southwesterly direction, threading its way through rocky gorges. Here it receives the Gunig Su. Beyond Palu, the valley of the Murad is more open. Approximately 10 miles east-northeast of Kharput, the Murad receives its most important affluent, the Peri Su, which drains the entire Dersim region. The Murad joins the Kara Su at a point not too far from Keban Maden. The length of the Murad from its source to its junction with the Kara Su is 415 miles, while that of the Kara Su is 275 miles. Although considerably longer than the Kara Su, the Murad Su has never had the commercial or historical importance of the Kara Su, probably because of its narrower and more confined course. It is perhaps for this reason that the Kara Su rather than the Murad Su has usually been regarded as the main stream.

Beyond the point of the confluence of the two rivers, the Euphrates flows in a southwesterly direction past the lead mines at Keban Maden. Here it swerves around the Musher Dagh, forming a great bend, and is joined first by the Karu Chai and later, about 7 miles farther on, by the Tokma Su. Beyond this point, it pierces the Taurus, running into the deepest and the wildest gorges of its entire course. It then runs southeast until it comes close to the sources of the Tigris and then turns abruptly and flows in a south-westerly direction, leaving the mountains a few miles above Samsat (Samasota).

The Euphrates receives only two important tributaries after this point, the Balikh and the Khabour. These tributaries do not concern us much because for the most part they flow into non-Kurdish lands,[13] the only exception being the upper reaches of the Khabour and its affluents the Jubjub, the Zergan, and the Jaghjagh, which have their sources in the southern slopes of the Karaja Dagh and the Tur 'Abdin.

Biogeography

The Armenian Plateau north of Lake Van is for the most part treeless because much of the area is covered with rather recent volcanic overflows. There are, however, a few ex-ceptions, notably the Soghanli Mountains in the north. South of Lake Van, in Kurdistan proper, despite the fact that the land has suffered greatly from centuries of deforestation and neglect, vegetation is much more luxuriant. In many areas in this part of Kurdistan, the mountains are covered with a variety of dwarf oak, the bearer of the gallnut of com-merce. Other trees found in this area are the birch, the poplar, and the willow. The ma-jority of the trees are deciduous, although pine and fir are found in some localities.

Fruits of the temperate zone—including grapes, figs, apples, pears, apricots, pome-granates, peaches, and mulberries—as well as nuts are found in abundance all over Kur-distan. Wheat, millet, barley, maize, and rice are grown, as well as tobacco, which is one of the area's main cash crops. Licorice is also found in many parts of Kurdistan. Vegeta-bles grown in the area include eggplant, gourd, spinach, okra, and green beans, as well as most other vegetables usually found in temperate zones. In the springtime, this area is particularly rich in wildflowers such as daisies, buttercups, roses, and anemonies, and in the upland pastures there are various kinds of alpine gentians, irises, ranunculus, tulips, and primroses.

Domestic animals found among the Kurds include fat-tailed sheep, cattle, horses, mules, goats, water buffalo in certain areas, dogs (especially the *tanjiy,* which is greatly beloved by the Kurds, and a type of very wild *kocher* or shepherd dog), and poultry, in-cluding turkeys and chickens. Among the wild animals of Kurdistan are the wolf, bear, snow leopard, lynx, fox, jackal, ibex or wild goat, wild sheep, moufflon, wild boar, stone martin, gray squirrel, and reptiles—including turtles, various kinds of snakes, and very large lizards. Birds found in the area include the red-legged and the gray partridge as well as a giant partridge known as *ur keklik,* sand grouse, stork, bustard, snipe, and vari-ous kinds of birds of prey such as the eagle. Among the fish found in Kurdistan are trout in mountain streams, a type of inland salmon, carp, and the remarkable biz found in the Greater Zab.[14]

Climate. Kurdistan has a continental climate, with long cold winters and hot dry summers. The continentality is especially pronounced north of Lake Van, the Armenia proper of pre-World War I times. In this area, winters are so severe that most of the houses in which the peasants dwell are mere underground hovels. The town of Erzerum, sometimes known as the "Siberia of Turkey," has a six-month winter with an average

2. Mountains near the Kurdish province of Van (Turkey). Courtesy of Burhan Elturan.

temperature below 15 degrees Fahrenheit. The temperature has been known to fall below −17 degrees Fahrenheit every night for three weeks. Absolute minimums of −30 degrees have been recorded, and on the higher plateaus such figures as −40 degrees Fahrenheit are not unknown. Another extremely cold area is the Norduz basin, south of Lake Van, which in winter is practically abandoned. Summers are hot and arid, particularly toward the north and east. Maximum summer temperatures exceed 100 degrees Fahrenheit and often rise as high as 110 and 120 degrees in certain valleys.[15]

Mineral Resources. Kurdistan is rich in mineral resources. The existence of a number of minerals has been reported by travelers and others in various parts of Kurdistan. However, because in many cases neither the quality nor the quantity of these minerals has been established, I concentrate here on exploited mineral deposits. Chrome is found at Gulman, west of Lake Van. The Gulman ores account for 60 percent of the total Turkish output of chrome. Copper is mined at Ergani Madeni (Arghana Maden) near the headwaters of the Tigris. Lead and zinc blende is found at Balya Madeni and at Kevan Madeni. These mines have been worked for some time, and the ore that remains is reported to be of low grade. Lead and zinc are sometimes found together, with small quantities of gold and silver or with copper, as at Ergani Madeni. Sulphur is found throughout the area; asbestos is found at Kars.

Oil is found at Baba Gurgur near Kirkuk in Iraq, and in the Naftkhana-Naftisha region along the Perso-Iraqi frontier. It is also found in a number of other scattered localities such as Naftdagh near Salahiya (Kifri) in Iraq, in the neighborhood of Zakho in Iraq, and along the Bohtan Su in Turkey. Coal of varying qualities is also reported. Bituminous coal is found near Salahiya and Sharanish in Iraq. Various kinds of building stones, including granite, limestone, marble, and lime, are found all over Kurdistan. Numerous mineral and thermal springs are scattered throughout the area. Rock salt is found at various localities near Tuz Khurmatu, and gypsum abounds in the lower hills of Iraqi Kurdistan.[16]

Population

Estimates of the size of the Kurdish population vary greatly. Lack of agreement on this matter is not new. There were considerable discrepancies among the figures given by various sources before and immediately after World War I.[17] Despite the fact that the Kurds are better known today than they have ever been in the past, the size of the Kurdish population continues to be a controversial issue. This has been particularly noticeable in the daily press, where estimates have varied not only among different newspapers,[18] but among different issues of the same paper as well.[19]

This results partly from the fact that until the 1950s no reliable population figures existed for the countries inhabited by the Kurds. The governments of these countries, besides being reluctant to give out such information, have tended to minimize the size of their Kurdish populations.[20] Kurdish nationalist sources, in contrast, have tended to exaggerate the number of the Kurds. Another factor that contributes to this problem is the lack of agreement as to what constitutes a Kurd. For example, Kurdish nationalists claim such groups as the great Lur confederation as Kurds, whereas the Persian government denies that the Lurs are Kurds. Experts are still divided on this issue. More often than not, however, the figures for the Kurdish population of Persia exclude members of the Lur confederation—namely, the Lurs, the Bakhtiaris, and the Mamasani. Similar disagreement has existed with regard to the groups speaking the various Dimli dialects—namely, the Zazas of Turkey, the Hawraman of the Perso-Iraqi frontier, and the Gurani of Persia, although this controversy has gradually diminished, and these groups have come to be accepted as non-Kurmanji-speaking Kurds.

British official C. J. Edmonds, one of the leading authorities on the Kurds, writing in the 1950s, placed the total number of Kurds, including those in Syria and the Soviet Union, at more than 5 million.[21] He stated that the number of Kurds in Iraq could be accurately estimated at 1.1 million, constituting from one-fifth to one-sixth of the country's total population. According to Edmonds, the number of Kurds in Iran was greater than in Iraq, but their proportion of the total population was considerably lower. He estimated the number of Kurds in Turkey at 2.5 million.[22]

The following Kurdish population figures were given by W. J. Elphinston:[23]

Turkey	1,500,000
Iraq	800,000
Iran	600,000
Syria	250,000
Soviet Armenia	20,000
Total	3,170,000

Pierre Rondot took issue with these figures, which he considered to be excessively low.[24]

Robert Zeidner in 1959 estimated the number of Kurds in these countries as follows:[25]

Turkey	2,000,000
Iran	750,000
Iraq	700,000
Syria	250,000
Armenian and Azerbaijan S.S.R. (up to)	100,000
Total	3,800,000

In contrast to the relatively low estimates given by Elphinston and Zeidner, we have the following figures given by the Kurdish League in 1949:[26]

Turkey	3,800,000
Iran	3,000,000
Iraq	1,200,000
Total	8,000,000

In 1947, Lucien Rambout gave similar figures for the three countries, as well as the percentage of Kurds in relation to the total population:[27]

TABLE 1.1

Percentages of Kurdish Population

Country	Kurds	Percentage
Turkey	4,000,000	25
Iran	3,500,000	23
Iraq	1,000,000	28

Lucien Rambout (pseud. Father Thomas Bois) estimated the number of Kurds in Syria at 250,000 and the number in the Soviet Union at 160,000, bringing his total to 8,910,000.

The following table shows the Kurdish population figures given in the 1937 and 1953 editions of the *Great Soviet Encyclopedia*:[28]

TABLE 1.2

Kurdish Population—*The Great Soviet Encyclopedia*

Country	1937	1953
Turkey	1,700,000	2,500,000–3,000,000
Iran	1,200,000	2,000,000–2,500,000 (including 300,000 in Khurasan)
Iraq	500,000	1,200,000
Syria	200,000	300,000
USSR	80,000	45,866
Afghanistan and Pakistan	—-	200,000
Total	3,680,000 (3½ to 4 million)	7,245,866 (7 million)

The total population figure given in the later edition was almost twice as large as that given in the 1937 edition. It is interesting to note that the article in which the larger figures appear was friendlier in tone toward the Kurds and less friendly toward the governments of the Kurdish-inhabited countries.

History of the Kurds

The Origins of the Kurds and the History of the Name "Kurd"

Despite the fact that the Kurds speak dialects akin to Persian, they are by no means a purely Iranian people. The area they occupy today has from the earliest times been the scene of a ceaseless ebb and flow of various peoples. Successive waves of conquerors, imperial armies, and savage hordes swept across these lands, and each left behind a trace, however faint, on the racial, linguistic, and cultural character of the inhabitants.

Evidence of these different accretions may be seen in the various physical types that are found among the Kurds with respect to such characteristics as head shape, hair and eye color, and build. The language also shows traces of various influences. The Semitic influence is unmistakable in the initial letters of such words as *hawt* and *asp,* and the Scythian influence is evident in such instances as the *te* ending employed in certain north Kurdish dialects in forming the plural—for example, *keleshte* (brigands).[29] Various religious beliefs imbedded in syncretic religions found among the Kurds, such as veneration of the sun among the Yazidis and of trees and stones among the Dersimlis, are further indications of this varied heritage.

The earliest inhabitants of Kurdistan were the ancient native peoples of the Zagros and the Eastern Taurus. Among the various inhabitants of the Zagros mountain range, three groups—the Guti, the Lullubi (Lullumi), and the Kashshu (Kassites)—may be cited as representative. All of these peoples were related to the Hallapi (Elamites). The earliest inhabitants of the Eastern Taurus were the Hurrians, who were also thought to be related to the Elamitic group.[30]

The development of the Kurds' Iranian character was at first a slow and gradual process. The first Indo-European incursions in western Asia began in the third millennium B.C. on a very small scale. It was not until the second millennium that Indo-Europeans appeared in force in that area. The Hittites, an Indo-European people, overran most of Anatolia, Armenia, Kurdistan, Mesopotamia, and the Levant. The Iranization of the Zagros and the Taurus mountain ranges was brought about by the appearance of the Medes, the Persians, and other Iranian peoples.

Perhaps one of the best clues to the racial origins of the Kurds may be found in the etymology and history of the name "Kurd." G. R. Driver, in a remarkable study, tried to trace the philological connections of this word. The results of his study have found general acceptance among scholars, with the exception of what he believed to be the earliest mention of the Kurds on a clay tablet of the third millennium B.C.[31]

Xenophon's famous account of the Kardoukhoi in his *Anabasis* is one of the earliest references we have to the Kurds. From then on, this word appears in slightly different forms in various Greek and Roman writers. The name "Kardakes" we find applied to a class of Asiatic mercenaries who seem to have been recruited from the districts inhabited by the Kardoukhoi. According to Driver, a scholiast commenting on Strabo said that the Kardakes were so called "because they lived by theft; for *Karda* means 'manly' and 'warlike.' "[32] It is interesting to note that in Assyrian, *qardu* means "strong" or "hero" and *qaradu* means "to be strong."[33] This name form corresponds almost exactly with "Beth Qardu" or "Ba Qarda" found in Syriac and Arabic sources. Beth Qardu refers to the lands between the Tigris and Jabal Judi. Not too far from this area lay Pactyca of the classical writers, where the Armenians and the inhabitants of Pactyca, according to Herodotus, formed the thirteenth Satrapy of the Persian Empire.

Another interesting name is "Khaldi," which Professor Vladimir Minorsky has described as having "a certain consonantal resemblance" to the name "Kurd." The Khaldi, who established the Vannic Empire, first emerged around the end of the ninth century B.C. and maintained themselves as a considerable power until the appearance of the Armenians toward the seventh century B.C. In their heyday, the Khaldi controlled most of Armenia and northern Kurdistan and contended, often successfully, against the Assyrian Empire. The famous mountain stela of Keleshin between Rawanduz and Ushnu is a Vannic relic, indicating the southern thrust of this people.[34]

Even after the disappearance of the Khaldi as a power, their name survived in the toponomy of the region around Lake Van—for example, Khilat (Akhlat), Chaldiran, Chaldir, and so on. Minorsky points out that parallels have been sought north of the Caucasus; thus, the Georgians are called Kharthv-eli (in Savanian, Khyard; in Mingrelian, Khort-u).[35]

Whether the Kardoukhoi or the Kardu were Semites or an ancient indigenous people, they lived in the same area where Kurds are found today. The conclusion that the Kardu and the Kurds must be the same, in the words of Professor Minorsky, became "axiomatic at the beginning of the twentieth centry."[36]

Another name by which the inhabitants of this area were known is "Kyrti" or "Kyrtioi," whom Strabo mentioned as dwelling in Little Media and in Persia. The Arabs, too, have mentioned the Kurds as living in these two regions. The Arabs called these people "Kurd" or "Akrad" (sing. Kurdi). This is the same nomenclature as that used by the Sassanians. In the *Karnamak-i Artakhshir-i Papakan,* there is a reference in which the name-form "Kurd" (pl. Kurdan) is found; the Kurdish king Madig is called "Kurdan Shahi Madig."[37]

Minorsky has drawn attention to the fact that the name "Kurd" has been used since very early times as a synonym for "nomad." He quotes the Arab historian Hamza al-Isfahani as saying, "The Persians call the Daylamites the 'Kurds of Tabaristan,' as they call the Arabs the 'Kurds of Suristan.' "[38] From this, he concludes that the Arab authors, in speaking of the Kurds, did not limit the name to the Kurdish-speaking people only, but applied it to all the Iranian nomads.

Confining himself to the Kurmanji dialects, Minorsky has pointed out the basic unity underlying Kurmanji despite its great diversity. This unity is never in doubt when the various Kurmanji dialects are compared with Persian or with the various northwestern Iranian languages. According to Minorsky, this unity must have existed before the dispersion of the Kurds, at a time when they lived in compact communities. The Kurds speak one of the northwestern Iranian languages, which he believes to be primarily that of the Parthians and to a certain extent that of the Medes. His conclusion is that the Medes and the Parthians played an important role in shaping the character and the composition of the Kurdish race and language.[39]

Minorsky has discussed the political situation in the Middle East during the ninth century B.C., when we hear for the first time of the incursions in force of Iranian elements into this area. There were first the two rival powers of Assyria and Urartu. The regions along the eastern mountainous frontier were inhabited by a number of non-Iranian peoples, such as the Kharkhar, the Ellipi, and so on. A number of small powers existed farther east—namely, the kingdom of Parsus, south of Lake Urmiya; to the east of it, the kingdom of the Mannians; and, finally, to the east of the Mannians, the Medes. In the seventh century B.C., the region was disturbed by a sudden incursion of nomads. The Cimmerians, fleeing before their enemies the Scythians, overwhelmed the regions south of the Caucasus, sweeping away the Vannic kingdom of Urartu and thereby enabling the Assyrians to expand eastward. Soon after the arrival of the Cimmerians, their pursuers the Scythians arrived on the scene and for a brief period succeeded in ruling the various kingdoms south of Lake Urmiya, in particular the Mannians and the Medes. The Medes eventually succeeded in emerging as the dominant power in this area after carrying out a massacre of Scythian chiefs. Media soon was strong enough to form an alliance and to attack Assyria, causing its downfall. The fall of Assyria created a vacuum that the Medes and various Iranian or Iranianized elements proceeded to fill. However, the arrival of the Armenians on the scene and their occupation of the area north of Lake Van limited the expansion of the Iranians to the area south of the lake.[40]

The Kurds and the Muslim Conquest

The Kurds appear to have steadily gained power and influence during the Sassanian period. Toward the close of this period, they expanded into most of the mountainous borderlands of western Persia and succeeded in consolidating their power in these areas. The Arab conquerors found them in possession of many of these border regions, where the Kurds resisted the passage of the first Arab armies into Persia and later, after the Arab conquest had become an accomplished fact, continued to be a dangerous rebellious element.

The Kurdish people emerged from historical obscurity after the Arab conquest, for it was the Arab writers who for the first time gave us a wealth of information about them. The Kurds' initial fierce resistance during the early phases of the Arab invasion and their continued contumaciousness undoubtedly contributed to their prominence in the early annals of the Arabs. Our knowledge of the Kurds is owing to an even greater extent, however, to the spirit of intellectual curiosity generated by Islamic civilization, which has given us a vast geographical literature oftentimes containing surprisingly accurate accounts of various lands and peoples.

The Kurds apparently came in contact with the Arabs for the first time after the occupation of Takrit in northern Iraq and of Hulwan on the western edge of the Iranian plateau in A.H.15/A.D. 637. Three years later the Kurdish ruler of al-Zawzan (the region north of the present Iraqi border) is reported to have paid *kharaj* (land tax) to the Arab conquerors and to have been confirmed in his authority by them. The Arabs fought the Kurds in A.D. 639, when the latter went to the aid of al-Hurmuzan, the Persian governor of al-Ahwaz, in southern Persia. The Arabs captured the district of Shahrizur in A.H.22/A.D. 643 after a bloody war with the Kurds. The Kurds are reported to have taken part in a number of uprisings at this time, the most notable of which was the rebellion of al-Khirit near al-Ahwaz in Fars, where Kurds made common cause with Persians and Christians. At this time, forcibly converted Kurds were apostasized en masse.[41]

During the caliphate of the Umayyad 'Abd al-Malik ibn Matwar, the Kurds partici-pated actively in the great rebellion of 'Abd al-Rahman ibn al-Ash'ath. The latter is re-ported to have been in alliance with the Kurds of Saburan in Fars in A.H. 83/A.D. 702. The Umayyad governor of Iraq, al-Hajjaj ibn Yusuf al-Taqafi, punished the Kurds of Fars for causing disturbances in that province in A.H. 90/A.D. 708. In the year A.H. 117/A.D. 735, the Kurds became involved in the dynastic quarrels of the Umayyads, sid-ing with Caliph Marwan II against Sulayman ibn 'Abd al-Malik, who was defeated.[42]

A Kurd is linked with the foundation of the 'Abbasid dynasty, one of the most mo-mentous events in Islamic history. Abu Muslim al-Khurasani, the leader and military commander of the 'Abbasid-'Alid forces, who in a series of battles routed the Umayyad armies and succeeded in overthrowing the Umayyad dynasty, is said to have been of Kurdish descent.

Throughout the long history of the 'Abbasid dynasty, the Kurds proved to be one of the most difficult elements to rule. The Khazar invasion of Armenia in A.H.147/A.D. 764 touched off a number of Kurdish rebellions. In the year A.H. 220/A.D. 835, during the reign of al-Mu'tasim, a Kurdish rebellion was led by Ja'far ibn Faharjis in the region of Mosul (al-Mawsal). The Khariji rebel Musawir was joined in the year A.H. 252/A.D. 866 by the Kurds of Mosul. During the great Zanj rebellion, which almost caused the down-fall of the 'Abbasid Empire, the Kurds, under their leader Muhammad ibn 'Abd Allah ibn Hazarmard, allied themselves with the rebels. In the rebellion of the partly Kurdish Khariji leader Daysam ibn Ibrahim, the rebels, who were mostly Kurds, seized Zarbayjan in A.H. 327–28/A.D. 938.

Kurdish Dynasties

The emergence of native Kurdish dynasties in the ninth, tenth, and eleventh cen-turies A.D. is part of a general phenomenon that manifested itself throughout the Iran-ian lands of the eastern caliphate. This sudden upsurge of Iranian energy, which brought Khurasanians, Daylamites, and Kurds to the seats of authority, created a pat-tern that, for all its different local coloring, was similar in inspiration and composition. Professor Minorsky has aptly described this period of Iranian revival and ascendancy as "the Iranian intermezzo," for, as he points out, it formed the transition between two mo-mentous periods of Islamic history: the collapse of Arab domination and the rise of Turkish power.[43]

The Shaddadid dynasty was founded by Muhammad ibn Shaddad ibn Qartaq in the year A.H. 340/A.D. 951 after the collapse of the power of the Musafarid rulers of Azerbayjan. The Shaddadids ruled in eastern Transcaucasia in the lands enclosed by the Kur and the Araxes rivers. One branch of the Shaddadids had its capital at Ganja and at the ancient Armenian capital of Dvin (Arabic, Dabil). There were ten rulers in the Ganja branch of the Shaddadids. The rule of this dynasty was ended in A.H. 468/A.D. 1075 by the Seljuk sultan Alp Arslan. A later branch of the family ruled at Ani, another ancient Armenian capital. There were seven Ani rulers, and their dynasty lasted from about A.H.465/A.D. 1072 to A.H.596/A.D. 1199.[44]

The Marwanid dynasty was founded by the Kurd Bad (or Badh) Abu Abdullah al-Hussayn ibn Dustak al-Harbukhti, a native of the Bahasna Mountains near Khizan. The rise of this prince to prominence started in the year a.h. 374/A.D. 984, when, upon the death of the Buwayhid prince ʿAdud al-Dawla, he seized the city of Mayyafariqin and held it, together with the rest of the province of Diyarbakr, against the Buwayhid Samsam al-Dawla and against the sons of Nasir al-Dawla the Hamdanid. Bad, who was killed in a battle with the Hamdanids, was succeeded by his maternal nephew Abu ʿAli al-Husayn ibn Marwan ibn Lakak al-Harbukhti. The latter, who established himself at Diyarbakr, may be said to be the first Marwanid ruler. His domain included Nasibin, Jazira, and Tur ʿAbdin.

The most brilliant member of the Marwanid family was Nasir al-Dawla Abu Nasir Ahmad, who ruled for almost fifty-one years, from A.H. 401–402/A.D. 1010 to A.H. 453/A.D. 1061. Historians tend to agree that he was a just and enlightened ruler. He built mosques, hospitals, and bridges and was a patron of poets and men of learning. The Marwanid dynasty, which had five rulers, came to an end in A.H. 476/A.D. 1083.[45]

The Hasanwayhid dynasty was founded about A.H. 348/A.D. 959 by Hasanwyah (Hasanoya) ibn Hasan, chief of the Barzikani (Barzinji) tribe, who started his career by cooperating with Rukn al-Dawla, the Buwayhid. The Buwayhids, however, seem to have coveted the domains of the Hasanwayhids, which included a large stretch of territory from Khuzistan to Shahrizur. There were in all five princes of this house, whose rule lasted until A.H. 488/A.D. 1095.[46]

Another Kurdish dynasty was that of the ʿAnnazids, who ruled from A.H. 381/A.D. 991 to A.H. 511/A.D. 1117. It was founded by Abu al-Fath Muhammad ibn Annaz, who established his capital at Hulwan. The ʿAnnazid state occupied the frontier region between Iraq and Iran. There were seven ʿAnnazid rulers.[47]

The greatest and the most renowned of all Kurdish dynasties was that of the Ayyubids. It was founded by Salah al-Din Yusuf ibn Ayyub ibn Shadi, the Saladin of the Crusades. The dynasty took its name from Salah al-Din's father, Najm al-Din Ayyub. All sources seem to agree on the history and origins of the Ayyubid family. They were natives of Dvin and apparently were in the service of the Kurdish rulers of that town, the Shaddadids. Salah al-Din's grandfather, Shadi ibn Marwan, is reported to have left Dvin, his native town, with his two sons, Asʿad al-Din Shirkuh and Najm al-Din Ayyub, for Baghdad. From there, he journeyed to Takrit, where his son Ayyub became the commander of the town. In the year A.H. 532/A.D. 1137–38, twenty years after Shadi's departure from Dvin, Salah al-Din was born in Takrit, Iraq.[48]

Salah al-Din's father and uncle left Takrit as the result of an incident, to enter the service of Nur al-Din Zangi, the atabek of Mosul, under whom they had held the Takrit appointment. After many years of soldiering in Syria and acting as an agent for Zangi, Salah al-Din was appointed vizier of the Fatamid caliph al-'Adid in Egypt in succession to his uncle Shirkuh.[49] Salah al-Din seized the opportunity arising from the sickness of al-'Adid, proclaimed the dying caliph deposed, and ordered the khutba (sermon) to be read in the name of the 'Abbasid caliph of Baghdad. This coup had the effect of placing Egypt under the nominal suzereignty of Baghdad, while making Salah al-Din the master of Egypt. Having thus created a basis of control for himself, he moved into Syria, bringing under his power most of the country that was not under the rule of the crusaders. It was during this period that he felt strong enough to organize and lead the Muslim forces against the Crusaders.

Salah al-Din's career reached its culmination in the battle of Hittin in A.H.583/A.D. 1187. It was this battle that broke the power of the Crusaders and paved the way for the surrender of Jerusalem.[50] Salah al-Din died six years later, in A.H. 589/A.D. 1193. Before his death, he divided his vast empire among his sons and brothers. However, soon after his death, family quarrels broke out. His brother al-Malik al-'Adil succeeded in bringing most of the Ayyubid realms under his rule, but he repeated Salah al-Din's mistake by dividing his territories among his own sons: al-Kamil received Egypt, al-Mu'azzam received Damascus, and al-Fa'iz received Iraq. Al-Fa'iz was in turn succeeded first by his brother al-Awhad and later by al-Ashraf. Only Aleppo continued to be held by Salah al-Din's descendants.[51]

The Mongols and the Kurds

The Mongol invasion, because of its sudden and violent character, probably created greater destruction and dislocation in Kurdistan than the Turkish invasions, although its effects were not as permanent. The Mongols appear to have known of the Kurds' war-like character even before reaching Kurdistan. It is interesting to note that the great Khan Mangu gave the following instructions to his brother, Hulaghu Khan, who was despatched to western Asia with the object of conquering the caliphate: "Treat well all those who obey! Crush all rebels! Raze to the ground all citadels and fortresses on your way. . . . March from Turan to Iran and when you finish them, march on to Iraq: exterminate those Lurs and Kurds and destroy their strongholds of Kerdeh-Kuh and Lembeh-Ser, where those people are always worrying travellers by their brigandage."[52]

The havoc wrought by the Mongol invasion in Kurdistan was of such a character that, according to various sources, many sections of Kurdistan were depopulated by massacres and migrations. Many of the tribes of Shahrizur are reported to have left for Egypt as a result of the Mongol invasion. This flight from the Mongols carried some Kurdish tribes as far west as Algeria. According to Ibn Khaldun, two Kurdish tribes named Lawin and Badin went to Algeria, where they were well received by the Caliph al-Murtadi of the Almohades.[53] The interval between the decline of Mongol power and the rise of the Safavids saw the rise and fall of the two Turkomen dynasties, the Ak Koyunlu (the White Sheep dynasty) and the Kara Koyunlu (the Black Sheep dynasty) in

Kurdish lands, and the eruption of Timur Lang (Timerlane), which rivaled the Mongol invasion in its destructiveness.[54]

The Kurds Since the Sixteenth Century

After the rise of the Ottoman and the Safavid empires in Turkey and Persia, respectively, the Kurds and their country became a bone of contention between these two powerful states. The Safavids, who had succeeded in wresting most of northern Kurdistan from the Turkomen dynasties, were soon compelled to give up their Kurdish acquisitions to the Ottomans. The battle of Chaldiran in A.D. 1514 marks a very important date in Kurdish history. Although the Ottomans succeeded in checking Safavid power, they failed to destroy it. As a result of this defeat, the Safavids lost the greater part of Kurdistan. Fighting between Turkey and Persia continued intermittently throughout the next three centuries, as a result of which the Kurds suffered greatly. Not only was their homeland devastated by the fighting, but their services were enlisted by both antagonists.

After the battle of Chaldiran, the policy adopted by the Ottoman sultan Selim the Grim toward the Kurds stood out in marked contrast to that of the Persian shah Isma'il. The latter reportedly imprisoned eleven leading Kurdish chiefs who had come to reaffirm their allegiance to him and seriously alienated the Kurds by imposing upon them Azerbayjani Turks as governors.[55] The sultan, in contrast, displayed greater generosity and farsightedness in dealing with the Kurds. To the able Kurdish statesman Idris Bidlisi he entrusted the organization of Kurdistan and the integration of the Kurdish autonomous principalities into the Ottoman imperial system. The very wide powers given to Idris Bidlisi are evident from a *farman* (royal decree) issued by the sultan in the year A.H. 921/A.D. 1515.[56]

In A.D. 1639, the Treaty of Zuhab was concluded between Sultan Murad IV and Shah Safi al-Din, defining the frontier between the Turkish and the Persian empires.[57] This treaty perpetuated the division of Kurdistan between the two countries.

The amicable relations that had existed between the Kurds and the Ottomans under Sultan Selim I soon deteriorated. It seems that the Ottoman government, no longer fearing Persian power, disregarded the conditions in accordance with which the Kurds had thrown in their lot with the Ottomans and had agreed to cooperate with them. From 1650 to 1730, the Ottomans suppressed most of the autonomous Kurdish principalities in the Diyarbakr-Van area. This process of reducing the Kurdish principalities was completed during the middle half of the nineteenth century.

The overthrow of the Safavid dynasty and the usurpation of the Persian crown by Nadir Shah in 1736 brought new vicissitudes to the Kurds. Not only did this conqueror use the Kurds on a large scale in his military expeditions, but his numerous wars with the Ottoman Empire caused much destruction and loss of life. Among measures he adopted was the transportation of thousands of Kurdish families to Khurasan with the object of protecting Persia's eastern frontier against the incursions of the Turkomen.[58]

The interlude of confusion and disorder that followed Nadir Shah's death in 1747 brought to the fore a remarkable Kurdish leader, Karim Khan Zand, who for nearly thirty years ruled Persia as regent of the empire. According to all accounts, he was an enlightened and merciful ruler, and throughout his rather long reign (1750–79) the country enjoyed a much needed respite from the violence and bloodshed of his predecessor.[59] Karim Khan was succeeded by the unfortunate Lutfi 'Ali Khan. The latter, after a protracted struggle with his minister Agha Muhammad Khan, the future founder of the Qajar dynasty, fell victim to that minister's treachery.[60]

The Kurds do not seem to have fared well under the first Qajar ruler. A cruel and vengeful man, Agha Muhammad Khan tried to exterminate the whole Zand tribe and all those who had been associated with it.[61] However, it was not he, but one of his successors, Nasir al-Din Shah, who put an end to native Kurdish rule in the Ardalan and the Mukri country. The fact that the house of Ardalan was related to the royal family did not seem to make much difference.

The last Ardalani prince was Shulam Shah Khan, who succeeded to the dignity in 1865. After the death of this prince a few years later, Nasir al-Din Shah, exercizing his prerogatives as monarch and elder relative, barred the rightful heir from succession. In this manner, the political existence of the oldest Kurdish principality was brought to an end.[62] The Baba Miris, who ruled the Mukri country from their capital at Sawj Bulaq (Mahabad), shared a similar fate a few years later. They appear to have been set aside after Shaykh 'Ubayd Allah's invasion of Persia (see chapter 4).[63]

Strange as it may seem, the suppression of these two Kurdish principalities caused little if any excitement in Persia, whereas similar measures in Turkey had very different results.

Religion

Most Kurds are Sunnis of the Shafi'i rite. The majority of the Kurds were probably Zoroastrians before the introduction of Islam into Kurdistan.[64] Some of them were pagans, whereas others embraced Christianity. A number of Zoroastrian, Christian, and pagan beliefs and practices are still prevalent among the Kurds.

Christianity appears to have penetrated Kurdistan in the early centuries of the Christian era. Mar Mari of Urfa (died A.D. 226) is reported to have converted to Christianity the king and people of Shahgert, who "worshipped trees and sacrificed to the idol of copper."[65] We are also informed that Isho Yaba built a convent near Thamanin in the vicinity of Jazirat ibn 'Umar at the "spot where the Kurds had sacrificed to devils."[66] The Kurds who were converted to Christianity by Mar Saba (died A.D. 485) are described as having been previously worshippers of the sun. The Arab historian al-Mas'udi, writing in the fourth century A.H., mentioned Kurdish Jacobites and al-Jurqan in the neighborhood of Jabal Judi.[67] From the author of the *Pseudo-Majriti* (written circa fifth century A.H.), we learn the curious story of a Christian Kurd, obviously a convert, who wanted to become a magician.[68]

Even in more recent years, there are numerous indications that Christianity at one time had spread among the Kurds. According to a modern Kurdish writer, certain Kurdish tribes make the impression of the cross on dough prior to its being baked.[69] Wigram and Wigram inform us that during the annual migrations of the great nomad tribe of the Herki, members carry with them in a wooden box a sort of palladium that is supposed to be the head of Saint George.[70] Basile Nikitine, a leading expert on the Kurds, mentions the same story and adds that other Kurdish tribes, such as the Abdoi and the Nisanai, engage in similar observances.[71] According to Nikitine, many tribes in Bohtan, Midyat, Sasun, and other regions still retain memories of their ancient Christian antecedents. He maintains that in Sasun they are called "those who have denied the cross."[72]

The opening phrase of a recently discovered Christian prayer in the Kurdish language throws an interesting light on the antiquity of Christianity among the Kurds. In a brief notice, Minorsky has described this fragment and translated it into French. Although the copy of the manuscript in which this prayer was found dates to the early fifteenth century, Minorsky believes the original to be very ancient. According to him, it is written in a north Kurdish dialect and probably is from the Araxes River basin.[73]

The conversion of the Kurds to Islam appears to have been a rather slow process. With the exception of those regions where the Kurds came into early contact with the Muslim Arabs—including the tribes of Fars, Hulwan, Shahrizur, Jazirat ibn 'Umar, and Diyarbakr—there remained numerous isolated enclaves in the more inaccessible regions where the Kurds continued to adhere to their old beliefs, whether they be Zoroastrian, Christian, or pagan. Judging from a curious passage provided by Bar Hebraeus, the conversion of the Kurds to Islam was far from completed even by the beginning of the thirteenth century:

> And in the year six hundred and two of the Arabs [A.D. 1205] a race of the Kurds who were in the mountains of Madai (Media), and who are called Tirahaye, came down from the mountains, and wrought great destruction in those countries. And troops of the Persians were gathered together, and they met them in battle and many of them were killed. Now these mountaineers had not entered the Faith of the Muslims, but they had adopted the primitive paganism (of their country) and Magianism. When a Muslim fell into their hands they put him to death with cruel tortures.[74]

Writing in 1596, the author of the *Sharafnama* described the Pazuki tribe by saying, "And they do not adhere to any definite religious school nor do they follow the commandments to do what is right and abstain from what is forbidden."[75] Even in the nineteenth century a number of writers reported the existence of a tribe of Kurds, the Balaki in the Sasun highlands, who were neither Muslim nor Christian nor Qizilbash.[76]

The isolated nature of many regions in Kurdistan, the imperfect or nominal conversion of some of them in the early centuries of Islam, and the refuge afforded by the mountain fastnesses to various heretical or extremist groups may account for the numerous sects found among the Kurds. A brief discussion of the various religious sects in Kurdistan may provide a better understanding of the different religious and social ideas held by important segments of the Kurdish people.

The Yazidis

The Yazidis are a unique sect whose origins continue to be a mystery despite considerable research.[77] Yazidism is a syncretic religion that includes elements borrowed from Zoroastrianism, Manichaeanism, Islam, Christianity, Judaism, Sabaeanism, and Shamanism.

The Yazidis believe that the world was created by seven angels. The central idea in their religion appears to be the dualism between God and Malak Ta'us (lit., Peacock Angel) or Satan. According to them, God is a passive entity who is only the creator, not the preserver, of the world. Malak Ta'us is the active and executive organ of the divine will. Shaykh 'Adi, who is said to have attained divinity through transmigration, is believed to be one with Malak Ta'us. Contrary to popular belief, the Yazidis do not worship Satan, for Malak Ta'us is regarded as a fallen angel who, because of his repentance, will in due time be restored to God's favor. They deny the existence of evil and do not believe in punishment by hell. The Yazidis believe in their uniqueness and complete separation from the rest of humankind. They claim that, unlike other humans, they were not descended from Adam and Eve, but from a child named Shadid ibn Jarrah, who developed from the seed of Adam only, in a jar that was kept closed for nine months.

The Yazidis used to be very numerous and powerful, until about the early 1800s. Continuous and systematic Ottoman massacres greatly reduced their numbers. There are perhaps seventy thousand of them distributed in Iraq, Syria, Turkey, and the Soviet Union. The Yazidis' spiritual and temporal leader resides in the Shaykhan district of the Mosul province in Iraq, where the tomb of Shaykh 'Adi, the principal Yazidi shrine, is located.

The Sarlis

The Sarlis, who are found in the Mosul province of Iraq, are another sect with unusual religious beliefs.[78] They are reported to be monotheists and to acknowledge certain prophets, and they believe in death, resurrection, paradise, and hell. Sarlis neither fast nor pray. They are said to buy paradise from their chief religious dignitaries. Their enemies accuse them of holding a meeting at the beginning of each lunar year, at which time they kill a cock and eat it together; after the meal, in which both men and women participate, they are said to extinguish the lights and to engage in a ritual orgy.

The Qizilbash

The Qizilbash are an extreme Shi'a sect in Turkey who inhabit the region between Mush and the southwestern bend of the Euphrates, including the Dersim highlands.[79] The term *qizilbash* (red-head) is a term of opprobrium applied to them by the orthodox Muslim Turks. They call themselves "Yol Ushaghi" (Children of the True Path).

The Qizilbash believe in the unity of God and in his omnipotence and that he has "neither son nor companion." Although they believe in the resurrection of Christ, they regard him only as a prophet and identify him with 'Ali. They regard Adam, Noah, Abraham, Moses, Christ, Muhammad, and 'Ali as the greatest prophets. However, they see 'Ali as greater than Muhammad. They believe the twelve imams to be the twelve apostles under different names. The Qizilbash identify Hasan and Husayn, the two sons of 'Ali, with Saint Paul. They accept the New Testament, the Pentateuch, and the Qur'an. They have no religious book of their own, but receive their instruction from their sayyids, who are their religious as well as their temporal leaders. All of their sayyids claim descent from a certain Imam Bagkir, who was the reputed founder of their religion. According to tradition, Imam Bagkir was miraculously born of an Armenian virgin, the daughter of an Armenian priest. The Qizilbash revere trees, stones, and other natural objects. Each year on the first of January, they observe a sort of communion. After prayers, the sayyid blesses the bread, which is called *haq loqmase,* and distributes it to the communicants. Their enemies maintain that the purpose of these meetings is for the performance of ritual orgies.

The Ahli Haqq

The name "Ahli Haqq" means "the People of Reality" or "the People of Truth." Although they have frequently been referred to as the "'Ali-Allahi" (the defiers of 'Ali), this is a misleading name, stemming no doubt from the fact that traces of extreme Shi'ism are found among them. The central dogma of the Ahli Haqq consists of a belief in the successive manifestations of the divinity. These manifestations are seven in number and are enumerated in an elaborate table of theophanies. The first is that of Khwandagar, the creator of the world, who in pre-eternity was enclosed in a pearl; the second is 'Ali, and so on. However, the most important of all the seven manifestations is that of Sultan Sohak, the fourth avatar, who forms the central figure in the Ahli Haqq religion.

According to the Ahli Haqq, humans are of two types, good and evil. The first are created from yellow clay, the second from black clay. Metempsychosis (passage of the soul from one body to another) forms one of their chief articles of faith. The rites of the Ahli Haqq show extensive borrowings from various sources. Their syncretic religion clearly shows the influence of Gnostic, Manichaean, Zoroastrian, Hindu, Jewish, Christian, and Muslim elements. Many of the pagan beliefs found among them may represent ancient survivals. However, it is not improbable that some of these beliefs may have found their way among the Ahli Haqq via certain heterodox Christian and Muslim doctrines such as Isma'ilism in Islam and the Thonraki or Paulician heresy believed to have originated in Armenia. An interesting belief among the Ahli Haqq is that on the Day of Judgment, which is supposed to take place in the plain of Shahrizur in southern Kurdistan, all the sultans will be punished.

The Ahli Haqq is a religion of the lower classes and is found among nomads, villagers, and the poorer inhabitants of towns. Its adherents live principally in western Iran in the Guran country and in Luristan. However, they are also found in scattered communities in Persian Ayzerbayjan, Transcaucasia, Mazaindaran, Khurasan, Tehran, and Namadan. Important enclaves of the Ahli Haqq are also found in the Kirkuk, Sulaymaniya, and Mosul regions in Iraq, where they are known as Kaka'is.[80]

Kurdish Literature and Cultural Activities

Traditional Literature: Folklore and Poetry

The scope and significance of Kurdish literature have become increasingly evident as a result of continued research by European as well as native Kurdologists. Our awareness of both the written and the oral literature of the Kurds has undergone a profound change. A measure of the progress made in this direction may be gained from the fact that Alexandre Jaba in his *Recueil de notices et de récits Kourdes* (St. Petersburg, 1860) mentions the names of only 8 Kurdish poets, whereas 'Ala al-Din Sajjadi discusses 24 poets at considerable length and lists 212 others in his history of Kurdish literature, *Mejuy Edebe Kurdi* (Baghdad, 1952). The knowledge we have today of the richness and variety of Kurdish folklore affords a striking contrast to our ignorance of this matter in the mid-nineteenth century.

It is interesting to recall that James Fraser, a professional writer who traveled widely in Kurdistan in the 1830s, failed in his attempts to discover any evidence of belief in fairies or other supernatural beings among the Kurds.[81] Such is the volume and range of Kurdish folkloric material in our possession today, however, that a Soviet Kurdologist, according to Nikitine, describes its abundance as a case of "hypertrophy."[82] The Soviet source attributes the excessive development of this genre of Kurdish literature, at the expense of written literature, to the illiteracy that is almost universal among the Kurds and that in certain instances, as among the Yazidis, is a religious requirement imposed on all but a select few.

For our knowledge of Kurdish folklore we are greatly indebted to a number of writers who have brought to light a great deal of hitherto unpublished material. Among them are Basile Nikitine; Princes Sureya, Jaladet, and Kamuran Bedir Khan; Roger Lescot; Ereb Shamilov; 'Ala al-Din Sajjadi; and Thomas Bois.

Kurdish folklore in its various forms—stories, fables, fairytales, epics, lyrics, proverbs, anecdotes, charms, and riddles—embraces a great diversity of themes. Love, patriotism, war, and hospitality are favorite subjects. These themes of Kurdish folklore may be said to fall into three categories: (1) those that are the product of Kurdish experience; (2) those that are based on the folkloric heritage of the whole Middle East; and (3) those that are borrowed or adapted from neighboring peoples. Although the bulk of Kurdish stories, fables, and fairytales is still unrecorded, the collections we now have are no doubt fairly representative.

Kurdish storytelling is characterized by simplicity and oftentimes by a keen sense of humor. Some of the stories in our possession, such as the "Story of Suto and Tato,"[83] show considerable narrative skill and for all their grimness are relieved by a lively if raw humor. This story tells of fierce passions unleashed by a blood feud arising from the oppression of one tribe by another. The blood feud is carried on against a background of cruelty, treachery, and desperate courage. Few Kurdish stories are as revealing as this one, which, as Nikitine has pointed out, provides "a vivid picture of the Kurdish mentality."[84]

The story "Shaykh Soleyman,"[85] about a rogue and a thief who masquerades as a pious shaykh and ends by robbing the shrine of a saint, is at once an irreverent barb aimed at this class of religious men and an expression of undisguised admiration for robbery, even in the most reprehensible circumstances. For the bold and resourceful robber, nothing is sacrosanct, not even the shrine of a great saint. It is interesting to note how the thief tries to set at rest his robust conscience, and perhaps that of his followers, by the following rationalization of his act: if the saint be a true one, he certainly knows that the living have more use for the things of this world than do the dead; if he be a false saint, then I have nothing to fear.[86]

In the story "Hasan Beg, Mir of Hakkari, and the Good News of the Spring Bird,"[87] the magpie is praised above all the migratory birds of the spring, for unlike the others he is not merely a fair-weather friend. In the words of the *mir* (prince), "The dirty magpie is always with us, in good times and in adversity . . . a trustworthy friend, never fearing the cold. It is our friend, for in happiness and in sorrow it always equally shares our lot."[88] In this story, the magpie symbolizes the tribesman's deep attachment to his tribe and his loyalty to his fellow tribesmen. In Kurdish literature, the magpie is a recurrent symbol of a sober and sensible person.

"The Cock and the Fox" is a variant of a Persian fable of the same title.[89] It is an anticlerical story aimed at the shaykhs, the highly revered heads of the religious fraternities in Kurdistan. With charm and sly humor, it exposes the hypocrisy and rapacity of some shaykhs. The fox, pretending to be a sayyid, induces a cock, a huppe, a duck, and a magpie to accompany him on a pilgrimage to Mecca. Because of their blind confidence, all except the magpie fall victim to the wily fox. According to Nikitine, the cock in this story represents the credulous and much exploited peasant, the huppe is a well-to-do paterfamilias in search of profitable respectability, and the duck probably stands for a wild tribesman easily deceived by flattery. The magpie, a lowly vagabond, represents a shrewd and practical person who, because he places no confidence in the fox's words, is the sole survivor.

The ballad of the siege of Dimdim Kala is one of the most celebrated of Kurdish epics. It is the story of a desperate, unyielding band of Kurds who covered themselves with glory at the siege of the fortress of Dimdim near Urmiya in 1608. In defending the beleaguered fortress, the Kurdish chieftain Amir Khan and his faithful Baradost tribesmen held at bay the superior forces of the Safavid Shah 'Abbas I for several months, suffering and inflicting terrible casualties. The defenders continued to fight until every one of them was killed.[90]

Mame Alan is the most popular Kurdish epic. Of all the oral literature of the Kurds, it alone has the character of a true national epic. There is no standard version of this epic, although it is known all over Kurdistan, from Kurd Dagh to Lake Urmiya. Not only do versions differ from region to region, but each *dengbej* or Kurdish troubadour has his own version. *Mame Alan* is the only Kurdish epic in which the miraculous plays an important role and the events are ficticious and not historical. Lescot has suggested that the Kurds may have adopted this very ancient epic from another people, and he speculates about its possible Alanic origins.[91]

The great Kurdish poet Ahmadi Khani, desirous of creating a truly Kurdish national literature, chose the legend *Mame Alan* as the basis for his imposing *methnewi* (poem

consisting of rhyming couplets) called *Mem u Zin.* In recasting this legend, Khani followed Persian and Arabic models and gave it a thoroughly Islamic impress.[92]

Kurdish folksongs, like the folksongs of other peoples, are the lyrical expression of
the native pattern of life and activity, and the mood usually associated with it.[93] The *pe-
hizok* or autumn songs are sung by young men and women at the time of the nomads'
descent from their upland summer retreats *(zozan)* to the plains. Dance songs include
the *dilok,* sung to the accompaniment of drum and flute, and the *belite,* sung at student
circle dances. The *berdolavi* are sung by young women at the spinning wheel as they
weave their multicolored carpets. The *lori* are cradle songs noted for their freshness and
simplicity. Also popular among the Kurds are the *lawij,* usually short poems telling of
martial deeds, chivalrous exploits, and love affairs.

Certain schools train bards or troubadours who specialize in reciting the popular
legends and stories of Kurdistan. These bards are called *dengbej* in northwestern Kurdistan and *shair* (from the Arabic *sha'ir*) in the Mukri country and in southern Kurdistan.
The student bards, who are supposed to have beautiful voices, commit to memory their
vast repertories of songs, legends, and poems because most of them are illiterate and a
large proportion of Kurdish folk literature is still unwritten.[94]

Poetry constitutes by far the major portion of Kurdish written literature. This is
only natural among a people where illiteracy is so widespread, for the poet, unlike his
other literary confreres—the essayist, the critic, the playwright, and the novelist—does
not require an especially literate and cultured audience. The richness and variety of
Kurdish poetry is considerable, and, along with other forms of literature, it is now being
further developed and enriched by a Kurdish literary renaissance.

Kurdish poets have traditionally concerned themselves with the twin topics of ro-
mantic love and deep attachment to their native land. The seventeenth-century poet
Ahmadi Khani and the nineteenth-century Hajji Qadir of Koi are regarded as the two
greatest Kurdish poets. The former, a native of Hakari who lived and died in Bayazid,
was the author of the great epic *Mem u Zin* referred to earlier. To the Kurds, he is what
Firdawsi is to the Persians. He was also the author of a religious poem "Equide Imani"
and of a rhymed Kurdish-Arabic dictionary called *Nawbar* (Firstlings) intended for
children's use.[95] Hajji Qadir of Koi (1815–92) was known for his intensely patriotic
poems and for that reason is considered one of the fathers of Kurdish nationalism. Some
of his poems have a materialistic and agnostic flavor, which may account for his current
popularity in Kurdish leftist circles.[96]

Cultural Activities in Kurdistan

Iraq and Syria are the two most important centers of Kurdish cultural activities. The
political climate has militated against a similar development in Turkey and has greatly
reduced its scope in Iran. Despite the small size of the Kurdish community in Soviet Armenia and Azerbayjan, the Soviet Union encouraged and publicized Kurdish cultural
activities in that country.

In Iraq, where there is a large Kurdish population, cultural activity (as opposed to
political activity) by the Kurds has always been permitted, although perhaps not partic-

ularly encouraged. Since the early twentieth century, a vigorous cultural movement has flourished in Iraq in the Kurdish dialect of Sulaymaniya, which is closely allied to the Mukri dialect of Persia.

Until his death in 1950, Haji Tawfiq Peramerd of Iraq was the most prominent literary figure in Kurdistan. A poet, storyteller, and journalist, he was a man of varied interests and catholic tastes, and his work embraced literature, history, and politics. In the course of a long literary career, Peramerd produced a great number of poems, stories, essays, and some translations. His masterly rendition of Ahmadi Khani's great epic *Mem u Zin* into the Sulaymaniyan idiom, now the acknowledged literary vehicle of southern Kurdistan, is regarded as his finest achievement.[97] He was a talented poet with a whimsical sense of humor that endeared him to all those who knew him. For many years, he was the editor of *Jin*, the outstanding literary magazine in Iraqi Kurdistan.[98]

The prolific and industrious Husayn Husni Mukriyani, whom Edmonds has called the Kurdish Caxton, published for many years the literary and historical magazine *Zari Kurmanji* in Arbil, Iraq. His works, complete with woodcuts, were printed on a small hand press.[99] Colonel Tawfiq Wahbi, for a long time a senator and cabinet minister in Iraq, was a distinguished Kurdish scholar who wrote on history, folklore, lexicography, and religion. During World War II, he was associated with *Akhbar al-Harb*, a magazine published by the British embassy in Baghdad. This publication, noted for its clear and expressive prose style, paid particular attention to the coining of new technical words in Kurdish.[100]

Allah Sulayman, known as Guran, was perhaps the most gifted of modern Kurdish poets in Iraq. His most important work is *Buhusht u Yadigar* (Paradise and Remembrance). The learned Dominican Kurdologist Father Thomas Bois compares Guran's ode "The Blood Red Rose" to Shelley's "Ode to the Skylark." One of the most notable Kurdish literary achievements in Iraq is a history of Kurdish literature written by 'Ala' al-Din Sajjadi. Bois describes this work as a "monument of learning and culture."[101]

The Kurdish literary movement in Syria is a product of special circumstances. This movement, which has been flourishing since the early 1920s, owes its existence as well as its impulse and flavor to the presence of a large number of Kurdish émigrés from Turkey. The Kurdish nationalist organization Khoybun (Independence), which has had its headquarters in Syria since 1927, has served as a nucleus and a rallying point for Kurdish literary as well as political activity. The Bedir Khan brothers, Sureya, Jaladet, and Kamuran, have been its leading spirits. In addition to playing leading roles in the Kurdish nationalist movement, all three were capable writers in several languages.

The emir Jaladet Bedir Khan, who was a pioneer in the Kurdish literary movement in Syria, devised a simple and adequate Latin alphabet for his native tongue. Through his two publications *Hawar* and *Ronahi*, he succeeded in inducing the Kurds of Syria to adopt this alphabet. Under his own name and under the pseudonym Herikol Azizan, he wrote numerous literary, lexicographical, and grammatical studies in Kurdish and French.

His brother Kamuran Bedir Khan, who was professor of Kurdish at the École des Langues Orientales in Paris, also had for many years a very prolific and varied literary output. He translated the Qur'an as well as the Gospels of Saint Luke and Saint John into Kurdish. He also reportedly worked on a French-Kurdish dictionary. However, as Bois points out, he is primarily a poet of delicate imagery with a delightful sense of humor.

The most eminent of all Kurdish poets in Syria is Jegerkhwin, who is said to have been trained to be a mulla (clergyman) but abandoned religion for literature. His poetry, which Bois describes as vibrant and patriotic, deals with social and political subjects.[102]

The most noted literary figures among the Soviet Kurds were Vesire Nadyri, Atame Teir, Jassime Jalil, and Ereb Shamilov. Poet and storyteller Vesire Nadyri's works speak of the eternal friendship between the Kurds, the Azerbayjanis, and the Armenians, and sing the praises of the *kolkhoz* (collective farm) and of the Soviet way of life. A number of his poems are addressed to the "Great Stalin." Both Atame Teir and Jassime Jalil were translators. The former translated Pushkin, Lermontov, Tolstoy, and Gorky into Kurdish. Ereb Shamilov, who wrote several books in Russian, is celebrated for his biography entitled *The Kurdish Shepherd,* which was also translated into Arabic. In essence, Soviet Kurdish literature is very much like the literatures of other Islamic peoples who have inhabited that region.[103]

Kurdish literary activity in Iran has not been very impressive, in part because of the official discouragement of such activities, but also because of the great attraction that Persian literature has always had for the Kurds. The most noted contemporary Kurdish poets in Iran are Heyman and Hezar, who during the brief existence of the Mahabad Republic (discussed in chapter 15) were patronized by the republic's founder and president Qadi Muhammad. Mohammad Mokri, an official of the Iranian Ministry of Education, published a collection of Kurdish songs with a Persian translation. Shaykh Ayat Allah Kurdistani published *A History of the Kurds* in Kurdistan in the late 1950s.[104]

2

The Social Organization of the Kurds

Tribal and Nontribal Elements

The Kurdish people, roughly speaking, may be said to fall into two major classes, the tribal and the nontribal. The former, usually nomadic or seminomadic, for the most part lead a pastoral existence and are noted for their martial qualities; the latter, who form the bulk of the settled population, are peasants.[1] Despite the fact that the nontribal Kurds in most cases outnumber the tribal Kurds, it is the latter who constitute the ruling class.

Claudius James Rich, the first modern writer to mention the differences between these two classes of Kurds, wrote in 1836:

> I had to-day confirmed by several of the best authorities, what I had long suspected, that the peasantry in Koordistan are a totally distinct race from the tribes, who seldom, if ever, cultivate the soil; while, on the other hand, the peasants are never soldiers. The Clannish Koords call themselves Sipah, or military Koords, in contradistinction to the peasant Koords; but the peasants have no other distinguishing name than Rayah or Keuylees, in this part of Koordistan. A tribesman once confessed to me that the clans conceived the peasants to be merely created for their use; and wretched indeed is the condition of the Koordish cultivators. It much resembles that of a Negro slave in the West Indies; and the worst of all is, I have never found it possible to make these Koordish masters ashamed of their cruelty to their dependents.[2]

This dichotomy led a number of writers to conclude that the tribal Kurds represented a wave of conquerors who swept down from the mountains and subjugated the older native population. Rich, the first to speculate on this problem, asked, "May not these be the aboriginal inhabitants of these countries, who had been conquered by the fierce tribes of the mountains?"[3] Research in the twentieth century has tended to confirm the validity of this observation. According to Minorsky, "The settled Kurds seem very often to represent the older population who were conquered by the *ashirat* soldiers or accepted this domination to secure protection against their neighbours."[4] Barth

27

sheds an interesting light on this question in his discussion of the subjugation of the *miskin* villagers by the Hamawand tribesmen around the turn of the century.[5]

This division of the Kurds into the dominant tribal *('ashirat)* group and the subject peasant *(rayat)* group prevails throughout most parts of Kurdistan.[6] In the Sulaymaniya area, among both the Jaf and the Bilbas tribesmen, the peasant class is known as *guran*.[7] Among the Suran, the Bahdinan, and the Hakari tribes, they are known as *kurmanj*,[8] while among the Hamawand they are known as *miskin*.[9]

Tribal Organization and Institutions

The Tribe, the Clan, and the Lineage

There seems to be a certain degree of confusion regarding the terms used to denote various Kurdish tribal units. This confusion stems in part from the fact that not all of these terms are in general use throughout Kurdistan and in part from the fact that they sometimes are used loosely and interchangeably by the Kurdish tribesmen themselves.[10] A few examples taken at random suffice to indicate the confusing nature of the terminology involved.

The Balik tribe of the Rawanduz region apply the terms *'ashirat, taifa,* and *tira* to conform to the usual anthropological classification of tribe, clan, and lineage,[11] respectively, whereas the comparable terms in use among the Sanjabi tribe of Persian Kurdistan are *il, tira,* and *taifa*.[12] The terms in use among the Oramar and the Rikan tribes living along the Turco-Iraqi frontier are *'ashirat, ojagh,* and *mala*,[13] whereas the terms found among the Jaf tribe of southern Iraqi Kurdistan are *'ashirat, tira,* and *hoz*.[14]

In view of the fact that tribal organization is basically similar throughout Kurdistan, notwithstanding local differences in terminology, the following discussion deals primarily with the tribal organization of the Jaf confederation of southern Iraqi Kurdistan. According to Barth, the Jaf *'ashirat* or tribe is divided into a number of *tiras* or clans, which in turn are subdivided into a number of *hoz*. The *tira* approximates a maximal lineage and is the basic political group and land-owning unit.[15] The *hoz*, however, represents a simple descent group or lineage, all of whose members are descendants in the male line from the same ancestor. Thus, all the members of the tribal group Hoz-i-Kaka Hama are descended from a man named Kaka Hama. However, name forms indicating descent from a given ancestor are not exclusively applied to a *hoz*. The Hoz-i-Jarweiz, the family or the house of Jarweiz, for example, is a *tira* because of its organization as a political group.[16]

Barth discusses the process by which a branch of a *tira* may split off and form a new group. The new offshoot, according to him, will continue to trace its descent from the parent group, but will maintain its separateness and independence. Such an offshoot, for example, is the Benajut group, a branch of the Shaykh Isma'ili *tira*. However, a group of related *tiras*, such as the Shatri, will continue to associate with one another on a footing of complete equality, a fact that emphasizes their common descent as "sons of one father." These *tiras* maintain a certain amount of political cooperation. When faced with important decisions such as war, the chieftains of the various *tiras* meet in council. Agreement is reached by discussion, but the council as a body has no formal powers.[17]

The Khel

The *khel* is a tribal unit organized for economic purposes. The *tira* holds grazing rights in common, but does not usually camp out as one unit. Rather, it divides itself into a number of camps, each of which is called a *khel.* The latter is normally a lineage segment and is held together by economic and lineage ties.[18] It is led by an elder who is informally elected and is granted authority because of his influence and prestige.

According to Barth, a *khel* usually consists of a number of households, varying between twenty-three and thirty, each occupying a separate tent. Cattle are herded in flocks of about five hundred head, and each flock is tended by a herdsman. Wealth varies greatly within a *khel,* some households owning as many as two thousand animals, others as few as fifty. In cases where one person does not own enough animals to constitute a normal herding unit, composite herds are formed along kinship lines, with fathers, brothers, and other relatives combining their livestock. Hired shepherds, laborers, and other individuals may form part of a *khel* without being members of the tribe. Poor relatives are oftentimes exploited for this purpose.[19]

The *khel* of southern Kurdistan appears to be similar to the *oba* of certain parts of central and northern Kurdistan.[20] According to Nikitine, the number of animals in an *oba* varies between five hundred and ten thousand. He adds that an *oba* consists of from eight to fifteen tents. In southern Kurdistan, the number of tents constituting an *oba* varies between fifteen and twenty, and the number of sheep owned by such a unit ranges from one thousand to two thousand head.[21]

Tribal Leadership

Each *tira* is headed by a *ra'is* or *agha,* an inherited position. The *ra'is* or the *agha* class represents the nobility of the *tiras.* However, a strong bond of kinship ties the chiefs to the members of their *tiras.* There are relatively few cases of intermarriage with the noble lineage segment of other *tiras.* Endogamy, based on the principle of orthocousin marriage, is the rule within each noble family. Needless to say, this practice helps to strengthen the chief's position within his own clan.[22] Exogamous marriages are rare, and when they take place, they are often between the chief and some wealthy "commoner" within the *tira* itself.

The leaders of the Jaf belong to the *begzada* or the "princely house."[23] Barth states that often they are also represented as forming an independent *tira* of their own, but in fact they may be more properly described as a family or *hoz.* The *begzada* are divided into three branches: the Kaykhosro Begi, the Bahram Begi, and the Welled Begi. The Kaykhosro Begi and the Bahram Begi are both seventh-generation descendants of Zahir Beg, but the Welled Begi are further removed. All *begzada* are now settled and live as absentee landowners. Their relationship to the nomadic sections of the Jaf is unclear and difficult to assess.[24]

The Jaf *begzada* have a peculiar institution known as *pyshtmala* (around the house). This is an important means of reinforcing the controlling power of the *begzada* over the various *tiras.* The *pyshtmala* is made up of men drawn from all the Jaf *tiras.* Their duties

3. A Yazidi *agha*. From the Jebel Sinjar, circa 1935. From *The Yezidis: A Study in Survival,* 1987. Kegan Paul: London and New York. Courtesy of Kegan Paul International.

include guarding the *beg* or paramount chieftain and performing various tasks in his house. Barth compares this institution to the Viking *hird* in form and function. The fact that members of the *pyshtmala* are drawn from all the *tira*s has made them more amenable to discipline and has been a safeguard against factionalism and feuds.[25]

Political Concepts and Practices

We possess a number of valuable accounts of Kurdish political concepts and practices, which, despite their fragmentary nature, shed considerable light on Kurdish political thinking. It should be pointed out, however, that the autonomous Kurdish political system never developed beyond the tribal stage. Those Kurdish leaders who succeeded in founding such systems followed an Islamic rather than a Kurdish pattern of political organization. As a result, tribal-based institutions, rather than state-based institutions, have come to be the Kurdish political institutions par excellence. The extension of various alien administrations (Turkish, Persian, Iraqi, Syrian, and Russian) into Kurdistan, coupled with the continuing process of detribalization, may result eventually in the complete elimination of Kurdish political institutions. Study of these institutions may, however, provide some indication of current and future political trends in Kurdistan.

The character of Kurdish tribal institutions is reflected in the deliberative bodies that decide and pass on important tribal affairs; in the elective principle, which often plays a decisive role in the succession of chieftains; and in the nature of relations between the members of the tribe and their chiefs. One of the fullest and most interesting accounts is Rich's description of the conduct of public affairs among the great Bilbas confederation: "In the tribes which form the Bulbass nation, every man, even of the meanest rank, has a voice in public affairs. You may be settling business with them, when on a sudden some common fellow will start up and say, 'I do not agree with it!' and this is enough to spoil the whole affair in a moment." [26]

By way of illustration, Rich told the story of a Bilbas tribesman who objected to arrangements made for the cessation of hostilities between his tribe and the Baban principality of Sulaymaniya. At a meeting attended by representatives of both parties, all of the other Bilbas tribesmen agreed that the Bilbas chieftain should proceed to Sulaymaniya to negotiate with the Baban prince, while the latter's brother stayed as hostage with the Bilbas tribe. However, the arrangements were changed to meet the dissenting tribesman's objection.[27] From this, it appears that the individual Bilbas tribesman enjoyed what amounted to a *liberum veto*.

Various writers have emphasized the importance of councils in Kurdish tribal affairs. The chief, according to Nikitine, is assisted by a council of elders. The council's function is the settlement of disputes and the administration of justice in accordance with tribal customary law.[28] It deals with such questions as war, the settlement of feuds, the restitution of stolen property, and the arbitration of disputes concerning the abduction of women or grazing and irrigation rights. One of the severest punishments imposed by these councils is banishment from the tribe.[29]

Barth mentions an interesting practice found among the Shatri clans of the Jaf confederation in connection with the holding of council meetings. According to him, the chiefs of the various clans (*tiras*) meet in the tent of a rich commoner and not in the tent of a chief, so that no one of them shall have an advantage over the others.[30]

The community's will, as expressed either by councils of elders or by the public as a whole, often plays a decisive role in determining the succession of tribal chieftains. Although it is usual for the eldest son to succeed his father, primogeniture is not a rigidly established rule among the Kurds. Rich described succession among the Bilbas as follows: "When a chief dies, he is succeeded by the best or the bravest of his family, with the common consent of his tribe. If his eldest son is incapable, the best of the brothers succeeds." [31]

The situation among the Jaf appears to be substantially the same. Rich wrote:

4. Kurdish chiefs. Myron Bement Smith Collection. Freer Gallery of Art and Arthur M. Sackler Gallery Archives, Smithsonian Institution, Washington, D.C.: Gift of Katharine Dennis Smith. Photographer: Antoin Sevruguin.

"When the chief dies if his son is young, he does not succeed, as the clan could never be governed by a stripling. In that case the vacant chieftainship is filled by the brother or the uncle of the deceased Bey."[32] Succession in the Hakari principality was determined by the tribal council. Members of the council resorted to an unusual method to dispose of an unfit candidate. According to Major E. B. Soane, a member of the British administration in Iraq after World War I,

> A curious custom is told of in connection with the succession to the Khanate. This was, and is, hereditary, but if the Khan be not considered equal to his exalted post, a meeting of important men is called. If after deliberation the Khan is deemed unworthy, a pair of shoes is placed before him, and he is expected to don them and quit the room, thereby consenting to the transfer of the succession to the next candidate. The deposed Khan's lands and property are not taken from him.[33]

In at least one region of Kurdistan, the chieftainship appears to have been an elective office in which the representatives of the whole people participated. According to Kamuran Bedir Khan, "In the political life of Kurdistan we have even seen a republic in the region of Shirnakh, where the chief was elected by the people."[34]

Numerous writers have commented on the relationship between the Kurds and their chieftains. Some have maintained that the Kurdish tribesmen display toward their chieftains a blind and unquestioning obedience, risking their lives at their leaders' bidding without asking any questions. In 1918, Soane reported encountering a group of Kurdish warriors returning from a bloody engagement in the course of which some fifty men had been incapacitated. When he asked about the cause of the conflict, no one in the whole group seemed to know. "The chief told us to fight Hama Beg's men, and we did," he was informed.[35]

The Kurds' devotion to their religious leaders or shaykhs is as great if not greater than their devotion to their secular leaders. However, the shaykh's role has assumed such great importance in modern times that I give it detailed treatment in a separate section of this chapter.

In discussing the relationship between the Kurds and their leaders in 1921, Major W. R. Hay, also of the British administration in Iraq, divided the Kurdish chieftains into "good *aghas*" and "bad *aghas*." The first, he said, have the interest of their tribesmen at heart and are true fathers to their people, whereas the second rule their followers with a heavy hand, exploiting and oppressing them whenever they have a chance to do so.[36]

Hay mentioned that chieftains in the remoter districts identify themselves more closely with their followers than do those located close to government centers.[37] The significance of this distinction lies in the fact that the regions lying near government centers are occupied mainly by nontribal Kurdish peasants, whereas the inhabitants of the remoter districts are tribally organized nomadic and sedentary Kurds. Damaluji, who discusses the same issues in the Bahdinan region, attributes the settled Kurds' docility and submissiveness to the fact that they are tied to the land, which is the source of their livelihood, and are thus unable to escape the heavy hand of the chieftain by moving to a different locality.[38] It is clear from Damaluji's text that he had in mind primarily those Kurds among whom tribal organization had been weakened.

Tribal Sentiment

One of the most striking features of Kurdish tribal life is the peculiar tenacity of Kurdish tribal sentiment.[39] On numerous occasions, it has proved even stronger than religious sentiment. Although this tendency at first glance may appear to be rather unusual for the Middle East, it actually is not as uncommon as it may seem.[40]

Before World War I, the Great Artoshi group of Kurdish nomads and the Tyari Christians, both of whom according to tradition are of common descent and occupied the left bank of the upper reaches of the Zab, often fought against the Nestorian Christians and Muslim Kurds who occupied the right bank of the same river. These two confederations were known as Baski-i-Chep (the Left Wing) and Bask-i-Rast (the Right Wing), respectively.[41] Earlier, at the time of the suppression of the Kurdish principalities, the Christian Armenian and the Muslim Kurdish highlanders of Sasun fought side by side against the Ottoman armies under Rashid Muhammad Pasha until they both were overwhelmed.[42]

Perhaps the most striking example of tribal sentiment transcending religious loyalties is provided by the Muslim-Christian federation of Hakari, which flourished during the early part of the nineteenth century.[43] In the Hakari emir's absence, the Nestorian patriarch administered the principality, sitting in judgment on Christians and Muslims alike, and even receiving the sultan's envoys. The latter point is of great importance, for it means that this was no mere local arrangement, but a fact known to and accepted by the highest authorities.

The Blood Feud

As in all tribal communities, the blood feud is widespread throughout Kurdistan. Its pattern and intensity vary from one place to another and are influenced by a number of factors. It is strongest in the more purely tribal areas and weakest in regions where, for various reasons, the process of detribalization is most advanced and the influence of the external administration is greatest.

There is no doubt that the kinship structure of the closely knit endogamous tribal community tends to promote the blood feud. The tribal group regards itself as a single unit and is so regarded by outsiders—a fact that engenders the idea of collective responsibility, with the consequent practice of retaliation against the offender or any member of his group by any member of the victim's group. According to Leach, "The motif of the blood feud may be summarized by the phrase that 'a man's wrong must be avenged by his kinsfolk and his descendants,' and we may note at once that a system of small patrilocal nearly endogamous groups is peculiarly suited to perpetuate antagonisms of this kind."[44]

Nikitine lists *tola* (vengeance) as one of the three things that dominate the Kurd's thinking and determine the pattern of his loyalties and behavior.[45] The commission of murder is the signal for the beginning of a blood feud in conflicts concerning such matters as theft of animals, water or grazing rights, and, most serious of all, questions of honor involving women.[46] According to Nikitine, who wrote about the Kurds of central Kurdistan, the victim's family acquires the right of retaliation against the murderer, who is banished from the tribe for a period of five years or more. At the end of this period, provided a settlement has been made, the murderer may return to the tribe, with the elders' approval and the chieftan's confirmation. The victim's family, however, retains its right of retaliation.[47]

The chiefs lose no time in taking effective measures to settle a conflict before it assumes serious proportions. Blood feuds involving the chiefs themselves, however, are much more difficult to settle.[48] *Fasl* (settlement of the blood feud) entails the payment of blood money, known in Kurdish simply as *khwin* (blood).[49] In addition to blood money, it is customary for the offender's family to present the aggrieved party with a horse and to give away a girl in marriage to a member of the victim's family in order to allay feelings of vengeance *(tola)* and to unite the two families involved.[50]

The settlement of a blood feud is entrusted either to a person of prestige in the community or to a council of chiefs or elders. According to Hay, such a tribal council limits itself merely to arbitrating the case. The government, however, invariably insists that the council's decisions shall be binding.[51] A blood feud often flares up again even though a settlement has been made. An example is the resurgence of the feud between Suto Agha of Horamar and Tato Agha of Rekan. Despite the fact that Suto Agha had taken the initiative in settling the feud by giving away his daughter in marriage to Tato Agha, a few years later he had Tato's son-in-law and the latter's brother treacherously murdered while they were staying with him as his guests.[52]

An important practice connected with the blood feud is the granting of asylum (*pana*) to the offender. A breach of asylum by the offender is viewed seriously, and those guilty of it are liable to retaliation by the person granting the asylum, usually a person of influence. The settlement of a breach of asylum entails payment of a certain amount of money known as *wushir* as compensation for the dishonor and injury done to the granter of asylum.[53]

Barth writes of "the absence or very weak development of blood feuding patterns in Southern Kurdistan."[54] According to him, what obtains in that area is a form of revenge rather than the institutionalized type of blood feud governed by ideas of retaliation and equality and based on the concept of collective responsibilitiy.[55] Barth contrasts this situation with that of the Rawanduz area, where the blood feud still prevails. He attributes this difference to the retention of tribal organization in the Rawanduz area and the weakening of it in southern Kurdistan by the feudal Baban administration based on nonlineage principles.[56]

The basis on which Barth predicates his conclusion is open to question. Barth himself admits that the material from which he drew his conclusion is "very incomplete."[57] Furthermore, it appears that he had in mind mostly the nontribal areas in the neighborhood of Sulaymaniya. His conclusion probably would not apply to the tribally organized, seminomadic segments of the great Jaf confederation in the southeastern part of this region or to the Pizhdar confederation in the northeastern part. Moreover, it is doubtful that Baban rule permanently weakened tribal organization in southern Kurdistan. It is known that after the disappearance of the Baban feudal state, the area was plunged into a state of great instability, as a result of which the various tribal elements reverted to old tribal ways. In fact, Barth himself points out that the Jaf tribes became very powerful, assimilating remnants of other tribes, whereas the Hamawand embarked on a career of lawlessness and brigandage.[58] Soane described the Jaf, one of the major tribes of southern Kurdistan, as follows in 1918:

> The Jaf tribe (commonly spoken of as the Jaf Muradi) is a lawless, wild, savage, quarrelsome tribe, which fights fiercely on occasion. So much bad blood exists among the various sub-tribes, however, that any concerted action is practically impossible for them. The whole tribe is riddled with blood feuds, the consummation of which occupies a large part of the tribal time.[59]

The far-reaching consequences of the blood feud, and the manner in which it affects not only the two parties involved and their adherents but also the community as a whole, are perhaps best illustrated by the celebrated feud between the families of Bawil Agha and 'Abd Allah Pasha, two noble families of Rawanduz. This feud, which began some time before the British occupation of Iraqi Kurdistan, continued to smolder for a long time. In the early years of the British occupation, it seriously interfered with the administration of the region, creating difficulties of a very grave nature.

The appointment of Isma'il Beg, the grandson of 'Abd Allah Pasha, as governor of Rawanduz led the family of Bawil Agha to ally itself with the disaffected Surchi tribesmen, who eventually rose in rebellion and succeeded in driving out the British temporarily from most of the Rawanduz region.[60] We learn from A. M. Hamilton, an engineer in Iraq, that this feud was of general concern when he was in charge of building the great Rawanduz road in the late 1920s.

Isma'il Beg was eventually ambushed and killed while on his way to Rawanduz.[61] Another victim of the feud, according to Leach, was a nephew of Hamid Amin Agha of Dergala, related to both feuding families, who was killed in 1937. The last in the sequence of murders reported by Leach occurred in 1938.[62]

A significant aspect of this feud is the political character it has assumed with the passage of time. Leach states: "the affair has become entangled with all sorts of wider issues—Kurdish nationalism in particular. Accusations of being pro-British, or pro-Arab, or anti-Kurd were levelled at all and sundry, and in the limited time available I had no chance to unravel all the complex of personal antagonisms and rival interests involved."[63] In 1954, in a book written by a Kurdish writer, the feud was referred to in the course of a highly partisan discussion of Isma'il Beg's political activities.[64]

It may be fitting here to consider the notions of reprisal and revenge prevalent among certain Kurdish tribes. According to R. Thurnwald, "Reprisals also are executed on animals and even on inanimate objects such as tools and weapons."[65] For example, in 1853, Sir Austen Henry Layard gave an eyewitness account of a Yazidi snake-charmer who angrily bit off the head of a snake that had drawn blood from his seven-year-old son as the child was assisting him in his performance.[66] Fraser related the story of Muhammad Pasha of Rawanduz putting wolves to death, after inflicting lingering tortures, in revenge for killing a man.[67]

Although the existence of these practices among the Kurds on the individual level is interesting in itself, the manner in which such practices find expression on the collective level, when political issues are involved, is particularly significant. In this connection, an episode reported by Nikitine is revealing. A punitive Ottoman force, led by General Fadil Pasha against Shaykh 'Abd al-Salam of Barzan, was ambushed by the shaykh's *murids* (disciples), and most of its members were either killed or captured. Of the two cannons used by the Ottomans against the tribesmen, only one had functioned properly; the other had exploded at the initial stages of the battle and lay disabled and silent. After their victory, the *murids* swarmed around the damaged cannon, embracing it and calling it a true believer and a martyr *(shahid)* for having refused to make war against the shaykh. The other cannon, which was regarded as an infidel, was hurled into the valley and dashed to pieces in punishment. The crew of the "true-believing" gun were treated generously, given presents, and set free, but the crew of the "infidel" gun were treated rudely and kept as prisoners.[68]

Status

The concept of "office" in the Kurdish tribal system, as in all systems based on traditional authority, is not well developed. As a consequence, status assumes an overriding importance. I shall not dwell on the sociological nature of status here except to say that it derives from a number of sources such as descent, wealth, and possession of sacred powers. Status among the Kurds is emphasized daily in a number of ways. It is shown, for example, in the behavior of persons of equal or disparate status toward each other, such as in the etiquette of greeting and manner of address, and in the elaborate seating arrangements in chieftains' guest houses and other public meeting places.

An interesting custom prevalent in Kurdistan clearly shows Kurdish scrupulousness in stressing equality of status between persons of equal rank. We learn from Damaluji that when the two Naqshbandi leaders, Shaykh 'Abd al-Salam of Barzan and Shaykh Baha al-Din of Bamirni, met in 'Amadiya in 1905, they kissed each other's hands. This, he adds, is in accordance with custom.[69] The American missionary Justin Perkins gave a graphic description of this custom, which he witnessed near Rawanduz around 1850: "Of the simple, primitive manners which we observed among the Kurds on our way, their style of mutual salutation arrested our attention. When two men meet, they grasp each other's right hand, which they simultaneously raise, and each kisses the hand of the other."[70]

The Kurds are very sensitive with regard to precedence as an indication of status. According to Barth, "In Kurdish culture, as in most other cultures, the first in a sequence, and in fact precedence in general, is regarded as symbolic of status."[71] Indeed, history provides numerous instances of the importance the Kurds attach to precedence. We learn from the Kurdish historian Sharaf Khan of a dispute regarding precedence among Kurdish princes at the court of Iskander Pasha, the Ottoman viceroy at Van. Iskander Pasha appears to have regarded the matter so seriously that he referred it to the sultan Sulayman the Magnificent, who issued an imperial decree establishing the order of precedence among the princes concerned.[72] Similarly, Rich stated that the Mizuri chieftains enjoyed the privilege of hereditary precedence over all other chieftains at the court of the princes of Bahdinan.[73]

The deeply ingrained Kurdish concern for precedence, coupled with their respect for tradition, is demonstrated by the deference shown to members of princely houses that no longer retain the predominant position they once enjoyed. Speaking of the various leading families among the Herki, Nikitine says: "The most ancient family is that of Mala Shabe Agha at Shiwa Herki. It no longer possesses influence or wealth, but the prestige which it had formerly won, still remains; in all the assemblies of the Herki Kurds the first place is reserved for it."[74]

A conversation between British political officer Captain Woolley and Kurdish chieftain 'Abd al-Rahman Agha Khartawi in 1919, at the time when there was talk of establishing a Kurdish kingdom and the British were seeking likely candidates for king, is illuminating. After discussing the merits of the various Kurdish ruling houses, 'Abd al-Rahman Agha stated that apart from the family of Bedir Khan, the Kurdish chieftains were "too like the teeth of a horse, all on a dead level. One or the other may have the advantage in point of wealth or fighting power, but not in name nor in historical antecedents." [75] It should be pointed out that this tribal chieftain came from Bohtan, the region of the Bedir Khanids.

The Kurds' Everyday Life

Transhumance

The seasonal migrations of the nomadic and seminomadic tribes in Kurdistan are of the so-called vertical Persian type. At the end of spring, the tribes leave the hot plains and valleys and move to their summer camping grounds in various upland mountain areas *(zozan),*[76] where they spend the summer pasturing their flocks. They leave these upland pastures in the autumn and return to their winter camping grounds in the warmer lowlands.

Although the various tribes have their known summer and winter camping grounds, which generally are not disputed by other tribes, conflicts regarding camping grounds sometimes arise. A powerful tribe usually has the choice of the best summer and winter camping grounds because it is capable of maintaining its right.[77] Likewise, the right of passage to and from the mountains is usually established, but the seasonal migration is often an occasion for sharp clashes between the nomads and the settled tribes through whose lands they pass.[78] Clashes sometimes take place among various nomad tribes also.[79] These upland pastures are sometimes not far from a given tribe's winter camping grounds. Most of the region located between the Turco-Iraqi frontier and Lake Van is known collectively as Zozan. These upland pastures have an abundant water supply, such as the Merwanen and the Farashin uplands, for the entire area is a great watershed.[80]

After World War I, the seasonal migrations of many nomad tribes accustomed to spending the summer in Turkey and the winter in Iraq were completely interrupted because of the interposition of the Turco-Iraqi frontier in the path of their migrations. The cessation of nomad traffic between Turkey and Iraq originally resulted from the unfriendly relations existing between the two countries. However, the situation has continued unchanged even after the improvement of these relations, perhaps because of the growth of Kurdish nationalism in Iraqi Kurdistan.

Dwellings

Kurdish dwellings, other than those in urban centers, fall into two classes, those of the settled population and those of the nomads or seminomads. The settled populations live in small houses built of stone and mud, with roofs made of poplar beams and branches plastered over with mud. These houses are usually built on a slope, the flat rooftop of one house forming a front terrace for the house above it.[81] In certain parts of

5. A Kurdish village in Adiyaman (Turkey) showing typical Kurdish flat-roofed dwellings. Courtesy of Burhan Elturan.

Kurdistan, particularly in the Dersim highlands[82] and in parts of the Hakari highlands,[83] houses are reported to be built of stone and plaster and are fairly sturdy.

The nomads live in black tents made of goats' hair. Few Kurds live all year round in these tents. The majority may be termed seminomads who live in houses during the winter and in tents during the summer. In the summer months, many Kurds live in a summer dwelling known as *chardaq,*[84] which is a sort of open bower made of beams of wood covered over with branches.

Food

The Kurds' diet consists primarily of grain and milk products. The latter include cheese, various kinds of curdled milk (such as *du, mast,* and *mastao*), and clarified butter.[85] Lentil, barley, millet, maize, cracked wheat *(burghul),* and rice are the usual cereals consumed by the Kurds. Raisins form an important part of the Kurdish diet, comparable as a staple food to dates among the Arabs. According to Hay, staple foods among the Kurds consist of wheat bread, raisins, vegetables, curdled milk *(mast),* and *burghul.*[86] Barley bread is also widely consumed, especially among the Yazidis. In certain parts of Kurdistan, in out-of-the-way mountain regions where good farming land is scarce, acorns are ground and used as flour for bread, especially in times of scarcity.[87] Fruits and vegetables are eaten when available. A number of writers mention onions as an important item in the Kurdish diet.[88] Honey and manna are favorite foods. In recent years, tea has become an important commodity in Kurdistan.

6. An underground dwelling in the village of Mox in the province of Mush (Turkey). Courtesy of Burhan Elturan.

Meat is rarely eaten except by the wealthier Kurds.[89] Lamb is preferred, but goat's meat, beef, and poultry are also consumed. The Kurds eagerly seek game, such as gazelle in the plains and ibex and mountain sheep in the hill regions, and game birds, such as duck, partridge, quail, and sand grouse.[90] Many areas in Kurdistan abound with wild boar. Because Muslims, Yazidis, and Ahli Haqq are forbidden by their religion to eat pork, the presumption is that the Kurds do not eat this food. However, various reports indicate that members of all three groups occasionally violate this prohibition.[91]

The Kurd is reputed to be frugal in his eating habits.[92] Hay mentioned that in the Arbil region the Kurds he observed ate only two meals a day, at noon and in the evening—except for the wealthier Kurds, who also ate in the morning.[93] However, a Kurdish writer, discussing the eating habits of the Kurds of Bohtan, maintained in the early 1930s that they partook of six meals a day, the first one early in the morning and the last at bedtime, and that city-dwellers ate an additional meal.[94]

Clothing

Kurdish dress differs considerably from one part of Kurdistan to another.[95] This difference is reflected in the turban, the usual headdress for the majority of the Kurds. The Hakari and Mukri Kurds wear a large silk or cotton kerchief, with fringes, around a peaked cap topped by a tassel, so that the fringes fall over the eyes.[96] A very common type of turban found throughout central and southern Kurdistan consists of a silk kerchief wound around a skullcap.[97] Some Kurdish tribes adopt a headdress that bears little or no resemblance to the turban. The Jibranlis of northern Kurdistan wear a foot-long white felt hat, resembling a busby, around which a small piece of silk is tied,[98] whereas the Shikak wear a wool knit cap or hood surmounted by a pompom.[99] These are but a few examples of the Kurdish headdress. Although all Kurdish turbans may look alike to the casual observer, a Kurd can easily tell the tribe and the locality from which a person comes by the manner in which his turban is tied.[100]

The northern Kurds of the Armenian plateau, who are noted horsemen, wear tight-fitting jodhpurlike trousers.[101] Farther south, in central and southern Kurdistan, the usual type of trousers is the *shulwar*, bagging above the knees and narrowing at the ankles.[102] Here, too, particularly in the Bahdinan area and in certain parts of the Rawanduz region, the Kurds wear bell-mouthed trousers called *rang*, which are similar to those worn by sailors.[103]

Another item of Kurdish dress that shows considerable variety is the waistband or sash that the men wrap around their middles. Some of these sashes are several yards long and are intricately wound. Daggers, revolvers, and other things are often stuck into their ample folds.[104]

The long white sleeves of the Kurdish shirt are another peculiarity of Kurdish dress. The wearer ties the ends behind his back when working, eating, washing, or fighting.[105] The Kurds wear various types of jackets, including the sleeveless felt jacket popular throughout southern Kurdistan and the Zouavee-like jacket called *salta*.[106] In cold weather, they wear a thick felt overcoat.

Kurdish shoes are generally shaped to the foot, with upturned toes and no heels. They are usually made of buffalo hide. Shoes worn by the Kurds include the crimson kind known as *zergul* and the *kalik*, a buff-colored shoe with silk embroidery or woolen tufts. Some kinds have felt soles and are used for mountain climbing. High riding boots are worn by the northern Kurds of the Armenian plateau and by the Diza'i of the Arbil plain.[107] The Persian *giwah*, made of closely knit cotton or silk, with a hard sole, is also much in use. Knee-high woolen socks are worn at Ranya, at 'Aqra, and in the Rawanduz-Hakari region. They are usually held in place by woolen strings with pompoms.

In the regions where Kurds and Arabs meet, such as in southern Kurdistan and upper Jazira, south of the Karaja Dagh and the Tur 'Abdin, the Kurds adopt the Arabs' flowing robes, some of them even discarding the Kurdish turban for the Arab *kufiya* and *iqal*.[108]

The Status of Women

Most writers seem to agree that Kurdish women enjoy a remarkable degree of freedom in comparison with many Arab women, which is evident in a variety of ways. The Kurdish woman, unlike many Muslim women, is not secluded and does not wear the veil. She mingles freely with men and displays none of the timidity or coyness of women accustomed to seclusion.[109] During feasts, weddings, and other celebrations, Kurdish men and women dance together.[110] Soane observed that this is unusual among Islamic people, who as a rule are conservative in such matters. He pointed out that in this respect the Kurds are more like the people of eastern Europe than the people of the Middle East.[111] It is not unusual for the Kurdish woman, acting as the head of her household in her husband's absence, to receive men as guests.[112] This freedom is rarely abused. The

7. Kurdish woman. Myron Bement Smith Collection. Freer Gallery of Art and
Arthur M. Sackler Gallery Archives, Smithsonian Institution, Washington,
D.C.: Gift of Katharine Dennis Smith. Photographer: Antoin Sevruguin.

Kurdish woman is chaste. Prostitution is unknown among the Kurds; in fact, many writers have noted that there is no word for "prostitute" in the Kurdish language.[113] In the severely puritanical atmosphere of Kurdistan, death is the usual punishment for any
breach of the moral code.[114]

The Kurdish woman is the mistress of her home. Her influence in the family circle is
considerable, and her counsel is heeded and respected.[115] According to Hay, "Most chiefs
are to a greater or less extent under the thumb of their womenfolk, who, I think, exercise
a great deal of influence for good and do much to prevent their husbands from making
fools of themselves."[116]

8. A Kurd from the Hawraman area in native dress. Only the members of one Christian family in Kurdistan continue to make the type of handwoven pants worn by this Kurd. Photographer unknown/Courtesy of Susan Meiselas, *Kurdistan: In the Shadow of History.*

Kurdish women among both the nomadic and the sedentary tribes perform many arduous tasks.[117] However, as Soane pointed out, they are not mere drudges who do all the work while their husbands spend their time in idleness. There is a remarkable division of labor between men and women. The men are usually busy in the fields, tending the flocks, tilling the land, taking care of the fruit trees or the tobacco patch, or carrying the produce to the neighboring markets, while the women are engaged in drying fruits and tobacco, weaving carpets, and performing various household duties.[118] Barth confirms this view:

The household is economically independent, and consists typically of one elementary family: husband, wife, and their children. Among these, the economic roles are distributed along the same lines that will be familiar from rural Europe. It should be unnecessary to enumerate these in detail. The male finds most of his work in the fields; his is also the privilege of looking after the horse. The other animals are tended by the women, who do the milking and preparing of food, and other household duties, including mud plastering of the house interior every fall. The roof on the other hand is kept in repair by the man. In the busy season the women also assist in the fields, especially during the grain harvest and in tobacco picking.[119]

Many Kurdish women are fine riders and excellent marksmen. Among the more warlike tribes they often fight with great bravery alongside their men.[120]

Women have often attained positions of great power and influence in Kurdistan, some of them even being recognized as chiefs of their tribes.[121] A brief discussion of a number of Kurdish women who have attained positions of great authority among their people gives some idea of their status in Kurdish society.

According to Cuinet, who was writing in the late nineteenth century, Halima Khanim of Hakari was the sovereign ruler of Bash Kals until she was compelled to surrender the town to the Ottoman authorities after their suppression of the Bedir Khan rebellion in 1845.[122] Around 1909, Fatma, a young Kurdish woman of thirty-six, became chief of the Ezdinan tribe after the death of her second husband, who had succeeded his brother (Fatma's first husband) as hereditary ruler of the tribe upon the latter's death; she was known throughout the tribe as *kralitsa* (the queen).[123] Maryam Khanim, of the famous family of the shaykhs of Nehri, displayed real qualities of leadership at a particularly critical period during World War I. It was with her that the advancing Russian army of the Caucasus negotiated regarding its passage through the tribal territories controlled by her family. Nikitine, who was a political advisor attached to the Russian army, pays high tribute to her dignity and wisdom, and testifies to her authority over her followers.[124]

For many years, Adila Khanim, wife of Othman Pasha Jaf, was the real power in control of Jaf affairs. Both during her husband's lifetime, when she acted as his counselor and representative, and after his death, when she assumed responsibility in her own right, she wielded great influence in the Shahrizur plain and the neighboring Turco-Persian frontier regions. It was mainly owing to her sound judgment that the commercial life of Halabja was revived and a semblance of law and order introduced into the distracted province.[125] Hafsa Khan, cousin and sister-in-law of Shaykh Mahmud, was another great lady of southern Kurdistan. It is reported that her initiative in saving the lives of a number of British prisoners during Shaykh Mahmud's rebellion was responsible for the Kurdish leader's death sentence being commuted and later for his being granted a reprieve.[126]

Finally, there is the Yazidi princess Mayan Khatun, a remarkable woman of great energy and ability, who has been the most influential person among the Yazidis for the past half century. She shared in the management of Yazidi affairs with her husband, 'Ali Beg, the amir of the Yazidis, until his murder in 1913. Her influence and prestige continued undiminished during the lifetime of her son, Sa'id Beg, whom she completely overshadowed, and of her grandson, Tahsin Beg, whose guardianship she assumed after his father's death in 1949. According to Damaluji, this adroit and resourceful woman has been the most feared and respected figure among the Yazidis.[127]

Marriage

Marriage among the Kurds is governed by Muslim law and practice and by local Kurdish custom. Although as Muslims the male Kurds are permitted to marry four wives, only tribal chieftains and some wealthy landowners are able to do so; the average Kurd is monogamous.[128] As a result of the freedom of movement enjoyed by the Kurdish woman, who goes unveiled and mingles freely with men, marriage often is the result of love rather than merely a family arrangement.[129] Generally speaking, the Kurd is an affectionate and devoted family man. Divorce, like polygyny, is rare among the Kurds as a whole and is more frequent among the wealthier class.[130]

When a Kurdish man wishes to marry, he sends an elderly male relative or friend, usually a person of prestige, to ask for the hand of the girl of his choice. His representative discusses the matter with the girl's father, extols the prospective groom's merits, and fixes the brideprice.[131] The brideprice is a certain sum of money that the bridegroom pays to the bride's father or guardian. Several writers imply that the brideprice is retained by the bride's father or guardian.[132] According to Kamuran Bedir Khan, however, this money is the marriage dowry and is withheld for a certain period by the bride's family as a guarantee of the husband's good conduct and is usually given to him after a number of years.[133] Damaluji uses the Islamic term *sadaq* for this sum of money, but does not specify who retains it.[134] In addition to the brideprice, it is customary for the bridegroom to present the bride and her father or both of her parents with certain gifts. Hay mentioned that a certain sum of money would be settled on the bride in the case of divorce.[135]

The marriage ceremony consists of a simple reading of the pertinent Muslim formula by a mulla (clergyman). Weddings are important occasions for feasting and celebrations in which the whole community participates. A custom falling into disuse entails posting the *brazava* (best man) at the door of the nuptial chamber and having him fire a shot announcing the consummation of the marriage.[136] According to Nikitine, this shot is fired by the husband himself.[137] A matron, the *berburi,* who serves as companion to the bride, is charged with showing the "tokens of virginity" to the parents and friends of the married couple.[138]

Orthocousin marriage, especially to the daughter of a paternal uncle, is considered to be the ideal marriage among the Kurds,[139] particularly in tribally organized communities where the patrilineal system underlies the social structure. This pattern of marriage, which is connected with the feud and with political power in general,[140] provides certain economic and political advantages to both parties. The nephew pays little or no brideprice to his uncle, and the latter profits from the political support of a colineage male, a factor of great importance in the power alignments that develop during a feud.[141] Although orthocousin marriage is a practice common to Islamic societies throughout the world,[142] its prevalence among the Kurds does not necessarily reflect an Islamic origin.[143]

A type of marriage known as *zhin-ba-zhin* (woman for woman), in which two men marry each other's sisters, is frequently encountered among the Kurds. It is normal in such cases for the parties concerned to dispense with the brideprice, an arrangement that is financially advantageous to both men.[144] Endogamous marriages are more prevalent in tribally organized communities, as already mentioned, whereas exogamous marriages are much more common among detribalized sedentary populations in both urban and rural areas.

Marriage among the Kurds is governed by Shafi'i Muslim law. The father has full authority to give away his virgin daughter in marriage without her consent, whether or not she has attained her majority. It is, however, considered commendable for him to seek her consent. According to Shafi'i law, a marriage contract is valid only if concluded between the bridegroom and the bride's guardian *(wali)*. In case of the father's death, the guardianship passes to the nearest male agnatic relative; her grandfather, if living, takes precedence over her brother. It should be pointed out that only the girl's father and grandfather have the authority to give her away in marriage, and for this reason they are known as her "coercive guardian" *(wali mujbir)*.[145]

However, local custom sometimes interferes with the father's or guardian's authority as defined by religious law. In fact, the interference often is so effective that the legal provisions not only are drastically modified, but sometimes are completely held in abeyance. For example, in the Barzan region, according to Jiyawuk, marriage takes place when two persons desirous of matrimony go before the shaykh of Barzan and confess their love. The shaykh then sends them to a mulla, who performs the marriage ceremony "whether or not the father or the guardian approves." Jiyawuk, however, adds that marriage in most cases takes place with the guardian's approval.[146]

Abduction provides further instances in which the father's or other guardian's authority is circumvented. This circumvention is sometimes achieved by invoking another legally valid provision that has the effect of nullifying the guardian's authority. According to Damaluji, although abduction is not countenanced in some parts of Kurdistan, it is widespread throughout most of the area.[147] He points out that it is usually the result of mutual love and connivance on the part of the couple involved, coercion being rare.

According to Damaluji, the usual practice is for the abductor to take the woman a distance of at least two *marhalas* (states), where the couple is married. In accordance with Shafi'i law, the father's authority as marriage guardian ceases to be effective beyond this distance. Peace is usually established with the girl's family through the mediation of notables after the payment of the *sadaq* or bridal gift. In addition to the *sadaq*, the man pays a certain amount of money called *haqq kriti* as compensation for the disgrace or dishonor resulting from the abduction. Peace among the two parties is sometimes impossible to establish when social equality *(kifa'a)* does not exist, and large-scale violence may ensue.[148]

The abduction of married women, which is rare, is regarded as extremely disgraceful.[149] Damaluji tells of an interesting practice in this connection. In order to avoid the stigma of adultery, recourse is sometimes made to a legal subterfuge, through which divorce from the first husband and marriage to the second is accomplished with the aid of certain venal mullas. The mulla asks the woman to abjure Islam and embrace Christianity or Judaism, whereupon she is regarded as being automatically divorced from her husband by reason of her apostasy. On the next day, the mulla calls upon her to re-embrace Islam, after which she and her second husband are properly married.[150] In the region of Ushnu, according to Nikitine, when a married woman or a girl is abducted, the abductor is obliged to pay her husband or father a sum of money known as *déwitané,* a word derived from *déwit,* meaning "inkhorn."[151]

Childbirth

When a baby is to be born, the women of the neighborhood, in particular the elderly women, come to assist, acting as midwives during the delivery.[152] According to Barth, the mother and the newly born baby, especially if it is a boy, are guarded for seven days and nights from a certain evil spirit called the *shaoa.* The *shaoa* is believed to be an old childless woman who is envious of the birth of children, baby boys in particular. In order to protect the baby boy from the *shaoa,* a knife, a large needle, or an onion leaf is placed in his crib. Although it is believed that the *shaoa* does not concern herself as much about female infants, a knife or an onion leaf is often used in the case of girls as well.[153]

According to Nikitine, who wrote about central Kurdistan, a newborn baby boy is guarded for the first six days by the attending women and relatives. The vigil is especially important at night against the evil spirit called *shesheh,* a name that Nikitine says is derived from the Kurdish word *shesh* (six). It is believed that the *shesheh* seeks to kill the newborn baby and his mother, so fire and light are used to exorcise the evil spirit. During these six days, a piece of cloth blessed by a noted shaykh is placed in the house to ward off the evil.[154]

Boys are circumcised any time before the age of puberty. The ceremony usually is performed by a barber, often on more than three boys at a time. It is customary that the wealthiest father pays all the expenses.[155] Some Kurds also practice the circumcision of females *(khafd).*[156]

The Shaykhs

The increasingly important role the shaykhs have come to play in the social and political life of Kurdistan calls for a discussion of their place in Kurdish society. Even a cursory glance at Kurdish history reveals that shaykh leadership has been the most consistently successful type of leadership among the Kurds for more than one hundred years, especially since the disappearance of the last autonomous Kurdish principality. Moreover, an understanding of the shaykh's personality and the nature of shaykhship *(mashyakha)* throws considerable light on the Kurdish character. Special attention is given here to the shaykh as a religious and political leader.

The Origins and Emergence of the Shaykhs

The early history of the founders of the shaykhly families of Kurdistan shows them to be men of remarkable qualities. However dissimilar they may have been as individuals, their character, temperament, and energy set them apart from the majority of their contemporaries. It is perhaps this similarity that accounts for a certain pattern that is discernible in their emergence as religious and political leaders.

In the mid-1930s, Pierre Rondot traced the history of a number of shaykhly families and determined the salient features of this pattern. According to his findings, these families are usually outsiders who settle in a certain locality, gather adherents, establish a reputation for piety, and contract matrimonial alliances with powerful families.[157] The numerous gifts they receive from their followers enable them to amass considerable wealth and property, thus further enhancing their power and influence.[158] Rondot's conclusions confirm the results obtained by other writers who have studied various individual shaykhly families.

Almost without exception, the founder of the shaykhly line is an outsider. He is neither a member of the tribe nor a native of the locality where he first attains fame. According to Rondot, this migratory tendency, which is such a recurrent phenomenon in the shaykhs' early history, proves the truth of the saying, "No Prophet has honor in his own country."[159] The following examples indicate how common this tendency is among the great as well as the minor shaykhly families.

The shaykhs of Nehri in the Shamdinan district of Turkey claim descent from Shaykh 'Abd al-'Aziz, son of Shaykh 'Abd al-Qadir al-Gaylani of Baghdad,[160] whereas the shaykhs of Barzinja in the Sulaymaniya district of Iraq trace their ancestry to two brothers who came to Kurdistan from Persia about six centuries ago.[161] Among the lesser shaykhly families, the shaykhs of Khalan and Zhinu-i-Shaykh of the Rawanduz district of Iraq are descended from a shaykh who came from the Lahijan district of Persia.[162] The shaykhs of Palu in Turkey trace their descent to an ancestor originally from the Sulaymaniya region.[163]

One of the first things a shaykh does after settling in a new locality is to establish a reputation for piety and good deeds. The constant praying, fasting, and humility of these devout men tend to greatly impress the Kurdish mountaineer, who is inured to lawlessness and lusty living.[164] According to an observer who lived for many years among the Kurds, "Asceticism sometimes adds still more to the reputation of a sheik. One sheik was reputed to have fasted forty days for nine successive years, subsisting each day on one fig and a little water."[165]

The founders of the shaykhly family of Khalan and Zhinu-i-Shaykh established a hospice for the succor of travelers overcome by the intense cold in the mountain pass leading to Khalan.[166] "In this way," according to Hay, "they acquired a wide reputation for piety and good works."[167]

The shaykhs frequently use their good offices for the amicable settlement of disputes. Rich gave an interesting example in connection with the struggle for power among members of the Baban family of Sulaymaniya.

When Mahmood Pasha finally determined on submitting to the Turks a short time ago, he went to Shaykh Khaled, the great saint of Sulimania, accompanied by his uncle, Abdullah Pasha, and his two brothers, Osman and Suliman. These three swore allegiance to Mahmood; and, as they foresaw that the Prince of Kermanshah was likely to attempt gaining over one of them, to set him up against the Pasha and the Turkish interest, they took an oath on the sword and the Koran and by their divorce,[168] that whatever letters might come to either of them from Persia or Turkey, they should open them at Shaykh Khaled's house, and in the presence of the whole party who then made the agreement.[169]

The gathering of adherents is another activity that the shaykh pursues with determination and singleness of purpose in his new domicile. More often than not, the prospective adherents are tribeless persons in need of protection. The Barzan family of shaykhs provides perhaps the most striking example of the protection afforded by the shaykhs to the tribeless peasantry. Their rise to power is closely associated with their role as champions of the cause of the Zibar peasantry against the unjust exactions of the *agha*s of the region. As a result of a series of bloody wars waged against these *agha*s, the Barzani became virtual masters of the entire Zibar region.[170] Even in more recent times, according to Barth, many of the followers of the Barzani shaykhs are tribeless persons of the *miskin* class.[171]

The shaykh, however, often counts powerful persons among his adherents. Rich stated that Mahmud Pasha and most of the prominent members of the Baban family were at one time among the followers of Shaykh Khalid al-Naqshbandi.[172] The great influence that Shaykh 'Ubayd Allah had over Kurds of all classes was made abundantly clear during his invasion of Persia. Great chieftains, with thousands of their followers, placed themselves under his command. Hamza Agha, chief of the powerful Mangur tribe, when hard pressed at one point during the fighting, sent a letter to Shaykh 'Ubayd Allah begging for men and rifles. He began the letter by addressing the shaykh as "Your Highness" and closed it with the plea, "I trust you will not forget me in your prayers."[173]

The matrimonial alliances that the shaykh forms upon settling in a new locality are extremely important because of the prestige and powerful connections they may give him. These marriages are of the same nature as all royal and aristocratic alliances, which are often based on power considerations.

The first matrimonial ties that the shaykh establishes are usually with the village headman or with a minor tribal chieftan.[174] Later, as the shaykhly family gains in power and prestige, it seeks to ally itself through marriage with the more exalted families. When the latter accept the family as equals, powerful alliances are formed. In this manner, two of the greatest and most revered religious families of Kurdistan, the Shamdinan and the Barzinja shaykhly families, established matrimonial ties with the celebrated Bahdinan princes of 'Amadiya.[175] An interesting account of the negotiation and conclusion of such a marriage was given by Hay, whom Shaykh Muhammad Agha of Walash[176] requested to be a member of the deputation that he sent to ask for the hand of the sister of Shaykh 'Ubayd Allah of Khalan and Zhinu-i-Shaykh.[177]

The political importance of these matrimonial alliances cannot be overestimated.

Through the wise and skillful use of such marriages, Shaykh Saʿid Barzinja was able to check the power of the turbulent Hamawand tribe and ultimately to dominate it. According to Soane,

> Subsequent to the events of 1881, when the Hamavends so nearly succeeded in taking Sulaimania and destroying the family [of the Barzinja Shaykhs], Shaykh Saʿid realized the importance of the tribe and its possible use as a weapon. In order to gain control over it, he, by a series of judicious marriages, bound it to him. . . . This policy succeeded so well that in 1908 the tribe found itself unable to disobey the shaikhs, when ordered to declare itself in rebellion.[178]

In 1944, when the shaykhs of Barzan were almost in a state of open rebellion against the Iraqi government, they concluded a marriage alliance with the Zibar *aghas*, for generations their rivals and bitter enemies. As a result of this astute move, their power, according to Longrigg, was "redoubled."[179]

One of the most widely accepted truisms is that wealth is a form of power. In a primitive environment such as that of the Kurds, where power underlies the whole fabric of society and permeates the people's activities, wealth is a great motivating force, and it looms very large in the calculations of a power-conscious individual. Consequently, the acquisition of wealth becomes one of the chief preoccupations of a shaykh upon settling in a new community.

The possession of wealth enables the shaykh to attract and hold his adherents, to feed and arm his retainers, and to take care of the numerous suppliants who flock to his hospice seeking aid and protection. The shaykh's wealth is derived mainly from gifts showered upon him by his followers, great and small. It is customary, although it is not obligatory, for a follower who visits a shaykh to offer him a small present.[180] However, the great chiefs and princes are the principal sources of these gifts.

According to Barth, the wealth of the Barzinja shaykhs may be traced to gifts of land and villages received primarily from the Baban family.[181] He goes into some detail regarding the growth of this wealth and the various means employed in its acquisition:

> From the modest beginning in Baban times, the family's economic power was progressively enhanced. The possibilities inherent in the Ottoman practices of land registration seem to have been utilized. After closer relations had been established with the Sultan, the Shaikhs were able to gain control over numerous villages by buying the land at very low rates from the government. A major source of revenue that made this type of transaction possible was the ownership of the Bazaar (Market district) of Suleimani (even today, [one-quarter] of the Bazaar belongs to the Shaikh family vs. [one-quarter] municipally owned).[182]

The shaykh's ownership of villages and lands gives him great power over the villagers and tenant farmers. The protection afforded them by living on the shaykh's property and the sense of close association with a holy person make them among the shaykh's most loyal adherents. Such villages often become important strongholds of shaykhly power. It is significant that on the eve of his invasion of Persia, Shaykh 'Ubayd Allah was active in purchasing numerous villages along the Turco-Persian frontier.[183]

The Influence of the Shaykhs

The majority of those who have come in contact with the Kurds agree that the average Kurd is tolerant or indifferent in matters of religion, though much prone to be under the shaykhs' influence. Professor Minorsky has pointed out that the Kurds are not given to extremist views, but are greatly persuaded by the shaykhs of the various orders.[184] According to Cuinet, "Although the Kurd is greatly disposed by his nature to religious tolerance, he is, by reason of his ignorance and simplicity, easily driven to fanaticism, the more so because of his strong belief in the miraculous."[185]

The unlettered Kurd's predilection for the miraculous, which places him so completely under the shaykhs' sway, was the theme of a similar comment by a British administrator with an intimate knowledge of the Kurds in the 1920s: "The Kurd is, in general, not devoutly religious, but his simple and superstitious nature makes him particularly susceptible to the influence, whether for good or for evil, of his holy shaikhs."[186]

Rich, writing in the 1830s, left us a memorable description of the veneration of the people of Sulaymaniya for Shaykh Khalid al-Naqshbandi, the great founder of the Khalidiya branch of the Naqshbandi order in Kurdistan.

> There is a great Mahometan saint living in Sulaimania. His name is Shaykh Khaled; but the Koords think it profanation to call him by any other name than *Hazret i Mevlana,* or the holy beloved one; and talk of his sayings as being *Hadeez,* or inspired. . . . All the Koords call him an evlia or saint; and a great many of them almost put him on a footing with their Prophet. Osman Bey, who with the Pasha and almost all the principal Koords are his *mureed*s or disciples, told me that he was at least equal to the famous Mussulman saint, Shaykh Abdul Kader.[187]

Rich emphasized the great regard in which Shaykh Khalid was held by informing us that no less a person than the pasha of Sulaymaniya himself "used to stand before him and fill his pipe for him."[188]

Time and again the *murid*s have shown an utter disregard for their lives in responding to their shaykhs' call in the course of the various uprisings led by these holy men. The followers of the shaykh of Barzan, known as the "madmen" (*diwana*), for example, are reported to be so completely devoted to the shaykh as to be willing to jump off the edge of a precipice if he should order them to do so.[189] However, it should not be imagined that this "blind obedience,"[190] as some writers have called it, is easily won. The leader's valor, astuteness, and prestige, as well as his ability and readiness to defend the interests of his followers, are extremely important for maintaining his hold on them.

The Shaykhs' Charismatic Personality

The shaykhs are believed to possess sanctity and certain supernatural qualities that endow them with miraculous powers (*karamat*).[191] Thus, they are regarded as holy men and looked upon with considerable awe and veneration. Their followers, as Cuinet pointed out in 1891, believe them to be in communication with the spirits of the saints of Islam and even with God. They deem them invulnerable and attribute prodigies to them. The shaykhs' prayers are regarded as sovereign remedies against all maladies. Their followers swear by the shaykhs' heads and dare not break vows thus made.[192]

One of the earliest and most interesting descriptions of the supernatural power attributed to these holy men was given by Rich, who reported the following statement made to him by a *murid* of Sultan Hassan, a celebrated dervish:

> "The Sultan, sir," said he, meaning the dervish, "understands everything by miracle. If you spoke to him in your own language he would understand you, though he never learnt it; and he knows every science without having read: nay, he knows even what passes in your mind; and when you have the intention of consulting him, he will answer you without your having spoken a word. He knows that we are now talking about him, and he will appear to people in dreams, or even in actual presence, though they may be in India or Persia."[193]

These supernatural powers may be based on hereditary charisma, which is shared by the family of the bearer of the charisma, in particular his closest relatives, or based on personal charisma, which inheres in the individual by virtue of certain qualities that set him apart from other men.[194]

Writing of the Barzinja shaykhs, Barth points out: "As descendants of the Prophet, the Shaikh family is considered to be vested with certain supernatural powers, derived secondarily from the sainted ancestor Kaka Hama. This gives Shaikh Mahmud the specific power to make amulets that protect the bearer from bullets and knives."[195] In addition to possessing hereditary charisma that attaches to him by virtue of his birth, Shaykh Mahmud also possessed personal charisma. Barth claims that it is difficult to separate the two and maintained that the former stems in part from the latter. Of the shaykh's personal charismatic powers, he says, "He is attributed with the ability to read a person's thoughts and character; he knows before a word is spoken for what purpose a person has come to him."[196]

Shaykh Mahmud's fearlessness, coupled with the fact that he survived many fights, gave him the reputation of being indestructible. According to the statement by one purporting to be an eyewitness, Shaykh Mahmud, unlike other mortals, could not be harmed by bullets: " 'Before God,' said the witness, 'I have seen bullets pass right through his body and kill the man behind him, yet the Shaikh remained unharmed. He cannot be killed in war.' "[197]

A shaykh's authority is never questioned by his followers once his reputation for sanctity and charismatic powers has been established. He tolerates no opposition and demands nothing less than complete submission to his will. Devotion to him must be absolute and unquestioning. He regards the recognition of his charismatic authority as a duty incumbent upon his followers. He imposes new obligations and demands all sorts of sacrifices from them.

The numerous calls to arms that the shaykhs have made since the memorable invasion of Persia by Shaykh ʿUbayd Allah have usually fallen on eager and willing ears. The shaykhs, hard taskmasters that they are, have rarely been failed by their adherents, who have responded to their shaykh's orders with a rare and frightening devotion, performing what is required of them with unquestioning obedience and with an enthusiasm that has often culminated in prodigious acts of valor.

The shaykh oftentimes resorts to the appointment of *khulafa* (sing., *khalifa*, "successor") in order to spread his fame and consolidate his influence at home as well as beyond the confines of his own territory. The appointment involves a ritual initiation into the *tarika* (Sufi religious order), and it confers upon the *khalifa* a certain amount of the shaykh's powers. The *khalifa* represents the shaykh during the latter's lifetime and even after, and is usually located in places or countries that are rather remote from the parent hostel where the appointing shaykh resides.[198]

The phenomenal spread of the Naqshbandi order in Kurdistan, to the detriment and partial eclipse of the Qadiri order in that area, may be attributed to the personality and proselytizing zeal of Shaykh Khalid and his initiative in supporting *khulafa*. Among the numerous *khulafa* appointed by Shaykh Khalid were Sayyid ʿAbd ʿAllah of Nehri[199] and Shaykh Taj al-Din of Barzan.[200] Both men founded what have amounted to dynasties that have greatly influenced events in this part of the world.

Secure as the shaykh's authority is among his followers under normal circumstances, it cannot long endure lack of success. As Weber has pointed out, the failure of a charismatic leader's powers results in the disappearance of his charismatic authority.[201] The downfall of Shaykh Khalid and his flight from Sulaymaniya offer a striking example of the loss of charismatic authority. Rich, who happened to be in Sulaymaniya at that time, provided a vivid account of the shaykh's sudden flight. He described how the shaykh was reviled by his former followers after his disappearance and contrasted this attitude with the veneration and esteem formerly shown him by the Kurds. Rich gave this significant reason for his downfall: "He lost his consideration on the death of the Pasha's son. He said he would save his life, and that he had inspected God's registers concerning him."[202]

3 The Suppression of the Semiautonomous Regimes in Kurdistan

Background

By the beginning of the nineteenth century, the weakness of the Ottoman Empire had become apparent to all. The European powers lost no opportunity to profit by it, and the subject races, sensing their masters' declining fortunes, were beginning to stir. The Turks themselves were painfully aware of their predicament. In recent years, their weakness had been such that more than once they had to choose between disaster or the pusillanimous mollification of friend and foe alike, both foreign and domestic.

But the Turks were a people with a centuries-old military and imperial tradition. They were not yet completely destitute of the qualities that had given them greatness as a nation, nor had men of strong resolve and great ability been exhausted among them. Sultan Mahmud II, despite early failures and disappointments, had succeeded in imposing comprehensive civil and military reforms that were intended to resuscitate the empire and raise it to its former greatness. One of the most important points in Sultan Mahmud's program of reform was the liquidation of the powerful hereditary princes and *derebey*s (lords of the valley) who had been showing increasing signs of being unreliable and dangerous vassals.

By the third decade of the nineteenth century, Sultan Mahmud II appears to have decided to suppress the semiautonomous hereditary regimes in Kurdistan. This was not merely an attempt to punish recalcitrance and to reassert Ottoman authority. It was rather a determined attempt to reconquer these territories and to bring them under direct Ottoman control. With this end in view, Rashid Muhammad Pasha, *wali* (governor) of Sivas and a former grand vizier,[1] was sent to Kurdistan with a formidable army. The *wali* of Baghdad, 'Ali Rida Pasha,[2] and the *wali* of Mosul, Injeh Bayraqdar Muhammad Pasha,[3] were instructed to put their forces at his disposal in case of need. After Rashid Muhammad Pasha's death, his task was completed by Hafiz Pasha[4] and others who saw to it that no powerful emir or *derebey* remained to challenge the sultan's authority in Kurdistan.

As the chosen instrument for the suppression of the Kurdish princes, Rashid Muhammad Pasha accomplished many things. The most important of them, no doubt, was the capture and removal to Istanbul of Muhammad Pasha, the "One-Eyed Pasha" of Rawanduz, who was the first of the great Kurdish princes to be overthrown and, at that time, the strongest. As we shall see in the next section, Rashid Muhammad Pasha resorted to diplomacy rather than to war in dealing with the powerful ruler of Rawanduz.

Rashid Pasha's other achievements included putting an end to a serious mutiny in Mardin,[5] the suppression of the Milli confederation in upper Mesopotamia,[6] the capture and dispatch of the great Shammar chieftain Sufuk to Istanbul, the punishment of the Yazidis of Sinjar and the Turkomen of Tal A'far,[7] and the subjugation of the Sasun-Motkan region—a task that Hafiz Pasha was to bring to a successful conclusion.

In this difficult highland region, Rashid Pasha had to cope with the combined forces of a number of powerful Kurdish chiefs. Rajab Beg of Hazo, Husayn Agha of Ilijeh, Temir Beg of Haini, and Mirza Agha of Banuka, chief of the Silivan tribe, put up a determined resistance and appear to have been faithfully supported by their Kurdish and Armenian subjects. After their defeat, most of these chieftains were banished to Adrianople in European Turkey.[8] Rashid Muhammad Pasha died of cholera in Diyarbakr in 1836.[9] He was succeeded by Hafiz Muhammad Pasha, who, among other things, completed the pacification of this area. Hafiz Pasha attacked and subdued Haji Zilal Agha of Nerjiki, one of the last powerful chiefs remaining in this region, and inflicted a similar fate on the Kharzan tribe.[10]

Muhammad Pasha of Rawanduz

The Rise of Muhammad Pasha of Rawanduz

Muhammad Pasha was no doubt the most illustrious of the long line of the Soran princes.[11] Very little is known of the early history of this remarkable man prior to his emergence as a conqueror. He was born in Rawanduz in A.H. 1198/A.D. 1783 and received his education from Mulla Ahmad ibn Adam, a noted local Kurdish religious dignitary.[12] At the age of thirty-one he succeeded his father, Mustafa Beg, during the latter's lifetime in the year A.D. 1814.[13] This fact has given rise to the conflicting reports regarding his assumption of power. According to some accounts, his aged and infirm father, realizing that he was no longer capable of coping with the onerous task of ruling the wild and turbulent principality, asked his son to take over. According to others, the son forced his father to relinquish his position in his favor.[14] So strong was this suspicion that he was accused of having cruelly blinded his father in order to attain this end—an accusation rejected by a British doctor who attended the old prince.[15] The voluntary retirement of Mustafa Beg is now generally accepted.[16]

The young *mir*'s restless ambition, aggressive spirit, and unflinching determination were soon felt by all those who had the misfortune to be in his way. The first to suffer were the men around him, including some of his closest relatives.[17] His treasurer-general, 'Abd Allah Agha, who had held the same job under his father and was recommended by the latter, was accused of plotting with Muhammad Pasha's uncles, Tamir

Khan Beg and Yahya Beg, and was executed.[18] Muhammad Pasha lost no time in undertaking a punitive expedition against his uncles.

On the first day of Muharram, A.H. 1230 (A.D. December 14, 1814), he marched against Hodiyan in pursuit of his uncle Tamir Khan Beg, who hastened to shut himself up in the fortress of Shaytaneh. After withstanding about four weeks of siege, the fortress was stormed on January 10, 1815, amid scenes of great carnage. Tamir Khan and his son Mahmud Beg were captured and executed. Having thus disposed of one uncle, Muhammad Pasha turned his attention to the other. He attacked and captured the fortress of Sidakan, where his uncle Yahya Beg and the latter's son 'Uthman Beg had taken refuge, and killed both of them. During this same expedition, he attacked the fortress of Rost, killing the ruler.[19]

After the elimination of these dangerous rivals, the *mir*'s authority was unchallenged throughout the principality, and he was thus free to turn his attention to his immediate neighbors. He attacked and subdued the Baradost, the Shirwan, the Surchi, the Khoshnaw, and the Mamish tribes in rapid succession.[20] The fate of some of the defeated tribal chieftains demonstrates his determination to crush all those who had the temerity to oppose Muhammad Pasha's designs. Thus, he is said to have put to death the chiefs of the Mir Mahmali, the Mir Yusifi, and the Pusht Gali, the three major subdivisions of the Khoshnaw confederation.[21] Similarly, he is reported to have killed Hamza Agha, the paramount chief of the Mamish, and wiped out most of that chief's immediate family.[22]

Muhammad Pasha appears to have been determined to possess himself of the whole region located between the two Zab rivers from the Tigris to the Persian frontier. In the course of achieving this aim, it was inevitable that he would clash with the Babans, who were the only external power in the region. In A.D. 1822, he occupied Harir, the ancient capital of the Soran principality, expelling its Baban ruler. The same fate overtook Koi Sanjaq in October 1823 and Ranya in Jamada ath-Thani in February 1824. Both Arbil and Altin Copru had fallen by September 1823. These conquests resulted in the Lesser Zab River becoming the boundary between the *mir*'s domains and the Baban principality, as it had been previously. The *wali* of Baghdad, 'Ali Rida Pasha, who was not in a position to stop the *mir,* bowed to the inevitable, recognizing the *mir*'s conquests and conferring upon him the rank of pasha.[23]

The Conquests of Muhammad Pasha of Rawanduz

The attack on the Yazidis. The second phase of the *mir*'s career begins with his conquests and depredations in the Greater Zab region, which started as a punitive expedition against the Yazidis of the Shaykhan. This expedition is said to have been touched off by the murder of 'Ali Agha al-Balti, chief of the Alkoshi, a subdivision of the Mizuri tribe, by the Yazidi chieftain 'Ali Beg.

The Yazidis and the Mizuris had been feuding for years, and their leaders were known to be bitter enemies. One day 'Ali Beg sent word to 'Ali Agha expressing his desire for peace and friendship and inviting him to act as a *kiriv*[24] (sponsor) at the forthcoming circumcision of his son. The Mizuri chieftain responded favorably and a few days later arrived at the residence of the Yazidi prince at Ba'idhra accompanied by only a few retainers.[25] Whether 'Ali Agha came with such a small escort in order to demonstrate his trust in his host or out of disdain for him is not known.[26] Whatever induced him to do so, it proved to be his undoing. The Yazidi chieftain, finding his erstwhile enemy so completely at his mercy, treacherously had him murdered. He then called in forty Yazidi chieftains and had them stab the body of the Mizuri leader in order that the Yazidi people as a whole would share in the responsibility for the murder.[27]

For a time, it looked as though a large-scale tribal war was about to break out. The Mizuri tribesmen, upon hearing of the outrage, went wild with anger and began to gather for a great raid against Ba'idhra. Meanwhile, thousands of Yazidi warriors flocked to their chieftain's residence in anticipation of the attack.[28] Trouble was averted when the pasha of 'Amadiya made known his opposition, and the raid was called off. This pasha, as the prince of Bahdinan, was the overlord of both the Mizuri tribe and the Yazidis, and the wishes of so powerful a person could not be ignored with impunity. Furthermore, the Mizuris no doubt feared that in flouting the will of the Bahdinan prince, who was suspected of complicity in the murder, they might find his forces arrayed against them.

A plea for redress by Mulla Yahya al-Mizuri, a noted religious dignitary and a cousin or nephew of the murdered chieftain, is said to have failed to move the Bahdinan prince. The latter, in declining to countenance punitive action against the Yazidis, is said to have blamed 'Ali Agha for having naïvely accepted the friendly overtures of the Yazidi chieftain and for having gone to visit an enemy in his own country without an adequate escort.[29] Mulla Yahya, disappointed and angry, is reported to have left 'Amadiya determined to avenge the murder of his kinsman. A man of great shrewdness and inflexible purpose, he succeeded before long in unleashing a tide of violence that brought death and devastation to the whole Bahdinan region, causing the downfall of the ruling dynasty and nearly exterminating the Yazidis of the Shaykhan.

Accounts vary as to the manner in which Mulla Yahya accomplished his purpose. According to one report, he sought the aid of the *wali* of Baghdad, who after hearing the mulla's grievances provided him with a letter to the pasha of Rawanduz. In this letter, he is said to have urged Muhammad Pasha to send a punitive force to chastise the Yazidis for their misdeeds.[30] According to another account, Mulla Yahya went directly to Muhammad Pasha, with whom he is said to have been on very friendly terms.[31] Whatever the truth of the matter, it was the ambitious "One-Eyed Pasha" of Rawanduz, then at the peak of his power, who proved to be the instrument of his vengeance.

Upon meeting Muhammad Pasha, Mulla Yahya is reported to have complained bitterly of the unjust murder of his kinsman by the Yazidi *mir* of the Shaykhan and of the excesses suffered daily by the Muslim population of Bahdinan at the hands of the Yazidis. He is said to have called upon the pasha to save the Muslims from the tyranny of their Yazidi oppressors. Mulla Yahya emphasized the fact that the Bahdinan princes were weak and decadent and made it quite clear that their principality, which was in a state of dissolution, was ripe for picking.[32] This plea to Muhammad Pasha was shrewdly calculated to flatter his vanity, appeal to his religious sentiment, and rouse his cupidity.

Whether Muhammad Pasha was genuinely moved by Mulla Yahya's request for succor and redress, or he merely regarded the mulla's grievances as a convenient pretext for invading the Bahdinan region is a matter that has never been satisfactorily ascertained. The important point is that Muhammad Pasha decided to march against the Yazidis. In order to give his expedition a religious character, he called upon his mufti (canon lawyer), Mulla Muhammad Khati, to issue a *fatwa* (legal opinion) declaring the enterprise a jihad (holy war).[33]

Muhammad Pasha crossed the Greater Zab at the village of Kellek[34] at the head of a large army in the year A.D. 1831.[35] After putting the inhabitants of this Yazidi village to the sword, he marched northward. The entire Yazidi-inhabited foothill country east of Mosul, from the Greater Zab to the Khabur River, was ravaged by fire and sword. Thousands of men, women, and children were hunted down and slaughtered, and whole communities wiped out. A number of the more fortunate Yazidis managed to take refuge in the neighboring forests and mountain fastnesses, and a few in their headlong flight succeeded in reaching such distant points as Tur 'Abdin, Jabal Judi, and Jabal Sinjar.[36] A mass of stragglers, fleeing in terror before their pursuers in the direction of Mosul, found the bridge of boats at that locality cut off and were overtaken and massacred at Koyunjik[37] on the east bank of the Tigris opposite Mosul.[38] There is no doubt that the losses suffered by the Yazidis were appalling.[39] The only survivors, other than those who fled, were a number of women and children who were carried into captivity—the women, according to Damaluji, having been spared on account of their good looks.[40]

Though the Yazidis suffered most, they were by no means the only ones to suffer. Christian communities lying in the path of the *mir*'s army or located within striking distance of his forces were massacred and despoiled. The village of Alqosh was sacked, and a large number of its inhabitants put to the sword.[41] The neighboring monastery of Rabban Hormizd was attacked and plundered, and a great many of the monks, including the abbott, Gabriel Dambo, were put to death. A large quantity of ancient manuscripts was destroyed or irretrievably lost.[42] The same fate overtook the monastery of Shaykh Matta.[43]

The fate of 'Ali Beg, the Yazidi *mir* of the Shaykhan, can be told in a few words. According to Addai Scher, he was captured by Muhammad Pasha and taken to Rawanduz, where, after refusing to embrace Islam, he was put to death.[44] Damaluji writes that 'Ali Beg fled before the advancing Rawanduz forces and hid in the mountains of 'Aqra, but was captured a few years later by Injeh Bayraqdar Muhammad Pasha, the *wali* of Mosul, who had him decapitated at a place called Kir Muhammad Arab on the river Gomel.[45]

The invasion and overthrow of the Bahdinan principality. Having crushed the Yazidis with impunity—no objection having been made either by their immediate overlords, by the Bahdinan princes, or by the Ottoman government, the supreme suzerain of all—Muhammad Pasha now turned his arms against 'Aqra, a Bahdinan appanage. After a few days' siege, the fortress of 'Aqra, regarded as almost impregnable, fell to the besiegers, and the ruling prince, Isma'il Pasha, was forced to flee.[46] However, the Zibari Kurds continued to resist the Sorani invasion fiercely. The spirit of anger and bitterness of the conquered but unbowed Zibaris was strikingly shown in the contemptuous and supremely defiant attitude of a Zibari warrior, one Azo of the village of Sawti. When invited to enter the service of the pasha, who had no son, Azo is said to have replied that he would make him one![47]

Muhammad Pasha then marched against 'Amadiya, the principal town of Bahdinan, which capitulated after a brief siege. The capture of 'Amadiya and the flight of its ruler Sa'id Pasha enabled Muhammad Pasha to become master of the whole region from the Greater Zab to the Khabur River, including the two important centers of Dohuk and Zakho.[48] After the capture of 'Amadiya and the flight of Sa'id Pasha, Muhammad Pasha appointed Musa Pasha as governor of the Bahdinan capital. Musa Pasha, a relative of Sa'id Pasha who had been on bad terms with the latter, had offered valuable assistance to Muhammad Pasha at the time of his attack on 'Amadiya.[49]

Impelled by the momentum of his conquest, Muhammad Pasha seemed incapable of calling a halt to his reckless career of expansion. His next objective was the conquest of the rugged Bohtan principality that lay north of the Bahdinan region. He marched against Jazirat ibn 'Umar, which he occupied without much difficulty, and thus found himself at war with its ruler, the famous Emir Bedir Khan of Bohtan. He then struck out northward, spreading terror among the defenders of Husn Kayf and threatening both Nisibin and Mardin.[50] He laid siege to Azikh but failed to take it, owing in part to the inhabitants' fierce resistance and in part to disturbing developments at 'Amadiya.[51] He was forced to relinquish his conquests in this region and to hurry back to the rebellious town, where the former ruler Sa'id Pasha, supported by a popular uprising, had deposed Musa Pasha and compelled him to flee.[52]

Muhammad Pasha besieged 'Amadiya, and after a period of desperate fighting he succeeded in overpowering the beleaguered garrison. Having reconquered 'Amadiya, the infuriated pasha proceeded to wreak his vengeance upon the hapless inhabitants. Many of the leading men were put to death, and a large part of the population was decimated by famine and pestilence.[53]

This time the pasha made no pretense of sparing the inhabitants' sensibilities. He annexed the whole region to the Rawanduz state and appointed his brother Rasul Beg as governor in place of the rejected Bahdinan prince, Musa Pasha.[54] By this act, Muhammad Pasha put an end to the centuries-old existence of the Bahdinan state. Although Isma'il Pasha, the last Bahdinan prince, succeeded in reviving it for a while after the fall of Muhammad Pasha, it was finally suppressed by the Ottoman government shortly thereafter.

The Fall of Muhammad Pasha of Rawanduz

Muhammad Pasha was now fast approaching the end of his career. The Ottoman government, which had hitherto shown a strange lack of interest in the Kurdish conqueror's activities, was now beginning to be genuinely alarmed by his unbroken successes and apparently insatiable ambition. The grave implications of his unchecked progress were now too obvious to be ignored, particularly when viewed against what was happening in other parts of the empire.

The Ottoman government had been forced to overcome its inertia and indecision to meet the growing menace of Muhammad ʿAli of Egypt. The struggle with the Egyptian dynasty had no doubt claimed all of the sultan government's efforts and the energies. However, Ottoman preoccupation with Muhammad ʿAli did not mean a lack of awareness of another steadily growing danger. If anything, the struggle with Muhammad ʿAli awakened the government to the dangers of its ambitious and unruly vassals and strengthened its resolve to deal firmly with them. Furthermore, Sultan Mahmud II's reforms and new policies provided a clear proof of the central government's determination to put an end once and for all to the pretensions of the various regional rulers. The time was fast approaching when the Ottoman Empire would find itself free of the *derebey*s of Anatolia, the hereditary princes of Kurdistan, the semi-independent slave pashas of Baghdad, the emirs of Lebanon, and the pashas of ʿAkka.

Muhammad Pasha of Rawanduz is said to have been in touch with Ibrahim Pasha, the son of Egypt's Muhammad ʿAli and the brilliant commander of his forces, no doubt with a view to coordinating their operations against the Ottoman Empire.[55] If true, this connection must have only hastened the blow about to fall upon the Pasha of Rawanduz.

In 1834, Ottoman commander Rashid Muhammad Pasha appeared with large forces in northern Mesopotamia. The former grand vizier and *wali* of Sivas, who had been entrusted with the task of suppressing the Kurdish prince, advanced southward along the Sinjar-Tal Aʿfar road, punishing recalcitrant elements in both places. After crossing the Tigris at Iski Mosul, he proceeded to the Soran country, halting at the Harir plain. Here he was joined by two powerful columns, one commanded by Injeh Bayraqdar Muhammad Pasha, the *wali* of Mosul, and the other by ʿAli Rida Pasha, the *wali* of Baghdad.[56]

The Kurdish pasha of Rawanduz had withdrawn all his forces beyond the Rawanduz gorge, obviously with the object of making a last desperate stand in defense of his capital. He had in the meantime taken the precaution of occupying strongly fortified positions astride the gorge through which passed the only road to Rawanduz. Rashid Muhammad Pasha, realizing that his forces would incur great losses if they were to attack the *mir*'s impregnable positions, decided that diplomacy would accomplish more than war. According to one account the Ottoman commander, who was an old friend of Muhammad Pasha, advised him to avoid bloodshed and to come to terms with the government. Rashid Pasha reportedly gave the *mir* the most solemn assurances that if he were to cease his hostile activities and surrender to the government, he would be honorably treated and restored to his principality. Muhammad Pasha agreed to do so, went to discuss matters with the Ottoman commander, and then was seized and sent to Constantinople under a powerful escort.[57]

According to another account, Rashid Pasha succeeded in winning over a large number of Kurdish religious dignitaries, including Muhammad Pasha's own mufti, Mulla Muhammad Khati. The latter is credited with having issued a *fatwa* to the effect that those who bore arms against the army of the caliph were unbelievers and their wives were thereby divorced from them. The pronouncement of this anathema created a deep impression on the *mir*'s followers. Faced with this threat, most of his troops are reported to have abandoned the struggle. After this clever strategem, which shattered the morale of the Rawanduz forces, Rashid Pasha is said to have gotten in touch with the Kurdish leader suggesting that he surrender and come to terms with the Ottoman government.[58]

The sultan is said to have received the *mir* graciously upon his arrival in Constantinople and to have bestowed upon him the highest honors. According to Frederick Millingen's 1870 account, "The Koordish Pasha was acknowledged to be a man endowed with the greatest qualities, and one of the pillars that sustained the throne of the Sultan. The Porte decided to reorganize the whole of Koordistan, and named Muhammad Pasha Governor-General of that province, giving him the most unlimited power."[59]

It appears from this account that Rashid Muhammad Pasha lived up to the solemn pledges he had given the *mir*. Unfortunately for the Kurdish leader, however, Rashid Pasha died while the former was still in Constantinople. It was now time for the *mir* to return home. His departure was characterized by the same marks of imperial favor shown him upon his arrival at the Ottoman capital. He left Constantinople for home on an Ottoman ship bound for the port of Trebizond or Samsum on the Black Sea. The pasha of Rawanduz never reached home. According to one account, he was killed while still at sea, and according to another he was executed at Sivas.[60]

It is said that Muhammad Pasha's execution was arranged by 'Ali Rida Pasha, the *wali* of Baghdad. The latter reportedly informed the Porte (Ottoman government) that it would be impossible for him to establish peace and order in the Pashalik of Baghdad so long as the *mir* of Rawanduz was alive. It appears that Mr. Wood, the British consul at Damascus, had interested himself in Muhammad Pasha's fate. In the course of his travels, this official, who had been the dragoman to the British embassy in Constantinople, had met the Kurdish leader when the latter was still at the peak of his power.[61]

The End of the Bahdinan Principality

A few words are sufficient to describe the fate of Isma'il Pasha, the last independent prince of his line and the end of the once famed Bahdinan principality. It will be recalled that Muhammad Pasha of Rawanduz invaded Bahdinan twice: the first time to crush the Yazidis and no doubt to test the Bahdinan princes' reaction; and the second time to conquer the Bahdinan principality and to make it part of his ephemeral empire. Isma'il Pasha and Muhammad Sa'id Pasha were defeated, dispossessed, and forced to flee. Shortly thereafter, taking advantage of the absence of the *mir* of Rawanduz, Isma'il Pasha had succeeded in overpowering the *mir*'s agent, Musa Pasha, at 'Amadiya. But his triumph was short-lived. The return of the infuriated pasha of Rawanduz was to involve Isma'il Pasha in a fresh defeat and to subject his unfortunate capital to a new ordeal.

Isma'il Pasha, who had succeeded in escaping with his life, for some time did not dare to make another attempt to regain his power. After the suppression of Muhammad Pasha by the Ottoman government, however, the Bahdinan prince returned to 'Amadiya and possessed himself of his principality. But this repossession, too, was not to endure. The *wali* of Mosul, Injeh Bayraqdar Muhammad Pasha, marched on 'Amadiya with a large force and after a long siege succeeded in capturing it. Isma'il Pasha became a fugitive again.[62]

However, the prince did not despair of regaining his principality. Before long he was again in touch with the leading men of 'Amadiya and the surrounding countryside. Having gathered some followers, he wrote to the *wali* of Mosul requesting the latter to allow him to return to 'Amadiya, but the *wali* did not answer him. He then journeyed to Jazirat ibn 'Umar, where, apparently under the protection of Bedir Khan, he communicated with his followers and before long marched on 'Amadiya at the head of a considerable force and occupied it.[63]

As soon as the *wali* of Mosul heard of the prince's action, he began to make preparations for an attack on the town. Isma'il Pasha, alarmed at this news, began to take measures to defend himself. It was probably at this time that he appealed to the Nestorian patriarch Mar Sham'un for help. The latter, as we shall see, sent him three thousand of his followers, but was forced to withdraw them when asked to do so by the *wali* of Mosul.[64]

In the meantime, the *wali* of Mosul was on his way to 'Amadiya with a large army. In the ensuing battle, Isma'il Pasha was defeated and captured, and then exiled to Baghdad, where he continued to reside with the rest of his family.[65] Thus came to an end another Kurdish principality that in prestige and lineage had been second to none in Kurdistan.[66]

Bedir Khan Beg, the Emir of Bohtan

The Rise of Bedir Khan Beg

Bedir Khan Beg is no doubt the most renowned member of the Azizan family, the hereditary rulers of Bohtan. This princely family, mentioned by the Kurdish historian Sharaf Khan al-Bidlisi as one of the oldest ruling families in Kurdistan, claimed descent from 'Abd al-'Aziz, a son of Khalid Ibn al-Walid, the great Muslim commander and companion of the Prophet. According to Hartmann, these rulers, like the majority of their subjects, were at one time Yazidis.[67]

Bedir Khan Beg, who succeeded to his principality at an early age,[68] was not heard from for a number of years. His accession coincided with the beginning of a crucial period of Ottoman and Kurdish history, the period of reforms that culminated in the suppression of the semiautonomous Kurdish principalities. At the beginning, he obviously was not strong enough to participate in shaping the events of his time, but there can be little doubt that he was carefully watching the momentous developments taking place around him.

In 1853, Sir Austen Henry Layard mentioned a curious piece of information relating to the early history of Bedir Khan. He stated that Bedir Khan ruled in the name of Emir Saif al-Din Shir, the hereditary ruler of Jazira, and that for a long time he was very careful to conform to the requirements of the situation. According to Layard,

> Mir Saif-ed-din was the hereditary chief of Bohtan, in whose name Beder Khan exercised his authority. His son, Asdenshir (a corruption of Ardeshir) Bey, is now under surveillance amongst the Turks. So well aware was Beder Khan Bey of the necessity of keeping up the idea amongst the Kurds, that his power was delegated to him by the Mir,

that he signed most of his public documents with that chief's seal although he confined him a close prisoner until his death.[69]

It should be pointed out that the name of the prince whom Layard referred to as Saif al-Din Shir's son was not "Asdenshir," a corruption of "Ardeshir," but rather 'Izz al-Din Shir (Yazdan Shir).

If Layard's report is true, it sheds new and significant light on certain points that have hitherto been vague. First, his report indicates that the relatively uneventful early years of Bedir Khan's reign were spent in consolidating his power—in the circumstances a serious and no doubt difficult undertaking. Second, it helps to explain an important development that was to have direct bearing on Bedir Khan's defeat and downfall—namely, the sudden defection of 'Izz al-Din Shir at the time when Bedir Khan was engaged in a life-and-death struggle against the Ottoman forces. If Layard's statement concerning Saif al-Din Shir and his son 'Izz al-Din Shir is true, it would explain the action of the latter, who has often been branded as a traitor to the Kurdish cause.[70] He may have withdrawn his support because of Bedir Khan's treatment of his father.

The information about Bedir Khan Beg's early career, although fragmentary, is nevertheless of considerable interest. We hear that in 1838 he was readying troops for an attack on 'Abdul Agha, the brother of Khan Mahmud. In 1839, he was appointed an honorary captain in the Ottoman army and participated, as the head of a contingent of Bohtan troops, in the battle of Nizib in which Ibrahim Pasha of Egypt won a decisive victory over the Ottoman army.[71] After the Ottoman defeat, Bedir Khan retired with his men to Jazirat ibn 'Umar, where, taking advantage of Turkish weakness, he began to strengthen his forces.[72]

Bedir Khan was greatly helped in achieving this aim by a singularly fortunate set of circumstances. To the south, the recent eruption and suppression of Muhammad Pasha of Rawanduz, besides putting an end to the Soran principality, had permanently weakened the Bahdinan princes. The Yazidis of Shaykhan had been thoroughly crushed by the "One-Eyed Pasha" of Rawanduz, and the Yazidis of Sinjar had been cowed by the various expeditions sent against them and were no longer to be reckoned with as a power. To the north, the power of the Kurdish *derebeys* of the Sasun-Motki highlands had been broken by Rashid Muhammad Pasha and his successors. To the east, Nurallah Beg, the *mir* of Hakari, was no longer the powerful prince that his predecessors had once been. He was distracted by internal dissensions stemming from the rivalry between him and Sulayman Beg, the youthful prince he had displaced. This quarrel not only had seriously split his numerous vassals, but also had irreparably damaged their loyalty. Among other things, it had led to a permanent breach with Mar Sham'un, the leader of one of the most powerful single tribal blocks in the Hakari domains. Of the major remaining Kurdish principalities, the remotely located Babans still managed to exist, but, as events were to prove, they were to enjoy only one more decade of a precarious existence.

All this, no doubt, gave Bedir Khan a unique position as the only remaining traditional leader in the Kurdish world, but it also made him a marked man. Under the circumstances, it might seem unreasonable to suggest that the Bohtan prince was helped by the Ottoman government, which, in its hour of need, may have been forced to seek an accommodation with him. There are good grounds, however, for believing that an agreement was reached with Bedir Khan. Such a measure is not out of character with Ottoman practice, and it is unlikely that a man in Bedir Khan's position would have refused such an offer if made.

In the course of a conversation with Dr. Austin Wright and Mr. Edward Breath of the American Mission in Persia, who accepted an invitation to visit him in 1846, Bedir Khan freely admitted that eight years earlier he had made some kind of compact with the Ottoman government. According to their report,

> he told us that eight years ago, when he was weak and Turkey strong, he entered into an engagement with the latter; and that now, though the power had changed hands, he did not violate his word. . . . Eight years ago he was poor, without power, and little known. The Turkish government then took him by the hand; and now his wealth is incalculable.[73]

Whatever the nature of the agreement between Bedir Khan and the Ottoman government, this report indicates that a mutually profitable accommodation had been reached between the two. It is interesting to note that this agreement was reached at a time when the government's pacification of Kurdistan was progressing apace and its dangerous struggle with Muhammad 'Ali of Egypt was still unresolved. At a time of such grave dangers and heavy commitments, it no doubt served Turkey's purpose to have one less enemy. There is every reason to believe that these American visitors honestly and faithfully reported this interview with Bedir Khan Beg. The two men seemed to have been favorably impressed by the emir, and their report is often couched in terms of admiration and praise.

Bedir Khan's Character

There is no question that Bedir Khan is one of the great figures of Kurdish history. The manner in which he raised himself from comparative weakness and obscurity to become, in his heyday, the most powerful and illustrious Kurd of his time is sufficient proof that he possessed outstanding qualities. To the Kurds he no doubt typified the ideal Kurdish leader. He was intelligent, had a good presence, and was not without a certain charm of manner. He was distinguished by bravery, determination, ambition, and piety. In a man of a passionate and impulsive nature, these qualities, though excellent in themselves, are often easily distorted, for unless redeemed by a measure of restraint and moderation, bravery is apt to deteriorate into recklessness, determination into obduracy, ambition into fatuous pretension, and piety into intolerance.

That Bedir Khan at times was guilty of some of these faults cannot be denied. His cruel suppression of the mountain Nestorians is a poor reflection on his humanity and political judgment. This action not only caused much unnecessary bloodshed, but, as we shall see, also led to his downfall. A measure of restraint and a little reflection might have averted the tragedy and saved him for greater things. The fate of Muhammad Pasha of Rawanduz should have served as a warning and an example to him: a decade earlier that prince had paid with his life and his principality for the satisfaction of destroying the defenseless Yazidis.

Bedir Khan pursued his ambitions with audacious initiative and an unrelenting singleness of purpose. Like all men of destiny, he had a sense of mission and a deeply rooted conviction that he possessed special powers. His person as well as his activities were tinged with a charismatic quality. Seen in this light, much of his behavior that appears inexplicable becomes clear. His sternness and religiosity, his disregard for accepted norms, and his obliviousness to danger may be viewed as part of his charismatic personality. In his own eyes, as well as in the eyes of his followers, his success bore the stamp of divine approval.

This is how he appeared to his American guests when he was at the peak of his power:

> His power extends from the Persian line on the east to far into Mesopotamia on the west, and from the gates of Diarbekr to those of Mosul; and his fame is wide spread. While we were with him, nearly every chief in northern Koordistan came to make their respects to him, bringing him presents of money, horses, mules and other valuable property. Even the Hakkary Bey, higher in rank, and once more powerful than he, and Khan Mahmud, called by an English traveller "the Rob Roy of Koordistan," seemed to think themselves honored by being in waiting upon him. The idea of destiny, so strongly fixed in all Mussulman minds, does much to strengthen his power and palsy the arm lifted against him. The many spirited chiefs under him though restive and extremely impatient of restraint, dare not lift a finger in opposition to him: as, in their own language, "God has given him the power, and it is in vain for us to strive for it."[74]

It can be seen from this impression how well Bedir Khan's personality fits Max Weber's description of the charismatic leader. Some of his actions provide striking indications that he was a bearer of charisma. His treatment of the converted Yazidis is both interesting and significant. According to Wright and Breath,

> He has proselyted, either by argument or the sword, a large number of the Yezidees. He has about his person fifty or sixty of that people, who have adopted the Muslim faith. Though called slaves,[75] they are the best dressed, best fed, and in every way best treated persons in his service. They are like members of his own family, and regarded as his children, to the no small annoyance of those who were born Mussulmans, and who are consequently kept at a great distance from him.[76]

The preferential treatment accorded to the converted Yazidis suggests that Bedir Khan Beg was concerned primarily with "proving himself" rather than with the sensibilities of his Muslim-born followers.[77]

The American missionaries Wright and Breath were struck by the stern and puritanical manner in which the emir maintained law and order:

The guilty under his government find no escape. Bribery, favoritism, etc., which too often, in these countries, pervert the cause of justice, and nullify the form of law, are unknown here. One morning while we were with the Emir, a thief was brought before him, which right hand was amputated as soon as the evidence of his guilt was established. We travelled in the wildest parts of Koordistan with such security, that we could hardly realize our being in a region of which we had so often heard and read, as being the scene of robbery and murder.[78]

Bedir Khan Beg regarded himself as a truthful and righteous man. According to Dr. Wright and his companion, he laid great emphasis on his faithfulness to his pledged word. He told them: "Upon this you may rely, that when I give you my word as a friend, I am so indeed."[79]

Bedir Khan, like many other charismatic leaders, had a strong religious streak. This religiosity occupied an important part of his time and thinking. As Wright and Breath put it, "He spends a great deal of time in his devotions, is exact in fulfilling all the prescribed forms of his religion and often, in hours of business, is engaged in prayer."[80] It was no doubt because of this predilection for religion that a number of shaykhs succeeded in gaining great influence over him and appear to have been instrumental in inducing him to deal so ruthlessly with the non-Muslim Nestorians.[81]

The Factors Underlying Bedir Khan's Attacks on the Mountain Nestorians

Bedir Khan's invasion of the country of the mountain Nestorians and the ensuing massacres have a claim on our attention for a variety of reasons. For one thing, there were the appalling losses suffered by the victims as a result of a ruthless war of extermination, which in cruelty and wantonness rivaled the savage attack on the Yazidis by Muhammad Pasha of Rawanduz. Another reason for the importance of the invasion is that it invited foreign interference in Ottoman affairs. This interference, although short of armed intervention, afforded the great powers a chance to meddle in Ottoman affairs long after these events were over, but failed to provide the victims with a remedy. Last but not least, the attack on the Nestorians brought about the downfall of Bedir Khan by providing the Ottoman government with a pretext for attacking and overthrowing his principality.

Many attempts have been made to account for Bedir Khan's massacres of the mountain Nestorians. Some have ascribed them to the emir's bigotry, which was fanned, it is said, by the grasping, fanatical, and insecure Nurallah Beg of Hakari with the support and blessing of the shaykhs and other religious dignitaries; others have attributed the massacres to the rivalry between English and American missionaries; and a third group has traced them to a deeply laid plot by the Ottoman authorities. The disunity of the mountain Nestorians and what has been described as the imprudent activities of their patriarch Mar Sham'un have also been cited as major causes of the tragedy. The fact is that the invasion and the massacre of the Nestorians had several causes, and all of these elements no doubt contributed to it in varying degrees.

The conflicting interests of various individuals and factions resulted in a fierce struggle for power. Ancient hatreds, religious fanaticism, greed, and thirst for power—all served to exacerbate tempers and finally precipitated the invasion and the massacre. The Nestorian patriarch Mar Sham'un, who was anxious to maintain his authority over his own people, was extremely jealous of any external element that threatened to undermine his position among them. Thus, he distrusted and resented the American missionaries, who were represented to him as attempting to accomplish the very thing he feared. For the same reason, he was at odds with some of the leading members of his community, who in turn resented his pretensions. The English and American missionaries, who contended for spiritual mastery over the Nestorians, took sides in this struggle, the English supporting patriarchal authority and the Americans opposing it. Both did their best to malign each other, the English apparently doing so with greater success.

The *mir* of Hakari, Nurallah Beg, was eager to assert his authority over Mar Sham un, not only in his capacity as the patriarch's suzerain but also out of fear that the patriarch might side with his own rival, Sulayman Beg. The patriarch resented Nurallah's pretensions both because he wanted to be independent of the *mir*'s authority and because he was partial to Sulayman Beg. The latter, who was aware of Mar Sham'un's attitude, reciprocated his sentiments and secretly supported him in his struggle against their common adversary.

Nurallah Beg was exasperated by Mar Sham'un's hostility and insubordination but was not strong enough to deal with him alone. He therefore applied for assistance to Bedir Khan Beg, who was only too glad to become a patron and supporter of Nurallah Beg. This action ensured the adherence of the powerful Hakari principality to the vast Kurdish confederation then being formed by Bedir Khan. But this was not all. The contemplated expedition against the Nestorians offered Bedir Khan a rich source of plunder with which to reward the growing number of his followers and at the same time provided him with a rare opportunity to prove his religious zeal. Both of these matters were of vital importance to his prestige and future plans.

The pasha of Mosul, who coveted the Nestorian country, was interested only in adding it to his domains. Though fully aware of the dangers threatening the Nestorians, he did nothing to prevent the invasion, if he did not in fact help to precipitate it. The pasha of Erzerum, under whose political jurisdiction the Nestorian country was included, appears to have been neither less guilty nor less deeply involved in the Nestorians' tragic fate than was his rival, the pasha of Mosul.

In the background stood the Ottoman government, indifferent but not innocent, waiting for the tribal war to start. What happened to the victims was immaterial. The prospect of having one less unruly leader to deal with and a pretext to punish the others was not unwelcome to the Ottomans.

A more detailed examination of the various rumored causes of the massacre, besides enabling us to arrive at a sounder appraisal of their relative importance, will also afford a revealing glimpse into the state of affairs prevailing in central Kurdistan at that time.

The Nestorians' disunity. There is little doubt that the disunity of the Nestorians at the time of the invasion was one of the main factors that made the attack possible. It is well to remember that only a few years earlier the *mir* of Rawanduz, a no less re-doubtable chief than Bedir Khan, had failed in his attempt to invade the Nestorian country when he was met by the united efforts of these mountaineers.[82]

The Nestorians' subsequent disunity is strikingly demonstrated in the widespread opposition to their patriarch Mar Sham'un—a fact that in more than one way facili-tated the invasion. The differences between Mar Sham'un and the two leading men of Ashita, Shamasha (Deacon) Hinno and Kasha (Priest) Jindo, which led to the excom-munication of the former, are a case in point. After his excommunication, Shamasha Hinno is reported to have gotten in touch with Bedir Khan, assuring him of his alle-giance and support if and when the impending invasion took place. Bedir Khan, who was delighted by this defection, not only spared Ashita but also went out of his way to shower gifts and honors on Shamasha Hinno. The latter's colleague, Kasha Jindo, is re-ported to have made a similar offer to Nurallah Beg and to have been similarly rewarded by that chieftain.[83]

The Tkhuma, one of the leading Nestorian clans, also appear to have been alienated by the patriarch. These clansmen, who adhered to Nurallah Beg, so completely deserted the common cause that they participated actively in the decimation of their own brethren.[84] It is interesting to note that during Bedir Khan's second invasion of the Nestorian country, this clan was the principal object of his wrath.

Nestorian relations with the principal Kurdish leaders. The Nestorians in general and the patriarch in particular seem to have given offense to all the leading Kurdish figures involved in the invasion. Isma'il Pasha of 'Amadiya, Nurallah Beg of Hakari, and Bedir Khan Beg of Bohtan all harbored strong grievances against the Nestorians. This does not necessarily mean that in every case these grievances were the fault of the Nestorians or that they were primarily to blame.

1. *Isma'il Pasha of 'Amadiya.* Isma'il Pasha's grievance is said to have stemmed from Mar Sham'un's failure to go to that chieftain's assistance when he was hard pressed by Ottoman troops. Briefly stated, this is what happened: When Isma'il Pasha heard of the preparations of the *wali* of Mosul, Injeh Bayraqdar Muhammad Pasha, to attack 'Amadiya, he reportedly appealed to Mar Sham'un for help. The latter, without any hes-itation and with the knowledge and approval of his immediate overlord, Nurallah Beg, sent three thousand of his followers to Isma'il Pasha's assistance.[85] However, when the Injeh Bayraqdar heard of the matter, he is reported to have informed Mar Sham'un of his decision to subdue 'Amadiya and ordered him to withdraw his forces. The patriarch, not wishing to incur the displeasure of the Ottoman government by ranging himself against it, hastened to obey. This act on the part of Mar Sham'un greatly offended Isma 'il Pasha, who, no doubt, when the fate of the Nestorians was being decided, threw against them whatever weight he may have had.[86]

There is reason to believe that the other Kurdish chieftains may have equally re-sented the patriarch's action. According to a contemporaneous source, "The proposed expedition of the Hakary Koords against Amadiyah has proved an entire failure, in con-sequence, it is believed, of the refusal of the Nestorian Patriarch to cooperate, and that stronghold of Koordistan has now submitted to the besieging Turkish army."[87] Inasmuch as the Kurdish princes were acting in concert against the Ottoman government, it is not unlikely that they interpreted the patriarch's action as a hostile gesture directed against all of them.[88]

2. *Bedir Khan Beg of Bohtan.* Notwithstanding the various other reasons that impelled Bedir Khan to take action against the Nestorians, he is said to have been particularly incensed by a series of defiant acts on their part that set in motion a feud between the two parties. According to some reports, the Nestorians, in the course of one of their border forays, had killed two Kurds of Bohtan. In retaliation, Bedir Khan had killed four Nestorians. The latter, not to be outdone, maintained the same ratio, killing eight of the *mir*'s subjects. It was at this juncture that Nurallah Beg approached Bedir Khan Beg with his request for aid and joint action against the Nestorians.[89]

3. *Nurallah Beg of Hakari.* Whatever differences the Nestorians may have had with Isma'il Pasha or with Bedir Khan Beg were of a relatively superficial and impermanent nature. Their differences with Nurallah Beg, the emir of Hakari, however, were of a different character—deeper, more complicated, and more enduring. The Nestorian highlands formed part of the Hakari principality. Therefore, the *mir* of Hakari was the suzerain, and the patriarch of the Nestorians was his vassal. The relations between the two men were strained, as they are likely to be when the suzerain is weak but insists on asserting his prerogatives and the vassal is strong and yields to his master's demands only grudgingly and reluctantly.

The dispute was embittered by other complicating factors. Nurallah Beg, a distant relative of the previous emir of Hakari, appears to have succeeded to the chieftainship despite the fact that Sulayman Beg, the son of the deceased emir, was the next in line of succession. Nurallah Beg apparently spared the youth for fear of starting a blood feud, but he took good care to relegate him to an inferior and ineffectual position, giving him the title of *mudabbir* (manager of affairs) of Hakari. Mar Sham'un, who had known the former emir and had been closely associated with him, was still faithful to his memory and consequently was inclined to favor the young dispossessed prince—a fact that naturally roused Nurallah Beg's anger and suspicions.[90]

Nurallah Beg appears to have been haunted by the idea that Sulayman Beg might succeed one day in ousting him. Fearing that his vassals might desert him for his rival, he sought to keep them attached to his person by various means, including giving them lavish gifts. This expenditure constituted a heavy drain on his finances, and he was invariably short of money.[91] Nurallah Beg's pecuniary troubles served only to deepen his sense of insecurity and turned him into a grasping and suspicious person. Mar Sham'un appears to have been one of those upon whom the Hakari chief made ceaseless demands for taxes and contributions, which Mar Sham'un resented. The patriarch's resentment was such that he is reported to have ordered the cancellation of the annual gift sent by the people of Ashita to the Hakari emir.[92]

The role of the American missionaries. Another factor that seems to have roused Nurallah Beg's fear and jealousy was the appearance of the American missionaries among the Nestorians. He, like other Kurds, was opposed to the missionaries for fear that they might teach the Nestorians the superior learning and arts of the Europeans (the Americans were regarded by them as "Europeans"), which would eventually enable the Nesto-rians to prevail against the Kurds.[93]

Moreover, the Kurdish chieftains feared that the missionaries, like other Europeans, might be in touch with high places in Istanbul. If so, they therefore might be in a position to bring various matters to the Porte's attention—a likelihood that the Kurds did not relish because it might mean the appearance of Ottoman forces in their country.[94]

The mission house built by Dr. Ashahel Grant at Ashita was a source of much irritation. It was rumored that it was being built as a fortress to be used for aggressive purposes against the Kurds or as a bazaar intended to draw away business from Julamerk and other Kurdish centers with a view to enriching the Nestorians at the expense of the Kurds. Nurallah Beg himself brought up these charges in the course of a conversation with Dr. Grant. When the latter denied them, pointing out that the mission house was intended to be a school and a residence for the missionaries, Nurallah Beg asked Dr. Grant to give him a statement to that effect in writing, and Dr. Grant did so.[95]

Opposition to the mission building came from Turkish as well as Kurdish sources. In fact, we have it on the authority of Dr. Grant himself that the pasha of Mosul had been scheming to bring about his assassination.[96] The undue importance attached to the mission house by both the Kurds and the Turks, notwithstanding the missionaries' assurances to the contrary, suggests that it was one of the factors that contributed to the massacres.[97]

Several English missionaries seized on the mission house issue, among others, to fix upon American missionaries the responsibility for the massacres. According to these English sources, the building of the mission house aroused the fears and suspicions of both the Kurds and the Turks, while the proselytizing by the American missionaries promoted faction and disunity among the Nestorians.[98] Although there is probably some truth in these charges, they no doubt are oversimplifications induced by partisanship. Although the American missionaries' activities may have been one of the numerous causes of the massacres, they were by no means the only or even the most important cause. In his 1853 book *Discoveries in the Ruins of Nineveh and Babylon,* Layard refuted the allegations of the English missionaries, and it is quite clear from what he had to say that the English themselves were not entirely free from blame. Layard's comments concerning his discussion of this issue with Mar Sham'un shed an interesting light on the controversy:

> Old influences, which I could not but deeply deplore, and to which I do not in Christian charity wish further to allude, had been at work, and I found him even more bitter in his speech against the American missionaries than against his Turkish or Kurdish oppressors. He had been taught, and it is to be regretted that his teachers were of the Church of England, that those who were endeavoring to civilise and instruct his flock were seceders from the orthodox community of Christians, heretical in doctrine, rejecting all the sacraments and ordinances of the true faith, and intent upon reducing the Nestorians to their own hopeless condition of infidelity. His fears were worked on

by the assurance that, ere long, through their means and teaching, his spiritual as well as his temporal authority would be entirely destroyed. I found him bent upon deeds of violence and intolerant persecution, which might have endangered, for the second time, the safety of this people as well as his own. I strove, and not without success, to calm his unreasonable violence.[99]

It is clear from this description that the American missionaries were the object of unfair accusations. However, although there is no doubt that they were a group of pious and dedicated men, their well-meaning but misdirected zeal led to a great deal of trouble for themselves and for others. Being convinced of the superiority of their beliefs and the righteousness of their intentions, they embarked on their missionary work with little or no awareness that their activities might be misrepresented, misunderstood, or resented by those among whom they labored. They should have anticipated and avoided difficulties with the patriarch. A man in the patriarch's position could not be expected to abandon the tenets and practices of the ancient church he headed and to yield his spiritual and temporal authority without a struggle. It certainly would have been better to work with him rather than in spite of him.

Similarly, the appearance of the American missionaries in the wild mountains of Kurdistan was a strange and unprecedented development that raised deep doubts and suspicions in Kurdish minds. Nor did it have the Ottoman authorities' approval. In the circumstances, it might have been more feasible, as Dr. Grant himself stated at one point, to have entrusted missionary work among the mountain Nestorians to native persons.[100] Moreover, the size and location of the mission building appears to have been ill chosen. In an April 1845 letter to the *Missionary Herald,* Thomas Laurie and Dr. Azariah Smith mentioned that it was built on the site of an old structure known among the Kurds as the "castle,"[101] a fact that no doubt accounts for the agitation caused by its construction. Upon inspecting the ruins of the mission buildings, Layard, a zealous defender of the American missionaries, commented, "They stand upon the summit of an isolated hill, commanding the whole valley. A position less ostentatious and proportions more modest might certainly have been chosen; and it is surprising that persons, so well acquainted with the character of the tribes amongst whom they had come to reside, should have been thus indiscreet."[102]

The role of the Ottoman government. One should not overlook the possibility that the Ottoman government sought to bring about a clash between the Kurds and the Nestorians, both of whom had for a long time been unruly subjects. Such a clash, in addition to weakening both antagonists and perhaps eliminating the Nestorians, would provide the Ottoman government with an excellent pretext for interfering in Kurdish affairs.

The attitude of the *wali* of Mosul at the time of the invasion of the Nestorian country by Bedir Khan's forces provides serious grounds for questioning his goodwill and intentions. It is significant that his forces, which were stationed along the borders of the Nestorian country, well within striking distance of the Kurdish forces then engaged in massacring these unfortunate people, should have remained inactive. Notwithstanding repeated assurances of protection made to Mar Sham'un, Injeh Bayraqdar Muhammad Pasha actually participated in blockading the Nestorian country instead of aiding the Nestorians, thus making the invaders' task easier.[103] In fact, there seems to be little reason to doubt his complicity. His uncertain attitude and dubious activities are often referred to in the American missionaries' letters both before and after the massacres. He reportedly was exultant at the news of the destruction of the Nestorians and shared in the spoils taken from them.[104]

Bedir Khan's Two Attacks on the Mountain Nestorians

The first invasion and massacre of the Nestorians took place in A.D. July 1843. Although the Tiyari and the Diz clans were the principal targets, many other Nestorian communities suffered. The invading forces, though led by Bedir Khan Beg, appear to have had the approval and support of the *wali* of Erzerum, whose province encompassed the Hakari region.[105] According to the *wali* of Mosul, these forces were collected from Van to Rawanduz and from the Tigris to the Persian frontier. He put the total size of the attacking force at one hundred thousand men, although the Nestorians themselves are said to have estimated it at seventy thousand.[106]

It is needless to go into the appalling losses suffered by the Nestorians or to describe the havoc wrought in their country. Much of this has been described in detail by Layard and others, including the American missionaries.[107] Those who survived the fury of the attacking tribesmen were carried into captivity as slaves. Very few succeeded in escaping to Mosul or Urmiya.[108] Strong protests by the British government, coupled with the personal exertions of the British ambassador, Sir Stafford Canning, were responsible for the liberation of many of the captives.[109]

The second invasion of the Nestorian country took place in 1846 and was directed primarily against the Tkhuma, who during the first invasion had allied themselves with the invading forces. This time Ashita, which had been spared in the first invasion, was also attacked and put to the sword. As in the case of the first invasion, extensive devastation and slaughter were reported.[110]

The Fall of Bedir Khan

England, supported by France, protested vigorously to the Porte, demanding that an end be put to the extermination of the Nestorians and that Bedir Khan be removed. The two European governments are said to have given promises of assistance to the Porte. Thus, at the insistence and with the support and blessing of these two great powers, the Porte finally decided to suppress Bedir Khan—an action it had long contemplated.[111]

This, however, was not an easy task. Bedir Khan had succeeded, over many years, in building up a vast Kurdish confederation through a series of alliances with a number of Kurdish chieftains, including those of Hakari, Van, Muks, and Bidlis.[112] Bedir Khan also succeeded in inducing the rulers of such remotely located regions as Kars and Ardalan to join his confederation.[113] His forces were well trained and well equipped, and he is reported to have established a rifle and munitions factory at Jazirat ibn 'Umar.[114]

9. The Bedir Khan family: *(seated left to right)* Emin Ali Bey (father of Jaladet, Kamuran, and Sureya), Ali Shamil Pasha, and Bahri; *(standing left to right)* Murat Ramzi Bey, Hasan, Miqdad Midhat Bey, and Kamil, ca. 1880. Photographer unknown/Courtesy of Saif T. Badrakhan. *Kurdistan: In the Shadow of History.*

An army was sent against Bedir Khan, but he had no difficulty in defeating it. After this success, he decided to sever all connections with the Ottoman Empire. He proclaimed the independence of his state and coined his own money, which bore the inscription "Bedir Khan, the Emir of Bohtan."[115]

Now that the menace of Muhammad 'Ali Pasha of Egypt had receded, the Ottoman government was able to turn its attention and the force of its arms against Bedir Khan and his confederation. A large army under the supreme command of Marshal Osman Pasha, assisted by Generals Omar Pasha and Sabri Pasha, was sent against him. The first important battle between the Ottoman army and the forces of Bedir Khan, fought in the neighborhood of Urmiya, is reported to have gone in Bedir Khan's favor. However, the defection of Emir 'Izz al-Din Shir, a relative of Bedir Khan and one of his leading army commanders, enabled the Ottoman army to occupy Bedir Khan's capital, Jazirat ibn 'Umar. This development forced Bedir Khan to hurry westward with his forces with the object of recapturing his capital, which he attacked and reoccupied, expelling 'Izz al-Din Shir and his Turkish allies.[116]

This success, however, was short-lived. The Ottoman army returned to the attack, and despite stubborn resistance Bedir Khan was compelled to vacate Jazirat ibn 'Umar and to take refuge in the fortress of Evra (Urukh).[117] In the meantime, Khan Mahmud, who was hastening to Bedir Khan's assistance, was intercepted and defeated at Til (also

Tila and Tilo), near the junction of the Bohtan and Tigris rivers, by Ottoman forces supported by Yazidi fighters.[118]

From his beleaguered fortress, Bedir Khan defied the combined forces of the Ottoman army and Emir 'Izz al-Din Shir for eight months. However, with supplies and ammunition greatly depleted, he was forced to sue for peace. His offer to surrender on condition of honorable treatment was accepted, and he was removed to Constantinople and later exiled to Candia in Crete.[119] He was allowed to be accompanied by his family and by about two hundred of his personal followers. It was with these followers that he succeeded in putting down the rebellion of the Cretan Greeks in 1856.[120] In recognition of this service, he was allowed to return to Constantinople and from there was sent to Damascus, where he resided until his death in 1868.[121] Bedir Khan left numerous descendants, many of whom were to be closely associated with the Kurdish nationalist movement in later years.[122]

After the defeat and exile of Bedir Khan, the Ottoman government turned on his former allies and subdued them one after the other. Khan Mahmud, who had been forced to surrender, was put to death after undergoing many tortures and indignities.[123] Nurallah Beg of Hakari, despite protracted resistance, was captured and sent into exile.[124] Sharif Beg of Bidlis, who appears to have resisted the longest, was finally captured and banished in 1849.[125]

After the removal of Bedir Khan, 'Izz al-Din Shir ruled in his place as the emir of Bohtan. Less than a decade later, at the time of the Crimean War, 'Izz al-Din Shir revolted against the Turks. He was suppressed and overthrown after desperate resistance.[126]

4

Shaykh 'Ubayd Allah of Nehri

Background: The Emergence of the Shaykhs as National Leaders

The suppression and eventual elimination of the hereditary semi-independent Kurdish principalities in the Ottoman Empire was followed by lawlessness and disorder throughout Kurdistan. The reasons for this state of affairs are not hard to find. The Ottomans had inaugurated the Tanzimat system with the intention of imposing a centralized system of administration. Although they succeeded in achieving the first aim, centralization, they failed, on the whole, to accomplish the second, administration. The government's inability to penetrate into the more inaccessible parts of Kurdistan, combined with its failure to exercise effective control over most of the misruled and disaffected provinces of the empire, rendered the new system of administration inoperative.

As a result, large segments of the territories of the former princes of Baban, Soran, Bohtan, Bahdinan, and Hakari were abandoned to the depredations of numerous petty tribal chieftains. These petty chieftains, hitherto effectively held in check by the powerful princes, were now at liberty to engage in all forms of lawlessness. It was not long before unchecked violence, bordering on chaos, became endemic in many of these areas, such as the Hamawand country in the heart of the Baban principality and the Zibar country in the Hakari-Bahdinan region.

This state of affairs was the outcome of the Ottoman government's failure to fill the vacuum created by the liquidation of the powerful native Kurdish leadership. The only solution the government seems to have had for coping with the situation was the periodic dispatch of punitive expeditions against the troublemakers. These expeditions often included large tribal contingents—frequently a source of the breakdown of law and order. For the most part, they failed to achieve their objectives, and most of the troubled areas were never permanently pacified. More often than not, they resulted in further violence and bloodshed and increased intertribal strife. This situation could not be tolerated for long, for insecurity was rife, trade was at a standstill, and large sections of the country were either ruined or in a state of decay.

The stage was set for the emergence of a new type of leader. Everywhere in the old seats of authority of the former Kurdish princes, the strange, unfamiliar figure of the shaykh arose to cast a new shadow of supreme authority over the disturbed land. For the first time since the overthrow of the Kurdish princes, a power greater than that of the petty feuding chieftains made itself felt.

Thus arose the shaykhs of Shamdinan, who, under Shaykh ʿUbayd Allah, dominated parts of the areas formerly under control of the princes of Bohtan, Bahdinan, and Hakari in Ottoman Turkey and Ardalan in Qajar Persia. The shaykhs of Barzinja came forth to claim the patrimony of the Baban princes, and the shaykhs of Barzan gained control over parts of the Hakari-Bahdinan principalities. Other shaykhs, less powerful than they but no less revered by their followers, such as the Qadiri shaykhs of Brifkan and the Naqshbandi shaykhs of Bamirni, succeeded in gaining control of parts of the Bahdinan principality.

The rise of the shaykhs to a position of national leadership among the Kurds not only shows the great reverence in which the shaykhs were held on account of their religious character, but also indicates that after the overthrow of the great Kurdish princes, there were no secular leaders among the Kurds capable of commanding sufficient power and prestige to fill the vacant seats of authority. The readiness with which the Kurds accepted the shaykhs as leaders shows the extent to which they felt the need to fill the power vacuum left by the disappearance of the princes. It also reveals the psychological vacuum that had created in the Kurdish national mind. Since Bedir Khan's surrender to the Ottomans in 1847, absence of a paramount figure embodying all the virile ideals of a tribal society was both unnatural and incomprehensible to the Kurds. It did violence to their system of values and left unfulfilled one of their most deeply felt psychological needs. The Kurds, like most primitive and warlike people, are inveterate hero worshippers. This intensely parochial people, still largely in their heroic age, yearned for one of their own kith and kin to wield supreme authority among them.

The Rise of Shaykh ʿUbayd Allah

As indicated earlier, the rise of Shaykh ʿUbayd Allah marks the emergence of a new type of leadership among the Kurds. He was the first and probably the greatest of the religious-secular leaders of Kurdistan. A number of circumstances combined to raise ʿUbayd Allah to a position of supreme leadership among his people. As noted, the suppression of the Kurdish princes had ushered in an era of disorder and economic distress throughout the Kurdish lands of the Ottoman Empire. Things became even worse as a result of the Russo-Turkish War of 1877–78. The havoc wrought by that war in the northeastern provinces of the empire resulted in unprecedented social and economic dislocation in that part of Kurdistan. A population harassed by violence and insecurity and decimated by famine and pestilence looked in vain for a savior. With the government apparently incapable of providing the urgently needed relief, the Kurdish people, perhaps now more than ever before, yearned for a leader of their own.

It was at this point that Shaykh ʿUbayd Allah appeared on the scene. A scion of the powerful shaykhly family of Shamdinan and son of the greatly revered Shaykh Sayyid Taha, he inherited his family's immense religious prestige upon succeeding his uncle, Shaykh Salih, as head of the Naqshbandi order of Shamdinan. To the sorely tried and despairing population, he seemed God sent, and indeed he believed himself to be so. The shaykh's subsequent success may be attributed in large measure to his unshakable conviction that the existing state of affairs had become intolerable and that he was the man called upon to bring about a new order of things. There is no doubt that the shaykh conceived of himself as a man with a mission and that he was so regarded by the numerous followers and adherents who flocked to his banner.

Shaykh ʿUbayd Allah combined in his person the role of a national leader devoted to the interests of his people with that of a devout Muslim bent on reestablishing the pristine purity of Islam in his homeland. It was his firm belief that corrupt governments and wicked persons had caused widespread suffering and distress throughout Kurdistan and that it was his duty to establish justice, to suppress lawlessness, and to put an end to evil in all its forms. The appearance in those troubled times of a leader who spoke with the voice of a prophet and the authority of a prince and who seemed to be deeply concerned about the welfare of his compatriots had an overwhelming effect on the Kurdish people. Sanctified by the memory of his sainted ancestry as well as by his own piety, he awed his countrymen by the force of his personality and roused them to acts of desperation by the passion of his words.

The role that the shaykh so fervently wished to assume was unexpectedly thrust upon him by the Russo-Turkish War of 1877–78 and by the events that followed in its wake. His appointment by the sultan-caliph as commander of the Kurdish tribal forces charged with the defense of the northeastern provinces of the empire had far-reaching effects on the subsequent course of events in Kurdistan and was perhaps decisive in his emergence as both an Islamic and a Kurdish leader—a role that no other person had assumed since the great Saladin of Crusades fame! Certainly, this appointment left no doubt as to his paramount position in Kurdistan. As an official act, it had the effect of an investiture, conferring upon him what had been denied to any other Kurd since 1847.

Shaykh ʿUbayd Allah, having found himself in a position of supreme command over a large number of his compatriots, could not easily relinquish his newly assumed role when the war was over. Fate, as it were, had beckoned to him, and from now on he, as with all men of destiny, was the instigator as well as the instrument of inexorable forces. In the short space of a few years, he became the acknowledged Kurdish leader of his time.

A number of late-nineteenth-century writers noted the importance of the religious element in the shaykh's rise to power. "A chieftain named Shaykh Obeidallah," Lord George Curzon wrote, "acquired a great reputation for personal sanctity . . . and gradually came to be looked upon as the head of Kurdish nationality."[1] Major Trotter, British consul-general in Erzerum and a contemporary of the shaykh, mentioned the great veneration in which he was held by his compatriots: "It is certain that the most influential man in Eastern Kurdistan is the Shaykh Ubeydullah, and amongst the frontier Kurds his person and authority are held more sacred than those of the Sultan."[2] The shaykh's religious position is well summed up in the words of S. G. Wilson: "Next to the Sultan and the Sherif of Mecca, he was the holiest person among the Sunnis of Kurdistan. Thousands were ready to follow him, not only as a chief, but as the Vicar of God."[3] According to a friend who knew Shaykh ʿUbayd Allah well the shaykh regarded himself as the third most important man in ecclesiastical rank in Islam, in addition to being "the civil monarch of the Kurds."[4]

Shaykh ʿUbayd Allah's Personality and Character

Although we possess considerable data on Shaykh ʿUbayd Allah's character and personality, it is not an easy task to portray adequately this strange and complex man. Of his physical appearance, only the scantiest account has come down to us. One of the few descriptions we have of him is by Dr. James P. Cochran, the American missionary and physician who attended him during his illness at the his home in Nehri. Cochran, who had so much to say about the shaykh's character and personality, said little about his personal appearance: "The Shaykh is fifty-three years old, rather prepossessing in his appearance and manner. He dresses in flowing robes of broadcloth, and wears a white turban."[5]

The shaykh appears to have created a favorable impression on most of those who knew him or knew of him. All sources seem to be agreed with regard to his great piety, integrity, and devotion to duty. According to Dr. Cochran, "His character stands out in clear contrast with that seen in the Persian officials as well as Turks. He, or his son, see personally all who come to them on business, no matter how trivial it may be. . . . From early morning to late at night he and his Heir Apparent are employed in the interests of Government and people."[6] The shaykh's abstemious nature and frugal habits apparently impressed the American missionaries. Cochran referred to the shaykh's simple home life and pointed out that "no alcohol ever enters his town,"[7] and Wilson described him as "simple in dress and food."[8]

Probity and an impartial if stern sense of justice characterized the behavior of this forbidding patriarchal figure. "As a lawgiver and judge," Wilson wrote, "he was noted for his virtue, as well as for his impartial justice."[9] In view of the corruption and venality that were so rife in Qajar Persia and Ottoman Turkey, it is remarkable that Shaykh ʿUbayd Allah should have insisted on and succeeded in imposing high standards of honesty and integrity among his followers. No doubt at times he must have been unduly harsh in imposing such standards on a people hitherto unaccustomed to them. According to Cochran, "They say he is a just Ruler and Judge. He never takes bribes nor allows his officials to do so. Death is the punishment given to any who break the law."[10]

However, it seems that the shaykh did not make any clear-cut distinction between his will and the law. Opposition to his will often brought swift and summary punishment. Once, upon being informed that a number of his followers had robbed a village despite his promise of protection, Shaykh ʿUbayd Allah had the unfortunate robbers crucified.[11] Perhaps Cochran had this incident in mind when he described the shaykh as a just judge and a kind ruler over his people "if they do his will—otherwise very cruel."[12] It should be kept in mind, however, that such cruelty was not unusual at that time in Kurdistan.

Although stern and exacting toward his own people, the shaykh often displayed a surprising degree of tolerance and open-mindedness toward others. A number of mis-

10. Dr. Cochran with Kurdish chieftain (unidentified). Photographer unknown/Courtesy Roswell O. Moore family. *Kurdistan: In the Shadow of History.*

sionaries who knew Shaykh 'Ubayd Allah noted this quality with great admiration. Speer commended him as "a man of wide and tolerant sympathy" and referred to his friendly attitude toward foreigners and his fair treatment of Christians. He told how the sultan had asked the shaykh, when he was a prisoner in Constantinople, to write a description of the conditions of the people in Kurdistan.

> The Shaykh wrote in his paper a great deal about the Nestorian Christians there, praising them as the best subjects of the Sultan. The Sultan objected to such language, and

three times returned the letter for correction. Finally the Shaykh said, "I don't know much about politics, but I do know something about truth telling, and this is the truth."[13]

The shaykh as a great religious leader apparently was deeply learned in what are known in the Muslim countries as the religious sciences.[14] We learn from Dr. Cochran that he was well read in Arabic and Persian literature and that among other things he read the Bible, a copy of which was sent to him by the doctor himself. Like most educated Kurds, he probably knew a great deal of Kurdish folklore and literature. Cochran paid warm tribute to his intelligence and thirst for knowledge: "He seemed to enjoy conversing on all subjects with me. During the week that I stayed at his house, I had many very pleasant talks with him. He was very much interested in hearing about the new inventions and other wonders of the Western world."[15]

Shaykh 'Ubayd Allah's Aims and Activities

The Unification of the Kurds and the Formation of a Kurdish State

The shaykh's primary aim was to unite the Kurds and to set up an independent Kurdish state. We do not know precisely when he formed this resolve, but we do know that it was greatly influenced by the events that accompanied and followed the war of 1877–78. The rise of the mystic and puritanical zealot to a position of supreme leadership among his people in those troubled times seems to have brought about a profound and abiding transformation in his own thinking. To him, it was a sign of divine favor that vindicated his righteousness and confirmed his belief in the charismatic quality of his leadership. The experience of wielding great power must have radically changed the nature and scope of the shaykh's ambitions. As the old parochial interests of a local leader gave way to a more comprehensive concern for the welfare of a whole nation, the idea of a united and independent Kurdistan took shape and came to dominate his thinking.

Many competent observers held this opinion. British vice-consul Clayton stated: "I am inclined to believe that he has a comprehensive plan for uniting all the Kurds in an independent state under himself."[16] William Abbott, British consul-general in Tabriz, writing at the time of the Kurdish invasion of Persia, summarized the shaykh's intentions as follows: "His project is to place himself at the head of a Kurdish Principality, and to annex the whole of Kurdistan both in Turkey and Persia."[17] A similar opinion was expressed by Trotter, who mentioned the extent of the shaykh's territorial ambitions: "There can be little doubt that this man's one object is to rid the country of the Sultan's officials and set himself up as ruler of Kurdistan, i.e., of the southern portion of the Van and the northern portion of the Mosul Vilayet (province), and as much further in every direction as he can extend his influence."[18]

Mr. Thomson, British minister in Tehran, discussed the shaykh's plans for setting up an independent Kurdish principality and the means by which he intended to accomplish this end:

There seems to be no doubt from these and from the proclamations and correspondence which he has lately sent to various Kurdish Chiefs along the line of the Persian border that his design is to detach the entire Kurdish population from their allegiance to Turkey and Persia, and to establish under his own authority a separate autonomous Principality, and that for the attainment of this object he is endeavouring by threats and promises to incite all the Kurdish tribes to join him in open warfare with this country [Persia].[19]

This, then, was the task to which Shaykh 'Ubayd Allah addressed himself and to the realization of which he bent all his energies with much tact and considerable political insight.

The need to unite the Kurds in an independent state appears to have urged itself upon him with the force and the persistence of an obsession. The compelling reasons for uniting the Kurds were mentioned repeatedly in his correspondence and declarations: (1) the racial, cultural, and linguistic similarity of the Kurdish people, which marked them off as a separate nationality; (2) the widespread lawlessness in Kurdistan stemming from Turkish and Persian misrule and resulting in the ill-repute of the Kurdish nation; and (3) the fear of Armenian ascendancy in Kurdistan.

The basic similarity of the Kurdish people. In order to gain a deeper insight into Shaykh 'Ubayd Allah's thinking, it is important to understand his concept of Kurdish nationalism and the ideas he held on this matter. The shaykh seems to have been firmly convinced that the Kurdish people constituted a separate nationality. He regarded them as being sufficiently similar in race, language, and way of life, as well as holding many other things in common, to have a distinct identity of their own. In a letter to Dr. Cochran, he wrote, "The Kurdish nation, consisting of more than 500,000 families, is a people apart. Their religion is different (to that of others), and their laws and customs are distinct."[20]

This statement certainly leaves no doubt as to his deep conviction of the basic unity of the Kurdish people. The shaykh's contention that the Kurds' religion was different from that of others is extremely significant. It indicates the extent to which nationalism depends on exclusiveness and difference. Both the Turks and Persians, whom Shaykh 'Ubayd Allah had in mind when he made this statement, are Muslims like the Kurds. The majority of the Kurds are Shafi'i Sunnites (Sunnis), whereas the Turks are Hanafi Sunnites and the Persians are Twelver Shi'ites (Shi'is). Thus, in order to emphasize the complete distinctiveness of the Kurds, the shaykh magnified denominational differences and made this extravagant claim, which is especially untenable in the case of the Turkish Kurds, who, like them, are Sunnites.

The ruinous effects of Turkish and Persian misrule. The deterioration of law and order after the suppression of the semiautonomous Kurdish regimes and after the war of 1877–78 assumed such proportions that organized government became impossible over large areas of the northeastern provinces. Although the majority of the law-abiding population continued to suffer the depredations of the lawless elements, the authorities seemed either unable or unwilling to check the violence and the ruin that threatened to engulf the land.

There is no doubt that this intolerable state of affairs was one of the most powerful influences in determining the course of the shaykh's future actions. It was not long before the whole of Kurdistan heard his protest. He attributed the distracted conditions of the country to misgovernment by the Turks and the Persians, and criticized the sultan's and the shah's officials for their corruption and ineptitude. He even ventured to challenge the right of both the Ottoman and the Persian governments to rule in Kurdistan. This challenge was not confined to words. As we shall see, he took up arms, first against Turkey and then against Persia.

One of the most striking aspects of Shaykh 'Ubayd Allah's condemnation of the lawlessness in Kurdistan was his deep concern over the ill-repute that it had brought upon the Kurdish name. In a letter addressed to Iqbal al-Dawla, the Persian governor of Urmiya, the shaykh on the eve of his invasion of Persia pointed out that the Kurdish nation suffered an undeserved reputation for lawlessness because no distinction was made between the innocent and the guilty. He accused the Turkish and Persian governments of having neither the will nor the power to govern their Kurdish subjects properly, with the result that the latter had lost all respect for their rulers.[21] The shaykh then informed the governor, "In view of this state of affairs, both the Persian and Turkish Kurds have resolved to unite and form a single nation, and keep order among themselves, and they undertake to bind themselves in writing that no disorder shall take place in their country."[22]

In a letter addressed to Dr. Cochran shortly after the invasion, the shaykh dwelt more fully on the abuses of the Turkish and Persian governments that had led him to undertake these military operations. He again expressed his concern over the reputation of the Kurdish nation, which he attributed to the malice and misgovernment of these two powers:

> It is known among all nations as mischievous and corrupt. This is how Kurdistan has been depicted. If one person from among them does an evil deed, a thousand peaceable and orderly persons gain an ill repute. Be it known to you for certain that this has all been caused by the laches of the Turkish and Persian authorities, for Kurdistan is in the midst between these two countries, and both Governments, for their own reasons, do not distinguish between good and evil characters.[23]

The shaykh went on to cite the depredations of two Kurdish tribes, the Shikak in Persia and the Herki in Turkey. He blamed the lawlessness of these tribes on the Persian and Turkish governments, which he maintained were either unable or unwilling to control them.[24] According to the shaykh, the Kurds and their leaders had become convinced of the futility of continuing to put up with this state of affairs: "The Chiefs and Rulers of Kurdistan, whether Turkish or Persian subjects, and the inhabitants of Kurdistan, one and all are united and agreed that matters cannot be carried on in this way with the two Governments, and that necessarily something must be done, so that European Governments, having understood the matter, shall inquire into our state."[25]

At this point, Shaykh 'Ubayd Allah demanded that the Kurds should be allowed to control Kurdistan, arguing that it would serve the cause of law and order: "We want our affairs to be in our own hands, so that in the punishment of our own offenders we may be strong and independent, and have privileges like other nations; and respecting our offenders, we are ready to take upon ourselves that no harm or damage shall accrue to any nation." [26]

It is evident from the foregoing that the desire to establish law and order in Kurdistan occupied a very important place in the shaykh's thinking. His insistence that the formation of a Kurdish state was the only remedy for lawlessness is significant, even if regarded as a pretext. The prospects of establishing a just and orderly government under Persian or Turkish rule seemed so remote at the time that the demand by the Kurds to set their own house in order seemed to be fully justified.

Fear of Armenian ascendency in Kurdistan. Fear of Armenian ascendency in Kurdistan appears to have been one of the most powerful reasons behind the shaykh's attempt to unite the Kurds. The Treaty of Berlin had given rise to a great deal of talk about Armenian ambitions in the eastern provinces, the most likely region for the establishment of a Kurdish state. Disturbing rumors to the effect that the great powers were about to grant the Armenians a status above that of the Kurds gained wide currency. These fears stemmed from Article 61 of the Treaty of Berlin, which promised the Armenians certain "improvements and reforms" and guaranteed their "security against Circassians and Kurds." [27] The Turks, as we shall see, were suspected of spreading these rumors among the Kurds and arousing Kurdish opposition to the reforms from motives of their own.

The arrival of British military consuls in Kurdistan increased Kurdish anxieties. Vice-consul Clayton reported, on the authority of certain Nestorian sources, that "the Kurds have been profoundly moved by the advent of European Consuls at Van. They regard the event with mixed feelings, partly of resentment and partly of fear, because they do not know what it may portend for them." [28] According to these sources, the Kurds would react adversely if anticipated measures did not materialize. "If they see no result ensue, it is to be feared that they will be encouraged in their evil ways." [29] There were certainly indications that the Kurds' apprehensive mood was turning into surly defiance. Clayton stated that Kurds in the vicinity of Mush and Bidlis "defiantly tell those that they maltreat and rob to go and make their complaints to the foreign Consuls." [30]

A remark made by Shaykh ʿUbayd Allah to an Ottoman official clearly reflected this mood: "What is this I hear, that the Armenians are going to have an independent state in Van, and that the Nestorians are going to hoist the British flag and declare themselves British subjects? I will never permit it, even if I have to arm the women." [31] The shaykh's attitude is not difficult to understand. He opposed the reforms because they foreshadowed the end of his dream of a Kurdish state and because he believed them to contain the seeds of a future Armenian state in which the Kurds would be reduced to an inferior status.

Winning the Cooperation of Local Christians

Despite the shaykh's opposition to the reforms, his approach seems to have been both reasonable and shrewd. No doubt he realized that the reforms were the direct outcome of the sad plight of the Christian populations, but he was unwilling to see the whole Kurdish nation penalized for that unhappy state of affairs. He certainly was aware of the ravages inflicted by certain lawless Kurdish elements upon the peaceful inhabitants of Kurdistan. It will be recalled that the shaykh, on various occasions, had denounced these marauders, whose depredations were onerous to Christian and Kurd alike. The continued failure of the Ottoman and Persian governments to establish law and order had convinced him of the futility of relying on them for a solution.

Shaykh ʻUbayd Allah seems to have come to the conclusion that the only way out of this difficulty lay in the elimination of Turkish and Persian influence and in closer cooperation between the Kurds and the local Christians. Although determined to render the reforms inoperative, the shaykh strove to make them unnecessary. With this object in mind, he tried on numerous occasions to establish contact with local Christian leaders. He was reported to have approached the Nestorian patriarch Mar Shamʻun, as well as the chief Armenian ecclesiastic in the Van-Hakari area and urged them both to join him against the Ottoman and Persian governments.[32] In return for their cooperation, he promised to protect the local Christians.

It should be pointed out here that there is no real contradiction between the shaykh's declared intention of opposing any preferential treatment given to the Armenians and Nestorians and his attempts to win them over to his side. In pursuing the latter policy, he had several objectives in mind. By persuading the Armenians and Nestorians to cooperate with him, he would ensure a united home front and have greater material and manpower at his disposal for the anticipated struggle with Turkey, while at the same time obviating the ascendancy of non-Kurdish elements in the area. Moreover, in being associated with the local Christians as their ally and protector, he hoped to gain the sympathy and support of the Christian powers in Europe. He would then be in a position to establish Kurdish hegemony over the entire area under his own aegis. The shaykh's promise of protection to the Christians was thus but a small price for all the benefits he expected to reap.[33]

The Armenians received Shaykh ʻUbayd Allah's offer of cooperation with considerable wariness and caution.[34] Besides their reluctance to become involved in an insurrectionary movement, they regarded the project as a Turkish-inspired plan designed to rob them of the privileges promised them in the Treaty of Berlin. The Nestorians, too, hesitated to commit themselves. Later, however, when the shaykh launched his attack on Persia, his forces included a contingent of mountain Nestorians led by a bishop, and his military band of musicians was entirely composed of these people.[35] Moreover, an Armenian notable named Simon Agha, charged with liaison duties, accompanied the shaykh's forces in order to ensure the protection of the Armenian populations lying on the route of the invading army.[36]

Winning European Support

Shaykh ʻUbayd Allah seems to have had considerable insight into the nature of power politics and diplomacy. He apparently attached great importance to making his legitimate aims known to the representatives of the great powers and to European public opinion in general. Wilson said of the shaykh: "He cultivated foreigners, and sought to enlist the public opinion of the world on his side."[37] In a letter to Dr. Cochran, the shaykh expressed the hope that the European governments would inquire into the state of affairs in Kurdistan.[38] He realized that winning the support of England was especially important, inasmuch as that country was responsible for carrying out the reforms provided for by the Treaty of Berlin. His unceasing efforts to cultivate the friendship of the American missionaries and his open profession of friendship for the Christians of Kurdistan were perhaps designed to achieve this end.

ʿUbayd Allah's judicious selection of friends among the American missionaries stood him in good stead, for it was through them that he succeeded in establishing informal relations with British representatives.[39] The American missionary Dr. Cochran, for instance, proved to be not only a valuable link with British consular officials, but also a trustworthy and sympathetic spokesman. The striking similarities between a highly favorable report on the shaykh and his movement, written by Dr. Cochran to the Board of Presbyterian Missions,[40] and an anonymous report received by the British consulgeneral Abbott in Tabriz[41] prove Cochran's authorship of this report beyond any doubt.

This is not to say that Shaykh ʿUbayd Allah was an unprincipled opportunist who tried to exploit his American friends and deceive the British authorities. On the contrary, there is ample evidence that he was most scrupulous in keeping his pledged word. He demonstrated the sincerity of his promises by his protection of the Christian population of the Urmiya plain throughout his campaign in Persian Kurdistan. Another indication of the shaykh's sincerity and goodwill, as we shall see later, was his decision to delay his attack on Urmiya at Dr. Cochran's request.

The Shaykh's Aims and Policies as Stated by His Khalifa

Perhaps the best statement of the aims and policies of Shaykh ʿUbayd Allah was made by Shaykh Muhammad Saʿid, ʿUbayd Allah's *khalifa* and brother-in-law, at a conference held outside Urmiya at the time of the Kurdish siege of that city. The primary purpose of the conference was to explain the shaykh's objectives to British consulgeneral Abbott. The conference was attended by the American missionaries, the Nestorian metropolitan of Naw Chia, and several followers of Shaykh ʿUbayd Allah, probably including the Armenian notable Simon Agha.

Shaykh Muhammad Saʿid declared that ʿUbayd Allah, if successful, undertook to suppress brigandage, restore order within the borders of Turkey and Persia, place Christians and Muslims on a footing of equality, promote education, and allow churches and schools to be built. According to Abbott, the *khalifa* went on to say:

> All the Shaykh wanted was the moral support of the European Powers, especially England, for whom he had the greatest friendship and regard. The Shaykh asked to be put on his trial. If he failed to organize Kurdistan, and to establish there a stable Government, then he was prepared to be judged by the tribunal of Europe, and to abide by the consequences.[42]

The Kurdish League

Soon after the reform provisions[43] of the Treaty of Berlin became known in Kurdistan, rumors circulating among the people hinted at the unpleasant shape of things to come and predicted dire consequences for the Kurds. This hitherto politically indifferent people reacted with unexpected vigor to what they believed constituted a threat to their future existence as a nationality. Before long, a movement was afoot throughout the eastern provinces to organize the Kurds and to coordinate their efforts in opposing the introduction of the dreaded reforms. This unprecedented political activity, which centered around Shaykh 'Ubayd Allah, came to be known as the Kurdish League.

At first, this attempt to reverse the decisions of the great powers, as set forth in the Treaty of Berlin, appeared as futile as it was audacious. For an amorphous mass of unlettered, disunited, and feuding mountaineers to succeed where Turkey had failed seemed most unlikely. The eventual success of this movement was owing to a number of factors, not the least of which was Turkey's reportedly benevolent attitude. Turkey had been suspected of instigating and supporting Shaykh 'Ubayd Allah's efforts to mobilize the Kurds. Early reports of Turkish-Kurdish cooperation are rather confusing and do not give a clear picture of the events then taking place in Kurdistan. Even usually well-informed British sources were not in agreement concerning the nature and extent of Ottoman support of Kurdish political activity.

The British consul-general in Tabriz, Mr. Abbott, in a dispatch to the British foreign secretary, criticized the Ottoman authorities for their leniency toward Shaykh 'Ubayd Allah, who only a year earlier had taken up arms against the government: "The Turkish Government, instead of inflicting upon the Shaykh the punishment due to a rebel, heaped favors upon him, and he is now carrying out his ambitious project with apparent impunity."[44] Abbott attributed this conciliatory policy to the fact that the shaykh was "carrying out the wishes of the retrograd party in Turkey."[45] Consul-General Abbott concluded his dispatch by emphasizing the necessity of watching 'Ubayd Allah closely.

Another British official, Major Trotter, consul-general in Turkish Kurdistan, took a different view of the situation. He expressed serious doubts as to the likelihood of official Turkish support for 'Ubayd Allah's activities on the grounds that such a policy would be incompatible with Turkey's own interests and security. According to him, the idea of Turkish-Kurdish cooperation was merely a figment of the imagination of certain organs of the press in Constantinople. In a dispatch to Mr. Goschen, British minister in that city, Major Trotter wrote: "I cannot believe that the Turkish Government could be guilty of such folly as to organize a League which, if once formed, must inevitably be directed against the Government itself."[46] He pointed out that the Ottoman government's policy had always been to set one tribe against another. He went on to cite the example of recent Kurdish rebellions that were suppressed with the aid of friendly Kurdish chieftains.

No doubt Major Trotter's skepticism regarding Turkey's role in the formation of the Kurdish League was prompted by commonsense considerations. Such considerations, however, do not always prevail in the councils of nations. Turkey had just emerged from a disastrous war that had cost it much in blood, treasure, and territory. The reforms, a humiliating reminder of defeat, threatened the Turks with further territorial losses. Seen in this light, Turkey's support of a Kurdish league, dedicated to the nullification of the reforms provision, is not difficult to understand.

Major Trotter, notwithstanding his refusal to believe in the existence of a Turkish-supported Kurdish league, was aware of "a certain amount of agitation amongst the Kurds, with reference to the once much talked-of question of Armenian autonomy." [47] His description of the climate of opinion then prevailing in Kurdistan was both accurate and revealing: "It is very possible that if exceptional privileges were granted to the Armenians, from which Turks and Kurds were excluded, the Kurds might combine against the Christians and against the Government, which introduced such innovations." [48]

Despite the fact that these two British officials disagreed on the matter of Turkish support of the Kurdish movement, Trotter shared Abbott's apprehensions concerning the dangers inherent in Shaykh ʿUbayd Allah's activities. He concluded his dispatch to Mr. Goschen with the following remarks: "If the Porte were wise in their own interests, it would seize the present opportunity of crushing the Shaykh, who, as long as he remains in his native country, will continue to be a thorn in their side." [49] Major Trotter's statement was evidently based on the presumption that Turkey was unaware of the full import of the shaykh's political activities and was certainly not a party to them. Later developments and fuller information do not bear out his view of the situation, for, as we shall presently see, Turkey was more deeply involved in the Kurdish movement than Trotter realized at the time.

A report submitted by Nestorian Monseigneur Krimian to the Armenian patriarch throws some light on the formation of the Kurdish league and its aims. Turkey's responsibility for the creation of the league and its motives for pursuing this policy were stated in no uncertain terms: "A Kurdish League is about to be formed at the instigation of the Central Government, which desired to stifle the Armenian question by raising a new one, that of the Kurds." [50] The report went on to point out the means by which the government intended to achieve this end: "The Ottoman Government, to raise the prestige of the Kurdish race in Europe, are making extraordinary efforts to provoke simultaneous insurrectionary movements in Turkey and Persia, where the Leaguers wish to create for themselves a second center of operations and of control, between Asma and Salmast." [51]

According to Krimian's report, "The soul of this League is the Ottoman policy, the Shaykh Ebedullah [ʿUbayd Allah] its nominal center; Bahri Bey its assiduous emissary." [52] The latter statement, however, fails to give an adequate picture of the situation, for, as we shall see, the shaykh was not a mere tool of Ottoman policy, as this statement seems to imply. Regardless of the Turkish government's part in the creation of the Kurdish League, the shaykh's role as its leader is of fundamental importance. This statement may have been a deliberate attempt on the writer's part to place the onus of responsibility on the Ottoman government, or it may have indicated the writer's ignorance of the true nature of Shaykh ʿUbayd Allah's role and activities.

The important role assigned in this report to Bahri Beg as the Ottoman government's emissary is of particular significance because it sustains Monseigneur Krimian's thesis of Ottoman sponsorship of the Kurdish League. Bahri Beg, a son of the great

Prince Bedir Khan, is said to have been contacting various Kurdish chieftains, "employing promises, entreaties and threats" with the object of uniting them all under Shaykh 'Ubayd Allah. According to the monseigneur's report, Bahri Beg had been sent by the Ottoman government to Hakari as the official bearer of the decoration that it had conferred upon the shaykh. However, the real nature of his mission is not clear. At times, he spoke as a government representative with wide powers, but at other times he acted as the shaykh's agent and supporter.[53] On one occasion, he is reported to have said, "I will write the Shaykh to go to Constantinople; if he resists, I will, on my return, march against him with the Imperial Troops." [54] Yet, according to the same source, as soon as Bahri Beg reached the shaykh, he summoned to him not only Kurdish chiefs from Armenia, but those from Persia as well. Many chiefs, the report maintained, allied themselves with Shaykh 'Ubayd Allah, although some were still unwilling to join him "in spite of all the efforts of Bahri Bey." However, the prediction was made that these chiefs would eventually go over to the shaykh.

Bahri Beg's mission as merely an official bearer of a decoration seems incompatible with his deep involvement in Kurdish affairs. If the utterances and activities attributed to him in the Armenian report are true, then the Ottoman government must have entrusted him with a much more important mission than the mere bearing of decoration. Of course, the possibility remains that in cooperating with the shaykh, he was doing so without the Turkish government's approval. But, in that event, it certainly was a strange coincidence that the government should have chosen as its representative to the shaykh a son of the great Prince Bedir Khan, whose prestige and renown were unrivaled throughout Kurdistan.

The Shaykh's Rebellion in Turkey

In 1879, Shaykh 'Ubayd Allah took up arms against Turkey. It was a cautious rising, in which the shaykh appeared to take no chances. This rebellion, as we shall see, was in many ways the model on which he patterned his subsequent invasion of Persia.

According to the *qaimmaqam* (deputy commissioner) of Gevver, 'Ubayd Allah aimed at forming "an independent Principality of the country inhabited by the Kurds, undertaking to pay as tribute the amount now levied in taxes by the Turkish Government." [55] The *qaimmaqam* believed that the shaykh chose this particular time to press his demands for independence because of the weakness of the Turkish administration in Kurdistan as a result of the war of 1877–78.

It appears that Shaykh 'Ubayd Allah had been suspected for some time of planning a rebellion. According to Vice-Consul Clayton, he had been preparing for the uprising for some two years.[56] It was rumored at the time of the rebellion that the *wali* of Van had received a warning from Diyarbakr a year earlier concerning the shaykh's intentions, but that he had not taken the warning seriously.[57] Perhaps the shaykh's restive mood was reflected in the fact that earlier that year he had written to the *wali* of Van "demanding decorations and other rewards for his services during the late [Russo-Turkish] war." [58]

There were many other indications that the atmosphere in Kurdistan was becoming increasingly tense, and preparations of a warlike nature were evident in the area. It was reported that the Hakari district was entirely in the shaykh's power[59] and that he was in communication with Mar Sham'un, the Nestorian patriarch, as well as with a number of influential Muslims in the city of Van.[60] According to the American missionary Dr. Reynolds, the Nestorians, hitherto very friendly to the missionaries, had suddenly become hostile.[61] Another significant development was that the Kurds were making large purchases of corn in Van.[62]

Shaykh 'Ubayd Allah reportedly was well supplied with good rifles. He was believed to have made considerable purchases of firearms at Koi through an agent at Urmiya.[63] The shaykh's forces were also said to be in possession of rifles originally provided to the Kurdish tribes by the Porte during the Russo-Turkish War. Consul-General Abbott mentioned that very few of the twenty thousand rifles issued to the Kurds at that time had been returned, despite the government's demand for their restitution: "It is not improbable that Shaykh Obeidoolluh and his adherents are now using against the Turkish Government many of these same weapons, originally provided for its defense."[64] The *wali* of Van reported that the shaykh had four thousand men under his orders and that armed Kurds continued to come across the frontier from Persia.[65]

The rebellion was evidently touched off when a group of Herki Kurds who had plundered a village were punished by the *qaimmaqam* of Gevver. When the news of this reached Shaykh 'Ubayd Allah, he sent word to various Kurdish leaders "urging them to revolt, saying that there was no longer any Turkish Government, and that he intended in eight days to march on 'Amadia."[66] Among those contacted was Shaykh Muhammad of Beridchan, who is said to have lost no time in reporting the shaykh's intentions to the *wali* of Mosul.

Five days later a battalion of government troops, dispatched from Mosul, arrived in the neighborhood of 'Amadiya. A force of nine hundred Kurds, assembled by Shaykh 'Ubayd Allah and placed under the command of his son 'Abd al-Qadir, attacked the Ottoman force and was defeated.[67] This seems to have been the decisive engagement, for although desultory fighting and indecisive skirmishing continued at various places, the Kurds knew that they were beaten. When they became aware of the government's determination and ability to suppress armed rebellion, the uprising soon petered out.

While the shaykh's son and his followers were in the field and his emissaries were secretly urging the various chieftains to rebel, Shaykh 'Ubayd Allah himself had wisely kept in the background, temporized with the government, and generally maintained an attitude of aloofness.[68] He now sent a letter to the *wali* of Van protesting his innocence, expressing his displeasure at what had happened, and affirming his loyalty to the government. "Inform the Government," he told the *wali*, "that I am more faithful than ever."[69] He is also reported to have "summoned his son Abd-ul-Kader to his presence, in order that he might compel him to make his submission to the Government."[70]

The Ottoman government's attitude toward Shaykh 'Ubayd Allah is rather puzzling. Although orders had been received from Istanbul stressing the necessity of dealing firmly with the rebels, and although high Ottoman officials such as the *walis* of Van and Mosul distrusted the shaykh and knew of his ambitions,[71] the central government displayed much restraint and forbearance in dealing with him. The *wali* of Van, both during the rebellion and after, showed him great consideration. Even the Ottoman grand vizier sent the shaykh a friendly telegram urging him to come to terms with the local authorities. This telegram was delivered to him in person by the mufti of Van on behalf of the government.[72] The *qaimmaqam* of Gevver, who had incurred the shaykh's displeasure by punishing a group of plundering Herki, was removed from his post.[73] Later, after the suppression of the rebellion, the shaykh was received in Van with great pomp. It appears that one of the shaykh's demands for a final settlement of his differences with the government was a salary of twenty thousand piastres a month. According to Trotter, the *wali* of Van recommended that this salary should be granted.[74]

Strangely enough, this unsuccessful rebellion marked the beginning rather than the end of Shaykh 'Ubayd Allah's political career. Soon after these events, he became the acknowledged leader of a vast Kurdish nationalist movement aimed at the creation of an independent Kurdish state. His followers and emissaries were busy throughout Kurdistan gaining new adherents for his cause.

The Ottoman government, which certainly must have been aware of 'Ubayd Allah's activities and ambitions, maintained a friendly attitude and helped rather than hampered his efforts. The government evidently either did not dare punish such a powerful and holy person or regarded him as a potential ally capable of performing valuable services in the future. Even when his activities culminated in the armed invasion of Persia, the Ottoman government, as we shall see, continued to defend the shaykh and to protest his innocence. This fact no doubt supported Persia's contentions that the Turks were behind Shaykh 'Ubayd Allah's movement.

The Kurdish Invasion of Persia

Causes of the Invasion

The origins of the Kurdish invasion of Persia may be traced in part to the Russo-Turkish War of 1877–78. As mentioned earlier, it was during this war that the Turks took the fateful step of arming thousands of Kurdish tribesmen with modern weapons. Shaykh 'Ubayd Allah was the leader of the largest contingent of these tribesmen in a jihad against Russia.[75] However, these forces did not for long constitute a problem for the Russians, who soon succeeded in defeating and dispersing them.

The arming of the Kurds, which had grave consequences for Turkey, was to have even graver consequences for Persia. The Kurdish warriors retained both their weapons and, what is perhaps even more important, the spirit of the jihad. The invasion of Persia demonstrated that it was just as easy to turn these tribesmen against the Shi'i Muslim Persians as it had been to turn them against the Orthodox Christian Russians. In fact, during Shaykh 'Ubayd Allah's rebellion in Turkey, his men had not hesitated to fight even the army of the sultan-caliph, the titular head of all Sunni Islam.

The reform provisions of the Treaty of Berlin, an outcome of the war of 1877–78, may be regarded as another indirect cause of the invasion. The rumored ambitions of the Armenians in the eastern provinces produced unprecedented unity among the Kurds, a people notorious for their disunity and lack of cohesion. It will be recalled that this was how the Kurdish League, a militant nationalist movement, had come into being. For reasons already discussed, the league appears to have had the sympathy, if not the active support, of the Turkish government. The shaykh lost no time in making use of the league to extend his influence and to consolidate his power throughout Kurdistan. By the time the question of the reforms had receded into the background, 'Ubayd Allah had emerged as the unquestioned Kurdish leader of his time. His prestige enhanced and his ambitions undiminished, he now felt that the time was ripe for the realization of his life-long dream of an independent Kurdish state. Having tried and failed in Turkey, he now turned his attention to Persia.

No doubt Persia's weakness was one of the main factors that made it such an inviting target. The comment of an observer close to the scene of these events is interesting: "It is possible that the Shaykh's recent move into Persia may have been made under the impression that the Persian Government was more rotten than that of Turkey, and that it would be easier to obtain independent authority there than in Turkey. This once obtained, he would use his greatly increased power against the Ottoman officials."[76]

There can be little doubt that what finally induced the shaykh to embark on his hazardous undertaking was Persia's feebleness, coupled with the detestation felt toward that country by the Sunni Kurds in general and by the shaykh's devoted *murid*s and dervishes in particular on account of the predominant Shi'i faith in Persia.

Shaykh 'Ubayd Allah stated the immediate causes of his invasion of Persia in a letter to Dr. Cochran dated September 25, 1880.[77] In this letter, he enumerated Kurdish grievances against Persia—wrongs suffered by him and by other Kurds. These complaints include the brutal murder of a number of Kurds and the ill-treatment of others, the imposition of heavy fines and exactions on certain Kurdish chieftains, the abduction of Kurdish women by Persian officials, and the spread of violence and lawlessness with consequent injury to the welfare and good name of the Kurdish nation. These acts, in the shaykh's opinion, constituted the casus belli of the conflict with Persia.

The Shaykh's Forces and Their Equipment

Even a short spell of fighting, regardless of the results, is sufficient to have a telling effect on the cohesiveness and discipline of a tribal force. Unless this force is rigidly controlled and sternly disciplined, success produces practically the same results as a setback. A defeat invariably ends in mass desertions and a rout, and a victory oftentimes deteriorates into an orgy of plunder and excesses. The spoil-laden tribal warriors, physically and mentally encumbered by their newly acquired wealth, are apt to disperse and slink away to their homes at the first opportunity. Thus, in a tribal war, the strength and composition of tribal forces are in a constant state of flux. Even when a tribal force is successful, the numbers of those forsaking the struggle may be as great as the numbers of fresh arrivals drawn by the prospect of quick enrichment. These facts, coupled with the lack of reliable figures, make it extremely difficult to give an accurate estimate of the total number of Kurdish forces participating in Shaykh 'Ubayd Allah's invasion of Persia.

Considering the weakness of the Persian forces in Azerbayjan at the time of the invasion, the shaykh's men were relatively well armed, as to both the quantity and the quality of their weapons. As mentioned earlier, much of the war material in the hands of the invading Kurds had been procured during the war of 1877–78, when the shaykh had been placed in charge of large tribal forces. The equipment that the tribesmen retained after their defeat and dispersal by the Russians included large quantities of Martini rifles and cartridges.[78]

According to an Armenian source, Shaykh ʿUbayd Allah's Kurdish League, on the eve of the invasion of Persia, had at its disposal "4,000 Martini rifles, of which 200 were of Persian and the remainder of Turkish origin."[79] According to Nikitine, of the twelve thousand men who attacked Urmiya, one thousand were armed with new-type rifles.[80] The shaykh apparently had his own facilities for meeting part of his needs for military supplies. The Persian ambassador in Constantinople described the shaykh as "the possessor of an important manufactory of cartridges."[81] The fact that the shaykh was well provided with arms and ammunition and continued to receive military stores is attested to by the reported capture of 160 camel loads of rifles and cartridges by Taymur Pasha Khan in the Baradost region in November 1880.[82]

Military Operations

Shaykh ʿUbayd Allah's only official intimation of his decision to invade Persia is a cryptic reference to his son's "going to Sawj Bulaq," which appears in the vaguely worded opening paragraph of one of the shaykh's two letters addressed to Dr. Cochran on the eve of his momentous undertaking. The letter begins: "I send Mollah Ismaʿil to explain, confidentially, as I have explained to him, the state of affairs here, and I specially request that you will inform the English Government of the facts of the case of Kurdistan, and respecting the going of my son to Sawj Bulaq."[83] As later events were to prove, the shaykh's emissary was to inform Dr. Cochran confidentially that the shaykh's son was "going to Sawj Bulaq," but at the head of an army!

In early October 1880, Shaykh ʿUbayd Allah's Kurdish warriors crossed the Persian border. According to contemporary reports, his army consisted of three contingents. One force was commanded by his cadet son ʿAbd al-Qadir, who moved in the general direction of the southern shores of Lake Urmiya toward Sawj Bulaq.[84] The second force, under the shaykh's eldest son Shaykh Siddiq, was stationed at Mergaver, "apparently to protect Abdul-Kader's retreat."[85] The third force, commanded by Shaykh Muhammad Saʿid, ʿUbayd Allah's brother-in-law and one of his *khulafa,* was said to number five thousand men.[86]

ʿAbd al-Qadir's force, on its way to Sawj Bulaq, was joined by Kurdish contingents from the Ushnu and Sulduz areas. Soon afterward they were joined by the Mangur Kurds under Hamza Agha and other chiefs who declared that they had sworn on the Qurʾan to fight until death. They captured Sawj Bulaq without resistance after the governor and garrison had been given safe conduct to leave the town. Upon Sawj Bulaq's fall into Kurdish hands, its chief Sunni ecclastic issued a *fatwa* (legal opinion)[87] declaring a jihad against the Shiʿis.[88]

Shaykh ʿAbd al-Qadir's next objective was Miyanduab. He seems to have sent a number of messengers to that town with the object of getting supplies and sounding out the inhabitants. The messengers were seized and put to death, a response that so enraged the shaykh that he decided to attack the town immediately.[89] Fearing reprisals, half of the inhabitants concealed their goods and valuables and fled. The other half, about three thousand men, women, and children, were massacred when the town was sacked by ʿAbd al-Qadir's forces.[90] The surrounding countryside as far as Binad and Maragha was ravaged by fire and sword.

The destruction of Miyanduab proved to be an empty victory, for the majority of the warriors, loaded with plunder, thereafter scattered and went back to their homes. Furthermore, it stiffened the Persians' resistance and did great damage to the shaykh's cause as a whole. According to Wilson, "This scattering proved that the Kurds were not capable of regular warfare. The massacre was not only a crime, it was an error; for it aroused the Persians to the resistance of despair, and destroyed whatever sympathy may have been felt for the Kurds."[91]

Shaykh ʿAbd al-Qadir next turned his attention to Maragha, after whose capture his forces were reported to have reached the neighborhood of Tabriz.[92] This marked the end of Shaykh ʿAbd al-Qadir's advance.

In the meantime, Shaykh Siddiq, who was reported to be threatening Urmiya with one thousand men,[93] was joined by fresh forces led by his father, Shaykh ʿUbayd Allah himself. The total number of this combined force, which now proceeded to besiege Urmiya, was estimated at eight thousand men.[94] After a few days of indecisive fighting, the inhabitants of the beleaguered city, who had heard of the fate of Miyanduab, decided to sue for peace. Accordingly, a number of notables and religious dignitaries communicated with Shaykh ʿUbayd Allah and offered to surrender the city provided he would promise to spare the inhabitants. The shaykh agreed, and a date was set for the surrender of the city.[95] When the appointed time arrived, however, the Persian authorities requested a delay. This the shaykh at first refused to grant, but he was persuaded to do so by Dr. Cochran, who, as we have seen, was on friendly terms with the Kurdish leader.[96]

The Persian authorities took advantage of the delay to strengthen the city's defenses. Knowing that a relief column was on its way to Urmiya, the governor, Iqbal al-Dawla, decided to resist the shaykh.[97] When the Kurds finally launched their attack, they were repulsed with heavy losses. This severe setback seems to have broken the spirit of ʿUbayd Allah's forces, for before long they were retreating in utter confusion toward their mountains.[98]

Thus ended the siege of Urmiya after ten days of great fear and uncertainty. The shaykh's failure at Urmiya marked the end of the Kurdish invasion of Persia. Soon the invaders were falling everywhere before the advancing Persians. Turkish army units, stationed along the Turco-Persian border, were cooperating with the Persian army by cutting off the retreat of the Kurdish forces.[99]

Shaykh ʿUbayd Allah, who succeeded in making his way to Naw Chia, was finally conveyed to Constantinople in July 1881 as the result of considerable pressure that the great powers exerted on the Porte. It is interesting to note that on his way to the capital, the shaykh was everywhere given a hero's reception.[100] After a few months' residence in Constantinople, he escaped and made his way back to his mountain home at Nehri. In deference to European public opinion, the Turks sent a force against the shaykh and de-manded his surrender. Realizing the hopelessness of the situation, 'Ubayd Allah gave himself up and this time was exiled to the Hijaz, where he died in 1883 at Mecca.[101]

The Aftermath of the Invasion

The Persian suppression of the shaykh's invasion probably surpassed in its savagery the excesses of the Kurdish invaders. Kurds and Sunnis were as mercilessly hunted down and butchered by the Persian soldiery as Persians and Shi'is had been by the Kurdish tribesmen. The indiscriminate nature of Persian retaliation is indicated by the fact that although a remarkably small number of the Nestorians of the Urmiya plain lost their lives as a result of Kurdish depredations, Persian forces massacred large numbers of Kurds.[102]

The Kurdish invasion and the measures taken to suppress it wrought havoc in northern Persia. In addition to heavy loss of human life, some of the richest of Persia's lands were completely laid waste. The Urmiya plain, known as "the garden of Persia," was devastated. This catastrophe was so great that all Persia was to feel its effects for many years to come. Stack, writing in 1882, mentions that while traveling through the province of Fars in southern Persia, he learned that "the people were paying a relief im-posed on account of the Kurdish invasion of Azarbiajan."[103] The impact of the invasion was such that, in the words of one of the American missionaries, Mrs. Mary Shedd, "Until the World War, all events in Urumia dated from the 'coming of the Shaykh.' "[104]

After the defeat of the Kurds, the position of the American missionaries in Urmiya became precarious because of unfounded charges of their complicity in the Kurdish in-vasion. The missionaries had maintained friendly relations with Shaykh 'Ubayd Allah, so the Persians accused them of having encouraged and supported him. Prompt and firm British diplomatic action, as we shall see, saved the missionaries from a very uncer-tain fate.

International Aspects of the Kurdish Invasion of Persia

Establishment of Diplomatic Relations Between the United States and Persia

One of the most important international repercussions of the Kurdish invasion of Persia was the establishment of diplomatic relations between the United States and that country. The U.S. government's attention was focused on Persia as a result of the dan-gers to which the American missionaries were exposed during and after Shaykh 'Ubayd Allah's invasion. U.S. congressman Rufus Robinson Dawes of Marietta, Ohio, whose sis-ter Mrs. Sarah J. Shedd, was one of the members of the Urmiya mission, took a special interest in the matter. He brought it to the attention of Secretary of State Evarts in a let-ter dated November 20, 1880. Dawes informed Secretary Evarts of the great peril in which the missionaries found themselves as a result of the recent events in Persia and suggested that the United States should ask the Persian government to extend its protec-tion to these American citizens. He concluded his letter by pointing out that his sister and her family were included in this party of missionaries.[105]

The contents of this letter were communicated to James Russell Lowell, U.S. minister in London, who in turn communicated with Lord Granville (George Leveson-Gower), British foreign secretary, requesting him to use the good offices of the British representative in Persia for the protection of American citizens there. Congressman Dawes then turned his attention to "secure passage by Congress of some measure for a better protection of American citizens in Persia."[106] Dawes found it necessary to engage in a great deal of lobbying in order to achieve his objective, for the public was uninformed on the matter, so there was no public opinion to support such a measure. In the meantime, the missionaries themselves continued to urge Dawes to work for the establishment of diplomatic relations between the United States and Persia.[107]

The first step taken by Congressman Dawes was a resolution that he introduced on February 6, 1882, calling for the establishment of U.S. diplomatic representation in Persia. In this resolution, he spoke at length about the commercial advantages of such representation and stressed the importance of that country as a future market for American products. One week after the introduction of this resolution, on February 13, 1882, it was passed by unanimous vote of the House of Representatives.[108] Finally, on August 3, 1882, five days before the adjournment of Congress, the House met to consider the bill (H.B. 6743) authorizing the establishment of diplomatic relations. The bill was passed by both houses on August 5, 1882, after an amendment had been added by the Senate. Mr. S. G. W. Benjamin was appointed as the first American diplomatic representative to Persia, with the title of chargé d'affaires and consul-general.[109] His designation was later changed to that of minister.

The Attitudes of the European Powers

Shaykh ʿUbayd Allah's movement had far-reaching international repercussions. The very nature of his undertaking, the invasion of Persia, constituted a grave international problem. It was inevitable that this invasion would involve Turkey, whose subject he was and from whose territory he had launched his attack. Russia, deeply interested in the internal affairs of both Turkey and Persia, saw in the shaykh's movement an attempt to disturb the status quo in an area of vital importance to Russia. England, in contrast, was deeply interested in maintaining the integrity of the Ottoman Empire and viewed with alarm the progress of events that threatened to range Russia on the side of Persia and thus involve Turkey in a hopelessly unequal struggle. Even Austria, far from the scene of these events, was diplomatically involved.

Russian promises of aid to Persia. Shaykh ʿUbayd Allah's invasion of Persia was bound to draw Persia closer to Russia for a number of reasons. Persia's humiliation at having its territory violated, its authority flouted, and its subjects massacred was so deeply felt that the Persians were willing to clutch at anything that promised vengeance and redress. The resentment and despair they felt as a result of their initial inability to stem the tide of the invasion and the excesses committed by the invaders against Persian citizens, as Persians and Shiʿis, kindled the fires of sectarian fanaticism in Persian breasts. The fact that the invasion was planned and organized on Turkish territory by a Turkish subject could not fail to make Persia suspect official Turkish participation in the shaykh's movement. Lord Curzon described well Persia's mood at this time: "The Shah appealed to Russia for help, to England for counsel, and to Turkey for amends."[110]

Russia was close at hand and in a position to render immediate help. The Persians were confident of Russian assistance, not only because of traditional Russo-Turkish animosity, but because the shaykh's movement threatened to rob the Russians of some of the fruits of their victory in the war of 1877–78. For this reason, the Russians, no less than the Persians, saw the hand of Turkey in the Kurdish eruption. Moreover, they felt that the new disturbances might lead to greater British influence in the eastern provinces, where, under the Treaty of Berlin, Great Britain was already charged with supervising the reforms. Another cause of Russia's opposition to the Kurdish movement was its desire to keep its hold on Persia by continuing to play the role of Persia's ally and protector.

Finally, the Russians feared that the movement might have adverse effects on the Kurdish populations in the newly acquired provinces of Kars and Ardahan. They certainly did not relish the idea of a revival of *muridi*sm in a region so close to the turbulent Caucasus. Shaykh 'Ubayd Allah, who had led Kurdish volunteers against Russian forces only two years earlier in the Russo-Turkish War, was a leader of the Naqshbandi, like the famous Caucasian rebel Shamil.

Although determined to put an end to the Kurdish venture in Persia, in case the Persians proved incapable of coping with the situation, the Russians refrained from any action that might offend the British or rouse their anger. They continued to follow closely the course of events in the troubled area and to take all the necessary precautions, but they were careful not to take any hasty or ill-considered measures that might precipitate a conflict with Turkey. They kept in close touch with the British while quietly concentrating troops along the Caucasian border.

Mr. Plunkett, the British diplomatic representative in St. Petersburg, was instructed to sound out the attitude of the Russian Foreign Office. On November 3, 1880, he reported that the Russian counselor, Baron A. G. Jomini,[111] attributed the Kurdish disturbances along the Turco-Persian frontier to Turkish machinations and feared that they might result in serious complications. In a dispatch to the British foreign secretary, Plunkett hinted at the possibility of Russian intervention. He made it quite clear that the Russian government might find itself more directly "interested in the matter than it happily was at present"[112] should the disturbances extend to the Russian frontier.

Three days later the Russian newspaper *Bereg* echoed these sentiments in plainer language. It no doubt expressed the official Russian attitude when it said:

> The Kurds have risen against Persia. Has not Turkey perhaps a hand also in the game? Does not the Porte perhaps hope to bring about a new state of affairs, which she could use as a pretext for not complying with the decision of the Berlin Conference as far as concerns Armenia? Perhaps the diplomats at Stanbul intend to make use of the Kurds in the same way as they did the Albanians in the Montenegrin affair. All these questions will perhaps shortly be answered.[113]

The newspaper went on to discuss the various commercial and political interests that both Russia and England had in Persia. It referred to the Anglo-Russian understanding that had existed before the Crimean War and called for a resumption of the friendly relations that had existed between the two countries prior to that war. It pointed out that "in reality no reasons exist which should necessitate any antagonism between Russia and England in Central Asia."[114] The newspaper mentioned the good relations existing between Russia and Persia, citing Persia's recent request for military assistance against the Kurds. It explained, however, that in case the conflict should assume a more serious aspect and extend to the Russian frontier, Russian troops would be "allowed to maneuvre on Persian territory in order to quell the revolt of the marauders."

Britain's reaction to Russia's policy. Great Britain seems to have been deeply concerned about the reports of Russia's offer of military assistance to Persia. Mr. Plunkett was instructed in a telegram from the British foreign secretary, Earl Granville, to report on the truthfulness of these rumors. Plunkett informed the foreign secretary by wire that he had again called at the Russian Foreign Office and discussed the matter with Baron Jomini. According to Plunkett, Jomini had informed him that it was the shah who had expressed to the Russian minister at Tehran the desire for Russian assistance in restoring order among the Kurdish tribes. Plunkett reported that the Russian emperor, "on hearing of this request, had at once acceded to it, with the express reservation, however, that on no account would Russian troops be authorized to follow the Kurds on to Ottoman territory."[115] Baron Jomini pointed out that the latest news from Kurdistan was so much better that Russian assistance in all probability would no longer be needed. Notwithstanding this fact, he said, steps were being taken to assemble the necessary troops on the frontier in case they should be required later. Jomini did not reveal the number of troops involved.[116]

Prince Andrei Lobanov-Rostovsky, the Russian ambassador in London, discussed the subject of Russian military assistance to Persia in the course of an interview with the British foreign secretary. The prince was reported to have stated that the shah had asked the Russian emperor for military assistance and had pressed him to place Russian forces at the disposal of the Persian government. According to Lobanov-Rostovsky, "This the Emperor had, however, declined to do, though he had agreed to allow some troops to concentrate on the frontier."[117]

Russia continued to pursue her conciliatory policy toward England. According to Granville, the Russian ambassador had been instructed to give assurances to the effect that the emperor, "while ordering his troops to approach the frontier, was determined to prevent them, as far as possible, from crossing it, as His Majesty would not intervene directly on behalf of the Persians, for fear of exciting international susceptibilities." Prince Lobanov emphasized that it was Russia's intention to remain within its own borders and "not to advance either into Turkish or Persian territory."[118] To these assurances the British foreign secretary gave a brief and meaningful response. According to his own account, "I replied that this was undoubtedly a most important end to observe."[119]

Soon after the spread of rumors that the Russians were about to send military aid to the Persians, there were reports of Russian troop movements. British consular officials were immediately reporting every scrap of information regarding the strength, composition, and destination of Russian troops in the Caucasus.[120] The highest estimate of Russian troops mentioned in this connection was six thousand.[121]

The Russians, however, tried to minimize the number and importance of these troops. Russian sensitiveness to this matter, even at a time when the Kurdish rebellion was being put down by the Persians, is well illustrated in Plunkett's report of a conversation with the Russian foreign minister M. de Giers. Plunkett suggested that in view of the improved situation in Kurdistan, further concentrations of Russian troops would not be necessary. In response, "M. de Giers merely replied that too much importance had been attached to the couple of regiments which Russia had thought right to move to Nakchevan."[122]

The Reforms as a Factor in Turkey's Attitude toward the Shaykh

There is certainly nothing far-fetched about the suspicion of official Turkish support for Shaykh 'Ubayd Allah's movement. Though the shaykh's and the Ottoman government's aims were ultimately incompatible, they were similar up to a point and identical in at least one respect. Both were unalterably opposed to the reforms envisaged in Article 61 of the Treaty of Berlin and in the Convention of Defense Alliance, to be discussed presently.

Perhaps a brief consideration of the motives that impelled the Turks to oppose these reforms would provide a clearer understanding of the Turkish attitude toward the shaykh. The Turks, who had a deep-seated aversion to all foreign-sponsored projects, regarded the reforms as only a means to an end, a prelude to further and more active foreign intervention. Since the beginning of the nineteenth century, foreign intervention in various forms had embroiled the Turks in a series of disastrous wars that had cost them the major part of their Balkan possessions. They could not forget that their latest disaster, the war of 1877–78, had been made possible by the reform-minded Constantinople conference. At this conference, the great adroitness and consummate diplomatic skill of Russia's ambassador to the Porte, General Nikolai Ignatiev, had succeeded in maneuvering Turkey, with the full approval of the great powers, into a position where it must either submit to excessive and unacceptable demands for reforms or go to war with Russia unaided.[123]

Turkey's strong opposition to these reforms did not stem solely from the desire to spare the eastern provinces the fate that had overtaken its Balkan possessions. In fact, the Turks' attitude toward the two areas was considerably different. They seem to have resigned themselves to the loss of their possessions in the Balkans, where, since the beginning of the nineteenth century, the process of alienation had been set in motion by the various intense Balkan nationalisms, backed by Russia's great military power. The warlike and largely Christian populations of the Balkans—linked to Russia either by ties of Orthodoxy, as in the case of Greece and Romania, or by both Orthodoxy and a common Slavic origin, as in the case of Montenegro, Bulgaria, and Serbia—had no counterpart in the eastern provinces. Here the only important non-Muslim element was the unwarlike Gregorian Armenians, a non-Slavic and non-Orthodox people. Because of the long tradition of Muslim dominance in these areas, the Ottomans regarded these provinces as an inalienable part of the Muslim homeland, of which they considered themselves the proper guardian.

Another point of considerable importance is that where Turkey faced Persia, a state weaker and more effete than itself, Turkey no doubt entertained hopes of making up for the losses it had sustained in Europe. Often beaten and constantly on the retreat before the stronger European powers, the Ottomans probably had never despaired of wresting Turkic-speaking Azerbayjan and Sunni-professing Persian Kurdistan from Persia.[124]

Of all the great powers, only Great Britain was interested in the execution of Article 61 of the Treaty of Berlin. Neither Germany nor Austria showed any interest in the fate of the sultan's Asian subjects, and France and Italy regarded the matter as of special interest to England only. Russia was hostile to the idea of the reforms, not only because it did not relish the prospect of a regenerated Turkey, but also because it feared that this British sponsored project might lead to a dangerous increase of British influence in these sensitive regions bordering on its Caucasian provinces. England, in contrast, was deeply interested in seeing the reforms introduced and saw them as the only means of saving the Ottoman Empire and of making the latter an effective barrier to Russia's southward march. The collapse of the Ottoman Empire would endanger the Straits, Suez, Aden, and Hormuz, which controlled not only the entrance to the Mediterranean, the Red Sea, the Indian Ocean, and the Persian Gulf, but also the approaches leading to England's Indian empire and worldwide trade. Thus, of all the signatories of the Treaty of Berlin, only England seemed to regard the reforms as a matter of vital concern.

In fact, England attached so much importance to the reforms that it had been careful enough to insert a clause regarding them in the Convention of Defense Alliance of June 4, 1878,[125] which it had secretly signed with Turkey almost a month before signing the Treaty of Berlin. This convention provides an interesting clue to Turkey's attitude toward the reforms. The sultan undertook to introduce reforms and to permit the British occupation of Cyprus in return for Britain's pledge to resist by force of arms Russia's retention of Batum, Ardahan, and Kars, if Russia were to attempt to take any additional territories belonging to the sultan.

It is one of those ironic facts of history that although Britain's unbending attitude at the Berlin conference forced Russia to give up Erzerum, Bayazid, and the valley of Alaskherd, as well as the hinterland of Batum, Britain failed to prevent Russia from retaining Batum, Ardahan, and Kars. Needless to say, the sultan was deeply disappointed. Britain's failure to keep the Russians out of the three places specifically mentioned by name in the convention appears to have shaken the sultan's confidence in Britain's ability or willingness to abide by its solemnly given pledges.

It is not improbable that because of Britain's failure to live up to its treaty obligations, the sultan felt that he was no longer bound to carry out his part of the bargain. We know that the British ambassador to the Porte, Sir Henry Austen Layard, had instructions from the British foreign secretary to use his great influence with the sultan to persuade him to acquiesce in the loss of Batum.[126] We also know that the sultan balked at issuing the *farman* (royal decree) authorizing the British occupation of Cyprus. Before giving his consent, the sultan had tried to insert a clause in the act of ratification of the convention, giving himself sovereign rights with respect to any reform that might be introduced within his dominions in Asia.[127] Only after considerable delay was Layard successful in securing the exchange of ratifications without the proposed addition.

British influence continued to deteriorate in Turkey. By the end of 1879, scarcely a year after the conclusion of the Russo-Turkish War, the Porte abandoned even the pretense of following British advice.[128] There were several reasons for this change. The Russo-Turkish War had generated strong antiforeign sentiment among the Turks, which was directed against all of the European powers. Great Britain, in particular, had become suspect because its policies and actions during the past two years had been ambiguous and disappointing to the Turks. The Porte had become suspicious of Britain because it was uncertain of that country's motives and intentions. Thus, British failure to defend Turkish interests, as promised in the defense alliance, induced certain influential Turkish circles to accuse Britain of having concluded that agreement merely with the object of grabbing Cyprus.

Furthermore, Great Britain's vital concern in the maintenance of the integrity and continuity of the Ottoman Empire and ceaseless efforts to achieve that end made it the object of suspicion and resentment on the part of the sultan and his retinue. This suspicion was not entirely without grounds. At one time, the British were so anxious to maintain Ottoman integrity that they even considered establishing a protectorate over Turkey.[129] Lord Salisbury, who had a comprehensive plan for the security and regeneration of Turkey,[130] wished to obtain the sultan's approval "while the fear of Russia was still upon him [the sultan]."[131] He was aware that time was of the essence in this matter. He believed that the sultan, who was suspicious by nature and susceptible to the influence of his corrupt and venal entourage, would decline to give his approval as soon as he was in a position to do so. In a letter to Sir Henry Layard, Salisbury wrote: "Our power of insisting upon it will diminish with each succeeding month."[132]

The British realized that the sultan's absolute powers, which were manipulated by those close to him, presented an insurmountable obstacle to any reforms. In their search for a formula to curb these powers, they aroused the suspicion of the sultan and his circle. An article in the *Phare du Bosphore* accused the British government of trying to take away from the sultan his sovereign rights in Asia Minor. It is noteworthy that various Turkish newspapers reproduced this article at the time.[133]

The sultan's fears concerning the fate of the eastern provinces were not unfounded. Recent developments in Bosnia, eastern Rumelia, and Egypt, where foreign powers had assumed direct administrative responsibility while recognizing the sultan's nominal sovereignty, had demonstrated his inability to maintain effective control over these areas.[134]

Another reason for Turkey's mounting resentment against England was the latter's refusal to extend financial aid to Turkey. At one time, Turkey seemed willing to do anything to obtain such a loan. But the sultan's repeated requests for a British loan went unheeded, a fact that greatly irritated the Ottoman government. The sultan himself is reported to have said, "Let Her Majesty's Government help us find money, and I will pledge myself that this and other reforms they require of us will be forthcoming." [135] He even went so far as to say that he was willing to name an English undersecretary of state to the Ministry of Finance. [136] Deeply embittered by these rebuffs for financial aid, the Porte behaved in a manner that is not difficult to understand. England's continued refusal to grant a loan to Turkey, despite the latter's repeated assurances of willingness to come to any terms, may have been owing to the chaotic state of Turkish finances and Britain's fear of the collapse and dissolution of the Ottoman Empire, as well as to its lack of confidence in Turkey's intentions.

Thus, the Turks, who were against the Treaty of Berlin reforms from the very beginning, grew more and more opposed to them as their relations with England deteriorated. [137] It is quite possible that the Ottoman government's strong opposition to the reforms was largely responsible for its indulgent attitude toward Shaykh 'Ubayd Allah. The shaykh's activities, as Monseigneur Krimian pointed out, served to defeat the reforms and to divert attention from the Armenians to the Kurds. Moreover, from Turkey's point of view, the shaykh's invasion of Persia not only constituted a resumption of his successful antireform activities in Turkey, but also may have held the possibility of bringing Kurdish-inhabited territory in Persia under Turkish control.

5 The Impact of the Young Turk Revolution on Kurdish Nationalism

The Committee of Union and Progress and the Young Turk Revolution

No proper discussion of Kurdish political history, or for that matter of the political history of any other Ottoman ethnic group, is possible without some mention of the Young Turk Revolution of July 1908. It had profound effects on the destinies of the peoples and the countries that composed the Ottoman Empire.

The revolution was the culmination of many years of clandestine activity, both in Turkey and abroad, by the Committee of Union and Progress (CUP).[1] CUP adherents were men of diverse national origins, often with conflicting aspirations.[2] Despite their differences, however, they were united by their common admiration for Western institutions and their intense dislike of the sultan-caliph Abdul Hamid II. The leading members of the organization, who had fled Hamidian tyranny and settled in Europe, became imbued with Western social and political ideas. They were particularly influenced by the egalitarian and libertarian ideals of the French Revolution, doctrinaire nationalism, and Comtian positivism.[3] As a secret conspiratorial organization, the CUP was influenced by a number of European secret societies, especially the Carbonari, the International Macedonian Revolutionary Organization (IMRO), and the Freemasons.[4]

Kurds or persons of Kurdish ancestry played an important role in the committee from its inception. Two of the four founding members of the first CUP, Ishak Sukûti[5] and 'Abd Allah Jawdat,[6] were Kurds. Later on, other prominent Kurds joined the movement and became deeply involved in its activities. In 1895, a number of Young Turks were apprehended and sent into exile, including Sukûti, who was exiled to Rhodes, and Jawdat, who was exiled to Tripoli.[7] Another Kurd, Shaykh 'Abd al-Qadir of Nehri, the son of Shaykh 'Ubayd Allah, was implicated in the CUP's abortive plot to overthrow Sultan 'Abdul Hamid II in 1896 and was exiled to Mecca.[8]

Meanwhile, other Kurds continued to participate in the CUP. The Young Turk Liberal Congress held in Paris in 1902 was attended by 'Abd al-Rahman Bedir Khan and Hikmet Baban, members of two noted Kurdish families.[9] After the revolution, a number of Kurdish members of the CUP occupied positions of great importance. Among them were Isma'il Haqqi Baban,[10] who became minister of public instruction, and Sulayman

Nadif,[11] who became *wali* of Baghdad. The former, in particular, is reported to have at one time wielded great influence in the councils of the Young Turks.

The Young Turk Revolution was precipitated by the Anglo-Russian agreement of June 1908, concluded at the Baltic city of Reval (Tallin) between King Edward VII and Czar Nicholas II. The two rulers were said to have reached a comprehensive understanding with regard to Turkey and to have elaborated plans for the imposition of reforms as well as for the eventual dismemberment of the Ottoman Empire.[12] CUP members were stunned by the news and decided to act quickly. In a desperate attempt to forestall the implementation of this agreement, a sudden coup by Young Turk army officers forced the sultan to restore the Constitution of 1876 as a prelude to the introduction of large-scale reforms. In doing so, they wanted to demonstrate to the world Turkey's willingness and ability to set its house in order by voluntarily initiating reforms, making foreign intervention unnecessary.[13]

The revolution was greeted with jubilation and optimism throughout the empire. With the CUP's blessings, Turks, Albanians, Arabs, Armenians, and Kurds pledged themselves to forget past differences and to work together for the common good and well-being of the Ottoman fatherland. At last, Turkey seemed to be at the threshold of a new era of brotherhood and solidarity.

But this was not to be. As soon as the initial surprise of the revolution had passed, it was evident that forces hostile to the Young Turks were at work, both at home and abroad. On October 5, 1908, at Russia's instigation, Bulgaria declared its independence. Two days later Austria-Hungary announced the formal annexation of Bosnia and Herzegovina.[14] The attitudes of England and Germany were not very clear, but the former was allied with Russia, and the latter with Austria.

At home, ominous rumblings were audible as the spirit of opposition gained in strength. The Reactionary Party, consisting mostly of irreconcilable elements loyal to the sultan, bided their time while preparing to seize power. The Liberals were disillusioned with the Young Turk regime and expressed strong resentment of the new rulers' authoritarian character. The various national groups, which had greatly increased the scope of their political activities, were clamoring for greater freedom and autonomy.

The intensification of nationalist activity in the critical months that followed the revolution presented a serious challenge to the CUP's authority and a grave threat to the integrity of the empire. The separatist tendencies inherent in the various nationalist movements were a source of great anxiety to the Young Turks. They feared that these movements, if left unchecked, would lead sooner or later to demands for local autonomy, followed by foreign intervention and the usual loss of territory through secession or annexation. Bitter experience had made the pattern familiar. The loss of Bulgaria and Herzegovina was too recent to be forgotten.

The counterrevolution of April 1909 brought things to a head. Adherents of the sultan, in a bid to seize power, rose up in Constantinople (Istanbul) and succeeded in liquidating many CUP members in that city. When the sultan failed to punish the offenders, Turkish army units stationed in Macedonia marched into Istanbul under Mahmud Shawkat Pasha, crushed the revolt, and deposed the sultan.[15]

After putting down the counterrevolution, the Young Turks resolved to stamp out all opposition. Henceforth, all those who disagreed with them were ruthlessly silenced or eliminated. The Reactionaries, the Liberals, and particularly the nationalists, all felt the heavy hand of the CUP. With the crushing of opposition elements, the Young Turks simultaneously launched their program of forcible Turkification and the creation of a highly centralized administrative system.

Thus, the Young Turks' brief honeymoon with the various non-Turkish Ottoman nationalists came to an end. The recently established political clubs and societies were closed down, newspapers were banned, and nationalist activity in general was prohibited under pain of severe punishment. These repressive measures succeeded only in establishing an outward calm. The various nationalist movements were driven underground, but repression seemed only to strengthen their determination to resist Turkish domination.

The Rise of Kurdish Political Organizations

The revolution of 1908 caused deep political stirrings among the various Ottoman peoples. The various nationalisms, long dormant or silent, were suddenly awakened and became articulate. It was in that year that the first Kurdish political society or club, Kurdistan Ta'ali ve Terakki Jam'iyati (Society for the Rise and Progress of Kurdistan), known as the Kurdish National Committee, was founded in Istanbul. Its founders were Emir Amin 'Ali Bedir Khan, General Muhammad Sharif Pasha, Shaykh 'Abd al-Qadir of Nehri (son of Shaykh 'Ubayd Allah), and the Damad marshal Dhu al-Kifl Pasha.[16]

The Kurdish National Committee, according to Elphinston, supported the CUP "in return for certain guarantees."[17] The Young Turks, however, appear to have reneged on their promises when they embarked on their indiscriminate suppression of the various nationalist movements. Amin 'Ali Bedir Khan and General Sharif Pasha were condemned to death and had to flee the country.[18] Amin 'Ali's eldest son, Sureya Beg Bedir Khan, who had returned to Istanbul after the revolution and resumed the publication of the Kurdish nationalist newspaper *Kurdistan,* was likewise compelled to seek refuge abroad.[19]

At about the same time, a cultural organization, Kurd Nashri Ma'arif Jam'iyati (Society for the Propagation of Kurdish Education), was established, and an elementary school for the education of the children of the Kurdish colony in Istanbul was opened in the Chenberli Tash quarter of that city. The school was placed under the direction of Emir 'Abd al-Rahman Bedir Kahn. The Young Turks closed down this society, the school, and the Kurdish National Committee in 1909, when they embarked on their policy of Turkification.[20]

In the year 1910, Kurdish students in Istanbul formed the Hivi-ya Kurd Jam'iyati (Kurdish Hope Society). The organizers included Khayali of Motki, 'Omar and Qadri of the family of Jamil Pasha Zade of Diyarbakr, Fuad Temo Beg of Van, and Zaki Beg of Diyarbakr. The society continued its activities up to the outbreak of World War I, when it was compelled to suspend operations. However, it reappeared after the war and resumed its work until the occupation of Istanbul by the Kemalists. The Hivi Society published a paper under the name *Rouj Kurd* (Kurdish Day).[21] After the armistice, Sureya Beg Bedir Khan formed the Committee of Kurdish Independence in Cairo.[22] Likewise, after the Armistice of Mudros, a number of Kurdish leaders founded Kurdistan Ta'ali Jam'iyati (Society for the Rise of Kurdistan) in Istanbul; it was known as the Kurdish National Committee. This society, which was headed by Shaykh 'Abd al-Qadir, included a number of prominent Kurdish leaders: Amin 'Ali, Murad, Khalil Rami, and Kamuran Bedir Khan; Hikmat, Husayn Shukri, Fuad, Mahmud, and 'Ali Baban; Akram Beg Jamil Pasha Zade of Diyarbakr; Amin Zaki Beg and Mustafa Pasha of Sulaymaniya; and a number of well-known men from Dersim, Kharput, and Malatya.[23]

A new society, the Kurd Tashkilati Ijtima'iya Jam'iyati (Kurdish Social Organization Society), was formed by the Emirs Amin 'Ali, Jaladet, and Kamuran Bedir Khan; Kemal Fewzi; Akram Beg Jamil Pasha Zade; Dr. Shukri Muhammad; and Memdouh Selim Beg.[24] Another society whose existence was recorded at this time was the Kurd Millet Firqasi (Kurdish National Party).[25]

The Shaykhs and Kurdish Nationalism after the Young Turk Revolution

Kurdish nationalist activities were becoming increasingly evident throughout Kurdistan. Ideas circulated by clandestine nationalist publications were augmented by word of mouth. News and rumors with a political and nationalist flavor were fast becoming favorite topics of conversation at Kurdish gatherings.

The task of propagating a forbidden and unfamiliar idea among an overwhelmingly illiterate people with ill-defined loyalties was not an easy one. The difficulties encountered were many, and the risks involved were considerable. Some recipients of illegal nationalist publications did not hesitate to turn them over to the authorities in order to prove their loyalty to the Ottoman government.[26] However, it should not be assumed that this practice was common or that in all cases it was dictated by self-seeking or lack of patriotism. No doubt some among those guilty of this practice may have regarded Kurdish nationalist activity simply as a form of treasonable agitation directed against the lawful authority of the sultan-caliph and the Islamic state.

Nationalist ideas eventually found their way into the *takiyas* (gathering places for specific religious orders), where they gained powerful supporters in the Kurdish shaykhs. This development was of great significance in the history of Kurdish nationalism. For a number of reasons, the importance of the *takiyas* as centers for the dissemination of nationalist ideas can scarcely be exaggerated. The ideas emanating from these focal points found ready and wide acceptance among the Kurds, for they bore the stamp of the shaykhs' great learning and unimpeachable religious authority. Moreover, the shaykhs' religious character and influence gave the *takiyas* relative immunity from interference and harassment by the authorities.

The shaykhs, who as a class represented an important segment of the Kurdish elite, were ardent nationalists. Unlike the largely Turkified urban Kurdish elite, they were closely associated with the Kurdish masses and identified themselves with them. Fur-

11. Kamuran, Sureya, and Jaladet Bedir Khan. Photographer unknown/ Courtesy of Joyce Blau, The Kurdish Institute of Paris.

thermore, by both training and conviction they stood for the traditional Islamic state as opposed to the modern secular state envisaged by the Young Turks. Consequently, they distrusted the new rulers in Istanbul, whose ideas and policies they regarded as the culmination of the un-Islamic innovations of Sultan Mahmud II, a particularly unpopular figure among the religious orders.[27] The overthrow of 'Abdul Hamid (1876–1909) by the Young Turks was another source of deep resentment, for in the eyes of the shaykhs, 'Abdul Hamid's pro-Kurdish and pan-Islamic policies had made him the ideal sultan-caliph. Thus, from the beginning, the shaykhs were cast in the role of an opposition to the new regime, on political as well as on religious grounds.

Although the majority of the shaykhs were sympathetic to the Kurdish nationalist cause, not all of them dared reveal the true nature of their feelings. Those who felt strong enough to do so expressed their support for the nationalists and participated openly in nationalist activities. Others less powerful were anxious not to compromise themselves by either word or deed and confined themselves to hoping secretly for nationalist success.

The influence of Kurdish nationalist ideas on the shaykhs' political thinking is perhaps best reflected in a petition submitted in the form of a telegram to the Porte and the Ottoman Parliament in Istanbul by a number of Kurdish notables and shaykhs from the Bahdinan region.[28] This petition, which requested the introduction of certain reforms in Kurdistan, was principally inspired by Shaykh 'Abd al-Salam of Barzan and Shaykh

Nur Muhammad of Dohuk, at whose home it was written. The petitioners requested the following reforms: (1) the adoption of Kurdish as the official language in the five Kurdish *qadas* (administrative districts); (2) the adoption of Kurdish as the language of instruction in the Kurdish areas; (3) the appointment of Kurdish-speaking *qaimmaqams* (district deputy commissioners), *mudirs nahiyas* (subdistrict officers), and other officials; (4) the administration of law and justice in accordance with the Shari'a (Muslim canon law) in view of the fact that Islam was the state religion; (5) the positions of *qadi* (religious judge) and mufti (canon lawyer responsible for delivering formal legal opinions) to be filled by adherents of the Shafi'i school of law; (6) taxes to be levied in accordance with the provisions of the Shari'a, and the abolition of all taxes in excess of or incompatible with the amounts established by the Shari'a; and (7) taxes collected for exemption from labor service to remain in effect, provided they were set aside for the repair and maintenance of roads in the five Kurdish *qadas*.[29]

The proposed reforms clearly sprang from an unmistakable nationalist impulse, colored by the religious character of its principal authors. The first, second, third, and seventh points are expressions of Kurdish nationalism, whereas the fourth, fifth, and sixth points reflect a religious sentiment. The fifth point is especially significant, for it is here that the nationalist and religious elements meet and merge into each other. The provisions concerning the appointment of *qadis* and muftis of the Shafi'i school, the sect to which the majority of the Kurds belonged, was tantamount to demanding the recognition of the paramountcy of this sect in the Kurdish area. This, of course, would have meant the establishment of a Kurdish national church.

Basically there was nothing new about these objectives. Former generations of Kurds had given serious thought to the ideas of reform, local autonomy, and even independence. The memory of Shaykh 'Ubayd Allah, the last great leader of Kurdish nationalism, who at various times had sought to advance these goals, was still fresh in the minds of many Kurds. It was perhaps inevitable that the weakness of the Ottoman state and its uncertain fate should have caused Kurdish leaders, among others, to think seriously of their own national future.

The Young Turks disliked the shaykhs as thoroughly as they were disliked by them. This mutual hostility was accompanied by mutual contempt. Time was to show how grossly the two parties underestimated each other and how much sorrow to themselves and to their people could have been avoided by more understanding and a greater measure of forbearance. Defiance of Turkish nationalism was soon to end in personal tragedy for a number of the Kurdish shaykhs, and Turkish harshness was soon to demonstrate the implacable nature of their antagonists.

The Growing Conflict Between the Kurds and the Turks

Causes of the Conflict

The deterioration of Kurdish-Turkish relations after the Young Turk Revolution and up to the outbreak of World War I can best be seen in the series of conflicts that took place between the Kurds and the Ottoman government during that period. Before we turn to these events, however, it may be useful to review briefly the principal causes that led to the estrangement between the two peoples.

1. The Young Turks' attitude toward the caliph and toward religion in general shattered a myth greatly cherished by the Kurds and destroyed the most powerful bond between them and the Ottoman state. Moreover, with the fall of 'Abdul Hamid, the Kurds lost a powerful patron and a privileged position, for he had used the great prestige and power of his office to grant honors and privileges to the shaykhs and tribal chieftains whose followers made up the Hamidian regiments.

2. The Young Turk policies of administrative centralization and forcible Turkification were bound to result in discord and strife. Administrative centralization meant the extension of Ottoman authority into regions where such intrusion was bitterly resented. Similarly, the Kurds naturally resisted the policy of forcible Turkification, which aimed at the suppression of all non-Turkish nationalities, because it clashed with the basic premises upon which their society was established.

3. The series of diplomatic and military defeats suffered by the Young Turk regime undermined the very basis of Ottoman authority. It engendered sedition and encouraged the Kurds' desire for a separate existence.

4. The Young Turk Revolution, which had the effect of awakening the national aspirations of the various non-Turkish Ottoman peoples, failed to live up to its early promise. Corruption and misrule, coupled with a policy that vacillated between high-handedness and weakness, served only to exasperate the Kurds and goad them into rebellion.

5. These serious causes of conflict were greatly aggravated by the intensification of Kurdish nationalism and by Russia's determined bid to win over the nationalists as well as the disaffected Kurdish tribal leaders.

The Uprising and Murder of Shaykh Sa'id Barzinja

The first signs of the impending conflict between the Kurds and the Young Turks appeared shortly after the initial success of the Young Turk Revolution. In 1908, Shaykh Sa'id Barzinja of Sulaymaniya instigated a rebellion of the Hamawand tribe in defiance of the Young Turks and in support of the sultan.[30] According to British major E. B. Soane, "The object here was clearly rebellion against the new Majlis [Parliament]. The Shaikhs [of Barzinja] were naturally royalists, and were supported by Sultan 'Abdul Hamid's good will, if not active military assistance, in this move."[31]

This rebellion, coupled with the complaints of the Sulaymaniya merchants who were suffering from Shaykh Sa'id's oppression, led the authorities in Istanbul to take action. The shaykh was induced to proceed with a number of his relatives to Mosul, where he was detained. In May 1909, in the course of an anti-Kurdish riot, the aged shaykh was murdered on the threshold of his house.[32] This act, whose authors remained undiscovered, plunged the Sulaymaniya region into a state of anarchy. His enraged family, in particular his son Shaykh Mahmud, who succeeded to the shaykhship, retaliated by inaugurating a reign of terror in the town of Sulaymaniya and by unleashing the

Hamawand tribe on the countryside. As a result, the economic life of the region was brought to a virtual standstill.[33]

The Hamawand continued in a state of rebellion until July 1910, when Nadim Pasha, then the *wali* of Baghdad, reached an agreement with them and accepted their nominal submission. Nadim Pasha's policy of conciliation, however, appears to have been abandoned upon his recall to Constantinople in April 1911, whereupon the Hamawand reverted to their former lawlessness. The subsequent enrollment of some Hamawand tribesmen in frontier companies patterned after the Hamidiyah regiments was not too successful, and the Hamawand were reported to have been still in a state of rebellion at the outbreak of World War I.[34]

The Uprising and Death of Ibrahim Pasha of the Millis

Perhaps the most dramatic action by a Kurdish leader in support of the deposed sultan was that taken by Ibrahim Pasha, chief of the Milli confederation and general of the Hamidian regiments. When the news of the fall of 'Abdul Hamid reached him in April 1909, Ibrahim Pasha marched upon Damascus at the head of fifteen hundred Kurds and occupied the city in the name of the sultan. However, he soon was forced to withdraw. On his way back to his stronghold at Viranshahr, he was killed in the area of Jabal 'Abdul 'Aziz during an engagement with Shammar tribesmen who had been sent by the Young Turks to harass his retreat.[35]

Incidents Involving Other Kurdish Leaders

Measures adopted by the Ottoman government in the face of growing Kurdish restiveness and intransigence served only to alienate the Kurds further. For example, at the end of 1910, the government attempted to collect taxes from the Jaf, the most powerful tribe of southern Kurdistan, who had not paid them since the advent of the Young Turks. Mahmud Pasha, the paramount chieftain of the tribe, was called to Mosul and kept there for almost a year. He eventually was released, but the matter was never satisfactorily settled.[36] In 1912, Mustafa Pasha, chief of the Bajalan Kurds in the Khanaqin region, who was suspected of pro-British leanings, was detained for some time in Baghdad as a political suspect.[37] In the same year, Sulayman Bedir Khan was killed by the Turkish police in Bohtan in the course of disturbances, which led to an attempt at reconciliation between the Young Turks and the Kurdish nationalists.[38]

Kurdish Intransigence and the Balkan Wars

The grave events of the first and second Balkan wars, culminating in a series of humiliating defeats for the Ottoman forces, placed unprecedented strain on the already attenuated allegiance of the Kurds. According to an official British report, when the Bulgarian army took the great fortress of Adrianople (Edirne) by storm on March 26, 1913, and Istanbul itself seemed threatened with a similar fate, a number of Kurdish tribes seem to have decided to put an end to the Ottoman connection. The Milli, the Karakacheli, the Kitkan, and the Barazi tribes reportedly agreed to form a confederation with the object of declaring their independence in the event of the fall of Istanbul to the

Bulgarians.[39] This plan did not materialize because the Bulgarian army failed to press its attack, and the war was brought to an end through the mediation of the great powers. It is interesting to note, however, that a false report announcing the fall of the capital induced 'Abd al-Qadir ibn Derai, chief of the Karakacheli, to take action. He and his followers attacked and plundered the town of Birijik and crossed the Euphrates with the intention of extending their operations, but had to retire when their allies failed to support them.[40]

Kurdish Response to Russian Overtures

Russia, Turkey's neighbor and enemy, was not likely to overlook the Kurds' restiveness and increasing estrangement. Since the turn of the century, the Russians had been following with great interest the growing disaffection of the sultan's Kurdish subjects and for a number of years had been seeking to win them over, with varying degrees of success.[41] The attitude of the majority of the Kurds toward Russian blandishments was well summed up in the following observation by Gertrude Bell, who was with the British Office of the Civil Commissioner in Iraq during World War I:

> Before the war the attitude of the Kurdish tribes towards Russia all along the eastern frontier of Turkey was not clearly defined, but on the whole it may be said that while there existed a fundamental suspicion of Russia, resulting in a reluctance to respond to her overtures, Ottoman misrule tended to force the Kurds against their will into her arms. Thus chiefs in the Mosul area, such as the shaikh of Barzan, after holding out for several years against Russian invitations, were in the end obliged to seek refuge in Russian territory, and in the spring of 1914 it was rumoured that the Hamawand, Jaf and Dizai, despairing of receiving from the Ottoman Government the reforms they desired, were prepared to call in Russian aid.[42]

The Russians, as we shall see, were to figure prominently both in the revolt of Shaykh 'Abd al-Salam II of Barzan and in the insurrection at Bidlis.

The Conflict Between the Barzani Kurds and the Turks

Shaykh 'Abd al-Salam II of Barzan

Perhaps the most formidable Kurdish leader the Ottoman government had to deal with during this period was Shaykh 'Abd al-Salam II of Barzan (hereafter 'Abd al-Salam). Shaykh 'Abd al-Salam's conflict with the Young Turks was a culmination of the struggle between the shaykhs of Barzan and the Ottoman authorities. The government was bound to resist firmly the Barzan shaykhs' determined attempts to establish their hegemony over the Barzan-Zibar region, at a time when the Turks had largely succeeded in suppressing the powerful Kurdish principalities.

The Barzan shaykhs had succeeded in overcoming their enemies with their desperate bands of *murid*s. The religious fervor of these *murid*s and their blind obedience to the shaykhs had been such as to earn them the appellation *diwana,* or "madmen."[43] The strange religious beliefs that frequently circulated among the Barzanis caused periodic outbreaks of religious extremism, which inevitably led to violent clashes with their neighbors as well as with the government. The first such outbreak[44] occurred during the time of Shaykh 'Abd al-Salam I, who was proclaimed as the Mahdi[45] by his followers. An even more serious outbreak occurred after his son Muhammad had succeeded him as shaykh of Barzan.[46]

These heterodox and extremist movements were fraught with dangerous implications for the government, and it could not but view them with the gravest concern. Over and above the fact that they led to serious disturbances and presented a challenge to the state's authority, they constituted a dangerous deviation from Islamic orthodoxy. In the politicoreligious system of an Islamic state, which the Ottoman Empire claimed to be, religious nonconformity is tantamount to treason. It was therefore the duty of the Ottoman sultan, who claimed the caliphal authority, to suppress all such offenses and to punish the offenders.

Scholars have suggested various causes of the conflict between Shaykh 'Abd al-Salam and the Ottoman government. Damaluji attributes it to the intrigues of the Zibar *agha*s, the hereditary enemies of the Barzan shaykhs. After suffering a series of crushing defeats at the hands of the Barzanis, the Zibar *agha*s set themselves to the task of rousing the government against their powerful rivals.[47] With the aid of local Ottoman officials, according to Damaluji, they eventually succeeded in turning the government against the Barzan shaykhs. He also mentions two other contributing factors that helped precipitate the conflict—namely, the odium attached to Barzani religious extremism and the growth of Kurdish nationalism. The latter undoubtedly stiffened Shaykh 'Abd al-Salam's attitude toward the Young Turks, and it induced the Young Turk regime to take stern measures against him.

Writing in 1922, W. A. Wigram and Sir Edgar T. A. Wigram attributed the conflict to the machinations of a Mosul notable, Sabonji Pasha, who, with the aid of corrupt and unscrupulous officials, sought to possess himself of a number of villages belonging to Shaykh 'Abd al-Salam. The shaykh's determination not to give up his property, according to the Wigrams, was to have serious consequences, for soon charges of conspiring against the government were brought against him, and a punitive force was sent into his territory.[48]

Jiyawuk contends that 'Abd al-Salam's conflict with the government was caused by the latter's attempt to undertake a comprehensive census of the population and livestock in the Barzan region. The shaykh and his people strenuously opposed this measure, which eventually led to an armed conflict with the government.[49]

No doubt any or all of these factors may have contributed to the outbreak of hostilities between the government and Shaykh 'Abd al-Salam. The long-standing feud between the Zibar *agha*s and the shaykhs of Barzan is a historical fact, and to this day it has continued to plague the relationship between the two families.[50] Similarly, a Mosul notable's attempt to obtain Barzani villages with the help of government officials is a plausible reason; practices such as this were common enough in Ottoman times.[51] Furthermore, the reported Barzani opposition to the proposed census was in keeping with the attitude of most tribes in the Middle East. Tribesmen have always resisted or reluctantly submitted to census taking because of their fear that it might lead to conscription and increased taxation. These fears may have gained much substance from the Young Turks' avowed policy of administrative centralization.

The tragic outcome of this conflict, whatever its causes, was to influence the course of events in the Barzan country long after the Turks had ceased to hold sway there. In fact, it is not an exaggeration to say, as Damaluji has implied, that all the subsequent Barzani rebellions have largely grown out of these unfortunate events.[52]

Turkish Attempts to Suppress Shaykh 'Abd al-Salam

Shortly after the fall of 'Abdul Hamid and the coming of the Young Turks to power, General Muhammad Fadil Pasha Daghistani, commander of the Ottoman forces in the Mosul *wilayat* (province) and acting *wali*, ordered Shaykh 'Abd al-Salam to appear before him in Mosul to answer charges of conspiring against the government. Urged by his followers not to comply with the order for fear that he might fall into a trap, the shaykh sent an evasive answer indicating his inability to go to Mosul at the specified time because of personal affairs.[53] The *wali* responded by attacking the shaykh with a force of six thousand troops, including tribal levies drawn from a number of neighboring Kurdish tribes. A fierce war followed, as a result of which the shaykh's followers inflicted considerable casualties on the Ottoman forces. However, the government's superior power prevailed in the end. Barzan village was stormed; the shaykh's residence and *takiya* were destroyed; the commander of his forces, Faqi 'Abd al-Rahman, was killed; and his family was captured.[54] The shaykh was compelled to flee in disguise to the Hakari mountains, where he sought refuge with the Tiyari highlanders.[55]

After his appointment as *wali* of Baghdad, Nadim Pasha, in accordance with his prudent and conciliatory policy, exonerated the shaykh, restored him to his former position, and awarded him an indemnity for damages suffered as a result of the punitive expedition sent against him.[56] Colonel Safwat Beg, a Turkish officer who was a sympathetic supporter of the shaykh, appears to have played an important role in bringing about the reconciliation.[57]

This respite, however, proved to be only short-lived, for shortly after Shaykh 'Abd al-Salam had come down from the Hakari mountains and established himself at the village of Bab Sefan in the Mizuri Juri region, Nadim Pasha was recalled to Istanbul. The shaykh's old antagonist, General Muhammad Fadil Pasha Daghistani, ordered him to present himself at Barzan village. When the shaykh pointed out that the destruction of his home in that village made it impossible for him to go there, the general marched against him. In the ensuing battle, which took place in the gorge of Bab Sefan, the shaykh's *murids* inflicted a crushing defeat on the government forces, capturing two regiments.[58]

After his victory, the shaykh submitted a petition to the government expressing his loyalty, protesting his innocence, and requesting the removal of Daghistani. The fait accompli of the shaykh's victory, combined with Colonel Safwat's efforts on his behalf, induced the government to respond favorably to his request. He was once again exonerated, and the general was transferred to Baghdad as a divisional commander.

After these events, the shaykh proceeded to Barzan village, rebuilt his house, and established a school for children. The government speedily met his request for a teacher and sent a qualified person from Mosul. It also appointed a *qaimmaqam* to administer the Barzan region.[59]

During the next two years, Shaykh ʿAbd al-Salam's relations with the government and with his neighbors appeared to be friendly and harmonious. However, he was on particularly good terms with Shaykh Sayyid Taha II of Shamdinan, whose activities were a source of grave concern to the Ottoman government. It was reported that Sayyid Taha, after a visit to Russia, had established himself at the village of Rajan in Russian-occupied Persian Kurdistan and had placed himself under Russian protection. It is not surprising that the Ottoman authorities should have viewed the friendship between these two powerful leaders with suspicion and alarm and closely watched their activities. Some of the messages exchanged between the two men were clearly treasonable. In one of these messages, Shaykh ʿAbd al-Salam reportedly said, "The day is coming when the Kurds will need powerful support, and such support is sure to come from the Russians."[60]

Safwat Beg, the shaykh's ardent supporter, who earlier had warned him against Ottoman perfidy and advised him not to go to Mosul, went so far as to suggest that the shaykh and he should follow the example of Sayyid Taha and ʿAbd al-Razzaq Bedir Khan and go over to the Russians.[61] These activities and contacts did not for long remain unknown to the government. Fadil Pasha Daghistani, who had never ceased to warn the government against both the shaykh and Safwat Beg, lost no time in accusing the two men of disloyalty and sedition.[62]

The new *wali* of Mosul, Sulayman Nadif, who was a zealous Young Turk, appears to have been bent upon suppressing all those who were opposed to the ideas and policies of the new regime.[63] No doubt he regarded men such as the shaykh as anachronisms who had no place in the new scheme of things. One of his first acts was to call on Shaykh ʿAbd al-Salam to appear before him in Mosul. When the latter did not comply, he was declared a rebel, and a force of regular troops and tribal levies was sent against him. A month of stiff fighting followed, in the course of which many soldiers and *murid*s were killed. The shaykh was defeated and fled across the frontier to Urmiya, where he entered into relations with the Russians.[64]

The Capture and Execution of Shaykh ʿAbd al-Salam II

Early in 1914, while traveling in the neighborhood of the Turco-Persian frontier on his way to visit Simko Agha, paramount chief of the Shikak tribe, Shaykh ʿAbd al-Salam was waylaid and captured by a band of Shikaki tribesmen, who turned him over to the *wali* of Van in the hope of receiving the price that the Ottoman authorities had placed on his head.[65] The shaykh was sent under heavy escort to Mosul, where, after spending some time in prison, he was hanged with three of his followers.[66] According to Damaluji, Sulayman Nadif executed the shaykh without obtaining the necessary authorization from Istanbul.[67]

At about the same time, the *wali* moved against other Kurdish shaykhs in the Mosul region. Despite his great age, Shaykh Nur Muhammad of Dohuk, who had participated with Shaykh 'Abd al-Salam in drawing up the petition of reforms mentioned earlier, was brought to Mosul and thrown into jail, where he eventually died. It seems that Sulayman Nadif had intended a similar fate for Shaykh Baha al-Din of Bamirni but was prevailed upon to leave him alone.[68]

The Revolt of Bidlis

In 1913, a serious Kurdish rebellion, led by a number of religious leaders, broke out in the Bidlis region.[69] Fifteen years later a well-known Turkish writer charged the Russians with instigating this rebellion, which he claimed was to be a prelude to Russian intervention. According to this writer, "The revolt of Bidlis, staged by the local Russian consul, which was to have been followed by Armenian massacres, to create a pretext for active Russian intervention, was only averted by a mere chance."[70]

The Kurdish rebels, who seem to have achieved important initial successes, are reported to have reached the outskirts of the town of Bidlis.[71] Powerful reinforcements rushed there by the government succeeded in crushing the rebellion.[72] The leader of the rebellion, Shaykh Salim, was forced to seek asylum in the Russian consulate, where he remained until Turkey's entry into World War I. Upon the outbreak of hostilities, the Turks broke into the consulate, captured the shaykh, and publicly hanged him.[73]

6 *Russia's Kurdish Policy*

It was fairly evident since the beginning of the nineteenth century that Russia's conquest of the Caucasus would sooner or later bring that country into contact with the various peoples living in the frontier regions of Turkey and Persia. The most important and numerous of these peoples were the Kurds. The first significant Russian contact with the Kurds took place during the first decade of the century as a result of the Russo-Persian conflicts of 1804–12. The crushing defeats suffered by the Persians in the battles of Arpatch (1807) and Aslanduz (1812), which culminated in the humiliating Treaty of Gulistan in 1813, must have greatly enhanced the Russians' prestige among the Kurds.[1]

In 1828, the Russo-Prussian war brought to an end more than a decade and a half of peaceful Russo-Persian relations. However, the speedy defeat of the Persian forces soon compelled Persia to sue for peace, which was established by the Treaty of Turkmanchai of 1828. This treaty was a severe blow to Persia, for it not only eliminated that country as a power in Caucasian affairs, but also marked the beginning of Persian capitulations.[2] As might be expected, these Russian successes made a profound impression on the Kurds. Sir James Fraser, who spent a night as a guest of some Kurds in northwestern Persia a few years after these events, reported an episode that reveals the contempt in which the Kurds had come to hold their Persian masters.[3]

The Policies of Prince Paskevich

Prince Ivan Paskevich may be said to have laid the foundation for Russia's policy toward the Kurds. He seems to have been the first Russian official to have recognized the immense strategic importance of the Kurdish lands, which lay astride the approaches to the Ottoman Empire and the rest of Southwest Asia. Consequently, he placed great value on maintaining friendly relations with the warlike Kurds. This approach was reflected in his plan for the conquest of Anatolia. One of the three prerequisites on which he based this plan was reaching an understanding with the Kurdish tribal chieftains of the Armenian highlands and the upper Euphrates valley.[4]

With the outbreak of the Russo-Turkish War of 1828–29, Prince Paskevich, who appears to have given the matter considerable thought, proceeded to implement his well-laid plans. He was quick to seize upon and exploit the discontent provoked among the conservative and feudal elements by the reforming policies of the Ottoman sultan Mahmud II (1808–59). Many of the Kurdish chieftains, in particular those who inhabited the remote frontier regions and who led a virtually independent existence, deeply resented these policies, which they regarded as impious innovations as well as unwarranted encroachments on their hereditary rights.[5]

Through the judicious use of Muslims in his service, Paskevich succeeded in winning over many Kurdish chieftains.[6] For example, Husayn Agha, the khan or paramount chieftain of the Erivan Kurds, joined the Russians upon the outbreak of hostilities and served them well throughout the campaign. Husayn Agha's services were not limited to the three thousand cavalrymen he put into the field; in addition, his great prestige and power were used to influence other Kurdish chieftains, and his efforts were often of decisive importance. For example, he persuaded the pasha of Mush, who had received instructions from the Ottoman authorities to ready a great cavalry force of about twelve thousand, to remain neutral.[7]

Commenting on Husayn Agha's activities, William Monteith said in 1856: "He subsequently proved an efficient ally of Russia against his own people; and it was principally owing to his power and influence that the Pasha of Moush had been induced to enter into a treaty of neutrality with the Russians—a treaty he had strictly adhered to, though he did not allow his men to join those of Husayn Agha in their advance into Turkey."[8]

Paskevich also seems to have astutely exploited religious and racial antagonisms, for he made use of both Armenians and Yazidis. Hasan Agha, a leading Yazidi chieftain, was one of the most faithful Kurdish chieftains in his service.[9]

On June 23, 1829, upon the arrival of Paskevich at Copru Koi, where most of the Russian forces were concentrated, he received Kurdish chieftains from the Agri Dagh (Ararat) and Bingol regions.[10] He appears to have been welcomed wherever he went. According to Monteith, "He was everywhere received with loud acclamations, in which the Kurdish Beys joined with all their hearts, saying 'Take Erzeroum and you will be willingly joined by all our tribes.' "[11]

Paskevich's success in establishing friendly relations with the Kurds paid handsome dividends. Monteith pointed out that the number of Kurds serving with the Russian army was much greater than the number serving with the Turks.[12] In addition to the active military support rendered by some Kurdish tribes, other tribes aided the Russian forces by providing them with food and supplies when they passed through Kurdish territories.[13]

However, Paskevich's hold on the Kurds' loyalties was as tenuous as that of their Ottoman rulers, and the Kurds are reported to have vacillated between the two combatants. According to one source, "The Kurds remained a doubtful factor, and Paskevich deserved credit for the skill of his policy toward them. Their neutrality gave Paskevich all the advantages which Napier enjoyed nearly forty years later in Abyssinia, where a passive but potentially dangerous mountain population allowed a relatively small force to advance."[14]

The Kurds and the Russo-Turkish Wars

The war of 1828–29 marked a turning point in Russo-Kurdish relations. The wise and skillful policies pursued by Paskevich toward the Kurds during that conflict established a pattern that was followed with considerable success throughout the subsequent Russo-Turkish wars.[15] The outbreak of the Crimean War revealed the deep inroads Russia had made on the loyalties of Turkey's Kurdish subjects. During this conflict, two Kurdish regiments fought on the side of the Russians against the Ottoman army,[16] and a serious rebellion led by Emir 'Izz al-Din Shir (or Yazdan Shir) broke out in the Bohtan region.[17] Similarly, during the war of 1877–78, some Kurdish contingents participated in the military operations of the Russian army on the Caucasian front.[18] As this war was drawing to a close, Husayn Pasha and Osman Pasha, sons of the great Emir Bedir Khan, rose in rebellion against Turkish authority, overran most of the Bohtan region, and successfully held it for about nine months. Their rebellion was brought to an end only through duplicity, after force of arms had failed.[19]

The success that attended Russian arms during the Russo-Turkish wars created a deep impression on the Kurds. In an attempt to explain Russia's irresistible power and the inevitability of its triumph, the 'Alawi (Qizilbash) Kurds of the Dersim highlands, adherents of an extreme Shi'i sect, believed that the Russians were fighting with 'Ali's sword, which he had entrusted to them.[20]

However, it would be a great mistake to suppose that the Russians won over the Kurdish people as a whole. The majority of the Kurds and their leaders remained loyal to the sultan and fought on the Turkish side, both as regular soldiers and as members of irregular tribal forces. In the war of 1877–78, many Kurds, like other Ottoman subjects, served willingly in the Ottoman army, and large tribal forces were led by Kurdish shaykhs, such as Shaykh 'Ubayd Allah and Shaykh Nasir of Tello.

During World War I, the Kurds certainly rallied to the Turks despite Russian efforts to the contrary. In this choice, they were greatly influenced by pan-Islamic propaganda and the Ottoman declaration of jihad, as well as by the skillful activities of German agents and the great prestige of German arms.

Czarist Russia's Armenian Policy

Czarist Russia did not have a Kurdish policy in the same sense that it had an Armenian policy. No doubt Russian sympathy and support for the Armenians, on the one hand, and the incompatibility of Armenian and Kurdish interests, on the other, precluded such a possibility. Consequently, for many years Russia did not have a long-range Kurdish policy with well-defined goals. Yet it often found itself, particularly in times of war, constrained to win over the Kurds or at least to ensure their neutrality and often succeeded in doing so. Czarist Russia's dealings with the Kurds were usually confined to temporary accommodations with various tribal chieftains, designed to achieve certain limited objectives. However, the prolonged struggle with Turkey eventually induced the Russians to seek a more comprehensive understanding with the warlike Kurdish tribes that lived in compact masses along vital military routes leading into Turkish territories.

Russia's policy toward the Kurds, however, did not assume definite shape until the latter part of the nineteenth century. It was just beginning to emerge as a coherent and purposeful policy when it was rudely upset by two developments stemming from World War I—namely, Turkey's call to the holy war and the Russian Revolution. In order to gain some idea of the nature of Russia's attitude toward the Kurds and the gradual emergence of its Kurdish policy, a brief discussion of its Armenian policy is perhaps necessary.

Russia's Support of the Armenian Cause

The Armenian question, which plagued Russo-Turkish relations during most of the nineteenth century and the early part of the twentieth century, was skillfully developed into a valuable instrument of Russian foreign policy. According to Lobanov-Rostovsky, Russia's Armenian policy was pursued with two primary aims in mind. The first was the protection of the Armenians, motivated by humanitarian considerations as well as by considerations of domestic policy.[21] The second aim was to eliminate any possibility of intervention by a rival power on behalf of the persecuted Armenians—an intrusion dangerously close to Russia's Caucasian provinces.[22] To these two aims should be added a third: the weakening of Turkey and the eventual separation of the Armenian provinces in eastern Turkey, after the pattern already established in the Balkans.

Russia's espousal of the Armenian cause was astutely employed to further its designs on Turkey. It provided a convenient pretext for intervention and offered a means of exerting continuous pressure on the Porte. In order to have a free hand in dealing with Turkey, Russia skillfully utilized its support of the persecuted Armenians to influence European public opinion in its favor.

Championing of the Armenian cause also elicited the sympathy and support of Armenians everywhere. In the first place, it assured Russia the loyalty and devotion of its own Armenian subjects, who inhabited much of the frontier region bordering on Turkey. Second, it made the Armenians in Turkey look on Russia as their savior and induced a number of their leaders to make common cause with her. Third, it won the support of the influential and articulate communities of the Armenian diaspora in the United States, England, France, Italy, Egypt, and a number of other countries.

It would be misleading, however, to attribute only selfish and ulterior motives to Russia's espousal of the Armenian cause. The truth is that the Russian masses and even the czarist government were motivated by genuine humanitarian and Christian ideals. Like Spain at the other extremity of Europe, Russia had never lost the crusading spirit generated during centuries of domination by conquerors of an alien race and religion. It is well to remember that it was in large measure owing to the intense religious feeling of the Russian masses that the grand dukes of Moscow changed from the tax gatherers of the khan to champions of Russian orthodoxy. To lose sight of this fact is to misunderstand one of the fundamental forces in Russian history.

Causes of the Change in Russia's Policy Toward the Armenians

Russia's policy toward the Armenians began to undergo a significant change shortly after the war of 1877–78. This change was brought about by a series of developments that followed the war and that, at least for the time being, greatly influenced Russia's policy toward the Ottoman Empire and its various national minority groups. Russia's relations with the great powers, the Nihilist threat at home, and difficulties in dealing with its Bulgarian and Armenian protégés contributed in varying degrees to this change. A brief discussion of these issues may help us to better understand Russia's attitude toward the Armenians and their cause.

In order to preserve the peace, then gravely menaced by the various problems arising out of Russia's victory over the Ottoman Empire in the war of 1877–78, Otto von Bismarck suggested that the powers meet in conference at Berlin. Russia suffered a severe diplomatic defeat at the Berlin conference, where the Concert of Powers, presided over by Bismarck, largely succeeded in depriving it of the fruits of victory. There was nothing new in England's traditional policy of maintaining the territorial integrity of the Ottoman Empire against Russian ambitions, but Austria-Hungary's attitude and Bismarck's conduct before and during the conference were far from reassuring. Russia must have felt isolated as it confronted not only England, but also its two former associates in the Dreikaiserbund, Germany and Austria-Hungary, who obviously believed that the bund no longer served their purpose.[23] The manner in which Russia had been robbed of its hard-won victory was received with resentment and disappointment throughout the empire.[24]

Grave domestic troubles added to the bitterness of Russia's diplomatic defeat. The wave of Nihilist terror that had abated during the war was now renewed with increased violence, culminating in the assassination of Alexander II in 1881. This event made a deep and lasting impression on his son and successor, Alexander III, and caused a violent reaction among the Slavophiles and other conservative elements, who, moved by deep patriotic fervor, rallied to the new sovereign. Western democracy was assailed, and liberalism was denounced as foreign and unwholesome. A return to the pure and undefiled native institutions was vigorously advocated by such men as Constantine Pobedonostsev, formerly tutor and now political mentor of Alexander III.[25]

All of Russia's vicissitudes were now attributed to Europe. Perfidy and betrayal abroad as well as terrorism and regicide at home were the penalty for contact with European civilization. In the words of Bernard Pares, "Russia under Alexander III sulked," and, one should add, turned away in revulsion from Europe. Henceforth, autocracy and orthodoxy in their Russian form were to be the two pillars upon which czardom was to rest. Consequently, the salvation of the empire demanded the elimination of everything that was non-Russian and non-Orthodox. In order to achieve this end, the various national and religious groups were subjected to a policy of forcible Russification. This policy, inaugurated during the reign of Alexander III, was not completely abandoned by Nicholas II.[26]

The refractory attitude displayed by some of the nationalities whose cause Russia had so steadfastly championed against the Turks gave it serious cause for concern. The sharp rebuff Russia suffered in 1885 at the hands of the Bulgarians, damaging alike to its interests and prestige, was the result of a strident nationalism that had been assuming an increasingly defiant character.[27] Similarly, Armenian resistance to the Russification policies was an unmistakable manifestation of nationalistic self-assertion.[28]

Needless to say, the behavior of both the Bulgarians and the Armenians was a source of deep disappointment to the Russians, who could not but regard it as gross ingratitude. Bulgaria, which was to have served as Russia's bridge to Istanbul, had become a barrier instead. But Bulgaria was already in existence, and Russia's exertions on its behalf were beyond recall. Armenia, still unredeemed and struggling to be, was not so fortunate. This time the Russians were resolved not to allow an Armenian national state to stand between them and other key parts of the Ottoman Empire to the south. Russia's resentment over the turn of events in Bulgaria and Armenia was well summed up in the words of the Russian chancellor Prince Lobanov, who said: "We don't want an Armenian Bulgaria."[29] The growth of terrorist and revolutionary activities among the Armenians in Turkey, at a time when Russia itself was convulsed by similar activities, may have further prejudiced the czarist authorities against the Armenians and their cause.

The policies aimed at the Russification of the Armenians culminated in the Decree of 1903, which provided for the confiscation of the property of the Armenian national church and the closing down of Armenian schools—measures that the Armenians bitterly resented. The massacres and countermassacres in which the Armenians and the Tatars of Baku became involved during the first decade of the twentieth century have been blamed on the deterioration of relations between the Russians and their Armenian subjects.[30] However, this unhappy phase of Russo-Armenian relations did not last long. International developments seem to have convinced both parties that it was in their interest to resume their former amicable relations.

Russian Initiatives for Armenian Reforms

On October 10, 1912, the viceroy of the Caucasus, Count Illarion Ivanovich Vorontsov-Dashkov, urged the czar to pursue an active Armenian policy. In a report submitted to his government, he said: "An open intervention for the protection of the Turkish Armenians, is essential particularly in the present time . . . to prepare before hand a sympathetic population in those localities which as things are at present may easily find themselves willingly or unwillingly within the sphere of our military operations."[31]

A little more than a year before the outbreak of World War I, Russia took the initiative in reopening the question of reforms in Turkish Armenia with the European powers. France and Britain expressed sympathy for Russia's position and declared their willingness to support the project, but Germany seems to have joined the other powers only with the greatest reluctance. Throughout the negotiations that followed, Germany is reported to have vigorously defended Turkey's point of view and to have emphasized that the powers "ought not to lose sight of the interests of the Kurds."[32] After lengthy deliberations, the Armenian convention, embodying a watered-down version of the Russian proposals, was finally signed in 1914.[33]

The Emergence of a More Aggressive Russian Policy toward the Kurds

Toward the turn of the century, Russia appears to have finally embarked on a bolder Kurdish policy that had the twofold aim of winning over the Kurds and turning them against their Turkish and Persian rulers. Money, arms, and promises were used to spread disorder and foment rebellion. Thus, both the plundering forays of Simko Agha of the

Shikak into Turkish territory[34] and the rebellion at Bidlis[35] are said to have been insti-gated by the Russians.

The rise of Kurdish nationalism offered an unprecedented opportunity for Russian political activity among the Kurds, which was eagerly seized upon and wisely exploited. Russia greatly encouraged the Kurdish national movement,[36] and disaffected Kurdish leaders did not hesitate to seek Russian aid and asylum.[37] Kurdish nationalism provided a convenient foil for many Kurdish leaders' pro-Russian activities. The same activities that only a few decades earlier would have been regarded as little less than treasonable now acquired a certain heroic and ennobling character in the eyes of many Kurds.

After the Russian occupation of Persian Azerbayjan, the gradual penetration of Kurdistan was carried out from such Russian-dominated centers as the Urmiya[38] and the Maku-Koi regions.[39] As Russian activities gained in momentum from 1910 onward, an increasing number of Kurdish chieftains from the frontier regions and beyond looked to the Russians for support.[40] As Longrigg points out, "The Sayids of Neri, Shaykh 'Abd as-Salam of Barzan, the Jaf leaders, and the Assyrian Maliks and bishops were not alone in maintaining touch with them."[41]

The ultimate objectives of this policy are not very clear. 'Abd al-Razzaq Bedir Khan is reported to have gone to St. Petersburg around 1909 with a project for an independent Kurdish state.[42] Unfortunately, we possess no information regarding official Russian re-action to his project. Basile Nikitine, former Russian consul in Urmiya and a leading au-thority on the Kurds, asserts that the Russian government never endorsed this plan. In a letter to the editor of the *Manchester Guardian* in 1950, he emphatically denied that his government ever intended to set up an independent Kurdish state.

In this letter, Nikitine maintained that czarist Russia could scarcely be said to have had what might be regarded as a Kurdish policy. In support of this contention, he ex-plained that during World War I the Russian Caucasian army "had no accurate maps of Kurdistan, no knowledge of the Kurdish language, and so on."[43] Furthermore, he pointed out that as a Russian consul at Urmiya, he never received any instructions as to how to deal with the Kurds. He concluded his argument by stating: "I rather believe that, contrary to the case of the Armenians, and in a way the Nestorians, our Foreign Office, as well as the Vice-regency in Tiflis, had no definite Kurdish policy."[44]

A different view was expressed thirty years earlier by Major E. W. C. Noel, a British intelligence officer who was a keen student of Russian activities in the Middle East and one of Britain's leading Kurdish experts. In a report dated July 1919, Major Noel claimed that he came across certain Russian official documents in Tiflis during the war that shed a curious light on certain aspects of Russia's policy in Kurdistan: "From the documents I had access to at the Russian General Staff at Tiflis in 1917, I gained the impression that it was intended to use the Kurds as a counterpoise to the Armenians, and that there was no intention of giving the Armenians much of a say in matters appertaining to those areas claimed by Armenia, but which were predominantly Kurdish."[45]

Writing at a time when Russia was still suffering from the ravages of war and revo-lution, Noel emphasized the possibility of its recovery and the revival of its interests in

Kurdistan. He pointed out that in the past Russia had greatly encouraged the Kurdish national movement, and he predicted that it would pick up the threads of its old policy as soon as it was in a position to do so. Russia's abiding interest in the region, according to him, was demonstrated by the demands of Admiral Kolchak's representatives in Paris for a mandate over Armenia.

So certain was Noel of the inevitable revival of Russian interest in Kurdistan that he urged his government to lose no time in establishing the British position in that region: "In view of the close connection between Mesopotamia and Kurdistan and the many Kurds who are included in our Mesopotamian administration it would seem of great importance that we should forestall Russia in Kurdistan, by contributing to a solution of the question which will circumscribe her field of action there."[46]

The Impact of Soviet-Turkish Relations on the Soviet Union's Kurdish Policy

The Soviet Union's attitude toward the Kurds in the period following World War I was influenced by a number of international considerations. Fear of the Allies, in particular Great Britain, and suspicion of their intentions were strong in Russia. Kemalist Turkey was assailed by similar fears and suspicions. The dangers faced by the two regimes brought them together, inaugurating an era of goodwill and cooperation mutually advantageous to the two countries. The Soviet Union provided Kemalist Turkey with greatly needed material and moral support.[47] And Turkey's friendship with Russia, at a time when the latter had few friends, greatly enhanced Soviet prestige in the Muslim world.[48] Moreover, the friendship of a strong nationalist Turkey afforded protection of Russia's southern flank.

This friendship, however, solid as it may have appeared on the surface, was not without its inner stresses and strains. The Lausanne Conference, where Turkey was so ably served by Russia's Chicerin, was to reveal the basic incompatibility of the two states' aims and purposes. The Russians were disappointed and angered by the fact that the Turks had negotiated separately on the Straits at the conference. The Soviet demand that the whole issue be renegotiated by a subcommittee went unheeded, and the Turks ignored Soviet references to the Soviet-Turkish treaty of March 16, 1921. In the early part of February 1923, Ismet Pasha (Inönü), the chief Turkish delegate, delivered a speech at the conference in which he announced Turkey's agreement to the demilitarization of the Straits and declared them open to ships of all nations.[49] The Soviet reaction was not slow in coming. The Third International launched an attack on the Turkish government, accusing it of persecuting the Communists in Turkey.[50]

This, however, was only a temporary setback. Other developments were soon to bring the two countries together again. The award of the Mosul *wilayat* to Iraq by the League of Nations on December 15, 1925, was followed two days later by the signing of a new Russian-Turkish treaty.[51] Another event that paved the way for a resumption of close relations between the two countries was the Kurdish rebellion of Shaykh Sa'id in the early spring of 1925. The Kurdish issue was of great importance to Turkey, and the Turks suspected Great Britain of having instigated the rebellion. In this, it seems that both the Russians and the Turks thought along similar lines. Fischer has summarized the Soviet views on Great Britain's use of the Kurds as a tool of British policy:

> Moscow believed that Great Britain's policy at the time inclined towards the establishment of an independent or semi-autonomous Kurd state, or that the English, at any rate, were using the Kurds to further their own ends in the Near East, and to sow discord between Persia and Turkey. The Moscow Izvestia of October 6, 1927, definitely charged that British gold was responsible for Kurd raids from Turkey into Persia and from Persia into Turkey. Angora shared the view, and the Anatolian Press aired it. In general, Moscow is convinced that British agents employ recalcitrant tribes in all these Eastern countries as a means of applying pressure on constituted governments and thus effecting London's or Delhi's policies.[52]

Fischer goes on to say that the Russians tried to bring this point home to both Turkish and Persian statesmen and that the Soviet press warned against the dangers of enmity between Turkey and Persia resulting from Kurdish border incidents instigated by the British.[53]

No doubt the Soviet Union profited from Turkey's fears of British support for Kurdish nationalism. Russo-Turkish relations continued to be amicable, and, insofar as the Kurdish question was concerned, the Soviet Union lost no opportunity to display its solicitude for Turkish interests. As described in a subsequent chapter, the Russians offered their good offices to mediate Turkish-Persian difficulties stemming from the Kurdish revolt of Agri Dagh (Ararat) in 1930. During the 1930s, however, despite continued outward friendliness, the two countries' divergent policies gradually caused them to drift apart. The fears that had exercised Turkish minds ever since the end of World War I began to abate as Turkey became more confident and more certain of Western nations' goodwill. This changed attitude was in conformity with the policies of westernization pursued by Turkey since the establishment of the republic.

The Montreux Convention of 1936, which did not coincide with Russian interests, indicated once more that Turkey and Russia did not see eye to eye on the vital issue of the Straits. The Turks were drawing closer to the Kurdish-inhabited states of Iraq and Iran (formerly Persia), a trend that culminated in the conclusion of the Sa'adabad Pact in 1937. The Russians deeply resented this step. A sizable Muslim bloc near the borders of Russia's Asiatic and largely Muslim provinces would not fail to arouse its suspicion and fears. The Russians regarded the Sa'adabad Pact, which among other things aimed at curbing Kurdish uprisings, as a coalition sponsored and directed by Britain against the Soviet Union.

In the meantime, the Soviet Union was beginning to show an increasing interest in the Kurds. Soviet scholars devised a modern Latin alphabet (later changed to Cyrillic) for the Kurdish language, and steps were taken to create a vigorous literary and cultural movement among the Kurds of the Soviet Union. In July 1934, a congress of Kurdologists was held in Erivan.[54]

The Kurds, who had hitherto been neglected by the authorities in both Soviet Azerbayjan and Soviet Armenia, began to assume a new importance. According to a Soviet source, the two Transcaucasian republics had failed not only to further the Kurds' material and cultural well-being, but also "to have grasped the importance of the Kurds within the framework of a far-sighted Soviet policy in the Middle East."[55] In 1936, the Armenian Communists were severely castigated by the government for their negligence with regard to the Kurds living within the Armenian Soviet Socialist Republic and were accused of racist and chauvinistic practices.[56]

However, not until the outbreak of World War II and the Russian occupation of northern Iran did Russia show its hand in Kurdish affairs. After the war, contact with the disaffected Kurds and the restless energies and ambitions unleashed by the resurgence of Russian power after the defeat of the Axis induced the Russians to resume their old Kurdish policy.

Russia's interest in the Kurds was undoubtedly given great impetus by the deterioration of Russian-Turkish relations that began during the latter part of World War II and continued after the war. In the spring of 1945, the Soviet Union denounced the Soviet-Turkish Treaty of Friendship and Neutrality. Shortly thereafter, the Soviets advanced unofficial territorial claims on certain regions in Turkey's eastern provinces and demanded a revision of the Montreux Convention. These developments, coupled with the Soviet Union's open support of Kurdish nationalism, no doubt induced Turkey to take the lead in the formation of the Baghdad Pact with Iraq and Iran. This move completed the estrangement between the Russians and the Turks.

The Soviet Union, which had long been aware of the importance of the Kurds, was now determined to use them as a disruptive element against the pro-Western governments of Turkey, Iraq, and Iran. The Kurds' disenchantment with the West in general and with England in particular, coupled with their dislike of the three Baghdad Pact states, where the majority of the Kurds lived, naturally played into Soviet hands. The Russian attitude during the Barzani rebellions in Iraq (chapter 13) and the establishment of the Mahabad Republic in Iran (chapter 15) left no doubt as to future Russian intentions in this region.

7

The Kurds and World War I

The Effects of the War on the Kurdish People

World War I brought much suffering and severe losses to the Kurdish people. Because the Kurdish homeland happened to be located along the borders of the Ottoman and the Russian empires and thus lay in the path of the two contending armies, a large part of these lands became a battlefield from the earliest months of the war. This was true not only of Turkish Kurdistan and of those Kurdish lands lying within Russian territory, but of Persian Kurdistan as well.[1] The theater of operations extended from Sari Kamish in the north to Khanaqin in the south and from the Mukri country in the east to Erzerum and Erzinjan in the west. Many regions in this area changed hands several times, with disastrous results to the inhabitants. Both sides appear to have been guilty of excesses. This was not surprising, considering the passions animating the combatants. The zeal generated by the jihad among the Turkish forces was matched by a similar sentiment among the Armenian and Assyrian auxiliary units serving with the Russian army.

The war made heavy demands on Kurdish manpower. The number of Kurds engaged in the war is not easy to determine. However, some idea of their numbers may be gained from the following estimate made by the Kurdish historian M. A. Zaki, who held high rank in the Turkish army.[2] According to him, two armies, the Eleventh Army with headquarters at Mamurat al-'Aziz (Elazis) and the Twelfth Army with headquarters at Mosul, were made up entirely of Kurds. In addition, most of the officers and men of the Ninth Army, based at Erzerum, and the Tenth Army, based at Sivas, were Kurds. The Kurds also provided 135 squadrons of reserve cavalry as well as a number of frontier units and full complements of gendarmerie and security forces.[3] Many Kurdish tribal volunteers responded to the jihad, including those who fought under Shaykh Mahmud and other Kurdish leaders in the battle of Shu'ayba in southern Mesopotamia.[4] Large tribal forces served against the Russian army, both in Turkey and in northwestern Persia. Zaki estimated the total Kurdish battle casualties at three hundred thousand.[5]

The number of Kurds who perished from war or massacre was equalled, if not surpassed, by the number of those who perished from cold, famine, and pestilence. The Turkish army operating in Kurdistan lacked adequate supplies and means of transportation and lived off the local population. The military authorities compelled the people to sell them foodstuffs and other provisions at very low prices, often paying for them in valueless paper money and at times resorting to outright confiscation.[6] As a result of these practices, many Kurdish farmers and shepherds fled to remote areas with their produce and their flocks. Thus, the flow of provisions to the cities and villages was cut off, which led to scarcity and starvation among both civilians and members of the armed forces. The Second, Third, and Sixth Ottoman armies suffered greatly from famine and disease, the Third Army in particular being decimated by an epidemic of typhus.[7] The civilian population suffered to an even greater extent. In 1917, the Sulaymaniya region experienced a severe famine, which was reported to have resulted in the death of 70 percent of the inhabitants and soldiers in that area.[8]

The conduct of military operations in both Turkish and Persian Kurdistan was characterized by extreme ruthlessness, and the combatants showed little if any concern for the life and property of the native populations. The widescale destruction and the misery of the people were intensified by the changing fortunes of war. The alternating advances and retreats of the two contending armies were invariably accompanied by murder, rapine, and destruction. Many regions throughout Kurdistan were laid waste and their populations decimated.

A few examples give some idea of the great losses that the Kurds sustained during the war. When the Russians penetrated into the Bayazid-Aleshkird region in northern Kurdistan in December 1914, only one-tenth of the population is said to have survived the fury of the Armenian units attached to the Russian army.[9] After the outbreak of the Russian Revolution and the collapse of the Russian army in 1917, armed Armenian bands, freed from the restraining influence of their Russian officers, massacred large number of Kurds in the Erzerum-Erzinjan region.[10] Other regions in northern Kurdistan, such as Van, Bidlis, and Mush, met with a similar fate.

Another area that suffered greatly during the war was the Shamdinan-Rawanduz region of central Kurdistan. Of the one hundred villages of the Balik tribe, all but three or four were burned to the ground, and within the thirty-odd villages of the Rawandek section of the Baradost, "neither man, woman or child remained."[11] For the Baradost tribe as a whole, fifty-two of the eighty-one Baradost villages existing before the war were destroyed by the Russians or the Turks, and the tribe's 1,080 families were reduced to 157.[12] The Kuwaruk tribe, which numbered 150 families before the war, was said to have been reduced to only 7 families by 1919.[13] It was also reported that of the 250 houses in Nehri, only 10 were left standing, while of the 2,000 houses in Rawanduz, only 60 remained by the end of the war.[14] This grievous loss of life resulted as much from famine, typhus, and the great influenza epidemic of 1919 as from military operations.[15]

The population of Khanaqin and the surrounding countryside, which had sided with the Turks in opposing the Russian advance in 1916, suffered many hardships during the Russian occupation of that region from April to June 1917.[16] Flocks and foodstuffs were seized, farming and irrigation interfered with, and individuals molested and their property looted. As food became scarce and famine and brigandage mounted, large numbers of persons fled to the Turkish-occupied zone.[17] Various contemporaneous British sources attributed the conduct of the Russian troops in the Khanaqin region to the collapse of their morale as a result of the revolution at home.[18]

At the end of June 1917, the Russians evacuated the Khanaqin region, and it was immediately reoccupied by the Turks. The latter, who employed unusually harsh methods in obtaining food and other necessities, completed the ruin of this area.[19] The defeat of the main Turkish forces north of Baghdad, which led to a general Turkish withdrawal, brought the British forces to Khanaqin in December 1917. There they found the population in extreme distress. According to an official British source, "In no part of Mesopotamia had we encountered anything comparable to the misery which greeted us at Khaniqin. The country harvested by the Russians had been sedulously gleaned by the Turks, who, when they retired, left it in the joint possession of starvation and disease."[20]

Despite Persia's neutrality, Persian Kurdistan became a battlefield shortly after the outbreak of hostilities between Russia and Turkey. As a result of the harsh methods used by both armies, whole regions were devastated, and the inhabitants were reduced to abject misery. Many of those who were not slain in the course of the fighting were deprived of food and shelter, and thousands of persons died of starvation and disease. The following description gives some idea of the plight of Persian Kurdistan during the war:

> The villages had been gutted by passing armies, Russian and Turkish, the roof beams and all wooden fittings torn out and used as fuel, and the rain and snow of the winter had completed the destruction of the unprotected mud walls. The fields lay untilled, and if any of the husbandmen remained, it was because they were too greatly extenuated by hunger to flee. But in fact there was no sure refuge for those who took flight. Not only in Persian Kurdistan but the whole Persian empire was in the grip of famine.[21]

At the end of the war, after four years of unchecked violence and destruction, the whole region was on the verge of ruin. Thousands of sick and starving Kurds poured into Urmiya in search of food and shelter. So pitiful was the condition of these refugees that even their erstwhile bitter enemies, the Assyrians, were moved to give them what help they could and to plead their cause before the American Relief Committee. According to an American eyewitness, "Assyrians shared their homes and small allotments of grain with starving, penitent Kurds, and all the Assyrian prelates from the Patriarch and Metropolitan down to the parish priest, have united in petitions to the Americans, asking that relief be sent to the suffering Kurds, friendly and hostile alike."[22]

Considerable uprootings of Kurdish populations took place during the war. In addition to those Kurds who fled from their homes in Turkish Kurdistan at the approach of the Russian army, large-scale deportations appear to have been organized by the Ottoman authorities. An imperial decree signed by Sultan Muhammad V outlined a scheme for the deportation and resettlement of the Kurds. In accordance with this scheme, the Kurds were to be broken up into small groups and settled in specified zones in the Turkish-speaking *wilayat*s of western Anatolia, where their numbers were not to exceed 5 percent of the total population. The Kurdish notables and chiefs were to be settled in cities or towns, and all connections with their followers were strictly prohibited.[23]

According to Bletch Chirguh, the records of the Turkish refugee administration indicate that seven hundred thousand Kurds were forced to leave their homes. Kurdish sources report that the majority of these persons died of hunger, cold, and disease before reaching their various destinations.[24]

The Activities of Kurdish Nationalists during the War

The outbreak of World War I, even more than the Young Turks' repressive measures, proved to be a powerful check to Kurdish nationalism. The Kurdish national movement in Turkey faded into the background as the great conflict, in which the Kurds early became involved, made greater and heavier demands on their energies and resources. Their deep involvement in the tragic fate of the Armenians left them no choice but to close ranks with the Turks in order to face the common dangers of the war. However, a small band of Kurdish nationalists living in exile continued to work for an independent Kurdistan. Some of them turned to England and others to Russia, the two great powers then at war with the Ottoman Empire.

In December 1914, General Muhammad Sharif Pasha offered his services to the British expeditionary forces in Mesopotamia, evidently with the object of obtaining some assurances with regard to the future of Kurdistan. His offer was declined because the British at that time did not envisage military operations in so remote an area.[25] General Sharif Pasha, as we shall see, was to renew his contacts with the British at the end of the war.

Members of the Bedir Khan family, especially 'Abd al-Razzaq Beg and Kamil Beg Bedir Khan, maintained close and cordial relations with the Russians. Some time after the Young Turk Revolution, 'Abd al-Razzaq Bedir Khan, who happened to be in Paris, is reported to have sounded the Russians with regard to their intentions in Kurdistan.[26] It appears that in 1916 Kamil Bedir Khan was actively engaged in pleading the Kurdish national cause in Tiflis, before the Grand Duke Nicholas, viceroy of the Caucasus and commander in chief of the Caucasian front.[27]

During the Russian occupation of eastern Turkey in 1917, Kamil and 'Abd al-Razzaq Bedir Khan had been appointed *walis* of Erzerum and Bidlis, respectively.[28] 'Abd al-Razzaq, who again became prominent in Kurdish national affairs after the war, was reported to have been poisoned by the Turks in Mosul in 1918,[29] whereas Kamil was reported to be still in Tiflis in September 1919.[30] Another member of the same family, Sureya Beg, eldest son of Amin 'Ali Bedir Khan, was engaged in Kurdish nationalist activities in Cairo, where he published the newspaper *Kurdistan*, no doubt with British approval and support.[31]

Some time before the war, Shaykh Sayyid Taha II appears to have entered into formal relations with the Russians. He is reported to have traveled in Russia and to have been fluent in the language of that country.[32] After spending some time in Novo Rossiisk, the shaykh apparently returned as a Russian protégé and established himself at the village of Rajan in Persia, just across the Turco-Persian frontier.[33] According to an official British report, Shaykh Sayyid Taha was not only friendly with Russian consular officials, but "there was at one time an idea that he might be used as the figurehead of a nominally independent Kurdistan under Russian auspices."[34] According to another official British report that discussed Sayyid Taha's pro-Russian activities before the war, "even then he was working for Kurdish independence under Russian protection, as the Russians were more capable of keeping order than the Persians."[35] During the war, however, Sayyid Taha's desire to curry favor with both sides led to his being imprisoned at different times by both the Turks and the Russians.[36] Because he managed to keep on good terms with the Germans, the Russians doubted his loyalty and in retaliation destroyed his house at Nehri when their forces crossed the Turco-Persian frontier in 1916.[37]

Nikitine has informed us that toward the end of 1917, he received a message from the Istikhlas e Kurdistan (Society for the Deliverance of Kurdistan) in the form of a letter from Sayyid Taha. In this letter, Nikitine was requested to arrange a meeting between Sayyid Taha and the Russian military commanders in order to draw up a plan for common action against the Turks with a view to liberating Kurdistan.[38] An official British source referred to the connections of Sayyid Taha and his uncle, Shaykh 'Abd al-Qadir, with Russian diplomatic agents in Tehran and Tiflis. It went on to say that the two shaykhs "in the early days of the conflict had done all in their power to overthrow the strategy of Von der Goltz on the Persian frontier."[39]

Sharif Pasha's Views on the Future of Kurdistan

It will be recalled that in December 1914 General Muhammad Sharif Pasha sought unsuccessfully to reach an understanding with the British expeditionary forces in Mesopotamia. Despite this rebuff, he did not give up his hope of Anglo-Kurdish cooperation. In June 1918, at a time when the outcome of the war was still uncertain, Sharif Pasha contacted Sir Percy Cox,[40] the chief political officer of the British forces in Mesopotamia, and proposed the adoption by the British of a bold and imaginative policy with regard to the Kurds. These proposals, if adopted, would have provided the basis for a unique relationship of interdependence between the British and the Kurds. In fact, in 1936, Sir Arnold Wilson described Sharif Pasha's recommendations as an intelligent anticipation of the mandate system.[41]

In discussing this matter with Cox, Sharif Pasha strongly urged that the British should take immediate steps to rally the Kurds by announcing a constructive policy with regard to Kurdish aspirations. He pointed out that to achieve this end an official declaration of British intentions concerning the Kurds' future was of the utmost importance.[42] The British, he suggested, should give the southern Kurds guarantees of autonomy under British protection, and British officials should be deputized to assist in the administration of the country and in controlling its finances.[43] Sharif Pasha advised against annexations—a view consistent with repeated British pronouncements during the war—and advocated the establishment of British-protected autonomous states in Kurdistan, Mesopotamia, and elsewhere.

The Kurdish leader emphasized the importance of setting up a working administration in the occupied zones of both Mesopotamia and Kurdistan and thus facing the forthcoming Peace Conference with a fait accompli. In his opinion, to let matters drift until such time as the Peace Conference was convened would be sheer political folly, for it would be certain to invite confusion and uncertainty throughout the occupied zones. Sharif Pasha urged that the British should do for the Kurds what they proposed to do for the Arabs of Mesopotamia.

In October 1918, Sharif Pasha wrote the British authorities, pointing out that the political situation had taken a turn for the worse as a result of the Turks' success in fostering hatred between the Kurds and the Armenians. The main task, according to him, was to bring about a reconciliation between the two peoples based on the mutual recognition of the legitimate claims of both nationalities. For this purpose, he recommended the immediate establishment in London of a committee consisting of Kurdish and Armenian representatives.[44] Although such a committee was never formed, Sharif Pasha himself, as we shall see, succeeded in coming to terms with Armenian leaders at the Peace Conference.

Kurdish Activities at the Peace Conference and in Istanbul

Kurdish nationalist organizations chose General Sharif Pasha to represent the Kurds at the Peace Conference. This task was particularly difficult, for before any progress could be made, it was necessary to overcome the strong anti-Kurdish bias animating the representatives of the victorious Allies—a legacy of the Armenian massacres. Sharif Pasha appears to have pleaded the cause of his people so well and to have conducted himself with so much dignity and tact that he succeeded in gaining the sympathy of the Western powers and the friendship of the Armenians. Before long, a Kurdo-Armenian accord was reached between Sharif Pasha, acting in behalf of the Kurds, and Boghos Nubar Pasha and Avetis Aharonian, acting in behalf of the Armenians.[45]

These developments alarmed the Turks, who lost no time in trying to come to terms with the Kurds. They decided to deal directly with the source of the trouble—the Kurdistan Ta'ali Jam'iyati (Kurdish National Committee). According to a Kurdish source, the Turks invited the Kurdish National Committee to designate three delegates to participate in studying the Kurdish question and to help in formulating the necessary decisions.[46] A special council was formed for this purpose. It was composed of Ibrahim Effendi al-Haydari (minister without portfolio and former Shaykh al-Islam), Abouk Pasha (minister of public works and former minister of war), and 'Awni Pasha (minister of the marine), as representatives of the Ottoman government; and Shaykh 'Abd al-Qadir of Nehri and the emirs Amin 'Ali and Murad Bedir Khan, as representatives of the Kurdish National Committee. After some deliberations, the council decided on the following points:

1. The recognition of a large measure of autonomy in Kurdistan.

2. The immediate promulgation of laws resulting from the foregoing decision.

3. The unimpeded execution of all obligations flowing from these laws.

4. The Kurds to undertake to continue being a part of the Ottoman Empire and to continue to recognize the suzerainty of the sultan-caliph.[47]

An official British publication gave a different account of these events. It stated that the Turks did not invite the Kurdish National Committee to send delegates to discuss the Kurdish question, but rather summoned them to explain their activities and to state on what authority they were negotiating with the British in Constantinople on matters pertaining to Kurdistan. The Ottoman officials, according to this report, pointed out that such matters were within the competence of the Porte, which they maintained was in a position to grant a large measure of autonomy to the Kurds.

Rif'at Beg, a spokesman for Shaykh 'Abd al-Qadir, who was not present at the parley, is said to have replied that the Kurds had acted in accordance with the principles of President Woodrow Wilson, which gave every nationality the right to work out its own salvation. The Kurds, he stated, were convinced that Great Britain was the only power that could assure the freedom and security of Kurdistan, and for that reason they had started these negotiations. Rif'at Beg expressed his doubts with regard to Turkey's ability to grant autonomy to the Kurds in view of its own uncertain future. At this point, Abouk Pasha is said to have jumped up angrily and told the Kurdish spokesman that the Ottoman government was stronger than ever, that it had decided not to relinquish one foot of its territory to anyone, that orders had been issued to the Turkish Caucasian army to oppose all foreign armies, and that the repatriation of Armenian refugees was not being allowed. At this point, 'Awni Pasha reportedly cut short Abouk Pasha's outburst.[48]

The Treaty of Sèvres

In the meantime, Sharif Pasha's efforts at the Peace Conference seemed to be bearing fruit. Although subject to many disappointing conditions, Kurdish national aspirations finally gained official recognition and endorsement in the abortive Treaty of Sèvres, signed in August 1920. This treaty, which provided for the establishment of a Kurdish national state, is regarded as a milestone in Kurdish history.

Section 3 (Articles 62–64) of the Treaty of Sèvres dealt with Kurdistan.[49] Article 62 provided that "a Commission sitting at Constantinople . . . shall draft within six months from the coming into force of the present Treaty a scheme of local autonomy for the predominantly Kurdish areas lying east of the Euphrates, south of the southern boundary of Armenia as it may be hereafter determined, and north of the frontier of Turkey with Syria and Mesopotamia, as defined in Article 27, II (2) and (3)."[50] This article also provided for the protection of the Assyro-Chaldeans and other racial and religious minorities. It stipulated that in order to ensure this protection, a commission composed of British, French, Italian, Persian, and Kurdish representatives should be formed to "decide what rectifications, if any, should be made in the Turkish frontier where, under the provisions of the present Treaty, that frontier coincides with that of Persia."[51] Article 63 provided for the acceptance and execution of the provisions of Article 62 by the Turkish government.[52]

Article 64 of the Treaty of Sèvres indicated when and how the Kurds could apply to the Council of the League of Nations, indicating their desire to gain independence from Turkey:

> If within one year from the coming into force of the present Treaty the Kurdish peoples within the areas defined in Article 62 shall address themselves to the Council of the

League of Nations in such a manner as to show that a majority of the population of these areas desires independence from Turkey, and if the Council then considers that these peoples are capable of such independence and recommends that it should be granted to them, Turkey hereby agrees to execute such a recommendation, and to renounce all rights and title over these areas.[53]

Finally, Article 64 provided that following Turkey's renunciation of its rights and title over these areas, the principal and Allied powers would raise no objection to "the voluntary adhesion to such an independent Kurdish State of the Kurds inhabiting that part of Kurdistan which has hitherto been included in the Mosul vilayet."[54]

The Treaty of Sèvres, as we shall see, was stillborn. It was swept aside by a resurgent Kemalist Turkey and in 1923 was superseded by the Treaty of Lausanne.

8 *The Situation of the Kurds in Turkey, Persia, and Syria after World War I*

The Situation in Turkey

The signing of the armistice of Mudros in 1918 was the signal for a sudden recrudescence of the Kurdish nationalist movement in Turkey. This development resulted not only from the efforts of Kurdish nationalists returning from exile or resident in Turkey, but also from active Turkish support.

The resumption of Kurdish nationalist activity in Turkey and Turkish-controlled Kurdistan had immediate and far-reaching effects. It greatly augmented the power of Kurdish nationalist forces everywhere, giving a new meaning to the activities of Kurdish intellectuals, as well as to the efforts of Kurdish dignitaries in seeking local hegemony over certain parts of Kurdistan.

Diverse elements, hitherto at cross-purposes and with conflicting loyalties and irreconcilable interests, banded together with the avowed purpose of establishing Kurdish independence, or at least a form of Kurdish autonomy. The motives and objectives of the different adherents of the movement were as many and as varied as the individuals and groups involved. Dedicated nationalists, ambitious dignitaries, persons fearful of retribution for their part in the Armenian massacres, embittered former CUP members, army officers, and even Arab nationalists desirous of including Kurds in the projected Arab state—they all had their own reasons for supporting this movement.

Sources of Support for the Kurdish Movement

The Kurdish movement derived its strength and inspiration from two different sources. One of them was a pro-Turkish and pan-Islamic party animated by religious sentiment and supported by pan-Islamic elements. It worked in close cooperation with Turkish officials and was actively anti-British. The other source was neither pro-Turkish nor motivated by religious considerations. It sought complete Kurdish independence and was supported by pan-Kurdish nationalists. Despite the basic cleavages existing between the two groups with regard to ultimate aims, they ignored these differences and carefully avoided an open breach.

The pan-Islamic party was unalterably opposed to the idea of an Armenian state, for its members felt that the establishment of such a state would result in an irretrievable loss of Turkish territory and the creation of a bitterly hostile neighbor. The party hoped to defeat this project by organizing massive popular opposition, and for the realization of this end it spared no effort. When its primary aim of preventing the establishment of an Armenian state seemed doomed to failure, its members did not hesitate to give their full support to the idea of an independent Kurdish state, which was clearly the lesser of two evils. An independent Kurdish state not only might serve as a valuable counterpoint to a resurgent Armenia, but might even obviate its creation altogether. Moreover, an independent Kurdistan need not be more than a convenient temporary arrangement, to be followed by reunion with Turkey at some future date.

The pan-Kurdish nationalists were not as opposed to Armenian independence as were the pan-Islamic elements. Many among them were willing to recognize Armenian aspirations, provided that Kurdish aspirations would receive similar recognition. In fact, some of the leaders of the pan-Kurdish nationalists, as we shall see, sought to form a common front with the Armenians.

The Activities of ʿAli Ihsan Pasha

In northern Kurdistan, soon after the signing of the armistice, the Kurdish nationalist movement appeared in the form of a large-scale agitation. The movement is said to have been organized and directed by influential Turkish officials and CUP members with the object of embarrassing the Allies. ʿAli Ihsan Pasha, former commander of the Turkish Sixth Army, is believed to have been the chief organizer of the movement in the regions north of the British-occupied zone. The results of these activities soon became evident. In January 1919, CUP members were reported to be at Kharput, urging the Kurds to demand independence at the Peace Conference. At about the same time, ʿAli Ihsan Pasha appears to have been actively engaged in suppressing anti-Turkish elements at Diyarbakr and elsewhere.[1] He is said to have incited the Barazi tribe in the Seruj region to attack the Kitkan for their pro-British attitude, and to have imprisoned a chief of the Karakacheli.[2] He reportedly succeeded in winning over neighboring chieftains by supplying them with money, arms, and equipment to be used against the British should the latter attempt to extend their zone of occupation.[3] It appears that ʿAli Ishan Pasha was so successful that an antiforeign attitude prevailed wherever he managed to extend his influence.[4]

Jazirat ibn ʿUmar, where ʿAli Ihsan Pasha was reported to have been active at the beginning of February 1919, was another center of unrest. Here, as elsewhere, he set in motion a movement calculated to combat British influence and to prevent British occupation. A number of influential Arab and Armenian notables were detained, traffic was interfered with on the Tigris between Jazirat ibn ʿUmar and points south of the armistice line, and Kurds were being recruited and armed in flagrant defiance of the armistice terms. Kurds disregarded orders from Istanbul enjoining the enforcement of the terms of the armistice with the tacit approval, if not at the behest, of the local Turkish authorities.[5]

The situation was getting out of hand so rapidly everywhere in the regions north of the armistice line that the Turkish government was forced to take action. On February, 21, 1919, 'Ali Ihsan Pasha was removed as a result of the disturbances, which he not only seemed "unable or unwilling to suppress," but was in fact suspected of fomenting. A number of his friends and followers faithfully and efficiently continued his work, however.[6]

'Ali Ihsan Pasha was no ordinary malcontent; he was a Turkish patriot and a soldier. He clearly and accurately estimated the Allies' difficulties and proceeded to exploit the situation to his country's advantage. In as much as he had signed under protest the armistice terms dictated to him by Sir John Marshall (see chap. 11), it is not surprising to find him engaged in thwarting Allied designs on parts of his country beyond what he had so reluctantly yielded to a resolute and unrelenting victor. 'Ali Ihsan's ulterior motives in fomenting unrest are perhaps best described in the words of a contemporary official British report: "Though in fact, he is working in favour of an independent Kurdistan, it would seem that he only does so to embarrass the Allies; what he really wishes is to discourage them from taking over the control of Kurdistan whereupon he will do his utmost to bring it again under Turkish rule."[7]

Attempts to Form an Anti-British Resistance Movement among the Kurds

At this time, the Kurdish movement in Diyarbakr was led by a certain 'Ali Beg, who formed a party for "Turco-Kurdish independence." This party's aim seems to have been to prevent the Kurds from coming under any foreign power in case they were not to be included in the new Turkish state. 'Ali Beg reportedly was trying to obtain government permission to publish a newspaper for the purpose of fostering this idea.[8]

Early in March 1919, leading notables from Severek approached the Turkish authorities and the leaders of the local branch of the CUP at Diyarbakr with the object of taking joint measures to resist foreign occupation. As a result, a plan was agreed upon in accordance with which Turkish troops and the neighboring Kurdish tribes would cooperate in defending the Severek-Diyarbakr-Urfa region. With this purpose in mind, they released Mahmud ibn Ibrahim Pasha, paramount chieftain of the Milli, and 'Abd al-Qadir ibn Der'ai, chief of the Karakcheli, who were in prison on charges of disloyalty to the government. They offered to restore Mahmud to his position as paramount chief of the Milli confederation and to make him the most powerful Kurdish chieftain east of the Euphrates if he would agree to lead his forces and the neighboring tribes in driving the British garrison out of Urfa and across the Euphrates.

Mahmud agreed and sent letters to various tribal chieftains, including the Badelli and Dukurli Kurds and the Juhaysh Arabs, inviting them to mobilize and join in the campaign. After some hesitation, the two Kurdish tribes decided to participate.[9] Other Kurdish chieftains, however, had considerable misgivings. On March 12, 1919, the chief of the Kitkan Kurds and a number of important chiefs under his influence met the British military authorities at Arab Punar, where they discussed the situation and decided to form an anti-Turkish league.[10]

In an effort to strengthen Mahmud's hand, Turkish troops were reported to be joining the Milli Kurds, and the Turkish military authorities were said to have presented

Mahmud with two or three field guns in addition to undisclosed amounts of small arms. All these measures failed to save Mahmud's movement from collapse. His most important allies, the Karakacheli, were not all of one mind with regard to the alliance. Mustafa of the Karakacheli quarreled with his cousin, 'Abd al-Qadir ibn Derai, over the question of joining their bitter enemies, the Milli. The attempt by the authorities at Severek to mediate was of no avail. It was soon apparent that owing to dissensions and lack of cohesion, Mahmud's movement was doomed, and the confederacy so laboriously brought together fell to pieces.[11]

An attempt to bolster the resistance movement in the Mardin region failed to achieve its purpose. Shaykh 'Abd al-Qadir of Nehri, president of the Committee for Kurdish Independence in Istanbul, in cooperation with Shawkat Beg, a member of the Administrative Council of Mardin, was reported to have sent emissaries among the tribes urging them to oppose foreign intervention. Except for the few chieftains who expressed their adherence to the suggestion, however, the majority seemed to be indifferent. These activities were strongly supported by Kan'an Beg, commander of the Turkish Fifth Division at Mardin.[12]

At about this time, 'Ali Batti, chief of the Haverkan, was reported to have met with 'Abd al-Rahman, chief of the Shernakhli, and Ramadan, chief of the Salahan, and these three Kurdish leaders reached an agreement to oppose future British advances. There were reports that other chiefs were also being contacted for this purpose.[13]

In and around Urfa, the situation appears to have been rather ambiguous. During the second week of March 1919, one Mahmud Beg, a Kurdish notable of Urfa and a fervent Turkophile, inaugurated a campaign against the interference of Christians such as the British, in the affairs of Muslim states. At the same time, two CUP leaders, Severekli 'Ali Effendi and Baghdanli Sayyid Beg, were said to be engaged in rousing the tribes in the neighborhood of the town and organizing a force to fight the British. The chiefs of the neighboring tribes were reported to be coming to Urfa to make protestations of their loyalty to the Kurdish cause.[14]

The Kurdish Club's Aims and Activities

By this time, the Kurdish Club was already established and functioning at both Diyarbakr and Mardin.[15] The town notables who organized and directed the club's activities appear to have been a group of corrupt and self-seeking individuals, according to British major E. W. C. Noel. He maintained that many of them were active members of the CUP and that after Turkey's defeat they joined the Kurdish National Party at the bidding of the Turks, who held out to them the attractive prospect of Kurdish autonomy under Turkish protection.[16]

In Diyarbakr, as elsewhere, the Kurdish Club directed its activities toward two objectives. First, it set itself to the task of curbing British influence and opposing British intervention, for which purpose a force of Turks and Kurds was enrolled and held ready to go into action. Second, it sought to combat Armenian activity and to frustrate Armenian ambitions. With the latter object in mind, the mufti of Severek had been induced to issue a *fatwa* in accordance with which it was made lawful to kill those Armenians who, before the Allied authorities in Aleppo, had accused Muslims of participation in the massacres of 1915. Once more the Armenians became subject to molestation as a fresh wave of popular hatred mounted against them.[17]

The Turkish government, which was officially opposed to these activities, ordered the arrest of a number of important Kurdish Club leaders. These leaders sought refuge with neighboring Kurdish tribes, among whom they proceeded to spread the idea of Kurdish independence. Despite these arrests, the anti-British and anti-Armenian campaign continued to be waged by other members of the club with even greater zeal. In fact, they went so far as to invite "all patriotic Kurds to join in the Kurdish Club." On March 21, 1919, members of the Kurdish Club called a meeting that was attended by a deputation of prominent Kurdish chiefs and other dignitaries, including the chief of the Serkuji, the chief of the Hazo, the mufti of Severek, and two notables of Derek. At this meeting, it was decided to defend Mardin and Diyarbakr against British intervention at all costs.[18]

The activities of the Kurdish Club in Mardin were being directed by seven leading notables. Inasmuch as their chief objective was to prevent the British occupation of Mardin, they concealed their plans from the local Christians. They sought to induce as many persons as possible to sign a document to the effect that all the inhabitants of the town—Kurds, Turks and Christians—were unanimous in desiring an autonomous Kurdistan. Many individuals, including Mar Elias, patriarch of the Jacobites, refused to sign, evidently so as not to compromise themselves with the Turkish authorities in the future. The wording of the statement had to be changed to read that the signers, being Ottoman subjects, did not wish for British interference. The patriarch left for Istanbul (formerly Constantinople) after signing the document.[19]

The Liquidation of the Kurdish Club

International developments, in particular the spread of President Wilson's ideas of self-determination, induced the members of the Kurdish Club to adopt a more independent attitude vis-à-vis the Turks. Major Noel commented with sarcasm and evident distaste on the effect that the Wilsonian principles produced on the Kurds:

> The tantalising version of President Wilson's doctrine that everybody should do as he liked, has slowly dawned on their horizon with all its alluring possibilities, and erstwhile Turco-Kurds are now convinced that if they shout loud enough, President Wilson will hear them and allow them to mismanage Diarbakr by themselves, and to continue to fatten on the Christian property that they stole during the massacres, without even having to share the spoil with the Turks.[20]

The increasingly defiant attitude of the Kurdish leaders alarmed the Turkish authorities, who regarded the club's activities with growing disfavor and finally decided to liquidate it. The Greek occupation of Izmir (Smyrna) provided them with ample material for agitation, and it was fully utilized. Greek atrocities in that town were blamed on the British, and the Kurds were asked to apply the analogy of Izmir to Diyarbakr, where the arrival of the British would be followed by the arrival of Armenian troops.

A great deal of fanaticism, in addition to legitimate alarm, was aroused among the people. Members of the Kurdish Club, many of whom were implicated in the Armenian massacres of 1915 and were fearful of punishment, hoped for another massacre that would do away with the last witnesses to their past misdeeds. The Christians, thoroughly frightened by these developments, sent a deputation to Major Noel at Mardin to beg for British intervention.

The Turks, seeing that their propaganda had overshot its mark, took quick measures to rectify the situation. Their intention had been to stir public opinion against the British rather than against the Christians. They also realized the possible repercussions of a fresh massacre. The Turkish authorities lost no time in exploiting the situation to their advantage. The Kurdish Club was made the scapegoat, and in this way an unwanted and inconvenient organization, which had begun to show itself opposed to Turkish sovereignty, was suppressed. The Kurdish Club was disposed of in dramatic fashion. Guns were mounted on the citadel, troops were called out, club leaders were arrested, and the club itself finally closed on June 4, 1919.[21]

The Situation in Persia

Effects of the Sultan's Pan-Islamic and Pan-Kurdish Policies

After the armistice, the Kurdish nationalist movement spread to Persian Kurdistan, where it found enthusiastic adherents. According to Noel, many Kurds of Sulaymaniya left for Persia shortly after the cessation of hostilities to preach the idea of a united Kurdistan.[22]

This was the culmination of a sequence of events originally set in motion by Sultan 'Abd al-Hamid's pan-Islamic and pro-Kurdish policies. The pan-Islamic policy, based on the concept of the universal character of the Ottoman sultan-caliph's authority, was often employed with consummate skill by 'Abd al-Hamid as an instrument of foreign policy calculated to influence the decisions of the great powers. The pan-Kurdish policy was designed to win over the warlike Kurds, whom 'Abd al-Hamid wished to use as a barrier against possible Russian aggression and as a check against Armenian ambitions.

These policies fell on fertile soil in Persian Kurdistan, a region greatly coveted by Turkey. The Persian Kurds had responded enthusiastically to the Ottoman ruler's overtures. As Sunnis, they deemed it their duty to give allegiance to the sultan-caliph, while as Kurds they were flattered and gratified by the patronage of such an august person. These astutely conceived policies were continued by the Ottoman government even after the overthrow of 'Abd al-Hamid and played a decisive role in bringing together the Kurds of Persia and the Kurds of the Ottoman Empire.

Largely as a result of these policies, the Persian Kurds were twice brought under Ottoman control—namely, during the Turkish occupation of 1906–11[23] and during World War I. On both occasions, their territories were practically assimilated into those of their more numerous kinsmen living within the Ottoman Empire. Thus, thanks to persistent Turkish efforts, the Kurds of Persia were drawn into the mainstream of Kurdish life.

The Growing Desire for an Independent Kurdistan

The question of Kurdish independence was beginning to exercise the minds of responsible leaders in Persian Kurdistan even before the end of World War I. In July 1918, one of the leading chieftains of the Mukri tribe of the Sawj Bulaq (Mahabad) region is reported to have discussed a scheme for an independent Kurdish state under British protection with Lieutenant-Colonel R. L. Kennion, British consul at Kirmanshah, when the latter was on tour near Sakiz.[24] The Mukri chieftain is said to have pointed out that once the Kurds were free to act for themselves, they would seek to reach a peaceful settlement with the Armenians through the good offices of the British government.[25] In fact, he appears to have made it clear that a free Armenia in the northern provinces of Turkey would be acceptable to the Kurds providing the Kurds were allowed to set up their own independent state south of the Armenian state and north of the Arab state.[26]

A little less than a year later the two important Kurdish leaders who were in Persian Kurdistan, Isma'il Agha (Simko) of the Shikak and Shaykh Sayyid Taha of Nehri, were known to be working closely together on a plan for the inclusion of the Persian Kurds in an independent Kurdish state.

In March 1919, Sayyid Taha came to Baghdad with the object of obtaining the support of the British authorities for such a scheme, but he failed to achieve his purpose. British civil administrator Gertrude Bell wrote an interesting description of Sayyid Taha's reaction to the failure of his mission: "When it was explained to him that he could expect no help from us in realising this project as far as the Persian Kurds were concerned, he expressed great disappointment and observed that the separation of Persian Kurdistan from Persia was certain to come even if we withheld our consent." [27] Notwithstanding Sayyid Taha's disappointment, he is reported to have stated his willingness to help the British in every possible way in establishing an independent Kurdish regime.[28]

Simko Agha acted almost simultaneously. In early May 1919, he addressed a letter, couched in friendly terms, to Sir Arnold Wilson, acting civil commissioner in Mesopotamia, whom he had known before the war. Notwithstanding the real object of his letter, he spoke at length of a personal matter. He seemed to be greatly perturbed by a recent attempt on his life, which he blamed on a Persian official, and it was upon this incident that he dwelt most.[29] Simko Agha's subsequent activities are dealt with in a later section.

The Causes of Unrest in Persian Kurdistan

At the end of the war, Persian Kurdistan was reported to be in a state of turmoil bordering on chaos. The confusion was such that even British official sources found it difficult to know what was actually happening there. Needless to say, British authorities in Mesopotamia viewed this state of affairs with grave concern, fearing the spread of serious disorders to neighboring regions under their control.[30]

Responsible British officials attributed this unrest to two major factors: (1) the

Kurds' determined opposition to the repatriation of the Assyrian and Armenian refugees, which was believed to have been fostered by a pan-Islamic movement centered at Tabriz and backed to some extent by Persian officials; and (2) the Kurds' intense dislike for the "emasculated Persian rule," which was too weak to maintain law and order.[31]

In February 1919, the question of revolt against Persian rule was discussed at a meeting attended by a large number of Kurdish chieftains in Persia. These leaders reportedly decided that such a revolt should be carried out, but that no action should be taken until the attitude of the great powers toward the Persian Kurds and the repatriation of the refugees had been ascertained.[32]

Agitation and disorder appear to have continued unabated in Persian Kurdistan. On May 23, 1919, the Kurds were reported to have seized the governor of Salamas and to have besieged Koi. This outbreak was attributed to rumors that the British and the Persians were on the point of repatriating the Christian refugees. In an attempt to prevent the repatriation, the Kurds reportedly appealed to Javid Beg, commander of the Eleventh Caucasian Division of the Turkish army, and to Haydar Beg, *wali* of Van and a former member of the CUP, who had an anti-Christian and anti-British reputation.[33]

At that time, there were conflicting reports regarding the activities of Simko Agha. According to one source, he was collecting a force with which to oppose the repatriation of the Christians.[34] Strangely enough, however, the Spanish vice consul at Salamas, who was an Armenian by birth, claimed that Simko Agha did not take part in the movement aimed at preventing the return of the Christian refugees and, in fact, maintained a friendly attitude toward them.[35]

The general tension in this region was increased by the *wali* of Van's distribution of arms to the Herki tribesmen, by the local Persian governor's favorable attitude toward the antirepatriation movement, and especially by the attitude of the Persian heir apparent *(wali-'ahd)*,[36] who was known for his pro-German and pro-Turkish sympathies.[37]

The Activities of Simko Agha

The rise of Simko. Isma'il Agha, better known as Simko,[38] paramount chief of the turbulent Shikak tribe inhabiting the Turco-Persian frontier regions near Kotor, was one of the most remarkable personalities to emerge in Kurdistan during the war.[39] He succeeded his brother, Ja'far Agha, who was treacherously murdered in Tabriz on orders from the *wali 'ahd*.[40] Ambitious, cunning, and ruthless, Simko for a number of years held undisputed sway over a large portion of Persian Kurdistan from Kotor to Bana. By adding nationalism to brigandage, he managed to become not only a hero among his own people, but also a thorn in the side of Persia and a power to be reckoned with by Turkey and by the British administration in Mesopotamia.

Simko, at various times during and after the war, had allied himself with and fought against the Russians, Turks, Armenians, Assyrians, and Persians.[41] He first gained notoriety by his treacherous murder of the Nestorian patriarch Mar Sham'un, shortly after concluding an alliance with him.[42] This act is said to have been instigated by a Persian official.[43]

In view of these various developments, it was perhaps inevitable that Simko, the most powerful figure in Persian Kurdistan, should have placed himself at the head of a movement for the autonomy of the Persian Kurds. In October 1921, he moved his headquarters to the old Mukri capital of Sawj Bulaq (Mahabad), where he was reported to have begun the publication of *Independent Kurdistan,* a newspaper intended to serve as a mouthpiece for Kurdish aspirations.[44]

At about this time, the Soviet government reportedly mediated with the Persian government on behalf of Simko, recommending that autonomy be conceded to the Kurds.[45] The Soviets were then on friendly terms with Persia, with whom they had earlier that year concluded the now famous treaty of February 1921.

The Persian government, whether because of the reported Soviet mediation or because of its preoccupation with the task of pacifying the disaffected elements in various parts of the country,[46] maintained a truce with Simko during the first half of 1922. It even tried to come to terms with him by holding out the prospect of granting a measure of autonomy to the Persian Kurds.[47] Simko, however, appears to have become impatient. Taking advantage of the still unsettled condition of the country, the Kurdish leader decided to strike a decisive blow for the realization of his dream.

The rebellions of Simko Agha. In the summer of 1922, Simko declared himself in open rebellion against the government and marched on Maragha. His occupation of that town coincided with a revolt among the kindred Lurs, with whom he appears to have been in secret agreement.[48] The Persian army, commanded by Riza Khan, the future shah of Persia, fell first upon the rebellious tribes of Luristan, crushing their revolt. It then turned on Simko and succeeded in defeating and dispersing his forces. He fled across the frontier into the Kurdish zone of Iraq.[49] In the operations against Simko, Turkey rendered valuable support to the Persian army by sending powerful units to the Turco-Persian frontier.[50] This action on the part of Turkey marked the end of Simko's cooperation with the Turks.

Simko's defeat appears to have been complete, as indicated by his unheralded arrival at Dera near Arbil at the end of October 1922, accompanied by only a few followers.[51] C. J. Edmonds, who conferred with him a few days later at the village of Bahirka, states that Simko seemed less resentful against the Persians than against the Turks, who had pretended to support him but had turned against him.[52]

The Kurdish leader expressed his disappointment and surprise at the British refusal to support him against the Persian government. The latter, he pointed out, was cooperating with the Turks, who were openly engaged in warlike activities against the British. According to Edmonds, Simko stated that "he had come in the hope of finding us ready to champion the cause of Kurdish freedom against two governments hostile to us; if he was wrong he had no wish to demand asylum but would make his way to his tribes and do his best alone."[53]

Simko probably had expected British support in return for services that he had rendered three months earlier in July 1922 during the anti-British rebellion of Karim-i Fatta Beg in Sulaymaniya. At that time, Simko, in cooperation with Sayyid Taha, had prevailed on the Persian tribes not to support the rebellion and consequently had greatly helped to relieve the pressure on Babakir Agha, pro-British chief of the Pizhdar

12. Simko in Sulaymaniya. Photographer unknown/Courtesy of Rafiq
Studio. *Kurdistan: In the Shadow of History.*

tribe, who had fled into Persian territory when hard pressed by hostile members of his tribe.[54]

After Simko's flight into Iraq, Major Noel appears to have tried unsuccessfully to bring Simko, Sayyid Taha, and Shaykh Mahmud together with the object of forming an alliance to frustrate Turkish designs.[55] On January 8, 1923, Simko paid a visit to Shaykh Mahmud in Sulaymaniya, where he was received with a parade of troops and a salute of seven guns, and the day of his arrival was proclaimed a public holiday. The local newspaper, *Rozh-i-Kurdistan*, described him as "the doughty champion of Kurdistan, His Excellency Isma'il Agha Simko." However, no agreement was reached between the two leaders.[56]

The defeat and murder of Simko. In December 1923, upon tendering expressions of loyalty to the Persian government, Simko was granted unconditional pardon.[57] In 1926, he again rose in rebellion but was severely defeated near Dilman and fled with about one hundred followers to Iraq, where he sought asylum. The Iraqi government refused Persian demands for his extradition on the grounds that extradition of political offenders was not permitted under the Extradition Law of Iraq. However, Iraq agreed to the dispatch of a Persian official to conduct negotiations with Simko.[58] By the end of 1927, however, the Persian government had taken no such action, and Simko continued to reside in Rawanduz, where he was described as "a menace to good order on both sides of the frontier."[59]

In May 1928, Simko voluntarily left Iraq for Turkey.[60] A little more than a year later, in July 1929, he reappeared in Iraq, establishing himself at a point near the Perso-Turkish-Iraqi frontier with fifty followers. When informed that his continued residence in Iraq would be contingent upon his remaining in a place designated by the Iraqi government, he again withdrew to Turkey, where he remained for the rest of the year in the mountainous districts west of the Rubar-i-Haji Beg River.[61]

It appears that Simko's peregrinations came to an end when he received an official letter from Tabriz offering him full pardon and the governorship of Ushnu. Simko proceeded to Ushnu, where he was installed as governor and for three days received homage from the neighboring Kurdish tribes. Then he received a message that an important Persian official was coming to pay him a visit. Accompanied by a number of Kurdish chiefs and their followers, Simko set out to meet him. After waiting for a long time at the designated place, they were informed by a mounted messenger that the official would not be able to reach Ushnu that day because his car had broken down. Simko and his party returned to Ushnu, and as they approached his home, members of the Persian army, stationed on the neighboring roofs, opened fire on them from all sides. Simko and twelve other Kurdish chiefs, together with their followers, were killed. A British report mentioned that Simko had been warned of treachery by some of his men but had refused to heed their warnings.[62]

The Situation in Syria

The Position of the Kurds in Syria

The situation of the Kurds in Syria after World War I was greatly influenced by developments in Turkey. Nationalist activity among the urban Kurdish populations of Damascus, Aleppo, and other Syrian towns was an echo and an extension of Kurdish nationalist activity in Turkey.

This was also true of the Kurdish tribes in Syria. The newly drawn frontier line did not mean much at the time to the Kurdish tribesmen in the northern frontier regions of the country, for although the new frontier in many cases placed members of the same tribe under two different administrations, French and Turkish, it separated but did not actually sever the two segments.[63] The Syrian Kurds in these regions continued to be in touch with their kinsmen in Turkey (often members of the same clan) and were subject to the same influences.

Thus, the Kurdish tribes in northern Syria were as much influenced as were their kinsmen in Turkey by such centers of Kurdish activity as Urfa, Severek, Mardin, and Jazirat ibn 'Umar. Like the Kurds of Iraq and Persia, the Kurds of Syria felt the impact of Kurdish nationalist agitation emanating from Turkey and in fact contributed to it.

On March 19, 1919, Yusuf Haydar and Khayr al-Din al-Zerguli, the owners of the Damascus newspaper *al-Mufid*, printed a long article on Kurdish independence entitled "An Open Letter to the Kurds of North and South Kurdistan." The propagandistic nature of this article was evident from the fact that free copies of the newspaper were distributed in the streets of Aleppo. The article began by lamenting the Kurds' political indifference and reminded readers of President Wilson's words about "the removal of the yoke of bygone days from the necks of nations, the yoke which stifles progress." After referring to the Arab revolt and the Arabs' bid for independence, it called on the Kurds to bestir themselves and claim their patrimony, a free Kurdistan, which should include Erzerum, Van, Bidlis, Kharput, Diyarbakr, Mosul, and many other places where a total of 3.5 million Kurds lived. Unknown agitators distributed pamphlets containing this article in Aleppo, Midiat, Azekh, Goyan, the country north of Zakho, Nisibin, Jazirat ibn 'Umar, Shernakh, Mosul, the Zab country, and elsewhere.[64]

Notwithstanding the Syrian Kurds' participation in the Kurdish national movement, it should be pointed out that they differed in one important respect from the Kurds in Turkey, Iraq, and Persia. Syria had neither the numerous self-contained Kurdish communities of those countries nor any focal centers of Kurdish tribal life and tradition comparable to Bidlis, Diyarbakr, and Jazirat ibn 'Umar in Turkey; Sulaymaniya, Rawanduz, and 'Amadiya in Iraq; and Sinna, Sawj Bulaq, and Urmiya in Persia. It was perhaps for this reason that Syrian Kurdistan failed to produce any Kurdish national figure of the stature of Shaykh Mahmud in Iraq, Simko Agha in Persia, or Shaykh Sa'id in Turkey. The most prominent leaders of the Syrian Kurds were the Bedir Khan brothers, originally Kurds from Jazirat ibn 'Umar in Turkey, who, although of princely descent, were intellectuals rather than the traditional type of Kurdish leader with mass tribal support.

The situation in Syrian Kurdistan was not as explosive as it was in Iraqi Kurdistan and Persian Kurdistan, nor did it lead to the series of disturbances that took place in those two regions. Even in later years, Syrian Kurds, as we shall see, were to remain more quiet than their kinsmen in Turkey, Iraq, and Persia. However, the area has not been without its small share of trouble.

The Kurds and the French Occupation of Syria

The French appear to have won the Kurds' confidence soon after their occupation of Syria. In February 1921, when friction between France and the Kemalists culminated in armed clashes, Milli Kurds cooperated with the former in repulsing a force of Turkish irregulars that tried to wrest Dair al-Zor, on the upper reaches of the middle Euphrates River, from the French.[65]

At this time, the French seem to have toyed with the idea of setting up a Kurdish principality comprising Urfa, Ras al-'Ain, Mardin, Nasibin, and Jazirat ibn 'Umar, under a son of Ibrahim Pasha Milli.[66] They abandoned the idea, however, and before the year was out, they had reached a comprehensive understanding on many unresolved issues with the Turks. This understanding was embodied in the Franklin-Bouillon agreement of October 20, 1921. In accordance with this agreement, the French consented to withdraw from Cilicia and other territories claimed by Turkey, besides undertaking to give the *sanjaq* of Alexandretta a special administrative regime. However, this settlement did not affect the stabilization of the situation along the Turco-Syrian frontier, particularly in the Jazira province, the region of greatest Kurdish concentration in Syria. The Mixed Commission in 1925 and a Franco-Turkish agreement in February 1926 failed to settle all the points at issue between France and Turkey. Not until 1930 was the eastern portion of the Syrian frontier delimited in a final manner.[67] The latter settlement formally gave to Syria the Jazira province, which the French had held and administered ever since their occupation of the country.

Soon after the French had supplanted Faysal's Arab regime in Syria, they had taken steps to settle and develop this rich province.[68] By various means, they encouraged Arab, Kurdish, Circassian, Armenian, Jacobite, Syrian Catholic, and later Assyrian settlers to settle and cultivate the province. Such towns as Hassetche (Hassaka), Qamishli, and Amuda were populated and became flourishing centers. The French, from the very beginning, appear to have tried to cultivate and retain the goodwill and friendship of the Jazira Kurds, no doubt as a counterweight to the Arabs in the area. The Kurdish and Arab tribes, for many hundreds of years, had contended for possession of this region, and around the turn of the century this struggle had culminated in a bitter conflict between the Kurdish Milli confederation of Ibrahim Pasha and the great Arab Shammar tribe.

The Khoybun and Other Activities of Kurdish Émigrés in Syria

Kurdish émigrés in Syria, under French patronage, were allowed to engage in extensive nationalist activity and to establish in Damascus and Beirut some of the leading Kurdish political and cultural centers.[69] These émigrés, for the most part Kurds from Turkey who had taken refuge in Syria and were bent on continuing their struggle against the Turks, undertook the organization and leadership of the Syrian Kurds. Developments in Turkey after World War I greatly helped these émigré leaders in the accomplishment of their objectives. What residual pro-Turkish feeling had remained in the Jazira after the French occupation had disappeared after the Kurdish revolt of 1925 and subsequent revolts in Turkey.

The most important activity of the Kurdish émigrés in Syria was the formation in 1927 of the Khoybun (Independence), an organization whose primary aim was to promote the Kurdish national cause and to direct Kurdish activities against the Turks. It actively participated in organizing the Agri Dagh rebellion in Turkey in 1930. The Khoybun established centers of Kurdish nationalist activity in a number of cities outside of Syria, including Cairo, Paris, Detroit, and Philadelphia.[70] It was particularly active in Paris.

The establishment of the Khoybun laid the foundation for close cooperation between the Kurds and the French in Syria. The fact that the French allowed the Khoy-bun—for many years the most articulate Kurdish nationalist organization—to use Syria as a base for its operations induced the Kurdish nationalist leaders to do their best to create a strong pro-French attitude among the Kurds of Syria. This relationship was to prove profitable to both the Kurds and the French and was not marred by any serious differences. At the time of the Agri Dagh revolt of 1930, probably in response to Turkish representations, the French requested Emir Sureya Bedir Khan to leave Syria for France, where he continued to reside and to engage in nationalist activity until his death in 1938.[71] During World War II, as we shall see, the French authorities asked the Khoybun to refrain from engaging in anti-Turkish activities, and the latter consented to do so.

Kurdish Disturbances in the Jazira in 1937

Soon after the conclusion of the Franco-Syrian Treaty of 1936, tension mounted in the Jazira province when, in accordance with the provisions of that treaty, French officials in Jazira were replaced by Syrians. Important segments of the population, encouraged by local French officials, resented this step and demanded as a minimum that local officials be appointed from among the local population. The Kurds of Hassetche resorted to open violence in the Jazira in June 1937 as a result of the appointment of Syrian officials from outside the province. These disruptions were put down with the help of French military forces. Shortly thereafter, the Christians of Qamishli and other centers in the Jazira renewed the disturbances, combining violence with demands for a special administrative regime that would guarantee equal rights irrespective of race or religion.[72]

These outbreaks, which reached a peak in August 1937, deteriorated into communal clashes. A number of Christians from Amuda were killed by the followers of a pro-government Kurdish chieftain. French troops were called out to quell the disturbances, and order was restored. Agitation for a separate regime in Jazira continued, however, and a number of incidents occurred, culminating in December 1937 in the kidnapping of the Jazira governor by a separatist group from Hassakz. In the meantime, Cardinal Tapouni, the head of the Syrian Catholic Church, was actively engaged in promoting the cause of the separatists in Paris and Rome.[73] This, however, was a passing phase, and before long things returned to normal.

9 Disturbances in the Mosul and Arbil Divisions of Iraqi Kurdistan after World War I

By the spring of 1919, the violently anti-British and anti-Christian Turkish propaganda began to bear fruit in Iraqi Kurdistan, particularly in those parts of the Mosul *wilayat* nearest the agitation centers of Shernakh and Jazirat ibn 'Umar. The British were represented as infidels who were determined to fasten an unjust and alien tyranny over the Kurds with the object of enslaving them in their own selfish interests as well as in the interests of the native Christians, their coreligionists. Religion, patriotism, and native customs were invoked against the conquerors.

Tension in the border regions appears to have reached such intensity that all the Christian communities between Jazirat ibn 'Umar and Zakho were reported to have been placed in a position of great danger. In fact, anti-Christian disturbances are said to have broken out in several localities.[1] It is quite plain that British administration in the wild northern borderlands of the Mosul *wilayat* did not start under the most favorable conditions. Even if circumstances had been better, it is doubtful that the Kurds, inured for centuries to Ottoman ways, would have taken with alacrity to the unfamiliar ways of the newcomers.

The Outbreak in the Zakho Area

The British appear to have had ample proof of subversive Turkish activities, but they were either unwilling or unable to put a stop to them. On March 19, 1919, letters sent by 'Abd al-Rahman Agha of Shernakh, an influential chieftain who claimed authority over a large tribal confederation, were intercepted by the British. In these letters, 'Abd al-Rahman Agha urged Kurdish chieftains located within the British zone to expel the foreigners. He asserted that the movement he was advocating was officially recognized and supported by the Turkish government, which in turn enjoyed the approval and support of various individuals and committees in Constantinople, Cairo, and Paris that were working for the establishment of a Kurdish state.[2] At about the same time, Turkish officers reportedly visited Shamdinan with the object of inducing the local leaders to join the movement, but were coldly received. One Turkish officer is even believed to have penetrated into the Mosul *wilayat* with a similar mission.[3]

The Goyan, a turbulent tribe living in an inaccessible mountain region north of

Zakho, were the first to act. They had already been guilty of a series of lawless acts per-petrated against the Christians of the neighboring villages and were finally induced to take the audacious step of challenging the occupying power itself.

Captain A. C. Pearson, the assistant political officer at Zakho, who is said to have been making earnest efforts to put an end to Goyan depredations, finally received word from their chieftains that they were willing to come to terms with the British. With this end in mind, he set out to meet the Goyan chieftains, accompanied by a Goyan escort. He was ambushed and murdered on April 4, 1919, while on his way to the meeting place. Ac-cording to British official sources, the circumstances of Pearson's death leave no doubt as to the premeditated nature of his murder and the complicity of his Goyan escort.[4]

The British were aware of the grave implications of this development. They no doubt feared that this incident might inaugurate a wave of violence against British offi-cers throughout the area—a fear that soon proved to be only too well founded. An offi-cial report reflected their dilemma and anxiety as they sought to find some effective means of coping with the situation. They inevitably thought of their Turkish predeces-sors and the measures they were likely to have taken in a similar situation. According to the report,

> During the latter part of the Turkish regime, the Turks had not failed, if their officials were assaulted, to take the most drastic measures. Under our rule this was the first case which had occurred, and the tribes naturally look upon it as a test of the vigour and strength of our Government and as a measure of the extent to which we could be defied with impunity.[5]

The report went on to speak of the various alternatives that the British considered in dealing with the matter. The dispatch of a punitive expedition against the Goyan, to-gether with the occupation of Jazirat ibn 'Umar, was considered and dismissed. This plan had obvious advantages, but it had its disadvantages, too. It is true that the Goyan would be punished and that the military occupation of Jazirat ibn 'Umar would extir-pate intrigue in one of its most active centers, completely turning the position of the turbulent tribe and isolating it. But the Goyan lived for the most part outside the limits of the British zone, and such an expedition would constitute an invasion of Turkish ter-ritory. This fact, coupled with the difficulty of the terrain and the lack of adequate forces and supplies, seemed to outweigh any advantages the plan may have had.[6]

The possibility that the Turks might be called upon to punish the offenders was considered, but was rejected as unfeasible. It was known that the disturbances were largely a result of Turkish intrigue and that as a consequence the Turks could not be ex-pected to cooperate wholeheartedly or effectively. Moreover, it was felt that to invoke Turkish help in suppressing the Goyan might be regarded as a sign of British weakness in the region—an impression they wanted to avoid at all costs.[7]

Having considered and rejected the foregoing alternatives, the British authorities eventually decided on bombing as the most practicable means of dealing with the

Goyan. Although the first attempts did not produce the desired results, subsequent bombings appear to have succeeded in subduing the unruly tribesmen.[8]

The Outbreak at 'Amadiya

The next outbreak against the British occurred at 'Amadiya. Here, as at Zakho and indeed throughout the British-occupied zone, Turkish propaganda used the same arguments to promote sedition and unrest. According to Bell, the British extended their administration to the 'Amadiya region in January 1919, when they moved a detachment of troops to within four miles of the town of that name.[9] In March, an assistant political officer was appointed to administer the region from the town of 'Amadiya. In June 1919, the British decided to withdraw their troops to the Suwara Tuka Pass some eighteen miles west of the town. This left the assistant political officer, Captain D. Willey, together with Lieutenant H. Macdonald and Sergeant S. R. Troup, who were in charge of the local levies, and two Indian telegraph clerks, completely isolated in the town.[10]

The British withdrawal, as we shall see, was to end in tragedy for the British officials at 'Amadiya and to endanger the British position in the northern part of the Mosul *wilayat.* However, it would be a mistake to exaggerate the importance of this event. Although it encouraged and may have even hastened the disturbances that broke out soon after at 'Amadiya and in the surrounding countryside, it certainly was not responsible for the people's insurrectionary mood. A delicate situation had existed for quite some time, and the explosive elements of which it was compounded had been in the making ever since the arrival of the British. Various factors had brought about this situation.

The Attitude of the 'Amadiya Kurds toward the British

The Kurds, who had for several centuries identified themselves with the Ottoman state and tradition, undoubtedly resented the coming of the British to their country as conquerors representing an alien religion and culture. The average Kurdish chieftain, inured to Turkish ways, must have found British administrative policy and practice uncongenial, annoying, and often unpalatable. Although the British administrators seemed patient, understanding, and anxious to win the people over, they insisted on collecting taxes and were determined to assert their authority. Their officials were efficient, dedicated, and apparently incorruptible, but meddlesome.

Whatever merits the new order possessed, and whatever benefits it promised to confer, there were many whose interests had been better served under the old scheme of things—in particular the powerful chieftains who previously had enjoyed a semi-independent status. In Ottoman times, the Kurds of these regions had been left to their own devices, except on those occasions when an ambitious sultan or overzealous official felt inclined to assert the state's power. But these bursts of Ottoman energy, besides being rare occurrences, were usually ill-conceived and badly executed, achieving little besides large-scale devastation. More often than not, they degenerated into ineffectual half-measures, with the situation invariably reverting to what it had been before the initiation of military operations. (The only exception was the series of campaigns undertaken to overthrow the Kurdish principalities during the first part of the nineteenth century.) Such government authority as normally penetrated into the remote Kurdish valleys was so emasculated that the chieftains had no difficulty in turning it to their own advantage.

The Effects of British Administrative Measures

Probably the major source of disaffection among the 'Amadiya Kurds was the series of unpopular administrative measures introduced by the new occupying force. These measures included the raising of local gendarmes, the collection of taxes, the advance of cash and seed grain directly to needy cultivators instead of through the tribal chieftains, and the repatriation of the Assyrian refugees.[11] These measures appear to have roused the suspicion and hostility of the powerful town notables and the neighboring tribal chieftains. Not only were they regarded as unwarranted interference in local affairs, but they seemed to threaten the very basis on which rested the powers and the privileges of these men.

There is no doubt that these measures contributed greatly to the mounting resentment against the British, and they may, in fact, have been directly responsible for the outbreak at 'Amadiya. Understanding the effects of these measures on the Kurds clarifies the nature of Kurdish grievances against the British.

The gendarmes. The Kurdish chieftains appear to have resented the raising and stationing of local gendarmes within their region. They must have sensed that the creation of such a force would make deep inroads on tribal loyalties. By joining this government-controlled force, the tribal recruit automatically transferred his allegiance from his tribe to the government. The tribe not only lost valuable manpower, but lost it to a potential enemy—the government—whose interests did not always coincide with those of the tribe or its chieftain. Moreover, the chieftains must have known that the levies were being formed for the purpose of asserting and maintaining the new administration's authority. These powerful robber barons felt that the presence of this force in their midst imposed severe restraints on their freedom of action. They realized that as long as this force remained within striking distance, they were no longer free to engage in violence or to profit by it. Raiding, feuding, and blackmailing were fast becoming hazardous undertakings.

Taxes. The Kurds, like most of the people of the Middle East, have traditionally resented the payment of taxes.[12] The persistence of this attitude has resulted in large measure from the fact that taxes have frequently been imposed without regard to the taxpayers' financial capacity and, more often than not, collected by harsh and unscrupulous methods.[13] Tribal communities throughout the region, probably because of their ability to resist the government, have been notorious for their reluctance to pay taxes. The British authorities' insistence on levying and collecting taxes accounts for some of the resentment felt against the new scheme of things in the 'Amadiya region.

Advances of cash and seed. Advances of cash and seed grain to the tribesmen constituted another source of dissatisfaction with the British. By making such advances directly to needy cultivators and not through the chieftains, the British incurred the latter's resentment. To the tribal leaders, this new and dangerous arrangement threatened to undermine their authority and to eliminate them as a dominant class in the affairs of their region.

Whereas in Ottoman times the common tribesman had been accustomed to turn to his chieftain for favors and assistance, he was now being encouraged to turn directly to the government. This British policy tended to deprive their leaders of their traditional role as intermediaries between the government and the people, upon which their influence and power had largely rested.

The repatriation of the Assyrian refugees. The repatriation of the Assyrian refugees roused the fears and suspicions of the ʿAmadiya Kurds. The Kurds of this region had waged long-standing feuds with the Assyrians.[14] They were now apprehensive that the British, who were helping the refugees to return to their homes, would eventually enable the Assyrians to gain the upper hand and to avenge themselves upon the Kurds. Turkish propaganda, coupled with the boastfulness and wishful thinking of both the Armenians and the Assyrians, was largely responsible for the widespread belief that Christian domination of the Kurds was imminent.

The ʿAmadiya Uprising and British Punitive Action

The fears and suspicions created by these issues ripened into deeply felt grievances under the influence of Turkish agitation and intrigue. The difficulties besetting the British in this turbulent region are shown by an incident that occurred at the beginning of the new administration. Soon after the British occupation of ʿAmadiya, the assistant political officer, Captain Willey, came into conflict with some of the leading citizens of the town. A standing feud between two leading notables, which had split the town into two warring factions, seems to have so gravely threatened the maintenance of law and order that Captain Willey felt compelled to interfere. He is said to have disarmed the two factions and to have taken cash security from both, with a view to ensuring their good behavior in the future. The impartial severity of his actions so incensed both factions, however, that they joined forces against the British.[15] After months of Turkish threats, incitement, and cajolery, the Kurds of ʿAmadiya resolved to raise the standard of revolt and to eject the British by force of arms. "The *Aghas*," according to civil commissioner Sir Arnold Wilson, "took secret counsel, and in their blindness saw no better course open to them than violence."[16] The conspirators included the chief men of ʿAmadiya and the surrounding districts, spearheaded by the leaders of the two feuding factions in that town. On the night of July 14, 1919, a number of men scaled the walls of the house in which the assistant political officer and his companions were sleeping and killed Willey, Macdonald, and Troup. The levy guards who tried to stop the attack were also killed.[17]

The British acted quickly and vigorously. The Eighteenth Division stationed at Mosul was immediately ordered into action and punitive measures were set in motion. One brigade from the Eighteenth Division under General Nightingale was assembled at Suwara Tuka, the outpost to which British troops had been withdrawn three months earlier, and a second brigade under General Woolridge was dispatched to Zakho. General Cassels, an officer who had distinguished himself during the later stages of the Mesopotamian campaign, was entrusted with the conduct of military operations. The

13. A typical Kurd, Iraq. Postcard, Iraq, circa 1960. Photographer unknown/Courtesy of Joyce Blau, Kurdish Institute of Paris. *Kurdistan: In the Shadow of History.*

British commander in chief instructed him to comb the entire countryside with the object of punishing the rebels and asserting the now badly shaken British authority.[18]

An early attempt by the British to reach 'Amadiya met strong Kurdish resistance, indicating that several tribes were involved. Consequently, no important move was made until the punitive force was ready for action and the necessary troop dispositions had been made, which took about a fortnight to complete. By the end of July 1919, the force was ready to embark upon its task. On August 1, 1919, a large village in the 'Amadiya region was captured, and some of the leading rebel chieftains and a substantial number of rifles of Turkish origin fell into British hands. Punitive operations were continued into the neighboring valleys, and the Kurds are reported to have sustained considerable casualties. Several chieftains known to have been directly responsible for the murder of the British officers were tried and executed. The Ser ʿAmadiya plateau and the villages and districts beyond were overrun, and punishment was inflicted on the Barwari tribes who had been involved in the outbreak at ʿAmadiya.[19] The town of ʿAmadiya was captured on August 8, and a number of notables described as "minor offenders" were arrested.[20]

It must not be supposed that these successes were obtained easily or without reverses. The Kurds fought bravely and tenaciously, and on a number of occasions displayed the daring and pugnacity for which they are noted. For example, while the British were busy pacifying the ʿAmadiya region, a tribal force composed of Guli tribesmen and other elements from the region west of the Khabur made a surprise attack on the British position at Suwara Tuka. Although they were eventually driven off, they gave the defenders some anxious moments and succeeded in inflicting considerable casualties.[21]

Toward the end of August, as military operations were being brought to a successful conclusion in the ʿAmadiya region, the British decided to turn their attention to the offending tribes west of the Khabur. Consequently, General Woolridge was sent against the Guli, who had led the attack on Suwara Tuka. By the middle of September 1919, while operations in this sector were still in progress, most of the important hostile elements in the ʿAmadiya region had made their submission.

It was at this time that the Goyan, who had been guilty of murdering Captain Pearson in April, made a series of bold attacks in the neighborhood of the Guli country, where General Woolridge was still engaged in pacifying the tribe. In the face of this new provocation, the British decided to carry the punitive operations into the Goyan country. General Nightingale's brigade was ordered to this sector and entrusted with the task of chastising the turbulent tribe. The column penetrated into the heart of the Goyan country, where Karoar, the principal village, was captured and partly burned in retaliation for Pearson's murder. This final punitive measure brought the three-month campaign to a conclusion.[22]

The Outbreak in the Zibar-Barzan Region

The third outbreak against the British occurred in the Zibar-Barzan region and was to engulf ʿAqra, the largest town in the area. This region, it will be recalled, had been the scene of much strife and bloodshed in Ottoman times. The periodic wars between the Barzani shaykhs and the Zibar *agha*s and the involvement of the Ottoman government in these wars, usually on the side of the Zibar *agha*s, had turned this region into one of the most turbulent areas under Turkish rule. Only five years earlier the Ottoman *wali*, Sulayman Nadif, brought one phase of the long, drawn-out contest with the Barzan shaykhs to an end by hanging Shaykh ʿAbd al-Salam, the head of the Barzani family.

When the British moved into the area, they found themselves facing the same problems that had plagued their Turkish predecessors. Wishing to preserve, at any cost, the precarious peace in the turbulent frontier regions and mindful of the unpleasant consequences of favoring one party over another, the British seemed resolved to adopt an attitude of complete impartiality toward the two antagonists. Events, however, soon proved the futility of their hopes.

When the British took over the Mosul *wilayat* and proceeded to extend their administration to the various districts and subdistricts, they attached the Barzan country to 'Aqra. This action appears to have been greatly resented by Shaykh Ahmad of Barzan, the brother and successor of Shaykh 'Abd al-Salam, who regarded 'Aqra as a stronghold of Zibari influence. At one time, Shaykh Ahmad even indicated a strong desire to move into the Rawanduz region—a move discouraged by the British. In order to obviate the occurrence of untoward incidents between the Barzanis and the Zibaris, the British forbade Faris Agha of Zibar from crossing the Zab into Barzani territory.

These efforts to hold the balance between the two antagonists incurred the resentment and the hostility of both parties. The Turks were not slow to profit by this development. They used their good offices to compose the differences between Faris Agha and Shaykh Ahmad, and the two men were temporarily reconciled. Thus, at a single stroke, the Turks succeeded in gaining both sides to their cause.[23]

In the meantime, the Turks continued their efforts to oust the British from the Mosul *wilayat* by every possible means. In the winter of 1918–19, reports of an imminent Turkish invasion of the region were rife. Enver Pasha was reported to have arrived at Van at the head of large reinforcements consisting of Turkish troops and Russian deserters. He was represented as having been in touch with Suto[24] Agha of Oramar, the Barwari chieftains, and other elements hostile to the British.[25]

At this time, too, Sharifian agents from Syria are reported to have been active among the Kurdish tribes of this region. Although they apparently gained nothing of consequence for their master's cause, there can be no doubt of the tension and unrest created by their appearance. What they offered was both tempting and intriguing. The possibility of becoming once more part of an Islamic state appealed to the Kurds' religious sentiment, and the prospect of a loose and ineffectual control from so distant a capital as Damascus promised to leave them undisturbed in the enjoyment of their traditional privileges.[26] The shape of things to come in the Sharifian state, as represented by the Sharif's emissaries, was a poignant reminder of the severed Ottoman connection and served only to make the Kurds more keenly aware of their loss.

It was against this background that Mr. J. H. H. Bill succeeded Colonel G. E. Leachman as political officer of the Mosul division in October 1919. Soon after assuming his new duties, Bill proceeded on a tour of inspection to the Zibar district with the object of acquainting himself with the region's various problems. In the course of his tour, he imposed fines on Faris Agha and Babakir Agha, two leading Zibari chieftains, whose followers had been guilty of shooting at members of the gendarmerie. The two chieftains appear to have been greatly offended by this punishment and appealed to Shaykh Ahmad of Barzan for help. In response to their appeal, Shaykh Ahmad sent his brother, Mulla Mustafa, with some twenty men. The Barzani contingent, together with Faris Agha, Babakir Agha, and their followers, amounting in all to about one hundred men, ambushed Mr. Bill's party near Bira Kapra, Babakir Agha's village. Mr. Bill, Captain K. R. Scott, and two of the four gendarmes who accompanied them were killed. The other two gendarmes, who were Zibari tribesmen, went over to the attackers and were spared.[27]

The Zibari and Barzani tribesmen, now in an exultant mood, attacked and looted

'Aqra. During the next two days, the tribesmen quarreled over the loot, and the Barzanis returned home. According to British sources, several local chiefs expressed their loyalty to the government and offered to send help. The townspeople were greatly relieved when a force of Kurdish levies commanded by Captain F. C. Kirk, assistant political officer at Batas in the Rawanduz region, arrived at 'Aqra on November 9, 1919. We are also informed that there were no signs of hostility toward the punitive column that made its appearance shortly thereafter in the Zab River valley. The villages through which the column passed are reported to have displayed white flags in token of their peaceful intentions and to have been fearful of their *agha*s and happy at the sight of the government forces.[28]

The punitive column burned the houses of the Zibar chiefs in reprisal for the murder of the British officers and their escort and, crossing the Zab, inflicted the same punishment on the Barzanis. The villagers in this region, as in the 'Amadiya region, are said to have been unmolested. The rebel chieftains apparently failed to rouse the neighboring tribes, owing mainly to the loyalty of the leading man in the 'Aqra region, 'Abd al-Qadir Agha of Shush.[29]

The four rebels—Faris Agha and Babakir Agha of Zibar, along with Shaykh Ahmad of Barzan and his brother Mulla Mustafa—fled into the mountains and were outlawed. It is interesting to note that this outbreak failed to create any immediate repercussions in the neighboring regions. According to both Gertrude Bell and Arnold Wilson of the British civil administration, "No sympathetic disturbance took place in Amadiyah, and Sayyid Taha of Shamdinan refused to listen to the suggestion of the *qaimmaqam* of Nehri, where the Turks kept a small garrison, that he and Situ of Oramar should cooperate on behalf of the Zibaris. His attitude caused the *qaimmaqam* uneasiness as to his own safety, and he left Nehri for Bashqala."[30]

Whether or not the Turks were directly responsible for this outbreak, once more a general uprising failed to materialize in the Mosul *wilayat*. In commenting on the outbreak, Wilson stated: "All evidence goes to show that the murder of the two British officers was not planned beforehand, but followed upon one of the sudden fits of anger which are typical of Kurdish temperament. But, once accomplished, it gave the signal for rebellion."[31]

Suto Agha, a treacherous and cruel chieftain from the wilds of the Harki-Oramar region, provided a grim postscript to these events. The wily chieftain, who appears to have convinced the *qaimmaqam* of Nehri of his devotion to the Turkish cause,[32] availed himself of the disturbances in the Zibar-Barzan region to settle some old scores. In the words of an official British report, "Situ of Oramar, who had a long standing feud with Abdul Wahab of Raikan, took advantage of the Aqrah disturbances to capture him, under the guise of friendship, and cut his throat."[33]

The Outbreaks in the Arbil Division and in the 'Aqra District of the Mosul Division

The State of Affairs in the Arbil Division

The Arbil division was the last Kurdish region to succumb to the wave of disturbances that broke out among the Kurds of the Mosul *wilayat* shortly after the signing of the armistice with Turkey. Whereas the Kurds rose in rapid succession to challenge the authority of the new government in the Zakho region (April 1919), the Sulaymaniya region (May 1919),[34] the 'Amadiya region (July 1919), and the Zibar-Barzan region (November 1919), it was not until August 1920 that the Kurds of Arbil followed suit.

There were political, geographic, and economic reasons for this lag. Owing to the comparative remoteness and inaccessibility of the Arbil division, it was only natural that the Turks should concentrate most of their disruptive efforts on the nearer and more important Mosul division. The Zakho, 'Amadiya, and Zibar-Barzan regions, because of their close proximity to the Turkish agitation centers at Jazirat ibn 'Umar, Shernakh, and Nehri, were easy to reach and rouse. As regards the uprising in the Sulaymaniya division, there is no doubt that it was attributable to a Kurdish nationalist sentiment, however vague or undeveloped, as well as to Shaykh Mahmud's ambitions and strong leadership. The Arbil division was sadly lacking in both respects. Also, the Kurds of the Arbil division had suffered the ravages of war to a greater extent than their brethren to the north and south and needed more time to recover.

Although the Kurds of Arbil remained quiet, they were not indifferent to the momentous events taking place around them. Captain W. R. Hay, the British political officer who was in charge of the Arbil division and whose courage and tenacity enabled him to withstand and eventually to stem the tide of rebellion in his division, commented on the effects of the various outbreaks on the Kurds of Arbil. According to him, "The revolt of Shaykh Mahmud, in May 1919, was the beginning of the reaction in northern Mesopotamia, and though it ended in failure it showed that it was possible to defy the new Government, and sent out waves of unrest over the country."[35]

The impact of Shaykh Mahmud's rebellion appears to have been particularly strong in the Koi Sanjaq district and among the Khoshnaw tribes.[36] In his 1921 account of these events, Hay also emphasized the unsettling effects on the Arbil division of the murder of the British officers at Bira Kapra. According to him, highway robbery and lawlessness in general increased greatly after that event.[37] Similarly, the outbreak at Tal A'far created much excitement in the town of Arbil, and malcontents were emboldened to preach rebellion openly.[38]

The Threatened Attack on Arbil

By the early summer of 1920, the state of political ferment throughout British-occupied Mesopotamia was beginning to assume an alarming aspect. By the middle of August, the disturbances, which began in the south at the end of June, had spread to Diyala, Kirkuk, and Arbil. On August 12, 1920, Captain Hay was attacked in the Rawanduz gorge and narrowly escaped with his life.[39] On September 3, 1920, Captain F. C. Kirk was forced to leave Koi Sanjaq. The levies under Captain Littledale withdrew from Rawanduz and Batas to Arbil. On September 8, Sir Arnold Wilson, the acting civil high commissioner, arrived by plane in Arbil. His visit was calculated to boost the morale of the town's local officials and leading citizens and to discourage the tribal forces that had been threatening to attack.

Wilson's visit produced the desired result and enabled the town to hold out until the arrival of the British military forces several days later. However, Arbil owed its delivery primarily to three men: Khurshid Agha, paramount chieftain of the Diza'i tribe, who had promised to defend the town and had called out his tribesmen and threatened to fight the would-be attackers; Ahmad Effendi, the mayor of Arbil, whose ceaseless exertions to maintain law and order in the town contributed to the stabilization of the situation; and finally, Captain Hay, the political officer whose courage and good sense inspired confidence and enabled those elements loyal to the administration to continue united in their resolve to weather the storm.[40]

In the preceding sections, I have discussed the various causes of the emergency growth and rapid spread of the insurrectionary spirit among the Kurds. It is of interest at this point to mention an observation made by Wilson, who attributed some of these troubles and disturbances to what he described as "itinerant mischief-makers." According to him, "There were many such on the move at this period. Some were Bolshevik emissaries who combined the fiercest zenophobia with a passion for the rights of man in general and for the support of lawbreakers in particular. Others were adherents of Shaykh Mahmoud, and cherished hopes that he would be returned to power."[41]

The Outbreak of the Surchis in the Mosul and Arbil Divisions

The Surchis of the Mosul Division

The Surchis of the Mosul division had been guilty of participation in looting the town of 'Aqra at the time of its capture by the Zibari-Barzani forces at the end of 1919. Punitive measures had been contemplated against them at the time, but the column sent to punish the Zibaris was ordered to leave the Surchis alone so long as they remained quiet. However, their peaceful conduct was deceptive, for in April 1920 they took up arms at the instigation of the Zibaris. The outbreak, though sudden, was not unexpected. It was known as early as January that trouble was brewing, when Faris Agha of Zibar, accompanied by an armed following, came to Bajil with the object of inducing the Naqshbandi Shaykh 'Ubayd Allah to participate in an attack on 'Aqra. At the time, trouble was averted by an air attack on Bajil, which compelled the Zibaris to flee before they had a chance to carry out their designs.[42]

The Surchis are said to have been willing to submit to the government, but Zibari intrigue and the Surchis' own distrust of the government apparently held them back. Though they remained quiescent during February and March, their smoldering hostility, fanned by Turkish propaganda, could not be kept under control for long. In April 1920, they ambushed and destroyed a military convoy bound for 'Aqra. This act of open defiance was followed a few days later by an attack on 'Aqra itself. The local gendarmes commanded by a British sergeant succeeded in holding off the attackers until the arrival of reinforcements twenty-four hours later.[43]

After these events, there could be no doubt about the Surchis' attitude and intentions. A punitive column sent against them met with no resistance. Bajil, Kelati, and Susnawa, the three main Surchi centers in the Mosul division, were destroyed, but no leaders were encountered or captured. The latter appeared to have fled to inaccessible mountain regions upon the approach of the punitive column. During the next few months, things quieted down, except for a few skirmishes fought against Zibari and Surchi raiding parties in the vicinity of 'Aqra. The introduction of a system of military patrols in the area succeeded in putting an end to hostile activities by the Surchis. They gave no further trouble until the eruption of their kinsmen, the Surchis of the Arbil division, in August 1920.[44]

The Surchis of the Arbil Division

The situation in Arbil was greatly aggravated at this time when a strange set of circumstances brought together tribal malcontents, a number of desperate men involved in blood feuds against the government representative at Rawanduz, and a band of outlaws into a formidable and dangerous combination against the government. The tribal malcontents for the most part consisted of the Surchis of the Arbil division located at the Harir plain. Those involved in the blood feuds were the brothers of Yusuf Beg, who had been strangled under mysterious circumstances,[45] and Nuri, the son of Bawil Agha, whose brothers had been shot, it was said, on orders by Isma'il Beg, the British-appointed governor of Rawanduz.[46] The outlaw band was a group of highwaymen headed by Hamada Chin in the neighborhood of the Spilik Pass.[47]

After his attack on Major Hay in August 1920 in the Rawanduz gorge, Nuri Bawil Agha had crossed the Zab and taken refuge with the Surchis of the Mosul division. From his refuge, he was able to bring about the uprising that culminated in the expulsion of the British from the Rawanduz and Batas districts of the Arbil division and came close to driving them out of the town of Arbil and the rest of the division. The majority of the shaykhs of the 'Aqra Surchis joined their kinsmen of the Harir plain in the uprising. The situation became extremely dangerous when the neighboring Khoshnaw, hitherto friendly to the British, were induced after some hesitation to throw in their lot with the rebels. As pointed out earlier, more dangerous developments were averted by the steadfastness of a handful of persons at Arbil who succeeded in holding the roused tribes in check until the arrival of relief forces from Mosul and Kirkuk.[48]

Having been foiled in their attempt to seize Arbil, the greater part of the Surchi forces crossed the Zab at Girdmamik into the 'Aqra region. Here they lost no time in attacking the Assyrian refugee camp at Jujar. This serious blunder was to cost them heavily in lives and prestige. The Surchis, joined by sections of the 'Asha'ir al-Saba' tribe, attacked the Assyrian camp in the evening. The attack was repulsed with heavy losses, and the Assyrians, pursing their attackers, drove them in the direction of the Zab, where many were killed or drowned.[49]

This event, besides dealing a severe blow to the Surchis' prestige, had a salutary effect on the neighboring tribes from the British point of view. In fact, Wilson stated that it may have been responsible for the peace that prevailed in the Mosul division at a time when British authority was being challenged over most of British-occupied Mesopotamia.[50]

In November 1920, the Assyrian repatriation movement was said to have broken the power of the tribes of the Zibar-Barzan region through whose territories it happened to pass.[51] By the end of 1920, the Surchi shaykhs—Qaiyun, Shikak, and Mazo—were reported to have accepted the terms offered them and to have made their submission to the authorities at Mosul. Shaykh 'Ubayd Allah of Bajil, who went to Mosul with the intention of making his peace with the government, reportedly rejected the terms offered him upon finding that instead of being appointed governor of his district, he was required to pay a fine. Shaykh Raqib of Sardaria, who was reported to be busy trying to establish himself as shaykh in the Harir plain, did not bother to make any overtures to the British.[52] In January 1921, Wajji, one of Shaykh 'Ubayd Allah's sons, made his submission, and his example was followed by his father in September of the same year.[53]

10 Shaykh Mahmud and the Rise and Fall of the South Kurdish Confederation in Iraqi Kurdistan after World War I

The British Advance into Southern Kurdistan

In March 1917, the British occupied Baghdad, an action that soon brought the British military forces in Mesopotamia into close proximity to the southernmost tribes of Kurdistan. Initially, however, political considerations had militated against the extension of British influence into this sector.[1] Thus, throughout the whole period of the Russian occupation of the Khanaqin region, which lasted from April to June 1917, the British maintained only the most tenuous contacts with certain Kurdish tribal elements, in particular Mustafa Pasha, paramount chieftain of the Bajalan tribe.[2] The Turks reoccupied Khanaqin after its evacuation by the Russians and remained there until the British occupied it in December 1917.[3] It was only after the British occupation of Khanaqin at that time that they actually came in direct contact with the Kurds.

British Contacts with the Kurdish Tribes

Having established themselves in Khanaqin, the British proceeded to consolidate their position. They lost no time in coming to an understanding with the Bajalan, with whom they had already been in touch, and they gradually began to extend their influence over the neighboring tribes. Toward the end of September 1917, the British got in touch with Shaykh Hamid Talibani and learned from him that his tribes and other neighboring tribes had successfully resisted Turkish demands for assistance and supplies. The Talibani chieftain, who had concentrated his forces in the Gil district northeast of Tauq, was joined by mounted forces from other tribes. Shaykh Hamid could count not only on his own tribesmen, but on his allies, the Daudis, as well.[4]

At first, the British appear to have aimed merely at maintaining friendly relations with these tribes and inducing them to deny the Turks grain and other badly needed provisions. They succeeded in doing this, but they refrained from encouraging these tribes to take offensive action against the Turks, presumably because they were not in a position to provide any help.

In the spring of 1918, the British drive gathered momentum, and Kifri, Tuz Khurmatu, and Kirkuk were occupied in rapid succession. These advances enabled the

British to establish closer contact with Shaykh Hamid Talibani.[5] Now Kurdish troops were employed for the first time against the Turks. A Kurdish contingent consisting of some two hundred Dilo, Bajalan, and Suramiri tribesmen went into action against the Turks along the upper Diyala (Sirwan) in April 1918.[6]

The British then turned their attention to the transfrontier region east of Khanaqin, which had for some time been a hotbed of anti-British intrigue. This strategically important region, which lay astride the important Baghdad-Kirmanshah road and commanded the lines of communication between Mesopotamia and Persia, was distracted by ceaseless strife and widespread lawlessness. German and Turkish agents, Persian Democrats, and local tribesmen were doing their best to make things as uncomfortable as possible for the British, who were in occupation of the region. Various forms of harassment, such as the destruction of British military installations, raids on isolated parties, and the disruption of lines of communication, were carried out with varying degrees of success. The British, aided by friendly local tribesmen, did their best to foil these attempts.

It was at this time that hostile sections of the Bajalan and the Guran were reported to have destroyed and removed much of the machinery of the Anglo-Persian Oil Company at Chia Surkh near Khanaqin, while a group of unfriendly Kalhuri tribesmen waylaid and attacked a British survey party. The Sinjabi chieftain, 'Ali Akbar Khan, at the head of Sinjabi and Gurani henchmen, was actively interfering with the passage of supplies to Khanaqin. In April 1918, Kalkhani and Kalhur tribesmen, supported by the British column, succeeded in defeating and dispersing the forces of 'Ali Akbar Khan, who had been cooperating with the Persian Democrat Sulayman Mirza and at the same time intriguing with German and Turkish agents.[7] After the capture of Sulayman Mirza by a British column and his dispatch to Baghdad, 'Ali Akbar Khan continued his close contacts with German and Turkish agents. He was last reported to be intriguing with the German agent Von Drueffel with the object of getting the Sinjabis and other kindred tribes armed with rifles for action against the British. He had fled after being wounded in the clash with the British and eventually appears to have lapsed into innocuous inactivity.[8]

Shaykh Mahmud's First Overtures to the British

Upon the successful completion of the British operation that led to the capture of Sulayman Mirza, Major Goldsmith, the political officer in charge of Khanaqin, proceeded on a tour of inspection of the surrounding countryside. It was at this time that Shaykh Mahmud, who was destined to play such an important part in the history of southern Kurdistan, was first heard from. According to an official British report, "It was on this tour that Shaikh Mahmud of Sulaimaniyah sent his representative to meet the political officer asking to be authorised to act as representative of the British Government at Sulaimaniyah, pending our arrival."[9]

The Kurds were obviously impressed by British successes and decided to join the winning side. The British received letters from the Hamawand, the most noted fighting tribe in southern Kurdistan, who declared their readiness to offer whatever assistance

was needed of them. At a meeting of Kurdish notables held at Sulaymaniya, it was decided to set up a provisional Kurdish government under Shaykh Mahmud and to adopt
a friendly attitude toward the British.[10] According to Sir Arnold Wilson, the acting civil
commissioner,

> Shaykh Mahmud himself wrote "on behalf of all the Kurdish people on either side of
> the frontier," offering to hand over the reins of Government to us or to officiate as our
> representative under the protection of the glorious British flag. The people of Kurdis-
> tan, he said, were delighted with our successes, and, freed by the valour of our troops
> from Turkish despotism, looked forward to prosper under our rule as Iraq had pros-
> pered. He concluded by asking for an assurance that in no circumstances would we per-
> mit the restoration of Turkish authorities in Kurdistan.[11]

The British Withdrawal from Kirkuk

According to Wilson, when the British decided to evacuate Kirkuk in May 1918, he
was obliged to inform the Kurds that the British were leaving the neighborhood of the
town because of the hot weather and that they hoped to be back soon. As he put it, "I accepted Shaikh Mahmud's proposal that he should act as our representative, if he could
do so, and actually drew up a public proclamation on the subject."[12] This proclamation
was never issued, for Kirkuk, evacuated by the British on May 24, was promptly reoccupied by the Turks.[13] At the same time, a Turkish force was dispatched to Sulaymaniya,
which was reoccupied and placed under martial law. Shaykh Mahmud was arrested and
sent to Kirkuk, where he was jailed. Notables belonging to the shaykh's party were imprisoned or fined, and all those associated with his movement suffered a great loss of
face and "were covered with ridicule."[14]

No doubt some individuals suffered the full force of Turkish retribution,[15] but in
general the Turks seemed to have displayed an unusual degree of leniency and moderation. They wisely refrained from harsh and vindictive measures. Not wishing to risk a
tribal upheaval whose consequences they were not in a position to cope with, they did
not harm Shaykh Mahmud. After a period of detention in Kirkuk, he was released and
allowed to return home.[16] There were no exactions and no forcible seizures of tribal
property. Provisions needed by the army were paid for in cash, and tribal levies were
duly given their salaries. The conciliatory attitude adopted by the Turkish authorities
did much to reconcile the tribes to them. Such was the effect of Turkish behavior on the
people that many joined the Turks voluntarily, although we are informed that some
were pressed into their service by force.[17]

The British withdrawal from Kirkuk appears to have been brought about by the deterioration of the military situation in Transcaucasia and the assumption of additional
heavy responsibilities in Persia by the British military command in Mesopotamia. These
developments had led to the diversion of all available means of transportation to the
Persian Road.[18]

The withdrawal from Kirkuk dealt a severe blow to British prestige in Kurdistan and
indeed throughout Mesopotamia, and the British continued to suffer from its effects

long after they had won World War I. The Kurds, who had declared themselves for the British in such an overt manner, were now assailed by doubts and suspicions. Their faith in British power and British promises was badly shaken. Wilson described the reaction of Kurdish leaders to the British retirement from Kirkuk and emphasized the unpleasant effect of the lavish promises of support that certain political officers had made to them:

> It seemed clear to them that the assurances of support, freely given by some irresponsible officers, and implicit in the more cautious advances made at Kirkuk by Bullard and at Kifri by Longrigg, were not to be relied on: we were, it seemed to them, playing the Russian game of using unsophisticated tribesmen as cats'-paws. Their leaders, some of whom, including the principal Hamawand chiefs, were on the way to Kirkuk when the withdrawal took place, returned to their homes in high dudgeon. They felt that they had been betrayed by us: we had induced them to show their hand to their enemies the Turks, and had left them in the lurch. The Hamawand leaders, in particular, never forgave us, and remained hostile to us for many years after.[19]

The Turks, as might be expected, exploited the British withdrawal from Kirkuk to the utmost. They attributed it to the Allies' critical position on the western front and described it as a prelude to the evacuation of Mesopotamia. According to Wilson, Turkish propoganda used with telling effect the theme of "perfidious Albion" exploitating other people to fight its battles. His book cites a Turkish propaganda leaflet that gave a long list of disasters suffered by those who allowed themselves to become the dupes of the British, threatened dire consequences for those who had abandoned the Turkish cause, and promised great rewards to those who had remained steadfast in their loyalty to Turkey.[20]

Wilson maintained that he had no inkling of the decision to abandon Kirkuk, stating emphatically that neither he nor the political officer on the spot, Major Reader W. Bullard (later Sir Reader Bullard), had been informed that the occupation was not to be permanent. He in fact flew out to Kirkuk a few days after the occupation of that town by the British to discuss a number of urgent problems and to enlist the sympathy and support of the tribes, with a view to protecting British lines of communication and ensuring the flow of supplies, in particular meat, to the troops.[21] The profound effects of this British debacle on the Kurds was immediately apparent, for whereas all British efforts to raise a force of Kurdish levies during the following summer failed, the Turks succeeded in recruiting a large Kurdish cavalry force that they employed against their adversaries in Persia.[22]

The Introduction of the Tribal System in Southern Kurdistan

In the autumn of 1918, the Ottoman *mutasarrif* (commissioner) and the garrison in Sulaymaniya surrendered to Shaykh Mahmud, thus officially terminating Ottoman administration in that region. The withdrawal of Turkish forces and officials left the Kurdish leader in sole control of Sulaymaniya and the surrounding countryside. Shortly thereafter, Shaykh Mahmud sent letters to the British authorities in Baghdad requesting that Kurdistan not be excluded from the list of liberated peoples.[23]

The fact that Shaykh Mahmud was politically the strongest personality in the region, coupled with his willingness to cooperate with the British occupation authorities, induced the latter to deal with him. Because the alternative to cooperating with him was to provide sufficient force to garrison Sulaymaniya and maintain order in the outlying mountainous districts, and the means to do this were then not available, the British accepted the shaykh's proposal with relief.

Major E. W. C. Noel, an officer who had much experience with the Bakhtiaris and other Persian tribes, was chosen for the task of inaugurating the new administration in southern Kurdistan.[24] The instructions issued to Noel on the eve of his departure to Sulaymaniya provide some indication of British intentions and expectations:

> You have been appointed Political Officer, Kirkuk Division, with effect from November 1st. The Kirkuk Division extends from the Lesser Zab to the Diyalah and north-east to the Turco-Persian frontier. It forms part of the Mosul Wilayat, the ultimate disposal of which is under the consideration of His Majesty's Government. For the present it must be considered as falling within the sphere of military occupation and administration of this force, and you should proceed on this assumption in your dealings with local chiefs, bearing in mind that it is improbable that the military authorities will see their way to detach troops permanently to Sulaimaniyah or to other places east of our present line. It should be your object to arrange with local chiefs for the restoration and maintenance of order in areas outside the limits of our military occupation, for the exclusion and surrender of enemy agents, and for the supply of commodities needed by our troops. You are authorized to incur such expenditure as may be necessary to the end, subject to previous authority, where practicable, in cases of large sums, and on the understanding, which should be made clear to the chiefs, that any arrangements you may make are of necessity provisional and subject to reconsideration at any time. You are authorized to appoint Shaikh Mahmud as our representative in Sulaimaniyah, should you consider this expedient, and to make other appointments of this nature at Chamchamal, Halabja, &c., at your discretion. It should be explained to the tribal chiefs with whom you enter into relations that there is no intention of imposing upon them an administration foreign to their habits and desires. Tribal leaders will be encouraged to form a confederation for the settlement of their public affairs under the guidance of British political officers. They will be called upon to continue to pay the taxes legally due from them under Turkish law, modified as may be found necessary, for purposes connected with the maintenance of order and the development of their country.[25]

Major Noel arrived in Sulaymaniya in the middle of November 1918 and was enthusiastically received. He immediately proceeded to put into effect a new system of administration, which it was hoped would prove acceptable to the people. Shaykh Mahmud was appointed *hukmdar* or governor of the district and head of the new South Kurdish Federation. Other Kurdish officials, working under the guidance of British political officers, were entrusted with the administration of the various minor subdivisions. Tribal chieftains were entrusted with the government of their own tribes and made responsible to the British authorities through Shaykh Mahmud. They were recognized and paid as government officials.[26]

There is little doubt that the newly established system of government in southern Kurdistan owed much to British colonial experience in India and elsewhere. The nature of the duties and obligations envisaged between the British government and the South Kurdish Confederation pointed to a relationship of dependence and paramountcy such as that which existed between the British Crown and the treaty states in India.[27] The new system of administration in southern Kurdistan was obviously based on the principle of indirect rule.[28] It was in many respects reminiscent of the Sandeman system and in particular the Bruce or the Maliki system, which grew out of it.

The Sandeman System

The Sandeman system, named after Sir Robert Sandeman,[29] was the form of administration that the British had applied in Baluchistan with the object of bringing this wild trans-Indus mountainous region within the system of the British Indian empire. This system, consisting of a subsidized tribal regime headed by a paramount native ruler, the khan of Kalat, was a triumph for the so-called forward policy.[30] The twin objects of this policy were held to be the protection of the inhabitants of the Sind borderland from the depredations of the turbulent hillmen, who enjoyed a privileged sanctuary in their rugged mountain country, and the strengthening of India's defenses against foreign invasion.

The Sandeman system has been criticized for being too dependent on the personal influence of one man—a criticism that appears justified. It has also been criticized on the ground that the granting of subsidies or allowances constituted a form of blackmail. However, the British historian C. Collin Davies has pointed out that these allowances cannot be described as blackmail because they were paid in return for onerous services rendered by the recipients, such as the guarding of trade routes and mountain passes and the implementation of *jirgah* (tribal council) decrees.[31]

The Bruce or Maliki System

The Bruce or Maliki system is the name given to the Sandeman system as applied among the Mahsuds of the northwest frontier region of India by the commissioner of the Derajat, R. I. Bruce.[32] This system proved to be a complete failure for several reasons. First, it failed to function among the more democratic Mahsuds because their *maliks* (chieftains) did not possess the authority that the Bruhui and the Baluchi chieftains possessed in Baluchistan. For this reason, Bruce's hope that Mahsud chieftains he appointed would succeed in controlling the tribes, in return for subsidies, failed to materialize. Second, he introduced the system without first militarily dominating the Mahsud country as Sandeman had done in Baluchistan. Furthermore, the Mahsuds, unlike the Baluchis, had always been dominated by powerful religious leaders under whose influence they often took up arms against the British in sympathy with or at the bidding of their Muslim kinsmen in Afghanistan.[33]

The Failure of the Bruce System in Southern Kurdistan

The new system of administration introduced by the British in southern Kurdistan was similar in many ways to the Bruce or Maliki system among the Mahsuds. The rapid deterioration and eventual failure of this system in southern Kurdistan left no doubt that it was as unsuitable for that region as it had been for the Mahsuds in India's northwest frontier. It is perhaps significant in this connection that the Kurds are similar to the Mahsuds in a number of respects. The Kurds, like the Mahsuds, have always been passionately attached to their freedom and have forever been in conflict with those who have tried to control them. Similarly, since the days of Shaykh 'Ubayd Allah, the Kurds, like the Mahsuds, have been dominated by their religious leaders, the shaykhs, rather than by their secular chieftains, the *agha*s. In British-occupied Kurdistan, skillful Turkish pan-Islamic propaganda succeeded in turning many Kurds against the British. Thus, the Kurds, like the Mahsuds, were instigated to rise against the British by a neighboring Islamic state and, like them, did so under the leadership of religious dignitaries.

It is interesting to note that Bruce, writing almost twenty years before the British came into direct contact with the Kurds, compared them to the Mahsuds. In defending the Mahsuds, he quoted a long passage from Lord Curzon's *Persia and the Persian Question,* in which Curzon defended the Kurds against charges of brutality, contumaciousness, and unreliability. After quoting Curzon, Bruce concluded, "If we substitute for the name of Kurds that of Mahsud Waziris this account would apply with equal correctness to the other." [34]

It could be argued that the new administrative system in Kurdistan might have worked had the British employed adequate forces to impose it, or had Shaykh Mahmud, the chosen instrument for its implementation, continued to cooperate with them. It is quite evident, however, that both of these suppositions ignore the fundamental nature of the situation. So far as the British were concerned, the provision of adequate forces to impose the new administrative system would have been self-defeating, for they had resorted to the system precisely to avoid the employment of large forces in the region. By installing a system of government acceptable to the people, the British hoped to eliminate the need for a costly and difficult undertaking. It should be borne in mind that Great Britain at that time was engaged in demobilizing its forces in Mesopotamia and that consequently neither the manpower nor the material was readily available. The contention that the system might have worked had Shaykh Mahmud cooperated also speaks poorly for the soundness of the system, for if the success or failure of a system of government is to depend on one man's attitude, the system cannot be a sound one.

Shaykh Mahmud's Appointment as *Hukmdar*

In order to gain firsthand knowledge of the situation in southern Kurdistan and to bolster up the British position in that region, the acting civil commissioner, Sir Arnold Wilson, proceeded to Sulaymaniya by air on December 1, 1918. A meeting was held with some sixty leading chieftains. The assembled chieftains came mostly from southern Kurdistan, but included a number from the Sinna, Saqqiz, and Hawraman (Awraman) regions of Persia. This meeting was followed by lengthy talks with Shaykh Mahmud and other leading men, in which the various aspects of the political situation were discussed.

Wilson reported the gist of these conversations. According to him, the Kurds were determined to resist the return of the Turks by force of arms. Although the Kurdish chieftains recognized the need for some form of British protection, they seemed unable to arrive at a unanimous agreement as to the means by which it should be achieved. Some chieftains declared themselves to be in favor of an effective British administration in Kurdistan, whereas others voiced opposition to the scheme; some insisted that Kurdistan should be administered from London and not from Baghdad. In their eyes, London evidently had taken the place of Istanbul. According to Wilson, a few of the assembled chiefs informed him confidentially that they would never accept the leadership of Shaykh Mahmud, but he added significantly that they were unable to suggest an alternative.[35]

After much discussion, Shaykh Mahmud handed Wilson a document signed by some forty chieftains. This document ran somewhat as follows:

> His Majesty's Government having announced their intention to liberate the Eastern peoples from Turkish oppression and to grant assistance to them in the establishment of their independence, the chiefs, as the representatives of the people of Kurdistan, beg Government to accept them also under British protection and to attach them to Iraq so that they may not be deprived of the benefits of that association. They request the Civil Commissioner of Mesopotamia to send them a representative with the necessary assistance to enable the Kurdish people under British auspices to progress peacefully on civilized lines. If Government extends its assistance and protection to them, they undertake to accept its orders and advice.[36]

In answer to this plea, Acting Civil Commissioner Wilson handed Shaykh Mahmud a letter that confirmed and supplemented the main points raised in the document. At the same time, the letter served to set the final official seal on Major Noel's earlier appointment of the shaykh as *hukmdar* of southern Kurdistan. I have not been able to locate the full text of this document, which apparently provided the legal basis for the establishment of Shaykh Mahmud's authority in southern Kurdistan. However, the gist of this letter appears in the following abbreviated form in a number of sources:

> In return he [Shaykh Mahmud] was given a letter stating that any Kurdish tribe from the Greater Zab to the Diyala (other than those in Persian Territory), who of their own free will accepted the leadership of Shaikh Mahmud, would be allowed to do so, and that the latter would have our moral support in controlling the above areas on behalf of the British Government, whose orders he undertook to obey.[37]

The two documents—the statement signed by the chieftain and the letter from Wilson—whether viewed singly or taken together, do not constitute a formal agreement between two equal and sovereign parties. Whatever Shaykh Mahmud or the other Kurdish leaders may have thought of this new arrangement, no doubt the British regarded it merely as a loose working compact of a temporary nature, entered into with a powerful local magnate with certain short-range objectives in view. Nowhere in either of the two documents is there any clear-cut mention of the sources and nature of the shaykh's powers.

The first document was signed by some forty tribal chiefs who referred to themselves as "the representatives of the people of Kurdistan." The implication is that Shaykh Mahmud and the rest of the assembled leaders were acting in the name of the Kurdish people. Indeed, the shaykh himself always maintained that his power stemmed from the people and that he had a mandate from all the Kurds of the Mosul *wilayat*. However, it appears that the British regarded this assertion as an unwarranted pretension, and they firmly set their face against the recognition of such a claim. The acting civil commissioner not only ignored it, but pointed out that such powers as the shaykh was to have were being conferred upon him by the British government. In fact, Wilson's letter made it painfully clear that the shaykh could continue to enjoy British support only so long as he continued to do their will in his capacity as British agent.

A number of other matters were discussed during Wilson's visit to Sulaymaniya. Shaykh Mahmud is said to have requested that British officers be put in charge of all government departments and of the levy force then being formed. He stipulated that subordinate staff, whenever possible, should be Kurdish and not Arab.[38] The townspeople and the tribesmen of Kirkuk and Kifri declined to join the proposed state under Shaykh Mahmud and instead asked for direct British administration. Shaykh Mahmud did not insist on their inclusion.[39]

The representatives of the Kurdish tribes of Persia, who had asked to join Shaykh Mahmud's South Kurdish Confederation, were informed that this was not possible. It was explained to them that Britain's international obligations made it impossible for the British government to lend its support to such a project. They were enjoined to remain loyal Persian subjects and to maintain friendly relations with the South Kurdish Confederation. They seem to have been satisfied by this explanation and are said to have accepted the situation cheerfully.[40]

Major Noel, who had been sent to Arbil and Rawanduz with the object of inducing the tribes in those areas to join the South Kurdish Confederation under Shaykh Mahmud, succeeded in his mission. The Kurds in those parts were reportedly anxious to share in the peace and prosperity of Shaykh Mahmud's state, which was to have British protection and financial backing.[41]

Shortly thereafter, political officers were appointed to Koi Sanjaq and Ranya, and the system of administration introduced at Sulaymaniya was extended to that area as well as to the Rawanduz region. The main task in the Rawanduz region was to cope with the terrible ravages of war. Rawanduz and the neighboring countryside had been reduced to a state of abject misery as a result of the successive battles waged there by the Turks and the Russians and the famine and pestilence that had followed in their wake. Immediate steps were taken to deal with the situation. Grain was shipped from Arbil, poverty relief was started, agriculture was encouraged, and a modicum of law and order was established. The task proved to be much more difficult in the more mountainous and inaccessible regions to the north of Rawanduz.[42]

The Shaykh Consolidates His Power

Shaykh Mahmud was determined from the beginning to consolidate his hold over the whole region brought under his control as *hukmdar*. With this end in view, he spared no effort to gather all the threads of authority into his own hands. He sought to ensure the loyalty of many tribal chieftains through a judicious distribution of funds and favors. The use he made of large subsidies made available to him by the British government and the manner in which he employed the authority vested in him as *hukmdar* to enhance his own position among the tribes were well known to the British. One report written in 1919 pointed out:

> Also, allegiance to Shaikh Mahmud as Hukmdar of the state had conditions which made him—thanks to the funds of H. B. M.'s Government—at once a popular figure and a royal road to prosperity. Following allegiance came allowances in ready cash—rare sight in those days—and the system whereby the tribal chief assessed his own goods and those of his tribe without the critical eye of a government official.[43]

While seeking to attach the tribes to himself, the shaykh succeeded in infiltrating and controlling the new administration. He filled the various posts with his own relatives and adherents and carefully excluded all those he did not regard as faithful followers and supporters.[44] His followers held all important posts in the new government. Thus, the chief of police of Sulaymaniya and the judge of the Sulaymaniya religious court, among others, were the shaykh's appointees.[45] Even the Kurdish levies, the only effective force then in the process of being formed in southern Kurdistan, were made to swear an oath of personal allegiance to Shaykh Mahmud.[46]

Shaykh Mahmud benefited from a singularly favorable set of circumstances. The British needed his support almost as much as he needed theirs. According to Bell,

> Without the full measure of co-operation and assistance which he was giving us, it would have been necessary to bring in a strong garrison, which at the time was out of question. From the political point of view it was of great importance that we should maintain order in the area, and at the time should avoid the appearance of using force for this purpose.[47]

Shaykh Mahmud was no doubt aware of his importance to the British. To what extent he believed they were willing to back him we do not know, but he did not hesitate to give the impression that they "were ready to establish his Governorship, if necessary, by force."[48]

Under the exigencies of the moment, certain influential elements within the new administration had to sweep aside whatever opposition they may have had to the exten-

14. Shaykh Mahmud (center) with his followers in Sulaimania, circa 1919. Photograph: A. T. Wilson. Courtesy of the Royal Geographical Society, London.

sion of Shaykh Mahmud's authority. The Kurds, who had suffered greatly from the war, were eager for a respite, and the British, the new power in the land, seemed determined to extend the benefits of their administration under the shaykh's leadership. Thus, objections were stilled, and the new regime was accepted throughout the area almost without demur. Major E. B. Soane described the Kurds' reaction to the establishment of the new state under Shaykh Mahmud:

> Nevertheless so anxious were the Kurds at the time for peace, so reduced by privation, that they were ready to sign any document or make any statement to procure tranquility and food. Thus tribe after tribe which hitherto had been barely cognisant of Shaikh Mahmud or at best had known him as an unworthy descendant of a good man, signed the stereotyped memorial praying for inclusion in the new state *under Shaikh Mahmud,* the clause they imagined the British Government to have made essential for reasons of its own.[49]

Criticisms of the Tribal System as Applied in Southern Kurdistan

In an official report, Major Soane strongly criticized the newly adopted administrative system. In a section entitled "Note on the Tribal System of Administration," he seized on what he regarded as the unwholesome aspects of the new system and described its evils point by point. In the first paragraph, he set down the two protagonists' intentions and expectations. He left no room for doubt that the British, who propounded the system and were backing it, and Shaykh Mahmud, the chosen instrument for its implementation, were at cross-purposes.

[A] system of administration which one may call the Tribal System, was adopted. It was considered by the Political Officer in charge that this would best meet the national aspirations and preserve the characteristic features of Kurdistan. It was considered by Shaikh Mahmud equally desirable to institute the tribal system as by that means he could more easily bribe or threaten the chiefs, could more readily centralise the control in himself and more rapidly attain the position of absolute power which was his aim. The system of direct government by officials, which naturally tends to disintegrate tribes and create a democratic and industrious homogeneous population, was by no means to his taste. As the principal adviser of the Political Officer, he therefore encouraged the revival of the tribal system which was—in Sulaimaniyah—moribund.[50]

Although it is quite evident that Soane's pet aversion was Shaykh Mahmud, whose motives he searchingly questioned and for whom he reserved his most scornful gibes, he by no means spared the system or those who inspired it. In this, as in all other official communications, Soane never minced his words. Neither the requirements of official decorum nor fear of disciplinary action ever induced him to temper his language or moderate his attitude.[51]

Having described the attitude of the British authorities and the Kurdish leader, Soane proceeded to describe the process by which the evils of this system were compounded. He pointed out in no uncertain terms that the new system was ill-conceived, reactionary, and impracticable.

Revival of the tribal system was therefore a retrograde movement. Already South Kurdistan had become largely detribalised and a measure of prosperity, in consequence, had been its lot in pre-war times. Now, the Political Officer, accepting the views expressed by Shaikh Mahmud, devoted his energies to re-tribalising. Every man who could be labelled as a tribesman was placed under a tribal leader. The idea was to divide South Kurdistan into tribal areas under tribal leaders. Petty village headmen were unearthed and discovered as leaders of long dead tribes. Disintegrated sedentary clans in the hot countries of Kifri were told to reunite and remember that they had been once tribesmen. Tribal chiefs were found for them. Revenue was to be paid on the estimation of this chief. Law was to be administered by this chief, who only must recognise Shaikh Mahmud as Hukmdar (and benevolent despot) of Kurdistan, and in return he should be subsidised. Ideal for the clansman but fatal for trade, civilisation and tranquility. It proved so; the records of the Acting Political Officer at Sulaimaniyah show a long hard fight against the natural results of the system. A tribal criminal had but to throw himself at the feet of his local chief, an offender of greater magnitude to prostrate himself before Shaikh Mahmud, to gain forgiveness and even favour. Any kind of offence could be atoned for by absolute submission to Shaikh Mahmud who immediately arranged matters with the tribal chief nominally responsible for the offender.

The people themselves—the breath and blood of the country—were thus given over, bound hand and foot, to a clique of chiefs now empowered to bleed and depress them.[52]

The net result of the introduction of this system was to fasten a corrupt and oppressive regime on the population. Soane described well its promotion of evil and injustice: "The tribal system was an idealistic one, and like so many idealistic schemes, it broke down when brought into contact with dishonest and mundane human nature. Its effects were to grant the lawless more latitude, . . .and the people less chance for achieving independence of petty oppressors, in short, it fostered and fathered the detrimentals and depressed the beneficial democratic elements."[53]

Soane stated that British political officers had detected the flaws and the drawbacks of the system from its very inception, and he cited a report submitted by Captain (later Brigadier) S. H. Longrigg, assistant political officer in Kirkuk, dated November 29, 1918. The gist of Longrigg's report was that despite the acceptance of the system by a large number of Kurds, it was apt to be resented by those whose interests it did not serve. He pointed out that some may have resented it to the point of wishing the old effendis (Turkish officials) were back. Moreover, Longrigg expressed fear that the Kurd under the new system might prove to be the equal of the Turk as an oppressor.[54] He even hazarded the opinion that the new regime might, if referred to the peasants, be rejected. He concluded his comments on the regime by saying, "it avowedly sacrifices democracy to nationality, for better or worse. It will be easy, though not pleasant, to be deaf to small, probably legitimate cries against our nominee."[55]

In another report submitted by Longrigg a month later (December-January 1918–19), he again discussed the tribal system, referring to it as an experiment. After pointing out the dangers inherent in placing the tribesmen at the mercy of their chieftains, he mentioned what he regarded as the advantages of the system. According to him, it fostered a national feeling in the Kurd, removed the tribesman from the corrupt and baleful influence of the officials, and reduced to one the number of possible offenders against justice and liberty.[56]

It is interesting to consider another British officer's opinion concerning the newly introduced tribal system. R. S. Jardine, at the time assistant political officer at Kifri, reported:

> The tribal system of the Qadha [district] is in a state of dissolution—a process fostered by the policy of the Turks since Hurriyah[57]—in some cases the village headman acknowledges no one but the Political Officer as his superior. This seems to simplify work of revenue collection, but makes administration of justice and law and order more difficult than it is in places where the tribal system persists in its primitive form. In several parts of the district I have managed to maintain the tribal system of responsibility for law and order, but all attempts to maintain it for revenue collection merely led to preposterous delay in its collection or intolerably unfair treatment of the Fallah [peasant]. But in spite of this the tribal system is worth a good trial.[58]

It will be noted from this report that even those political officers who were not as strongly opposed to the tribal system as Soane also had considerable misgivings as to the justice and the wisdom of its introduction. No doubt the British resorted to the tribal system as a temporary expedient. In the absence of an adequate number of trained administrative personnel and a sufficiently large force capable of coping with the difficult task of maintaining law and order in the newly occupied regions, they were compelled to devise a system of government that enabled them to employ a handful of their own officers in a supervisory administrative capacity.

The British needed, or imagined that they needed, the support of native leaders so badly that they did not hesitate to go to great lengths to win them over. In order to ensure their cooperation, British officials went so far as to acquiesce in unjust deals at the expense of the people as a whole. Many powerful tribal leaders and wealthy landowners were left undisturbed in the possession of lands to which they had no clear title. In fact, in many cases they had no claim to lands in their possession other than forcible seizure. Bell summed up this problem in a few revealing sentences:

> From the first a certain anxiety had been visible among the aghas lest British control should lead to awkward questions as to land ownership, there being in most cases no title except forcible possession. Though the power of agha and saiyid was contrary to the interests of the bulk of the population, it was impossible at the moment to put a curb on it, and in order to allay the fears of the ruling class the Tapu registers were not sent to Baghdad, where they would have been subjected to inconvenient scrutiny, but allowed to remain temporarily at Sulaimaniyah.[59]

In the light of subsequent developments, it is quite evident that these concessions proved to be utterly useless, for it was the very class to whom these concessions had been made that rose against the British a few months later.

The Deterioration of Relations Between Shaykh Mahmud and the British

The Shaykh's Resentment of British Restrictions

Now that Shaykh Mahmud had obtained the position he had so eagerly sought, he made no attempt to conceal the fact that he wanted all the privileges but none of the obligations that went with them. Notwithstanding the fact that his appointment as *hukmdar* had been made contingent on certain conditions, he appears to have regarded these conditions as unwarranted limitations on his authority. The area over which he was allowed to exercise control was restricted to the region lying between the Greater Zab and the Sirwan (Diyala) Rivers, and his authority as a ruler was greatly abridged by being subordinated to the British. The shaykh was unwilling to accept what he regarded as vexatious servitudes designed to curb his influence and to interfere with his freedom of action.

In a work written many years after these events, Edmonds discusses Shaykh Mahmud's reaction to the restraints and restrictions placed on his authority and points out what made the whole situation both incomprehensible and unacceptable to a person of his temperament and mentality. "He resented the restriction of his authority to the district just described. Even in Turkish times, as an official citizen, he had terrorized the town through his gangs of roughs and, now that he was officially the Ruler, he was quite incapable of understanding the restraints put upon him even by Noel's mild advisory regime."[60]

Bell, leaving no doubt as to Shaykh Mahmud's stand on this matter, asserted that the shaykh's attitude was strongly influenced by the men around him. According to her, these men, instead of urging upon him a more moderate and sober approach, encouraged him to adopt a defiant attitude.

> Shaikh Mahmud was not prepared to accept from us, any more than he had accepted from the Turks, a limitation on his authority. He was surrounded by interested syco-phants who filled his head with extravagant ideas and encouraged him to style himself ruler of the whole of Kurdistan. He interfered constantly in local administration and flooded the administrative departments with his relations and hangers on.[61]

Although Shaykh Mahmud was glad to receive British support and a British subsidy, he was obviously determined not to submit to any restrictions. At the beginning, he was careful to conform outwardly to the requirements of British policy, but he seems to have made up his mind to pursue his aims in his own way. Thus, he bent all his energies to increasing his power and spreading his influence throughout Kurdistan, evidently unmindful of what the British might think or do. Within a comparatively short time, he succeeded in increasing his power and extending his influence to such a degree that the British felt compelled to take immediate measures to stop the trend before the situation got completely out of their hands.

Hardly a month had passed since the installation of Shaykh Mahmud as *hukmdar* by the acting civil commissioner when the British found themselves faced with the necessity of making a painful reappraisal of the whole situation in southern Kurdistan. "By the end of December," stated the identical texts of two official reports, "doubts were beginning to arise as to the wisdom of allowing the power of Shaikh Mahmud to increase to too great an extent."[62]

It may seem strange and even paradoxical that the British should have been so disturbed by the growing power of a man they had supported and subsidized and whom they had helped to make the first ruler of a quasi-autonomous Kurdish state. Insofar as this discussion is concerned, it is immaterial to determine whether or not Shaykh Mahmud owed his position to the British and, if so, to what extent. What is important is what the shaykh thought about this situation. It is almost certain that he did not regard the British as his benefactors and consequently did not feel beholden to remain faithful to them. In his dealings with them, he appears to have adopted an opportunistic policy. He availed himself of whatever moral or material support they had to offer and continued to cooperate with them as long as this approach was profitable.

He worked feverishly to increase his power and extend his influence not only within the confines of the South Kurdish Confederation, but wherever it was possible for him to do so. Although he did not actually seek an open breach with the British, he was now less careful about keeping up appearances. Evidently obsessed by the idea of strengthening his position, he flouted his agreements with the British and ignored the recommendations of the political officers. He seems to have come to the conclusion that there was little if anything to be gained by further cooperation with them. Furthermore, he must have believed he had become so strong that the British would not dare to challenge his power and that he could therefore do what he liked with impunity.

It seems strange that Shaykh Mahmud, so soon after his assumption of power, should have adopted a course of action that was bound to involve him in conflict with the British. For whatever reasons he may have wanted to rid himself of the British connection, there can be no doubt that he acted too hastily, showed little tact, and did not give much thought to the inevitable outcome of an unequal struggle. British officials, in particular those with pro-Kurdish leanings who had their hearts set on the creation of a south Kurdish autonomous state, were baffled, disappointed, and angered by the shaykh's actions. These men apparently never forgave him for having so rudely shattered their expectations. Their references to him are fraught with invective bordering on vilification. The most charitable things they said of him is that he was a madman or a child.

In 1928, in an attempt to seek an explanation for Shaykh Mahmud's behavior, G. M. Lees rendered a harsh verdict on the shaykh's character:

> The evil reputation of Shaikh Mahmud for treachery and dishonesty was well known, but as his interests and ours appeared to coincide there seemed to be no occasion for him to play us false. Unfortunately he was trusted too implicitly and allowed too complete control of his large subsidy. Intoxicated by his sudden acquisition of power and wealth, Shaikh Mahmud's ambitions soon commenced to soar beyond their prescribed limits and he had visions of himself, as eventually king of a united and independent Kurdistan.[63]

Wilson said of Shaykh Mahmud: "In ignorance, but not in innocence, he was a child, with great ambitions and much natural cunning. He was given to sudden fits of passion and outbursts of cruelty, which suggested to so cool an observer as Soane that he was not always responsible for his actions."[64]

The Impact of Ideas and Events on Shaykh Mahmud

Other British writers have expressed similar opinions of Shaykh Mahmud. Whatever the truth of these charges, other things must have influenced the shaykh's attitudes and actions. In order to gain a proper understanding of Shaykh Mahmud's thinking and arrive at a just appraisal of his behavior, we should take all the factors involved into consideration.

Shaykh Mahmud's thinking was dominated by the idea that the Kurds—those of southern Kurdistan at any rate—were entitled to a state of their own and that he was the rightful head of such a state. The idea of a Kurdish state had been fostered by various Allied declarations during and after the war and by the general climate of opinion then prevalent among leading Kurds everywhere, whereas the idea of his leadership stemmed from a sense of personal mission and from the preeminence in southern Kurdistan of the Barzinja family.

Shaykh Mahmud owed his position largely to the high veneration in which his family was held. The prestige of three of his immediate forebears in particular cast an aura of sanctity about him. His great-great-grandfather, Shaykh Ma'ruf of Node, was noted for his vast religious learning and for his victory over the reknowned Naqshbandi shaykh Mawlana Khalid in a miracle-working contest.[65] His great-grandfather, the hallowed Haj Kak Ahmad, was the most celebrated saint and miracle worker of southern Kurdistan.[66] Finally, his own father, Shaykh Sa'id, had enjoyed considerable power and prestige as the friend and protégé of Sultan 'Abdul Hamid and was regarded as having died a martyr's death. Shaykh Sa'id was cast in that role after his assassination by a Mosul mob and for a long time was the symbol of the grievances of the Barzinja family and their followers against the Ottoman government.[67]

This family, as mentioned elsewhere in this study, had been the most persistent and the most powerful claimants to local hegemony since the fall of the Babans. Shaykh Mahmud, though not the eldest member of the dominant node branch of the Barzinja family of sayyids, was its recognized head and, as such, the focus of all the veneration and homage accorded to this holy family. As the head of the Barzinja family and as a charismatic leader in his own right, the shaykh felt that he had the strongest claim on the leadership of southern Kurdistan.

For this reason, Shaykh Mahmud had always insisted that he held a mandate from the Kurds of the Mosul *wilayat* and even from important segments of the Kurds of Persia. If he were really convinced of this fact, as he appears to have been, he must have regarded the limitation of his rule to only a portion of the area he claimed and the subordination of his authority to the British as flagrant and unjust abuses of his rights.

Evidence is not lacking that the shaykh firmly believed in the justness of his claims and his right to pursue them. Sir Arnold Wilson, who visited Shaykh Mahmud while the latter was recovering from severe wounds received in the battle of the Bazyan Pass, left us a memorable picture of the Kurdish chieftain. Writing in retrospect almost a decade after his meeting with Shaykh Mahmud, Wilson commented:

> I had seen him in office in Sulaimani on three occasions; I had seen him in hospital when, with a magnificent gesture, he denied the competence of any military court to try him, and recited to me President Wilson's twelve points, and the Anglo-French Declaration of 8th November 1918, a translation of which in Kurdish, written on the fly leaves of a Qur'an, was strapped like a talisman to his arm.[68]

This indeed is a vivid portrayal not so much of a rebel Kurdish chieftain as of the spirit and temper of the times in Kurdistan. The documents that the shaykh carried about his person and to which he appealed in defense of his actions were no doubt well chosen. However, these represented only two of the many factors influencing not only the shaykh but countless other men of his generation. It is to these forces that we must now turn if we want to understand a man who, after having unsuccessfully challenged the might of an empire and failed, spoke with such a righteous tone to one of its chief representatives.

Shaykh Mahmud's conduct becomes explicable only when viewed against the bewildering state of affairs in British-occupied Mesopotamia. The welter of new and unfamiliar ideas, the discordant claims of rival groups and competing ideologies, the currents and cross-currents of political intrigue, and the rumors and uncertainties of the times were sufficient to tax the minds and unsettle the hearts of most men. The various declarations of Allied war aims, such as the Anglo-French Declaration of November 8, 1918, and President Wilson's Fourteen Points, in particular the twelfth point, which applied the doctrine of national self-determination to the non-Turkish subjects of the Ottoman Empire;[69] Turkish agitation with its pan-Islamic and pro-Kurdish overtones; Sharifian propaganda, primarily pan-Arab in the Arabic-speaking regions, but pan-Islamic in the Kurdish-speaking regions;[70] Kurdish nationalist activities emanating from various sources and in various guises;[71] the communist revolutionary ferment percolating into the region after the upheaval in Russia:[72] all these served only to accentuate the hopes and fears of the moment and to increase the general confusion. In the midst of it all stood the British, hesitant and irresolute, their still unknown intentions viewed with doubt and suspicion.

Then there were the many conflicting rumors and reports. Although some may have been the work of idlers and wishful thinkers, others were clearly inspired by interested quarters, but all had one thing in common—they were given credence and eagerly circulated by the gullible public. There was talk of Armenian ascendancy;[73] of Arab domination;[74] of revived Turkish military power;[75] of a French takeover of the Mosul *wilayat*;[76] and of the imminent British evacuation of Mesopotamia—all of which had some basis in fact.

In the north, the future of the Mosul *wilayat* was still in doubt, and the Turks were menacingly clamoring for its return to them. Many of the more remote mountain regions in the disputed province were either lightly held by the British or were simply no-man's-land where the Turks still ranged at will. In the Arab-inhabited areas of the south, the situation was tense despite the outward calm. British intentions with regard to the future of the Mosul *wilayat* and, indeed, the rest of Mesopotamia were vague and ill-defined, and British policies often seemed tentative and provisional.[77] While a feeling of great uncertainty prevailed throughout the land, demobilization got under way, and the vast British military establishment, so laboriously assembled during the war, began to vanish before the people's incredulous eyes. The departure of thousands of troops certainly did not inspire confidence when so many issues, some of which were of a purely military nature, remained unresolved.[78]

To persons such as Shaykh Mahmud who had much at stake, what had been a nagging uncertainty now appeared as a distinct possibility. It must have been at this time that he decided to establish contact with the Turks, for he was soon reported to have been in touch with the Turkish agitation center at Shernakh as well as with the unruly

Goyan tribe.[79] In order to assess the wisdom, if not the rectitude, of his action, it is only fair to point out that a person in Shaykh Mahmud's position was bound to drift farther away from his British partners unless and until what he regarded as their declining fortunes should take a turn for the better.

Serious miscalculations on the shaykh's part were aggravated by his inordinate ambition and his advisors' fatuous promptings. He ignored the advice of his British mentors, flouted their wishes, and generally adopted an attitude of stubborn intransigence. A reckless and politically unsophisticated man, he apparently did not ponder the consequences of a clash with a great power. The men around him, instead of counseling moderation and a more sober approach, only goaded him into pursuing extravagant objectives.

It is not improbable that the shaykh might have succeeded in achieving most if not all of his aims had he adopted a more moderate and tactful approach. The British were too weary to invite trouble and too wise to lose a valuable friend. They faced so many problems in Mesopotamia and throughout the world that they had neither the desire nor the resources to seek anything but a peaceful solution whenever possible.

The British Curtailment of the Shaykh's Authority

The British were by now convinced that they could no longer trust Shaykh Mahmud and that unless they took drastic measures to curb his authority, their whole position in Kurdistan would continue to be gravely threatened. "It was by this time clear," stated Wilson, "that we could not prudently lend our active support to Shaykh Mahmud's pretentions to the hegemony of any considerable group of tribes, and, this being the case, it was generally agreed that it was necessary to modify our policy in Southern Kurdistan by the introduction of some sort of administration on lines similar to those in force elsewhere in Iraq." [80]

Early in March 1919, Acting Civil Commissioner Wilson called a conference in Baghdad with the object of discussing the latest developments in southern Kurdistan. The conference was attended by a number of experts, including Soane, Noel, Leachman, and A. L. Gordon-Walker. After a thorough discussion of Shaykh Mahmud and the whole situation in southern Kurdistan, they agreed "that Shaykh Mahmud's power should be gradually curtailed, but, if possible, in such a way as to avoid an open breach." [81] To this end, two important decisions were reached: first, that Soane should replace Noel as political officer in Sulaymaniya and, second, that a number of tribes and districts that had hitherto been under the shaykh should be allowed to secede.[82] The appointment of Soane was a clear indication that the British intended to deal drastically with the shaykh, for Soane was known for his intense dislike of the Barzinja family in general and of Shaykh Mahmud in particular—a feeling that, as mentioned earlier, he was never at pains to conceal.[83]

Immediate steps were taken to implement the decisions adopted at the conference. Soane was dispatched to Sulaymaniya, and while on his way to that town he stopped at Kifri and Kirkuk with the object of setting in motion the process that was soon to lead to the removal of various districts and tribes from under the shaykh's authority.[84]

The Jaf, who happened to be at their winter quarters in the Kifri region, are reported to have been unanimous in their desire to separate from Shaykh Mahmud and to be placed under direct British conrol.[85] Captain G. M. Lees, who had been selected to serve as assistant political officer in charge of Jaf affairs at Halabja, arrived in the Kifri region about the middle of March, where he lingered for a few days. While there, he paid the chieftains of the various Jaf subsections the monthly subsidies that they had hitherto received from Shaykh Mahmud, and he deducted these amounts from the shaykh's total subsidy. This action left no doubt in the minds of the Jaf that the British had changed their attitude toward the Kurdish leader and that a new policy was now in effect.[86] In March 1919, the Kirkuk and Kifri regions were detached from the South Kurdish Confederation of Shaykh Mahmud and established as a new division.[87] The Halabja district, while remaining part of the Sulaymaniya division, was now brought under direct British control.

It was now clear to all that the shaykh had lost the confidence of the British and that in due course he would lose whatever moral and material support he still enjoyed. This man, who but a short time earlier had been proclaimed the leader of southern Kurdistan to whom all loyal Kurds should rally, was now being represented as a fatuous pretender whom all should abandon. This development made a deep impression on the southern Kurds. His rivals and those hostile to him had viewed with grave misgivings the shaykh's role as the hegemon of southern Kurdistan and had accepted his assumption of power with considerable reluctance. These persons now hailed the decline of his power as a vindication of their earlier attitude toward him. However, in the eyes of his supporters and followers, including his numerous relatives, the shaykh was a wronged man who now more than ever roused their sympathies and elicited their allegiance.

The curtailment of the shaykh's authority was apparently accomplished without any untoward incident. The fact that his enemies welcomed it and the shaykh and his supporters did not oppose it led Soane to report rather prematurely on its salutary effects on Sulaymaniya and the surrounding countryside. According to him, Shaykh Mahmud's influence was declining fast, and as the advantages of law and order made themselves felt, the townspeople as well as the tribes were becoming favorably impressed by the new state of affairs.[88]

Unfortunately, the calm was deceptive and the optimism unwarranted. How bitterly the shaykh resented the diminution of his power and how strenuously he was to oppose it were soon to be demonstrated. It was, indeed, unrealistic to expect a man of Shaykh Mahmud's temperament and character to give up his ambitions, yield his powers, and suffer humiliation and loss of face without a struggle. In an official report that appeared a year after these events, Soane denounced in scathing terms the shaykh's behavior at the time. According to him, the shaykh hampered just administration and by various arbitrary means sought to belittle the British government and its officials. The shaykh gathered around him a band of malcontents and evildoers and began to contemplate plans for avenging himself upon the British government.[89] It was thus in anger and defiance that he received the British challenge to his power.

The Rebellion and Defeat of Shaykh Mahmud

The Capture of Sulaymaniya by the Shaykh's Forces

While the British were seriously thinking of reaching an accommodation with Shaykh Mahmud,[90] he struck suddenly in a desperate bid to regain his waning power and prestige.[91] A tribal force composed mostly of Hawramani and Meriwani tribesmen from across the frontier in Persia, led by Mahmud Khan Dizli[92] but acting under the orders of Shaykh Mahmud, appeared before Sulaymaniya in the early hours of May 23, 1919. It succeeded without much difficulty in routing the levy force sent to oppose it. The tribal force was joined by other followers of the shaykh from Sulaymaniya and the neighboring districts, as it moved to take possession of the town. Major F. S. Greenhouse, who was in charge during Soane's absence, and a number of other British officers were captured and imprisoned.[93]

Shaykh Mahmud declared himself ruler of all Kurdistan, seized the treasury,[94] raised his own flag,[95] and appointed his own administrative officials.[96] The telegraph line to Kirkuk was cut, and messengers with dispatches sent by Greenhouse were intercepted.[97] The first news of these happenings in Sulaymaniya reached the outside world through Lees, the assistant political officer at Halabja.[98] Lees himself had to flee his post and take refuge at Khanaqin after narrowly escaping capture or a worse fate.[99]

Soon after the outbreak, the shaykh's men captured a Sulaymaniya-bound government convoy from Kifri. The spoils, which included money, rifles, and horses, were a valuable addition to the shaykh's slender resources.[100] This indeed was an auspicious beginning, but the shaykh was soon to score a more significant success.

The British Reverse at Tasluja Pass

Upon learning of these developments, the British decided to take countermeasures. As a preliminary step, the officer commanding the Kirkuk garrison was instructed to send a detachment as far as Chamchamal on the main Kirkuk-Sulaymaniya road. Although the instructions made it clear that there was to be no advance beyond that point, the officer in command, obviously underestimating the Kurds' fighting qualities and the difficult terrain, decided to disregard his orders. He ordered a small force consisting of mounted troops, levies, armored cars, and Lewis guns mounted in Ford vans to push as far as the Tasluja Pass, twelve miles from Sulaymaniya. The force, compelled to retreat, was pursued by the Kurds over a distance of twenty-five miles and badly mauled. It sustained severe casualties and lost four armored cars and nineteen Ford vans.[101]

The shaykh's success had an immediate and electrifying effect throughout southern Kurdistan. In Wilson's words, "This 'regrettable incident' confirmed the now general belief of the inhabitants of Southern Kurdistan that we were no longer able to control events; the rebellion spread across into Persian territory, and several tribes arose against the Persian Government, proclaiming themselves partisans of Shaikh Mahmud and of his scheme for a free and united Kurdistan."[102]

The Shaykh's Defeat at the Bazyan Pass

The British were now fully aware of the gravity of the situation. By now, all southern Kurdistan knew that the shaykh had outwitted the British in Sulaymaniya and overpowered them at the Tasluja Pass. The British realized that their hold on a vital part of the occupied territories was seriously threatened and felt that unless they took urgent and decisive measures to eliminate the shaykh, he might yet succeed in arousing the whole country against them. "The Commander-in-Chief," explained Wilson, "realized that the impression of British helplessness must be removed forthwith." [103] The task of forming and leading a punitive force against Shaykh Mahmud fell to Major-General Sir Theodore Fraser, commander of the Eighteenth Division at Mosul. This force, which was assembled at Kirkuk, consisted of two brigades of infantry supported by cavalry, armored cars, and an air force unit. Another column was to move against Sulaymaniya from Khanaqin.[104]

General Fraser's force arrived at Chamchamal on June 15, 1919, and on June 17 the whole force moved up to the village of Takiya Kak Ahmad, some three miles from the Bazyan Pass.[105] In the early dawn of June 18, infantry units began to scale the almost perpendicular heights on both sides of the Bazyan,[106] and other forces soon began to pound it with heavy guns. As the shaykh's forces rushed to defend the Bazyan Pass against the main British force now pouring through the narrow gap, they found themselves assailed from all sides. The units that had earlier scaled the western face of Bazyan were now pouring down the other side. Before long, the shaykh's forces were surrounded and overwhelmed. The shaykh's defeat was complete. Forty-eight of his men were killed, more than one hundred were captured, and the rest had dispersed and fled.[107]

Thus ended the battle of the Bazyan Pass of June 1919, one of numerous battles fought at this strategic point.[108] Though merely an incident in British imperial history, Shaykh Mahmud's rebellion is a milestone in the history of Kurdish nationalism. It may in fact have had some bearing on the behavior of the Dilo, Zanganah, Daudi, and other Kurdish tribes in the southern part of the Kirkuk division who, a year later, at the time of the dangerous insurrection in the Arabic-speaking regions of Mesopotamia, erupted against the occupation authorities.[109]

After the battle of the Bazyan Pass, the British spent anxious hours looking for Shaykh Mahmud. He was finally found severely wounded. According to Edmonds, who accompanied Fraser's force as a political officer, "It was most important that he should not either die before he had been identified by a Kurdish personality, or escape; and any legend of a miraculous disappearance might cause untold trouble later." [110]

Another matter of concern for the British at this time was the fate of the captive British officers in Sulaymaniya.[111] Although thus far these officers had been unharmed, it was feared that they might be killed if the news of the shaykh's defeat became known in Sulaymaniya.[112] Consequently, a small cavalry force was ordered to proceed to Sulaymaniya immediately. The force accomplished its mission with success, arriving in the town before word of the disaster at Bazyan had reached the townspeople. The prisoners were freed and the town occupied.[113]

The Conviction and Reprieve of Shaykh Mahmud

Soon after Shaykh Mahmud recovered from his wounds, he was tried by a court-martial, found guilty, and sentenced to death. However, the British commander in chief, Sir George MacMunn, commuted his sentence to a long term of imprisonment. By a further act of clemency, this sentence was changed to banishment to India in 1921.[114] Wilson wrote in 1936 that although he understood at the time the reasons that had induced the commander in chief to adopt this clement attitude, he was opposed to the decision on practical grounds. He was afraid that as long as Shaykh Mahmud was alive, there could be no real hope for tranquility in the Sulaymaniya region.[115] A few years later Sir George MacMunn explained the extenuating circumstances that had inspired his act of clemency:

> Shaikh Mahmud was brought home a prisoner from the Bazian Pass. I had him tried, and he was sentenced to death. I knew he was an infernal scoundrel, and people wanted me to hang him, but I thought there was no fair ground for such action. The general delay in settling the future of Iraq had been so great as to be quite enough to confuse any man. Shaikh Mahmud owed no temporary allegiance to the British. When he engineered the coup d'etat he did not kill the four or five British officers he had in his hands, and I did not think it would be playing the British game fairly to shoot him.[116]

These measures, as subsequent events were to prove, failed to achieve any permanent results. Despite certain signs of superficial improvement, the situation remained as uncertain as ever. Even two years after these events, stability, the major British objective in southern Kurdistan, seemed unattainable. Evidently in desperation, the British resorted to a rather unexpected solution. They pardoned Shaykh Mahmud, brought him back to Sulaymaniya, and reinstated him for a second time as *hukmdar,* only to resume the struggle a few months later. The story of this futile experiment is told in chapter 11. In the meantime, it is necessary to examine the causes of the failure of the shaykh's first rebellion, which culminated in his defeat at the Bazyan Pass.

Reasons for the Failure of the Shaykh's Rebellion

Poor organization and inadequate resources seem to have been largely responsible for the failure of the rebellion. According to one source, captured correspondence revealed a number of facts of particular military importance. First, the shaykh's whole force appears to have been organized into a single battalion comprising four companies. At the same time, his mobility may have been limited by lack of a strong cavalry force.[117] Second, shortly after the outbreak of the rebellion, Shaykh Mahmud apparently failed to pay the levies—which engendered considerable dissatisfaction and resulted in numerous attempts to evade military service.[118] Third, the shortage of ammunition was a serious problem, as indicated by a captured order forbidding the expenditure of even a single round of ammunition without prior authorization, under pain of severe punishment. According to this order, shooting of any kind was strictly forbidden until the machine guns had opened fire.[119] A fourth point, not specifically mentioned by the foregoing source but certainly implied, was the question of morale.[120] Although the shaykh and a number of his followers fought with great bravery and determination, it is doubtful that the whole force was imbued by a similar spirit. In fact, the ill-paid British-trained levies are said to have made a point of holding out their rifles for inspection after the battle to show their captors that the guns had not been fired.[121]

The strength and composition of the shaykh's forces provide a reasonably reliable index of his power and popularity at the time of the rebellion. Besides his own followers in and around Sulaymaniya,[122] his numerous Barzinja relatives, and their adherents,[123] the shaykh was joined by various tribal elements.[124] These elements included the Hawramanis (Awramanis) under Mahmud Khan Dizli;[125] the Meriwanis[126] under Mahmud Khan of Kanisenan;[127] most of the Hamawands under their paramount chieftain Karim-i Fattah Beg;[128] the Mika'ili section of the Jaf;[129] the Jabbaris under their chief Sayyid Muhammad Jabbari;[130] the Shaykh Bizainis under one of their chieftains, Faris Agha;[131] a section of the Isma'il Uzairis;[132] a contingent of the Shuwans under 'Azza-i-Sharif Jalal;[133] and other lesser elements such as the followers of Shaykh 'Abd-Allah of Askar in the Qala Sewka (Aqjalar) district.[134]

Despite this imposing array of tribal names, the support received by the shaykh was both deceptive and disappointing. The number of those who joined him and stood fast by him was never more than a few hundred. With a few notable exceptions, their loyalties appear to have been uncertain and their support haphazard and short-lived. The narrow loyalties so characteristic of tribally organized societies militated against any sustained, large-scale military effort. Riven by intertribal antagonisms, the Kurdish tribesmen have rarely been able to form a united front against a common enemy. As a matter of fact, the concept of a common enemy must often have seemed to the average tribesman to be a contradiction in terms, for that would mean that the enemy in question is both his enemy and his enemy's enemy—a situation that is diametrically opposed to tribal wisdom that finds expression in the well-known adage "My enemy's enemy is my friend."

There have been times, of course, when the Kurds of a whole region have put aside their differences and forgotten their feuds to make common cause against an external opponent. But such combinations have been the exception rather than the rule. Moreover, these alliances have never lasted long enough to accomplish their purpose against the superior arms and organization of their powerful antagonists.

Shaykh Mahmud, as we have seen, had called on the southern Kurds to fight the British in the name of Kurdish nationalism and Islam. This was to be a national struggle and a jihad. To the majority of the Kurds, however, nationalism was a new and unfamiliar concept, and for this reason it failed to achieve the desired result. Jihad, in contrast, was by now only too familiar as a hopeless cause. The Kurds had just witnessed the failure of a similar call to arms by a person far greater and more powerful than the shaykh. The call to jihad by the sultan-caliph, backed as it was by the armed might and vast resources of the Ottoman Empire and its allies, had failed against the same enemy, the British, after four years of war.

The shaykh was bound to fail in mobilizing southern Kurdistan unless he succeeded in breathing a new spirit into his fractious compatriots. This he evidently was unable to do; he failed to reconcile and win over his rivals and those opposed to him. The Jaf and the Pizhdar, the two most powerful tribal confederations of southern Kurdistan, remained hostile and offered active support to his British antagonists.[135]

"The unsubstantial character of Shaikh Mahmud's rebellion," reported Bell in 1920, "was proved by the fact that out of a potential backing of many thousands, his active supporters numbered no more than 300."[136] Although Bell's low estimate may have been a deliberate attempt to minimize Shaykh Mahmud's importance, there can be no doubt that the number of his supporters was far below what it might have been. Other than his *murid*s (among whom his word had the force of religious law) and those who were closely bound to him by ties of kinship or interest, the number of those who rallied to the shaykh's cause was not impressive.

11 *Shaykh Mahmud's Second Rebellion*

Background

The fate of the Mosul *wilayat* was settled only after a bitter struggle in which the British, the Turks, and the native Arabs and Kurds participated. It will be recalled that the modern state of Iraq came into being with the Mosul *wilayat* as one of its constituent parts, although the Mosul issue was still controversial. The Mosul question was the outcome of a number of developments that profoundly influenced the course and trend of events not only in the *wilayat* of that name but throughout the whole Middle East. It is to these developments that we now turn our attention.

On May 9, 1916, the Sykes-Picot Agreement was reached between Great Britain and France.[1] It provided for the partition of the Ottoman Empire into various zones and spheres of influence. Russia at first opposed this plan, but later, after introducing certain conditions, agreed to it.[2] It was largely in accordance with this early blueprint that the Asiatic provinces of the Ottoman Empire were fragmentized and balkanized.

On October 30, 1918, the armistice signed at Mudros put an end to hostilities between the Turks and the Allies and thus set the stage for an event that was deeply to influence the fate and destiny of the people of the Mosul *wilayat*. This event took place in the city of Mosul on November 7, 1918, in the course of a conference attended by British and Turkish military representatives. The British commander, General John Marshall, despite the objections of the Turkish commander, General ʿAli Ihsan Pasha, insisted that the terms of the Mudros armistice required the Turks to evacuate the whole of the Mosul *wilayat*. In the face of his victorious opponent's unrelenting attitude, ʿAli Ihsan Pasha signed, under protest, the terms dictated to him.[3] It was by this fait accompli that the Mosul *wilayat* was established as a part of Iraq.

On January 28, 1920, the Kemalists announced the National Pact, a declaration largely based on decisions reached earlier at the congresses of Sivas and Erzerum. This document embodied Kemalist views with regard to the fate of the former provinces south of the armistice line of 1918 and made it quite clear that all the districts inhabited by a non-Arab Muslim population were to be regarded as an integral part of Turkey. There is no doubt that this latter reference was intended to apply to the Mosul *wilayat*, which was largely inhabited by a non-Arab Muslim population—the Kurds. The National Pact thus marked Turkey's first determined bid to retrieve the Mosul *wilayat* since its acceptance of the British terms at Mosul on November 7, 1918.[4] It also marked the beginning of Turkish agitation that was to plunge that province into turmoil for the next few years until the final settlement of the issue by the Anglo-Turkish-Iraqi Treaty of 1926.

Next in this sequence of events was Britain's acceptance in April 1920 of the mandate for Iraq—a step that made the British, with the approval of the League of Nations, responsible for both the Arab and the Kurdish parts of the country. It was in this capacity that Britain was to oppose Turkish claims to the Mosul *wilayat* at the League of Nations and at Lausanne and to prevent its forcible seizure by a revived Turkey.

The Allies, bent on the dismemberment of the Ottoman Empire and totally unmindful of the National Pact that the Kemalists had announced six months earlier, forced the sultan's weak regime to sign the Treaty of Sèvres on August 10, 1920. Articles 62, 63, and 64 of this treaty provided for the establishment of a Kurdish national state. Though nullified shortly thereafter by Kemalist victories and eventually cast aside and supplanted by the Treaty of Lausanne, the Treaty of Sèvres is nevertheless a milestone in the history of Kurdish nationalism, for this was the first time that the Kurdish dream of independence was enshrined in an international document.

In England, a separate Middle East Department, designed to deal with the problems of the area, was set up in the Colonial Office. This department assumed responsibility for the administration of Iraq and was charged with determining the nature of the future government of that country. In March 1921, shortly after assuming office, Winston Churchill, the new secretary of state for colonies, called a conference in Cairo to determine the future course of British policy in the Middle East.[5] Many important decisions were adopted at this conference, including the decision to support the candidature of Emir Faysal for the throne of Iraq. Faysal, who subsequently arrived at Basra in June 1921, was proclaimed king on August 23, after a referendum that purportedly gave him 96 percent of the total votes cast.

Before that, on November 11, 1920, a provisional national government had been formed under the presidency of Sayyid 'Abd al-Rahman al-Naqib. This development had a disquieting effect on the Kurds, for it aroused their fears of future domination by an Arab government in Baghdad. In order to allay these fears, the British high commissioner issued a statement on May 6, 1921, that was to be brought to the Kurds' attention by British political officers in the Mosul, Kirkuk, and Sulaymaniya divisions.[6]

The statement began by informing the Kurds that the high commissioner was aware of Kurdish apprehensions regarding their political future and their desire for an autonomous regime. It referred to the economic ties connecting the Kurdish areas with Iraq and apprised the Kurds of the high commissioner's desire to ascertain their wishes concerning these matters. Finally, without in any way indicating when or how the Kurds' wishes were to be ascertained, it proceeded to outline proposals for the administration of the Kurdish areas, "should they prefer to remain under the Iraq Government." Then, a proposed three-point administrative program was set forth.

The first point pertained to the formation of a Kurdish sub*liwa* (subprovince) comprising the four Kurdish *qada*s (districts) of the Mosul division—namely, Zakho, 'Aqra, Dohuk, and 'Amadiya. This sub*liwa* was to be placed under a British assistant *mutasarrif (liwa* governor), and the *qaimmaqam*s (district deputy commissioners), for the time being British, "would be replaced by Kurds or Kurdish-speaking Arabs acceptable to the Kurds" as soon as suitable men were available. The sub*liwa* would be subject both financially and judicially to the government in Baghdad—which would give it the right to send representatives to the constituent assembly. Administratively, the *qaimmaqam*s would be subject to the assistant *mutasarrif,* and all administrative appointments would be made by the British high commissioner after consultations with local authorities.

The second part of the program dealt with the administration of Arbil, Koi Sanjaq, and Rawanduz. It stated that the high commissioner would try to "associate British Officials" with the administration of the three districts. The appointment of government officials, it was promised, would be made with due consideration to the people's wishes.

The third and last point pertained to the Sulaymaniya division. Sulaymaniya was to be given the status of a *mutasarriflik* (subprovince), governed by a *mutasarrif* in council. The *mutasarrif,* who was to be appointed by the high commissioner, would be provided with a British political officer at Sulaymaniya who would act in this capacity. The *mutasarrif* in council would be delegated such powers as the high commissioner saw fit to delegate after consultations with him and with the Council of State.

The referendum held late July 1921 to determine the validity of Faysal's choice as king of Iraq produced two noteworthy developments. Sulaymaniya refused to participate, and Kirkuk did so reluctantly, accounting, it was said, for the 4 percent negative vote. It is equally significant that no representative from either of these two *liwa*s attended the accession ceremonies held in Baghdad on August 23, 1921.[7]

It is apparent from the foregoing discussion that the situation with regard to the Mosul *wilayat* was extremely complicated. The Kurds in particular were in an unenviable position. Emboldened by such promising developments as President Wilson's Fourteen Points, the Anglo-French Declaration, and the Treaty of Sèvres, and, in turn, encouraged and rebuffed by the British and cajoled and threatened by the Turks, they were at a loss as to what path they should pursue. Edmonds has well summed up the perplexing situation in which the Kurds found themselves during the period under discussion:

After the signature of the Treaty of Sèvres the Turks had not unnaturally redoubled their efforts to impress upon all the inhabitants of the wilayat that it was not worth the paper it was written on: there were threats of large-scale invasion, clandestine correspondence with leaders of urban society, secret missions to tribal malcontents, open incitements to rebellion, warnings to "traitors," and, pervading all, the religious appeal for loyalty to the Sultan who was also Caliph. The principal targets of this propaganda, the Kurds, now found themselves torn by every kind of conflicting emotion: loyalty to their religion, respect for and fear of the might of their late masters, dreams of an independence obtainable only with a support which the British seemed unwilling to give, impatience with the restraints imposed by the authority actually governing them, a lively realization that economically they were bound hand and foot to Baghdad, and reluctance to accept subordination, even with a measure of autonomy, to an Arab Kingdom.[8]

Turkish Agitation and Disorder in Iraqi Kurdistan

Major Soane, the British political officer for the Sulaymaniya division, had managed to maintain a remarkable degree of tranquillity, even during the difficult period of Shaykh Mahmud's rebellion.[9] His successor, Major H. A. Goldsmith, seemed to be doing just as well when a sudden rash of disturbances shattered the deceptive tranquillity in the Sulaymaniya division as well as in other parts of British-administered Kurdistan. These disturbances were known to have been instigated by the Turks.

In the winter of 1921–22, Mahmud Khan Dizli, who was in touch with Turkish agents, began a series of depredations in the Halabja district and his activities had to be checked by force. However, he remained a potential source of trouble until an agreement was reached with him at the end of May 1922.[10] One of the lesser insurgents continued to give trouble until he was defeated and his forces dispersed by a combined operation carried out by the levies and the British Royal Air Force (RAF) after an attack at Bani Banok in the neighborhood of Halabja.[11]

Early in the spring of 1922, the Turkish government took a drastic step, which was to inaugurate a period of Turkish forward policy in Iraqi Kurdistan and to throw the entire region into a state of ferment for many months to come. On March 17, 1922, the Turkish government appointed a certain agent, Ramzi Beg by name, as *qaimmaqam* of Rawanduz and sent him forthwith to that district. Toward the end of May, shortly after his arrival in that town, he started an intensive campaign among the tribes, using threats and blandishments. He spoke of the imminent arrival of large Turkish forces whose object was to wrest Sulaymaniya, Kirkuk, and Arbil from the British.[12] About the middle of June 1922, Ramzi Beg was followed by a certain Colonel 'Ali Shafiq al-Misri, who was popularly known as Özdemir. The latter made it known on his arrival that his mission was the reconquest of the Mosul *wilayat*.[13]

By the end of May 1922, the activities of the Turkish agent bore fruit. Impelled by some personal grudge, Sayyid Muhammad, chief of the Jabbari tribe, who it will be recalled was one of the partisans of Shaykh Mahmud in the rebellion of 1919, attacked and wounded the *mudir* (subdistrict officer) and called on his followers to rise against the government. His action appears to have appealed to Karim-i Fattah Beg, leader of a large section of the unruly Hamawand tribe and another 1919 rebel.

Karim-i Fattah Beg began his antigovernment movement in a rather unusual manner. He started by sending threatening letters to the assistant political officer, Captain Bond. Later he seemed to change his attitude and pretended that he regretted his earlier action. He invited Captain Bond and Captain Makant, who was in charge of the local levies, to meet him at a village in the neighborhood of the Bazyan Pass on June 18. Despite warnings by friendly chieftains, the two men considered it their duty to accept his invitation. Upon reaching the meeting place, the two officers were completely deceived by the cordial reception that the Hamawand chieftain accorded them and were shot in the back while riding by his side.

Having thus challenged the British administration's authority in this flagrant manner, Karim-i Fattah Beg now joined the insurgent Jabbaris.[14] For more than a month the levies and the RAF scoured the country in search of him, but he appears to have successfully eluded his pursuers. By the end of July 1922, he was reported to have gone north and joined the Turks.[15]

In the meantime, the levies that had arrived in the Pizhdar region in pursuit of the fleeing Hamawand chieftain, found the pro-British Pizhdar chief, Babakir Agha, sorely pressed by the hostile section of his tribe. The presence of the levies in the Pizhdar region redressed the balance of power and helped Babakir Agha to reestablish his authority over his tribe. The situation in that region was further stabilized by the intervention of Simko Agha of the Shikak, and his ally, Sayyid Taha of Nehri, in favor of the administration. These two Kurdish leaders are said to have warned the chieftains of the Persian Kurds across the frontier against lending their support to the rebellious elements in Sulaymaniya.[16]

The Situation at Ranya

The situation at Ranya had been steadily deteriorating owing to the presence of Özdemir and his organization at Rawanduz, on the one hand, and of 'Abbas-i Mahmud, leader of the hostile section of the Pizhdar, in the nearby Pizhdar region, on the other. Aware of the inherent dangers of the situation, the political officer, C. J. Edmonds, had been making earnest appeals for the dispatch of military forces to punish the recalcitrant elements before matters got out of hand. His appeals had gone unheeded, but conditions in that region, which continued to be serious, had not grown worse.[17]

However, the situation at Ranya was adversely affected by another recent development. The arrival of the Hamawand chieftain Karim-i Fattah Beg among the Turks encouraged them to hope for tribal cooperation. In pursuance of this aim, they sent small parties of Turks southward in the direction of Ranya, where they were joined by the hostile Pizhdar tribesmen of 'Abbas-i Mahmud and by the Hamawand tribesmen of Karim-i Fattah.[18] As part of an overall plan to rouse the tribes, Özdemir had sent letters to all the leading men of the Nawdasht area urging them to join his forces. This tactic conformed to the pattern of propaganda applied with such conspicuous success earlier in the Rawanduz region.[19]

On July 27, 1922, Colonel E. C. T. Minet and his Sulaymaniya levies arrived suddenly in the Darband. Karim-i Fatta Beg had crossed the Zab at Dukan and was hurrying toward Rawanduz. Minet had lost no time in setting out after the Hamawand chieftain in the hope of being able to intercept him before he reached his destination, but the report turned out to be premature.[20]

The arrival of the Sulaymaniya levies at the Darband appears to have had a salutary effect on the wavering tribes in the neighborhood of Ranya, and for the time being the situation was stabilized. However, this respite was destined to be of short duration.

Shortly thereafter Colonel Minet decided that he should retire to Sulaymaniya in order to "refit and recuperate." He did so with the bulk of his force, leaving behind a detachment with one hundred rifles and four machine guns.[21]

Meanwhile, Karim-i Fatta Beg succeeded in arriving at Rawanduz with a contingent of his Hamawand tribesmen. The Turks, encouraged by this new accession to their power, which greatly enhanced their prestige as well as their offensive capabilities in the region, lost no time in hastening their preparations for the descent upon Ranya. "By the 12th," said the political officer at Ranya, "it was clear that we were back where we had been before Minet's arrival and that the crisis was upon us."[22]

The political officer again made frantic appeals for the dispatch of ground troops and for the initiation of air operations against tribal forces now being readied by the Turks for the forthcoming advance on Ranya. Finally, on the evening of August 17, 1922, the political officer was informed by telegram that a force to be called "Ranicol" (Ranya Column) was being formed with the object of going into action against the Turco-Kurdish forces in the Ranya region. However, it was many days before Ranicol materialized. When it did, its strength was considerably below that originally promised. Ranicol, which had established its headquarters at Darband-i Ramkan on August 29, was attacked in the early hours of the morning of August 31 by Özdemir's forces.[23]

The column commander's indecision and poor leadership apparently were largely responsible for the ensuing defeat. By the end of the day, finding that the force was incapable of holding on to its position at the Darband, the commander ordered a retreat. But because he had issued conflicting orders to his subordinate at Ranya during the day, that town had been lost to the enemy, and he had to retire to Koi Sanjaq instead. What was intended to be an orderly retreat was soon turned into a rout by the pursuers, who swarmed down from the neighboring hills to direct damaging fire on the flanks and rear of the retreating force. After suffering many casualties and losing most of its equipment, Ranicol was in headlong flight in the direction of Koi Sanjaq. It was saved by the timely appearance of the RAF, which bombed and machine-gunned the attackers and forced them to give up the pursuit.[24]

Soane stated a year later that Turkish successes in the Ranya region were greatly assisted by the British government's uncertain policy in Kurdistan as well as by Simko's defeat in northern Persia, which induced many of his followers to seek employment with the Turks.[25] No doubt many factors weighed heavily in favor of the Turks. Yet there is no question that their defeating Ranicol (despite its relative unimportance from a military point of view) was a notable achievement. The fact that a small force with very limited resources succeeded in rousing a large part of the Kurdish countryside and was able to defeat a British-led force in British-controlled territory is a tribute to the skill, courage, and organizing ability of a handful of Turkish officers. A British official report attributed the sudden deterioration of the Ranya situation to fantastic rumors regarding the imminent arrival of great Turkish forces. This, no doubt, must have convinced many waverers that it was to their advantage to join the anti-British movement.[26] The Turks, of course, had set these reports in motion.

The Evacuation of Sulaymaniya

The foregoing events in the Ranya region appear to have induced the British to take precipitate action in Sulaymaniya. Fearing that their enemies, now in control of the Ranya and the Pizhdar regions, might make a sudden descent on Sulaymaniya, the high commissioner ordered the evacuation of the town in order not to risk the lives of British and other officials.[27]

Before leaving the town, the political officer, Major Goldsmith, had entrusted the administration of the division to the Elective Council, which had been associated with him in accordance with the high commissioner's announcement of May 6, 1921. The council had in turn chosen Shaykh Qadir, Shaykh Mahmud's younger brother, to be president. The latter, who had been in Baghdad, had been permitted to return to Sulaymaniya a few days earlier. With this transfer of authority went the handing over of the contents of the treasury and the armory.[28]

Members of the Barzinja family, who had been clamoring for the shaykh's return, were informed that in view of their abstention from participation in the recent disorder, Shaykh Mahmud was being allowed to proceed to Baghdad and that the future administration of their province would be settled after his arrival. This, then, is how the situation had developed on the eve of Shaykh Mahmud's return to Sulaymaniya.[29]

The rout of the British column in the Ranya area, coupled with the precipitate evacuation of Sulaymaniya, had greatly encouraged the Turks and their adherents. Before long, a Turkish reconnaissance party appeared on the Lesser Zab and threatened to disrupt British lines of communication. Prior to that, a small Turkish force had occupied Koi Sanjaq and then moved on to occupy Taqtaq on the Lesser Zab. In the former place, the Turks had appointed a *qaimmaqam* and in the latter a *mudir nahiya* (subdistrict officer).[30] The Shaykh Bizaini tribe, located on both banks of the Lesser Zab on the main road between Kirkuk and Koi, were reported to have thrown in their lot with the Turks.[31]

The Turks now contemplated other ambitious moves. 'Abbas-i Mahmud Agha, chief of the hostile Pizhdar faction, was sent at the head of a tribal force and a number of Turkish regulars to threaten Sulaymaniya. The notables of Sulamaniya, however, prevailed on the Pizhdar chieftain to halt his advance in the Surdash area pending the arrival of Shaykh Mahmud.[32] Preparations were also said to have been set in motion for an attack on 'Aqra.[33] However, before a month had passed, determined action by the RAF and British levies initiated a series of countermeasures that were to restore British control throughout the disaffected areas.

The Reinstatement of Shaykh Mahmud

The Shaykh's Unrealistic Plans and Expectations

By the spring of 1922, the situation in Iraqi Kurdistan had deteriorated to such an extent that the British decided once more to turn to Shaykh Mahmud, who, it will be recalled, had been exiled to India after the failure of his rebellion in 1919. We are informed that Shaykh Mahmud's adherents, led by his influential Barzinja relatives, had for some time been agitating for his return and reinstatement.[34] However, this movement does not seem to have had the necessary support throughout the Sulaymaniya division. In the south, the Jaf Begzada are reported to have viewed the possibility of the shaykh's return and reinstatement with grave misgivings. In the north, among the Pizhdar, as we have seen, a group led by Babakir Agha was strongly opposed to the shaykh, whereas another group led by 'Abbas-i Mahmud Agha strongly supported him.[35]

Whatever the nature of local popular sentiment toward Shaykh Mahmud may have been, it appears that the British had been toying with the idea of his return and reinstatement many months before the matter became a public issue.[36] In the preceding autumn, he had been brought from India to Kuwait, where, as it were, he was being held in readiness for his forthcoming assignment. In the meantime, his brother, Shaykh Qadir, had proceeded to Sulaymaniya, where, as mentioned earlier, he had been chosen president of the Elective Council.

On September 12, 1922, Shaykh Mahmud arrived in Baghdad. In the course of the negotiations that took place there, Shaykh Mahmud undertook not only to prevent the Turks from occupying the town of Sulaymaniya, but also to expel them from other parts of the division. He also agreed not to interfere in the affairs of the Kirkuk and Arbil divisions. In return, both the British and the Iraqi governments would do everything in their power to assist the shaykh in rallying Kurdish national sentiment. With King Faysal's permission, a number of Kurdish officers from the Iraqi army were seconded for service with Shaykh Mahmud to help him organize his levy forces.[37]

Shaykh Mahmud, who traveled by easy stages to Sulaymaniya, arrived at his destination on September 30, 1922, accompanied by Major Noel, the British officer who was to serve as his advisor. Along the route to Sulaymaniya, Shaykh Mahmud was acclaimed by tribal deputations amid scenes of great enthusiasm. In Sulaymaniya, where he took over the presidency of the Elective Council from his brother, he was greeted as the ruler of Kurdistan. The local press described Major Noel as some sort of a consul.[38] By conferring diplomatic status on the Shaykh's British advisor, the Sulaymaniya nationalists no doubt sought to emphasize the independence of the Kurdish enclave under Shaykh Mahmud and its separateness from Iraq.

On October 10, 1922, Shaykh Mahmud issued a decree announcing the formation of an eight-member cabinet.[39] The cabinet members included Shaykh Qadir, his brother, as prime minister; Salih Zako Saliqiran, a member of a renowned local family, as minister of national defense; Haj Mustafa Pasha, a former Ottoman general, as minister of national education; and 'Abd al-Karim Alaka, the leading Christian notable of Sulaymaniya, as minister of finance.[40] The shaykh also issued postage stamps and published a newspaper, *Rozh-i Kurdistan* (Sun of Kurdistan).[41] An official British report pointed out that tribal chieftains from both sides of the border enjoyed great influence in the shaykh's administration and added sarcastically: "It was, perhaps, not without significance that the Ministry of Justice remained unfilled."[42]

The Growing Discord Between the Shaykh and the British

Before long, serious friction developed between Shaykh Mahmud and the British. It was perhaps inevitable. He had been brought back on condition that he would take what he was offered, and he had agreed. Finding himself once more in a position of authority, he could not resist the glittering prize that, in the midst of all the chaos around him, seemed within his reach. The shaykh was a man with a deep sense of mission, a nationalist who believed himself to be the pioneer and the paladium of a future Kurdish state. He was ambitious and headstrong and on occasion showed that he could be egotistical and unscrupulous.[43]

Shaykh Mahmud was not unaware of the implications of his reinstatement. Whether the British had bowed before a popular demand for his return, or whether they were too weak to control Kurdistan without him, his reinstatement clearly proved that they must have regarded him as the most important personality in southern Kurdistan. The Turks had recently made remarkable headway against the British, and the latter seemed powerless to stop them. The situation was confused, unsettled, and dangerous. Now that the shaykh was back, the question boiled down to this: Was he going to hold down the country for such a trifling reward as the governorship of Sulaymaniya and its environs? After all, he was incurring serious risks by opposing the Turks, who still seemed formidable and who spoke confidently of coming back. If he were going to run such great risks, he might just as well play for high stakes.

The uncompromising attitude of the Arab rebels in southern Iraq had paid handsome dividends recently. It is true that the rebellion had been put down, the rebel demands for an Arab government had been met, and no important rebel leader had suffered. If the shaykh were to play his hand right, there was much to be gained: for the Kurds, an independent state; for himself, a kingship and immortal fame.

Had he had any doubts about himself, they must have been dissipated by his reinstatement and by the tumultuous reception given him by the tribal deputations. In addition, there were the Kurdish nationalists around him, embellishing his dreams and goading him into action. These thoughts must have exercised the shaykh's mind shortly after his arrival in Sulaymaniya, for he soon began showing signs of being difficult and of casting covetous eyes on the neighboring Kurdish regions in whose affairs he had promised not to interfere.

Shaykh Mahmud's restless ambition and his impatience to grasp more power than he had been allowed soon became manifest. In November 1922, he assumed the title of shah or king of Kurdistan.[44] He now claimed authority over all Kurdish areas within Iraq. According to an official British report, he did so regardless of the fact that neither Arbil nor Kirkuk nor the Kurdish *qada*s (districts) in the Mosul division had expressed any desire to submit to his rule. The report admitted that the Kurdish tribes of Kifri in the Kirkuk division had declared their adherence to Shaykh Mahmud, but it pointed out that the tribes in question had been induced to do so by the prospect of the complete absence of any restrictions under his rule.[45]

15. Shaykh Mahmud with gunners. Photographer unknown/Courtesy of Giw Mukryan.
Kurdistan: In the Shadow of History.

Hardly a month had passed since the shaykh's reinstatement when he was discovered to be in touch with the Turks. The capture of dispatches sent by Özdemir to Turkish military headquarters at Jazirat ibn 'Umar revealed the nature of his negotiations with the Turks.[46] Özdemir, while addressing the shaykh in flattering terms, was very careful not to commit himself in any way. In the words of an official British report, "He evaded every request to make a pronouncement in favour of Kurdish autonomy, and in writing to a Turkish Committee formed in Kirkuk he gave frequent assurances that his Government had no intention of favouring the pretensions of Shaikh Mahmud. He was in fact using him merely as a pawn in the game, the object of which was to recapture the Mosul wilayat with or against the wishes of the inhabitants."[47]

Shaykh Mahmud probably thought that he could serve his interests best by playing the Turks against the British. But moderate persons in Sulaymaniya viewed with alarm his intrigues with the Turks. Many of them are reported to have been alienated from him by the arbitrary methods of his rule and by his unpredictable behavior. Some of the most influential members of the shaykh's own family, who but a few months earlier had been pressing for his return, seemed now convinced that he was incapable of directing the affairs of the province.[48]

By this time, the British apparently despaired of working successfully with Shaykh Mahmud. In November 1922, a delegation from Sulaymaniya came to Baghdad in response to an invitation from the British civil high commissioner. The object of the invitation was to reach an agreement with the shaykh regarding his position and the future relationship of Sulaymaniya to the rest of the country. Progress in the negotiations was declared to be impossible because of the shaykh's extravagant claims, and the delegation returned to Sulaymaniya with nothing accomplished.[49]

The Changed Situation of the Kurds in Iraq

The Effects of the Lausanne Conference

The future of the Kurds in Iraq and thus the very nature of the Kurdish question in that country were to be profoundly influenced by the negotiations then in progress at Lausanne. The Treaty of Sèvres, it will be recalled, had provided for an autonomous Kurdish state in eastern Anatolia. At the same time, it had provided for the inclusion of the Iraqi Kurds in the proposed Kurdish state. Under that treaty, their connection with Iraq was of a temporary nature and could be terminated after the passage of one year, subject to the fulfillment of certain conditions,[50] by their adherence to the projected Kurdish state. In the Treaty of Lausanne,[51] which was to supersede the Treaty of Sèvres, the whole idea of creating a Kurdish state was abandoned. This change radically altered the position of the Kurds in Iraq and necessitated a reconsideration of the whole question of their future relationship with that country.

Increasing attention was now being given to the idea of integrating the Kurdish areas into the newly created Iraqi state. The Turks, of course, strongly resisted this idea. A bitter struggle over these areas ensued between Turkey and Great Britain at Lausanne and in the League of Nations. It was this struggle that formed the substance of the celebrated "Mosul question." The Turkish delegates at Lausanne pressed for the return of the Mosul *wilayat* to Turkey on the basis that the majority of the inhabitants were non-Arab. This demand was countered by the argument that the majority of the inhabitants—namely, the Kurds—were not Turkish either and that "economically and strategically these areas were too closely welded with Iraq to suffer amputation."[52]

The British now sought to find a modus vivendi whereby both Kurds and Arabs would live amicably under the same crown. Faysal is said to have been willing to "extend to the Kurdish provinces within Iraq a full measure of local autonomy," but it was for the Kurds themselves to decide in what manner it was to be exercised. On this matter, there does not seem to have been general agreement among the Kurds.[53]

The Anglo-Iraqi Declaration of December 24, 1922

Faced by the Turks' unrelenting attitude, on the one hand, and by Shaykh Mahmud's growing nationalist agitation, on the other, the British and Iraqi governments decided to make a policy declaration designed to placate and if possible to win over the moderate and still uncommitted Kurdish public opinion. In the words of the high commissioner's report, "The moment seemed ripe for a definite pronouncement on the part of the British and Iraq Governments which should curb Shaykh Mahmud's ambitions and at the same time give assurance to the moderate party to the effect that their legitimate aspirations would not be neglected."[54] With this end in view, the following declaration was issued on December 24, 1922, with the prior approval of King Faysal and his cabinet:

His Britannic Majesty's Government and the Government of the Iraq recognize the rights of the Kurds living within the boundaries of the Iraq to set up a Kurdish Government within these boundaries, and hope that the different Kurdish elements will, as soon as possible, arrive at an agreement between themselves as to the form which they wish that Government should take, and the boundaries within which they wish it to extend, and will send responsible delegates to Baghdad to discuss their economic and political relations with His Britannic Majesty's Government and the Government of the Iraq.[55]

Edmonds more than hints in his later comments on this declaration that it was not made seriously or in good faith. As a political officer, he was one of those officials entrusted with making the declaration known to tribal chieftains, shaykhs, and other leaders of Kurdish public opinion. He has left us a record of his reaction after translating the declaration to Shaykh 'Abd al-Karim of Qadir Karam: "This text, in particular the use of the words 'Kurdish Government' rather than 'Kurdish administration' and the absence of any geographical definitions, went far beyond anything which the previous attitude of the Iraqi Government, indeed of the High Commission, had led me to expect, and I translated it orally to Abdul Kerim with some misgiving. In Baghdad, however, they had felt no such qualms and had published it simultaneously in an official communiqué."[56]

The Activities of Sayyid Taha of Nehri

Prior to Shaykh Mahmud's reinstatement, Sayyid Taha had been one of those considered for the job. However, the rapid march of events and Sayyid Taha's sudden departure to Persia had militated against the further consideration of the matter. At the end of October 1922, Simko Agha of the Shikak and his associate Sayyid Taha had arrived suddenly in Arbil after Simko's defeat by joint Turco-Persian military operations. The position and circumstances of the two men were quite dissimilar. Simko, who was a Persian subject, was soon reconciled to his government and returned to Persia, where before long he was again in trouble. But his story has already been told.[57]

Sayyid Taha of Nehri, a grandson of the famous Shaykh 'Ubayd Allah, was a Turkish subject and owned property in Iraq in the neighborhood of Rawanduz. Consequently, his position in Iraq was quite different from that of Simko.[58] He was soon in touch with the British authorities in Iraq with a view to lending his support for the expulsion of the Turks from the Rawanduz region.

It is evident from his statements that Sayyid Taha was resolutely opposed to the Kemalists and that he had neither the desire nor the hope of reaching an understanding with them. He declared his intention of rallying the tribes against them in the Rawanduz region, where he had considerable influence. Sayyid Taha asked for and received rifles, ammunition, and money in order to organize armed tribal opposition to the Turks. Other British arrangements entered into with him included putting under his disposal a contingent of Kurdish volunteers to be released from the Iraqi army with the object of strengthening his tribal forces.[59]

Exceptionally heavy rains apparently prevented Sayyid Taha from undertaking any military operations. Nevertheless, rumors of his impending action apparently produced the desired result on the tribes of the Rawanduz region. His presence in the region reportedly aided the RAF in compelling the Turks to evacuate Ranya, thus leaving the pro-administration Babakir Agha in control of the Pizhdar. According to the high commissioner's report, the anti-Mahmud forces in Sulaymaniya welcomed the emergence of Sayyid Taha as a new force in Kurdish politics that offered some hope for counteracting their opponent's activities.[60]

The role Sayyid Taha hoped to play did not materialize for a number of reasons. In addition to the heavy rains that rendered military operations impossible, it seems that the Ordinance Department had issued him old equipment, much of which had to be discarded as unserviceable. He also overestimated his influence among the tribes, for even the Herki, upon whom he particularly counted, displayed no special enthusiasm for his cause. Moreover, Sayyid Taha's plan of action apparently did not meet with British approval. According to Edmonds, "He seemed to have no plan for his own activities and to be counting on indiscriminate bombing, not only of hostile targets but also of tribal chiefs who hesitated to cooperate with him."[61]

Sayyid Taha was appointed *qaimmaqam* of Rawanduz in April 1923. It is interesting to note that this appointment, which was sponsored and pressed for by Sir Henry Dobbs, the high commissioner at the time, was opposed by the Iraqi government and a number of British officials.[62]

Shaykh Mahmud's Cooperation with the Turks

In the meantime, the situation in Sulaymaniya deteriorated, and the prospect for an improvement seemed dimmer than ever. Shaykh Mahmud was reported to have suddenly found himself in desperate need of funds. Within the first three weeks of his arrival in Sulaymaniya after his reinstatement, the shaykh squandered most of the large amount of money he found in the treasury on gifts to visiting tribal chieftains and on the upkeep of their retainers. By collecting the excise duty on tobacco in addition to the tithe, he soon discovered a means to replenish his empty treasury. The tobacco merchants, rather than have their trade brought to a standstill, submitted to this imposition. The shaykh was reported to have succeeded in collecting 150,000 rupees by this means.[63]

Having become financially self-sufficient again, Shaykh Mahmud spurned the advice of moderate elements who, some time earlier, had urged him to adopt a more amenable attitude toward the British. He now reverted to his earlier stand. Not only did he refuse to attend a conference at Kirkuk, but the two delegates he sent on his behalf on January 23, 1923, displayed such an unbending attitude that nothing was accomplished. They were sent back to Sulaymaniya with the understanding that negotiations would be conducted only in accordance with the terms of the recent Anglo-Iraqi Declaration.[64]

A rapid series of developments followed. At the end of January 1923, Turkish officers visited Shaykh Mahmud in Sulaymaniya, where a plan for a concerted tribal attack on Kirkuk and Koi Sanjaq was formulated. Contacts were established with the Shi'i ulama of Karbala and Najaf, while the Turkish Committee in Kirkuk began to make feverish preparations for the forthcoming rebellion.[65] Özdemir, on his part, planned to follow up the attack on Kirkuk by an attack on Arbil. With this end in mind, he apparently got in touch with a Persian army commander across the border in order to obtain the latter's agreement concerning the passage of his forces across Persian territory and the recruitment of Kurdish tribal irregulars from Persia.[66]

British Action to Forestall the Shaykh's Rebellion

Fearful of the consequences, the British high commissioner decided on immediate action. The tribal opponents of Shaykh Mahmud from among the Hamawand, the Pizhdar, and the Jaf were contacted and put in a state of readiness.[67] On February 16, 1923, a conference was called in Baghdad to discuss the situation in Sulaymaniya. The conference, which was attended by British civil and military officers, ended by adopting the following plan of action:

> (1) On the 21st the High Commissioner would telegraph to Mahmud instructing him to come to Baghdad; (2) Failing his compliance a force of aircraft would demonstrate over Sulaimani and drop notices announcing his dismissal and giving him five more days within which to report in Baghdad together with all the members of the Administrative Council; (3) Two companies of the 14th Sikhs would be moved by rail to Kingirban and ferried thence by air (a novel operation at that time) to Kirkuk, to reinforce the Levies as a precaution against any impulsive drive in our direction; and (4) The barracks and Mahmud's headquarters at Sulaimani would be bombed if he refused to leave the town.[68]

No time was lost in implementing all four points. Edmonds conveyed the high commissioner's message to Shaykh Mahmud on the evening of February 20. The shaykh asked for an amplification, but Edmonds informed him that he was not authorized to discuss his superior's instructions.[69] According to the high commissioner's report to the Colonial Office, Shaykh Mahmud not only failed to comply with the message instructing him to proceed to Baghdad, but continued to elaborate his plans for the forthcoming attack on Kirkuk.[70] By February 22, Sikh forces had been successfully conveyed by rail and plane to Kirkuk. On February 23 and February 24, British planes dropped proclamations over Sulaymaniya to the effect that Shaykh Mahmud, who had failed to carry out his duties, had been dismissed.[71] On the evening of February 24, Shaykh Mahmud made a last minute attempt to reach a reconciliation with the British. However, several hours of negotiation by telegram with Edmonds failed to produce the desired result.[72]

Shaykh Mahmud apparently tried to gain time by hinting that he had decided to resign, but he was reported to have dispatched a column of levies to Chamchamal with the object of threatening Kirkuk.[73] He was ordered to leave Sulaymaniya by March 1, and the inhabitants were warned that, unless he complied, action would be taken against the town. The order went unheeded, and on March 3, 1923, government buildings in Sulaymaniya were bombed from the air.

The bombing of that town coincided with the arrival in Kirkuk of a deputation from Sulaymaniya that included Shaykh Qadir (Shaykh Mahmud's brother) and Haj Mustafa Pasha. Upon learning of the latest developments, members of the deputation spent a long time communicating with Shaykh Mahmud by telegram, urging him to leave the town. Shaykh Mahmud appears to have yielded to these appeals, for he was reported to have left Sulaymaniya in the early hours of March 4, 1923, accompanied by some two hundred levies and the contents of the treasury.[74] He was said to have taken refuge in the mountains of Surdash, north of Sulaymaniya. There he was visited by Özdemir, who reportedly urged him to recapture the town.[75]

In the early part of March, some of Shaykh Mahmud's followers concentrated in the vicinity of Sulaymaniya were located and dispersed by air action.[76] The shaykh nevertheless remained defiant and unrepentant. According to reports, he established headquarters at the great Jasana Cave in the Surdash area and billeted his forces in the neighboring villages, where he continued to collect revenue and to exercise his authority as previously.[77]

At the time of his flight from Sulaymaniya, Shaykh Mahmud had not forgotten to take the municipal printing press, which he soon put to good use. On March 8, 1923, he began the publication of a newspaper, *Bang-i Haqq* (the Voice of Truth or Voice of Reality).[78] This paper, which replaced *Rozh-i Kurdistan* as Shaykh Mahmud's official organ, stated that it was printed at the "General Headquarters of the Army of Kurdistan." Its contents comprised a single item, a proclamation of a jihad or holy war.

It was becoming increasingly evident that unless Shaykh Mahmud and his followers were dislodged from their hideouts in the Surdash area and dispersed, not only would Sulaymaniya continue to be at his mercy, but Kirkuk also would be constantly menaced. The British realized that under these circumstances it would be impossible to reestablish peace and stability in the area. However, it was quite clear that no matter what measures might be adopted in the Sulaymaniya-Kirkuk region, no permanent settlement could be achieved here or elsewhere in Kurdistan unless Özdemir's challenge was met and overcome. Shaykh Mahmud had been reduced to the position of a hunted fugitive, but Özdemir, who had been going from one success to another, was still on the march. Of the two, the latter was clearly the more formidable source of danger. For this reason, the British decided to deal with him first.

The Defeat of Özdemir

One of the decisions reached at the Cairo Conference was the transfer of the command of all British forces in Iraq from the army to the air force. This transfer was to take effect on October 1, 1922. The newly appointed air commander, Air Vice-Marshal Sir John Salmond, lost no time in adopting a number of measures that were to culminate in the defeat of Özdemir and the dispersal of his forces.[79]

Planes based at Mosul and Kirkuk unleashed a vigorous air offensive against the principal Shaykh Bizaini villages located along the middle course of the Lesser Zab River, as well as against the Turkish-held barracks at Koi Sanjaq. Levies under Colonel Minet, operating in close cooperation with the air force, found little resistance. By October 7, 1922, the Turks had abandoned Koi Sanjaq, and most of the Shaykh Bizaini chiefs made overtures for submission. The scene of air operations now shifted to the north, where hostile forces were subjected to continuous bombing from the air in the Ranya, Marga, and Pizhdar areas. The Shawur Valley, through which passed the main route connecting these areas with Rawanduz, was likewise constantly under heavy attack.[80] These operations continued during the autumn of 1922 and the following winter.

In March 1923, preparations were completed for strong ground forces to take the field against Özdemir. These forces consisted of two columns, Koicol (Koi Sanjaq Column) under Colonel Vincent and Frontiercol (Frontier Column) under Colonel Dobbin.[81] The two columns, supported by the air force, carried out a simultaneous outflanking movement against Özdemir's position at Spilik Pass. On the night of April 19–20, Özdemir abandoned his position at the pass. The town of Rawanduz, where Sayyid Taha was eventually installed as *qaimmaqam*, was occupied on April 22, 1923. Özdemir and his forces were not heard from again.

Further Operations Against Shaykh Mahmud

Having disposed of Özdemir, the British now decided to concentrate on Sulaymaniya and Shaykh Mahmud. Koicol was charged with the responsibility of reoccupying Sulaymaniya and undertaking such operations as were necessary to defeat Shaykh Mahmud, destroy his prestige, and punish the tribes that had rallied to his support. On May 8, 1923, proclamations were dropped from the air over Sulaymaniya informing the people of the government's decision to reoccupy the town.[82]

Shaykh Mahmud had returned from the Pizhdar region, where he had tried unsuccessfully to rouse the tribes in the rear of Koicol at the time of its operations against Özdemir. The shaykh now sent a letter to the column commander warning him against advancing to Chamchamal. On the following day, Shaykh Mahmud left his headquarters in the direction of Sulaymaniya with the object of resisting the advancing column. However, upon learning that the column had already advanced beyond the Tasluja Pass, the only easily defensible point between the Bazyan Pass and Sulaymaniya, he ordered a hasty retreat in the general direction of the Persian frontier.[83] He was later reported to have retired to Piran, a village located two miles on the other side of the Persian border.[84]

When Koicol reached Sarchinar on the outskirts of Sulaymaniya, it was met by the town notables, who had been asked on the previous day to be there. The column stayed at Sarchinar for one day while Edmonds, in his capacity as political officer, went to Sulaymaniya, where he set up a responsible governing body. Ahmad Beg-i Taufiq Beg was entrusted with the civil administration; Shaykh Qadir was made responsible for public security; and the former members of the police force, together with a former chief of police, were rehired. After receiving the submission of tribal and other deputations, Edmonds left the town and joined Koicol, which on May 17 proceeded to the Rawanduz region to punish the Shilana tribe.[85]

Early in June the Iraqi prime minister and the British high commissioner attended a conference held in Sulaymaniya to discuss the situation with the local notables. The negotiations broke down when the high commissioner was unable to give assurances to the Kurdish leaders that troops would remain in the town until the situation had been stabilized and restored to normal. In retrospect, Edmonds hints that the main reason for the breakdown in the conversations was the fact that the Iraqi side had made no concessions to Kurdish sentiment.[86]

On June 14, members of the temporary council resigned when Edmonds informed them that the British force was due to leave Sulaymaniya in three days. Terrified citizens who had reason to fear the return of Shaykh Mahmud began to make frantic preparations to leave the town.[87] Having thus resigned themselves to the abandonment of Sulaymaniya, the British now sought to establish a scheme that they called the "Cordon Sanitaire," whereby Shaykh Mahmud would be barred from interfering in the affairs of the neighboring areas.[88]

As might be expected, Shaykh Mahmud's followers entered the town soon after the retirement of the British force, but he himself did not return until July 11. Salih Zako Sahliqiran was succeeded by Majid Mustafa as commander of Shaykh Mahmud's force, which was still known as the "Kurdish national army." Having acquiesced in Shaykh Mahmud's return to Sulaymaniya, the British now sought to define his position and to indicate the limits of his jurisdiction. Edmonds addressed the following letter to him:

> H.E. The High Commissioner has heard that you have returned to Sulaimani and has ordered me to inform you that he has made arrangements for the administration of the qazas of Ranya, Qala Diza, Chamchemal, Halabja, Qara Dagh with Sangaw, and for the nahiya of Mawat and that you must not interfere in any way with the above mentioned districts, or with the villages appertaining to the Saiyids of Sargelu. If (which God forbid) you act against these instructions and interfere in the said districts or intrigue against the Government in other ways, the most drastic action will be taken against you. For the present, provided that you do not interfere with the above-specified districts and provided that you do not commit hostile acts, His Excellency does not intend to take action against you.[89]

Notwithstanding this warning, the shaykh had begun to interfere in the affairs of the areas mentioned in the letter. Consequently, his headquarters at Sulaymaniya were bombed, and this was followed by an outbreak of brigandage on the neighboring highways in sympathy with the shaykh.[90] The British punitive gesture does not seem to have daunted the shaykh, for he soon was again trying to extend his influence beyond the prescribed limits. In the meantime, he continued to write to Edmonds and to the high commissioner protesting his innocence and loyalty and insisting that he was misunderstood.[91] To his followers and those around him, he was careful to spread a line of propaganda calculated to maintain his hold on them. According to Edmonds, "His favorite line of propaganda was to the effect that the pronouncements made and the action taken against him had all been for purposes of international tactics, and that he was going to be restored to authority in due course."[92]

Seeing that past admonitions had been of no avail, the government decided to bomb the shaykh again, and his headquarters were attacked from the air on Christmas day 1923. In order to keep him in line, air demonstrations were continued over Sulaymaniya for a number of months.[93]

Shaykh Mahmud's continued insurgence finally convinced the high commissioner that there was no alternative to the reoccupation of Sulaymaniya. The town was duly occupied about the middle of July 1924. The forces employed in the reoccupation, which later were entrusted with garrison duties, consisted of an Iraqi army column, a force of police, a detachment of Assyrian levies, and the RAF. The administration of the region was entrusted to a British political officer, A. J. Chapman, who took over his duties as a *mutasarrif* under the Iraqi government, but was actually accountable to the high commissioner, from whom he took his orders.[94]

Shaykh Mahmud remained at large, making sudden forays against the outlying districts, harrying government forces, receiving or imposing taxes whenever he was able to do so, and flitting back and forth across the Persian border.[95] This state of affairs continued until he was forced to give up the struggle and retire to Persia. Shortly thereafter, in June 1927, he made his submission, was pardoned, and was allowed to return to Iraq where his confiscated property was returned to him.[96]

12 *The Kurdish Rebellions in Turkey*

The 1925 Revolt by Shaykh Sa'id of Piran

The Kurdish revolt of 1925 came at a very crucial period of modern Turkish history. The previous few years had been crowded with grave dangers and epoch-making achievements. In less than half a decade, the Turks had gained a resounding military victory over the Greeks, successfully defied the Allies at Constantinople and elsewhere, scored a brilliant diplomatic victory at Lausanne, and carried out an ambitious program of comprehensive reforms at home. Yet, for all their confidence, the leaders of the new Turkey must have had their fears. If this period was one of enthusiasm, accomplishments, and great expectations, it was also one of transition, uncertainty, and anxiety. Much remained to be done; dangers looming ahead had yet to be encountered and overcome; tasks begun had yet to be completed; ambitions deeply cherished were yet to be attained, and hard-won gains consolidated. Much of what had been achieved was still in a tentative stage. Foes abroad and a growing opposition at home presented serious threats even to the most solid accomplishments.

Notwithstanding all this, the leaders of the new Turkey were in an exultant and expansive mood. They faced the world and their country with defiant confidence and a grim resolve. Success had emboldened them to make a determined bid for the rich Mosul *wilayat*—a former province of their lost empire. But Mosul was in British hands, and the British were determined not to give it up. The impetus of Turkish successes had not spent itself yet, and there was grave danger that the Turks might precipitate a conflict over the disputed province. This question, taken up at the Lausanne Conference, caused so much friction that participants decided by mutual agreement to shelve it for a period of one year.

Relations Between the Kurds and the Turks

During this period, Turkish-Kurdish relations had been steadily deteriorating. The Turks were closely watching the Kurds, who formed the largest non-Turkish racial group left in Turkey after the war and who for this reason constituted a serious threat to the new state's national unity. They were fully aware that a powerful body of Kurdish opinion favored the formation of a separate Kurdish state. During World War I, prominent Kurds had contacted both the British and the Russians with such an end in view. Little had been accomplished at that time, in part because of the general postwar confusion and Allied preoccupation with the Armenian problem. After the war, as we have seen, the Kurds had patched up their differences with the Armenians, and representatives of the two sides had appeared together at the Peace Conference. In fact, at the time of Turkey's defeat and weakness, the Turks themselves, fearful of losing the eastern provinces to the Armenians, had done much to foster Kurdish nationalist aspirations and to encourage the Kurds to demand the creation of an independent Kurdish state in eastern Asia Minor. These vociferous Kurdish demands had borne some tangible results, for in the Treaty of Sèvres, provision had been made for the formation of such a state. But then came the miraculous Turkish revival under Mustafa Kemal, and the Turks first discouraged and later proscribed Kurdish nationalism.

Shortly before the outbreak of the Kurdish rebellion of 1925, Kurdish tribal leaders, intellectuals, and other nationalists had been exiled to western Anatolia, and the use of the Kurdish language had been prohibited.[1] These measures, coupled with the opposition of the largely conservative Kurdish religious and tribal chieftains to the new reforms—which among other things included the suppression of the caliphate and the abrogation of the Shari'a (Muslim canon law)—were no doubt crucial factors in the outbreak of the rebellion.

The rebellion, which began just at the time when the Mosul dispute had reached a critical stage, was destined to have a great bearing upon the conflicting claims of Great Britain and Turkey to that province. It greatly weakened Turkish claims to the largely Kurdish-inhabited province and all but undermined the Turkish government's position. In contrast, it gave peculiar cogency to British contentions and provided invaluable support to the British position—a fact that naturally roused Turkish suspicions and induced them to accuse the British of having fomented the rebellion. Insofar as Kurdish nationalism is concerned, the rebellion could not have occurred at a more opportune time. It dramatized Kurdish nationalist aspirations when all eyes were riveted on the Kurds of the Mosul *wilayat*. Although the rebellion failed to achieve its aims in Turkey, it saved the great Kurdish enclave in Iraq from Turkish domination.

The Outbreak of the Rebellion

The rebellion broke out in March 1925, at the time when the League of Nations Commission was conducting an inquiry in the Mosul *wilayat* south of the so-called Brussels Line to determine whether the inhabitants preferred to remain with the newly created Iraqi state or whether they were in favor of retroceding to Turkey. The outbreak came, as Toynbee pointed out a couple of years later, well to the north of the disputed territory, "in certain districts in which Turkish sovereignty was not at that time contested by any foreign power."[2]

Shaykh Saʿid of Piran, a leader of the Naqshbandi order of Dervishes, led the revolt.[3] Shaykh Saʿid enjoyed great influence in the surrounding regions, not only because of the hereditary sanctity that attached to him, but also because of the matrimonial alliances he had concluded with the neighboring Kurdish chieftains, particularly with the Zazas of the Dersim highlands.[4]

A number of writers have asserted that although Shaykh Sa'id was the titular leader of the rebellion, he was but one of many who conceived the idea and put it into practice. According to them, it was the outcome of a carefully laid plan devised by a number of Kurdish nationalists. The plan for the rebellion was confided to Colonel Khalid Beg, one of the chiefs of the great Jibranli tribe.[5]

The date for a general uprising had been set for March 21, 1925. However, the rebellion broke out prematurely on March 7—fourteen days earlier than had been intended.[6] This inadvertent change of the rebel timetable greatly upset Kurdish military plans. Not only were the various centers of resistance unaware of the outbreak of hostilities and therefore unable to rise simultaneously, but officers designated to direct military operations in specified sectors were unable to join their units in time.[7]

The rebellion spread rapidly, and the rebels advanced on a number of key towns. They succeeded for a time in occupying Kharput but failed to capture Diyarbakr, Arghana, Malatya, and other centers.[8] The rebellion seems to have lost its initial impetus after these reverses. However, even though the spread of the rebellion had been checked, it was still far from being under control. At the high altitudes where much of the fighting was taking place, it was still too early in the season to permit the movement of large masses of men and heavy equipment. Mountain passes were blocked with snow, and the few poor roads were usable only under the greatest difficulties.[9]

The Suppression of the Rebellion

Considerations of strategy and logistics pointed to the necessity of finding an access to rebel territory, protected as it was by impassible mountain barriers. The answer lay in using the Baghdad Railway, a section of which lay in Syria. Consequently, the Turkish government requested permission from the French authorities in Syria to use the Syrian section of the line for the conveyance of Turkish troops and supplies. Permission was granted in accordance with Article 10 of the Franco-Turkish Agreement of October 20, 1921.[10]

In the last week of March 1925, a Turkish counteroffensive was unleashed against the insurgents.[11] The Turkish General Staff's plan appears to have envisaged a vast encircling movement designed to prevent the Kurds from dispersing and later regrouping themselves into small mobile bands capable of waging guerrilla warfare.[12] The Turks succeeded in bringing the main rebel force to battle on April 8, 1925. In a decisive engagement fought in the Chapuqjar district, the rebel army suffered a severe defeat.[13] Shortly thereafter, on April 12, Genj was taken, Shaykh Sa'id and thirty-four of his principal supporters were captured, and the rest of the rebels laid down their arms.[14]

The suppression of the rebellion was accompanied and followed by summary trials, mass deportations, and harsh punitive measures[15] calculated to break the spirit of Kurdish resistance and to extirpate the last vestiges of opposition to Turkish rule. It seems that these measures were designed to be a lesson never to be forgotten. The actual number of persons killed or deported and homes and villages destroyed probably will never

16. Shaykh Sa'id and his collaborators captured by the commanders of the 12th division of the Turkish army, and Isma'il Hakki Beg, the governor of Genc (standing behind wearing a fez). Courtesy of Malmisanij Tayfun.

be known. According to Kurdish sources, civilian losses amounted to 206 villages destroyed; 8,758 houses burned; and 15,206 men, women, and children killed.[16] Two years after the rebellion Sureya Bedir Khan alleged that one million Kurds were murdered or deported.[17] Five years later, Chirguh, in contrast, maintained that more than 500,000 were deported during the winters of 1925–26, 1926–27, and 1927–28, and that more than 200,000 of these deportees lost their lives in the course of their forcible removal to western Anatolia.[18] These same sources claimed that the Kurds suffered 2,400 battle casualties in killed and wounded, and the Turks suffered 50,000 in killed and wounded. The campaign is said to have cost the Turkish treasury 60 million Turkish pounds.[19]

The Trial and Execution of the Rebel Leaders

Special courts-martial known as Tribunals of Independence set to work following the suppression of the rebellion. The most celebrated of these tribunals was the one that tried Shaykh Sa'id and other rebel leaders. In the course of this trial, which opened at Diyarbakr on May 27 and lasted until June 28, the prosecutor and the presiding judge made a number of interesting points. The prosecutor began his indictment with the following words:

> The causes and origins of the latest revolution which broke out in the eastern provinces of the eternal Turkish fatherland are identical with those which in a not too distant past led to the rising of Bosnia and Herzegovina, bordered on three sides by non-Turkish and

non-Moslem races, with those which, in spite of the brotherhood of five centuries, led the Albanians to strike the Turks in the back during the Balkan war, the Turks who have always shown the greatest affection for their compatriots. The ideal and the aim which nurtured the Kurdish revolution are the same which corrupted Syria and Palestine.[20]

In summing up the case against the accused, the president of the court addressed them as follows: "Some of you induced by personal egoism, others by foreign counsel and political jealousies, but all of you motivated by the purpose to set up an independent Kurdish state, started the revolution. Upon the scaffold you shall pay the price of ruined homes and rivers of blood you shed."[21]

Upon the conclusion of the trial, on June 28, 1925, fifty-three Kurdish leaders were condemned to death, and the sentences were carried out immediately.[22] Besides Shaykh Sa'id, those condemned to death included Sayyid 'Abd al-Qadir, son of the famous Shaykh 'Ubayd Allah; a former senator and high Ottoman official; and eight other shaykhs. All Sufi *takiya*s in the eastern provinces were ordered closed.[23]

A brief and bloody postscript to the rebellion followed the execution of the Kurdish leaders at Diyarbakr. Fresh eruptions were reported at Bidlis and Mush and in the Shamdinan district of Hakari.[24] Shaykh 'Abd Allah, a son of Shaykh 'Abd al-Qadir of Nehri (who was among those executed at Diyarbakr), rose to avenge his father's death and was reported to have been successful at first. He was heavily defeated in August, however, and fled across the border into Iraq together with two hundred Kurdish families.[25] A son and a brother of Shaykh Sa'id were also forced to seek asylum in Iraq.[26] Repressive measures were extended to various Kurdish tribes in southeastern Turkey as well as to the remnant of Chaldean and Jacobite Christians in the same part of the country.[27]

Toynbee pointed out that although the Turkish government showed both energy and skill in putting down the rebellion, it displayed poor judgment and lack of political wisdom in dealing with the Kurds and their grievances afterward. The Turks made no concessions to Kurdish nationalist aspirations and resumed with renewed vigor the policies of centralization, Turkification, secularization, and westernization—the same policies that had led to the outbreak of the revolt.[28]

The Causes of the Rebellion of 1925

The Turkish government's viewpoint. The Turkish government portrayed Shaykh Sa-'id's rebellion as a reactionary and retrograde movement led by obscurantist and primitive religious and tribal leaders. These leaders, it maintained, were unwilling to give up their hereditary rights, which were threatened with extinction by Mustafa Kemal's progressive and forward-looking reforms. Official Turkish sources also claimed that the British had instigated the Kurdish rebellion, but this issue is dealt with later.

Whatever truth there may have been in these charges, it was quite obviously in the Turkish government's interest to emphasize the reactionary and religious rather than the nationalist aspects of the rebellion. It will be recalled that the Turkish government was at the time seeking the retrocession of the Mosul *wilayat*—an event that depended entirely on the consent and continued goodwill of the numerous Kurdish populations of that province and the approval of the League of Nations. The Turkish government's official acknowledgment of the nationalistic character of the Kurdish rebellion would have completely undermined Turkey's case. The Turks could not very well admit that Kurds north of the Brussels Line were engaged in a bloody struggle for their independence against the Turkish army, while contending that Kurds south of that line were eager to rejoin the Turkish state.[29]

The Turkish government had another significant motive for stressing the reactionary character of the Kurdish revolt. It gave the regime an excellent opportunity to deal a crippling blow to its opponents. All those who in one way or another were opposed to Mustafa Kemal and disapproved of him or his policies were accused of having conspired with the rebels. They were subjected to various repressive measures and even dragged before the notorious Tribunals of Independence. By this means, dissident voices were silenced and the opposition destroyed.[30]

The controversy over the nature of the rebellion. A number of writers seem to have accepted the Turkish government's viewpoint, not only with regard to the rebellion's reactionary nature but also with regard to the opposition's alleged connections with the rebels. According to August Ritter von Kral,

> It was proved that the leaders, under Siek Said from Genj, west of Lake Van, were in touch with the personal friends of the late Caliph and with the Pretender to the throne Prince Selim, who was living in Syria near the frontier. It was intended that the revolt, using the rallying cry "defend the imperilled faith," should spread like lightning throughout western Anatolia and finally lead to the occupation of the Capital, but it was not able to spread beyond the vilayets near its origin.[31]

Another writer was even more explicit. Speaking of the antireformist group, Sir A. Telford Waugh stated in 1930: "They formed a new party, which they called the Progressive Republican Party. The influence this party exercised may be gauged by a letter written to Sheikh Said, in which it is stated that Kiazim Kara Bekir's party will support the rebels. In fact, Sheikh Said's rebellion derived encouragement from the religious party."[32]

Gentizon, who wrote shortly after the suppression of Shaykh Sa'id's rebellion, appears to have regarded the revolt as a struggle between reaction and progress: "The profound causes which produced the Kurdish revolt are of an administrative and religious nature. The movement was at one and the same time a reaction of Kurdish feudalism against the state and a conflict between the old Turkey attached as it was to the old Islamic traditions and a new, secular and progressive Turkey."[33]

Gentizon pointed out that administrative difficulties grew out of the impact of Western-type reforms on a feudal, impoverished, and politically immature Kurdistan. He compared the Kurdish revolt to the counterrevolution of 1908 and called it an explosion of fanaticism. According to him, Shaykh Sa'id, who had waved the green banner of Islam, was determined to reestablish the Shari'a law.[34]

Rambout takes issue with Gentizon's assertions, pointing out that in the trial of Shaykh Sa'id and his companions, both the prosecutor and the court president made it clear that nationalism was an important motive in the rebellion.[35] As might be expected, most Kurdish and pro-Kurdish sources emphasize the nationalist rather than the religious and reactionary motives of the rebellion.

In 1927, Toynbee expressed serious doubts as to the possibility of knowing with any degree of certainty which of the two motives—the religious and the reactionary, on the one hand, or the nationalist, on the other—was the stronger. He pointed out the difficulty of forming an impartial opinion because of the fact that all or most of the information regarding the rebellion was at the time derived from Turkish sources, and the Turkish government had certain compelling reasons to minimize the nationalist and to magnify the religious and reactionary aspects of the uprising.

In the course of discussing this issue, Toynbee stated at one point: "There is, however, some evidence that the reactionary and fanatical impetus behind the Kurdish revolt was stronger than the national impetus."[36] But he almost reversed himself in the face of further and obviously more convincing evidence:

> On the other hand, it is noteworthy that the revolt did not spread among the Turkish population of Erzerum, Trebizond, and Samsun, who were almost as backward and reactionary as their Kurdish neighbours, and who not long afterwards (in November 1925) rose on their own account against the Angora Government's westernizing reforms. The view that the revolt and its suppression represented a conflict between the Kurdish and the Turkish nationalists, not a conflict between reaction and progress, is supported by the following piece of information which the writer of this survey received from a Turkish friend who is in a position to know the facts: "When the rebels entered Kharput all elements in the town opposed them under the leadership of Nuri Effendi, the candidate of the Progressive Party in a by-election. In fact, the Kurdish insurgents were driven out of Kharput, the day following their entry, by the notables and other inhabitants belonging to two different political parties. Considering that the vilayet of Kharput (Ma'muret l-Azia) is one of the most fanatical vilayets in Eastern Anatolia, the attitude of the inhabitants of this vilayet affords concrete evidence that the character of the revolt was not in the least religious, and that the (Turkish) opposition party had no relation whatever with the rebels."[37]

Toynbee, it should be pointed out, presented the results of his research on this matter in a more succinct and less detailed manner in another work.[38]

The role of both nationalism and religion in the rebellion. Despite the varying interpretations of the Kurds' motives, the Kurdish rebellion of 1925 was the outcome of both nationalistic and religious causes. The Kurds as a whole have generally been strongly attached to their nationality. The spread of modern concepts of doctrinaire nationalism among them and the emergence of a new generation of ardent nationalists rendered them all the more sensitive to any attempt at forcing them to renounce their nationality. For this reason, they resented and resisted the suppression of Kurdish nationalist activity and the prohibition of the Kurdish language. They opposed Turkification because, as the term implies, the Kurd was to be changed into a Turk; this, of course, was tanta-mount to bidding the Kurd to cease to be himself and to assume a new identity. The fu-tility of such an attempt in a time of rampant nationalism is too obvious to need any elaboration.

The Turkish governments' secularizing and westernizing policies, though not ob-jectionable to Kurdish intellectuals, were without any doubt very odious to the mass of the Kurdish people. The religious and tribal chieftains, in particular, were bitterly op-posed to these policies, which ran counter to their most cherished beliefs and threatened their hereditary privileges. In the eyes of devout Kurds, the suppression of the caliphate and the Shari'a law by the leaders of the new Turkey severed the ancient and deeply cher-ished bond of Islamic brotherhood between themselves and the Turks. They felt that they no longer had anything in common with the authors of these impious innovations, who by their own actions had cut themselves off from the rest of the faithful. What was incomprehensible to them was that this alien and renegade government was now telling them that henceforth they were going to be Turks, not Kurds, which was like telling them to renounce their nationality, adjure their faith, and join the company of the impi-ous and the iniquitous. They were not going to submit to such dictation.

Thus it was that a strong Islamic sentiment came to be an important ingredient of Kurdish nationalism. Although the majority of the nationalists may not have shared this solicitude for religion, there is little doubt that they encouraged and fostered the Kurds' religious identity, which promised to unite their compatriots at a time of great national crisis. That they lost no time in pressing this powerful ally into the service of their cause is perfectly understandable. It was not the first time that religion was being manipu-lated. The Turks themselves had often used it as an agent of both division and unity, ac-cording to the way it suited their purposes.

Charges of British Instigation

Another controversial matter was the charge that British intrigue was behind the Kurdish rebellion. This charge has been frequently repeated and widely believed. The Turks, as might be expected, were the first to voice it, but various sources later picked it up and gave it wide currency.

According to Armstrong, Mustafa Kemal in a fit of anger charged that the British were behind the rebellion and that they were providing the rebels with arms and sup-plies. He repeated these charges in the Grand National Assembly:

> But what made it worse was that England was behind it all, . . .England had always used the Kurds to injure Turkey; in the World War she had sent her agents, Lawrence and Noel, to rouse them to stab Turkey in the back; at the Treaty of Sevres she had promised to make them into a separate state; her agents had been found there again this time, arming and inciting the tribes.
>
> England wanted Mosul and its oil. The Kurds were the key to Mosul and the oil of Irak. She was using this backhanded blow to force Turkey to give up Mosul.[39]

Official Soviet sources supported this thesis at one time,[40] and various writers dealing with modern Turkey have alluded to it in their works.[41] Kurdish nationalists and British publicists as a rule have denied these claims.[42] It should be pointed out that the Turks have failed to produce any convincing evidence to substantiate their claims. Whatever the truth of the matter, there is no doubt that the British profited by the unhappy events in Turkish Kurdistan. Shaykh Sa'id's revolt and its suppression were certainly instrumental in deciding the Mosul dispute in favor of Britain.

The Kurdish League: Khoybun

The suppression of the Kurdish revolt of 1925 did not put an end to the Kurds' suffering or to the Turks' worries. The deportation of Kurds was accompanied and followed by various repressive and vexatious measures, while sporadic clashes continued to take place in the eastern provinces. By 1927, it was becoming quite clear from the frequency and magnitude of these clashes that the Kurds were preparing for another trial of strength.[43]

In the spring of 1927, a Kurdish National Congress met on one of the mountains of Kurdistan. The congress, initiated by Kurdish nationalists from Syria, was attended by delegates representing various tribal and urban organizations, as well as by delegates representing rebel fighters who had taken refuge in remote mountain fastnesses.[44] The delegates agreed on a number of comprehensive and ambitious decisions. They decided to dissolve all existing Kurdish nationalist organizations and to amalgamate them into one, the Khoybun (Independence); to continue the struggle "until the last Turkish soldier had left Kurdish soil"; to create a single command; to establish supply depots and munitions dumps; to put an end to Kurdish-Armenian differences; and to designate Kurd Ava at Agri Dagh as the provisional capital of Kurdistan. It was also decided to seek an understanding with the Persian government and the "sisterly" Persian nation and to maintain friendly relations with mandatory powers in Iraq and Syria.[45]

In October 1927, at a meeting held in Beirut, Lebanon, the formation of the Khoybun was officially announced.[46] Emir Jaladet Bedir Khan was elected the first president of the society.[47] In accordance with the agreement made at the Kurdish National Congress, the new organization superseded all the former Kurdish nationalist societies, which voluntarily dissolved themselves and merged to form the new Khoybun.[48] The Agri Dagh revolt was the direct outcome of Khoybun activities.

The Agri Dagh Revolt of 1930

The Khoybun appointed Ihsan Nuri Beg, subsequently known as Ihsan Nuri Pasha,[49] a former staff major in the Turkish army who had commanded a rebel contingent during the 1925 rebellion, as supreme commander of the Kurdish forces at Agri Dagh. It entrusted Ibrahim Pasha Haski Tello with civil administration.

By 1928, a miniature Kurdish state had been created at Agri Dagh. A small army of several thousand well-trained and well-equipped Kurdish fighters had been assembled, arsenals and supply depots established, and the Kurdish flag hoisted.[50] This obviously was the nucleus of the Kurdish state to be. The Turkish authorities could not long remain unaware of or indifferent to these ominous developments. Surprisingly enough, they decided to adopt a conciliatory attitude and initially resorted to negotiation rather than to the use of force.

Turkish Attempts at Conciliation

Deportations were stopped, and a new law was promulgated in accordance with which all Kurds who tendered their submission within three months from the date of the proclamation of the law were to be amnestied. Likewise, all deportees were to be permitted to return to their homes, and all Kurdish nationalists in Turkish prisons were to be pardoned. At the same time, Turkish authorities made various attempts to persuade the Kurds to come to terms. The *wali* of Bayazid was authorized to open negotiations with the rebels at Agri Dagh, and other Turkish officials were instructed to contact various Kurdish leaders with a view to reaching an amicable settlement. All these attempts, however, proved futile. Kurdish nationalists accused the Turks of bad faith, asserting that the Turkish government had no intention of making any concession to Kurdish nationalist aspirations and that it was merely playing for time and trying by devious methods to induce them to lay down their arms.[51]

Having failed to achieve any worthwhile results, the Turkish government decided to negotiate directly with Ihsan Nuri Pasha. With this end in view, it informed the Kurdish leader that an official delegation would wait on him at Shaykhli Copru, a frontier post thirty miles from Bayazid.[52] Ihsan Nuri accepted the invitation and went to the meeting at Shaykhli Copru with an escort of sixty mounted followers. At the meeting, which is said to have taken place sometime around the middle of September 1928, he was offered a general amnesty, which would include him and those under his command, as well as a number of personal benefits if he and his followers laid down their arms and left their mountain stronghold.[53] Kurdish writers claim that Ihsan Nuri turned down these offers because the Turkish delegation had completely ignored Kurdish national aspirations.[54]

The Suppression of the Revolt

Having despaired of reaching a settlement with the embattled Kurdish rebels at Agri Dagh, who represented a grave and growing menace, the Turks decided to resort to arms. In May 1930, two Turkish army corps, the Fourth and the Sixth, were concentrated in the neighborhood of Agri Dagh under the command of General Salih Pasha.[55] The Turks attacked on June 11, 1930, their aim being to destroy the Kurdish forces concentrated at Agri Dagh. On June 15, the Kurdish nationalist forces launched counteroffensives at Tendarek, Igdir, Erdjish, Sipan Dagh, Kagsimat, Shatak, Van, and Bidlis. The Turks, finding themselves suddenly called on to cope with the Kurdish attacks at so many locations, were forced to abandon their attack on Agri Dagh. Furious fighting continued at many points until about the middle of July. The Kurds claimed to have inflicted heavy losses on the Turkish forces.[56] Notwithstanding these claims, however, the Kurds gradually lost the contest.

In August and September 1930, the Kurds launched a series of new diversionary attacks against Turkish forces at various points far to the south of the main battle zone. Fighting is reported to have flared up at such places as Julamerk, Si'irt, Mardin, Severek, and Urfa. The most determined of all these attacks was a powerful thrust in the direction of Diyarbakr carried out by considerable Kurdish forces on September 2, 1930.[57]

This attack appears to have been the last major effort on the part of the Kurdish rebels. The impetus of the rebellion was spent by now, and the weight of superior numbers and resources began to tell. Having gained the upper hand, the Turks were not slow to press their advantage. They sought and destroyed the rebel forces all over the eastern provinces. Those who survived were compelled to flee and disperse, and Ihsan Nuri took refuge in Persia.[58]

The suppression of the revolt was accompanied and followed by drastic punitive measures, which are said to have included deportations, mass arrests, and summary executions.[59] Kurdish villages in the area were bombed and set on fire, and whole communities suffered heavy losses.

The Khoybun and its branches were very active in pleading the cause of the Kurds of Turkey before world opinion, and a delegation was sent to Geneva with the object of acquainting the League of Nations with the plight of their countrymen. The Second International (of the Internationale Ouvriere Socialiste [IOS]), then in session in Zurich, Switzerland, adopted a resolution protesting against the ruthless suppression of the Kurds in Turkey and the violation of the Treaty of Lausanne. The following is a translation of this resolution:

> The executive of the I.O.S. draws the attention of the world to the massacres by means of which the Turkish Government is seeking not only to reduce the Kurds struggling for their liberty but also to exterminate the peaceful Kurdish population that did not take part in the insurrection, and by which means they are seeking to inflict on the Kurdish people the fate of the Armenians without the public opinion of the capitalist countries protesting against this bloody barbarism.
>
> The executive, likewise, draws attention to the serious dangers to peace resulting from the violation of Persian territory by Turkish troops. This is a proof of the scandalous inadequacy of the international organization of the world whereby military forces are capable of penetrating into a territory of a feeble neighbor state without organized humanity being able to extend the necessary protection.
>
> In drawing attention to the dangers that may result from these events in Kurdistan the Executive invites world public opinion to protest at one and the same time against the violence committed by the Turkish oligarchy and against the indifferent silence of the capitalist governments toward the bloody crimes whose victim is the Kurdish people.[60]

The resolution went on to quote Articles 37, 38, 39, 40, and 44 of the Treaty of Lausanne in accordance with which Turkey had undertaken to protect its minorities.[61]

The Turco-Persian Conflict Arising out of the Agri Dagh Revolt

The Agri Dagh revolt led to serious differences between Turkey and Persia. There were charges and countercharges and much mutual recrimination. The Turks accused the Persians of actively supporting the rebels by allowing them to use Persian territory as a base for their operations against Turkey. The Persians denied the charges and countered by accusing the Turks of violating Persian territory. At one point, the situation threatened to develop into an armed conflict, but wiser counsels prevailed. The trouble stemmed from the fact that part of Agri Dagh, which the rebels had been using as their headquarters, was in Persian territory. It was therefore very easy for the rebels to slip across the rugged, unguarded frontier into Persia, where they presumably availed themselves of the immunity afforded by Persian territory to reorganize and obtain necessary supplies. The difficulty was solved by a territorial exchange involving principally the regions of Agri Dagh and Kotur.

The Soviet Union is reported to have offered its services as a mediator—a step, no doubt, motivated by the desire to preserve peace in regions so close to its southern borders.[62] It must have viewed with deep concern the prospect of the outbreak of hostilities between its two southern neighbors over territory contiguous to its Caucasian provinces. It is interesting to note that in making this offer, the Russians were reverting to an old role. For more than seventy years, from 1843 to 1914, Great Britain and czarist Russia had acted, despite many interruptions, as the mediating powers in an effort to settle the vexed question of the Turco-Persian frontier.[63] Britain was no longer associated with Russia in this endeavor, not only because of the changed nature of Anglo-Russian relations, but also because Turkey, one of the two parties to the dispute, would almost certainly have refused a British offer to mediate. The dispute in question had grown out of the rebellion of Agri Dagh, and the Turks were once more accusing the British of having instigated the new Kurdish outbreak.[64]

The Kurds' Position in Turkey after the Revolt

Perhaps the most adverse result of the Agri Dagh revolt, insofar as the Kurds of Turkey were concerned, was the Turkish government's enactment of a repressive law placing the eastern provinces and their Kurdish inhabitants under severe disabilities. A law promulgated on May 5, 1932, created four zones in Turkey, three of which were in Kurdistan. One of these zones was completely evacuated and declared forbidden territory "for sanitary, material, cultural, political, and strategic reasons as well as in the interest of public order."[65] The tribes were declared to be devoid of a legal personality. Consequently, all rights they hitherto enjoyed—including even those based on judgments, decrees, and other legal documents—were rescinded. Likewise, the powers of tribal chieftains and religious shaykhs, together with the various organs and institutions appertaining thereto, were declared abolished, regardless of whatever documents or traditions they were based on. All property formerly regarded as belonging to these organizations or institutions was to revert to the state, and its distribution to new settlers was subject to the decisions and decrees issued by the government. This law also provided for the deportation of tribal chieftains, shaykhs, and other notables living in the eastern provinces to certain designated zones. All those whose mother tongue was not Turkish were under serious handicaps.[66] This, then, was the legal denouement of the Agri Dagh rebellion of 1930. Before long, the wisdom of these measures was to be put to a severe test.

The Dersim Revolt of 1937

In January 1937, a serious revolt broke out in the Dersim highlands. The inhabitants of this isolated and inaccessible region, who speak the Zaza dialect and are adherents of extreme Shi'i tenets, had not participated in any of the previous Kurdish revolts. As Shi'is, they were indifferent to the abolition of the caliphate and were certainly not in sympathy with the religious doctrines propagated by the Sunni Kurdish shaykhs. The intrusion of Turkish secular laws and Turkish arms shattered the linguistic, religious, and geographic isolation that had hitherto checked the spread of Kurdish nationalism among the Dersim Kurds.[67]

The Causes of the Revolt

In January 1937, the publication by the Turkish government of a law designed to enforce assimilation appears to have greatly incensed the Dersim Kurds, and they called mass meetings to discuss the new law. Eventually they decided to send a delegation with a letter of protest to the Turkish military governor, expressing the people's opposition to the new law. According to Kurdish sources, the Turkish governor arrested the emissaries bearing the letter of protest and executed them a few days later at Elazio. In retaliation, the Kurds attacked a convoy of police cars and kidnapped the policemen. This act marked the beginning of the Dersim revolt.[68]

This rebellion, which was led by a religious chieftain, eighty-two-year-old Sayyid Riza of Dersim, blazed for two years, causing heavy losses for both the government and the rebels.[69] In discussing the causes of the revolt, Elphinston has said, "it would appear that the Turkish government policy had, in the first place, antagonized the Kurdish patriarchal feudal leaders; in the second place, it had led to the opposition of the religious leaders, and finally, the Kurdish people themselves had been aroused by the fear that they might lose their separate racial identity."[70] According to him, although these three reasons would seem to be the most obvious and the most tangible, it would be a mistake to attribute the revolts exclusively to them. Behind all these revolts lurked the spirit of nationalism.[71]

The Suppression of the Rebellion and Its Aftermath

Little is known about the conduct of military operations against the Dersim Kurds. Military censorship was extremely tight at the time of the revolt, and for many years afterward the whole of the Dersim (Tunceli) was a restricted area where travel was prohibited and the flow of news was strictly controlled. According to available information, a formidable Turkish force was assembled in the neighborhood of Dersim in May, prior to the initiation of military operations.[72] Strategic points were occupied, and the weight of modern armaments, including aircraft, was brought to bear on the embattled Kurds. The defenders fought desperately but were forced to retire to upland fastnesses with their flocks and families after the destruction of their villages.[73] Despite government claims that the army had the situation under control,[74] according to Elphinston, the Kurds took to guerrilla warfare and continued to defy the army for many months, so that military operations "lasted well into 1938."[75]

The rebels, having reached the limit of their endurance after almost two years of ceaseless fighting, decided to lay down their arms. Sayyid Riza, together with a number of leaders and their families, surrendered to the Turkish army. The leaders were tried and hanged, and large-scale deportations were set in motion.[76]

The Kurds have charged that the Turks resorted to the most inhuman methods to punish the rebels, both during and after the rebellion.[77] There are no official figures to indicate the number of those killed during the rebellion or deported afterward. One source put the number of those who lost their lives at forty thousand;[78] another source put the number of those deported at three thousand families.[79]

The Turks have claimed that religious and reactionary elements among the Dersim Kurds were responsible for the rebellion. According to an article that appeared in *Le Temps* shortly after the outbreak of the rebellion and that seemed to reflect Turkish official thinking, the rebels, before taking up arms, addressed some sort of an ultimatum to the government. In this ultimatum, they reportedly asked the government to withdraw all military forces from the region; stop the construction of various means of transportation such as roads, bridges, and railroads through their territory; reduce taxes; and allow them to retain their arms.[80]

After the suppression of the Dersim rebellion, Jalal Bayer, the then Turkish minister of the interior, was reported to have declared in the Turkish National Assembly that the Kurdish problem no longer existed and that the brigands had been forcibly civilized. According to Elphinston, that statement has remained the official Turkish attitude toward the Kurds, who are still referred to officially in Turkey as "Mountain Turks."[81] The Dersim *wilayat,* or Tunceli, as it is officially called, was declared a closed area and placed under tight military control. In the winter of 1945, the Turkish National Assembly debated this special system of administration in force in the Tunjeli *wilayat* and then put it to a vote. The vote reportedly resulted in a decision prolonging the period for which this system of administration would be in effect.[82]

Signs of a New Turkish Policy toward the Kurds

A year later, in 1946, when the same issue was again brought before the Turkish National Assembly, the result was different. This time the Assembly passed a law terminating the special administrative regime that had been in force in the Tunjeli *wilayat* since the 1937 rebellion.[83] This development seemed to herald a new trend. On March 28, 1947, in the course of an address to university students, the Turkish prime minister paid tribute to the Kurds as good citizens, laying special emphasis on their loyal service in the army.[84]

Despite the fact that many of the old restrictions and handicaps were retained, for the first time in many years Turkish voices were raised to demand justice for the "inhabitants of the East." In 1948 and 1949, the injustices and misdeeds of government functionaries in the eastern provinces were freely discussed in both the Assembly and the press. Some of these discussions were of a general nature and dealt with such matters as maladministration, official negligence, and incompetence, whereas others were more specific and dealt with particular cases.

In 1948, the relatives of thirty-three persons who had been shot down without trial on orders of the subprefect of Bayazid in 1943 brought the matter before the Grand National Assembly. After being debated in the Assembly, it became something of a cause célèbre. The prime minister, Hasan Saka, criticized the shortcomings of the administration in the eastern provinces, pointing out that the inhabitants had been subject to many abuses and that their economic and cultural welfare had been sadly neglected.[85]

Ahmad Emin Yalman, the eminent Turkish journalist, took the occasion to write a sobering article about the necessity of carrying out basic reforms in the region. Some of the points he raised in this article are of particular interest. He stated that none of these provinces was regarded as a colony; that they all formed part of Turkey and enjoyed equal rights; that the Constitution made no distinctions whatsoever between the citizens on account of their religion, race, or other matters; that historical precedent demonstrated that discrimination based on ethnic grounds was inadmissible; that from the point of view of the country's general interests, misused zeal, whether employed in the service of particular interests or of personal passions, did not contribute to the maintenance of public order or to the achievement of public welfare. He then declared:

> As a result of the arbitrary act committed in the name of national security the regime of special administration in force in the eastern provinces has come to be a source of misfortune for this heroic part of the country. For decades the eastern provinces have not known a period of tranquillity. Troubles and revolts have been endemic—a fact that has compelled the government to make sacrifices and to resort to violent measures.
>
> But when the situation in the eastern provinces is considered in the light of fairness, it will be found that the basic reason for these permanent troubles does not lie in the intrigues of foreign powers, nor does it lie in the reactionary tendencies of the population, but that it is the direct outcome of evil administration.
>
> In general the population of the eastern provinces is composed of hard-working people, of disciplined citizens with respect for the law. In recent times Soviet radio broadcasts have reserved an important place for Kurdish propaganda in their programs. We should not ignore the aspect that this question has assumed in Iran and Iraq. Of course, in Turkey there is no Kurdish question in the proper sense of the word.[86]

Yalman went on to say that maladministration and injustices had brought about separatist ideas. He emphasized the fact that the Turks had to guard against providing the enemies of the country, who desired to bring about its ruin, with the opportunity to do so. He concluded by saying, "In Turkey, given a just spirit and a competent administration, there is no problem that is insoluble."[87]

There is no doubt that the ideas and developments that followed in the wake of World War II were largely responsible for the tolerant spirit and liberal approach of many responsible Turks. The introduction of the two-party system in Turkey after the war, which in itself was a manifestation of the new influences at work, greatly helped to mitigate the official attitude toward the Kurds. Under the two-party system—unlike the days when Turkey was ruled by one dominant group and popular support was of no consequence—the candidates of the two competing parties had to woo the electorate.

The Democratic Party, the new party eager to seize power, was particularly active in seeking Kurdish votes. Lord Kinross (Belfour) tells of a conversation he had with a former member of the Turkish Parliament who had represented the People's Party:

> He was critical also of the attitude of the Democrats towards the Kurds. In the past it was the Turkish policy to dominate these rebellious highlanders by force. Today the policy was to educate them, particularly in the Turkish language, and thus gradually to assimilate them into the Turkish community. A firm hand, however, was still required. Turbulent Kurdish Sheikhs had been periodically exiled by the People's Party, to other parts of Turkey. But the Democrats, for electoral reasons, were now allowing them to return. They were also encouraging manifestations of reaction, religious and sartorial, of which he disapproved. The veil was returning. The Kurds in the villages were being allowed, once more, to wear their traditional headdress, instead of the uniform cloth cap; and in Diyarbakr the youth of the city was tending to revert in its costume to the broad baggy trousers of the *ancien regime:* a far cry from the days when Ataturk's police would forcibly cut out the seat of men's trousers with a large pair of scissors. . . . All this, my host considered, was most dangerous.[88]

A more just and equitable treatment of the Kurds in the years immediately following the war seemed to hold some promise for a more enlightened approach to the Kurdish problem in Turkey. In conformity with the new postwar trend, the Turkish government was reported to have adopted a number of measures intended to improve the material well-being of its Kurdish subjects.

In 1946, a British writer reported favorably on developments in the Kurdish areas of Turkey, where a program of agrarian reform and rural welfare was said to have been successfully launched. Young political officers, apparently drawn from the Turkish army, were apparently doing a good job among the Kurds. The standard of health, according to this source, was higher in the Kurdish areas of Turkey than it was in the neighboring countries.[89]

These developments seemed to augur well for the future. However, the issue that has always constituted the Kurds' major grievance in Turkey remained unresolved, for the Turkish government still refused to recognize the Kurds as a separate nationality or to allow them freedom to pursue their own cultural activities.

13 *The Barzani Rebellion of 1931–1932*

The Barzani rebellion of 1931–32 remains in some ways an obscure phenomenon. The sequence of events in the Barzan region of Iraq, which culminated in open rebellion in the late summer of 1931, is not clearly known and has been the subject of much contention and debate.

The Iraqi government, which undoubtedly was in possession of much significant information, appears to have steadfastly set its face against any public discussion of the rebellion. In fact, there is every reason to believe that the Baghdad authorities not only shied away from openly discussing the causes and nature of the rebellion, but also endeavored to suppress many pertinent facts. Official pronouncements, while vigorously denouncing Shaykh Ahmad of Barzan as a rebel and disturber of the peace, contained only vague hints as to the nature of the offenses of which he was presumed to be guilty.

The extremely delicate and explosive nature of the issues involved no doubt prompted this official reticence. The strange beliefs and practices attributed to the Barzanis were not only heterodox and heretical, but in the eyes of all good Muslims constituted a flagrant relapse into polytheism and apostasy—offenses of the most serious nature in Islamic society. Against such offenders, it is Muslims' duty to wage war until the former have been induced to return to the Islamic fold or are annihilated.

To have publicly leveled such grave charges at the Barzanis not only would have inflamed public opinion against them, but also would have placed them outside the pale of Islam and obligated the government to fight them to a finish. Committing itself to the pursuance of such a harsh and uncompromising policy would have placed the government in an extremely awkward position and would have rendered an eventual settlement virtually impossible. Moreover, the bond of religious solidarity in Islam is so strong that no responsible Muslim group or government would ever sanction such a drastic step unless forced to do so by extreme necessity. The desire to maintain the unity of the Muslim community has always been so strong that Islam has traditionally been more tolerant of its aberrant members than has any other religion.

Another important consideration that may have induced the government to resort to a policy of vagueness and ambiguity was of a totally different nature. The implication of the Assyrians' part in the rebellion—who according to conflicting reports were represented first as the antagonists of the Barzanis and later as their allies and supporters—called for particular precautions. Whatever part the Assyrians may have had in the Barzani rebellion (and it appears to have been of negligible importance), popular feeling against this non-Muslim minority has always been intense in Iraq. The government therefore may have thought it unwise to discuss the various issues pertaining to the rebellion, lest in so doing it might unwittingly jeopardize Assyrian lives and property throughout the country.

Causes of the Rebellion

Those who have dealt with the Barzani rebellion of 1931–32 fall, roughly speaking, into two groups or schools of thought. One group, consisting mainly of former British officials in Iraq, maintains that the real cause of the rebellion should be sought in the strange and complex personality of Shaykh Ahmad of Barzan and the religious excesses he sanctioned. They assign primary importance to the religious factor, attributing to the shaykh a large share of the responsibility. These persons make no attempt to hide their disapproval of Shaykh Ahmad, who, casting himself in the dual role of rebel and religious zealot, threatened to dissipate their patient and arduous labors of many years. Consequently, the shaykh emerges from their pages as an irrational individual, deserving pity, perhaps, but not sympathy.

The second group of writers, consisting mostly of Kurds with strong nationalist inclinations, along with a few Arabs, yield to the average Muslim's predilection to forgive and forget the past lapses of an aberrant fellow believer who is once again safely back within the fold. These writers pass lightly over the religious aspect of the rebellion and, as we shall see, tend to assign a large share of the responsibility to the Assyrians.

It should be kept in mind that the shaykhs of Barzan are leaders of the Naqshbandi order. Writing of this order, Edmonds has pointed out, "It is also accepted as orthodox, but, whether owing to the absence of any highly respectable Superior like the Naqib of Baghdad in the neighbourhood or owing to something in its teaching, uneducated members of this order in Kurdistan seem to be particularly prone to manifestations of eccentricity."[1]

Damaluji, who has discussed the Sufi orders in Kurdistan at some length, mentions that corruption had crept into the beliefs and practices of some of them. It is interesting to note that he singles out the Barzani shaykhs to prove his point:

> In the time of Shaykh ʻAbd al-Salam I, the grandfather of Shaykh ʻAbd al-Salam II . . . the order was corrupted, its very nature being tampered with and changed. The adherents began to view their shaykhs in a light that Islam does not permit. The basic reason for these corrupt beliefs may be ascribed to their deep-seated ignorance as well as to their isolation in the remote and inaccessible mountains where they lived. Their isolated existence, cut off as they are from the outside world, coupled with their boundless devotion to their shaykhs, resulted in their deifying and worshipping of these men.[2]

Events in the Years Preceding the Rebellion

British sources have discussed the strange events leading to the Barzani rebellion with more candor and in greater detail than most other writers. According to W. C. F. Wilson, a British administrator of many years' service in Iraq, Shaykh Ahmad dominated the Barzan region with the aid of his brothers and an armed band of several hundred of his adherents. He was so greatly venerated that he came to be regarded as a god. A fervent devotee of the shaykh, one Mulla Jug by name, is reported to have traveled throughout the Barzan region claiming that Shaykh Ahmad was God and that he, Mulla Jug, was his prophet. Mulla Jug appears to have been an eloquent and effective speaker, and his preaching won him many followers. His fame, we are informed, began to surpass even that of his master. This fact, according to Wilson, induced one of the shaykh's brothers to put Mulla Jug out of the way.[3] This episode seems to have been followed by fantastic developments. In Wilson's words,

> Up to that time the Koran had been revered, but now the Shaikh issued orders for the destruction of all copies to be found. He also withdrew the ban on the eating of pork, for wild pigs were plentiful in Barzan. Armed missionaries were sent out beyond the Barzan bounds, and villages which refused to accept the Shaikh were burned and a number of the male inhabitants put to death. This state of affairs could not be allowed to continue, and the Iraq Government was forced to take action in conjunction with the Royal Air Force.[4]

This, then, is one account of the strange happenings that took place in the Barzan region before the outbreak of the rebellion in 1931. Wilson, whose article appeared in April 1937, gave no dates, but stated at one point that the events he was describing had taken place five years earlier.[5]

Stephen H. Longrigg, another former British official with a long record of service in Iraq and an acknowledged authority on the country, gives a similar account of these events. According to him, trouble began to brew in the Barzan region as early as 1927:

> The place of Shaykh Mahmud as leading Kurdish disturber of the peace was taken in the same year, 1927, by Shaykh Ahmad of Barzan in whose territory Iraqi troops had recently manoeuvred. This half-witted Dere Bey, obscurely prompted by some resentful megalomania, now proclaimed himself Almighty and gained some converts by the preaching of a devoted Mulla. But the reaction of horrified listeners led to a scuffle in which lives, including his brother's, were lost. It was followed by an intervention of police and the reinforcement of the Army garrison at Bilih, near Barzan. The new religion died out; but the Shaykh, talking and writing war and sedition to all who would listen and spreading rumours of Assyrian trespass, remained a menacing figure.[6]

These two accounts, it will be noticed, differ in a few minor respects. Whereas Longrigg maintains that one of Shaykh Ahmad's brothers lost his life in the course of a scuffle involving Mulla Jug, Wilson asserted that it was the mulla himself who was eliminated by one of the shaykh's brothers. The shaykh's lifting of the ban on the eating of pork, mentioned by Wilson, does not appear in the passage from Longrigg because that event did not occur until four years after the events of 1927 that culminated in the demise of Mulla Jug. Longrigg mentioned it among the events that took place during 1931.

The quotation from Longrigg contains two interesting points that may have had some bearing on Shaykh Ahmad's subsequent claims and grievances. The first point, mentioned in the initial sentence of the quotation, pertains to the maneuvers of the Iraqi army in Barzan territory; the second point, mentioned in the last sentence, alludes to rumors concerning Assyrian trespass.

The Presence of Army Units and Assyrian Settlements

The shaykh no doubt resented the presence of the Iraqi army in Barzan territory. He probably regarded it as a threat to his hitherto unchallenged authority in the region and an unwelcome prelude to tight government control. His reaction to the intrusion of the government's external authority into his region must have been similar to that of the various semi-independent princes and *derebeys*[7] of the Ottoman Empire when faced with a similar threat during the early part of the nineteenth century. No doubt Longrigg, who mentions the presence of the Iraqi army in the Barzan region in a casual and off-hand manner, must have had these thoughts at the back of his mind in his description of the shaykh as a *derebey*.

The shaykh, as we shall see, did complain about the Iraqi army's presence in the Barzan country—a complaint echoed by a number of writers sympathetic to the Barzani leader. In fact, it appears to have been one of his main grievances when he raised the standard of revolt.

That the shaykh's fears were not misplaced finds confirmation in some highly authoritative quarters. In 1933, Air Marshal Sir Robert Brooke Popham, who served in Iraq as chief of the RAF, stated: "In 1928, when I went to Iraq, I was shown on the map an area (Barzan) where the Iraq police had not yet penetrated. It was realized that sooner or later this would have to be brought under control. We meant to do so in due course by peaceful penetration."[8]

We now come to the other point alluded to in Longrigg's foregoing passage—namely, the shaykh's complaint regarding "Assyrian trespass." Regardless of the validity of his reasons, the shaykh had some grounds for making this charge against the Assyrians. The Barzani leader was aware that plans were being considered for the settlement of the Assyrians on the fringes of his country, and he may have been genuinely alarmed at the prospect of having such turbulent people as neighbors. Only a few years earlier, at the time of the ill-fated repatriation movement led by Agha Petros, Shaykh Ahmad had suffered heavy losses at the Assyrians' hands when he and his Zibari allies tried to prevent their passage through Zibari-Barzani territory on their way to the Hakari highlands. The shaykh was also aware of the government's determination to extend its authority into the Barzan country. The Assyrian levies and the Iraqi army had recently been hovering around his territories and in some cases had actually established permanent bases located within easy striking distance.

In the circumstances, it is not improbable that the shaykh may have connected the settlement of the Assyrians with the military activities taking place around him. If so, he must have regarded the recent army maneuvers as an ominous sign presaging some sinister design against himself and his people. Moreover, if we are to give credence to certain reports, his fears and suspicions may have been intensified by troublemakers anxious to see the Kurds and the Assyrians at each other's throats.[9]

There is every reason to believe that Shaykh Ahmad was little inclined to tolerate either the Assyrian settlement scheme or the penetration of his country by the government and its forces. Which of the two he regarded as the more serious threat to his still unchallenged authority is not too clear. Jiyawuk, a strong apologist for the shaykh, provides us with a clue.

According to Jiyawuk, Shaykh Ahmad addressed an appeal to King Faysal I in which he deplored the establishment of military strongholds in the Barzan region and tried to find out the reasons for this. If it was to protect the Barzanis, he asserted, the latter had proved in the past that they were fully capable of doing so themselves. However, if the army was in Barzan to help settle the Assyrians, he argued, it was being employed to enforce an unjust decision—a decision so patently unjust that he felt confident neither the king nor his ministers would support it.[10]

Despite the shaykh's elusive approach and his skillful efforts to parry one of the two points at issue, he left no doubt that he did not want to have the army in Barzan for any reason. Nevertheless, he wisely refrained from making an issue of the army's presence in his region and instead concentrated his efforts on the Assyrians. His protests against the settlement scheme had the ring of a legitimate grievance and were bound to gain him considerable sympathy and support in many quarters.

The Views of Kurdish Writers

Long after the shaykh himself had ceased to make an issue of the settlement of the Assyrians, a number of Kurdish writers revived the question, contending that it was one of the major causes, if not the major cause, of the Barzani rebellion of 1931–32.

Ardalan, one of the first to raise this issue, maintains that the whole affair stemmed from the British government's decision to settle the Assyrians in the Barzan region—a fact that the Barzanis deeply resented and strenuously opposed. According to him, when fighting broke out between the Assyrians and the Barzanis, the British called on the Iraqi government to interfere, thus precipitating the rebellion.[11]

Al-Brifkani has asserted that the settlement of the Assyrians in the Barzan country, coupled with Britain's desire to extend its influence over this strategically important frontier region, were the two real causes of the rebellion. According to him, the settlement scheme, which envisaged settling the Assyrians in the regions of Birazgird, Shirwan, Baradost, and Margasur, was by far the more important cause of the rebellion. The Barzanis, he states, decided to resist this policy, and, as a result, the Iraqi government initiated military operations against them.[12] Jiyawuk reiterates the same ideas, contending that the entire Barzani question stemmed from British attempts to force the Barzanis to give up their lands to the Assyrian settlers.[13]

However, the contention that the Barzani rebellion of 1931–32 occurred only because of the intended settlement of the Assyrians in the Barzan region is not convincing. Although it is perfectly true that both the Iraqi government and the British government as the mandatory power tried to find a home for the Assyrians in northern Iraq, a search for a suitable district large enough to provide a home for all the survivors of this broken nation proved futile. According to Longrigg, "The surviving community of some 20,000 souls could never be concentrated in a single enclave, since Iraq afforded none which was sufficient, cultivatable, and unoccupied."[14]

The inevitable result was the dispersal of the Assyrian community in the various parts of northern Iraqi Kurdistan. Consequently, settlements were established in the Dohuk, 'Amadiya, Barwari Bala, Barwari Zhayr, 'Aqra, Zakho, and Shaykhan regions, as well as in the Harir and Diyana regions of Rawanduz.[15] Attempts to establish Assyrian settlements in the Baradost region failed for various reasons, including the outbreak of hostilities between Shaykh Ahmad of Barzan and Shaykh Rashid of Baradost.[16]

It should be noted that these Kurdish writers advanced their thesis of Assyrian responsibility for the 1931 Barzani rebellion after the occurrence of the second Barzani rebellion of 1943–45, at a time when the Barzanis, defeated and dispersed, were suffering great hardships. The avowed aims of these writers were to plead the Barzanis' cause, to air their grievances, to emphasize the unjust treatment to which they had been subjected, to exonerate them of charges of rebellion and wrongdoing, and to win for them public as well as official sympathy. Their intentions were no doubt laudable, for the Barzanis—not entirely through their own fault—have been dogged for many years by tragedy and misfortune. Since Ottoman times, their grievances have been ignored, and their requests for redress have gone unheeded. Their troubles and difficulties have largely stemmed from lack of official understanding and sympathy.[17]

The Outbreak of the Rebellion

The precarious peace that had existed in Barzan since the disturbances of 1927 came to an end in the summer of 1931. A British administrative inspector had in the meantime visited Shaykh Ahmad and had duly warned him about the attitude of the Baghdad authorities.[18] Longrigg describes the fresh outbreak in Barzan as follows:

> In July of the latter year [i.e., 1931], he [Shaykh Ahmad] again lost his wits, accepted and imposed "Christianity," and ordered his scared followers to conform to his new faith by roasting and eating pork. A number of the horrified retinue obeyed; but a neighbor, Shaykh Rashid of Baradost, expressed his disapproval by raids which kindled all the fires of tribal warfare. Shaykh Ahmad's brother, Mulla Mustafa, and other well-wishers tried in vain by diplomacy to extinguish them; but he himself [Shaykh Ahmad], restored to the Muslim faith, led forays of unusual savagery into Baradost country.[19]

This, then, was the sequence of events that developed into a full-fledged rebellion, culminating in the interference by the Iraqi army and the British RAF. Whatever may be said of the shaykh's unusual conduct, he cannot be accused of unprovoked aggression against his neighbor. To the leader of a Sufi order such as the shaykh, these strange and extraordinary proceedings were perhaps a test of his powers and a demonstration of the charismatic authority that he, no less than his followers, believed he possessed. The fact that his followers complied when ordered to eat the forbidden meat may have resulted more from their recognition of this special power than from their fear of punishment.

Another source sheds significant light not only on Shaykh Ahmad and his rebellion but also on his assailant, Shaykh Rashid—also a Naqshbandi shaykh. Hamilton wrote in 1937 that Isma'il Beg, grandson of 'Abdullah Pasha of Rawanduz and one-time governor of that town, told him the following in the course of a conversation:

> Shaikh Ahmad is a young man with strange ideas about our Mohammedan religion. For a time he became half Christian and invited friendship with the Assyrians. At once propaganda was spread through Kurdistan saying that Shaikh Ahmad was plotting with the Assyrians to suppress all Mohammedans—lies, of course, but his fanatical neighbor, Shaikh Raschid, was encouraged by the mysterious political agent I have referred to, to attack the "Kaffar" [i.e., Kuffar] or unbelievers. He was told that their bullets would turn to water. He was actually silly enough to believe this and attacked Shaikh Ahmad. As you know, he got much the worse of the fight. Thereupon the Iraq Army was brought up "to bring peace to Kurdistan" as they said. The Army got into difficulties almost as soon as it arrived and was only saved from destruction by the intensive bombing of your R.A.F.[20]

This statement is a clear refutation of the contention that the shaykh was driven to rebellion on account of the Assyrian settlement scheme. On the contrary, he appears to have been completely reconciled with the Assyrians and to have definitely abandoned the charge he had made against them in 1927. As a matter of fact, one gathers that his heterodox beliefs and practices, coupled with his friendly attitude toward the Assyrians, led to his being regarded as half Christian and to his being assailed and execrated as an infidel.[21]

The statement that a "mysterious agent" had instigated Shaykh Rashid to wage war against Shaykh Ahmad is very interesting. As Isma'il Beg indicated in the passage, he had referred to this agent elsewhere in the course of his conversations with Hamilton.[22] Shaykh Rashid's credulity is strikingly illustrated by his naïve acceptance of assurances that if he attacked the "infidels," their bullets would turn to water and he could therefore do so with impunity.

The Government's Decision to Intervene

By November 1931, Shaykh Ahmad had inflicted such severe losses upon Shaykh Rashid that the Iraqi government decided to intervene, and the army was ordered into action despite the difficulties of a winter campaign.[23] The Iraqi government's decision to punish Shaykh Ahmad evoked considerable criticism. Isma'il Beg, in the course of his conversations with Hamilton, deplored the fact that before the army's attack on Shaykh Ahmad, the government had made no attempt to investigate the causes of the quarrel or to settle it amicably.[24]

Captain Philip Mumford, who served for seven years as British intelligence officer in Iraq, also blamed the Iraqi government for taking punitive measures against the shaykh. According to him, "There was another Kurdish chief powerful enough to cause the Iraq Government much uneasiness, Shaikh Ahmad of Barzan. This man was no worse than the average mountain chief in the backward areas, and the British, who had been responsible for him for the past fifteen years, had no reason to get rid of him. He was, however, attacked by the Iraq Government early last winter."[25] While blaming the Iraq government for initiating military operations against Shaykh Ahmad, Mumford criticized his own government for agreeing to use the RAF against the Barzanis and other Kurdish rebels.[26]

According to Jiyawuk, the Iraqi government's decision to take punitive action against the Barzanis was based on the following grounds, each of which he asserts was unfounded:

1. *Barzani refusal to agree to an annual sheep count.* Jiyawuk points out that whereas in Ottoman times the Barzanis had discharged their sheep tax obligations by paying an assessed lump sum each year, Shaykh Ahmad had agreed to pay this tax in the manner required by the Iraqi government. This system entailed that the flocks were counted each year and a certain sum levied per head of sheep. Jiyawuk asserts that the sheep count issue was raised merely as a pretext to punish the Barzanis.[27]

2. *Barzani opposition to the establishment of police posts in the Barzan region.* This contention too, according to the writer, was unsupported by facts. As mentioned earlier, Shaykh Ahmad had written to the king concerning this issue, and Jiwayuk provides the following text of shaykh's letter in support of his argument:

> If the object [of building these police posts] is to defend us against external aggression, we undertake to guarantee to the government that we shall defend our land even as we defended it at the time when the czarist army threatened to overwhelm Mosul. If, on the other hand, the object is to build fortresses to harass us, this we submit is an attempt to stir trouble, for we are more obedient to the august throne than others. We feel that unseen hands are busy behind the scenes trying to eject us from our lands with the intention of settling the Nestorians [Assyrians] therein—a fact that (we feel sure) our Lord the King and his revered government will not countenance.[28]

Despite this reassuring message, Jiwayuk says, the government declared the shaykh a rebel. He points out that the most striking proof of the shaykh's loyalty was demonstrated by his answer to Shaykh Mahmud of Sulaymaniya in 1930 when the latter envoked his aid against the government. "I deem it an honor to be a servant to your groom," he wrote, "but at the same time I cannot bring myself to wage war against the Muslim Arabs."[29] But the government, according to Jiyawuk, adamantly refused to listen to the shaykh's arguments and insisted on his submission—which the shaykh refused to give.[30]

3. *Barzani lawlessness and banditry.* Jiyawuk also rejects this charge, asserting that British insistence on the settlement of the Assyrians on the periphery of the Barzan region was responsible for the Barzanis' restiveness. Barzani attacks against the trespassing Assyrians should be blamed on the British, he says, because they were the direct outcome of British activities.[31]

4. *Shaykh Rashid's complaints against the Barzanis.* The complaints voiced by Shaykh Rashid of Baradost, a leader of the Naqshbandi order, against the Barzanis were used as a pretext to punish the latter. Shaykh Rashid, according to Jiyawuk, was one of the greatest enemies of the Barzani shaykhs because of repeated clashes that had taken place between the two sides concerning observances, adherents, and other matters pertaining to the Sufi order.[32]

5. *The Barzanis' heterodox beliefs and practices.* The government charged the Barzanis, says Jiyawuk, with heterodoxy. According to him, the government was induced to make this charge by the enviousness and intrigues of certain shaykhs who resented the fact that numerous adherents were flocking to the standard of the Barzani shaykhs.[33]

Military Operations Against the Barzanis

An Iraqi government communiqué, issued in November 1931, announced the initiation of punitive measures against Shaykh Ahmad of Barzan.[34] It stated that the shaykh, in a series of devastating attacks, had carried fire and sword to a number of peaceable, unoffending villages. It also mentioned an engagement that had taken place on November 9 between government and rebel forces, listing the casualties suffered by both sides. The communiqué ended on a confident note, stating that the government had taken effective measures to inflict condign punishment on the disturbers of public order and tranquillity.[35]

An Iraqi army force, which had apparently succeeded in penetrating deep into rebel territory, suffered a severe defeat in the neighborhood of Barzan village and was rescued only by the timely intervention of the British RAF. The shaykh, obviously awed by the results of the bombing and still protesting his loyalty, released the prisoners he had taken and withdrew from the Baradost region, the scene of the recent Barzani triumphs against Shaykh Rashid.[36] In this manner, the first phase of the campaign came to an end. Considerable losses, coupled with severe winter conditions, forced both sides to bring their military activities to a standstill.

In the early spring of 1932, as Iraqi army units moved again into Barzani territory, the British high commissioner warned the shaykh not to resist. The warning went unheeded, and the army column was attacked, resulting in heavy losses and a second defeat. Once again the RAF was called on to intervene, and the rebel forces were subjected to intensive bombings and soon dispersed. An Iraqi column advanced into the Barzan country under powerful air cover, and Barzan village and the surrounding countryside were occupied. This development was followed by a lull in the fighting, in the course of which the shaykh released a captured pilot, but attempts to reach a peaceful solution proved fruitless.[37]

Operations were resumed, and the Barzanis were subjected to relentless pressure from land and air. Many of the shaykh's followers were killed, and much of his territory occupied. Delayed-action bombs dropped by British planes made it difficult, if not impossible, for him to obtain supplies from the abandoned villages.[38] With his forces reduced, his mobility restricted, and his supplies depleted and running out, the shaykh was clearly at the end of his tether. In the summer of 1932, he suddenly gave up the unequal fight and sought asylum in Turkey.[39] He surrendered to the Turkish border guards and was immediately removed with his brothers and their families to Edirne (Adrianople) in European Turkey, where they were kept until arrangements were made for their return to Iraq. According to al-Brifkani, the Turks handed the Barzanis over to the Iraqi authorities in conformity with the extradition agreement in force between the two countries.[40] However, it is safe to assume that the Turks did so after receiving assurances that the shaykh and his brothers and followers would be spared.[41] Upon their arrival in Iraq, Shaykh Ahmad and his brother Mulla Mustafa were first exiled to Nasiriya on the lower Euphrates and later moved to Sulaymaniya in southern Iraqi Kurdistan.[42]

By the time the Barzani rebellion of 1931–32 was over, much blood and treasure had been wasted, and the Barzan region, the scene of military operations, was devastated and its inhabitants impoverished. By adding new grievances and grudges to the old, the rebellion placed heavy strains on Kurdish-Arab relations. Perhaps the most harmful outcome was the incalculable damage done to the Iraqi government's prestige. The fact that a few hundred ill-equipped men had been able to defeat regular troops more than once and had forced the government to seek the aid of the mandatory power was a development fraught with serious implications. Had there been any doubts about the government's power, there were none now. Its grave weakness and the extent of its dependence on foreign support were revealed to all eyes. Potential troublemakers might well have asked: Need a future rebel fear to challenge the Iraqi government after the departure of the mandatory power?

Further Disturbances in the Barzan Region, 1934–1935

In 1934 and 1935, a large force of Barzanis under the leadership of one Khalil Khushawi was responsible for widespread disorder in Iraqi Kurdistan. Whether or not this disorder was the last flicker of the Barzani rebellion is not quite clear. Longrigg treats it as a separate development that had no connection with Shaykh Ahmad's earlier rebellion: "This bandit," Longrigg says of Khushawi, "who for long defied the combined operations of Iraqis and Turks, dodged across frontiers from valley to valley and destroyed the villages of all who denounced him. Later in 1935 most of his followers were rounded up, and a dozen hanged; he himself vanished, to reappear in mid-winter and to be caught and shot in March 1936."[43]

Al-Brifkani maintains that this fresh outbreak was a continuation of Shaykh Ahmad's rebellion under new leadership. He asserts that the rebel force, which was led jointly by Shaykh Ahmad's maternal uncle Alu Beg and Khalil Khushawi, was largely composed of *diwana* fighters, the shaykh's fanatic adherents. Al-Brifkani points out that this uprising had well-defined aims, which seem to have been achieved after more than a year of fighting. According to him, when the government asked Alu Beg to cease hostilities, he agreed to do so on two conditions: (1) that he and his followers be allowed to reside at Barzan; and (2) that the government release Shaykh Ahmad and his followers from exile in Nasiriya. The government agreed to the first condition but offered a compromise on the second. Alu Beg and his followers were permitted to live in Barzan, and Shaykh Ahmad and his brother Mulla Mustafa were transferred to Sulaymaniya. This compromise, according to al-Brifkani, brought the Barzani rebellion of 1931–32 to an end.[44] Concerning Khalil Khushawi's fate, he says nothing.

14

The Barzani Rebellion of Mulla Mustafa, 1943–1945, and the Growth of Kurdish Political Organizations

The Escape of Mulla Mustafa

In the summer of 1943, Mulla Mustafa, Shaykh Ahmad's brother, escaped from Su-laymaniya and succeeded in making his way to the Barzan region by a roundabout route through Iran (formerly Persia). The mulla's escape appears to have been well planned. According to one source, he was assisted in his flight by Shaykh Latif Barzinja, a son of Shaykh Mahmud.[1] Mulla Mustafa is said to have received help along the way from a number of his followers living among the Mangur and the Mamish tribes in the Iraq-Iran frontier region.[2] His arrival at his tribal home set in motion a series of events that before long culminated in armed clashes with government forces.

Several reasons have been advanced for Mulla Mustafa's flight from Sulaymaniya, where he had been living in forced residence for the past seven years. A number of writers have stressed financial difficulties. The meager allowance provided by the government appears to have been quite inadequate to meet the bare needs of the exiled Barzani leaders with their families and numerous dependents.[3] The local authorities, headed by the Kurdish *mutasarrif* Shaykh Mustafa al-Qaradaghi, appear to have pursued a policy of harassment toward the Barzani leaders.

The Kurdish writer Ma'ruf Jiyawuk maintains that local sympathizers were prevented from extending financial help to the Barzani leaders. He states that in the course of an interview he had with Shaykh Ahmad, the Barzani chieftain complained bitterly of the hardships they had to undergo because of the government's inadequate allowance and its attitude. Shaykh Ahmad reportedly asked: "Is it right that Captain Lyon,[4] chief of the administrative inspectors in the north, comes to visit me and leaves money under my rug, while Shaykh (Mustafa) al-Qaradaghi does not permit people to help us and treats us with such severity, for no reason at all?"[5]

According to Jiyawuk, Shaykh Ahmad informed him that he had no knowledge of Mulla Mustafa's intentions prior to his escape. The shaykh believed, however, that two things had induced Mulla Mustafa to flee from Sulaymaniya, one involving the exhaustion of his personal funds[6] and the other an insult greatly damaging to his prestige.[7] Whatever the truth of these speculations, it is significant that a prominent Kurdish writer has given them currency. Prior to his flight, Mulla Mustafa was reported to have been in touch with Kurdish nationalist organizations.[8] If true, this may well have been the most important reason for his flight.

Mulla Mustafa's Conflict with the Iraqi Government

Upon his arrival in the Barzan country, Mulla Mustafa is reported to have requested the Iraqi government to grant amnesty to the Barzani exiles and to extend economic aid to the Barzani people.[9] There is no doubt that the economic situation in that area was desperate. At the time, there were rumors, eventually substantiated, that a state of famine existed in the Barzan country, to the point where the people had been reduced to eating acorns for lack of grain.[10]

The government's reply was to demand Mulla Mustafa's surrender and to instruct the police forces to pursue and capture him. He protested his loyalty to the government, but insisted on the fulfillment of his demands. When he failed to get a satisfactory response from the government, in exasperation he decided on armed rebellion.[11]

Mulla Mustafa's Attacks on Police Posts

The Kurdish leader began hostilities by attacks on police stations and successfully captured the stations at Shandeh and Khirzok. These successes, besides greatly enhancing his prestige, enabled him to acquire much needed arms and ammunition, and the number of his followers rapidly increased.[12] A regiment of mobile police was sent against him, but it was defeated.

The mulla continued his attacks on police posts until he had captured a large number of them. He refused to heed a message from Prime Minister Nuri al-Sa'id urging him to surrender. The message was sent through Shaykh Ahmad, who was still detained in Sulaymaniya.[13] An Iraqi army column dispatched against the rebel forces failed to achieve its purpose. The government tried to negotiate with Mulla Mustafa and offered him the choice of either crossing into Iran or living in the Pizhdar region in Sulaymaniya *liwa*, but he declined the offer and again demanded Kurdish rights.[14] Mulla Mustafa then received a stern warning from the British embassy, ordering him to cease his hostile activities and to arrive at an immediate understanding with the Iraqi government.[15]

The mulla, who had hitherto remained obdurate and seemed unwilling to come to terms despite recent Iraqi attempts to seek an amicable settlement, now showed signs of relenting. On December 25, 1943, Nuri al-Sa'id reshuffled his cabinet, the most significant change being the inclusion of Majid Mustafa, a prominent Kurd, as minister without portfolio in charge of Kurdish affairs.[16] This conciliatory gesture, coupled with continued British pressure, finally induced the rebel chief to suspend hostilities.

Mulla Mustafa was not easy to deal with, nor was he entirely to blame. A new and perhaps unexpected role had been thrust upon him by the forces he had set in motion. This man, who but a few months earlier had been only a fugitive with a grievance, now stood at the head of a movement as the champion of his people and the embodiment of their cause.

17. Mulla Mustafa. François Xavier Lovat/Courtesy of Kurdish Institute of Paris. *Kurdistan: In the Shadow of History.*

Mulla Mustafa's Demands

Mulla Mustafa, now in an expansive mood, is said to have presented the government with a number of demands:

1. The creation of an all-Kurdish province embracing the *liwas* of Kirkuk, Arbil, and Sulaymaniya, as well as the Kurdish *qadas* (districts) of Mosul—namely, Dohuk, 'Amadiya, 'Aqra, Zakho, Sinjar, and Shaykhan[17]—and the largely Kurdish *qada* of Khanaqin in Diyala *liwa*.

2. The appointment of a Kurdish official with cabinet rank to administer the newly created Kurdish province.

3. The appointment of a Kurdish undersecretary to each of the various ministries.[18]

4. The cultural, economic, and agricultural autonomy of Kurdistan in the widest possible sense, except in matters pertaining to the army and the gendarmerie.[19]

5. The dismissal or transfer from the Kurdish areas of officials known for bribery or misuse of authority.[20]

6. The adoption of Kurdish as an official language.[21]

Notwithstanding the extravagant nature of these demands, the government showed a sincere desire to come to terms with the Barzani leader and to remove the causes of disaffection in Kurdistan. Shortly after his appointment, Majid Mustafa left Baghdad for parleys with Mulla Mustafa, whom he met at Margasur. Agreement was reached on the following points:

1. Shaykh Ahmad, together with all the Barzani men, women, and children detained

with him in the town of Hilla (to which they had moved after being exiled to Sulay-maniya), would be released and allowed to return to Barzan.

2. Mulla Mustafa was to proceed to Baghdad to make his formal submission to the government.

3. The administration of the Barzan region was to be entrusted to officials noted for their honesty, integrity, and sense of justice.

4. There would be the opening of schools, the building of roads and police posts, and the provision of similar amenities conductive to the establishment of law, order, and prosperity.[22]

After reaching this agreement with Mulla Mustafa, the Kurdish minister proceeded on a fact-finding tour of the Kurdish areas. He investigated grievances, dismissed un-popular officials, and rushed food to the sorely tried Barzani tribesmen, now on the verge of starvation.[23] Upon his return to Baghdad, he submitted a comprehensive re-port to the Council of Ministers. Among other things, Majid Mustafa recommended the appointment of liaison officers between the government and the Kurdish tribes.[24] Sev-eral Kurdish army officers were assigned to fill this role.

The cabinet was divided in its attitude toward the Barzani movement. The Iraqi prime minister, Nuri al-Sa'id, is reported to have favored a sympathetic and conciliatory policy, but a number of his colleagues, alarmed by Mulla Mustafa's successes and in-censed at his demands, advocated a policy of unequivocal firmness.[25] These differences were still unresolved when the prime minister left for Palestine on January 9, 1944.[26]

The Council of Ministers' Decision

A little more than two weeks after the prime minister's departure, the cabinet made a determined attempt to settle the Barzani problem and the various issues stemming from it.[27] A Council of Ministers meeting, presided over by the deputy prime minister, Tawfiq al-Suwaydi, resulted in the Council of Ministers' decision of January 25, 1944. This decision, which obviously reflected the dominant sentiment among members of the cabinet toward the Barzani movement, consisted of the following points:

1. The reestablishment of administration in the *qada*s of Zibar, Rawanduz, and 'Amadiya and in the *nahiya*s (subdistricts) of Margasur, Shirwan, Mazin, and Barzan. The appointment of honest and capable officials, and, if necessary, the utilization of the services of Kurdish army officers as government agents and liaison officers.

2. The establishment of police posts in the Iraqi frontier regions and astride high-ways and crossings, and the expansion of police posts located in the vicinity of *nahiya* headquarters.

3. The building of roads and the establishment of police posts in Khalifan, Rayzan, 'Amadiya, Bileh, 'Aqra, Barzan, Margasur, Shirwan, Mazin, Diyana, and Kani Resh.

4. The immediate removal of Mulla Mustafa from the Barzan region and his settle-ment in the Piran country.[28]

5. The return of the exiled Barzani shaykhs to their homes and the government's ac-ceptance of Mulla Mustafa's coming to Baghdad to make his submission, at a time and

in a manner to be determined by the minister of interior and the Kurdish minister without portfolio.

6. The recovery of government arms and equipment captured by Mulla Mustafa and his followers, and the immediate initiation of steps to accomplish this task.

7. The government's approval of the principle of proclaiming a general amnesty for the Barzani rebel gangs with the exception of members of the armed forces and government officials who joined these gangs. The date for the issuance of this amnesty to be determined by the government at a later date.

The Council of Ministers' decision represented a victory for the anti-Kurdish faction in the cabinet, and it is significant that it was adopted during the absence of Nuri al-Sa'id, who, as mentioned earlier, favored a conciliatory approach to the whole problem.

Jiyawuk has criticized this decision as a hasty and unwise measure and has singled out a number of points that in his opinion constituted major errors of political judgment:[29]

1. The decision to employ Kurdish members of the Iraqi armed forces as liaison officers in the Kurdish tribal areas was a serious error with unfortunate results for all concerned. These men, through no fault of their own, became involved in the Barzani movement and were later executed for participating in the Barzani rebellion.

2. The decision concerning the immediate exile of Mulla Mustafa, at a time when efforts were being made to conciliate the rebellious tribesmen, was inopportune and ill-advised. It was certain to be resented and resisted by the tribesmen and was hardly conducive to the promotion of confidence in the government's goodwill.

3. The decision to recover government arms and equipment captured by the rebels was a well-nigh impossible demand. Although the Barzani leaders handed over all the arms they were in a position to collect from tribesmen subject to their authority, most of the equipment had fallen into the hands of lawless elements and was beyond recall.

4. The delay in granting an amnesty to the Barzanis continued to be an element of serious tension between the Barzanis and the government until the necessary law was passed in April 1945.

5. The decision not to extend the amnesty to Kurdish government officials and army officers who had joined the Barzani rebellion was a serious mistake. These men were thus rendered desperate and preferred to remain outlaws and die fighting rather than surrender and be hanged. Moreover, Shaykh Ahmad was not in a position to round up these men and hand them over to the government.

Attempts to Resolve the Barzani Problem

Upon his return to Baghdad on February 7, 1944, the prime minister resumed his efforts toward an amicable settlement of the Barzani problem. This was not an easy task, for although he was anxious to reconcile the rebellious Barzanis and to allay their fears, he no doubt was equally anxious to uphold the government's prestige and authority.

In the meantime, both sides seem to have made some progress toward reaching agreement on a number of points. Some government arms and ammunition captured by the Barzanis were handed over to the Iraqi authorities.[30] Shaykh Ahmad was allowed to return home to Barzan together with members of his family and those of his follow-ers who had shared his exile.[31]

Mulla Mustafa's Visit to Baghdad

On February 22, 1944, not long after Shaykh Ahmad's arrival in Barzan, Mulla Mustafa journeyed to Baghdad to make his formal submission to the government. The regent[32] received the mulla, accompanied by leading Barzani chieftains and by Fattah Agha Herki,[33] paramount chieftain of the great Herki tribe of nomadic Kurds. During this meeting, Mulla Mustafa asked for and was granted pardon and presumably made his peace with the government.[34]

Mulla Mustafa's visit to Baghdad failed to produce any lasting improvement in gov-ernment-Barzani relations, if indeed it did not further serve to exacerbate tempers on both sides. It deepened rather than dispelled the feeling of mutual antipathy and dis-trust. Arab nationalists deeply resented both the arrival of the Barzani leader in Bagh-dad, accompanied by an impressive retinue of tribal leaders and followers, and his cordial reception by high government officials. In the circumstances, it perhaps is not surprising that the appearance of large numbers of heavily armed Kurdish warriors on the streets of the capital assumed an ominous aspect. Many regarded it as a threat and an affront to the state's authority, and it provoked a violent press attack against the Barzanis that inflamed public opinion and hastened Mulla Mustafa's departure from Baghdad.[35]

According to one source, Mulla Mustafa was allowed to return to Barzan for the avowed purpose of collecting government military equipment captured by the Barza-nis. Instead, however, he is reported to have embarked on an extensive tour of the neigh-boring Kurdish regions with a view to consolidating his position among Kurdish tribal chieftains and notables and to winning them over to his cause.[36]

The Prime Minister's Proposals

Despite these unfavorable developments, Iraqi prime minister Nuri al-Sa'id contin-ued in his efforts to find a solution acceptable to both sides. He toured the Kurdish re-gions in May 1944, at a time when there were mounting signs of tension and uneasiness between Kurds and Arabs, particularly in the army.[37] In an attempt to meet some of the Kurdish demands, the prime minister agreed to the creation of Dohuk *liwa,* a new all-Kurdish administrative unit to be formed from the *qada*s of Dohuk, Zakho, 'Amadiya, 'Aqra, Sinjar, and Shaykhan in Mosul *liwa.* The Kurdish minister, Majid Mustafa, was to be entrusted with the appointment of Kurdish officials in the newly created *liwa.* Nuri also offered to make a number of other concessions—namely, the appointment of a Kurdish deputy director general in the Ministry of Education, the improvement of so-cial services in the Kurdish regions, the grant of agricultural loans, and a sympathetic re-examination of the tobacco monopoly, which was a perennial source of friction between the government and Kurdish tobacco growers.[38]

The prime minister, however, failed to win the support of his colleagues, and the idea of the projected Dohuk *liwa* proved unacceptable to the regent. As might be expected, this development led to a cabinet crisis, and Nuri al-Sa'id was forced to hand in his resignation on June 3, 1944. In the words of a British observer, "The anti-Kurdish feeling in much of the Baghdad political world had again prevailed; it was based, as ever, on the fear of separatism, on the certainty that indulgence in the north would be followed by equal or greater Shi'i demands, and on the crudely selfish ambitions of the Kurdish leaders."[39]

The Policies of the New Cabinet Toward the Barzanis

The cabinet of Hamid Pachachi, which succeeded that of Nuri al-Sa'id, did not carry out the outgoing prime minister's Kurdish policies. Opposition to these policies came mainly from the minister of interior, Mustafa al-'Umari, and the minister of defense, Tahsin 'Ali, whereas Prime Minister Pachachi and Foreign Minister Arshad al-'Umari endorsed Nuri al-Sa'id's policies.

In July 1944, shortly after the new cabinet had come into power, the minister of economics, Tawfiq Wahbi, who was a Kurd, was sent on a goodwill mission to Kurdistan. He is reported to have discovered considerable hostility toward the government among the Barzanis, who recently had greatly increased their strength through a marriage alliance with their traditional rivals, the Zibar *agha*s. This antigovernment feeling was soon demonstrated by Mulla Mustafa's defiant actions, which Longrigg has aptly, if somewhat spiritedly, summed up as follows: "On the Minister's departure Mulla Mustafa helped himself to Government grain stores, looted police posts, conducted a futile correspondence with the Mutasarrif of Mosul, and demanded from Baghdad the fulfillment of Nuri Pasha's promises—and a loan for himself."[40] Because of the Barzanis' desperate economic plight, the government distributed free grain and cloth in the disaffected regions, and an uneasy peace continued to be maintained throughout the winter of 1944–45.

On April 10, 1945, the Iraqi Parliament passed an amnesty bill granting pardon to all Kurdish offenders up to February 22, 1944, except for army officers who took part in the Barzani rebellion.[41] This gesture had a salutory and reassuring effect on the Barzanis. It did much to dispel their doubts about the government's goodwill. Mulla Mustafa and the minister of interior met in Mosul, obviously in an effort to reach a comprehensive understanding pertaining to a number of still unresolved issues. What agreement was reached, if any, is not known, but apparently in accordance with Barzani wishes, the Barzan district was detached from Mosul *liwa* and made a part of Arbil *liwa*.[42] In the meantime, the government, which had been slowly but steadily trying to fulfill its promises to the Barzanis, seems to have made a beginning toward launching an expanded program of social services. New schools and hospitals were planned, and work was actually started on a number of them.[43]

The Deterioration of Barzani-Government Relations

At the time, these favorable developments seemed to augur well for an amicable settlement of the whole Barzani question. But such a settlement was not to be, for deeper and more profound influences were at work. Mutual suspicion had no doubt undermined the basis of confidence between the government and Mulla Mustafa and had rendered any genuine and lasting understanding impossible. Any attempt by the government, however legitimate, to assert its authority or to regain prerogatives yielded under necessity only served to rouse the Barzani leader's suspicions. The very nature of his new role impelled him to consolidate and increase his gains, for his successful rebellion had imbued him with a sense of mission, a beguiling and dangerous acquisition more difficult to yield than power or fame. The government, alarmed at Mulla Mustafa's intransigence and fearful of the consequences, became increasingly adamant and unyielding. It seemed inevitable that the slender thread that held the government and the Barzani leader together would reach a breaking point under the cumulative weight of unresolved problems.

Barzani Resentment of the Government's Demands

It will be recalled that repeated government demands urging the Barzani leaders to hand over captured government military equipment had failed to produce the desired result. The government now renewed its demand. The Barzani leaders, who had handed over a quantity of arms and ammunition soon after the cessation of hostilities, maintained that they were unable to trace the rest because most of it had fallen into the hands of lawless elements who had fled to inaccessible mountain regions.

The government likewise renewed its demand for the surrender of Kurdish civil servants and army officers who had participated in the Barzani rebellion and who continued to live in the Barzan country after the cessation of hostilities. The exclusion of these persons from the amnesty of April 1945 indicated that the government was determined to press this issue.

The Barzani leaders apparently decided to ignore this demand, and no doubt they had good reason for doing so, for it failed to take into account the age-old tribal custom that requires the granting of asylum to whomever seeks it. Moreover, it ignored the fact that the Barzani leaders would naturally be unwilling to surrender those persons who, at the risk of their lives, had rallied to the Kurdish cause. Such an act of treachery and ingratitude would not only cover the Barzani shaykhs with infamy for the rest of their lives, but put an abrupt and inglorious end to their newly assumed role as the champions of Kurdish nationalism.

It is indeed surprising that the government should have made such a demand at all, for it is highly unlikely that these desperate men, knowing themselves to be doomed, would give themselves up without resistance, even if the shaykhs were willing to do the government's bidding. In the circumstances, it would have been necessary for the Barzanis to subdue their erstwhile supporters by force of arms in order to hand them over to the government. Some Kurdish writers seem to have regarded both of these demands as mere pretexts intended to annoy and harass the Barzanis and eventually to involve them in an armed conflict.[44]

The Government's Attitude toward Mulla Mustafa

The government viewed with alarm Mulla Mustafa's defiant attitude as well as his growing power and prestige, which made him preeminent in the affairs of his district and the neighboring regions. The following description of his activities at this time, even if grossly exaggerated, shows that there were some grounds for the government's apprehension. According to the *Times* of London: "Mulla Mustafa acted like an independent ruler. He arrogated the right to intervene in inter-tribal disputes, he interfered with the Government administration and distribution of supplies, he maintained numbers of armed men. He terrorized the building contractors and stopped the construction of police posts, schools, and hospitals. By the middle of 1945 his arrogance knew no bounds and the Barzani country was out of governmental control."[45]

The frequent trips that the mulla was making among the tribes also gave the government serious cause for concern.[46] These trips, which he obviously undertook with a view to consolidating his power, roused Kurdish nationalist sentiment and had a generally disquieting effect on the Kurds.

It should be pointed out that the Iraqi government's relations with Mulla Mustafa at this time were not those typical of a state toward one of its own subjects. No doubt the fact that he had attained great power and influence by force of arms and had come to be regarded as the leader of the Kurds, the second largest ethnic minority in the country, made him feel that he was entitled to a special position. However, there was no legal or constitutional basis for his being accorded such a position by the government. As far as the government was concerned, no matter how powerful he had become, he was a subject of the Iraqi state and sooner or later would have to yield whatever temporary advantages he had obtained as a successful rebel leader.

Another factor of considerable importance was that the Barzani shaykhs apparently believed that they could count on British support, a fact that no doubt stiffened their attitude vis-à-vis the Iraq government.[47] Despite the fact that the British and Iraqi authorities were in constant touch with Mulla Mustafa and his emissaries, tension mounted and the situation steadily deteriorated. The British continued to urge the Barzani chief to make his submission to the government, while he in turn continued to insist on the fulfillment of his demands.[48]

The Resumption of Hostilities and the Defeat of Mulla Mustafa

Iraqi army columns began to move to the mountainous regions of northern Iraq—a move that Mulla Mustafa viewed with misgiving. The British reportedly informed the Kurdish leader that he had nothing to fear from the army's movements, which were purely for the purpose of training the Iraqi armed forces in mountain warfare.[49] At this time, an unfortunate incident occurred that led to the resumption of hostilities. An attempt by the police force at Margasur to disarm Alo Beg, the maternal uncle of the Barzani leaders and one of the chieftains of the Shirwan tribe, resulted in the death of Alu Beg, one of his followers, and four policemen.[50] When Shaykh Ahmad heard of this incident, he is reported to have decided on armed conflict. He sent a message to his brother Mulla Mustafa, who was on a goodwill tour among the Bahdinan tribes, informing him of the details of the Margasur incident. Mulla Mustafa appealed to the British, asking them to use their good offices to stop the fighting that had already broken out in many localities.[51]

Three army columns converged on Barzan, while a police column marched from 'Amadiya, and the Turks hastened to seal off their frontier. Despite a setback, the three columns continued military operations successfully against the rebels. The use of tribal levies raised by the minister of interior proved particularly useful. It enabled the government forces to oppose Mulla Mustafa with the same type of seasoned mountain fighters as he was employing against them. Moreover, by pitting Kurd against Kurd, the government made it impossible for the rebel chief to rally the majority of the Kurds to his cause and thus dealt him a blow more severe than any military defeat.[52] Many of the tribal levies mobilized against Mulla Mustafa, it should be pointed out, were neighbors who "welcomed the chance to pay off old scores and be subsidized for doing it."[53]

In mid-September 1945, Mulla Mustafa suffered a grievous loss by the defection of Mahmud Agha Zibari.[54] A month later, hemmed in from every side, he managed to slip into Iran through the Keleshin Pass, accompanied by numerous armed followers.[55]

The Role of the Hiva Party in Mulla Mustafa's Rebellion

It appears that the Hiva (Hope) Party, first formed in 1935,[56] was revived and back in operation prior to Mulla Mustafa's 1945 rebellion. The Hiva is reported to have held a meeting in Barzan in the course of which party officers were elected, members enrolled, a constitution approved, and the name "Hiva" officially adopted. Barzan was to be the temporary headquarters. Two important decisions were taken at this meeting: (1) that the party should declare the autonomy of Kurdistan, and (2) that the party should not encumber itself by ties with any foreign power.[57]

A freedom committee was formed, and it adopted the following program:[58]

1. To bring about the union of the tribes. The first stage of this task to be limited to the unification of the tribes closest to Barzan. The program of unification to be steadily pursued until all the Kurdish tribes had been united.

2. To liberate Iraqi Kurdistan by political means.

3. To establish relations with other freedom-seeking parties.

4. To contact the diplomatic representatives of other governments, with a view toward enlisting their support.

5. To carry out widespread propaganda by means of publications.

6. To fight the colonial policies of Iraq.

7. To create a Kurdish army.

An important aim of the Hiva Party was to maintain liaison with other Kurdish parties and presumably with other non-Kurdish political organizations.[59] The Hiva proceeded to carry out this program.

We learn from several sources that Majid Mustafa, the Kurdish minister without portfolio, was in touch with Hiva members, who in turn appear to have been in touch with Mulla Mustafa.[60] Its members' activities amply demonstrated the vital role that the Hiva played in Mulla Mustafa's rebellion. The army officers appointed by Majid Mustafa to act as liaison between the government and the tribes are said to have been dedicated Hiva members entrusted with carrying out the party's instructions. Each one of them appears to have been charged with "strengthening the nationalistic spirit within the designated area of his jurisdiction."[61] These persons traveled widely among the tribes of 'Aqra, Shaykhan, Bahdinan, Baradost, Balikh, and other regions in an effort to unify the Kurdish tribes.[62]

In accordance with the Hiva program, an effective Kurdish fighting force seems to have been organized. When fighting again broke out in the summer of 1945, Mulla Mustafa was able to put into the field about five thousand tribal fighters. These contingents were drawn largely from the Barzani confederation, comprising the Muzuri Zhori, Muzuri Zheri, Berozhi, Shervani, Dolamari, and Baradosti tribes.

Close relations seem to have been established with Kurdish political organizations in Iran[63] and with the Khoybun in Syria.[64] Similarly, the Hiva was in touch with Iraqi Kurdish Communists, whose support and sympathy they enjoyed,[65] and with various foreign envoys in Baghdad. Hiva members were constantly in touch with the British embassy and in particular with the various British political officers in Iraqi Kurdistan.[66] They were also known to have contacted American diplomatic representatives on more than one occasion.[67] On August 20, 1945, during Mulla Mustafa's last rebellion, the Barzani Hiva leader addressed a letter to the British, American, Soviet, French, and Chinese envoys in Baghdad, as well as to the then prime minister of Iraq, Hamid Pachachi, complaining of oppressive measures taken by the Iraqi government against the Kurds and referring to the Atlantic Charter.[68]

The Hiva Party was disbanded after the defeat of Mulla Mustafa and his flight to Iran. The collapse of the Barzani movement generated a great deal of bitterness and recrimination among the Kurds. Majid Mustafa, the Kurdish minister, became the object of vehement attacks for his part in the negotiations between the Barzani leaders and the Iraqi government. Aspersions were cast on his integrity, and his motives as a peacemaker were seriously questioned. He was accused of having betrayed the Kurdish cause by giving the Iraqi government sufficient time to mobilize its resources and complete its military preparations. It was alleged that his professions of sympathy for the Barzanis were a mere pretense and that his real aim was to strengthen the hand of the British and Iraqi authorities.[69]

Majid Mustafa was represented as having carefully prepared the ground for his role of peacemaker by insinuating himself into the confidence of Kurdish students and intellectuals, in particular members of the Hiva Party.[70] It was said that his object in ingratiating himself with the Hiva was to dispel any suspicion of disloyalty to the Kurdish cause.[71] It has even been maintained that Majid Mustafa's activities caused a serious split in the party between those who believed him to be a loyal Kurd and those who doubted his sincerity.[72] No doubt the task of Majid Mustafa, like that of many peacemakers, was a difficult and thankless one. It should be pointed out that his critics gave no convincing evidence to substantiate the serious charges they made against him.

The Shurish and Rezgari Kurd Parties

After the collapse of the Barzani movement, the party organization of the Hiva was irreparably damaged, and the bulk of its membership split into small groups with no plan or program. However, a number of leftist members of the Hiva soon joined with other leftist elements to form the Kurdish Communist Party, known as Shurish (Revolution).[73]

In the absence of an effective Kurdish nationalist party, the Shurish succeeded in becoming the bulwark of Kurdish nationalism. It was mainly responsible for the creation of the Rezgari Kurd Party (Kurdish Deliverance Party), a larger organization of the national or popular-front type. None of the various groups that combined to form the Rezgari Kurd kept its former political identity except the Shurish, which continued to maintain its separate internal organization.[74] On the eve of the formation of the Rezgari Kurd Party, the Shurish issued a stirring appeal to the Kurdish people, urging them to rally to the new party and to give it their full support.[75]

The National Manifesto of the Rezgari Kurd Party

The Rezgari Kurd Party issued a manifesto setting forth its aims and objectives:

> *First.* Our highest aim is to unify and liberate Greater Kurdistan. Because the Party is located in Iraqi Kurdistan, we strive to safeguard Iraq from the influence of imperialism and reactionary governments, which are still among the greatest obstacles to national self-determination.
>
> *Second.* To endeavor to obtain administrative independence for Iraqi Kurdistan, an important step toward the realization of national self-determination for the Kurds.
>
> *Third.* To endeavor to end all kinds of persecution and discrimination suffered by the Kurds and other minorities.
>
> *Fourth.* To endeavor to establish and strengthen relations with Kurdish parties and centers outside Iraq, for the purpose of coordinating all efforts for the achievement of the highest aim—the right of national self-determination and ultimate liberation.
>
> *Fifth.* To endeavor to bring about a comprehensive reform of political, social, economic, and cultural problems by providing democratic rights and by raising the level of agriculture and industry, spreading education, and reviving Kurdish history and literature.
>
> *Sixth.* To bring the Kurdish language into general use in schools and government departments throughout the Kurdish regions.
>
> *Seventh.* To strive to explain the Kurdish cause to all nations, particularly the nations of the Middle East.
>
> *Eighth.* To strive to establish relations with democratic parties and organizations and to cooperate with them.
>
> *Ninth.* To seek to establish relations with the democratic nations with the object of combatting imperialism and reaction, and their agents, which are working for the revival of the Sa'adabad Pact, and to fight against all imperialistic and reactionary blocs that hamper freedom in general and the freedom of the Kurds in particular.[76]

The Rezgari Kurd Party gained rapidly in strength and soon became a political force of some importance, particularly among the Kurdish intelligentsia and youth. However, this new "national-front" party met strong opposition from several quarters. The British and Iraqi governments are said to have been greatly alarmed by its emergence. The British were apparently so disturbed that they sought to induce Kurdish religious leaders and shaykhs to issue *fatwas* (legal opinions) declaring it unlawful to join the new party.[77]

Kurdish Communists and the Rezgari Kurd Party

Kurdish Communists' participation in the Rezgari Kurd Party and their open advocacy of Kurdish national self-determination evoked severe criticism on the part of the Iraqi Communist Party in Baghdad. Their action in identifying themselves with the Rezgari was denounced as a divisive practice injurious to the cause of the Iraqi masses of whom the Kurds formed a part. This attack led to some heated exchanges between the Kurdish group and the Baghdad group of Communists.[78]

During the latter half of 1946, the Kurdish Communists left the Rezgari Kurd Party. However, they continued to collaborate with the Rezgari group, which now had changed its name to Barti Demokrati Kurd (Kurdish Democratic Party, or KDP) but continued to function as a "national front." Whether or not the Kurdish Communists' withdrawal from the Rezgari was influenced by the Baghdad Communists' attitude is not known. Laqueur maintains that the Kurdish Communists left the Rezgari not as a result of pressure by the Baghdad Communist group, "but rather in order to make it a more efficient instrument of directing non-communist groups by remote control, and at the same time to make it seem a 'safer' group in the eyes of the authorities, a stratagem which, incidentally, succeeded."[79] He points out that the KDP was hardly affected by the Iraqi government's anticommunist drive in 1948.[80]

15 *The Kurdish Republic of Mahabad*

The Anglo-Soviet invasion of Iran in September 1941 resulted in the collapse of Iranian authority throughout the tribal areas. In the Kurdish regions, one of the most serious consequences of this collapse was the Kurds' seizure of vast quantities of arms and ammunition abandoned by the Iranian forces fleeing before the advancing Russians.[1] Needless to say, this development gravely upset the balance of power between the government and the tribes in Kurdistan and was later to impede the government's task in reasserting its authority over that part of the country. The fact that the Persian Kurds, who nursed a deep sense of grievance against the shah's government, suddenly found themselves well armed and completely free from restraint created a situation fraught with dangerous possibilities.

Riza Shah's Tribal Policy

In order to understand the nature and source of Kurdish grievances against Iran, it is perhaps necessary to consider Riza Shah's tribal policy. For almost two decades, the Kurds had been forced to submit to the shah's harsh rule and his officials' corrupt practices with no hope of redress or remedy for wrongs suffered. Riza Shah's successful struggle against various rebellious tribes served as a prelude to his assumption of supreme power in Iran. He therefore knew from experience that their narrow tribal loyalties, their fighting qualities, and their social, economic, and political organization militated against the realization of his cherished dream—the creation of a modern nation-state. He viewed the tribes as an element of lawlessness and instability, a scourge to the settled population, and a thorn in the government's side. He therefore decided to break their power once and for all and to divert their restless energies into more peaceful channels.

Riza Shah's tribal policy struck at the very root of the tribal order, for he was bent on "destroying the tribal organization, preventing migration, and attempting to convert tribesmen into agriculturists."[2] This policy naturally led to a comprehensive assault on all aspects of tribal life. Riza Shah was merciless and unrelenting in his suppression of native institutions; not even native attire escaped his attention.[3] Unmindful of the violence done to the sensibilities of his Kurdish subjects and indeed to the very fabric of their traditional life, he was determined to carry out his policy regardless of the consequences. All resistance was savagely crushed. Tribal leaders were executed, poisoned, or exiled,[4] and even whole tribes broken up and deported.[5] A system of military strongholds linked by roads was introduced, and turbulent elements were gradually brought under control.[6] However, Riza Shah's "crude but effective"[7] policy triumphed only while he ruled.

The fact that this policy led to bloodshed and widespread misery resulted less from its aims than from the truculent and uncomprehending spirit in which it was undertaken. A more sympathetic and humane approach might have achieved better and more permanent results. But the vision, careful planning, and adequate human and material resources necessary for the success of so vast and ambitious an undertaking were sadly lacking. No wonder the project failed with disastrous results for the tribes and for the country as a whole. In the words of a well-known expert in Persian/Iranian affairs, "The tribal policy of Riza Shah, ill-conceived and badly executed, resulted in heavy losses in livestock, the impoverishment of the tribes, and a diminution of their numbers."[8]

The Effects of the Allied Occupation of Iran

The severe dislocation and drastic changes that followed the Anglo-Soviet invasion of Iran in World War II precluded the continuation of Riza Shah's tribal policy. The maintenance of a strong central authority, a condition necessary for the enforcement of such a policy, was manifestly impossible after the fall of Riza Shah's regime and the breakdown of organized government in the tribal areas. Moreover, even if the Iranian authorities had been in a position to pick up the threads of the former shah's policy, they were not free to do so. England and the Soviet Union would certainly not have countenanced any move on the Iranians' part that might arouse the tribes. Peace and tranquillity were essential if the uninterrupted flow of vital supplies to the Soviet Union was to be maintained. The two occupying powers were determined to subordinate everything to the successful prosecution of the war.

The Three Zones of Iranian Kurdistan

One of the curious results of the Allied occupation of Iran was the division of Iranian Kurdistan into three distinct zones—a Soviet zone, a British zone, and a Kurdish-held territory located between the two Allied zones. The Soviet zone stretched as far south as the neighborhood of Rizaiya, and the British zone extended some distance north of the Khanaqin-Kirmanshah road. The intervening territory had remained in Kurdish hands since the precipitate flight of the Iranian forces and the disintegration of civil administration.[9]

In all three zones, the Kurds showed an unmistakable tendency to break away from the now tenuous Iranian connection, or at least to obtain a certain degree of autonomy. They seem to have lost no time in making overtures to the Soviets soon after the latter's arrival in northwestern Iran. But the Soviet authorities, who at that time appear to have maintained an attitude of aloofness and noninterference in local matters, are reported to have discouraged these early overtures. According to a well-informed British authority, "In the north, Kurdish eyes were turned towards Russia. When the Russians entered Iran in 1941 hopes were aroused that they might assist the Kurdish independence movement, but their very correct behaviour quickly gave the Kurds to understand that any such hopes were vain." [10]

The absence of effective Iranian authority in the Kurdish areas induced the Soviets to deal directly with the Jalali, the Shikak, the Herki, and other Kurdish tribes inhabiting their zone. They do not seem to have made heavy demands of the tribes or to have unduly interfered in their affairs. An American observer close to these events stated, "The chiefs of these tribes were allowed to manage their own affairs by the Soviets, who only required that they maintain security and provide grain for the Red Army." [11]

Persian Kurdish chieftains reportedly approached the British embassy in Baghdad with a view to their inclusion in a "British zone," a move similar to others made in the past by Kurdish chieftains from Iranian Kurdistan. British refusal to consider the offer apparently convinced these chieftains of the futility of their mission, for no further attempts were reported.[12]

Political Developments in the Kurdish Zone

It was in the Kurdish-held middle zone that the first stirrings as well as the culmination of Kurdish political activity were to take place. Here, free from foreign occupation and unhampered by Iranian authority, the Kurds drank deeply of all the things they had been denied and boldly sought to gain their autonomy.

Hama Rashid, a chief of a section of the Bana Begzada, who had been a fugitive in Iraq for a number of years, ventured to cross the frontier into Iran. With the aid of a number of followers who rallied to his cause, he succeeded in establishing his authority as a semiautonomous chieftain in the Bana-Sardasht region.[13] Notwithstanding the fact that he was responsible for the death of a high-ranking Iranian army officer and was regarded as a rebel, the Iranian authorities were too weak to take any action against him. They recognized Hama Rashid as a semiofficial governor, paid him a salary, and charged him with maintaining order in the region.[14] At about this time, the Iranian government recognized another Kurdish chieftain, Mahmud Agha of Kanisenan, who had succeeded in extending his authority over the Meriwan region, as a semi-autonomous governor.[15]

In the summer of 1942, Hama Rashid clashed with Mahmud Agha. The latter sought and obtained assistance from Iran, and with the aid of two Iranian columns supported by light tanks he defeated Hama Rashid's forces and drove them across the frontier into Iraq.[16] The Iranian government, having rid itself of Hama Rashid, apparently lost no time in turning its forces against Mahmud Agha, who was compelled to follow his rival into Iraq.[17]

As a result of these events, by the autumn of 1945 the Iranian government was in control of all the Kurdish areas south of the Saqqiz-Bana-Sardasht line.[18] However, the government apparently was unable to reestablish its authority in what remained of the Kurdish-held zone—namely, the territory located between the Saqqiz-Bana-Sardasht line and the southern limits of the Soviet zone. It was in Mahabad (Sawj Bulaq), the principal town in this region, located within the areas inhabited by the Iranian Azerbai-jani, that the most important Kurdish political developments were to take place.

The Impact of Allied Propaganda

The revival of Kurdish nationalist activity in this region, which led to the formation of the Komala-i-Zhian-i-Kurd (Committee of Kurdish Youth) and culminated in the founding of the Kurdish Republic of Mahabad, received a powerful stimulus from the political ferment generated by World War II. Despite the fact that this region remained outside the British and Soviet occupied zones, there is no doubt that the people were greatly influenced by Allied wartime propaganda. It will be remembered that except for differences in terminology and emphasis, the two brands of Allied propaganda, Soviet and Western, stressed essentially the same themes. Thus, it was not possible for politi-cally unsophisticated peoples such as the Kurds to distinguish one from the other. Both Soviet and Western propaganda denounced the Axis for enslaving and exploiting other nations, extolled political freedom and the self-determination of peoples, and promised the inevitable overthrow of the tyranny of the strong over the weak.

These ideas could scarcely fail to produce a deep impression on the Kurds, who identified themselves with the forces struggling for the liberation of subject peoples. No doubt this attitude was influenced by the fact that two of the states with large Kurdish populations, namely Iraq and Iran, had briefly clashed with the Allies, and Allied inter-vention had been necessary to overthrow their pro-Axis regimes. Moreover, the Turks, despite their alliance with England and France and their government's desire to remain neutral, were known to hold traditional feelings of friendship toward the Germans. These facts undoubtedly served to promote Kurdish sympathy for the Allies.

The Occupying Powers' Attitudes toward the Kurds

Great Britain and the Soviet Union, the two great powers most deeply interested in this region, were aware of the problem posed by the Kurds, especially in Iranian and Iraqi Kurdistan. Turkey's sensitiveness with regard to the Kurdish question was well known to all of the combatants. German agents reportedly were busily engaged in try-ing to foment trouble among discontented Kurdish elements in Iran, Iraq, and Syria with the intention of pinning the blame on the British. In fact, German propaganda had already accused the British of causing unrest among the Iranian Kurds.[19]

The situation, therefore, was delicate and fraught with danger. During the crucial early years of the war, when the Germans had succeeded in reaching the northern Cau-casus, Britain and the Soviet Union were anxious not to do anything that might provoke Turkey into entering the war on the side of Germany. For this reason, both powers maintained an aloof attitude toward the Kurds during the first few years of the war.

But the two powers were not destined to pursue identical policies with regard to the Kurdish problem, or to any other question for that matter, for very long. As the German menace receded and the prospects of an Allied victory became more certain, the old unity induced by the fear of a common enemy began to wear thin. Each of the two powers seemed bent on following whatever policy was most compatible with its own national interests.[20]

Great Britain, which was bound by alliances to Turkey and Iraq, and which hoped to maintain friendly relations with Iran, naturally tended to uphold the status quo. In order to avoid any misunderstanding, it carefully refrained from showing any sympathy toward Kurdish nationalist aspirations.

The Soviet Union, in contrast, was not on particularly friendly terms with Turkey and had no diplomatic relations with Iraq, and its relationship with Iran was still ambiguous and far from reassuring. It thus had little to lose and much to gain by posing as the champion of Kurdish nationalism. Such a policy, by ensuring the friendship and devotion of a large warlike minority in all three countries, would eventually prove to be both a valuable instrument for exerting pressure in times of peace and a powerful weapon militarily in times of war. Furthermore, it was not only the Soviets who were desirous of promoting such friendship. The Kurds themselves, having despaired of British help, were ready to turn to a new patron.

As mentioned earlier, the Soviets at first did not seem too eager to show the Kurds any special marks of favor and adopted an attitude of aloofness and strict noninterference. The first signs of a change in the Soviet attitude toward the Kurds appeared in 1942. In that year, two significant moves were made, one by the Soviets and one by the Kurds. The Soviets for the first time invited a number of influential Kurdish leaders to a meeting in Baku.[20] At about the same time, three Kurdish officers of the Iraqi army are said to have contacted the Soviet occupation authorities in Iran and offered the armed help of their compatriots in the war against Germany.[21] Which of these two moves preceded the other is not quite clear. At any rate, the Soviets seem to have been still unwilling to take the Kurds under their wing, for in the spring of that year, when some Kurds raided villages west of Lake Urmiya, the Soviets did not hesitate to call the Iranian army and gendarmerie to deal with them. Later, however, they appear to have suffered a change of heart and did their best to frustrate the efforts of the Iranian security forces.[22]

The Komala

The Formation of the Komala

On August 16, 1943, a band of Kurdish nationalists founded the Komala-i-Zhian-i-Kurd in Mahabad. These persons consisted of small merchants and petty officials. In order to maintain the secret character of the organization, its total membership was kept below one hundred, and it was organized in cells. Semiweekly meetings were held in private houses, but no two meetings were successively held in the same house.[23] The Komala's intense nationalism was indicated by the fact that only persons born of a Kurdish mother and father were eligible for membership. The only exception was in the case of persons born of a Kurdish father and an Assyrian mother. This seems somewhat strange considering the vexed relations between these two peoples after World War I, but, in the words of the American observer Archie Roosevelt, Jr., it might have been "an indication of the present close relations between Kurds and Assyrians."[24]

Having firmly established itself in Iranian Kurdistan, the Komala lost no time in extending its activities into the neighboring Kurdish-inhabited countries. It became especially active in Iraq, where chapters were founded in Mosul, Kirkuk, Arbil, Sulaymaniya, Rawanduz, and Shakhwa. At least one chapter was reported to have been functioning in Turkey.[25]

Soviet Contacts with the Komala

In 1944, the number of Soviet political officers and agents was greatly increased in both Azerbayjan and Iranian Kurdistan. These men were Muslim for the most part and appeared to have been effective. A certain captain Jafarov, a Soviet Kurd attached to the Soviet consulate at Rizaiya, was said to have wandered freely among villagers and tribesmen dressed like one of them. Two other Soviet agents, Abdullahov and Hajiov, who ostensibly were engaged in purchasing horses for the Red Army, are said to have actually been charged with establishing contact with the Kurdish nationalist movement. A chance meeting between Abdullahov and a Komala member is said to have put the Soviets in touch with that organization. Before long, a Russian-speaking Komala member was appointed as a liaison officer between the Komala and the Soviet occupation authorities.[26]

The Soviet international propaganda agency Vsesoiuznoe Obshchestvo Kulturnoi s Sziazi s Zagranitsei (VOKS, Society for Cultural Relations with Foreign Countries) was at this time busily engaged in establishing various branches of the Iranian-Soviet Cultural Relations Society all over Iran. The Komala leaders asked this agency to establish a branch in Mahabad, which, significantly, was called the Kurdistan-Soviet Cultural Relations Society.[27]

In April 1945, at a ceremony held in the clubhouse of the Kurdistan-Soviet Cultural Relations Society, the Komala came into the open. The Soviet consul at Rizaiya and the VOKS chief in Azerbayjan were the guests of honor. The main item on the program was a play called *Daik Nishtman* (Mother Nativeland). An old woman representing Kurdistan was being abused and ill-treated by three ruffians—namely, "Iraq," "Iran," and "Turkey." The culmination of the play was reached when "Mother Nativeland" was rescued by the united efforts of her sons. The next scene was interesting. According to Roosevelt, "the audience, unused to dramatic representations, was deeply moved, and blood-feuds generations old were composed, as lifelong enemies fell weeping on each other's shoulders and swore to avenge Kurdistan."[28]

The Admittance of Qadi Muhammad to the Komala

It was at this meeting that Qadi Muhammad, the future president of the Kurdish Republic of Mahabad, was admitted to the Komala. Soviet officials reportedly were gratified at this development, for they apparently had been seeking a powerful figure who could lead the organization. Aware of the tribes' power, the Soviets had attempted unsuccessfully to induce one of the great tribal chieftains to lead the Kurdish national-ist movement. The Soviets reportedly had approached the three most powerful tribal chieftains of Iranian Kurdistan—Qarani Agha Ra'is-al-Asha'ir, chief of the Mamish; 'Amr Khan Sharifi, chief of the Shikaks; and Amir As'ad, chief of the Deh-bokris—with this offer in mind. All three men were said to have politely declined the offer.[29]

The Soviets, who persisted in their quest for a Kurdish leader, finally decided on Qadi Muhammad, the hereditary religious judge *(qadi)* of Mahabad and one of its lead-ing religious figures. Before long, they succeeded in gaining his confidence. Frequent visits to Qadi Muhammad and the attention generally lavished on him eventually led to a significant development. By bringing pressure to bear on the Iranian government, the Soviets succeeded in replacing the Dehbokri chieftain Amir As'ad, who acted as the gov-ernment representative in the area, with the *qadi's* cousin, Sayf Qadi, who thus became the local commander of the gendarmerie. This substitution was tangible proof of the value of Soviet friendship and an example of what could be accomplished in the future by such fruitful collaboration.

Before long Qadi Muhammad gained full control of the Komala. Some of the Ko-mala leaders appear to have anticipated this development. According to Roosevelt,

> Qazi [Qadi] Mohammad is said to have learned of the Komala only about a year after its formation when he sent emissaries discreetly offering his adherence. Komala leaders had decided not to admit him, fearing that because of his strong and authoritarian character and also because of the deference which they themselves had been accus-tomed since childhood to show him and his family, he would eventually dominate the party and end its democratic character. When at Soviet insistence the Komala finally did admit him there came about precisely the result they feared—one-man rule of the party.[30]

He not only tightened his control over the Komala, but also pursued a line of policy fa-vorable to the Soviet point of view. How far the *qadi* was willing to go along with the So-viets is evident from subsequent developments.

The Background and Character of Qadi Muhammad

Qadi Muhammad came from one of the most distinguished families in Iranian Kurdistan—the hereditary *qadis* of Mahabad. The family owed its preeminence not only to the piety and learning of its members, but also to the courage and patriotism that they had displayed in times of crisis. Members of the family more than once placed themselves at the head of their people and fearlessly assumed the responsibilities of leadership in times of great danger and uncertainty. Consequently, the people of Ma-habad and the surrounding countryside came to look on them as the acknowledged re-ligious and civil leaders of the region.

Qadi Muhammad's father, Qadi 'Ali, and one of his cousins, Qadi Mun'im, did much to mitigate the rigors of Russian military occupation during World War I, when famine, pestilence, and the ravages of war wrought havoc in northwestern Iran. Qadi 'Ali's paternal uncle, Qadi Fattah, took a leading part in organizing local resistance to czarist intervention in Azerbayjan during the disturbances that convulsed the country at the time of the constitutional revolution *(mashrutiya)* in 1905. He is said to have donned a shroud and invited the people to join in a a jihad against the czarist forces, by whom he was subsequently killed.[31]

Thus, it is not surprising that the people as well as the Iranian authorities held the family in high regard. Even Riza Shah, who was not noted for his friendly attitude toward religious dignitaries, is reported to have shown the family marks of special favor and to have been well disposed toward Qadi Muhammad's father. After the latter's death in the middle 1930s, Qadi Muhammad was appointed to the judgeship of Mahabad on the recommendation of the local civil and military authorities.[32]

No doubt Qadi Muhammad's learning and strength of character and the prestige of his family and office combined to give him a position of considerable power and influence in Mahabad. To the outside world, however, he remained completely unknown until events swept him into international prominence as the head of the Kurdish Republic of Mahabad. His sincerity, unaffected manners, and frugal habits left a favorable impression on foreigners who came in contact with him.

Among those who met Qadi Muhammad, none has given a more sympathetic description of the Kurdish leader than Archie Roosevelt, Jr. The picture of Qadi that emerges from Roosevelt's writings is that of a dedicated patriot and a cultured man of wide interests and tolerant views. Even after his rise to power, he displayed none of the intemperateness of the zealot, the haughtiness of a man of rank, or the harshness of one inured to rude surroundings. According to Roosevelt, "He seemed to be a man of deep convictions, backed with a rare courage and self-sacrifice, but tempered with broadmindedness and moderation."[33] When the Mahabad Republic later collapsed, Qadi Muhammad's response when he learned that he and his brother Sadr Qadi had been condemned to death was characteristic. He pleaded not for his own life, but for that of his brother, whom he believed to be a victim of gross injustice.[34]

The Democrat Party of Kurdistan

Soviet Plans for a Kurdish Party

By the summer of 1945, the Soviet Union decided to pursue a new policy in Iran aimed at encouraging the northwestern provinces to seek an autonomous or separate existence from the rest of the country. In order to prepare the ground for the implementation of this scheme, the Tudeh Party in Azerbayjan abolished itself, reappearing under the name of the Democrat Party of Azerbayjan. It adopted Azeri Turkish as its official language and demanded separation from Iran. It resorted to this maneuver, according to Roosevelt, in order to enable leftist elements to have a free hand in Azerbayjan without embarrassing the Tudeh in other parts of Iran. In his words, they could then "stage a revolution, declare the province independent, and possibly request incorporation in the

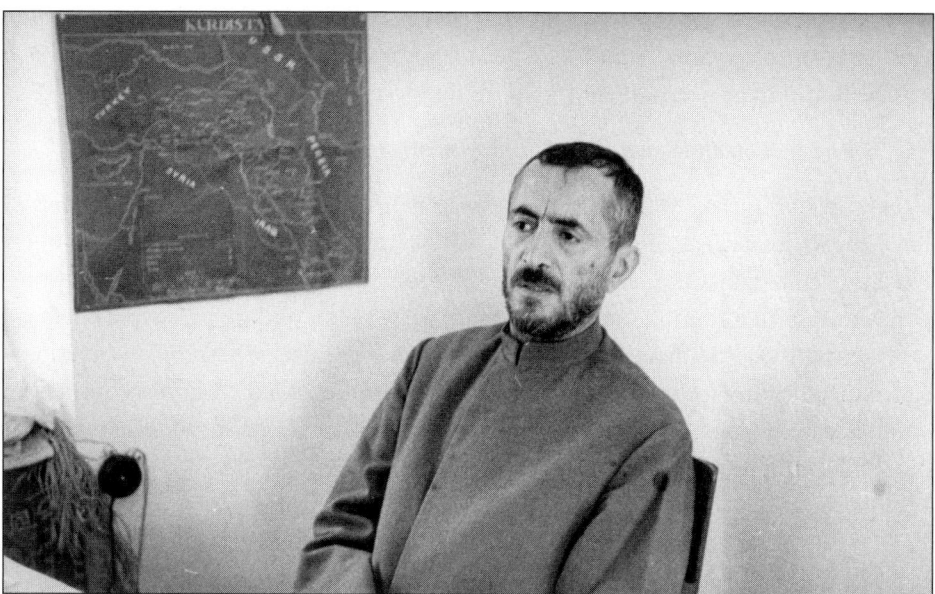

18. Qadi Muhammad in his office in Mahabad with map of Kurdistan behind him, 1946. Archibald Roosevelt/Library of Congress, Washington, D.C. From Susan Meiselas, *Kurdistan: In the Shadow of History.*

Soviet Union." [35] In December 1945, the DPA declared the formation of an autonomous government, Democratic Republic of Azerbayjan, in Tabriz.

The Soviet plan also entailed the formation of a new Kurdish party. As Roosevelt pointed out, the Kurds could hardly be expected to join a party dedicated to Azerbayjan nationalism. On September 12, 1945, Captain Namazaliev, Soviet commandant at Miyanduab, was reported to have summoned a number of Kurdish leaders, including Qadi Muhammad and Sayf Qadi, to a meeting with the Soviet consul in Tabriz. Upon their arrival in Tabriz, the Kurds were told to proceed to the railway station, where they were put on a train that took them to Baku. [36] After three days in Baku, during which time they were treated to tours, theatrical shows, and the opera, their sojourn culminated in a meeting with an important Soviet official. According to Roosevelt,

> On the fourth day they were ushered in to see Bagherov [Russian spelling, Bagirov], President of the Azerbaijan S.S.R. (Actually Chairman of the Praesidium of the Supreme Soviet of the Azerbaijan S.S.R.), who harangued them regarding the wrongs they had suffered under Reza Shah, and said that the Soviet Government would help the new Democrat Party, which was dedicated to freedom for the oppressed and which he strongly urged them to join. He condemned both the Tudeh Party, which he character- ized as a group of ineffective trouble-makers, and the Komala, which he said was started in Iraq under the auspices of British intelligence and was nothing but an instrument of British imperialism. Then, after a warning not to say anything about the trip, the Kurds were put on the train to Tabriz, where they were loaded into Red Army vehicles and driven off to their homes. [37]

This account shows that the formation of the Hizb-i-Dimokrat-i-Kurd (Kurdish Demo-crat Party) was Soviet inspired. The Kurdish leaders' trip to Baku in all likelihood was arranged with the object of giving them the necessary instructions.[38]

The Formation and Aims of the Democrat Party of Kurdistan

Upon his return to Mahabad, Qadi Muhammad called a meeting of Kurdish nobles, intellectuals, journalists, and members of Parliament to announce the formation of the Kurdish Democrat Party. He urged all Kurds to join the party and many did so.

A manifesto outlining the newly formed party's aims and policies was issued and was signed by Qadi Muhammad and a large number of Kurdish leaders. The manifesto stated that the Kurds wished to share in the benefits of the Atlantic Charter now that the world had been liberated from fascism. It went on to say that the Kurds sought nothing more than their human and constitutional rights, which Riza Shah had for so long de-nied them.[39] The party's program consisted of the following points:

> The Kurdish people in Iran should have freedom and self-government in the adminis-tration of their local affairs, and obtain autonomy within the limits of the Iranian State;
> The Kurdish language should be used in education and be the official language in administrative affairs;
> The provincial council of Kurdistan should be immediately elected according to constitutional law and should supervise and inspect all state and social matters;
> All state officials must be of local origin;
> A single law for both peasants and notables should be adopted and the future of both secured;
> The Kurdish Democrat Party will make a special effort to establish unity and com-plete fraternity with the Azerbaijani people and the other peoples that live in Azerbaijan (Assyrians, Armenians, etc.) in their struggles;
> The Kurdish Democrat Party will strive for the improvement of the moral and eco-nomic state of the Kurdish people through the exploration of Kurdistan's many natural resources, the progress of agriculture and commerce, and the development of hygiene and education; and
> We desire that the people living in Iran be able to strive freely for the happiness and progress of their country.[40]

The Republic of Mahabad: Its Aims and Policies

The Republic of Mahabad was established in January 1946, a month after the for-mation of the Azerbayjani republic.[41] Qadi Muhammad inaugurated the Kurdish Re-public at a meeting in Mahabad attended by tribal chiefs, leaders of the new Kurdish Democrat Party, Mulla Mustafa, and three Soviet officers. A national parliament of thir-teen members was formed, and Qadi Muhammad was elected president. The Republic of Mahabad was officially proclaimed in March 1946.[42] In April, officials of the two regimes signed a treaty stating that "the military forces of the signatory nations will as-sist each other whenever necessary."

On the day that the republic was proclaimed, Qadi Muhammad announced the opening of a high school for girls.[43] This was a significant gesture, for in this land of illiteracy the rudiments of education were lacking. The few schools that existed were not equipped to educate the Kurds in their own language, nor were they intended to do so. Education of girls was practically nonexistent. Legislation was passed instituting universal and compulsory elementary education. Children of the poor were to be given free instruction, clothing, food, and textbooks.[44] The absence of textbooks in the Kurdish language was one of the most pressing problems. "At first," claimed Roosevelt, "Kurdish teachers had to translate from Persian textbooks orally in the classroom, but shortly before the fall of the Kurdish Republic, textbooks in Kurdish had been printed for the primary grades."[45]

One of the most urgent needs was to provide the necessary means for the dissemination of information—required for political as well as for educational purposes. With this end in mind, the government started the publication of a daily newspaper and a political monthly periodical.[46] Two more magazines, *Havar* and *Hilale,* soon followed.[47] *Hilale,* a woman's magazine, began to appear in May 1946.[48] All these new publications were printed on a press obtained from the Soviet Union, which also provided the necessary newsprint.[49] An indication of the importance that Qadi Muhammad attached to the Kurdish language and literature may be gained from the fact that he had on his staff two young poets, Heyman and Hezar, who were allowed to publish their poems despite the paper shortage.[50] As might be expected, the material carried by the Kurdish newspapers and magazines showed strong Soviet influence. Roosevelt pointed out that "they contained a large proportion of Soviet material translated word for word into Kurdish."[51]

A few months after the establishment of the Mahabad Republic, a large number of Kurdish notables addressed a memorandum to the Iranian government in which they asked for the formation of a "Supreme Council of Kurdistan." They pointed out that the Kurdish question was not of interest merely to them, but to all Kurds throughout Iran. The Kurdish question, they went on, could not be resolved by a unilateral decision by the Iranian government. "Our step," the memorandum declared, "is evident of our sentiments of loyalty towards Iran. We hope the Government will not let this opportunity which we are offering to pass."[52]

Qadi Muhammad expressed his views on June 1, 1946, to a correspondent of the French press agency. "The Kurds," he said, "would be satisfied if the central government decided really to apply democratic laws throughout Iran, and recognized the laws now in force in Kurdistan concerning the education of the Kurd and the autonomy of the local administration and the army."[53] When the French journalist asked Qadi Muhammad about the danger of conflict with the central government and the possibility of foreign intervention, the Kurdish leader replied:

> The situation in Kurdistan is very different from that in Azerbayjan. Our country has never been occupied by Soviet troops, and since the abdication of Reza Shah, neither the Gendarmerie nor Iranian troops have penetrated into Kurdistan. We have therefore

practically been living in independence since that time. Further we shall never tolerate foreign intervention wherever it comes from. The question of Kurdistan is a purely internal affair which should be settled between Kurds and the Central Government.[54]

Qadi Muhammad then reviewed Kurdistan's past and stated that if the Kurds now claimed autonomy, it was because of the central government's indifference to their interests. "We do not desire to imitate either the Americans or the Russians," he said, "but we refuse to be in the position of animals of the civilized countries."[55]

Problems and Weaknesses of the Mahabad Regime

Elements of Division and Disunity

Mahabad was another sad reminder of the traditional lack of cohesion so characteristic of Kurdish political activity. Once more, at a time of national crisis, the Kurds failed to compose their differences and proved incapable of closing their ranks. The elements of division and conflict were many and varied. Self-seeking, rivalry, and intrigue prevented the various groups from reaching a common understanding. Conflicting interests were rendered irreconcilable and resulted in dissension and disunity.

The local tribes, on whose unity the whole future of the regime depended, were hopelessly divided into two conflicting camps, one in favor of the Mahabad Republic and the other opposed to it. Likewise, the various tribal groups and leaders from outside the region, such as Hama Rashid Khan of Bana and his followers, the Shikakis, the Herkis, and the Barzanis, were not all of one mind. As we shall see, they pursued their own ends to the detriment of the common goal.

These troubles were not the only ones that plagued the Mahabad regime and indeed Kurdish society in general. The long dormant Kurdish society, awakened by the din of a great war and the strident claims of rival ideologies, found itself divided into two groups fiercely vying with each other for the leadership of the Kurdish people: the traditional leaders and the emergent intelligentsia.[56]

The conservative elements—including the older generation, the majority of tribal chieftains, and the mercantile classes—viewed Soviet overtures with suspicion and for that reason were reluctant to accept Soviet support. They favored the gradual attainment of national aims and adopted a cautious and restrained attitude. The radical elements, including the younger generation and the intelligentsia, more idealistic and impetuous, were in favor of extreme measures. They were not only grateful for Soviet support, but oftentimes impatient to invoke it. No doubt this political dichotomy greatly aggravated the dissensions and the lack of cohesion among the Persian Kurds and hastened the collapse of the fledgling republic.

The tribal situation within the territorial limits of the Mahabad state was as follows: the three major tribes of the region—the Mamish, the Mangur, and the Dehbokri—were openly hostile to the Kurdish regime.[57] Qarani Agha, the aged chieftain of the Mamish, was one of the three Kurdish chieftains whom the Soviets had approached when they were seeking a leader of the Kurdish movement, but he had declined their offer. Qarani Agha and his son Mam ʿAziz, together with their allies the Mangur under Bayazid Agha, were so unalterably opposed to the Mahabad regime that the Soviet vice-consul at Rizaiya threatened to unleash the Barzanis against them. This threat was in fact carried out shortly thereafter, and Mam ʿAziz and a number of his followers found it necessary to flee to Iraq. This punitive action served only to exacerbate tempers and deepen antagonisms. Amir Asʿad of the Dehbokri, who also had declined the Soviet invitation to lead the Kurdish nationalist movement and was subsequently deprived of his position as the representative of the central government at Mahabad, maintained an attitude of uncooperative aloofness and would have nothing to do with the Kurdish republic.[58]

The Character and Activities of Some Key Kurdish Figures

A brief consideration of the character and activities of the men who influenced the course of events in Mahabad reveals some of the regime's inner weaknesses. These individuals played important roles in the various political and military developments; some of them held high posts in the Mahabad regime, and were responsible for a number of important decisions.

Hama Rashid Khan. Hama Rashid Khan of Bana was one of the turbulent leaders who attached himself to the Mahabad regime. As noted earlier, after his unsuccessful attempt to establish himself as a semiautonomous chieftain in the neighborhood of Bana in 1942, he was forced to flee to Iraq. His numerous clashes with the Iranian army and with other Kurds seemed to have had no aim other than advancing his own personal interests. He spent much of his time crossing and recrossing the Iran-Iraq frontier in pursuit of his ambitions or in search of personal safety. Hama Rashid, who was one of five recipients of the rank of "marshal" under the Mahabad regime, participated in the fighting that broke out in the Saqqiz-Bana-Sardasht region in 1942.[59]

Roosevelt made the following comments about this Kurdish leader:

> Hama Rashid was of dubious value to the Kurds, as he was continually carrying on secret negotiations with the Iranian army for his reinstatement as Governor of Baneh, and was suspected by both Kurds and Iranians of a mysterious connection with the British. In August, hearing that plans were being made in Mahabad to have him murdered, Hama Rashid fled back to Iraq.[60]

Zeru Beg Herki. Zeru Beg Herki was another such adventurer. A minor chieftain of the Herki tribe, he started his career at the end of World War I as a bandit and an ally of the famed bandit-rebel chieftain Simko Agha. After the latter's murder by Riza Shah, Zeru Beg fled to Iraq, where he continued to live in comparative obscurity until the Anglo-Russian invasion of Iran made it possible for him to return to that country. He ventured to cross the frontier after the collapse of Persian authority in northwestern Iran and succeeded in establishing himself in the Baranduz Valley, not too far from the Iran-Iraq frontier.[61] Zeru Beg was another of those created a "marshal" after the inauguration of Qadi Muhammad as president of the Kurdish Republic. He was also a member of the Kurdish delegation that signed the treaty concluded between the Azerbayjani Democrats and the Kurds of Mahabad on April 23, 1946. One of his last exploits was his precipitate flight to Ushnu after a number of his followers ambushed some Iranian soldiers while he was negotiating with the Iranian commander, General Homayuni. There he joined Mulla Mustafa just before the latter started on his epic flight toward the Soviet frontier.[62]

What exactly his value was to the Mahabad regime is not clear. He is reported to have succeeded in ingratiating himself with the Soviet authorities and to have been their favored protégé. Whether he used his Soviet connections to serve his people by acting as a link between them and the Soviet authorities or whether he employed them for his own self-aggrandizement is not known.

'Amr Khan Sharifi. The activities of a number of other Kurdish leaders raise some doubts as to their motives. A notable example is 'Amr Khan Sharifi, paramount chieftain of the Shikak tribe and one of the most powerful and highly respected men in Iranian Kurdistan. He seems to have made a favorable impression on several American observers. Roosevelt described him as "the grand old man of Kurdistan,"[63] and U.S. Supreme Court justice William O. Douglas, who was his house guest a few years after the fall of Mahabad, has paid him warm tribute.[64] Yet his conduct can scarcely escape the stigma of opportunism.

'Amr Khan collaborated with the Mahabad regime and continued to be one of its most influential members until shortly before its collapse. He served as the republic's minister of war and was one of the five persons invested with the rank of "marshal." He also was a member of the central committee of the Democrat Party of Kurdistan and was one of the signatories of the Azerbayjani-Kurdish Treaty of April 23, 1946.[65] His tribesmen joined the Mahabad forces and participated in military operations on a number of occasions. When it became clear that the fall of Mahabad was only a matter of time, 'Amr then withdrew his support and retired to his home at Zindasht to await developments.[66] A few years later, when asked about his reasons for joining the Mahabad Republic, he reportedly replied that he had done so in order to save his neck.[67]

Throughout the period of his association with the Mahabad regime, 'Amr Khan appears to have been in close touch with George Allen, the American ambassador in Tehran—a precaution no doubt induced by the same concern for self-preservation. Douglas has described how Amr Khan succeeded in extricating himself through the American ambassador's good offices. "When Amar Khan joined the Cabinet of Qazi Mohammad, he kept in touch with George Allen and threw his weight against the Soviet influence in that government. After the Mahabad Government fell, and Amar Khan stood in danger of being hanged along with Qazi Mohammad, George Allen pleaded Amar Khan's case before the Shah, winning both the case and Amar Khan's devotion."[68]

Haji Baba Shaykh. Duplicity and opportunism were commonplace at the time of the Mahabad Republic. Even the aged and greatly revered Haji Baba Shaykh, while serving as prime minister of the republic throughout its year-long existence, was in constant touch with the Iranian central government. By his own admission, he contrived to keep the Iranian government informed of whatever passed between the Soviet representatives and his own colleagues in the Mahabad regime.[69]

Qobad. Qobad, a son of the famous chieftain Simko Agha of the Shikak, is reported to have requested the Iranian government, through his kinsman 'Amr Khan Sharifi, to provide his tribesmen with arms in order to march against Mulla Mustafa and his followers.[70] The latter, who eventually succeeded in escaping to the USSR, were at that time desperately trying to avoid being encircled by the Iranian army. It is very unlikely that the Iranian government acceded to Qobad's request, for we know that 'Amr Khan himself took no part in the military operations then being conducted in the neighborhood of the Shikak country. In this connection, Roosevelt's remarks are revealing: "The Iranian army, evidently not wishing to incur obligations, had not informed Amr Khan of its projected move into Azerbaijan, and so by the time he had gathered his tribesmen to attack the Democrats, the war was over."[71]

The Role of the Barzanis

The Barzanis—desperate, irreconcilable, and with objectives of their own to pursue—were from the beginning a source of both strength and weakness to the Kurdish state, although they initially were received with open arms by Qadi Muhammad's regime. Soon after their arrival in Iran, they began negotiations with the Iranian government and agreed to give up their arms and settle down as political exiles. After failing to reach an agreement with the Iranian authorities, however, they changed their minds and rallied to Qadi Muhammad.[72] The Barzanis were the best trained and the best armed of the various tribal forces and had no difficulty in establishing themselves in a militarily predominant position. They contended successfully with the Iranian army, intimidated uncooperative tribes, and generally proved themselves to be the most effective fighting force in Iranian Kurdistan.

However, the sudden appearance of so considerable an agglomeration of power in the rather limited territory of the Mahabad Republic upset the normal power relationships among the tribes of the region. The arrival of the Barzanis no doubt was deeply resented as an unwarranted intrusion by "outsiders," particularly among those tribes whose interests were adversely affected. Notwithstanding the strength of the pan-Kurdish sentiment prevalent at the time and the nature of the Barzani "mission" in Mahabad, such interference in local affairs by an outside group must have seemed intolerable to the parochial-minded Kurd with his narrow tribal loyalties.

The presence of the Barzanis in the territories of the Mahabad Republic caused other resentments and difficulties as well. The feeding and provisioning of several thousand men were a heavy drain on the meager food resources of the region and must have resulted in considerable hardship for the local population.[73] However, the most serious problem connected with the presence of the Barzanis in Iranian Kurdistan appears to have been of an entirely different nature.

The Barzanis apparently did not see eye to eye with Qadi Muhammad and had a falling out with him not too long after their arrival in Iran. Shaykh Ahmad of Barzan claimed that things were brought to a head by the Barzanis' refusal to do the bidding of Qadi Muhammad, who wanted to send them on punitive expeditions against various recalcitrant tribes. The Barzani leader maintained that relations between him and Qadi

Muhammad deteriorated to such an extent that the latter bitterly denounced him before Soviet officials as a British agent. The eventual outcome of this clash, according to Shaykh Ahmad, was that he was sent to Shaytanabad, where he was forced to stay until the fall of Mahabad.[74]

The Causes of Tribal Opposition to the Mahabad Regime

Tribal opposition to the Kurdish Republic of Mahabad sprang from a variety of historical, political, religious, social, and economic factors.

Anti-Russian sentiment. The Mahabad regime obviously derived various benefits from its Soviet connection. As far as the Kurds were concerned, there is no doubt that the Soviet Union's great name and prestige impressed many Kurds and induced them to rally to the new state. However, this same connection served to alarm and antagonize an influential segment of Kurdish tribal leaders. The anti-Russian attitude of these men had been shaped by a long history of unpleasant relations.

Every time there had been a war between Russia and Persia or between Russia and Turkey, the Kurds had to face the Russians as deadly antagonists. Furthermore, because such a large part of the Kurdish homeland lay in the frontier regions of Russia's two southern neighbors, every fresh conflict brought great losses and untold suffering to the Kurds. For nearly two centuries, the Kurdish subjects of the shah and the sultan had been taught to regard the Russians as the infidel enemy par excellence.

World War I, in particular, had left a legacy of fear and distrust of Russia. That struggle, as a result of the Turkish declaration of a holy war, had kindled the fires of racial and religious hatred. The war on this front often deteriorated into massacre and countermassacre, each side trying to outdo the other. Anti-Russian feeling, as might be expected, was particularly strong among those elements in Iranian Kurdistan that had responded to Turkey's pan-Islamic propaganda,[75] who were a majority of the Persian Kurds. However, we should not forget that there were those who had been won over by the Russians.[76]

With the coming of the revolution in Russia and the establishment of the Soviet regime, a somewhat new attitude toward the Russians began to emerge. A suspicion of the Soviet government's antireligious policies was added to the Kurds' earlier anti-Russian and anti-Christian sentiment. No doubt this anti-Soviet sentiment was strongest among Kurdish chieftains and other landowning notables who feared the eventual loss of their power and property under a Soviet-type system.

The economic factor. Economics was another important cause of Kurdish resentment against the Mahabad regime. Kurdish cultivators, in particular tobacco growers whose livelihood depended largely on the Iranian market, suffered great financial losses when they found themselves cut off from the rest of Iran. As noted earlier, another hardship endured by the Kurds of Mahabad was that they had to share their depleted food supplies with a large number of Barzani warriors.[77]

Resentment of Qadi Muhammad's leadership. Finally, many Kurdish tribal leaders resented the rise of Qadi Muhammad to a position of supreme power by the rather unusual means of party machinery and the support of the urban population. Power in

Kurdistan, from time immemorial, had been concentrated in the hands of those who controlled the quasi-military organization of the warlike tribes. This control had been maintained by means of strong tribal and feudal ties. The Kurdish ruling class had traditionally been drawn from three groups: the hereditary princes, the shaykhs of the religious brotherhoods, and the tribal chieftains. All Kurdish leaders who ever entertained pan-Kurdish ambitions and dreamed of establishing their hegemony over the rest of their compatriots came from one of these three dominant groups. The careers of Prince Bedir Khan of Bohtan, Shaykh 'Ubayd Allah of Nehri, and Simko Agha of the Shikak, to mention only three such men, may be cited as examples.

Under the circumstances, it is inevitable that an aspirant to national leadership such as Qadi Muhammad was bound to be at a disadvantage. He was, it is true, a respected member of a greatly revered family in his own town of Mahabad, but he was only an urban religious dignitary and lacked both the prestige and the prerogatives of a member of one of the great ruling groups. As a national leader, he possessed none of the attributes of leadership that had caused thousands of supporters to flock to the standard of his predecessors. He had neither the aura of ancient authority that was once so unique a possession of the great hereditary princes, nor the aureole of sanctity that marked off the great shaykhs of the Qadiri and the Naqshbandi brotherhoods from other men, nor the power and fame of the chieftains who headed the great tribal confederations.

Notwithstanding all these handicaps, Qadi Muhammad succeeded for a while in becoming the supreme leader of his people. Of all the factors involved in his rise to power, none is more significant than his acceptability as a national leader to large segments of the Persian Kurds. This no doubt was a portent of deep significance whose social and political implications were only too apparent. It was a clear indication that the old social order was in a state of ferment and that the system of polity that it had sustained for centuries was in imminent danger of collapse.

This ferment was greatly accelerated by the upheaval of World War I and the events that followed it. The establishment of modern or modernized administrations in Turkey, Iran, and Iraq after that war gave a fresh fillip to the processes of settlement and detribalization, and quickened the pace of education, industrialization, and urbanization. The forces of change that had slowly but steadily been advancing into the remotest corners of Kurdistan since the turn of the century had left their mark everywhere. The old tribal and feudal loyalties, greatly weakened by the strains and stresses of a changing world, were gradually yielding ground before a new kind of loyalty. Modern doctrinaire nationalism, by supplanting and usurping the functions of these loyalties, was beginning to influence the nature and sources of power in Kurdistan.

However, subsequent events were to show that these emerging changes were not yet as far-reaching or as profound as they had been believed to be. The traditional strongholds of the old order proved to be still largely intact, and the majority of the tribal populations were only just beginning to feel the impact of the new ideas. Thus, when the two sides arrayed their forces and stood facing each other, the old shibboleths and the old loyalties proved stronger than the new.

A large number of the tribal chieftains in particular were unsympathetic to the new leader. As mentioned earlier, they feared and suspected his newly acquired power, which had not been attained in a traditionally recognized manner. To many, Qadi Muhammad's assumption of supreme power constituted an unprecedented deviation from established norms. They were scornful of his pretensions and jealous of his powers, and they regarded his espousal of Kurdish nationalism as a convenient foil for his ambitions. Perhaps they recognized the threat that the new leader represented to themselves as an elite social class.

The Fall of the Mahabad Republic and Its Aftermath

Probably the single most direct cause of the collapse of both the Azerbayjani and Mahabad republics was the Soviet Union's decision, made under intense pressure from the Western powers, to withdraw its military forces from Iran in May 1946. In view of the impending Soviet withdrawal, the Iranian government began to take more active military measures. More and more Iranian troops were put into the area, and Qadi Muhammad, who had only a handful of reluctant tribal levies to oppose them, was in a hopeless situation.

In December 1946, the Imperial Iranian army attacked the Azerbayjani Democrats and within 24 hours their resistance collapsed. The defeat of the Azerbayjani Democrat forces by the Iranian army at the Qaflankuh Pass on the night of December 10, 1946, marked the end of the Kurdish Republic of Mahabad, just as a year earlier the capture of Tabriz by the Azerbayjanis had been the signal for the creation of the Kurdish Republic. It is interesting to note that in his message of surrender to the Iranian prime minister, the Democrat governor of Azerbayjan announced that the Kurdish commander Sayf Qadi had been apprised of the situation and instructed to cease hostilities.[78]

Two days later Sadr Qadi, Qadi Muhammad's brother, proceeded to Miyanduab, where he met the Iranian commander General Homayuni. The object of Sadr Qadi's mission was to make arrangements for the peaceful occupation of the Mahabad region by the Iranian army. An agreement was subsequently reached in accordance with which the Iranian forces were to move into the region as soon as the Barzanis evacuated it.

After the Barzanis' withdrawal to Naqada, the Iranian army began to move in the direction of Mahabad, preceded by irregular tribal forces including contingents from the Dehbokris, the Mamish, and the Mangurs, three leading tribal groups hostile to the Kurdish regime. However, these forces were stopped near the town by a representative of Qadi Muhammad who pointed out that the agreement had provided for the occupation of Mahabad by regular Iranian troops rather than by tribesmen, whose presence it was feared would result in widespread disorder. This request was acceded to, and the tribesmen withdrew. The Iranian army entered Mahabad, and for a few days cordial relations existed between the army commanders and the Kurdish leaders.[79]

This honeymoon, however, soon came to an end. On December 17 and 18, many Kurdish leaders, including Qadi Muhammad and his cousin Sayf Qadi, were arrested and jailed. On December 30, Sadr Qadi was arrested at his home in Tehran and brought to Mahabad, where he was imprisoned with his brother, Qadi Muhammad. From all available evidence, the arrest of Sadr Qadi was an unjustified act of vindictiveness. Throughout the existence of the Kurdish republic, he had maintained a correct and nonpartisan attitude toward the regime headed by his brother. He was a member of Parliament and resided in Tehran. Throughout the year, he had left Tehran only when his services as a mediator had been required by the Iranian authorities.[80]

With the Kurdish leaders in prison, the Iranian army, now in complete control of Mahabad, invited all those who had complaints against the prisoners to present whatever evidence they possessed.[81] This move on the part of the Iranian authorities sealed the fate of the accused. That this proceeding was a kangaroo court was apparent from the statement of an Iranian source that the judges of Qadi Muhammad were men who had long sought to put an end to his power.[82]

The accusations brought against Qadi Muhammad included the misappropriation of eighty thousand rials from the treasury of Bukan, cooperation with Hama Rashid and the Barzanis, and the sending of fifty young men to the Soviet Union for military training.[83] Upon the completion of the trials, Qadi Muhammad, Sayf Qadi, and Sadr Qadi were condemned to death. Upon learning of his brother's fate, Qadi Muhammad was stunned by the injustice of the sentence and pleaded for his brother's life. His efforts were in vain, however, and at dawn on March 31, 1947, all three men were hanged in the square of Mahabad, which was heavily guarded by Iranian soldiers manning machine guns.[84]

Kurds everywhere received the fall of Mahabad and the execution of Qadi Muhammad and his companions with sorrow and resentment. In Turkey and Iraq, the public expression of Kurdish sentiment was not possible. In Iranian Kurdistan, which was under martial law, the people were sullen but quiet. However, violent rioting is reported to have broken out in Khurrumabad, the chief town of Luristan, on May 11, 1947, in protest against the executions at Mahabad.[85]

The tragic consequences of the fall of Mahabad for the Kurds and for the people among whom they lived were not yet over. As noted earlier, a number of Kurdish Iraqi army officers who had joined Mulla Mustafa at the time of his rebellion in Iraq had accompanied him to Mahabad after the collapse of that rebellion. The fall of Mahabad brought these officers back to Iraq, where they were arrested shortly after their arrival. On June 19, 1947, four of these officers—'Izzat 'Abd al-'Aziz, Mustafa Khushnaw, Muhammad Mahmud, and Khayrullah 'Abd al-Karim—were executed in Baghdad.[86]

The horror and dismay produced by these executions were enormous. This was the first time that Kurdish nationalists had been so dealt with in Iraq. The reaction produced by this event among the Kurds of Iraq and elsewhere was one of surprise, disappointment, and rage. Kurdish nationalism was neither weakened nor diminished by this blow. It proved instead to be a source of great strength to one group of Kurdish nationalists in particular. Now that members of the intelligentsia—the new force contending for leadership among the Kurds—could boast of martyrs, they spoke with authority.

The Kurdish émigré press widely publicized the execution of Qadi Muhammad and his companions in Mahabad and of the four officers in Baghdad. How the young ex-

19. Qadi Muhammad on the gallows, March 31, 1947.
Photographer unknown/Courtesy of Martin van Bruinessen.
Kurdistan: In the Shadow of History.

tremist Kurdish nationalists and leftists felt is perhaps best illustrated by the *Voice of Kurdistan,* a mimeographed publication by Kurdish students in Europe. The August 1949 issue of this publication dealt with the executions in Mahabad and Baghdad in two separate articles. The article "Eternal Glory to Qadi Muhammad" castigated the Americans (in particular President Truman), the British, the Turks, and the Iranians in vehement communist terminology. It poured the most bitter terms of hatred and anger on the Iranians, whom it described as "the Hashish-smoking monarchist Fascists."[87]

The execution of the Kurdish army officers was dealt with under the rubric "The Testament of Our Martyrs." This article purported to give the last words uttered by the officers just before their execution. The officers were said to have spoken with feeling of their families and of Kurdistan, stating the reasons that impelled them to take up arms in defense of their ideals. All the officers ended by shouting slogans, except for Mustafa Khushnaw, who expressed the hope that his life would serve as an inspiring example to his three small children. Muhammad Mahmud shouted, "Long live Kurdistan!" Khayrullah 'Abd al-Karim shouted, "Death to our enemies and long live Kurdistan!" and 'Izzat 'Abd al-'Aziz shouted, "Death to the imperialists and their vile agents!" [88]

A Comparison Between the Azerbayjani Democrat Regime and the Kurdish Republic of Mahabad

Some of the reasons for the failure of the Kurdish Republic of Mahabad may become more clear when it is compared with the Azerbayjani Democrat regime of Tabriz. Despite the fact that both of these regimes began, existed, and disappeared more or less at the same time and under similar circumstances, a number of significant differences are apparent.

Of the two regimes, that of the Azerbayjanis was the better organized and more politically experienced and had an older revolutionary tradition dating back to the Persian constitutional revolution of 1905–1909. These differences are perhaps best reflected in the types of men who assumed the leadership in Azerbayjan and in Iranian Kurdistan. Ja'far Pishevari, Dr. Javid, and other Azerbayjani leaders were sophisticated Communist intellectuals and seasoned party members who knew exactly what they wanted.[89] By comparison, the Kurdish leaders were simple, homespun men. Most of them were politically naïve and had little or no ideological orientation. The bourgeois and feudal mentality of the Kurdish leaders contrasted strangely with the Marxist thinking of the Azerbayjani leaders. Even Qadi Muhammad, the most learned and intellectual figure among the Kurds, was little more than a well-educated country cleric.

Another significant contrast can be drawn between the origins of Azerbayjani separatism, which gave rise to the Azerbayjani Democrat regime, and the Kurdish nationalist movement, out of which grew the Kurdish Republic of Mahabad. Azerbayjani separatism arose under the impact of Soviet and Turkish activities aimed at weakening the allegiance of the native population as a preliminary step to annexation. The more advanced and better-administered Soviet Azerbayjan had always exerted a strong influence on the kindred Iranian Azerbayjanis across the border. The Soviet, who no doubt always entertained the hope of drawing Iranian Azerbayjan into their orbit and eventually absorbing it, skillfully utilized all the opportunities afforded them by the ethnic, cultural, and geographical affinities existing between the two Azerbayjans.

The Ottoman Turks, in contrast, who at one time had been the keen rivals of the Russians in their desire to possess themselves of Iranian Azerbayjan, carried out intensive pan-Islamic and pan-Turanian propaganda (promoting the use of the central Asian languages, especially the Uralic-Altaic languages) prior to and during World War I, with great success. Thus, the centrifugal forces set in motion by Russia and Turkey had long been at work among the Azerbayjanis, who had more than once shown an unmistakable tendency to gravitate toward one or the other of these two rival states. The pro-Soviet movement led by the Azerbayjani Democrats in 1945–46 perhaps came closest to the realization of this long-cherished ambition of union with Russia.

The movement that led to the establishment of the Mahabad Republic was but the latest manifestation of the smoldering Kurdish nationalism that had periodically ignited in the various regions inhabited by the Kurds. The recurrence of these uprisings indicates that despite successive failures, the Kurdish desire for independence had never been completely stifled. These Kurdish outbursts, it should be noted, have been of a sporadic and local nature and have never assumed the character of a general conflagration. In fact, the Kurds have never combined in a unified uprising, even within any one of the several countries they inhabit. This no doubt resulted from the absence of a central organization capable of directing and coordinating Kurdish activities everywhere.

In addition to the superior organization of the Azerbayjanis and the greater experience of their leaders as compared with the Mahabad Kurds, their task was simpler—to bring about the annexation of Iranian Azerbayjan by the Soviet Union.[90] They were able to concentrate all their energies on this task and to pursue it with a remarkable singleness of purpose. The Mahabad regime's task, in contrast, was not as easy. They sought to form a nucleus for a much greater Kurdish state embracing all Kurdish lands. Although they were then struggling with the Iranian government, they knew that eventually they had to wrest the greater part of the future Kurdish state from Turkey, Iraq, and Syria.

A notable difference between the Kurdish Republic and the Azerbayjani regime was the former's comparative freedom from Soviet interference. Soviet agents were not as much in evidence in the territories of the Kurdish Republic as they were in Azerbayjan, and those that happened to be there operated in a more discreet and unobtrusive manner. Despite Kurdish denials, a Soviet representative apparently was stationed at Mahabad. The last official to act in this capacity, a man by the name of Asadov, was said to have remained at Mahabad up to the collapse of the regime and to have succeeded in fleeing to the Soviet consulate at Tabriz.[91]

The atmosphere prevailing in Mahabad was in sharp contrast to that which prevailed in Azerbayjan. Individual freedom was greatly abridged in Azerbayjan, and even terrorist methods were resorted to, whereas the Kurds enjoyed freedom from harassment by the authorities, and violence against dissenters was rare. An Iranian newspaper reporter who happened to be at the scene of these events praised the moderateness and benignness of Qadi Muhammad's rule. According to him, Qadi Muhammad put an end to looting and robbery, so the citizens of Mahabad enjoyed a brief period of peace and security. During the time that he was in office, only one person was reported to have been killed.[92]

Roosevelt made the following comparison between the two regimes:

> While terrorism reigned unchecked in Eastern Azerbayjan, in Kurdistan there were few if any political prisoners and only one or two cases of what may have been political assassination; though a number of Kurds not in sympathy with the regime did flee to Teheran. In the streets of Mahabad one could hear radio broadcasts from Ankara or

London, while in Tabriz to listen to these bought the death penalty. Whether the reason for this freedom was the moderation and liberalism of Qazi and his cabinet, or the presence of the tribes who would not tolerate violent action against persons connected with them, the net result was to make the regime popular at least among the citizens of Mahabad who enjoyed their respite from the exactions and oppression they considered to be characteristic of the Central Iranian Government.[93]

Another striking difference between the two regimes was revealed when both of them came to an end. In Azerbayjan, there was a strong popular reaction against the Democrat regime, whereas in Mahabad nothing of the sort took place. According to Roosevelt,

> Everywhere else in Azerbayjan, peasants, workers, and shopkeepers massacred the Democrats at the first indication of their collapse. This spontaneous reaction clearly indicated the hatred felt by the people for the regime. Yet in Mahabad, all passed peacefully, a circumstance especially remarkable in that elsewhere in Azerbayjan the secret police was strong and prepared for such emergencies, while Qazi Mohammad did not even have such an instrument. This fact would tend to confirm reports that Qazi Mohammad's regime was popular—at least in his own capital.[94]

The Question of Soviet Aid to Mahabad

The fierce passions generated by the rise and fall of the short-lived Kurdish Mahabad Republic died down within a decade, but the controversy concerning its nature and genesis has continued unabated. Some have contended that it was a purely Soviet-inspired venture, whereas others have insisted it was a spontaneous outgrowth of Kurdish nationalist sentiment. There is much to support both of these views.

The Mahabad regime received much of its impetus and inspiration from the Soviet Union, and many Kurds pinned their hopes for its ultimate success on continued Soviet sympathy and support. However, any attempt to discount Kurdish nationalist sentiment and to minimize the role played by the Kurds themselves would be both unfair and unrealistic. Whatever importance may be assigned to the Soviet factor, there is no doubt that the phenomenon of Mahabad would have been impossible without the powerful impulse of Kurdish nationalism.

At the time, much was made of Soviet help to the Mahabad regime. Reports of large-scale Soviet military aid and increased Soviet interference in Kurdish affairs began to appear in the Western press. These reports assumed a particularly alarming nature in the spring of 1946, at the time of the Kurdish attacks on Iranian garrisons at Bana, Saqqiz, Sardasht, and other points in Iranian Kurdistan.

In March 1946, the Soviets reportedly were training and arming the Kurds of Iran and smuggling arms to the Kurds of Iraq and Turkey. A number of Soviet officers were said to have joined the Iranian Kurds in an advisory capacity.[95] Additional reports claimed that the Soviets were continuing to provide the Kurds with advice, technical assistance, and supplies.[96] Early in April, news was circulated that the Kurds had received twenty tanks, four trucks, and an undisclosed number of mortars and other arms from a Soviet unit stationed at Miyanduab.[97] These reports, however, grossly exaggerated the extent of Russian aid to the Kurds. It is now clear that one of the principal reasons for the collapse of the Mahabad Republic was precisely the absence of such assistance. In fact, Qadi Muhammad's regime actually received little from the Soviets other than encouragement and unkept promises of help.

16

The Kurds and the Kurdish Question after the Fall of Mahabad

Kurdish Hopes and Expectations during World War II and After

Although this chapter deals with various developments that took place immediately after the fall of Mahabad, a brief discussion of certain issues that preceded that event is necessary here. Despite the fact that no promises were given to the Kurds during World War II similar to those given to the Arabs and other nationalities during World War I, the circumstances were such as to lead the Kurds to hope for certain benefits. These hopes no doubt were based on the fact that during the war the Kurds, in response to Allied solicitations, had remained quiet, even while one Kurdish-inhabited country, Iraq, had briefly been at war with Britain, and another, Iran, had found itself at odds with Britain and the Soviet Union and was occupied by them.

The French and later the British had asked the Syrian Khoybun, whose activities were usually directed against Turkey, to do everything in its power not to antagonize that country, and it had agreed to do so.[1] In fact, the Khoybun's loyalty to the Allied cause appears to have been such that, on the day that Tobruk fell to the Germans, the organization's president, Emir Jaladet Bedir Khan, is said to have called three times at the office of British colonel W. G. Elphinston to express his sympathy and unwavering devotion to the Allies.[2]

In Iraq, where the British wanted the Kurds to be quiet, the latter had lived up to expectations. The fact that in May 1941 the Rashid 'Ali regime in Iraq had sided with the Axis encouraged the Kurds in that country to hope for a reorientation of British policy in their favor. Shaykh Mahmud, who had fled from Baghdad after the outbreak of hostilities between Iraq and Britain, had toyed with the idea of starting a rebellion in Kurdistan against the Baghdad regime—an idea that had considerable support in Kurdish quarters, particularly among the younger generation. However, the rapid collapse of the Rashid 'Ali regime rendered such a move unnecessary and even undesirable.[3]

As mentioned earlier, an interesting development took place shortly after the Allied occupation of Iran. Kurdish officers from the Iraqi army, with a view no doubt toward ensuring future Russian support, were said to have approached Soviet army authorities soon after their arrival in Iran in 1941 and offered to form a Kurdish volunteer force to fight alongside the Red Army. This offer was declined.[4]

Because the Kurds had maintained a pro-Allies attitude throughout the war, in addition to having scrupulously refrained from engaging in political activity embarrassing to the Allies, they rightly or wrongly expected to be rewarded with at least a partial fulfillment of their national aspirations. Moreover, the Allies' anti-Axis propaganda had laid great emphasis on the coming liberation of the conquered peoples of Europe and Asia. The Kurds undoubtedly identified themselves with those nations to whom an Allied victory would bring a new deal.

The Barzani rebellion in Iraq and later the rise of the Mahabad Republic in Iran were to disabuse the Kurds of any illusions they may have entertained in this regard. British support to the Iraqi government during the Barzani rebellion and the Anglo-American attitude throughout the brief existence of the Mahabad Republic convinced the Kurds that it was futile to expect the West to support their desire for nationhood. The growth of Russian influence in the Middle East had induced the West to stand by the governments of Turkey, Iran, and Iraq, which meant that Kurdish interests could no longer be identified with those of the West. In order to cope with Soviet inroads in the region, the Western powers tried to avoid doing anything that might rouse the suspicions or hurt the sensibilities of the governments of the Kurdish-inhabited countries.

Disappointed and disenchanted with the West, the Kurds turned to the Soviet Union, upon whom they now pinned their hopes. Soviet backing for the Mahabad Republic, the asylum given to Mulla Mustafa and his followers in the Soviet Union, coupled with sympathetic and skillful Soviet propaganda, helped to turn the Kurds, especially the young and the idealistic among them, toward the Soviet Union. After the Barzani rebellion in Iraq and the fall of Mahabad in Iran, both Kurdish communism and Kurdish nationalism were driven underground. It was here that the two met and mingled.

The situation in the Middle East in 1945 was anything but reassuring. The Kurds, who were in a restive and expansive mood, were to raise the standard of revolt in Iraq before the year was out, and their brethren in Iran were busily engaged in laying the foundations for the future Republic of Mahabad. The Kurds' plans elsewhere, although they had failed to mature, remained a source of deep concern. The Azerbayjanis of Iran, more advanced and better organized than the Kurds of that country, were perfecting their plans for the creation of a state of their own. Autonomy was their immediate aim, but secession or even attachment to the Soviet Union may have been their ultimate goal.

The Soviet Union, which was backing the Kurds and the Azerbayjanis, renounced the Soviet-Turkish Treaty of Friendship and Neutrality in March 1945.[5] This ominous move was followed by a number of disturbing events. In August 1945, Mulla Mustafa was in open rebellion in Iraq. His defeat in mid-September and flight into Iran were soon followed by another disconcerting development. In November 1945, the Democrat Republic of Azerbayjan came into being. Turkey, alarmed by persistent reports of an imminent Kurdish rebellion and possible Soviet intervention, concentrated large forces on its Caucasian frontier—a move that brought a prompt Soviet protest.[6]

In 1946, the Kurdish-inhabited states were troubled by new alarms and fresh anxieties. The Kurdish Republic of Mahabad was officially proclaimed in March 1946 amidst great excitement throughout Kurdish lands.[7] The Soviet Union's failure to evacuate its forces from Iran on March 2, 1946, the date set for the evacuation, caused deep concern as to its ultimate intentions.[8]

The Iraqi government, apprehensive of a recrudescence of trouble in Kurdistan, began consultations with the Turkish authorities. In the early part of March 1946, the Iraqi foreign minister, Nuri al-Sa'id, was reported to be discussing possible Turkish-Iraqi collaboration, in the event of a future Kurdish uprising, with Turkish officials in Ankara.[9] The Iraqi prime minister, Tawfiq al-Suwaydi, spoke openly of involving the Anglo-Iraqi Treaty if a Soviet-backed Kurdish rebellion were to take place in Iraq.[10] In a statement published by the *New York Times,* he denied that Nuri al-Sa'id was in Ankara for any purpose other than the discussion of cultural and economic matters. Political negotiations in the circumstances, he stated, would have a disturbing effect on the international situation. However, he stressed the fact that the Sa'adabad Pact was still in force.[11]

In the meantime, articles denouncing Turkey's Kurdish policy began to appear in the Soviet press. An article signed by I. Vasiliev in the periodical *Trud* took Turkey to task for its repressive policy against the Kurds. It concluded by hinting that the Turkish-Iraqi Treaty of March 24, 1946, had a secret supplement providing for joint measures against the Kurds.[12]

In a note to Turkey on August 7, 1946, the Soviet Union proposed the revision of the Montreux Convention of 1936, suggesting that the defense of the Straits of Gibraltar be made a joint Soviet-Turkish responsibility. Turkey rejected this proposal, and the United States and Britain opposed it.[13]

Turkey, Iraq, and Iran, strongly supported by the West, particularly by the United States, succeeded in weathering the storm. The evacuation of the Soviet forces from Iran on May 8, 1946, greatly weakened the position of the Democrat Republic of Azerbayjan and the Kurdish Republic of Mahabad. As we have seen, both of these regimes collapsed before the end of 1946.

The events of the two preceding years, which had awakened the governments of the Kurdish-inhabited countries to the grave dangers threatening them, had helped bring Turkey, Iraq, and Iran together. The ever-present menace of Kurdish uprisings and Soviet intervention, kept alive by continued Soviet pressure, forced them to coordinate their efforts and to move closer to the West. The pro-Western orientation of these countries' policies, in turn, only served to exasperate the Soviets and to increase the vehemence of their attacks against them.

By 1950, the intensity of Soviet agitation reached alarming proportions. These verbal attacks, which were being increasingly concentrated on Iran and the United States, assumed a particularly menacing tone in the summer and fall of 1950.[14] Kurds were called on to assassinate Iranian officials, to commit acts of sabotage against the Iranian government, and generally to act as partisans. Comparisons with Korea were now frequently made by the Soviets, and the use of force was threatened.[15] This war of nerves, which greatly alarmed the governments of the Kurdish-inhabited countries, kept the Kurds in a state of ferment.

Turkey, Iraq, and Iran proved incapable of countering Soviet propaganda among the Kurds. They displayed neither boldness nor imagination in dealing with their Kurdish populations and seemed content with adopting a defensive attitude. Nor did the United States and Britain succeed in inducing these three countries to adopt a more sympathetic and conciliatory policy toward the Kurds. It was at this time that the uprising of the Jawanrudi tribe took place in Iran.

The Uprising of the Jawanrudi Tribe in Iran

Despite Iranian claims to the contrary, it is doubtful that the rebellion of the Jawanrudi tribe in Iran in September 1950 was motivated by any political aims. It probably was brought about by a combination of Iranian maladministration and Kurdish truculence. However, like many other Kurdish outbursts, it served to underline Kurdish grievances and thus inevitably assumed a political complexion. Besides focusing international attention on the Kurds, it provided fresh grist for the mills of nationalist and communist propaganda.

Official Iranian sources maintained that the uprising took place when the Jawanrudis, who had been ordered to disarm but refused to do so, proceeded to attack Iranian army garrisons. This action, according to Iranian sources, forced the Iranian government to undertake punitive measures. The Iranian government further claimed that the Jawanrudis were communist inspired and in proof cited the inflammatory Kurdish-language broadcasts emanating from Soviet radio stations.[16]

Kurdish sources, however, claimed that the uprising of the Jawanrudis was brought about by heavy Iranian exactions. The Kurds of Jawanrud and Shahabad were required to pay an additional 20 percent of their harvest as rent to the shah in addition to the usual taxes. This requirement, the government claimed, was in accordance with an old decree issued by Riza Shah Pahlevi that had declared all tribal lands in the regions of Jawanrud and Shahabad to be his private property. When the Jawanrudis refused to submit to these exactions, the Iranian army moved against them.[17]

The Jawanrudi tribe's rebellion and its suppression by the Iranian army provided fuel for Soviet attacks on the Iranian government and its Kurdish policy, at that time as well as several years later. In 1956, when Soviet attacks against the Baghdad Pact had reached a peak, a Soviet publication claimed that the Jawanrudi uprising had been a victim of that pact. According to this source, a few years prior to the initiation of military operations against the Jawanrudis, the Iranian government had granted them some degree of autonomy and had agreed not to station troops or police in their region. The Jawanrudis, pleased with these arrangements, had led a peaceful and law-abiding existence.

The Soviet publication argued that because the Jawanrudis occupied a strategic position astride the Iran-Iraq frontier, they were accused of causing unrest in the frontier region, and a punitive expedition was sent against them. After the outbreak of hostilities between the Iranian government and the tribe, the article maintained, those tribesmen who tried to flee into Iraq were forced to return because of the military measures adopted by Iraq in accordance with the Baghdad Pact. The article concluded by saying that "the extermination of the Kurdish people is one of the consequences of the Baghdad Pact."[18] It should be pointed out that the Baghdad Pact was not in existence at the time of the Jawanrudi uprising. Therefore, the statement that action by Iraqi frontier units was taken in accordance with the Baghdad Pact was not true.

The ratification of the Baghdad Pact in February 1955 served only to increase the Russians' fury against the member states. The Kurds, resentful of the pact, which they regarded as directed against their national aspirations, became more receptive to Soviet overtures.

The Iraqi Kurds' Drift toward Communism

The dichotomy in Kurdish political thinking, referred to in the preceding chapter, was becoming more acute. The ideas of the younger generation, led by impatient and extremist elements, found expression in the clandestine *Azadi* (Freedom), a communist newspaper that, among other things, advocated a united front with the Arabs. The older nationalists, largely conservative and restrained, published *Nishtman* (Fatherland), a publication that aimed at the attainment of Kurdish unity, asked for Kurdish rights, and called on the feudal and tribal leaders to change their ways.[19]

Sulaymaniya, which became the principal center of communist activity in Iraq, was well chosen for a number of reasons. Political activity in a remote provincial town was less likely to attract the attention of the central authorities in Baghdad. Sulaymaniya, for many years a citadel of Kurdish nationalism, had a long tradition of opposition to Baghdad. This strongly developed antigovernment sentiment, coupled with the fact that Sulaymaniya was more literate than any other Kurdish center, made it a promising field for communist proselytization. By invoking Kurdish nationalism, the Communists could pass for a variety of extreme nationalists—a cloak under which they could work with relative impunity. Furthermore, besides affording a safe base from which to operate, Sulaymaniya was conveniently located near an international frontier. Contacts with Communists in Iran and beyond were easy and unhampered.[20]

Insofar as the Kurds of Iraq were concerned, it was probably in Sulaymaniya that the effective alliance between Kurdish nationalism and Kurdish communism took place. It was here that the leadership of the Kurdish masses gradually began to pass from the *agha*s, shaykhs, and older nationalists to the intelligentsia. The continuous student-led disturbances in Sulaymaniya in 1948 provided a clear indication of the new trend.[21]

During the violent eruptions of January 1948 in Baghdad—an ominous portent of the approaching revolution of July 1958—Kurdish demonstrators who joined the rioting masses in the capital demanded the release of the Barzani leaders.[22] In Sulaymaniya, where rioting and disturbances appear to have become the order of the day, the demonstrators, who hailed the Russians and railed against the Arabs and the British, "chased an English teacher from the town and burned the British Institute."[23] In Kirkuk, demonstrators attacked the British consulate.[24]

How much of this unrest was owing to the spread of communism is difficult to determine even now. Referring to this period, Edmonds wrote:

> Many young Kurds, with a racial grievance added to feelings of frustration and discontent with the established order common to the youth of many countries besides Iraq, were tending to look to Russia for their inspiration; it was not that they knew or cared very much about Marxism, but rather that they were conditioned to lend themselves to activities inspired or directed from Moscow.[25]

Edmonds went on to say that Russia lost no opportunity to exploit the Kurds' discontent and to benefit from it.[26]

A similar view was expressed by another British source about a year after the uprisings: "There is, in effect, more discontent than Communism in Iraq. Kurdish students toy with it in the hope that the Kurds might thus be free of Baghdad rule, and it is here that left-wing activity is most noticeable."[27]

An article that appeared in 1951 in the French newspaper *Le Monde* dealt with the same subject. The Kurdish Communists, according to the author, had their roots in both the Kurdish nationalist movement and Iraqi communism. For this reason, they had constantly vacillated between the two poles of Kurdish nationalism and communist Kurdish-Arab binationalism. In the author's opinion, this vacillation accounted for Iraqi Kurds' frequent withdrawals from and return to the Communist Party. He expressed the belief that Kurdish communism was relatively strong in Iraq and cited a source according to which the Kurds constituted about 40 percent of the total effectiveness of the Iraqi Communist Party.[28]

This estimate seems somewhat high when compared to the most reliable population statistics of the time, which tell us that the Kurds of Iraq constituted between one-fifth and one-sixth of the country's population.[29] If the writer in *Le Monde* is correct, it would simply mean that even as far back as 1951, the Kurds' representation in the Iraqi Communist Party (40 percent) was approximately double their proportion of the total Iraqi population (17 to 20 percent).

The older Kurdish nationalists cannot be accused of having been idle while the Communists took over the leadership of the Kurdish youth. The odds were heavily against the nationalists because in the majority of cases the governments of the Kurdish-inhabited countries failed to accede to even a minimum of their demands. Yet nationalists persevered and continued to work for their cause as best they could. Having despaired of getting anything from their governments, they sought to solicit the aid of the Western great powers as well as various international organizations. The next section provides a record.

Notes and Memoranda Presented by the Kurds to Various International Bodies and Leading Statesmen

The outbreak of World War II revived Kurdish hopes and intensified nationalist activity. Kurdish nationalists presented a number of notes and memoranda to various international bodies and leading statesmen in which they aired Kurdish grievances and pressed Kurdish claims. A brief review of these communications gives an idea of the nature and extent of Kurdish activity in this field. These documents are summarized chronologically here.

1. Memorandum on the Kurdish question presented to the great powers on August 30, 1943.[30] This memorandum gave a concise review of Kurdish history, ethnic boundaries, population, race, language, religion, and so on. The most significant part was the last section, given in the English text but not in the French text, entitled "Why Should a Kurdish State Be Created?" Here the Allies were reminded of the Wilsonian principles, in accordance with which the Treaty of Sèvres had provided for the creation of a Kurdish state. The Allies were also reminded of the principles for which they took up arms against the Axis and were told that there could be no stability in the area unless the Kurds, oppressed by Turkey, Iraq, and Iran, were freed. This memorandum was prepared by the Bedir Khan group in Beirut.

2. Memorandum of March 30, 1945.[31] A new memorandum was presented in the name of the Kurdish League on March 30, 1945, to the heads of the delegations attending the San Francisco Conference. It reiterated Kurdish grievances and demands.

3. Letter accompanying the March 30 memorandum, submitted to the heads of the delegations at the San Francisco Conference on March 30, 1945.[32] In this letter, the heads of delegations were urged to use their influence and that of their governments toward the achievement of three ends: (1) to have the San Francisco Conference accept the principle of recognizing the right of peoples who have not yet acquired their independence to submit their claims before international assemblies; (2) to arrange for a plenary session of the San Francisco Conference to discuss the Kurdish question; and (3) to form a special international commission to be charged with studying and finding a solution to the Kurdish problem.

4. Letter accompanying the March 30 memorandum, presented to the great powers on March 31, 1945.[33] The letter stated that in accordance with the principles affirmed in the Atlantic Charter, an equitable solution of the Kurdish problem should be found now that the war for justice and liberty had been victoriously concluded.

5. Letter to the great powers submitted by Ihsan Nuri Pasha, commander in chief of the Kurdish national forces at Agri Dagh (Ararat) on July 21, 1945.[34] In this letter, Ihsan Nuri Pasha presented the Kurdish case and requested that representatives of the Kurdish people be allowed to present their claims at the San Francisco Conference, stressing the fact that not only organized states but national groups should be allowed to be heard.

6. Note presented to the foreign ministers of the great powers meeting in London on September 10, 1945.[35] This note protested the military operations initiated in August 1945 against the Barzani Kurds in Iraq and requested that the matter be brought to the attention of the ministers' governments as well as to the attention of the foreign ministers' conference.

7. Note presented to the great powers on November 26, 1945.[36] In this note, the Kurdish League again asked the great powers to find a just solution to the Kurdish problem.

8. Note addressed to the members of the United Nations on December 9, 1945.[37]

This note recalled previous notes and letters presented to various international bodies and reiterated the need for a settlement of the problem, which was important for the stability of the entire Middle Eastern area.

9. Telegram of December 24, 1945, addressed to the foreign ministers of the great powers meeting in Moscow.[38] This telegram was signed by Iraqi Kurdish leaders and stated that the rights of the Kurdish people and the promises made to them had not been fulfilled and that successive Iraqi governments had neglected the economic, cultural, and social interests of the Kurdish people. It went on to say that the Kurdish people were convinced that these governments had aimed at Arabicizing the Kurds and had not respected their rights as a separate nationality, and it demanded that they be granted internal autonomy within the Iraqi kingdom.

10. Appeal by the Rezgari Kurd Party (Kurdish Deliverance Party) to the United Nations Organization.[39] In this document, issued in the early part of 1946, the Rezgari Kurd Party demanded the liberation and unification of the Kurdish people and called for an end to their exploitation. The importance of an equitable solution of the Kurdish problem for the peace of the Middle East was again stressed.

11. Memorandum to the Anglo-American Sub-Committee of Inquiry on Palestine in 1946.[40] This memorandum from the Kurdish League referred to the ill-treatment of minorities in the Middle East, with special reference to the Kurds of Iraq.

12. Memorandum to the foreign ministers of the great powers meeting in Paris on June 26, 1946.[41] This memorandum, presented by the Kurdish League, reviewed the developments following World War I, alluding to the Treaties of Sèvres and Lausanne. It discussed the division of the Kurdish homeland between Turkey, Iran, Iraq, and Syria, and the Kurds' futile attempts during this period to regain their liberty. A breakdown of Kurdish population figures for Turkey, Iran, and Iraq was also given.

13. Note presented to the Four Foreign Ministers' Meeting in Moscow on March 10, 1947.[42] This note from the Kurdish League referred to the Kurds' various attempts to regain their rights, to the Kurds' despair, and to the danger of Kurdish youth being driven to nihilism. The foreign ministers were asked to intervene immediately in favor of the Kurds.

14. Note to General Marshall presented on March 31, 1947.[43] Among other things, this note from the Kurdish League objected to the aid given to Turkey by the United States.

15. Note addressed to the president of the United Nations Commission on the Rights of Man on July 30, 1947.[44] This note spoke of the oppression of the Kurds by the governments of Turkey, Iran, and Iraq. It described the destruction of the villages of the Barzani Kurds by the Iraqi army and the RAF and of the subsequent ill-treatment of the Barzanis in Iraqi concentration camps.

16. Memorandum of November 29, 1948.[45] This memorandum, prepared by the Kurdish League, was the most detailed statement of Kurdish complaints and claims. It was accompanied by a letter to Mr. Trygvie Lie, secretary-general of the United Nations, dated November 29, 1948.[46]

17. Note addressed to Mr. Ernest Bevin, British foreign secretary, on January 6,

1948.[47] This note was presented at the time when a new treaty between Great Britain and Iraq, to replace the Anglo-Iraqi Treaty of 1930, was being negotiated. It expressed the hope that a clause defining the Kurds' status in Iraq would be inserted in the new treaty. The note pointed out that the omission of such a clause from the treaty of 1930 had been detrimental to Kurdish rights. It reviewed the various events that followed the treaty of 1930 and the termination of the British Mandate in Iraq. (The final result of these negotiations led to the Treaty of Portsmouth.)

18. Letter by Muhammad Hilmi Beg in the name of the Kurdish National Democratic Party to Pandit Nehru on February 14, 1949.[48] This letter requested Mr. Nehru to include the Kurdish question on the agenda of the Asiatic Conference then meeting in New Delhi. A copy of this letter was also submitted to the Asiatic Conference.

19. Letter addressed to the president of the United Nations Commission on the Rights of Man on January 15, 1949.[49] This document referred to the previous note to the president of the commission on July 30, 1947, and to the unjust treatment of the Kurds in Turkey, Iraq, and Iran, emphasizing in particular the sad plight of the Barzanis in Iraq.

20. Letter submitted to the United Nations on March 3, 1956.[50] This letter restated the Kurds' grievances and urged consideration of their demands by the United Nations.

21. Address by the widow of Jaladet Bedir Khan before the Asian-African Solidarity Conference at Cairo in December 1957.[51] The text of this address was similar to the March 3, 1956, letter to the United Nations. It mentioned the maladministration and lack of social services in Kurdish areas, the lack of educational facilities for Kurds in their own language, and the suppression of Kurdish culture, especially in Turkey and Iran, but pointed out that the situation was somewhat better in Iraq. It stressed the Kurds' determination to obtain their liberty and the unification of their homeland, and refuted allegations that Kurdish revolts had been inspired by outside influences.

22. Letter addressed to United Nations secretary-general Dag Hammarskjold by the Society of Kurdish Students in Europe in October 1958.[52] In this letter, the society requested the secretary-general to place the Kurdish question on the agenda of the special session called to discuss Middle Eastern problems. It expressed the hope that Turkey and Iran would adopt a new policy toward the Kurds, inspired by the new Iraqi policy.

23. Letter addressed to Egyptian president Jamal 'Abd al-Nasir (Nasser) by the Society of Kurdish Students in Europe in October 1958.[53] This letter thanked President Nasser for inaugurating a broadcasting service in Kurdish from Cairo.

24. Letter to Premier Nikita Khrushchev by the Society of Kurdish Students in Europe in October 1958.[54] The letter expressed appreciation for the encouragement given to Kurdish cultural activities in the Soviet Union. It suggested that the Latin alphabet be used instead of the Cyrillic for Kurdish publications issued in the Soviet Union and that a Kurdish broadcast from Moscow be initiated. Copies of this letter were sent to the Soviet republics of Azerbayjan and Armenia.

Despite the numerous notes and memoranda submitted to the United Nations, the Kurds did not succeed in their attempts to have their case heard before that body. The nonexistence of a Kurdish state and the absence of a state willing to sponsor their case meant that there was no way in which the Kurdish question could be brought before the United Nations. Thus, when a petition was submitted to the secretary-general in 1948, together with the memorandum of November 1948 by a "Kurdish Delegation,"[55] their request was courteously declined and they were informed that they would have to search for a sponsor.[56]

Kurdish complaints previously addressed to the League of Nations had met with a similar fate. Sir Arnold Wilson, during a meeting of the Royal Central Asian Society on September 26, 1932, had remarked that "minorities in Iraq differed greatly from any other minorities in the world, in that there is no member of the League of Nations to bring up their claim or particular case at Geneva."[57]

It is interesting to note that despite their active support of Kurdish nationalism, the communist bloc countries, including the Soviet Union, made no attempt to sponsor the case of the Kurds before the United Nations.

Kurdish-Arab Relations: Rapprochement and Discord

While striving to win international recognition and perhaps international action favorable to their cause, the Kurds also tried to gain their Arab neighbors' sympathy and cooperation. Their peculiar circumstances, coupled with the existence of large Kurdish populations in Iraq and Syria, rendered such a course of action both desirable and necessary.

After the failure of the Barzani rebellion and the fall of Mahabad, the Kurds found themselves politically isolated. Keenly aware of the dangers of political isolation, they lost no time in advocating a closer relationship with the Arabs, which not only would benefit the Kurds in Syria and Iraq, but also would give the Kurdish people as a whole invaluable international support. Among other things, they hoped it might enable the Kurds to bring their case before the United Nations. The Kurdish wing of the Iraqi Communist Party and other kindred organizations were strong advocates of such a course of action.

Nor were the Kurdish nationalists behindhand in this respect. In the course of an interview in 1951 with the Paris correspondent of the Baghdad newspaper *al-Sha'b,* Emir Kamuran Bedir Khan dwelt on an Arab-Kurdish friendship, pointing to the kind treatment of the Kurds in Syria and Iraq. In those two countries, he stated, the Kurds enjoyed many rights and privileges denied to their kinsmen in Turkey and Iran. He pointed out that in the two Arab states, the Kurds were allowed to publish newspapers, magazines, and books in their language and to develop and preserve their own culture without any interference from the authorities. He stressed the fact that, despite certain differences between the Arabs and the Kurds in Iraq, the Kurds did not regard that country in the same light as they regarded Turkey and Iran.[58]

Four years later, in the course of my own conversation with Emir Kamuran, he elaborated on this issue. He said that it was most essential for the Kurds to cooperate with the Arabs, who were the only people in the Middle East who understood the Kurds and sympathized with the Kurdish point of view. He then pointed out that in the past the Kurds had journeyed to London, Paris, and other Western capitals to plead their cause.

"Now," he said, "we all know that that was a mistake. In the future we shall go to Baghdad, Damascus, and Cairo."[59]

Both sides appear to have recognized the need for understanding and close cooperation between the Kurds and the Arabs. From the point of view of some pan-Arab leaders, this would be a sound long-term policy; when the time came for the Arab countries to unite, the Kurds, if friendly, might refrain from causing any difficulties.

In a comprehensive article on the pan-Arab movement published by the widely read Egyptian magazine *al-Hilal* in 1943, 'Abd al-Rahman 'Azzam, later the secretary-general of the Arab League, made a strong plea for Arab-Kurdish friendship. 'Azzam paid high tribute to the Kurds, stressing the ancient Islamic ties existing between them and the Arabs and citing the great services rendered to Islam and the Arabs by Salah al-Din (Saladin) and other Kurdish commanders. He emphasized that the Arabs in Iraq should avoid at any cost giving offense to Kurdish sensibilities and declared that the Kurds are a loyal people who would never attempt to harm Arab aspirations.

The Kurds, according to 'Azzam, should never be made to feel that an Arab union is not in their interests. "The hopes and aspirations of Iraq," he stated, "should not envisage expansion at the expense of the Kurds. Rather, the Arab nation [once it was united] should leave it up to the Kurds to choose between joining it or becoming independent. If that [becoming independent] be their desire, there should be neither offense nor ill feeling [on the part of the Arabs]." 'Azzam then warned the Iraqis to guard against foreign intrigues and to beware of engaging in contention and argument with the Kurds and thus to avoid antagonizing them. He concluded his comments on Kurdish-Iraqi relations by saying, "The question is very simple and the choice lies with the Kurds. When Iraq becomes powerful it may even serve as a rallying point for this [kindred] eastern nation."[60]

No doubt both the Arabs and the Kurds were sincere in their desire for mutual understanding and cooperation, and the mutual expression of esteem and confidence seemed to augur well for the future. The fact that a good relationship between the Arabs and the Kurds, at that time, appeared not only necessary but also easy to achieve to the two proponents quoted here—an Egyptian Arab and a Syrian Kurd—is not difficult to understand. Egypt had no Kurds, and the small Kurdish population of Syria was relatively well treated in that country. However, the situation changed when Egypt, as the champion of Arab nationalism, united with Syria and, after the revolution in Iraq, made a determined bid to unite with that country but failed, largely owing to Kurdish opposition.

Friction between Arab and Kurdish nationalists had developed soon after the July 1958 revolution in Iraq. One of the earliest complaints was made by the Barzani exiles, whose return to Iraq from the Eastern bloc countries had been arranged through the United Arab Republic (UAR) ambassador in Prague. The Barzanis claimed that when they stopped in Egypt on their way home, they were subjected to harassment and discourteous treatment by the Egyptian authorities and that their departure was unnecessarily delayed. The Congress of Kurdish Students in Europe, held October 4–8, 1958, in Munich, was the object of a vehement attack by the Union of Arab Students in West Ger-

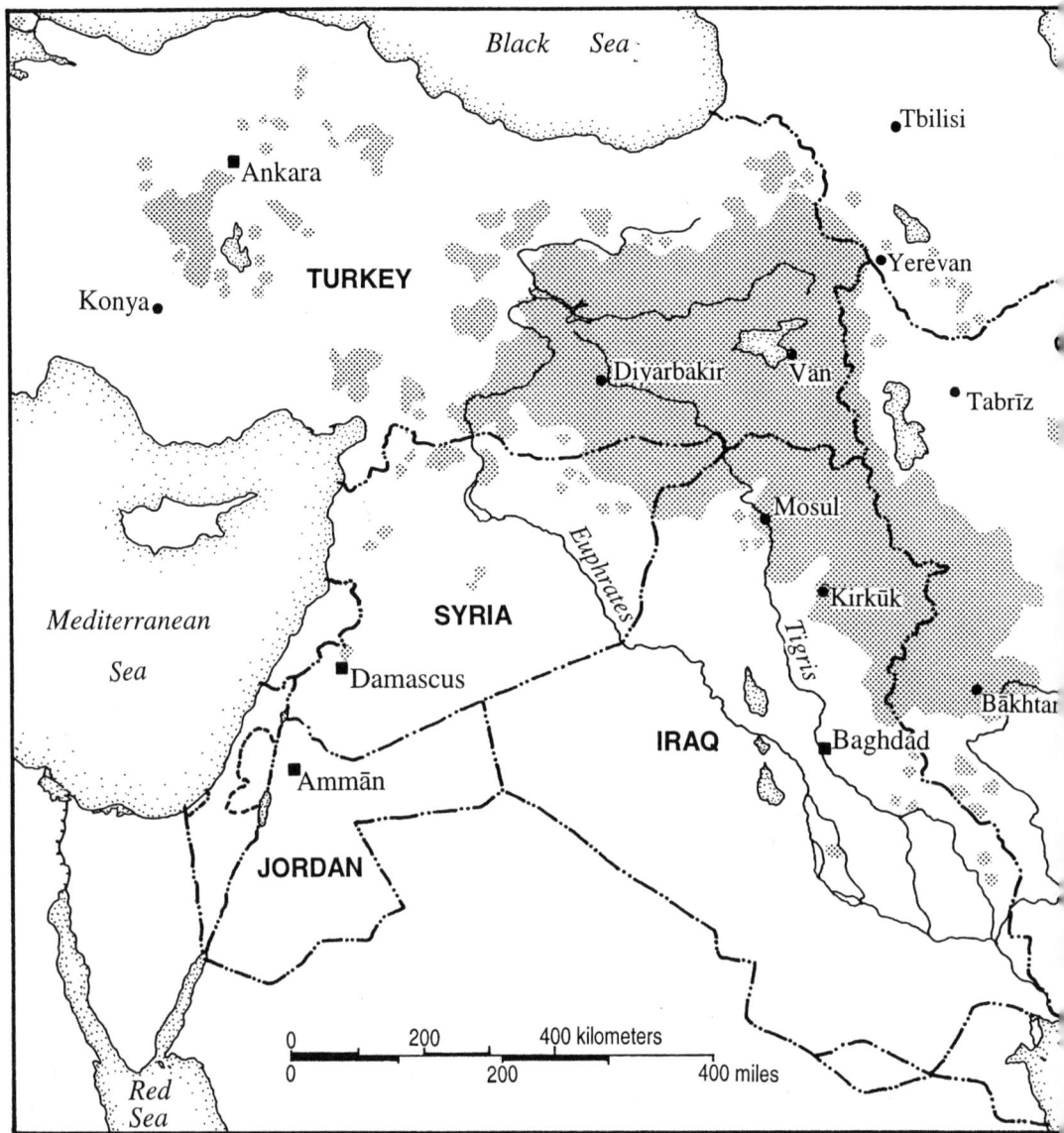

Kurdish areas in the Middle East.

many. The latter denounced the aims of the Congress of Kurdish Students as an offense and a menace to Arab nationality and called on Arab students to boycott it, threatening to punish those who did not do so.[61]

The gap between the Kurds and the Arabs therefore widened and became scarcely bridgeable. Arab nationalists in Iraq as well as in the UAR were bitterly opposed to the Kurds, who, together with the Communists and other leftists, were blamed for Iraq's rejection of union with the UAR. The conflict and contention between the two continued.

In a communication to the Iraqi Kurdish newspaper *Khabat* dated October 10, 1959, the Society of Kurdish Students in Europe disclaimed any connection with a man-

ifesto hostile to 'Abd al-Karim Qasim, the leading instigator of the 1958 revolution in Iraq and then the first head of the government it established (discussed in the next section), that had been broadcast by the clandestine radio station "The Voice of Free Iraq." The society accused this radio station of being a creature of Nasser and took it to task for attributing the manifesto to them. The society denounced Nasser, the UAR, the Ba'thists, and the radio station in the strongest terms, but paid warm tribute to Qasim and his regime.[62]

In the same communication, the Society of Kurdish Students in Europe accused the Egyptian magazine *Kuli Shay'* of falsification for publishing excerpts from a letter received from an Iraqi student in London. The letter writer, according to the Iraqi Society of Kurdish Students, denounced the society for its collaboration with the Society of Kurdish Students in Europe because of the latter's open advocacy of secession from Iraq. The society's communication decried this statement as an unfair imputation and went on to stress its members' deep loyalty to the Republic of Iraq and to its leader, 'Abd al-Karim Qasim. The communication then significantly stated, "This attitude of ours will remain unchanged as long as our Kurdish people continue to enjoy their rights and as long as the Republic will continue to pursue a democratic and emancipated course."[63]

The Kurds and the Republic of Iraq

The suddenness of the events of July 14, 1958, in Iraq, coupled with the impenetrable curtain rung down by the new revolutionary regime over the whole country, rendered speculation about many issues in Iraq, including the Kurds, very difficult. The frontiers were effectively sealed off, and all contact with the outside world was suspended. For the first few days, the meager news that leaked out pertained for the most part to the details of the upheaval and the state of internal order.

There is nothing to indicate that a favorable position for the Kurds in Iraq was envisaged either before or immediately after the July revolution. However, there can be no doubt that they greatly benefited from the struggle for power between the Qasim group and the Ba'thist-nationalist group. Had the latter group prevailed, it is more than doubtful that the Kurds would have enjoyed the rights and privileges they gained at the time.

A statement in a semiofficial publication lent substantial support to this view. It briefly surveyed the early postrevolution period in Iraq and the main issues involved in the struggle between Qasim and 'Abd al-Salam 'Arif, his first deputy, who, with his pro-Nasser Ba'th followers, was more stridently pan-Arab. It then went on to say:

> Some had wished to rouse the Kurds, the copartners in the Iraqi fatherland. However, the complete and undiminished recognition of Kurdish rights by Qasim barred their way and foiled their attempt. Kurdish leaders have unhesitatingly declared that had they themselves been in power, they could not have offered the Kurds more than what Qasim has offered them.[64]

It would seem from this statement and from the context that Qasim, rather than the other revolutionary leaders, was responsible for the Kurds' favorable position at that time and that the grant of rights and privileges to them came after, rather than before, the struggle for power between Qasim and his opponents.

Indeed, it is safe to say that a definite conciliatory trend was discernible from the very beginning. But how far the new revolutionary leadership, as it was composed immediately after the revolution, was prepared to go to meet Kurdish nationalist demands was uncertain. It is likely, however, that 'Abd al-Salam 'Arif and other extreme Arab nationalists would have refused to go as far as Qasim did. Finally, one cannot help wondering about Qasim himself. Did he from the very beginning intend to be as generous with the Kurds as he subsequently was, or was he forced to do so after the Kurds and the pro-Kurdish communist and leftist groups rallied to his support during the ensuing struggle for power?

No matter what answer may be given to this question, one thing seemed to be certain. Although there was a trend to conciliate the Kurds, no clear-cut Kurdish policy was formulated. This is not strange when one stops to think of the irreconcilable ideas held by the heterogeneous elements that had temporarily combined to overthrow the old regime.

After the violent events of July 14, 1958, the new revolutionary regime in Iraq lost no time in adopting a number of measures calculated not only to conciliate the Kurds, but also to win them over. A Kurd, Khalid al-Naqshbandi, was one of the three members of the Council of Sovereignty set up after the revolution.[65] The new cabinet included another Kurd, Baba 'Ali, a son of Shaykh Mahmud, as minister of communications and works.[66] Shaykh Latif, Baba 'Ali's brother, who had been serving a four-year term in prison, was set free. Shaykh Ahmad of Barzan, his son, and his nephew (his brother Mulla Mustafa's son), all of whom had been living in exile in the provinces, were pardoned and allowed to go home. A photograph showing Qasim standing beside a Kurdish officer who had been wounded in the fighting at the royal palace on July 14 was widely publicized.[67]

These gestures of goodwill were soon followed by a more concrete indication of the Kurds' changed position in Iraq. Article III of the Interim Constitution promulgated after the revolution stated: "The Arabs and the Kurds are regarded as copartners in this homeland, and their national rights are recognized within the framework of Iraqi unity."[68] Thus, for the first time since the formation of the Iraqi state, the Kurds found official recognition in the Constitution and were placed on an equal footing with the Arabs.

At the same time, there was much talk of Kurdish-Arab brotherhood and solidarity. Statements by Qasim and other authorities, speeches by members of visiting Kurdish deputations, as well as official press releases and radio programs spoke increasingly of the "Republic of the Arabs and the Kurds" and of the indissoluble unity of the two peoples.

Meanwhile, Mulla Mustafa, who had taken refuge in the Soviet Union after the fall of Mahabad, lost no time in sending telegrams to Qasim and to the Council of Sovereignty in which he expressed his felicitations and his desire to return to Iraq. The response was immediate and favorable, and the necessary arrangements were made with the UAR ambassador in Prague for the speedy return of Mulla Mustafa and his followers to Iraq. His arrival in Baghdad, where numerous Kurdish deputations from all over Iraqi Kurdistan flocked to welcome him, was the occasion for impressive celebrations.

Kurdish Opposition to Union with the UAR

Mulla Mustafa's return to Iraq coincided with the mounting tension between those who wanted immediate and complete union with the UAR and those who were against it. In fact, it is even possible that his return may have hastened the final rift between the two groups. The largest number of those who favored the closest and the most speedy alignment with the UAR was to be found among members of the rightest Istiklal (Independence) and the Ba'th (Revival) parties. The moderately leftist Hizb al-Difa' al-Watani al-Dimokrati (National Democratic Party) and the Communist Party viewed with distaste the abolition of parties and the curbs placed on all except authorized political activities in the UAR and thus were opposed to the idea of union.

The Kurds, who for obvious reasons had grave misgivings about joining a larger Arab state, were actively opposed to a close association with the UAR. Such a state, they feared, being predominantly Arab, would reduce them to a national minority of no great consequence.

The Kurds and the Fall of 'Abd al-Salam 'Arif

In the meantime, national as well as international attention was increasingly being focused on 'Abd al-Salam 'Arif, whose impetuosity and bluster had established him as a celebrated but highly controversial figure. 'Arif's impromptu speeches were wildly applauded by the delighted crowds, but dismayed the more thoughtful members of the public.[69] His statements on foreign and domestic issues alarmed responsible officials and frightened the well-to-do.[70] Moreover, his overbearing demeanor and imperious tone alienated a number of leading political figures as well as many of his fellow officers.[71]

The most serious of 'Arif's activities was his open advocacy of immediate union with the UAR and his close association with the Ba'thists. His stand, which was hailed by the pan-Arabs and bitterly assailed by their opponents, produced a deep cleavage and precipitated a power struggle for which neither he nor his followers seem to have been prepared.

The forces arrayed against 'Arif proved too formidable to cope with, particularly when Qasim decided to move against him. 'Arif was arrested on December 5, 1958, and delivered to the Mahdawi Court on December 27, charged with attempted assassination of the "sole leader" (Qasim) on October 11, 1958, and for inducing an uprising on December 4–5, together with other lesser charges. After a lengthy closed trial on February 5, 1959, he was condemned to death and dismissed from the armed forces. However, Qasim kept the court's verdict on his desk indefinitely without approving it. For the next three years, 'Arif remained in prison until his acquittal in the autumn of 1961, after the secession of Syria from the UAR.[72] 'Arif's fall dealt a severe blow to the Ba'thists and other groups with pan-Arab ideas and constituted a clear victory for the proponents of Iraqi unity. The latter included the Communists, the National Democrats, and the Kurds. Whatever Qasim's personal feelings may have been with regard to 'Arif's disgrace and fall,[73] he must have been glad of the chance to rid himself of an embarrassing associate, an unruly lieutenant, and a potentially dangerous rival.

Two episodes mentioned in the course of 'Arif's trial shed some light on his attitude toward the Kurds. The first pertained to Mulla Mustafa's return to Iraq and was reported by Colonel Wasfi Tahir, a bitter enemy of Colonel 'Arif. According to Tahir, when Qasim and Siddiq Shanshal, the then minister of guidance, were engaged in drafting an answer to Mulla Mustafa's telegram requesting permission to return to Iraq, 'Arif commented:

"Look at what these people are doing! Had I been entrusted with their task I would have simply wired two words, 'Go away! Go away!' " [74]

More serious than this, if true, was 'Arif's alleged behavior toward Shaykh Ahmad of Barzan, Mulla Mustafa's elder brother. According to a witness at his trial, 'Arif was rude and insulting to Shaykh Ahmad when the latter visited him to congratulate him on the success of the revolution and to express his thanks for being released from prison. 'Arif is reported to have told his guest something to this effect: "Be careful not to cause any disorders; otherwise we shall punish you severely." [75] The Barzani leader is said to have deeply resented this uncalled-for admonition.

It was reported at the time of 'Arif's fall that his fate had something to do with his opposition to Mulla Mustafa's return. Whatever truth there may have been in this report, one thing is certain: Kurdish influence under the new regime grew steadily after the overthrow of 'Arif. In fact, the Kurds were increasingly identified with the Qasim regime. On at least two occasions, they played a decisive role in defeating serious rebellions against Qasim. On both of these occasions, the Kurds made common cause with leftist and especially communist supporters of the regime.

The Role of the Kurds in the Mosul Rebellion

During the rebellion of Shamir tribesmen under the Arab Colonel 'Abd al-Wahhab al-Shawwaf in the spring of 1959, Kurdish tribal contingents, which were rushed to the support of army units loyal to Qasim and the popular resistance forces in Mosul, probably saved the day. The Kurds' intervention not only helped defeat hostile forces within Mosul, but also effectively cut off all outside help. The Kurdish forces in question included, in addition to Barzani fighters, tribesmen from the 'Amadiya region as well as from 'Aqra and Sinjar. According to an Iraqi journalist, more than five thousand Kurdish fighters were involved. [76] The Yazidi tribesmen from Sinjar, whose mountain home lies astride the main highway to the Syrian frontier and the Shammar encampments, appear to have played an important part in blockading the pro-Shawwaf forces.

After the Mosul rebellion, the Kurds and the leftists demanded and received credit for their signal services to the Qasim government. They were closely identified with the regime. The Barzani Kurds, together with other pro-Qasim leftist Kurdish elements, played an important role in quelling a dangerous uprising in the Baradost district of the Rawanduz region.

The Baradost Uprising of May 1959

The causes of the May 1959 Kurdish uprising in the Baradost district of the Rawanduz region have never been adequately explained. At the time when operations against the rebels were in progress, official information was meager. The Iraqi government, for obvious reasons, did not wish to publicize a revolt in Kurdistan at a time when the Kurds were being hailed as one of the regime's mainstays. Even after the revolt was over, official sources and the local press shed little or no light on this event. It was usually described as an imperialist-inspired revolt of feudal chieftains. [77] The foreign press, in contrast, regarded it merely as a revolt directed against the revolutionary regime in Iraq. [78]

This uprising, like the eruption of the Shammar Arabs at the time of the Shawwaf revolt in Mosul, was a belated reaction of the conservative and feudal elements against the July revolution. The suddenness of the revolution and the violence that accompanied it appear to have temporarily paralyzed all those opposed to the revolution and robbed them of the will to act at that time.

The three leading figures of the 1959 uprising, Shaykh Rashid of Lolan, his son-in-law Mahmud Khalifa Samad, and Shaykh Muhammad Siddiq, were closely associated with the old regime and thus were not well disposed toward the new one.[79] In addition to their opposition to the new revolutionary regime, the first two were bitter enemies of Shaykh Ahmad and Mulla Mustafa of Barzan. The violent clashes between Shaykh Rashid and the Barzanis had constituted one of the main reasons for the initiation of military operations against the latter in 1931–32. During the Barzani rebellion of 1943–45, Shaykh Rashid again ranged himself against the Barzanis and was this time joined by Mahmud Khalifa Samad.

Shaykh Muhammad Siddiq was too young to play any role in the events of 1931–32. In 1943, the shaykh, who was one of the most personable young Kurdish chieftains and who despite his youth was already a member of Parliament, managed not to become embroiled in the intertribal quarrels of the region. In the spring of 1943, I saw a great deal of Muhammad Siddiq in Arbil, and I remember well his criticism of the government for providing Mahmud Khalifa with money and arms to fight the Barzanis. At that time, he was very sympathetic to Mulla Mustafa and on bad terms with Mahmud Khalifa. The fact that he later decided to throw in his lot with Shaykh Rashid and Mahmud Khalifa indicates that he had a radical change of heart.

No doubt the unprecedented power and prestige that the Barzani family had enjoyed since the return of Mulla Mustafa from the Soviet Union had something to do with the uprising. Whether Shaykh Rashid and his son-in-law resorted to arms as a result of provocation or did so as a gesture of defiance against the regime that had so greatly exalted their bitter enemies above them was not clear. They rose in an armed insurrection despite the fact that the odds were heavily against them.

Barzani warriors, together with tribal contingents organized by the newly formed peasant societies, operated against the rebels as "popular resistance forces" in cooperation with units of the Iraqi army and air force.[80] The rebels were soon overcome, but the rebel chiefs, accompanied by a number of their followers, succeeded in fleeing across the frontier into Iran and Turkey. Shaykh Rashid himself, together with some members of his family and several hundred of his followers, crossed into Turkey.[81]

Thus ended the uprising of Shaykh Rashid. The Barzanis had at last succeeded in turning the tables on their stubborn adversaries. For the first time in three desperate encounters, they had the government on their side. They now inflicted on Shaykh Rashid what he had twice inflicted on them: defeat and exile.

For the second time in less than six months, the Barzanis had rendered a great service to the existing regime. Had Shaykh Rashid succeeded in holding his own even for a few months, he would have dealt a severe blow to the idea of Kurdish-Arab solidarity, one of the major pillars of the Qasim regime. His success, besides splitting the Kurds, would have cost Qasim much Arab support. The Barzanis were rapidly demonstrating that they were very valuable, if not indispensable, to the regime. The role of the leftists at the time of Shaykh Rashid's uprising should not be forgotten. Here, as in Mosul earlier, they did their best to defeat the anti-Qasim revolt. Their propaganda carefully emphasized Kurdish-Arab brotherhood and pointed out that Shaykh Rashid's rebellion was not a revolt of Kurds against the Qasim government, but rather a revolt by reactionary feudal chieftains and other remnants of the former regime.

The Disorder and Violence in Kirkuk

In the late summer of 1959, serious disturbances broke out in Kirkuk. When details of these events became known, it was revealed that atrocities of the most shocking nature had taken place. Qasim denounced the violence and its perpetrators in the severest terms, stating that in cruelty and barbarity the Kirkuk events surpassed anything done by Hulagu and Ghengis Khan. He went so far as to say that even the Zionist terrorists at Dair Yasin had not displayed such fiendish cruelty as that displayed by those elements who had taken the law into their own hands in Kirkuk.[82]

Qasim, who was visibly disturbed when making these statements, charged that similar bloodbaths had been intended to take place all over the country. He emphasized the fact that the government was in possession of vast incriminating evidence and that it intended to use all the power at its command to crush the conspirators.

Communist sources described the eruption of violence in Kirkuk as a struggle between the supporters of the regime and reactionary elements. However, fuller information left no doubt that racial hatred and personal animosities played an even more important role than ideological considerations. In Kirkuk, the Kurds and the Communists appear to have combined against the Turkomen.

The Kurds and the Communists had clearly overplayed their hands in Kirkuk. The signal services that both had rendered to the Qasim regime, both during the Shawwaf revolt in Mosul and during the uprising of Shaykh Rashid in the Rawanduz region, had enabled them to emerge as the guardians and staunch supporters of the new republican regime. The Communists, however, after the violent events in Kirkuk for which they were held responsible and Qasim's bitter denunciations of their actions, suffered a severe setback. A break between them and Qasim seemed imminent, and both they and the Kurds appeared to have lost their privileged position. Intrigues by pan-Arab elements culminating in an attempt on Qasim's life, however, brought about a gradual reconciliation between Qasim and the Communists and seemed to largely offset the bitterness engendered by their excesses in Kirkuk.

Although considerable odium came to be attached to the Kurds and the Communists, both of whom were often mentioned in connection with the unhappy events in Kirkuk, the Barzani leaders' reputation did not suffer. The Barzanis, who do not appear to have been involved in those events at the time, were careful to adopt an attitude of aloofness and noninterference afterward.

Kurdish Gains under the New Regime

Kurdish gains in Iraq were considerable and reflected the importance assigned to them by the new republican regime. All these gains, it will be recalled, were foreshadowed in the Interim Constitution, which recognized them as copartners with the Arabs within the framework of Iraqi unity. The spirit in which this recognition was carried out was as remarkable as the recognition itself. The idea of copartnership found significant expression in the new coat of arms of the Iraqi republic, where the Arab sword is matched by the Kurdish dagger.[83]

The Kurds' position immediately after the revolution can best be gauged by considering the gains they made with regard to their role in the government, their share of development projects and social services, and the cultural freedom granted them to develop as a separate nationality.

The Kurds' Role in the New Government

By and large, the Kurds' share of key government positions in the new regime was not too different from what it previously had been. However, their participation in the new government was established on a broader and more liberal basis, for two reasons. First, the new policy of the state toward the Kurds was fundamentally different from that of the old regime, in that it treated them as copartners and not as a minority group. Second, the peculiar circumstances obtaining in Iraq after the revolution forced Qasim and his regime to seek their support—a fact that greatly added to their weight in Iraq.

One of the earliest and symbolically most significant posts given a Kurd was the appointment of Khalid al-Naqshbandi as a member of the Council of Sovereignty. Needless to say, this appointment placed the Kurds, from the very inception of the new regime, on equal footing with the two other major Iraqi groups, the Sunni and the Shiʿi Arabs. Two cabinet posts were now held by Kurds, the ministry of communications by Hasan Talabani and the ministry of works and housing by ʿAwni Yusif.[84] These appointments, it should be pointed out, were in conformity with long-established practice. Under the old regime also, Kurds had traditionally held one or two cabinet posts.

In the foreign service, ʿAli Haydar Sulayman, a Kurdish career diplomat of ambassadorial rank, was retained and began serving as ambassador to the United States. Ismet Kattani was appointed as a member of Iraq's permanent delegation to the United Nations. Jalal Jaf was given the post of chargé d'affaires at Peiping. Kurds also began to hold important positions in the fields of education and religion. Dr. Siddiq Atrushi, a Kurd of Dohuk, held the post of director general of education, second in importance only to the minister of education. His brother ʿAbd al-Hamid Atrushi was mufti of Baghdad, the highest legal-ecclesiastical post among the Sunnis of Iraq.[85]

The Kurds were well represented on three powerful instruments of the new regime: the popular resistance forces (a paramilitary organization with branches throughout the country), the people's court, and the military prosecution board set up for the trial of members of the old regime as well as for the trial of the enemies of the

Republican regime. Colonel Bamerni headed the popular resistance forces; Colonel 'Abd al-Fattah Shali became a member of the people's court; and Adnan Babajan, a lawyer, was appointed a member of the prosecution board that assisted the military prosecutor-general.

Social Services and Rural Development

In accordance with the declared policy of the new regime, a stepped-up social and economic development program, designed to raise the standard of living and to improve living conditions throughout the country, was initiated and given top priority. Existing rural development projects and social services were expanded and speeded up. The main results achieved in Kurdistan up to July 14, 1959, included the following:

Housing. Several hundred new housing units were completed and others were begun at Sulaymaniya, Sarchinar, Darbandi-i Khan, and Arbil.[86]

Electricity. Electric power stations were built for the first time in certain localities. In other localities, existing facilities were either enlarged or replaced with new ones. Zakho, 'Aqra, Dohuk, Penjewin, Makhmur, Qal'a Diza'i, Kifri, Halabja, Rawanduz, and Shaqlawa benefited from this program.[87]

Water supply. New sources of potable water were made available for the population in various parts of Kirkuk, Arbil, Sulaymaniya, and Mosul.[88]

Health. A fully equipped and fully staffed hospital was scheduled to be completed before July 14, 1959, at Shakhwa. Plans were initiated for the establishment of child and mother welfare centers at Sulaymaniya and Kirkuk and for the building of a clinic in Sulaymaniya and a hospital in Mosul for the treatment of chest diseases. Two sanitariums for consumptives were planned for Arbil and Sulaymaniya.[89]

Town planning. Sulaymaniya, Kirkuk, and Arbil were included among the towns to undergo extensive changes in accordance with modern town planning.[90]

Rural revival centers. Rural revival centers were established at Arbil, Mosul, and Kirkuk to improve living conditions in the countryside.[91]

The textile industry. Work started on the construction of textile factories at Shahrizur and Sulaymaniya and on housing units for the employees of these factories.[92]

These benefits were offered or promised to the Kurds under the new government. It should be noted that some of these projects and improvements had been started under the old regime.

Encouragement of Kurdish Cultural Activities

Cultural freedom. Of all Kurdish gains under the new regime, those in the cultural field were the most spectacular and, to the Kurdish intelligentsia, were extremely gratifying. In fact, their gains in this field derived from and were complementary to their gains in the political field. Like their Arab "copartners," they were now free to develop their culture as a separate and equal nationality.

The Kurds had possessed cultural freedom under the monarchy, and they were free to use it without hindrance so long as they did not go beyond certain prescribed limits. However, the area where the cultural and the political mingled and merged and where no clear lines of demarcation existed was held to be questionable. Anything beyond that area was forbidden ground on which they were not allowed to tread. All this was changed after the revolution, and the latitude given the Kurds was considerably greater. They could vociferate about their culture and nationality as never before, but not in a spirit of hostility or ill will.

Education. In countries where education and similar matters are the state's responsibility, government initiative is imperative, not only because it sets the seal of official approval on any given undertaking in this field, but also because it is the only way to get things done. In response to Kurdish wishes, the new regime created a new directorate general for Kurdish education in the Ministry of Education and charged it with responding to the Kurds' educational needs.[93] As mentioned earlier, a Kurd was appointed as director general of education.[94] Another indication of the increasing official attention paid to Kurdish culture was the appointment of the well-known Kurdish poet Musa Hasan, better known by his pseudonym Jagerkhwin,[95] as professor of Kurdish at the University of Baghdad.[96]

Kurdish radio programs. Another significant development in the cultural field was the increase in the time allotted to the Kurdish program on Baghdad radio from two to four hours. The additional time came from the introduction of a new program in the Bahdinani dialect.[97] This development is both interesting and significant for a number of reasons. The Sulaymaniya dialect of Kurdish, in which an extensive literature began appearing, was previously the only officially recognized Kurdish dialect in Iraq and served as the accepted medium of expression throughout Iraqi Kurdistan. This dialect, closely related to Mukri Kurdish, was increasingly being used by the Mukri-speaking Kurds in Persia.[98] In fact, the preeminence of the Sulaymaniya dialect was so widely recognized that Kurdish broadcasts from the Soviet Union were in that dialect.[99]

The recognition of the Bahdinani dialect underscored Mulla Mustafa's influence and prestige and was indicative of the shift of Kurdish leadership in Iraq from the Sulaymaniya region, the center of the Barzinja shaykhs, to the Mosul region, the home of the Barzani shaykhs. However justified this move may have been, it was undoubtedly an expression of Kurdish particularism and possibly an indication of the Bahdinani Kurds' desire to break away from the tutelage of Sulaymaniya, which had for many years been the recognized Kurdish cultural center in Iraq.

It is interesting to speculate on the various possibilities inherent in the introduction of the Bahdinani radio broadcasts. Placed on an equal footing with the Sulaymaniya dialect, would the Bahdinani dialict become to northern Iraqi Kurdistan what the Sulaymaniya dialect had been to southern Iraqi Kurdistan? Such a distinction would be a serious drawback to the development of Kurdish nationalism, which in the past greatly suffered from the lack of a common language.

The Sulaymaniya dialect of Kurdish had been adopted as the vehicle of literary expression in important parts of Iraqi and Persian Kurdistan, so the possibility of its being adopted as the lingua franca of a large part of Kurdistan seemed promising. However, the establishment of two separate and equal Kurdish dialects in Iraq would, no doubt, tend to hinder the education of the illiterate Kurdish masses in that country. The process of duplication entailed in the task of developing two separate dialects into effective literary and scientific vehicles would result in the wasting of much time and effort.

The introduction of the Bahdinani dialect in the Baghdad radio program was apt to have repercussions outside of Iraq. The Turkish Kurds north of the Iraqi frontier and the Syrian Kurds in the Jazira province to the west speak dialects very close to the Bahdinani of northern Iraq. This means that the Kurds of Bohtan and Hakari, the two Kurdish regions in Turkey, and the Kurds of the Jazira province in Syria would be reached by the Baghdad radio broadcast. The Kurds of Iran, however, could be reached only through the Sulaymaniya dialect.

The Kurds' Attitude toward the Qasim Regime

The Kurds were enthusiastic about the new regime in Iraq and seemed very loyal to it. The rights and privileges they began to enjoy surpassed their wildest expectations. For this reason, it was with genuine sincerity that they began referring to the Republic of Iraq as "the Republic of the Arabs and the Kurds." The new regime in Iraq was felt to be so much their own that a writer chided 'Abd al-Hamid Saraj, the Syrian strongman who was reputed to be of Kurdish descent, for continuing to cooperate with Egypt's Nasser and called him a traitor to his Kurdish origin. Kurds throughout Kurdistan began increasingly to express their support and attachment to the new regime in Iraq as well as to 'Abd al-Karim Qasim, who was referred to as "the leader of the Arabs and the Kurds."

It is interesting to note that the attempt on Qasim's life brought measures of sympathy and protest not only from all over Iraqi Kurdistan,[100] but also from the Kurds of the neighboring countries. One such message, forwarded through "the well-known struggler Mustafa Barzani," came from "[t]he Kurdish strugglers in the Kurdistan that is annexed to Iran."[101]

The phrase "Kurdistan that is annexed to Iran" caught on and began to be frequently used by Iraqi Communists as well as by Iraqi Kurdish newspapers. What significance this phrase had and what it portended was not clear. Was this just another cliché enjoying a temporary vogue, or was Iraq preparing to play the role of claimant to neighboring Kurdish lands? This irredentist reference to Persian Kurdistan was rather puzzling.

✹ Conclusion

A strong sense of nationality has existed among the Kurds for a very long time. Although a people of mixed origin, the Kurds constitute a nationality that has proved its vigor throughout the ages. They have withstood the inroads of more numerous and highly developed peoples such as the Arabs, the Turks, and the Persians, and, despite certain affinities with the latter, they have succeeded in maintaining their separate identity. Their vitality has been demonstrated by expansion into non-Kurdish regions as well as by the Kurdicization of neighboring peoples.

Although no one dialect or language is common to all Kurds, the speakers of the various dialects and languages regard themselves as Kurds and are so regarded by each other. Despite the fact that among the Kurds there are Twelver Shi'is, 'Alawis (Qizilbash), Ahli Haqq, Kaka'is, and Yazidis, the majority of them are Sunnis of the Shafi'i rite.

Linguistically the Kurds may be divided into two major groups. The largest, most extensive group is the Kurds who speak Kurmanji or any of its related dialects and who, with few exceptions (notably the Yazidis), are Shafi'i Sunnis. This group represents the Kurds par excellence. The second group consists of the various Dimli-speaking groups, among whom are found the Kurds of Dersim, who are Zaza speaking and adherents of an extreme Shi'i doctrine, and the various Gurani-speaking enclaves in Iraq and Iran, such as the Guran tribe, the Bajalan, and the Kaka'is, all of whom are adherents of the Ahli Haqq doctrine, and the inhabitants of the Hewraman mountain area, who are Sunnis. Despite the fact that the latter group differs linguistically and religiously from the Kurmanji-speaking group, they believe themselves to be Kurds, and their Kurmanji neighbors do not contest this belief.

Despite the heterogeneous composition of the Kurds, in some cases attested to by various tribal traditions, they believe themselves to have a common ancestry. Some European scholars have claimed a Median ancestry for the Kurds, a claim that has found wide acceptance among Kurdish writers. Even though this belief may not necessarily agree with the facts (which, it should be pointed out, are very difficult to prove either way), it is the concept universally held among members of the group that matters. In this connection, some of the more highly developed nationalisms in the world offer a good parallel. The fact that the Prussians have many non-Germanic racial elements has not hampered them from playing a leading role in creating the German national state.

It is interesting to note that various Kurdish ruling families have pretended to an Arab descent and proudly displayed Arab genealogies—a fact no doubt because of the religious prestige that attaches to Arab descent among Islamic peoples. However, even those among them who have claimed such descent have never considered themselves anything but Kurds. Shaykh Mahmud, whose claim to be descended from the Prophet has been recognized by some leading genealogists, complained in a petition to the United Nations against being placed under an Arab government.

Of the various elements that go into the making of Kurdish nationality, probably the most important is a common social and economic organization. Although many racial strains have contributed to the making of the Kurdish people, and although there are varying degrees of differences in language and dialect among the various groups, a particular type of social and economic organization, comprising what has been described as a "mountain culture," is common to them all. This peculiar mountain culture is the product of environmental, geographical, and historical forces that have combined to shape the general configuration of Kurdish life and institutions. By and large, wherever this particular mountain culture is found coupled with the Kurmanji, the Dimli, or, according to some authorities, the Luri branches of the Iranian group of languages, the people are considered Kurds and the land Kurdistan. These elements, then, seem to be the two major components of Kurdish nationality.

The Kurds appear to have been aware of their separate national identity many years before Kurdish nationalism became a reality. Their feeling of solidarity and kinship has been demonstrated whenever they have come in contact with non-Kurds or whenever different groups of them come in contact with each other. Strange manifestations of Kurdish nationalistic tendencies are found among some of the heterodox Kurdish sects upon whom the hold of Islam has been greatly weakened. The Yazidis, adherents of a religion that seems to be connected with the remote Kurdish past, identify themselves very closely with the Kurdish national idea. "Oh Lord," they implore God in one of their prayers, "raise thou the Throne of Kurdistan high unto the heavens." It is noteworthy that the Yazidis believe that God speaks the Kurdish language, and another heterodox sect, the Ahli Haqq, places the scene of the Day of Judgment in the Shahrizur plain in southern Kurdistan.

That the Kurds were aware of their nationality as far back as the twelfth century is attested to by the maneuvering that led to the election of Salah al-Din to the vizierate. Nor was the idea foreign to Mulla Idris, the Kurdish advisor of Sultan Selim the Grim, who during the heyday of Turkish power forged the links of a Kurdish-Turkish partnership in a manner that ensured the preservation of Kurdish autonomy.

Muhammad Pasha of Rawanduz was similarly inspired by the idea of Kurdish nationality when he sought an accommodation with Ibrahim Pasha of Egypt with the object of acquiring the Kurdish provinces of the Ottoman Empire, and Emir Bedir Khan was impelled by the same motive when he declared his independence and extended his hegemony over a great Kurdish confederation of his own creation. It was certainly a nationalist impulse that was behind Shaykh ʿUbayd Allah's movement, and the shaykh was undoubtedly motivated by Kurdish nationalist sentiment when he declared in a letter intended for the eyes of the representatives of the British government, "We Kurds are a people apart."

During the nineteenth century, Kurdish national awareness grew rapidly with every fresh Kurdish outbreak. Although at times it may have seemed deceptively like modern nationalism, Kurdish national awareness did not actually reach this stage until the latter part of the nineteenth century, especially after Shaykh ʿUbayd Allah's movement. This movement, coupled with other developments and events within and without the Ottoman Empire, hastened the emergence and growth of doctrinaire nationalism among the Kurds. Kurdish national sentiment thus acquired a new motive power and became a political force of great importance in the affairs of the Middle East.

The spread of modern doctrinaire nationalism among the Kurds, an outcome of Kurdish intellectuals' active participation in nationalist activities, was in large measure a reaction against Armenian, Turkish, Arab, and Persian nationalisms. The emergence of a Kurdish nationalist press and the establishment of Kurdish clubs and societies gave a strong impetus to Kurdish cultural and political activities. Though somewhat haphazard and not too well coordinated at first, these early efforts laid the foundation for the development of Kurdish nationalism into a future mass movement.

World War I and its aftermath mark an important stage in the growth of Kurdish nationalism. The extent and intensity of nationalist feeling among the Kurds were profoundly influenced by the impact of such momentous developments as the overthrow of czardom and the outbreak of the Russian Revolution; the defeat and breakup of the Ottoman, Russian, and Austro-Hungarian empires; the fall of the House of Othman and the abolition of the caliphate, as well as the revolutionary ideas set in motion by these events; and the propagation of the Wilsonian principles of national self-determination.

The Arabs in the Hijaz, in Syria, and elsewhere seemed well on their way toward the achievement of their national aspirations. Even the Armenians seemed at the point of attaining a state of their own. These gains by former fellow Ottoman subjects, coupled with the vacuum of authority created in Turkish, Persian, and Iraqi Kurdistan after the war, raised Kurdish hopes and intensified Kurdish national expectations. The Kurds' aspirations, which had found recognition if not fulfillment in the Treaty of Sèvres, suffered a severe blow three years later at the Lausanne Conference.

The Kurds, now in a resentful mood, were rendered even more restive and unmanageable by the heightened impact of Western civilization in the years following the war—a development that they felt threatened to undermine their way of life. The Kurdish masses, with the encouragement of their leaders, were determined to resist this influence. The various Kurdish rebellions in Turkey, Iraq, and Iran, besides being violent manifestations of Kurdish nationalist sentiment, were also waged in defense of the Kurdish way of life. The extension of a central government's external authority into Kurdish lands, accompanied by the new and unfamiliar economic and technological processes of modern civilization, roused Kurdish resistance and increased the vehemence of Kurdish nationalism.

The aggressiveness of nascent Turkish, Persian, and Arab nationalisms gave rise to new grievances and apprehensions, for besides wounding Kurdish national pride, they threatened the Kurdish national identity with extinction. In 1952, Professor William Thomson, speaking of Turkey's attempt to denationalize and assimilate the Kurds, commented:

> But Iran is not registering the same success in its effort to denationalize the Kurds, and Iraq has conceded them a measure of self-determination. It is quite evident that the leaders of Turkey and Iran have forgotten, or do not consider applicable in their case, perhaps, the lesson of the Partition of Poland, which first raised the issue of nationality, and have not thought through the basis and justification of their own existence.[1]

During the period between the two world wars, the Kurds rose in a series of dangerous and bloody revolts in Turkey, Iraq, and Iran. Although some of these revolts were well organized and had well-defined political aims, others were no more than violent protests against some real or imagined injustice. Whatever the cause, every fresh outbreak seemed to fill the cup of Kurdish bitterness. Yet, strange as it may seem, the Kurds made no attempt at concerted action. The majority of Kurdish leaders, while talking about Kurdish nationalism, continued to busy themselves with matters of local or regional interest. Needless to say, this particularism militated against the creation of an all-Kurdish organization and rendered the coordination of Kurdish efforts impossible.

Kurdish revolts continued despite the fact that it must have been clear to the Kurds that they were incapable of prevailing against their adversaries unaided. Their only chance of success lay in outside help, and the only powers from whom they could hope to receive such help were Great Britain and France. This help never materialized, but both of these powers managed to retain the Kurds' friendship and confidence. In the late 1930s, responsible Kurds were beginning to resign themselves to the idea that Kurdish nationalist aspirations could not be attained short of a world conflict. No doubt many Kurds felt that the outbreak of World War II would provide the opportunity for which they had been waiting.

Allied wartime declarations and the whole tenor of Allied wartime propaganda once more raised the Kurds' hopes and led them to expect some consideration and perhaps a partial fulfillment of their national claims. In the meantime, they sought and received assurances of Soviet friendship and support. The rapid march of events was beginning to reveal a steady deterioration of Kurdish relations with the West, on the one hand, and a closer association with the Soviet Union, on the other.

On two crucial occasions, the attitude of the Soviet Union attitude toward the Kurds stood out in sharp contrast to that of the West. At the time of the Barzani rebellion of 1943–45, the British stood by the Iraqi government in opposition to the Kurdish rebels, and at the time of the rise and fall of the Mahabad Republic, both Britain and the United States supported the Iranian government against the Mahabad regime. On both occasions, the Soviet Union adopted a friendly and sympathetic attitude toward the Kurds, and in the case of Mahabad it was suspected of aiding and abetting the Kurdish nationalists. The Soviet Union's grant of asylum to Mulla Mustafa and his followers after the collapse of Mahabad and the open Soviet support and encouragement of Kurdish nationalist aspirations—made known to the Kurds through a sustained press and radio campaign, as well as through local communist parties' activities—served to draw the Kurds closer to the Soviet Union.

There is no doubt that the Kurdish question is one of the most vexed and dangerous problems confronting the Middle East today. It has, particularly since the end of the World War II, increasingly engaged the attention of interested governments as well as students of Middle Eastern affairs. Malcolm Burr, a British scholar, views the problem as essentially one of the adjustment of a people with a mountain culture to the conditions of the modern world. With the old Kurdish social and economic system in the process of crumbling, some way must be found of settling the Kurds and absorbing them into the modern economy. According to him, the various Kurdish rebellions represent the stand of brave, primitive men against the onslaught of alien and unfamiliar forces.[2]

Morgan Phillips Price, a British journalist and Labour member of Parliament in the mid-1940s, also saw the Kurdish problem as primarily a social and economic one, which he believed to be part of the whole nomad problem of the Middle East. According to him, "The people who handled it with success . . . are the Russians, because they have not treated it as a military problem of punitive expeditions but as an economic one related to the poverty of the tribes." In his view, although the punishment of brigands was sometimes necessary, as a policy it was useless.[3]

Also in the mid-1940s, H. M. Burton, a former British political officer in Iraq, believed that forcible detribalization of the Kurds was wrong and that a peaceful scheme of settling them had to be found. He maintained that the key to the settlement of the Kurds lay in the development of communications and the spread of education.[4]

According to Colonel W. G. Elphinston, a Middle East union composed of the Kurdish-inhabited countries would greatly contribute to the solution of the Kurdish problem. He advocated a customs and passport union that would eliminate frontier restrictions on the Kurds' movement from one country to another and would enable them to share in the resulting economic benefits. Elphinston voiced serious doubts concerning the feasibility of creating a Kurdish national state. In his opinion, geographic barriers would make a Kurdish state economically unsound.[5]

All these writers have stressed the social and economic aspects of the Kurdish question. Notwithstanding the importance of these factors, it must be kept in mind that nationalism, which lies at the root of the Kurdish question, is largely political and psychological in nature. Any adequate solution to the Kurdish problem must take these political and psychological factors into consideration.

Pierre Rondot, one of the best-informed authorities on Kurdish affairs, has repeatedly urged the West, in particular the United States, to take the lead in doing something for the Kurds. He has gone so far as to say that the Western powers in general, and especially Britain, have subordinated their Kurdish policies to their Arab policies.[6]

The 1958 revolution in Iraq, which brought the Kurds and the communists to the fore in that country, gave rise to an important question: whether Iraq would be used as a base for an active Kurdish nationalist movement and, if so, whether the Kurdish movement would be tinged by communism. Much depended on the attitude of the West as well as that of Turkey and Iran.

The materials analyzed for this study warrant the conclusions that the Kurds form a distinct nationality, that they have a strong consciousness of their Kurdish nationality, and that their national movement has deep roots in the convictions and aspirations arising from that nationality. The divisive factor of tribal loyalties tends to play a constantly diminishing role because of the impact of modern civilization, which is changing the cultural patterns in the whole Middle East.

The Kurds share, with other nationalities that have been under foreign control, the same aspirations for gaining the freedom to determine their own political future. The reactions of the Turks, the Iranians, and the Arabs to Kurdish aspirations will be important, but the Kurds' success or failure in achieving their aims will largely depend on the international situations in their part of the world.

As in other regions, the decisive factor will be the policies of the dominant world powers, who might either encourage Kurdish national aspirations or stand aloof from them. No one can foresee what these policies will be in the future.

This study has attempted to connect the Kurdish problem with the past policies not only of the Kurdish-inhabited states, but also of the great powers in order to demonstrate that no major country interested in the Middle East can afford to ignore the Kurdish problem or to avoid the formulation of a Kurdish policy as part of its overall Middle Eastern policy.

Appendix

✳

Notes

✳

Glossary

✳

Bibliography

✳

Index

 *Appendix*

The Treaty of Sèvres, Section 3: Kurdistan

Article 62

A commission sitting at Constantinople and composed of three members appointed by the British, French and Italian Governments respectively shall draft within six months from the coming into force of the present Treaty a scheme of local autonomy for the predominantly Kurdish areas lying east of the Euphrates, south of the Southern boundary of Armenia, as it may be hereafter determined and north of the frontier of Turkey with Syria and Mesopotamia, as defined in Article 27, 11, (2) and (3). If unanimity cannot be secured on any question, it will be referred by the members of the commission to their respective Governments. The scheme shall contain full safeguards for the protection of the Assyro-Chaldeans and other racial or religious minorities within these areas and with this object, a Commission composed of British, Italian, Persian and Kurdish representatives shall visit the spot to examine and decide what rectifications, if any, should be made in the Turkish frontier where, under the provisions of the present Treaty, that frontier coincides with that of Persia.

Article 63

The Turkish Government hereby agrees to accept and execute the decisions of both the Commissions mentioned in Article 62 within three months from their communication to the said Government.

Article 64

If within one year from the coming into force of the present Treaty the Kurdish people within the areas defined in Article 62 shall address themselves to the Council of the League of Nations in such a manner as to show that a majority of the population of these areas desires independence from Turkey, and if the Council then considers that these peoples are capable of such independence and recommends that it should be granted to them, Turkey hereby agrees to execute such a recommendation, and to renounce all rights and title over these areas.

The detailed provisions for such renunciation will form the subject of a separate agreement between the Principal Allied Powers and Turkey.

If and when such renunciation takes place, no objection will be raised by the Principal Allied

Powers to the voluntary adhesion to such an independent Kurdish State of the Kurds inhabiting that part of Kurdistan which has hitherto been included in the Mosul Wilayet.

Communiqué from the High Commissioner, May 6, 1921

The following communiqué from the high commissioner was published by the advisors in the Mosul, Kirkuk, and Sulaimani divisions on May 6, 1921:

"The High Commissioner has under active consideration the administrative arrangements to be made for the future of the Kurdish Districts in Iraq. It has been represented to him that apprehension exists lest the interests of the Kurds should suffer by subordination to the national Government established in Baghdad, and that, for this reason there is some demand for an autonomous regime.

"At the same time, the leaders of Kurdish opinion are understood to be fully alive to the economic and industrial ties connecting their areas with Iraq proper and to the inconveniences which separation might involve. In these circumstances His Excellency desires if possible, to obtain an indication of the real wishes of the Kurdish communities. Should they prefer to remain under the Iraq Government, he is prepared to recommend to the Council of State a solution on the following lines:

'One—As regards the Kurdish Districts of the Mosul Division which fall within this sphere of the British Mandate, a *Sub-Liwa* should be formed comprising the districts of Zakho, 'Aqra, Dohuk and 'Amadiya, with headquarters at Dohuk, the Sub-Liwa to be under a British Assistant Mutasarrif. Qaimmaqams for the time being should be British, but would be replaced by Kurds or Kurdish speaking Arabs acceptable to the Kurds as soon as competent men are forthcoming. This Sub-Liwa would be generally be subject, for all financial and judicial purposes, to the National Government at Baghdad and would then naturally send representatives to the Constituant Assembly; but for the purposes of general administration the Qaimmaqams would address the Sub-Mutasarrif while administrative appointments would be made by His Excellency, the High Commissioner in consultation with the local authorities.

'Two—The High Commissioner will endeavour to arrange to associate British Officials with the Administration of Arbil, together with Keui Sanjaq and Rawanduz, and will secure that in the appointment of Government Officials regard will be had to the wishes of the people. Details should be elaborated as soon as the situation admits.

'Three—Sulaimani will be treated as a Mutasarrifliq governed by Mutasarrif in Council; the Mutasarrif to be appointed by the High Commissioner and to have a British Advisor attached to him. Pending the appointment of a Mutasarrif the British Political Officer will act in this capacity.

'To the Mutasarrif and Council will be delegated such powers, including right of appeal to the High Commissioner, as may be approved by the High Commissioner, after consultation with the Mutasarrif in council on the one hand and the Council of State on the other.

'Qaimmaqams for the time being should be British to be replaced by Kurds as soon as competent men are forthcoming.' "

 *Notes*

Most of the *Encyclopedia of Islam* articles cited in this study are from the reprint of the original first edition, which was entitled *E. J. Brill's First Encyclopaedia of Islam: A Dictionary of the Geography, Ethnography, and Biography of the Muhammadan Peoples* (Leiden: E. J. Brill, 1913–36), 4 vols. and supplement. The reprint is entitled *E. J. Brill's First Encyclopedia of Islam, 1913–1936* (Leiden: E. J. Brill, 1987), 9 vols. References to the encyclopedia use the volume numbers from the reprinted edition, but the page numbers are the same in both the first edition and the reprint. A few articles cited in this study are from volume 9 of the reprinted edition, entitled *Supplement* (Leiden and London: E. J. Brill and Luzac, 1935). A few articles have been cited from *Encyclopedia of Islam, New Edition*, 11 vols. (Leiden and New York: E. J. Brill and Luzac, 1954–2003).

1. Geographical, Historical, and Cultural Background

1. *Kurdistan* is a relatively modern term used to denote lands inhabited by Kurdish-speaking peoples. This term was first used by the Seljuk Turks, who applied it to a province that forms only a small part of what is today known as Kurdistan. V. Minorsky, "Kurdistan," *Encyclopaedia of Islam*, 1st ed., 4:1130–32.

2. This description of the boundaries of Kurdistan is based on the following works: E. B. Soane, "Limits of Kurdistan," in *Report on the Sulaimania District of Kurdistan: With Some Notice of the Frontier Tribes of Turkey and Persia, and History of the Frontier Question of the Two Countries* (Calcutta: Superintendent of Government Printing, 1918), 1–3; Lucien Rambout, *Les Kurdes et le droit: Des textes, des faits* (Paris: Editions du Cerf, 1947), 1–2; map of Kurdistan in Muhammad Amin Zaki, *Khulasat Tarikh al-Kurd wa Kurdistan Min Aqdam al'Usur Hatta al-'An* (The Summary of the History of the Kurds and Kurdistan from the Most Ancient Times up to the Present), translated from the Kurdish into Arabic by Muhammad 'Ali 'Awni (Cairo: al-Sa'ada Press, 1939); map of Kurdistan published by the Kurdish League; F. R. Maunsell, "Kurdistan," *Geographical Journal* 3, no. 2 (Feb. 1894): 81–82.

3. William Bayne Fisher, *The Middle East: A Physical, Social, and Regional Geography* (London: Methuen, 1950), 303.

4. For the sake of consistency, in this discussion I have used the terms applied by the *Great Soviet Atlas* to the various Tauric mountain ranges in Turkey: Western Taurus (Zapadnyi Tavr); Central Taurus (Tsentral'nyi Tavr); Eastern or Armenian Taurus (Vostochnyi of Armianskii Tavr); and Inner Taurus (Vnutrenni Tavr).

5. L. Molyneux-Seel, "A Journey in Dersim," *Geographical Journal* 44, no. 1 (July 1914): 49–68.

6. Oswald stated that a fracture crosses Armenia, running from Karaja Dagh through Nimrud, Sipan, Tandurek, and Ararat to Shemakha in the Caucasus. Felix Oswald, *A Treatise on the Geology of Armenia* (London: Felix Oswald, 1906), 10. Twenty years earlier Clayton believed that there were underground connections between these volcanoes; E. Clayton, "The Mountains of Kurdistan," *Alpine Journal* 22, no. 97 (Aug. 1887), 296.

7. For an excellent study of the mountainous area south of Lake Van, see John Frodin, "La morphologie de la Turquie sud-est," *Geografiska Annaler* (Stockholm) 19 (1937): 1–28.

8. For a detailed description of the Hakari region, see W. A. Wigram and Sir Edgar T. A. Wigram, *The Cradle of Mankind: Life in Eastern Kurdistan,* 2d ed. (London: A. and C. Black, 1922), 262–310. Cf. Basile Nikitine, *Les Kurdes: Etude sociologique et historique* (Paris: Imprimerie Nationale Librairie C. Klincksieck, 1956), 30.

9. Fisher, 256.

10. Ibid.

11. Ibid., 258–59; George Babcock Cressey, *Asia's Lands and Peoples: A Geography of One-Third the Earth and Two-Thirds Its People* (New York: McGraw-Hill, 1951), 404; G. M. Lees, "The Middle East," in *World Geography of Petroleum,* edited by Wallace Everett Pratt (Princeton, N.J.: Princeton Univ. Press for the American Geographical Society, 1950), 164–65.

12. Vital Cuinet, *La Turqie d'Asie, géographie administrative, statistique, descriptive et raisonnée de chaque province de l'Asie Mineure,* vol. 2 (Paris: E. Leroux, 1891), 427–29; *Handbook of Mesopotamia* (London: Naval Staff, Intelligence Department, 1917–18), 1:22; R. Hartmann, "Dicle, Dicla," in *Islam Ansiklopedisi,* 3:582–85 (Istanbul: Milli Egitin Basimevi, 1955); Fisher, 340ff.

13. "Euphrates," in *Encyclopaedia Britannica,* 11th ed. (1910–11), 9:894–98. R. Hartmann, "Al-Furat," in *Encyclopaedia of Islam,* 1st ed., 3:118–20; Fisher, 340ff.

14. On the flora and fauna of the various regions of Kurdistan, see W. R. Hay, *Two Years in Kurdistan: Experiences of a Political Officer, 1918–1920* (London: Sidgwick and Jackson, 1921), 13–34; Molyneux-Seel, 49–50; Lees, "The Middle East," 192; E. Huntington, "The Valley of the Upper Euphrates River and Its People," *Bulletin of the American Geographical Society* 34, no. 4 (1902), 306–8; Walter B. Harris, "A Journey in Persian Kurdistan," *Geographical Journal* 6, no. 5 (Nov. 1895): 453–57; Rambout, 13–14; Kamuran Bedir Khan, "The Kurdish Problem," *Journal of the Central Asian Society* 36, parts 3 and 4 (July-Oct. 1949), 238–39.

15. L. Dudley Stamp, *Asia: A Regional and Economic History* (London: Nethuen, 1959), 81; Fisher, 309.

16. Fisher, 324–26; Soane, *Report on the Sulaimania District,* 14–15; Rambout, 14–15; K. Bedir Khan, 239.

17. The *Livre Jaune* published by the French government in 1892 estimated the number of Kurds in the Ottoman Empire at 3,012,879. In the official British publication *Armenia and Kurdistan,* the number of Kurds in the Ottoman Empire prior to World War I was estimated at about 1,500,000. Cf. C. W. Wilson and H. C. Rawlinson, "Kurdistan," in *Encyclopaedia Britannica,* 11th ed. (1910–11), 5:949–51, which places the figure at 1,650,000. For a detailed discussion of early Kurdish population figures, see Minorsky, "Kurdistan."

18. A number of newspapers, selected at random, give the following estimates of the total number of Kurds: *Chicago Daily News* (Mar. 20, 1946), 8 million; *Manchester Guardian* (Mar. 21, 1946), 2.5 million; *Times* (London) (May 6, 1946), 3 million; *Tribune des Nations* (Dec. 10, 1948), 9 million; *The Scotsman* (Jan. 9, 1951), 2.5 million; *New York Times* (Apr. 7, 1952), 3–6 million; *La Bourse Egyptienne* (Oct. 8, 1952), 4 million.

19. For example, *Le Monde* on December 4, 1945, estimated the total number of Kurds at 8–9 million, but on December 7, 1951, gave a population breakdown by country that totaled only 3,130,000.

20. Perhaps the most reliable figures on the Kurdish population of the Middle East up to 1960 were those for Iraq. In 1957, Edmonds estimated the Kurdish population of Iraq in a thorough and detailed manner, giving a breakdown by subdistrict, district, and province for the whole country on the basis of the general census of 1947. C. J. Edmonds, *Kurds, Turks, and Arabs: Politics, Travel, and Research in North-Eastern Iraq, 1919–1925* (London: Oxford Univ. Press, 1957), 438–40. Cf. C. J. Edmonds, "The Kurds of Iraq," *Middle East Journal* 11, no. 1 (winter 1957), 52; A. H. Hourani, *Minorities in the Arab World* (London: Oxford Univ. Press, 1946), 12–13; and Pierre Rondot, "La nation Kurde en face des mouvements Arabes," *Orient* 2, no. 7 (1958), 61. For Turkey, although no figures for the Kurds as such are given in the official census, 1,900,000 persons were listed as having Kurdish as their mother tongue.

21. C. J. Edmonds, "Middle East Focus on the Kurds," *Daily Telegraph* (London), July 22, 1958.

22. Ibid.

23. W. G. Elphinston, "Kurds and the Kurdish Question," *Journal of the Royal Central Asian Society* 35, part 1 (Jan. 1948), 41. The Kurdish population figures given in *The Middle East: A Political and Economic Survey,* 2d ed. (London: Oxford Univ. Press for the Royal Institute of International Affairs, 1954), are based on Elphinston's estimates.

24. Pierre Rondot, "La question Kurde dans l'Orient contemporain," *Bulletin Mensuel du Centre d'Etudes Kurdes,* no. 12 (1950), 4.

25. Robert Zeidner, "Kurdish Nationalism and the New Iraqi Government," *Middle Eastern Affairs* 10, no. 1 (Jan. 1959), 26.

26. Kurdish League, *Memorandum on the Situation of the Kurds and Their Claims* (Paris: Imprimerie Jean-Gap, 1948), 5. Figures very close to these were given in the "Memorandum on the Kurdish Question Presented to the Great Powers on August 30, 1943"; see *Bulletin du Centre d'Etudes Kurdes,* no. 6 (1949). Cf. "Memorandum Presented to the Minister of Foreign Affairs of the Great Powers Meeting in Paris on June 26, 1946," *Bulletin du Centre d'Etudes Kurdes,* no. 25 (1949). It is significant that the Kurdish League, as early as 1830, estimated the total number of Kurds at 8,387,280. Bletch Chirguh, *La question Kurde: Ses origines et ses causes* (Cairo: Paul Barbey, 1930), 8.

27. Rambout, 19.

28. "Kurdy," *Bol'shaia Sovetskaia Entsiklopediia,* 2d ed. (Moscow, 1953).

29. V. Minorsky, "Kurds," in *Encyclopaedia of Islam,* 1st. ed., 4:1132–55; V. Minorsky, "Les origines des Kurdes," in *Actes du XXe Congrès International des Orientalistes, Bruxelles, 5–10 Septembre 1938* (Louvain: Bureaux du Musson, 1940), 152.

30. For details, see Ephraim Avigdor Speiser, *Mesopotamian Origins: The Basic Population of the Near East* (London: H. Milford, 1930), passim.

31. G. R. Driver, "The Name Kurd and Its Philological Connexions," *Journal of the Royal Asiatic Society* 10 (July 1923): 393–403.

32. Ibid., 394.

33. Ibid. Cf. Minorsky, "Kurds," 1133.

34. Driver, "The Name Kurd," 394.

35. Adontz, *Armenia v epokhu Iustiniana,* 398, cited in Minorsky, "Kurds," 1133.

36. Minorsky, "Kurds," 1133.

37. Ibid.; see also Arshak Safrastian, *Kurds and Kurdistan* (London: Harvill Press, 1948), 16.

38. V. Minorsky, "The Guran," *Bulletin of the School of Oriental and African Studies* 11, no. 1 (1943), 75.

39. Minorsky, "Kurds," 1133–34. Cf. Janos Harmatta, "Studies in the Languages of the Iranian Tribes in South Russia," *Acta Orientalia* (Budapest) 1 (1951): 261–314.

40. Minorsky, "Les origines des Kurdes," 147ff.

41. Minorsky, "Kurds."

42. Ibid.

43. V. Minorsky, *Studies in Caucasian History,* Cambridge Oriental Series no. 6. (London: Taylor's Foreign Press, 1953), 109ff.

44. Ibid., 1–104; also E. Denison Ross, "Shaddad," in *Encyclopaedia of Islam,* 1st. ed., 7:246.

45. H. F. Amedroz, "The Marwanid Dynasty at Mayyafariqin in the 10th and 11th Centuries," *Journal of the Royal Asiatic Society* (Jan. 1903): 123–54; also K. V. Zettersteen, "Marwanids," in *Encyclopaedia of Islam,* 1st. ed., 5:309–10.

46. Minorsky, "Kurds," 1137.

47. V. Minorsky, "'Annazids," *Encyclopaedia of Islam, New Edition,* 1:512–13.

48. On the early history of Salah al-Din, see Minorsky, *Studies in Caucasian History,* 107–57.

49. Salah al-Din's appointment to the vizierate was arranged by Diya al-Din 'Isa, a Hakari Kurd. Ibid., 137–38; see also Stanley Lane-Poole, *Saladin* (New York: G. P. Putnam's Sons, 1901), and Morton Sobernheim, "Salidin," in *Encyclopaedia of Islam,* 1st ed., 7:84–89.

50. For a discussion of the organization of Salah al-Din's army, see H. A. R. Gibb, "The Armies of Saladin," *Cahiers d'Histoire Egyptienne* (Cairo) 3 (May 1951): 304–20.

51. For a comprehensive discussion of the Ayyubid dynasty, see Claude Cahen, "Ayyubids," in *New Encyclopaedia of Islam, 2nd Edition* 1:796–807.

52. Safrastian, 37.

53. Minorsky, "Kurds."

54. Ibid.; also V. Minorsky, "Ak Koyunlu," in *Encyclopaedia of Islam, New Edition,* 1:311–12.

55. Minorsky, "Kurds."

56. For the full text of this *farman,* see Zaki, *Khulasat Tarikh al-Kurd,* 184–90.

57. For a discussion of the vexed question of the Turco-Persian frontier, including a translation of the preamble of this treaty, see Edmonds, *Kurds, Turks, and Arabs,* 125–39.

58. For an authoritative biography of Nadir Shah, see Laurence Lockhart, *Nadir Shah: A Critical Study Based Mainly on Contemporary Sources* (London: Luzac, 1938).

59. Edward Granville Browne, *A Year Amongst the Persians: Impressions as to the Life, Character, & Thought of the People of Persia,* 3rd ed. (London: A. and C. Black, 1950), 94, 124. Nikitine, *Les Kurdes,* 178, 187.

60. Browne, *A Year Amongst the Persians,* 310ff.; cf. Nikitine, *Les Kurdes,* 169.

61. C. Huart and L. Lockhart, "Agha Muhammad Shah," in *Encyclopaedia of Islam, New Edition,* 1:246–47.

62. E. B. Soane, *To Mesopotamia and Kurdistan in Disguise. With Historical Notices of the Kurdish Tribes and the Chaldeans of Kurdistan,* 2d ed. (London: John Murray, 1926), 218 and 378–79.

63. Mirza Muhammad Djewad al-Kazi, "Studien aus dem Rechtsleben in Kurdistan," *Zeitschrift fur Vergleichende Rechtiswissenschaft* (Stuttgart) 22, part 3, (1909), 345.

64. Minorsky, "Kurds," 1151. According to Sir Mark Sykes, a number of Kurds he met informed him that their ancestors had been Zoroastrians before the advent of Islam. Mark Sykes, *The Caliphs' Last Heritage: A Short History of the Turkish Empire* (London: Macmillan, 1915), 425.

In discussing the spread of the Isma'ili and the Qarmatian heresies in the Muslim world, a well-known Muslim theologian points out the ready acceptance these ideas found among "wild Kurds and sons of Zoroastrians." 'Abd al-Qahir ibn Tahir al-Baghdadi, *Mukhtasar Kitab al-Farq bayna al-Firaq* (The Abridged Book of Differences among the Sects), edited by A. S. Hakim (Cairo: Matba'at al-Hilal, 1924), 141.

65. Hoffman, *Auszüge,* 270, quoted by Minorsky, "Kurds."

66. Minorsky, "Kurds," 1151.

67. Al-Mas'udi, *Muruj al-Dhahab,* vol. 3, 254, cited by Minorsky, "Kurds," 1135.

68. "A non-Arab man from among the Kurds went to a Babylonian shaykh and told him: 'Sir, I want you to teach me magic.' The master said: 'What is your religion?' The man answered: 'I am now a follower of the religion of Christ.' " See Helmut Ritter, *"Picatrix" das Ziel des Weisen von Pseudo-Magriti* (London: Warburg Institute, 1962), 316.

69. Ihsan Nuri, *Tarikh-e Rishe Nezhadi-ye Kord* (History of the Racial Origin of the Kurd) (Tehran: Sepehr Press, 1955), 117.

70. Wigram and Wigram, 162–63.

71. Basile Nikitine, "Les Kurdes et le Christianisme," *Revue de l'Histoire des Réligions* 85, no. 3 (May-June 1922), 155.

72. Ibid. Translations of non-English-language material are mine unless otherwise indicated.

73. According to Minorsky, this manuscript was found by the Georgian professor Abouladze in the library of the Armenian patriarchate at Echmiadzen in Soviet Armenia in 1937. In his opinion, there is no question as to the genuineness of the manuscript, which was copied under the auspices of the well-known historian of Timurlane, Th. of Mestoph (died 1446). The prayer, which is transcribed in the Armenian alphabet, reads as follows when transcribed into Latin letters: "P'ak'ej xode, p'ak'ej Zahm, p'ak'ej vemark, k'oy hati Xace esk'erma, rahmat-e-ma." It may be rendered in English as: "The pure [which is] also good, the pure [which is] also mighty, the pure [which is] immortal, [Thou] who came to the cross through [Thy] mercy and compassion for us." V. Minorsky, "Le plus ancien texte Kurde," *Bulletin Mensuel du Centre d'Etudes Kurdes,* no. 10 (1950): 8–10.

74. Bar Hebraeus, *The Chronography of Gregory 'Abu al-Faruj, the Son of Aaron, the Hebrew Physician, Commonly Known as Bar Hebraeus,* vol. 1, translated from Syriac by Ernest A. Wallis Budge (London: Oxford Univ. Press, H. Milford, 1932), 362.

75. Ameer Sharaf Khan al-Bidlisi, *Sharafnama: Fi Tarikh al-Duwal wa al-Imarat al-Kurdiya* (History of the Kurdish Governments and Princedoms), translated from Persian into Arabic with commentary by Muhammad Jamil Bendi Rozhbeyani (Baghdad: al-Naja Press, 1953), 359. Cf. Minorsky, "Kurds."

76. J. G. Taylor, "Travels in Kurdistan, with Notices of the Sources of the Eastern and Western Tigris and Ancient Ruins in the Neighborhood," *Journal of the Royal Geographical Society* 35 (1865), 28–29.

77. T. Menzel, "Yezidi," in *Encyclopaedia of Islam,* 1st ed., 8:1163–70, and the bibliography therein; Siddiq Damaluji, *al-Yazidiya* (The Yazidis) (Mosul, Iraq: al-Ittihad Press, 1948); F. Meier, "Der Name der Yazidis," in *Westöstliche Abhandlungen Rudolf Tschudi,* edited by F. Meier (Wiesbaden: Harrassowitz, 1954), 244–57.

78. J. H. Kramers, "Sarliyah," in *Encyclopaedia of Islam,* 1st ed., 7:174; also 'Abd al-Mun'im al-Ghulami, *Baqaya al-Firaq al-Batiniya fi Liwa al-Mawsul* (Remnants of Batini Sects in Mosul Province) (Mosul, Iraq: al-Ittihad Press, 1950).

79. The best discussion of the beliefs and practices of the Qizilbash is found in Molyneux-Seel, 49–68.

80. For details, see V. Minorsky, "Ahl-i Hakk," in *Encyclopaedia of Islam, New Edition*, 1:260–63; also W. Ivanov, ed., *The Truth-Worshippers of Kurdistan: Ahl-i Haqq Texts*, Isma'ili Society Series A, no. 7 (Leiden: E. J. Brill, 1953). For the best study of the Kaka'is in Iraq, see Edmonds, *Kurds, Turks, and Arabs*, 182–201.

81. Fraser stated: "I have been sadly disappointed, however, by these Koords in the matter of their superstitions—of faerie, witchcraft, and the like. . . . [T]hey either, so far as I could see, have but little genius for these things, or it comes little out. . . . [I]n such a country one would have expected to find a thousand picturesque superstitions and *diableries;* but all seems to be confined to the clumsy fancies of lucky and unlucky hours—the influence of the evil eye—a few omens drawn from such unpoetic accidents as sneezing once or twice when on the eve of an undertaking, &c &c." James Baillie Fraser, *Travels in Koordistan, Mesopotamia, &c. Including an Account of Parts of Those Countries Hitherto Unvisited by Europeans: With Sketches of the Character and Manners of the Koordish and Arab Tribes*, vol. 2 (London: Richard Bentley, 1840), 140–41.

82. Basile Nikitine, "La poésie lyrique Kurde," *L'Ethnographie* (Paris), no. 45 (1947–50), 39.

83. Basile Nikitine and E. B. Soane, "The Story of Suto and Tato," *Bulletin of the School of Oriental Studies* 3, part 1 (1923): 69–106.

84. Basile Nikitine, "Kurdish Stories from My Collection," *Bulletin of the School of Oriental Studies* 4, part 1 (1926), 121.

85. Ibid., 126–28.

86. Ibid., 128.

87. Ibid., 132–33.

88. Ibid.

89. Basile Nikitine, "Un sujet de fable: Variantes Kurdes et Persanes," *Revue d'Ethnographie et des Traditions Populaires* 3, no. 10 (1922): 129–40.

90. For a French version, see Alexandre Jaba, *Recueil de notices et récits Kourdes servant à la connaissance de la langue* (St. Petersburg: Eggers, 1860), 87–90. Jaba stated that the Kurdish poet Mala-i-Batie composed a poem celebrating this event.

91. Lescot's version of *Mamé Alan* is based on three main sources that he identified as Misho, a Kurdish troubador; Sebri, a Kurdish writer; and *Hawar*, a Kurdish magazine published in Syria. He also received much help from Prince Jaladet Bedir Khan. Roger Lescot, *Textes Kurdes*, vol. 2: *Mamé Alan* (Paris: Geunther, 1940), iii–xxiii.

92. For a brief synopsis of Khani's *Mem u Zin*, see Thomas Bois, "Coup d'oeil sur la littérature Kurde," *Revue al-Mashrig* (Beirut) 49 (Mar.-Apr. 1955): 201\#208>39.

93. For a discussion of Kurdish folksongs, see Thomas Bois, *L'ame des Kurdes à la lumière de leur folklore* (Beirut: n.p. 1946).

94. Nikitine, "La poésie lyrique Kurde," 51.

95. For a discussion of Ahmadi Khani's life and works, see 'Ala' al-Din Sajjadi, *Mejûy Edebî Kurdî* (History of Kurdish Literature) (Baghdad: al-Ma'arif Press, 1952), 189–213.

96. Ibid., 9–10; Bois, "Coup d'oeil," 210–11; and Zaki, *Khulasat Tarikh al-Kurd*, 359–60.

97. Ma'ruf Khaznidar, "Malhamat Mem u Zin" (The Epic of Mem u Zin), *Ar-Risalah al-Jadida* (Cairo) 1 (1971).

98. C. J. Edmonds, "A Bibliography of Southern Kurdish, 1937–1944," *Journal of the Royal Central Asian Society* 32 (Apr. 1945): 185–91; Bois, "Coup d'oeil," 218–19; Witold Rajkowski, "A Visit to Southern Kurdistan," *Geographical Journal* 107, nos. 3–4 (1946), 128.

99. Edmonds, "A Bibliography, 1937–1944," 185.

100. Ibid., 187.

101. Bois, "Coup d'oeil," 219.

102. Ibid., 223–29.

103. Ibid., 226–28.

104. Ibid., 222–23.

2. The Social Organization of the Kurds

1. Minorsky points out that Strabo had noted the presence of agriculturists among the Cyr-tii of Fars, who are believed to be one of the Kurds' ancestors. See Minorsky, "Kurds," 1133. Cf. G. R. Driver, "Studies in Kurdish History," *Bulletin of the School of Oriental Studies* 2, no. 3 (1922): 491–511.

2. Claudius James Rich, *Narrative of a Residence in Koordistan,* 2 vols. (London: James Duncan, 1836), 1:88–89.

3. Ibid., 153.

4. Minorsky, "Kurds," 1150.

5. Fredrik Barth, *Principles of Social Organization in Southern Kurdistan,* Universitets Etnografiske Museum Bulletin no. 7 (Oslo: Brødrene Jørgensen, 1953), 53ff.

6. Despite much evidence to the contrary, a learned Kurdish judge of Sawj Bulaq (Mahabad) argued against this view, probably from patriotic motives; as such, a division might seem to impinge on the unity of the Kurdish people. See al-Kazi, 329.

7. More than a century ago, Rich observed: "The Bulbassis have among them a people of dependents or peasants, who have no voice in their affairs, and are considered as a very inferior caste. This people are found scattered all over Koordistan, and are of no tribe or clan. The tribesmen call them Kelowspee or White Caps, and also Gooran. This latter name, which is the proper denomination of the people of Sinna, is applied by the clansmen as a term of reproach, and especially to timorous people." See Rich, 1:152–53. It should be noted that the name "Guran" does not always connote inferiority. The Kurdish historian al-Bidlisi lists the Guran as one of the four branches of the Kurdish people. Al-Bidlisi, 29. It is also the name of the powerful confederation of tribes occupying the mountains in the Karind-Zohab region astride the Kirmanshah-Baghdad road. Minorsky, who points out that the Guran were mentioned as a warlike tribe as early as the tenth century A.D., doubts that there is any direct relationship between the peasant population and the tribe that bears the same name. For an excellent discussion of the name "Guran," their origins, and their literature, see Minorsky, "The Guran," 75–103.

8. On the status of the Kurmanj among the Suran tribes of the Arbil region, see C. J. Edmonds, "A Bibliography of Southern Kurdish, 1920–1936," *Journal of the Royal Central Asian Society* 24 (July 1937), 488; for the Bahdinan tribes of the Mosul region, see Siddiq Damaluji, *Imarat Bahdinan al-Kurdiya Aw Imarat al-'Amadiya* (The Kurdish Princedom of Bahdinan or the Princedoms of 'Amadiya) (Mosul, Iraq: al-Ittihad al-Jadida Press, 1952), 123. A contemptuous reference to the Kurmanj in a tale of the Oramar-Hakari region indicates their inferior status in that part of Kurdistan. Nikitine and Soane, 103.

9. The origin of this word goes back to remote antiquity. In the laws of Hammurabi, it was applied to a class of people who occupied a status between that of slaves and that of persons enjoying full citizenship. According to L. W. King, it was a term applied to freemen who did not belong to the ruling race. It appears in Assyrian in the form *muskenu,* meaning "poor." The same word, with the same meaning, passed into Aramaic as *meskin,* into Hebrew as *misken,* into North

Arabic as *miskin* or *maskin*, into South Arabic and Ethiopic as *meskin*. From Arabic it passed into Italian as *meschino* and into French as *mesquin*. It occurs in both the Qu'ran and the hadith. Muslim interpreters have disagreed as to its precise meaning, the Malikis giving its meaning as "most needy" and the Shafi'is as "needy but not absolutely destitute." In Arabic, it also means "humble" or "miserable." Frants Buhl, "Miskin," in *Encyclopaedia of Islam*, 1st ed., 5:520. For a discussion of the position of the *miskin* peasants in the Hamawand country, see Barth, 53–59.

10. For instances of the loose usage of these terms by Kurdish tribesmen, see E. R. Leach, *Social and Economic Organisation of the Rowanduz Kurds*, London School of Economics and Political Science Monographs on Social Anthropology no. 3. (London: Percy Lund, Humphries, 1940), 14, and Barth, 37.

11. Leach, 13–14.

12. Mohammad Mokri, *'Ashayar-e Kord*, vol. 1: *Il-e Sanjabi Tarikhcheh Joghrafiya, Tireha* (Kurdish Tribes; vol. 1: The Sinjabi Tribe: Short History, Geography, Branches) (Tehran: Danish Bookstore, n.d.), 58–108 and passim.

13. Nikitine and Soane, 68–106.

14. Barth, 35–38.

15. Ibid., 36. Barth points out that each *tira* is headed by a hereditary chieftain or *ra'is* and that each of these tribal groups has traditional rights to certain pastures and camp sites. Ibid., 37.

16. Ibid.

17. Ibid., 37–38.

18. Ibid., 38.

19. Ibid.

20. It is strange that neither Barth, who wrote about the *khel*, nor Nikitine, who wrote about the *oba*, has identified the two with each other. Leach, who mentioned these two terms, asserted that the *khel* among the nomads corresponds to the *taifa* among the settled tribes. Furthermore, he stated that *hoba* (obviously *oba*) is a "small settlement of tents in one location," which according to him corresponds to the *gund* (village) of the settled tribes. Leach, 26–27.

21. For a detailed discussion of the *oba* and its significance, see Nikitine, *Les Kurdes*, 148ff.

22. Barth, 40.

23. Al-'Azzawi reports that according to a family tradition, the Jaf Begzada are of 'Alid descent. They trace their origin to Pir Khidr of Shahu, a mountain in the neighborhood of Jawanrud to which most Kurdish sayyids, including the Jaf, trace their origin. This connection seems to indicate that their ancestors were shaykhs who gradually became secular princes. See 'Abbas al-'Azzawi, *'Asha'ir al-'Iraq*, vol. 2: *al-Kurdiya* (The Tribes of Iraq; vol. 2: The Kurdish Tribes) (Baghdad: al-Ma'arif Press, 1947), 31.

24. Barth, 41.

25. Ibid.

26. Rich, 1:150.

27. Ibid.

28. Basile Nikitine, "Problème Kurde," *Politique Etrangère* 11, no. 3 (July 1946), 254. Cf. Rich, 1:152, who attributes the same functions to the councils of elders among the Bilbas and Jaf tribes.

29. Nikitine, "Problème Kurde," 254. See also his "La féodalité Kurde," *Revue du Monde Musulman* 60 (1925), 4.

30. Barth, 38.

31. Rich, 1:152.

32. Ibid., 1:112.

33. Soane, *To Mesopotamia and Kurdistan,* 374 n. 1.

34. K. Bedir Khan, 242. His account of the election of a chieftain in the Shirnakh region is interesting. The elders, who assembled for the purpose with prayer beads in their hands, filed past the various candidates. As they did so, they bowed respectfully before the candidate of their choice and placed their prayer beads at his feet, thus demonstrating the faith they had in him and the vote they had thus given him. *Bulletin du Centre d'Etudes Kurdes* 1 (1948), 12–13.

35. Soane, *Report on the Sulaimania District,* 40.

36. Hay, *Two Years in Kurdistan,* 62.

37. Ibid.

38. Damaluji, *Imarat Bahdinan,* 135.

39. Nikitine, "La féodalité Kurde," 5.

40. For a discussion of this question, including comparisons with various Middle Eastern mountain regions such as the Lebanese mountains, see Pierre Rondot, "Les tribus Montagnardes de l'Asie Anterieure: Quelques aspects sociaux des populations Kurdes et Assyriennes," *Bulletin d'Etudes Orientalis/Institut Français de Damas* 6 (1936), 5ff.

41. Iraq (British Administration), Office of the Civil Commissioner, *Administration Report of the Mosul Division for the Year 1921* (Baghdad: Government Press, 1922).

42. J. Brant, "Notes of a Journey Through a Part of Kurdistan, in the Summer of 1838," *Journal of the Royal Geographical Society* 10 (1841), 357–60.

43. Rondot, "Les tribus Montagnardes," 7ff.

44. Leach, 55.

45. According to Nikitine, these things are *tola* (vengeance), *mala* (tribe), and *keustan* (mountain country), which the Kurds equate with native land. Nikitine, "La féodalité Kurde," 4.

46. Cf. Leach, 55–56.

47. Basile Nikitine, "Quelques observations sur les Kurdes," *Mercure de France* 145, no. 543 (Feb. 1921), 669.

48. Hay, *Two Years in Kurdistan,* 73, and Leach, 56–57. Al-ʿAzzawi states that the murder of Muhammad Pasha Jaf by the Karam Waisi branch of the Shatiri clan led to such savage retaliation that most of the Karam Waisi were destroyed, not even women or children being spared. Al-ʿAzzawi, 2:41. The severity of the punishment meted out to this clan finds confirmation in Soane's account of its flight to take refuge with the Hamawand tribe. Soane, *Report on the Sulaimania District,* 15.

49. According to al-ʿAzzawi, the amount of blood money among poor-class Kurds in 1947 varied between twenty and forty pounds. Al-ʿAzzawi, 2:241. In 1921, Hay stated that "a Kurmanji or middle-class Kurdish farmer is valued at £90, one of his women at 45, and his leg or arm at say 20." Hay, *Two Years in Kurdistan,* 72. Cf. Leach, 56. It should be pointed out that *kurmanj* is a term applied to peasants in the Tawanduz area and not to middle-class Kurds.

50. Al-ʿAzzawi, 2:241. According to Hay, a girl is given away in marriage, as well as some livestock, in lieu of the blood money and not in addition to it.

51. Ibid., 72–73.

52. For a detailed account of this feud, see Nikitine and Soane, 69–102.

53. Al-ʿAzzawi, 2:242.

54. Barth, 73.

55. Ibid.

56. Ibid., 77.

57. Ibid., 73.

58. Ibid., 14.

59. E. B. Soane, *Notes on the Tribes of Southern Kurdistan* (Baghdad: Government Press, 1918), 20.

60. Hay, *Two Years in Kurdistan,* passim.

61. A. M. Hamilton, *Road Through Kurdistan: The Narrative of an Engineer in Iraq* (London: Faber and Faber, 1937), 270–309.

62. Leach, 57.

63. Ibid.

64. Ma 'ruf Jiyawuk, *Ma'sat Barzan al-Mazluma* (The Tragedy of Barzan the Oppressed) (Baghdad: al-'Arabiyah Press, 1954), 128–29.

65. R. Thurnwald, "Blood Vengeance Feud," in *Encyclopaedia of the Social Sciences* (New York: Macmillan, 1930), 2:598–99.

66. Sir Austen Henry Layard, *Discoveries in the Ruins of Nineveh and Babylon: With Travels in Armenia, Kurdistan, and the Desert* (New York: Harper and Bros., 1853), 2:257.

67. This story is probably pure legend intended to emphasize the Mir Kor's stern sense of justice. It is obvious from the story that the *mir*'s action was intended to frighten the villagers who witnessed the torture of the wolves into producing the real murderers. However, the concept of punishing the wolves for killing a man is in itself very significant. For details of the story, see Fraser, *Travels,* 1:66–67.

68. Basile Nikitine, "Les Kurdes racontés par eux-mêmes," *L'Asie Française* (1925), 153–54.

69. Damaluji, *Imarat Bahdinan,* 90.

70. Justin Perkins, "Journal of a Tour from Oroomiah to Mosul Through the Koordish Mountains, and a Visit to the Ruins of Nineveh," *Journal of the American Oriental Society* 2 (1851), 101. Perkins did not elaborate on the significance of this practice, nor did an anthropologist who quoted him later. Cf. Weston Labarre, "The Cultural Basis of Emotions and Gestures," *Journal of Personality* 16, no. 1 (Sept. 1947), 55.

71. Barth, 114.

72. Al-Bidlisi, 319. Cf. Damaluji, *Imarat Bahdinan,* 107.

73. Rich, 1:154.

74. Basile Nikitine, "Shamdinan," in *Encyclopaedia of Islam,* 1st ed., 7:303–6.

75. G. R. Driver, comp., *Kurdistan and the Kurds* (London: Royal Anthropological Institute, 1919), 22.

76. The summer pasture lands are known as *saran* (lit. peaks or mountain tops) in the Mukri country as *yaila* among the Turkish-speaking people of Persia/Iran and Asia Minor, and as *zoma* among the mountain Nestorians.

77. Around the turn of the twentieth century, the most powerful nomadic portion of the great Hartoshi (Artoshi) confederation, under its leader Hajji Beg, occupied the Farashin upland, the choicest pasture land in the whole *zozan* region. F. R. Maunsell, "Central Kurdistan," *Geographical Journal* 18, no. 2 (Aug. 1901), 124.

78. For a description of the havoc wrought by the nomads during their passage through the lands of the sedentary tribes, see Wigram and Wigram, 127–28, 159–60; Hamilton, 89–91; Hay, *Two Years in Kurdistan,* 79–80; Leach, 27; Damaluji, *Imarat Bahdinan,* 74.

79. An official British report described the unsettled conditions in the region of the Turco-Iraqi frontier as a result of intertribal warfare occasioned by the annual migrations. Great Britain, Office of the Civil Commissioner, *Administration Report of the Mosul Division for the Year 1921,* 8.

80. For an excellent description of this region, see Maunsell, "Central Kurdistan," 121–40.

81. Barth, 102; Leach, 48; Hay, *Two Years in Kurdistan,* 45–46; Basile Nikitine, "La vie domestique Kurde," *Revue d'Ethnographie et des Traditions Populaires* 3, no. 12 (1922), 334–35.

82. Molyneux-Seel, 49.

83. Bertram Dickson, "Journeys in Kurdistan" *Geographical Journal* 35, no. 4 (Apr. 1910), 375.

84. Hay, *Two Years in Kurdistan,* 46–47.

85. Ibid., 56.

86. Ibid.

87. Ibid.

88. C. Newin, "Le nombre des repas chez les Kurdes," *Hawar* 1, no. 13 (Dec. 14, 1932): 8–10; Damaluji, *al-Yazidiya,* 276.

89. Hay, *Two Years in Kurdistan,* 52–53; Leach, 30.

90. Leach, 29–31.

91. Damaluji, *al-Yazidiya,* 51; Ivanov, 97; and Hay, *Two Years in Kurdistan,* 29–30, 38. Cf. Wigram and Wigram, 281; and Fraser, *Travels,* 1:186–89.

92. Nikitine, "La vie domestique Kurde," 335; Major E. W. C. Noel, "The Character of the Kurds as Illustrated by Their Proverbs and Popular Sayings," *Bulletin of the School of Oriental Studies* 1, part 4 (1921), 83–84.

93. Hay, *Two Years in Kurdistan,* 56.

94. Newin, 8–10. This writer gave a detailed description of these meals.

95. V. Minorsky, "Sawdj Bulak," in *Encyclopaedia of Islam,* 1st ed., 7:186–92. Soane, *To Mesopotamia and Kurdistan,* 401.

96. Fraser, *Travels,* 1:86. Cf. Hay, *Two Years in Kurdistan,* 41.

97. M. Sykes, 582.

98. Bois, *L'ame des Kurdes;* see photograph facing page 20.

99. Cf. Hay, *Two Years in Kurdistan,* 41; Soane, *To Mesopotamia and Kurdistan,* 401; 'Ali Sido al-Gurani, *Min 'Amman ila al-'Amadiya* (From 'Amman to 'Amadiya) (Cairo: al-Sa'ada Press, 1939), 152.

100. Dickson, 362.

101. Wigram and Wigram, 9; Hay, *Two Years in Kurdistan,* 41; Henry Binder, *Au Kurdistan en Mésopotamie et en Perse, mission scientifique du Ministère de l'Instruction Publique* (Paris: Maison Quantin, 1887), 109–10; Fraser, *Travels,* 1:86; Sir Austen Henry Layard, *Nineveh and Its Remains,* vol. 1 (New York: G. P. Putnam, 1849), 206–7.

102. Al-Gurani, 152; Hay, *Two Years in Kurdistan,* 41.

103. Hay, *Two Years in Kurdistan,* 40; Hamilton, 137.

104. Hay, *Two Years in Kurdistan,* 42; Minorsky, "Sawdj Bulak."

105. Soane, *To Mesopotamia and Kurdistan,* 401; Wigram and Wigram, 9–10.

106. Hay, *Two Years in Kurdistan,* 41; Dickson, 362; Nikitine, "La vie domestique Kurde," 336–37.

107. Wigram and Wigram, 9; Soane, *To Mesopotamia and Kurdistan,* 401; al-Gurani, 41.

108. For a description of the dress of the Mukri Kurds, see Minorsky, "Sawdj Bulak"; Fraser, *Travels,* 1:86; and Soane, *To Mesopotamia and Kurdistan,* 401. On the Rawanduz Kurds, see Soane, *To Mesopotamia and Kurdistan,* 401; Hay, *Two Years in Kurdistan,* 40–42; Hamilton, 137–38 and photographs. On the Hakari Kurds, see Layard, *Nineveh,* 1:206–7; Binder, 109–10; al-Gurani, 152; and Wigram and Wigram, 112–13. On the Bahdinan Kurds, see Wigram and Wigram, 112–13;

Binder, 109–10; and al-Gurani, 152. On the Sulaymaniya region, see Rich, 1:86, and on the Armenian plateau region, see Dickson, 362.

109. K. Bedir Khan, 241; Bois, *L'ame des Kurdes*, 32; Soane, *Report on Sulaimania District*, 92–93; Nikitine, "Quelques observations," 671.

110. Bois, *L'ame des Kurdes*, 38–39; E. B. Soane, "The Southern Kurd," *Journal of the Central Asian Society* 9, part 1 (1922), 45.

111. Soane, "The Southern Kurd," 45.

112. K. Bedir Khan, 241; Nikitine, "Quelques observations," 671; Basile Nikitine, "Problème Kurde," *Politique Etrangère* 11, no. 3 (July 1946), 255; Soane, *To Mesopotamia and Kurdistan*, 397; Soane, *Report on the Sulaimania District*, 92–93; Layard, *Nineveh*, 1:153; Layard, *Discoveries*, 315.

113. Soane, *To Mesopotamia and Kurdistan*, 397; Nikitine, "Quelques observations," 670; Major E. M. Noel, *Diary of Major E. M. Noel, C.I.E., D.S.O., on Special Duty in Kurdistan, from June 14th to September 21st, 1919* (Basra, Iraq: Government Press, 1920), 10.

114. Soane, *To Mesopotamia and Kurdistan*, 397; Hay, *Two Years in Kurdistan*, 69–70; Leach, 56.

115. Soane, *Report on Sulaimania District*, 93; Nikitine, "Quelques observations," 670; Hay, *Two Years in Kurdistan*, 43; K. Bedir Khan, 241.

116. Hay, *Two Years in Kurdistan*, 43.

117. Soane, *Report on the Sulaimania District*, 93; Soane, *To Mesopotamia and Kurdistan*, 397.

118. Soane, "The Southern Kurd," 45.

119. Barth, 24–25.

120. Soane, *To Mesopotamia and Kurdistan*, 396–97; Jiyawuk, 24. Hamilton reports a fierce fight between the sedentary Surchi tribesmen of the Spillik Pass and the Herki nomads in the late 1920s, in which a number of Herki women participated. According to his informant, eleven men and four women were killed. Hamilton, 90.

121. Barth himself lists "low birth" as an impediment to leadership and cites the example of a certain Salim Beg, who was offered the position of ruler of southern Kurdistan by the Persian Nadir Shah but turned it down because he "knew his place." Barth, 121–22. However, it should be pointed out that Barth qualifies his theory by stating that neither "female sex" nor "low birth" is an absolute impediment to leadership because both may be offset by other factors.

122. Cuinet, 2:717.

123. H. A., "L'hospitalité Kurde," *Hawar* 1 (Aug. 8, 1932): 7–8.

124. Nikitine, "Quelques observations," 670; and Nikitine, "Problème Kurde," 255.

125. Soane, *To Mesopotamia and Kurdistan*, passim; G. M. Lees, "Two Years in South Kurdistan," *Journal of the Royal Central Asian Society* 15, part 3 (1928): 253–77; and Soane, "The Southern Kurd," 44–45.

126. Barth, 120–21. On Hafsa Khan, see note 111, chap. 10.

127. Damaluji, *al-Yazidiya*, 32–33, also 18, 20.

128. "Kurdistan," in *The Encyclopaedia of Missions: Descriptive, Historical, Biographical, Statistical*, 2d ed., edited by Edwin Bliss, Henry Dwight, and H. Allen Tupper (New York: Funk and Wagnalls, 1910), 530; Soane, *To Mesopotamia and Kurdistan*, 396; Hay, *Two Years in Kurdistan*, 44; Nikitine, "Quelques observations," 670; Leach, 21; Bois, *L'ame des Kurdes*, 31–32; and Damaluji, *Imarat Bahdinan*, 170.

129. K. Bedir Khan, 241; Soane, *To Mesopotamia and Kurdistan*, 237, 397; Damaluji, *Imarat Bahdinan*, 170.

130. Damaluji, *Imarat Bahdinan,* 170; K. Bedir Khan, 241; Bois, *L'ame des Kurdes,* 32.

131. Barth, 26; Hay gave an interesting account of his experience as a member of a deputation sent by a Kurdish *agha* to ask for the hand of a religious chieftain's sister. He discussed the brideprice and stated that some chieftains paid as much as five hundred pounds for a lady of high rank. Hay, *Two Years in Kurdistan,* 257–59, 44. Leach regarded this figure as too high; according to him, the brideprice was often exaggerated in order to flatter the woman. Leach, 44–45.

132. Barth, 28; Leach, 44–45; and Hay, *Two Years in Kurdistan,* 44.

133. K. Bedir Khan, 241.

134. Damaluji, *Imarat Bahdinan,* 169. According to Muslim law, the *mahr* or *sadaq* (bridal gift or dower) belongs to the wife. In pre-Islamic Arabia, the *sadaq* was given to the wife, but the *mahr* was given to her father or guardian. After the advent of Islam, the two were combined, and now the words *mahr* and *sadaq* are used interchangeably. There are two kinds of *mahr* according to Muslim law: *mahr al-mithl,* or unspecified *mahr,* which is commensurate with the bride's social position, wealth, and qualities; and *mahr musamma* or specified *mahr.* The latter, in turn, may be divided into two parts: *muqaddam,* which is prompt or immediate dower, usually payable before the consummation of the marriage; and *mu'ajjal,* or deferred dower, payable on the dissolution of the marriage by the death of the husband or by divorce. O. Spies, "Mahr," in *Encyclopaedia of Islam,* 1st ed., 5:137–38; and J. Schacht, "Nikah," in *Encyclopaedia of Islam,* 1st ed., 6:912–14.

135. Hay, *Two Years in Kurdistan,* 44. This "settlement" to which Hay referred is obviously the *mahr mu'ajjal* (deferred dower) mentioned in note 134.

136. Bois, *L'ame des Kurdes,* 39. Bois draws attention to the existence of the same practice among the ancient Hebrews, mentioned in Deuteronomy 22:15.

137. Nikitine, "La vie domestique Kurde," 342.

138. Bois, *L'ame des Kurdes,* 39.

139. Leach, 19–21; and Barth, 26ff.

140. Barth, 28.

141. Ibid.

142. For a good discussion of the practice of orthocousin marriage among the Arabs and the Semites in general and of the spread of this institution as a feature of Muslim social organization, see Brenda Z. Seligman, "Studies in Semitic Kinship. II. Cousin Marriage," *Bulletin of the School of Oriental Studies* 3 (1923–25): 263–79.

143. Barth doubts that the tendency toward endogamy in the area is a result of Islamic influences. He agrees with Lutzbetak *(Marriage and the Family in Caucasia)* that non-Islamic or pre-Islamic patterns of endogamy are found in the Middle East. Endogamy is known to have existed in Egypt, Sumer, Elam, Arabia, and Persia, where brother-sister marriage was a common feature of royal lineages, and in the Caucasian-Armenian area, where close-kin marriage is a basic fact of social organization. Barth, 136ff.

144. Ibid., 27.

145. Muhyi al-Din 'Abu Zakariya Yahya al-Hizami al-Nawawi, *Minhaj Al-Talibin: Manuel de Jurisprudence Musulmane selon le rite de Chafi'i,* (Methodology for the Seekers of Knowledge: A Manual of Muslim Jurisprudence According to the Rule of al-Shafi'i), vol. 2, Arabic text and French translation by Lodewijk Willem Van Den Berg (Batavia: Imp. du Gouvernement, 1883), 321–23; Schacht, "Nikah." Cf. Barth, 30.

146. Jiyawuk, 54.

147. According to Damaluji, this practice is particularly accepted by the Yazidis. See Damaluji, *Imarat Bahdinan,* 168, and especially his *al-Yazidiya,* 280–81.

148. Damaluji, *Imarat Bahdinan,* 168–69.

149. The running away of married women with men of their choice is much more prevalent among the Yazidis than among other Kurds. The reason, according to Damaluji, is to be sought in the inferior social status of Yazidi women, who are given away in marriage by their guardians when they are very young and often against their will to husbands who subject them to harsh treatment. Damaluji, *al-Yazidiya,* 281–82.

150. Damaluji, *Imarat Bahdinan,* 169–70. It is interesting to note in this connection that in both India and Indonesia, women wishing to dissolve their marriages resort to this subterfuge of divorce by temporary apostasy. In Indonesia, according to Schacht, there are cases of divorce by apostasy with the complicity of the Shari'a law courts. J. Schacht, "Talak," in *Encyclopaedia of Islam,* 1st ed., 8:636–40. For details on the situation in India, see As'ad 'Ali Asgar Fyzee, *Outlines of Muhammadan Law* (Calcutta: Oxford Univ. Press, 1949), 156–57.

151. Nikitine, "La vie domestique Kurde," 341.

152. For a detailed discussion of beliefs and practices connected with birth in central Kurdistan, see ibid., 339–40.

153. Barth, 112.

154. Nikitine, "La vie domestique Kurde," 340. The same beliefs and practices relating to the *shesheh* are found among the Nestorians of the Urmiya plain; see Basile Nikitine, "Superstitions des Chaldéens du Plateau d'Ourmiah," *Revue d'Ethnographie et des Traditions Populaires* 4, no. 14 (1923), 162ff. Among the mountain Nestorians, this evil spirit is known as Khwaraha; the child is similarly watched day and night and is protected by an onion and an iron woolcomb. Wigram and Wigram, 306.

155. Barth, 150.

156. H. Arakélian, "Les Kurdes en Perse," in *Verhandlungen des XIII Internationalen Orientalisten Kongresses—Hamburg, September 1902* (Leiden: E. J. Brill, 1904), 150.

157. Rondot, "Les tribus Montagnardes," 42–47.

158. Ibid.

159. Ibid., 44.

160. Ibid., 45. For a detailed history of the shaykhs of Nehri, see Nikitine, "Shamdinan."

161. Barth, 62.

162. Hay, *Two Years in Kurdistan,* 257. The shaykhs referred to here are Shaykh 'Ubayd Allah and Shaykh 'Ala' al-Din. Hay erroneously described them as "cousins," although the former was in fact the uncle of the latter. Leach, 8.

163. Rondot, "Les tribus Montagnardes," 46.

164. For the strenuous prayers and religious exercises in which the Sufis engage, see Louis Massignon, "Tarika," in *Encyclopaedia of Islam,* 1st ed., 8:667–72; Massignon, "Tasawwuf," in *Encyclopaedia of Islam,* 1st ed., 8:681–85; D. B. Macdonald, "Dhikr," in *Encyclopaedia of Islam,* 1st ed., 2:958; Macdonald, "Derwish," in *Encyclopaedia of Islam,* 1st ed., 2:949–51, and bibliographies therein.

165. S. G. Wilson, *Persian Life and Customs* (New York: Fleming H. Revell, 1900), 103.

166. Hay, *Two Years in Kurdistan,* 257. In Hay's time (1921), this village apparently was known by the name of Dar al-Aman (the Abode of Security). Leach pointed out that it is merely another name for Khalan. Leach, 8.

167. Hay, *Two Years in Kurdistan,* 257.

168. All three of these forms of oath taking are recognized in Muslim countries. When a man takes an oath pronouncing his divorce, his wife is automatically divorced from him unless within

four months by an act of expiation he renounces the oath. J. Pedersen, "Kasam," in *Encyclopaedia of Islam,* 1st ed., 4:783–85.

169. Rich, 1: 147–48; see also note 9 in this chapter.

170. Damaluji, *Imarat Bahdinan,* 131–32.

171. Barth, 83. The *miskin*s are the tribeless peasants inhabiting the Hamawand lands in the Sulaymaniya province.

172. Rich, 1:141.

173. Enclosure in No. 84, Letter from Mr. Thomson, British Minister in Persia, to Earl Granville, British Foreign Secretary, Teheran, Dec. 23, 1880, in Great Britain, *Correspondence Respecting the Kurdish Invasion of Persia, Turkey No. 5 (1881),* C. 2851 (London: H.M. Stationery Office, 1881), (hereafter *Turkey No. 5*).

174. Rondot, "Les tribus Montagnardes," 44.

175. Soane, *Report on the Sulaimania District,* 98. According to Soane, the Barzani shaykhs, after allying themselves with the 'Amadiya princes by marriage, reserved for their daughters and female relations the title of "khan," which only a member of the old families had a right to claim.

176. Shaykh Muhammad, the paramount chieftain of the Balik tribe, was not a religious dignitary. The name "Shaykh Muhammad" was given him at birth after a relative who was a real shaykh. Leach, 3.

177. Hay, *Two Years in Kurdistan,* 257–59.

178. Soane, *To Mesopotamia and Kurdistan,* 190. Also, Soane, *Report on the Sulaimania District,* 99.

179. Stephen H. Longrigg, *Iraq, 1900 to 1950: Political, Social, and Economic History* (London: Oxford Univ. Press for the Royal Institute of International Affairs, 1953), 326.

180. Barth, 84.

181. Ibid., 62.

182. Ibid., 63.

183. Enclosure 2 in letter from Consul-General Abbott to Earl Granville, Tabriz, July 13, 1880, *Turkey No. 5 (1881),* 9.

184. Minorsky, "Kurds."

185. Cuinet, 2:638.

185. Lees, "Two Years in South Kurdistan," 254. Cf. Hay, *Two Years in Kurdistan,* 38; and Safrastian, 92.

187. Rich, 1:140–41.

188. Ibid., 320.

189. Jiyawuk, 54.

190. Zaki, *Khulasat Tarikh al-Kurd,* 291; Damaluji, *Imarat Bahdinan,* 135; al-'Azzawi, 2:16. Cf. Hay, *Two Years in Kurdistan,* 65.

191. According to Macdonald, *karamat* are the miraculous gifts and graces with which God surrounds, protects, and aids his saints. He points out that the coincidence in derivation and in meaning between these *karamat* and the "spiritual gifts" of the early Christian Church (I Cor. 12) is most striking and can hardly be accidental. D. B. Macdonald, "Karama," *Encyclopaedia of Islam,* 1st ed., 4:744.

192. Cuinet, 2:638.

193. Rich, 1:141, footnote.

194. For a full discussion of the nature of charisma, charismatic authority, and the relation-

ship between the bearer of charisma and his followers, see Max Weber, *The Theory of Social and Economic Organization* (New York: Oxford Univ. Press, 1950), 358–92.

195. Barth, 63–64.

196. Ibid., 64.

197. Quoted by Hamilton, 201.

198. For the appointment of the *khalifa* among the Qadiri and Tijani orders, see T. W. Arnold, "Khalifa," in *Encyclopaedia of Islam,* 1st ed., 4:881–85.

199. Nikitine, "Shamdinan," 7:303–6.

200. Damaluji, *Imarat Bahdinan,* 65.

201. Weber, *Theory of Social and Economic Organization,* 360.

202. Rich, 1:320.

3. The Suppression of the Semiautonomous Regimes in Kurdistan

1. Rashid Muhammad Pasha, who was of Georgian origin, held the rank of *serasker* or marshal of the east in the Ottoman army and was commander in chief of the imperial army at the battle of Konia (October 1832), in which he was defeated and taken prisoner by Ibrahim Pasha of Egypt; Zaki, *Khulasat Tarikh al-Kurd,* 246.

2. The sultan had chosen Haji Muhammad 'Ali Rida, a Laz by race, to suppress Dawud Pasha, the last of the Georgian Mamluk rulers of Baghdad. He was *wali* of the Baghdad pashalik from 1831 to 1842. Stephen H. Longrigg, *Four Centuries of Modern Iraq* (London: Oxford Univ. Press, 1925), 264ff.

3. Muhammad Pasha, known as Injeh Bayraqdar, or the "Thin Standard-Bearer," ruled Mosul from 1835 until his death in 1843. Ibid., 283.

4. Hafiz Muhammad Pasha, a marshal of the Ottoman army, was a Circassian. He was Ottoman commander in the battle of Nizib (June 1839), in which Ibrahim Pasha of Egypt inflicted another decisive defeat on the imperial army. Zaki, *Khulasat Tarikh al-Kurd,* 251.

5. After the Egyptian defeat of the Ottoman army, Mardin appears to have been one of the first towns to revolt against the reforms, which were regarded as the source of all evil. The revolt occurred shortly after the battle of Konia, which took place in October 1832. See William Ainsworth, "Notes Taken on a Journey from Constantinople to Mosul, in 1839–1840," *Journal of the Royal Geographical Society* 10 (1841), 524.

6. Rashid Pasha attacked the Milli confederation in 1834. See Longrigg, *Four Centuries,* 286.

7. Ibid., 285.

8. It is interesting to note that Rajab Beg, Husayn Agha, and Temir Beg are said to have been usually at war with Mirza Agha, but they apparently composed their differences and fought together against the Ottoman army. The Armenians, who were treated on an equal footing with the Kurds, are reported to have fought well. Upon the submission of Mirza Agha, who was the strongest, the other *begs* submitted. For more details, see Brant, 358–60.

9. Zaki, *Kulasat Tarikh al-Kurd,* 246.

10. Brant, 376.

11. Muhammad Pasha is known among the Kurds as Mira Kora ("the Blind Prince") or Pashai Kora ("the Blind Pasha"). He suffered from an infection in one eye and should more properly be described in English as the "One-Eyed."

12. Al-Gurani, 130. Cf. Muhammad Amin Zaki, *Tarikh al-Duwal wa al-'Imarat al-Kurdiya fi al-'Ahd al-Islami* (The History of Kurdish States and Principalities during the Muslim Period), translated from Kurdish into Arabic by Muhammad 'Ali 'Awni (Cairo: al-Sa'ada Press, 1945), 207.

13. Ibid., 130.

14. Fraser, *Travels*, 1:64.

15. Dr. Ross, the physician of the British Residency in Baghdad, who journeyed to the fortress of Dumdum near Rawanduz where Mustafa Beg lived in retirement, found the old man to be incurably blind from natural causes. Ross dismissed as untenable the charge that the *mir* had blinded his father by the application of a steel pencil *(mil)* or by iron cups. Ibid., 1:72.

16. In addition to Fraser's account on this matter, see the following: Zaki, *Khulasat Tarikh al-Kurd*, 248; Zaki, *Tarikh al-Duwal*, 406; al-Gurani, 130; Longrigg, *Four Centuries*, 285.

17. The *mir* acquired such a sinister reputation that some writers did not hesitate to repeat rumors concerning his merciless treatment of his own brothers. According to Scher, upon Muhammad Pasha's accession to the principality, he killed off all his brothers with the exception of Rasul Beg. Addai Scher, "Épisodes de l'histoire du Kurdistan," *Journal Asiatique* 15 (Jan.-Feb. 1910), 133. Fraser stated that the *mir* disposed of several brothers, but he mentioned elsewhere (1:72) that the *mir* had four living brothers. Two of them, Tamir Khan and Sulayman Beg, were said to have been kept in chains in a remote fort; Ahmad Beg served as governor of Arbil; and Rasul Beg (later Pasha) was closely associated with the *mir* and was generally regarded as his successor.

18. Al-Gurani, 130.

19. Ibid.

20. Longrigg, *Four Centuries*, 285; Zaki, *Khulasat Tarikh al-Kurd*, 243; Zaki, *Tarikh al-Duwal*, 412; al-Gurani, 131.

21. Scher, 133. According to two writers, the descendants of the paramount chieftain of the Mir Mahmali continued to speak of the murder of their ancestor 'Uthman Beg by the *mir* and the subsequent defection of his son Mahmud Beg to the Ottoman government when 'Uthman Beg was attacked by imperial troops. See al-Gurani, 46, and al-'Azzawi, 2:133.

22. According to al-'Azzawi, Muhammad Pasha killed Hamza Agha, two of the latter's sons, two of his brothers, and four other relatives. Al-'Azzawi, 2:108. The *mir*'s ruthlessness in dealing with the defeated Mamish is well illustrated by Fraser, who happened to be in the region shortly after these events. He mentioned that forty Mamish chieftains, who had been kept in chains at Rawanduz after the reduction of their tribes, managed to escape during an outbreak of the plague in the town. According to him, most of these men were rounded up, and all of them together with their keepers were put to death. Fraser, *Travels*, 1:102. See also H. C. Rawlinson, "Notes on a Journey from Tabriz, Through Persian Kurdistan, to the Ruins of Takhti-Soleiman," *Journal of the Royal Geographical Society* 10 (1841), 32.

23. Al-Gurani, 131; Longrigg, *Four Centuries*, 285; Zaki, *Khulasat Tarikh al-Kurd*, 243.

24. Alexandre Jaba, *Dictionnaire Kurdo-Français* (St. Petersburg: Commissionaire de l'Academie Impériale des Sciences, 1879), 310. According to Jaba, the French equivalent of the word *kiriv* (transcribed by him as *qiriv*) is *parrain*, which in English would be rendered as "sponsor" or "godfather." Among the Yazidis, the *kiriv* is a person who acts as a sponsor at a circumcision ceremony. He holds the child in his lap during the circumcision operation, which is usually performed by a barber. The relationship thus created is called *kiriv khoni* or blood *kiriv*. *Kiriv*ship creates a strong bond between the sponsor's family and the circumcised child's family. The Yazidis attach great importance to this relationship and scrupulously observe the mutual obligations that grow out of it. Families bound by *kiriv*ship are expected to come to each other's aid in times of danger, to guard the honor of each other's womenfolk, and to extend financial assistance when needed. *Kiriv*ship may be established between a Yazidi and a non-Yazidi as well as between two

Yazidis. It is the only means by which an outsider may become associated with the Yazidis and thus gain partial admittance to the narrowly exclusive Yazidi community. Among the Yazidis, *kiriv*ship forms a barrier to marriage in that it places members of the two families within the prohibited degrees, usually up to five generations and in some cases even more. See Damaluji, *al-Yazidiya*, 64, 68.

25. Damaluji, *Imarat Bahdinan*, 43. See also Damaluji, *al-Yazidiya*, 461.

26. According to Damaluji, the Mizuri chieftain chose to have only a small escort out of arrogance and vanity. Damaluji, *Imarat Bahdinan*, 43.

27. Damaluji, *al-Yazidiya*, 461. Cf. Damaluji, *Imarat Bahdinan*, 43.

28. Damaluji, *al-Yazidiya*, 462; Damaluji, *Imarat Bahdinan*, 44.

29. Damaluji, *Imarat Bahdinan*, 44. Cf. Damaluji, *al-Yazidiya*, 462.

30. Damaluji, *al-Yazidiya*, 462. Cf. Damaluji, *Imarat Bahdinan*, 44–45 n. 1.

31. Mulla Yahya is said to have kept the *mir* of Rawanduz well informed on the state of affairs in Bahdinan and to have often encouraged him to invade it. Damaluji, *Imarat Bahdinan*, 44. Cf. Damaluji, *al-Yazidiya*, 462.

32. Damaluji, *al-Yazidiya;* Damaluji, *Imarat Bahdinan*, 44.

33. According to Damaluji, the person who issued the *fatwa* in question may well have been Mulla Yahya himself. Damaluji, *Imarat Bahdinan*, 45, and *al-Yazidiya*, 462. Cf. Zaki, *Khalasat Tarikh al-Kurd*, 243; al-Gurani, 60.

34. This village is also known as Kellek al-Dawasin. Damaluji, *al-Yazidiya*, 463; Damaluji, *Imarat Bahdinan*, 45. Al-'Azzawi refers to it as Yasin Kellek. Al-'Azzawi, 2:13.

35. The date of this event has variously been given as follows: Damaluji, in his *Imarat Bahdinan*, 45, gives the year A.H. 1247/A.D. 1831, but states in his *al-Yazidiya*, 463, that it took place "at the beginning of the autumn of the year A.H. 1248/A.D. 1832." Zaki, in his *Khulasat Tarikh al-Kurd*, 243, gives the date as A.H. 1247/A.D. 1831. Sulayman al-Sa'igh, *Tarikh al-Mawsil* (The History of Mosul) (Cairo: al-Salafiya Press, 1923), 1:306, gives the year A.H. 1247/A.D. 1831. Al-Gurani, 132, gives A.H. 1247/A.D. 1831; but Scher, 133–34, gives the date as March 9, 1832.

36. Al-Sa'igh, 1:307; Zaki, *Khulasat Tarikh al-Kurd*, 244.

37. Koyunjik is a series of vast mounds underlain by the remains of ancient Nineveh. *Koyunjik* is a Turkish word meaning "lamb." According to Wigram and Wigram, 102, the name signifies "the shambles of the sheep" and is supposed to refer to the massacre of the Yazidis at that place.

38. According to Layard, the bridge of boats had been removed because of the flood. Layard, *Nineveh*, 1:229. Other writers, however, say that the *wali* of Mosul, Sa'id Pasha, had deliberately cut off the bridge out of fear of the Rawanduz forces. See al-Sa'igh, 1:307; Zaki, *Khulasat Tarikh al-Kurd*, 244; Damaluji, *al-Yazidiya*, 463.

39. One source exaggerates Yazidi losses to the point of saying that not more than 5 percent of an estimated one hundred thousand persons survived the massacre. Damaluji, *al-Yazidiya*, 463.

40. Damaluji, *Imarat Bahdinan*, 45. The capture and sale of the Yazidis apparently became a widespread practice after these events. We learn from Layard that the British ambassador in Constantinople, Sir Stratford Canning, used his influence with the Ottoman authorities to stop the sale of the Yazidi captives. Layard, *Nineveh*, 1:203ff; Layard, *Discoveries*, 4.

41. According to Scher, 172 persons were killed, not counting women, children, and strangers. The date of the attack is given as March 15, 1832. Scher, 134. Cf. al-Sa'igh, 1:307; Damaluji, *al-Yazidiya*, 464.

42. Scher, 134; al-Sa'igh, 1:307; George Percy Badger, *The Nestorians and Their Rituals, with*

the Narrative of a Mission to Mesopotamia and Coordistan in 1842–1844, and of a Late Visit to Those Countries in 1850, 2 vols. (London: J. Masters, 1852), 1:265.

43. Badger, 1:265; Bar Hebraeus, 1:lix.

44. Scher, 134 and n. 3.

45. Damaluji states that according to the Salname or annual calendar of the Mosul *wilayat* for the year A.H. 1313, 'Ali Beg was executed in the manner described, together with a number of Janissary *aghas* and Kurdish chieftains. He gives the date of 'Ali Beg's execution as the year 1838. Damaluji, *al-Yazidiya,* 464, 468–69.

46. Longrigg, *Four Centuries,* 285; al-Sa'igh, 1:309; Damaluji, *Imarat Bahdinan,* 46.

47. Basile Nikitine, "Rawandiz-Ruiyndiz," *Encyclopaedia of Islam,* 1st ed., 6:913–14.

48. Longrigg, *Four Centuries,* 286; Damaluji, *Imarat Bahdinan,* 46.

49. Al-Sa'igh, 1:309; Zaki, *Khulasat Tarikh al-Kurd.*

50. Longrigg, *Four Centuries,* 286; Zaki, *Khulasat Tarikh al-Kurd,* 245; Damaluji, *Imarat Bahdinan,* 46.

51. Al-Sa'igh, 1:307.

52. Zaki, *Khulasat Tarikh al-Kurd,* 245; al-Sa'igh, 1:309.

53. Grant, who happened to be at 'Amadiya shortly after these events, spoke of the ruinous state of the town. According to him, out of 1,000 houses that the town boasted of before the advent of the Rawanduz Kurds, only 250 were still standing. See Ashahel Grant, *The Nestorians: Or, The Lost Tribes: Containing Evidence of Their Identity; An Account of Their Manners, Customs, and Ceremonies; Together with Sketches of Travel in Ancient Assyria, Armenia, Media, and Mesopotamia; and Illustrations of Scripture Prophecy* (London: J. Murray, 1841), 60–61.

54. Al-Sa'igh, 1:309; Zaki, *Khulasat Tarikh al-Kurd,* 244.

55. Al-Gurani, 132.

56. Longrigg, *Four Centuries,* 285; Zaki, *Khulasat Tarikh al-Kurd,* 245; al-Gurani, 132; Damaluji, *Imarat Bahdinan,* 47.

57. Zaki, *Khulasat Tarikh al-Kurd,* 247; Damaluji, *Imarat Bahdinan,* 47; Frederick Millingen, *Wild Life among the Koords* (London: Hurst and Blackett, 1870), 185–86; William Ainsworth, *Travels and Researches in Asia Minor, Mesopotamia, Chaldea, and Armenia* (London: John W. Parker, 1842), 1:323.

58. The foregoing account, according to al-Gurani, was given by the Kurdish historian Hussain Huzni Mukriani in his book *Mirani Soran.* See al-Gurani, 132–34. Zaki mentions this same account in an abbreviated form, stating that Muhammad Pasha was forced to surrender after a certain Kurdish religious dignitary, in the course of a Friday sermon, pointed out the illegitimacy of resisting the caliph's forces and pronounced such resistance anathema. See Zaki, *Khulasat Tarikh al-Kurd,* 247. The truth of this account was borne out by Fraser, who wrote more than 120 years ago and was a well-informed eyewitness of these events. According to him, "lingering remains of veneration for the successor of the Prophet and the head of their religion, forbade the Koords to oppose in arms the troops of the Sultan." See Fraser, *Travels,* 1:81–82.

59. Millingen, 186.

60. Ibid., 186–87; Damaluji, *Imarat Bahdinan,* 47–48; Zaki, *Khulasat Tarikh al-Kurd,* 247–48; al-Gurani, 134; Ainsworth, *Travels and Researches,* 323.

61. Ainsworth, *Travels and Researches,* 33.

62. According to Zaki, he fled to Nerwa, a village northeast of 'Amadiya. Zaki, *Khulasat Tarikh al-Kurd,* 248.

63. Ibid., 248–49.

64. Badger, 1:265.

65. Layard, *Nineveh,* 1:143–44.

66. The Kurds highly regarded this family, which claimed descent from the 'Abbasid caliphs. One of the best descriptions of the powers of the Bahdinan ruler and the ceremonial at his court in the early nineteenth century is given in Rich, 1:153ff. Cf. Damaluji, *Imarat Bahdinan,* 18–23 and 32ff.

67. R. Hartmann, "Djazirat B. Omar," in *Encyclopaedia of Islam,* 1st ed., 2:1030–31. For further information on the Bohtan region, see M. Streck, "Bohtan," in *Encyclopaedia of Islam,* 1st ed., 2:739–40.

68. According to Zaki, Bedir Khan Beg was a youth of eighteen when he became the emir of Bohtan. Zaki, *Khulasat Tarikh al-Kurd,* 250. Chirguh gives the year of Bedir Khan's accession as 1821 but does not indicate his age at the time. Chirguh, *La question Kurde,* 14.

69. Layard, *Discoveries,* 54.

70. Minorsky, "Kurds"; Chirguh, *La question Kurde,* 17; Nikitine, *Les Kurdes,* 134; Zaki, *Khulasat Tarikh al-Kurd,* 252, 262; Safrastian, 60; Damaluji, *Imarat Bahdinan,* 48–49. All these sources are agreed that 'Izz al-Din Shir was a relative of Bedir Khan. The last three sources accuse him of treason.

71. E. M. Noel, *Diary,* 53.

72. Ibid.

73. Dr. Austin H. Wright and Edward Breath, [a report on their visit to Bedir Khan as representatives of the American Mission in Persia], *Missionary Herald,* 42, no. 11 (Nov. 1846), 381.

74. Ibid.

75. The word *slaves,* which no doubt is the literal rendition in English of the Kurdish *ghulam,* is misleading. The expression *ghulam* is normally applied to a Kurdish chief's suite of armed retainers without any odium being attached to it. These men, in fact, served as the Kurdish emirs' personal guards. Nikitine, "La féodalité Kurde," 2.

76. Wright and Breath, 382.

77. Weber has pointed out that a charismatic leader gains and maintains his authority by proving himself. As a prophet, he must perform miracles; as a war lord, he must perform heroic deeds. "Above all, however, his divine mission must 'prove' itself in that those who faithfully surrender to him must fare well. If they do not fare well, he is obviously not the master sent by the Gods." Max Weber, *Essays in Economc Sociology,* edited by Richard Swedeberg (Princeton, N.J.: Princeton Univ. Press, 1999), 249.

78. Wright and Breath, 381–82.

79. Ibid., 381. This seems to contradict Layard's assertion that Bedir Khan, after giving solemn assurances to a great crowd of Nestorians who had taken refuge on an inaccessible crag that he would spare them, went back on his word and had every one of them killed or tossed into the valley below.

80. Ibid., 382.

81. Dr. Ashahel Grant claimed that at the time of his visit to Bedir Khan, on the eve of the latter's attack on the Assyrians, "some of the dervishes and moollahs, it was said, advised a war of extermination." Dr. Ashahel Grant, letter dated July 5, 1843, concerning his visit to Bedir Khan, *Missionary Herald,* 39, no. 11 (Nov. 1843), 434. Similarly, we learn from Layard that prior to Bedir Khan's second attack on the Nestorians, Sayyid Taha I was urging the emir to prove his religious zeal by shedding the blood of those unfortunate people. Layard, *Nineveh,* 1:193.

82. Thomas Laurie and Dr. Azariah Smith, letter concerning Bedir Khan and other matters, *Missionary Herald,* 41, no. 6 (Apr. 1845), 120. Cf. Perkins, 92.

83. Ibid., 118–19.

84. Ibid., 122.

85. Badger, 1:265.

86. Ibid.

87. Letter from Dr. Grant dated Sept. 12, 1842, *Missionary Herald* 39, no. 2 (Feb. 1843), 67.

88. The Kurds' attitude toward the Ottoman government, on the one hand, and toward their own chieftains, on the other, is graphically conveyed by an episode related by the American missionaries Laurie and Smith. According to them, upon their arrival at Ashita, after the second invasion of the Nestorian country, they went to see a young Kurdish chief who was acting as Bedir Khan's agent in that district. The Kurdish chief examined their credentials, consisting of a *farman* issued by the Porte, a document furnished by the pasha of Mosul, and a letter from Isma'il Pasha. He glanced at and cast down with contempt the first two, "but [elevated] the letter of Isma'il Pasha . . . to the forehead, and he [Bedir Khan's agent] rose as if the chief himself had been present in person." Laurie and Smith, 118.

89. Ibid., 122. Whatever truth there may be in this story, it is interesting to note that, like another one mentioned many years later, it attributes Bedir Khan's attack on the Nestorians to a desire for revenge. Apropos of these events, the writers stated, "It may or may not be true that the Badir Khan massacres were occasioned by many years of contumacy culminating in the extirpation of a village of Saiyids." See also Iraq (British Administration), Office of the Civil Commissioner, *Administration Report of the Mosul Division for the Year 1921,* 10.

90. Laurie and Smith, 121–22.

91. Ibid., 122.

92. According to Laurie and Smith, Nurallah Beg "neither overlooked nor forgot" this unfriendly gesture by Mar Sham'un. Ibid., 121–22.

93. Letter from Dr. Grant dated Dec. 26, 1842, *Missionary Herald* 39, no. 8 (Aug. 1843), 317–18; letter from Dr. Grant dated July 5, 1843, *Missionary Herald* 39, no. 11 (Nov. 1843), 435.

94. Only a few years earlier Nurallah Beg had been responsible for the murder of a German traveler and scholar by the name of Schultz on the suspicion that he was looking for buried treasure or precious metals, the discovery of which would bring the Ottoman authorities to the area. Layard, *Nineveh,* 1:179. See also Layard, *Discoveries,* 77.

95. Letter from Dr. Grant dated Dec. 26, 1842, *Missionary Herald* 39, no. 8 (Aug. 1843), 317–18.

96. Ibid., 318; see also letter from Dr. Grant dated April 18, 1843, *Missionary Herald* 39, no. 8 (Aug. 1843).

97. *Missionary Herald* 40, no. 3 (Mar. 1844), 82. This letter from Dr. Grant asserted that far from being the cause of the massacres, the mission house saved Ashita. Dr. Robinson cited this statement with approval in his introductory note to the American edition of Layard, *Nineveh,* 1:vii-viii. It should be pointed out that although Ashita was spared during the first invasion, it was not spared during the second. Moreover, Ashita apparently owed its deliverance during the first invasion to the fact that its two leading men allied themselves with Bedir Khan and Nurallah Beg, according to Laurie and Smith.

98. Badger, 1:260.

99. Layard, *Discoveries,* 424.

100. Letter from Dr. Grant dated Aug. 1843, *Missionary Herald* 40, no. 1 (Jan. 1844), 24.

101. Laurie and Smith, 118.

102. Layard, *Nineveh,* 1:156–57.

103. Letter from Dr. Grant dated July 5, 1843, *Missionary Herald* 39, no. 11 (Nov. 1843), 435–37.

104. Letter from Dr. Grant dated Aug. 1843, *Missionary Herald* 40, no. 1 (Jan. 1844), 23–24.

105. According to Grant, Bedir Khan acted under the orders of the *wali* of Erzerum, the Ottoman official directly responsible for the Nestorian country. This *wali* was rewarded for his pains with a decoration. See letters from Dr. Grant in *Missionary Herald* 39, no. 11, (Nov. 1843), 436, and 40, no. 1 (Jan. 1844), where Grant quotes the *wali* of Mosul, who insisted that the war against the Nestorians was carried out under the orders of the *wali* of Erzerum.

106. Letter from Dr. Grant dated Aug. 12, 1843, *Missionary Herald* 39, no. 12 (Dec. 1843), 453. According to Chirguh, the army led by the emir of Bohtan against the Nestorians amounted to a force ten thousand strong. Chirguh, *La question Kurde,* 16.

107. Layard put the number of those who lost their lives as a result of the massacres at ten thousand. Layard, *Nineveh,* 1:153. According to the American missionary Edward Breath, the number was seven thousand. Letter from Breath dated July 27, 1846, *Missionary Herald* 42, no. 12 (Dec. 1846), 407. According to Wigram and Wigram, a brother of Bedir Khan Beg, fearful of eventual economic distress if the massacres were allowed to continue unchecked, decided to bring the matter to his brother's attention in a graphic manner. One day he entered the emir's reception hall dressed as a Nestorian peasant carrying a shovel over his shoulder. All those present, including the emir, were baffled. "Mashallah!" said the emir, "what is the meaning of this masquerade?" The emir's brother then pointed out that if all the Nestorians were going to be wiped out as the emir seemed bent upon doing, every Kurd would be reduced to tilling the soil. He said that he therefore had decided to begin practicing his future trade. Wigram and Wigram, 318.

108. Letters from Dr. Grant, *Missionary Herald,* 40, no. 2 (Feb. 1844), 58; 40, no. 3 (Mar. 1844), 82–83; 40, no. 4 (Apr. 1844), 165; and 40, no. 5 (June 1844), 166.

109. Layard, *Nineveh,* 1:153.

110. Ibid., 1:189, 201.

111. Chirguh, *La question Kurde,* 16.

112. Ibid. These men were Nurallah Beg, Khan Mahmud, his brother Khan 'Abdul, and Sharif Beg, respectively. Nurallah Beg has already been mentioned in these pages, and Sharif Beg is dealt with later. Khan Mahmud, a remarkable individual, had risen from a position of comparative obscurity to become the most turbulent character in northern and central Kurdistan. He and his several brothers for a long time controlled most of the region south of Lake Van. His brother Khan 'Abdul, who had at one time been at odds with Bedir Khan but who eventually joined his confederation, was in control of the castle of Mahmudiya (Khosh Ab) and the surrounding countryside. Khan Mahmud himself had succeeded in capturing and occupying Van. J. Shiel, "Notes on a Journey from Tabriz Through Kurdistan via Van, Bitlis, Se'art, and Erbil, to Sulaimaniyah, in July and August, 1836," *Journal of the Royal Geographical Society* 8 (1838), 63–64; Brant, 386–88.

113. Chirguh, *La question Kurde,* 14.

114. Bletch Chirguh, *al-Qadiya al-Kurdiya: Madi al-Kurd wa Hadirihim* (The Kurdish Problem: The Past and the Present of the Kurds), Hoybun Publication no. 5. (Cairo: al-Sa'ada Press, 1930), 27.

115. Chirguh, *La question Kurde,* 16.

116. Ibid., 17.

117. Ibid.

118. Layard, *Discoveries,* 1:50.

119. Chirguh, *La question Kurde,* 17; [W. G. Elphinston], "The Azizan or the Princes of Bohtan," *Journal of the Royal Central Asian Society* 36, parts 3–4 (July-Oct. 1949), 250.

120. E. M. Noel, *Diary,* 53.

121. Ibid.; [Elphinston], "The Azizan", 250; Chirguh, *La question Kurde,* 17.

122. Although Bedir Khan is known to have left a very large family, reports have varied as to the number of his offspring. According to one source, he had forty sons and fourteen daughters. Letter from Major Trotter to the Marquis of Salisbury, dated Dec. 28, 1878, in Great Britain, Foreign Office, *Correspondence Respecting the Condition of the Populations in Asia Minor and Syria, Turkey No. 10 (1879),* Cmd. 2432 (London: H.M. Stationery Office, 1879), 12. According to Elphinston ("The Azizan," 250), he had sixty-five sons. According to E. M. Noel *(Diary,* 53), he had ninety sons.

123. Safrastian, 58–59.

124. Layard, *Discoveries,* 1:36; According to Layard, Nurallah Beg was banished to Candia, Crete.

125. Ibid., 1:35–36; Minorsky, "Kurds."

126. Minorsky, "Kurds"; Nikitine, *Les Kurdes,* 194; Zaki, *Khulasat Tarikh al-Kurd,* 255–56.

4. Shaykh 'Ubayd Allah of Nehri

1. George N. Curzon, *Persia and the Persian Question* (London: Longmans, Green, 1892), 1: 53.

2. Enclo. in No. 22, Trotter to Goschen, Therapia, Oct. 20, 1880, in Great Britain, *Turkey No. 5 (1881),* 17.

3. S. G. Wilson, *Persian Life and Customs,* 110. See also Robert E. Speer, *"The Hakim Sahib,"* the Foreign Doctor: A Biography of Joseph Plumb Cochran, M.D. of Persia (New York: Fleming H. Revel, 1911), 74.

4. Report by Dr. Cochran, June 1, 1880, to Board of Missions, quoted by Speer, 75. Cf. Enclo. 4 in No. 8, extract from letter to Consul-General Abbott, Urmiya, July 8, 1880, Great Britain, *Turkey No. 5 (1881),* 9. Although Dr. Cochran's name does not appear in the latter reference, a comparison of these two communications proves beyond any doubt that the latter, too, was written by Cochran.

5. Quoted in Speer, 79.

6. Enclo. 4 in No. 8, extract from letter to Consul-General Abbott, Urmiya, July 8, 1880, Great Britain, *Turkey No. 5 (1881),* 9.

7. Ibid.

8. S. G. Wilson, *Persian Life and Customs,* 110.

9. Ibid.

10. Enclo. 4 in No. 8, extract from letter to Consul-General Abbott, Urmiya, July 8, 1880, Great Britain, *Turkey No. 5 (1881),* 9.

11. Extract from letter by Dr. Cochran's sister, quoted in Speer, 96.

12. Letter from Dr. Cochran to his friend Mr. Clement, published in *Buffalo Commercial Advertiser,* July 26, 1880, quoted in Speer, 80.

13. Speer, 74–75.

14. They include Qur'anic exegeses, hadith, Muslim jurisprudence, Muslim religious literature, Sufi literature, and so on.

15. Extract from letter by Dr. Cochran's sister, quoted in Speer, 80.

16. No. 54, Clayton to Trotter, Van, Oct. 27, 1880, Great Britain, *Turkey No. 5 (1881)*, 33.

17. Enclo. 1 in No. 61, Abbott to Thomson, Urmiya, Oct. 7, 1880, in ibid., 47.

18. Enclo. in No. 22, Trotter to Goschen, Therapia, Oct. 20, 1880, in ibid., 16.

19. No. 61, Thomson to Earl Granville, Teheran, Oct. 31, 1880, in ibid., 45.

20. Enclo. 3 in No. 61, Sheikh Obeidullah ['Ubayd Allah] to Dr. Cochran, Oct. 5, 1880, in ibid., 47.

21. Enclo. 5 in No. 61, precis of letter from Sheikh Obeidullah to Ikbal-ed-Dowleh [Iqbal al-Dawla], governor of Urmiya, Sept. 15, 1880, in ibid., 49.

22. Ibid.

23. Enclo. 3 in No. 61, Sheikh Obeidullah to Dr. Cochran, in ibid., 47–48.

24. Ibid., 48.

25. Ibid.

26. Ibid.

27. The Treaty of Berlin and the secret Convention of Defiance Alliance Between Great Britain and Turkey, both of which deal with these reforms, are discussed in a later section of this chapter.

28. Enclo. 2 in No. 49, Clayton to Trotter, Van, Sept. 13, 1879, Great Britain, Foreign Office, *Correspondence Respecting the Condition of the Populations in Asia Minor and Syria, Turkey No. 4 (1880)*, C. 2537 (London: H.M. Stationery Office, 1880), 79 (hereafter *Turkey No. 4 [1880]*).

29. Ibid.

30. Enclo. in No. 30, Clayton to Trotter, Van, Aug. 19, 1879, in ibid., 53.

31. Enclo. in No. 7, Clayton to Trotter, Bashkale, July 11, 1880, Great Britain, *Turkey No. 5 (1881)*, 7.

32. At the time of the Kurdish rebellion in Turkey, Shaykh 'Ubayd Allah was said to have been in touch with Mar Sham'un. See Enclo. in No. 41, Clayton to Trotter, Van, Sept. 6, 1879, Great Britain, Foreign Office, *Turkey No. 4 (1880)*, 68. Later, during his invasion of Persia, the shaykh was reported to have contacted both Mar Sham'un and Ohannes Vartabed, the Armenian bishop at Bashkala. According to the latter, despite several pressing invitations from the shaykh "to come and see him and consult with him about the condition of the country and the steps to be taken," the bishop declined to meet him. See No. 68, Clayton to Trotter, Van, Nov. 2, 1880, Great Britain, *Turkey No. 5 (1881)*, 54.

33. According to Trotter, the shaykh's policy was "to conciliate the Christians about him, not out of love and regard for them but as instruments to carry out his desires." Enclo. in No. 22, Trotter to Goschen, Therapia, Oct. 20, 1880, in Great Britain, *Turkey No. 5 (1881)*, 17.

34. No. 68, Clayton to Trotter, Van, Nov. 2, 1880, in ibid., 54.

35. Enclo. 2 in No. 56, Abbott to Thomson, Tabriz, Nov. 7, 1880, in ibid., 40.

36. S. G. Wilson, *Persian Life and Customs*, 113.

37. Ibid., 110–11.

38. Enclo. 3 in No. 61, Sheikh Obeidullah to Dr. Cochran, Oct. 5, 1880, in Great Britain, *Turkey No. 5 (1881)*, 48.

39. The shaykh's desire to establish close relations with the American missionaries may have been owing to the fact that they spoke English and enjoyed British diplomatic protection, and thus were regarded as just another species of Englishmen. Thomas Laurie mentioned several instances in which both Kurds and Nestorians referred to Americans as Englishmen. For example, a contract for the purchase of land in the Nestorian country referred to Dr. Grant and his team of

American missionaries as "Hakim Grant, and . . . his associates, The English of America." Comparing Grant, who was noted for his piety, with Church of England missionaries, a Kurd said, "I see you are very different from other Englishmen; for you wish to maintain peace with all men." Thomas Laurie, *Dr. Grant and the Mountain Nestorians,* 3rd ed. (Boston: Gould and Lincoln, 1853), 266, 285.

40. Report by Dr. Cochran, June 1, 1880, to Board of Missions, quoted by Speer, 75.

41. Enclo. 4 in No. 8, extract from letter to Consul-General Abbott, Urmiya, July 8, 1880, Great Britain, *Turkey No. 5 (1881),* 9.

42. Enclo. 2 in No. 56, Abbott to Thomson, Tabriz, Nov. 7, 1880, in ibid., 39.

43. Article 61 of the Treaty of Berlin stated: "The Sublime Porte undertakes to carry out, without further delay, the improvements and reforms demanded by local requirements in the provinces inhabited by the Armenians, and to guarantee their security against the Circassians and Kurds. It will periodically make known the steps taken to this effect to the Powers, who will superintend their application." See Sir Edward Hertslet, *The Map of Europe by Treaty: Showing the Various Political and Territorial Changes Which Have Taken Place Since the General Peace of 1814* (London: Butterworths, 1875–91), 4:2796.

44. Enclo. in No. 2, Consul-General Abbott to Earl Granville, Tabriz, July 13, 1880, Great Britain, *Turkey No. 5 (1881),* 8.

45. Ibid., 9.

46. Enclo. in No. 22, Trotter to Mr. Goschen, Therapia, Oct. 20, 1880, in ibid., 16.

47. Ibid., 17

48. Ibid.

49. Ibid.

50. Enclo. in No. 6, letter from Monseigneur Krimian to the Armenian Patriarch, Van, June 20, 1880, in ibid., 6.

51. Ibid., 7.

52. Ibid., 6.

53. Safrastian, who makes no mention of Bahri Beg's official mission to the shaykh, informs us that Bahri Bey was very active in soliciting support for the shaykh's movement among the tribes. However, he does not give any source for this information. Safrastian, 81.

54. Enclo. in No. 6, letter from Monseigneur Krimian to the Armenian Patriarch, Van, June 20, 1880, Great Britain, *Turkey No. 5 (1881),* 6.

55. Enclo. 1 in No. 49, Clayton to Trotter, Van, Sept. 10, 1879, Great Britain, Foreign Office, *Turkey No. 4 (1880),* 78.

56. Enclo. in No. 41, Clayton to Trotter, Van, Sept. 6, 1879, in ibid., 68.

57. Ibid.

58. No. 41, Trotter to the Marquis of Salisbury, Erzerum, Sept. 19, 1879, in ibid., 67.

59. Ibid.

60. Enclo. in No. 41, Clayton to Trotter, Van, Sept. 6, 1879, in ibid., 68.

61. Ibid.

62. Ibid., 69.

63. Enclo. in No. 71, Abbott to Thomson, Tabriz, Sept. 25, 1879, in ibid., 101.

64. Ibid.

65. No. 49, Trotter to the Marquis of Salisbury, Erzerum, Sept. 27, 1879, in ibid., 77.

66. Enclo. in No. 41, Clayton to Trotter, Van, Sept. 6, 1879, in ibid., 68.

67. Ibid.

68. Enclo. 1 in No. 49, Clayton to Trotter, Van, Sept. 10, 1879, in ibid., 78.

69. Enclo. 3 in No. 49, Sheikh Ubaydullah to the *wali* of Van, dated twenty-second day of Ramadan, in ibid., 79–80.

70. No. 49, Trotter to the Marquis of Salisbury, Erzerum, Sept. 27, 1879, in ibid., 77.

71. Ibid.

72. Ibid.

73. Enclo. 1 in No. 49, Clayton to Trotter, Van, Sept. 10, 1879, in ibid., 78.

74. No. 73, Trotter to the Marquis of Salisbury, Erzerum, Oct. 18, 1879, in ibid., 102. A statement made by the Persian consul in Van is of interest in this connection. He maintained that the shaykh's rebellion was the result of Turkey's failure to pay him a promised subsidy. According to the consul, the shaykh was originally a Persian subject in receipt of a subsidy from the Persian government. Wishing to observe strict neutrality during the Russo-Turkish War, the consul withdrew this subsidy when the shaykh joined the Turks. The Ottoman government, which had promised him a "money payment," did not fulfill its promise, which irritated the shaykh and led to his disaffection. See Enclo. in No. 56, Clayton to Trotter, Van, Sept. 19, 1879, in ibid., 87.

75. According to Nikitine, the shaykh had about seventy thousand tribesmen from the Turco-Persian frontier region under his command. Basile Nikitine, "Les Afsars d'Urumiyeh," *Journal Asiatique* 34, (Jan.-Mar. 1929), 99.

76. Enclo. in No. 22, Trotter to Goschen, Therapia, Oct. 20, 1880, in Great Britain, *Turkey No. 5 (1881)*, 17.

77. Enclo. 2 in No. 61, Sheikh Obeidullah to Dr. Cochran, in ibid., 47.

78. Nikitine, "Les Afsars," 99.

79. Enclo. in No. 6, letter from Monseigneur Krimian to the Armenian Patriarch, Van, June 20, 1880, in Great Britain, *Turkey No. 5 (1881)*, 6.

80. Obviously this is a reference to the new breach-loading rifle. See Nikitine, "Les Afsars," 102–3. Consul-General Abbott also described the shaykh as "well supplied with Martini rifles." Enclo. 2 in No. 8, Abbott to Earl Granville, Tabriz, July 15, 1880, in Great Britain, *Turkey No. 5 (1881)*, 9.

81. Enclo. 1 in No. 74, memorandum from Persian ambassador in Constantinople to British chargé d'affairs, in Great Britain, *Turkey No. 5 (1881)*, 60.

82. Enclo. 2 in No. 70, Abbott to Thomson, Tabriz, Nov. 25, 1880, in ibid., 57.

83. Enclo. 4 in No. 61, Sheikh Obeidullah to Dr. Cochran, in ibid., 47.

84. S. G. Wilson, *Persian Life and Customs*, 111. Estimates of the size of this force vary considerably. Vice Consul Clayton reported that this force was estimated at twenty thousand men, but cautioned against placing reliance on this figure. See Enclo. 2 in No. 54, Clayton to Trotter, Van, Oct. 25, 1880, Great Britain, *Turkey No. 5 (1881)*, 32. Nikitine, quoting an unpublished Persian chronicle, gives the strength of the Sawj Bulaq force as between forty and fifty thousand. Nikitine, "Les Afsars," 95. According to Consul-General Abbott, this force, originally estimated at between ten and thirty thousand men, dwindled to fifteen hundred in the course of the campaign as a result of the men's return to their homes. Enclo. 2 in No. 56, Abbott to Thomson, Tabriz, Nov. 7, 1880, in Great Britain, *Turkey 5 (1881)*, 40.

85. Enclo. 2 in No. 54, Clayton to Trotter, Van, Oct. 25, 1880, Great Britain, *Turkey No. 5 (1881)*, 32.

86. No. 61, Thomson to Granville, Teheran, Oct. 31, 1880, in ibid., 45.

87. See D. B. Macdonald, "Fatwa," *Encyclopaedia of Islam*, 1st ed., 3:92–93.

88. S. G. Wilson, *Persian Life and Customs*, 111.

89. Enclo. 1 in No. 61, Abbott to Thomson, Urmiya, Oct. 7, 1880, in Great Britain, *Turkey No. 5 (1881),* 46.

90. S. G. Wilson, *Persian Life and Customs,* 111. Abbott estimated the number of Persians massacred at Miyanduab at two thousand. Enclo. 2 in No. 56, Abbott to Thomson, Tabriz, Nov. 7, 1880, Great Britain, *Turkey No. 5 (1881),* 40. According to Mrs. Cochran's letter of October 11, 1880, the number of persons killed in and around Miyanduab amounted to more than four thousand; Speer, 84. Lord Curzon, like Wilson, placed the figure at three thousand; Curzon, 1:553.

91. S. G. Wilson, *Persian Life and Customs,* 112.

92. No. 68, Clayton to Trotter, Van, Nov. 2, 1880, in Great Britain, *Turkey No. 5 (1881),* 54.

93. No. 61, Thomson to Earl Granville, Teheran, Oct. 31, 1880, in ibid., 46.

94. Enclo. 2 in No. 56, Abbott to Thomson, Tabriz, Nov. 7, 1880, in ibid., 39.

95. Nikitine, "Les Afsars," 101–2.

96. S. G. Wilson, *Persian Life and Customs,* 114; Speer, 86; Curzon, 1:553.

97. In organizing the defense of the city, Iqbal al-Dawla was greatly assisted by Bishop Cluzel, head of the French Catholic mission in Urmiya. It was mainly through the bishop's efforts that considerable sums of money were collected from the Urmiya merchants to defray the cost of the defense. See Nikitine, "Les Afsars," 103.

98. S. G. Wilson, *Persian Life and Customs,* 114; Speer, 90.

99. See S. G. Wilson, *Persian Life and Customs,* 117.

100. Curzon, 1:554; cf. S. G. Wilson, *Persian Life and Customs,* 119.

101. There seems to be some difference of opinion concerning the place where the shaykh died. Those who say he died at Mecca are Curzon, 1:554; S. G. Wilson, *Persian Life and Customs,* 122; and W. G. Elphinston, "The Kurdish Question," *Journal of International Affairs* 22, no. 1 (Jan. 1946), 94. But Zaki *(Khulasat Tarikh al-Kurd,* 120) indicates Taif, and Chirguh *(La question Kurde,* 18) gives Madina.

102. S. G. Wilson, *Persian Life and Customs,* 115–16.

103. Edward Stack, *Six Months in Persia* (New York, G. P. Putnam and Sons, 1882), 250–51.

104. Mary Lewis Shedd, *The Measure of a Man: The Life of William Ambrose Shedd, Missionary to Persia* (New York: George H. Doran, 1922), 45.

105. Rufus R. Dawes, comp., *A History of the Establishment of Diplomatic Relations with Persia* (Marietta, Ohio: E. R. Alderman and Sons, 1887), 5.

106. Ibid., 27.

107. Ibid., 25–26. See also letter from Joseph P. Cochran and W. L. Whipple to Hon. R. R. Dawes, Urmiya, July 6, 1882, and letter from Rev. Benjamin Labaree, Constantinople, Jan. 1882, to Hon. R. R. Dawes, Urmiya, July 6, 1882, ibid., 33–34.

108. Dawes, 27–33.

109. Ibid., 42–55.

110. Curzon, 1:557.

111. Baron A. G. Jomini held the position of senior counselor in the Russian Foreign Office from 1856 to 1888.

112. No. 29, Plunkett to Earl Granville, St. Petersburg, Nov. 3, 1880, Great Britain, *Turkey No. 5 (1881),* 20.

113. Enclo. in No. 28, extract from *Bereg,* St. Petersburg, Nov. 7, 1880, in ibid., 19.

114. Ibid.

115. No. 32, Plunkett to Earl Granville, St. Petersburg, Nov. 8, 1880, in ibid., 20.

116. Ibid.

117. No. 35, Earl Granville to Mr. Plunkett, London, Nov. 9, 1880, in ibid., 21.

118. No. 41, Earl Granville to Mr. Plunkett, London, Nov. 16, 1880, in ibid., 24.

119. Ibid.

120. Ibid., passim.

121. Enclo. 4 in No. 76, Abbott to Thomson, Tabriz, in ibid., 70.

122. No. 71, Plunkett to Earl Granville, St. Petersburg, Dec. 14, 1880, in ibid., 58.

123. Sir Henry Elliot and Gertrude Elliot, *Some Revolutions and Other Diplomatic Experiences* (London: J. Murray, 1922), 274–95.

124. These regions have often been a bone of contention between Turkey and Persia/Iran during the past four centuries. Ottoman armies overran much of these regions in their wars against the Safavids and later in their wars against Nadir Shah, but they were always ejected. Neither party ever adhered to the Treaty of Erzerum of 1847, which was supposed to have fixed the frontiers, and the frontier fluctuated throughout the nineteenth century. In 1905, taking advantage of Russia's temporary weakness after the Russo-Japanese War, Turkey occupied these provinces and was still in possession of them when the Balkan War of 1913 and Russia's renewed political and military vigor forced Turkey to evacuate them. Turkish troops were back in the same regions in 1917 after the collapse of the Russian armies during the revolution. See Minorsky, "Kurds." It is interesting to note the strong pro-Turkish attitude displayed during World War I by the people of Russian Azerbayjan, who, like the inhabitants of Persian Azerbayjan, are both Turkish speaking and Shi'i. See Firuz Kazemzadeh, *The Struggle for Transcaucasia* (New York: Philosophical Library, 1951), passim.

125. Article 1 of the Convention of Defensive Alliance states:

> If Batoum, Ardahan, Kars, or any of them shall be retained by Russia, and if any attempt shall be made at any future time by Russia to take possession of any further territories of His Imperial Majesty the Sultan in Asia, as fixed by the Definitive Treaty of Peace, England engages to join His Imperial Majesty the Sultan in defending them by force of arms.
>
> In return, His Imperial Majesty the Sultan promises to England to introduce necessary Reforms, to be agreed upon later between the two Powers, with the government, and for the protection of the Christian and other subjects of the Porte in these territories.
>
> And in order to enable England to make necessary provision for executing her engagement, His Imperial Majesty the Sultan further consents to assign the Island of Cyprus to be occupied and administered by England. See Hertslet, 4:2722–23.

126. So great was Layard's influence at one time that Reuez, the German ambassador, called him the "vice sultan." See William Newton Medlicott, *The Congress of Berlin and After* (London: Methuen, 1938), 114.

127. Ibid.

128. Ibid., 295.

129. See James Carlile McCoan, *Our New Protectorate: Turkey in Asia* (London: Chapman and Hall, 1879), passim.

130. Salisbury's plan was based on three essential points: a satisfactory military frontier in Europe, a military guarantee of the sultan's dominions by England and Austria, and internal reforms aimed at increasing the empire's efficiency, internal order, and prosperity. Insofar as the reforms were concerned, Layard was instructed to obtain a formal undertaking from the sultan

regarding the following points: *(a)* the institution of a gendarmerie in the Asiatic provinces, organized and commanded by Europeans; *(b)* the institution of central tribunals at a certain number of the most important Asiatic towns with jurisdiction over the lower courts and with at least one European lawyer of ascertained probity and learning; *(c)* the appointment of collectors in each *wilayat* who would be charged with the collection of revenue and the abolition of tithe farming. For further details, see Medlicott, 293.

131. Ibid., 292.

132. Ibid.

133. Ibid., 293.

134. Ibid., 295.

135. Ibid., 302.

136. Ibid., 306.

137. Ibid., 291.

5. The Impact of the Young Turk Revolution on Kurdish Nationalism

1. The CUP was founded in Istanbul in 1889 by Ibrahim Temo, 'Abd Allah Jawdat, Ishak Sukûti, and Mehmet Resit. Yusuf Hikmet Bayur, *Türk Inkılâbı Tarihi, Türk Tarikh Kurumu Yayınlarından* (The History of the Turkish Revolution) (Istanbul: Ma'arif Mataba'asi Press for the Turkish Historical Association, 1940), 1:66; İsma'il Hâmi Dânişmend, *İzahlı Osmanlı Tarihi Kronolojisi* (An Explanation of the Chronology of Ottoman History) (Istanbul: Türkiye Basımevi, 1955), 9:357. The first significant account of the early history of the Young Turks was given by Paul Fesch, who seems to have enjoyed their complete confidence. It is interesting to note that in discussing the founding of the CUP, Fesch mentioned Temo and Jawdat, who were then in Europe, and Sukûti, who was dead, but omitted the name of the fourth person, Resit, who was in Turkey at the time. Paul Fesch, *Constantinople aux derniers jours d'Abdul-Hamid* (Paris: M. Riviere, 1907), 369. See also Ernest Edmondson Ramsaur Jr., *The Young Turks: Prelude to the Revolution of 1908,* Princeton Oriental Studies, Social Science no. 2 (Princeton, N.J.: Princeton Univ. Press, 1957), 14–51. This is an excellent and richly documented study of the Young Turk movement prior to the revolution.

2. The disagreements that marred the Young Turk Liberal Congress, held in 1902 in Paris, provide some idea of the basic differences existing among the various factions. Ramsaur, 66ff.

3. These elements in Young Turk thinking are discussed by Ramsaur, passim.

4. For a discussion of the influence of the Carbonari, IMRO, and Freemasonry on the CUP, see ibid., 15, 101, and 103–9, respectively.

5. Ishak Sukûti (1868–1903) was a physician and political leader. He joined the CUP while a student at the Military College of Medicine in Istanbul. İbrahim Alâettin Gövsa, *Türk Meşhurları Ansiklopedisi* (Encyclopedia of Famous Turks) (Istanbul: Yedigun Nesriya, n.d.), 192; also Ramsaur, passim.

6. 'Abd Allah Jawdat: physician, poet, man of letters, and political thinker; one of the most brilliant and prolific writers of modern Turkey; born in Arabgir in 1869 of a Kurdish family. For an excellent and richly documented study, see K. Süssheim, "'Abd Allah Djewdet [Jawdat]," in *Encyclopaedia of Islam,* vol. 9: *Supplement,* 55–60.

7. Ramsaur, 26.

8. Fesch, 334; also Ramsaur, 33. According to Ramsaur, Shaykh 'Abd al-Qadir was exiled with twenty members of his family.

9. See list of persons attending the Young Turk congress in Fesch, 365 fn. 1; also *Pro-Armenia* 1 (Jan. 10, 1901), 30–31.

10. Isma'il Haqqi Beg was a member for Baghdad in the Mab'uthan (Parliament) and was closely associated with Tanin, the CUP mouthpiece. André Mandelstam, *Le sort de l'Empire Ottoman* (Paris: Librairie Payot et Cie, 1917), 24, 37.

11. Sulayman Nadif: politician, administrator, and noted journalist, who, despite being a full-blooded Kurd, was a zealous agent of Turkification. He served as *wali* of Mosul and later as acting *wali* of Baghdad. See Damaluji, *Imarat Bahdinan*, 98ff.; Jiyawuk, 56; Longrigg, *Iraq, 1900–1950*, 50; and Mandelstam, 277.

12. J. A. R. Marriott, *The Eastern Question: An Historical Study in European Diplomacy* (Oxford: Oxford Univ. Press, 1924), 431; William Miller, *The Ottoman Empire and Its Successors, 1801–1927* (Cambridge: Cambridge Univ. Press, 1934), 474.

13. Ibid., 62–63; Marriott, *The Eastern Question*, 431; Dânişmend, 355–56.

14. For details concerning the Bulgarian declaration of independence on October 5, 1908, and Austria's annexation of Bosnia and Herzegovina, see Miller, 478.

15. Ibid., 480–81.

16. Chirugh, *La question Kurde*, 19; Chirguh, *al-Qadiya al-Kurdiya*, 51; Basile Nikitine, "Kurdes," in *Dictionnaire Diplomatique* (Paris: Academie Diplomatique Internationale, 1933), 1:1201; Zaki, *Khulasat Tarikh al-Kurd*, 349–50. Although all the foregoing sources are agreed that the Kurdish National Committee was the first Kurdish political society, Muhammad 'Ali 'Awni, the translator of Zaki's book into Arabic, indicates in a footnote (p. 340) that a society known as Jam'iyat al-'Azm al-Qawi al-Kurdistaniya (Strong Kurdish Resolve Society) may have been the first.

17. W. G. Elphinston, "The Kurdish Question," *International Affairs* (London) 22, no. 1 (Jan. 1946), 94.

18. Ibid.

19. It appears that Tal'at Pasha tried to get Sureya Beg to join the CUP, but without success. See Driver, *Kurdistan and the Kurds*, 113.

20. Chirguh, *La question Kurde*, 19; Chirguh, *al-Qadiya al-Kurdiya*, 51; Zaki, *Khulasat Tarikh al-Kurd*, 350.

21. Chirguh, *La question Kurde*, 19–20; Chirguh, *al-Qadiya al-Kurdiya*, 52; Zaki, *Khulasat Tarikh al-Kurd*, 350; and Nikitine, *Les Kurdes*, 195.

22. Nikitine, *Les Kurdes*, 196.

23. Zaki, *Khulasat Tarikh al-Kurd*, 350; Chirguh, *La question Kurde*, 20; Chirguh, *al-Qadiya al-Kurdiya*, 52–53.

24. According to Zaki, the Bedir Khans and a number of their adherents split off from the Kurdistan Ta'ali Jam'iyati to form this new society. Zaki, *Khulasat Tarikh al-Kurd*, 350; Chirguh, *La question Kurde*, 20; Chirguh, *al-Qadiya al-Kurdiya*, 52–53. Cf. Nikitine, *Les Kurdes*, 196.

25. Zaki, *Khulasat Tarikh al-Kurd*, 350; Chirguh, *La question Kurde*, 20; Chirguh, *al-Qadiya al-Kurdiya*, 52–53; Nikitine, *Les Kurdes*, 196.

26. Damaluji, *Imarat Bahdinan*, 94–95.

27. Sultan Mahmud's reforms had led to the suppression of the Kurdish principalities in the first half of the nineteenth century. His annihilation of the Janissaries and the Bektashi order in 1826, coupled with his forward-looking but unpopular reforms, made his name anathema to the religious orders. It is said that after his death it was the Bektashi dervishes' custom to spit and utter a curse whenever they passed his tomb in Istanbul. John Kingsley Birge, *The Bektashi Order*

of Dervishes (London: Luzac, 1937), 79. A story is told of a dervish who, one day in 1837 while the sultan was crossing the Galata bridge, rushed at him with threats and insults, calling him *"giaour padishah"* (infidel sovereign) and accusing him of being a destroyer of Islam. John P. Brown, *The Darvishes: Or, Oriental Spiritualism* (London: H. Milford, 1927), 345–46; and Birge, 83.

28. Copies of this telegram were given to Shaykh 'Abd al-Qadir of Nehri (the son of Shaykh 'Ubayd Allah), Amin 'Ali Bedir Khan, and General Sherif Pasha—three leading Kurdish nationalists. According to Damaluji, this step was taken against the wishes of those signing the petition, who wanted to keep the telegram strictly official. We are informed that the giving of the copies was Shaykh 'Abd al-Salam's wish. Damaluji, *Imarat Bahdinan,* 96 fn. 1.

29. Ibid.

30. Shaykh Sa'id had come to have great influence over Sultan 'Abdul Hamid after having cured the illness of one of the sultan's favorite sons through prayer. Gertrude Lowthian Bell, *Amurath to Amurath,* 2d ed. (London: Macmillan, 1924), 249. Cf. Soane, *Report on Sulaimania District,* 98.

31. Ibid., 99–100.

32. For detailed accounts of Shaykh Sa'id's murder, see Bell, *Amurath to Amurath,* 249–50; Soane, *To Mesopotamia and Kurdistan,* 192; Soane, *Report on Sulaimania District,* 99–100.

33. Soane, *To Mesopotamia and Kurdistan,* 192ff., gives a detailed description of this situation; see also Soane, *Report on Sulaimania District,* 100–101.

34. E. J. R., *Precis of Affairs in Southern Kurdistan during the Great War* (Baghdad: Government Press, 1919), 1; Gertrude Lowthian Bell, *Review of the Civil Administration of Mesopotamia, 1914–1920* (London: H.M. Stationery Office, 1920), 43.

35. Elphinston, "The Kurdish Question," 94. For further details concerning Ibrahim Pasha's career and end, see Ewald Banse, *Auf den Spuren der Bagdadbahn* (On the Trail of the Baghdad Railway) (Weimar: A. Duncker, 1913), 76–94; M. Wiedemann, "Ibrahim Pasha's Gluck und Ende," *Asien* 8, no. 3 (1908): 34–37, 52–54; M. Sykes, 317–27; and Rondot, "Les tribus Montagnardes," 34–38.

36. E. J. R., 1; Bell, *Review of the Civil Administration,* 43. According to Longrigg, during Nadim Pasha's tenure as *wali* of Baghdad, Mahmud Pasha was invited to that city, where he was received with great honors and lionized. Longrigg, *Iraq, 1900–1950,* 57.

37. Even before the Young Turk Revolution, Mustafa Pasha had been in conflict with the Ottoman government and had been compelled to spend a number of years in Constantinople as a political exile. The charges of his pro-British sympathies were substantiated by his unequivocal support of the British cause after the capture of Baghdad. E. J. R., 1; Bell, *Review of the Civil Administration,* 43; Soane, *Notes on the Tribes,* 2.

38. Elphinston, "The Kurdish Question," 94–95.

39. Driver, *Kurdistan and the Kurds,* 30.

40. When required to explain his activities to the Ottoman authorities at Aleppo, 'Abd al-Qadir maintained that he was leading volunteers to the assistance of Turkey. The government accepted his explanation and ordered him and his force to assist in defending the capital. They apparently proved of little use in the front lines and were sent back home, "where they arrived laden with booty from Thrace." Ibid.

41. According to Longrigg, Kurdish notables were invited to Russia where they were well received. See Longrigg, *Iraq 1900–1950,* 58. Ahmad Emin Yalman points out that the Russians displayed feverish activity in Kurdistan prior to the outbreak of the war. See Ahmad Emin Yalman, *Turkey in the World War* (New Haven, Conn.: Yale Univ. Press, 1930), 209.

42. Bell, *Review of the Civil Administration,* 44.

43. Hay, *Two Years in Kurdistan,* 180. Cf. Nikitine, "Les Kurdes racontés," where they are referred to as "les fous."

44. For a description of this outbreak, see Nikitine, "Les Kurdes racontés," 150–51; Damaluji, *Imarat Bahdinan,* 90–91.

45. The Mahdi or the "Guided One" is an eschatological figure who is supposed to come before the end of the world, sword in hand, to destroy evil and tyranny, establish righteousness and justice, and restore the faith. According to one tradition, he is supposed to be of the family of the Prophet and to bear the name Muhammad, but according to another he is identified with Jesus. Mahdis supposedly have appeared in various Muslim countries in times of trouble and distress. For details on the concept of Mahdism and the various Mahdist movements, see D. B. Macdonald, "Mahdi," in *Encyclopaedia of Islam,* 1st ed., 5:111–15, and D. S. Margoliouth, "Mahdi," in *Encyclopaedia of Religion and Ethics,* edited by James Hastings, 8:336–40 (New York: Charles Scribner's Sons, 1917–30). On the persistence of Mahdist tendencies in Muslim countries, see H. A. R. Gibb, *Modern Trends in Islam* (Chicago: Univ. of Chicago Press, 1947), 153ff.

46. Nikitine, "Les Kurdes racontés," 150–51; Damaluji, *Imarat Bahdinan,* 91.

47. Damaluji, *Imarat Bahdinan,* 92, 131–33.

48. Wigram and Wigram, 139ff. It is interesting in this connection to note that Shaykh 'Abd al-Salam, in the course of a conversation with Damaluji, complained, "We have no villages to give the notables of Mosul as our enemies do. We are the sole defenders of our own interests." See Damaluji, *Imarat Bahdinan,* 92.

49. Jiyawuk, 55–56.

50. Damaluji, *Imarat Bahdinan,* 92–93, 131–33, has dealt most extensively with this struggle. Cf. Bell, *Review of the Civil Administration,* 73; M. Sykes, 323–25; Muhammad al-Brifkani, *Haqa'iq Tarikhiya 'an al-Qadiya al-Barzaniya* (Historical Truths Regarding the Barzani Problem) (Baghdad: Matba'at Sharikat al-Tiba'a wa al-Nashr al-'Ahliya Press, 1953), 7.

51. For details on such activities in the Bahdinan region of Kurdistan, see Damaluji, *Imarat Bahdinan,* 80–81.

52. Ibid., 99–100. According to Damaluji, the execution of Shaykh 'Abd al-Salam, which did violence to the Barzanis' deepest and most cherished beliefs, turned them into implacable enemies of all government authority.

53. Nikitine, "Les Kurdes racontés," 152. Cf. Wigram and Wigram, 139.

54. Nikitine, "Les Kurdes racontés," 152. Cf. Damaluji, *Imarat Bahdinan,* 97; and Wigram and Wigram, 139.

55. Nikitine, "Les Kurdes racontés," 152; Wigram and Wigram, 139.

56. Longrigg, *Iraq 1900–1950,* 58; Damaluji, *Imarat Bahdinan,* 97–98. See also the sources discussed in note 57.

57. Nikitine, who strangely enough does not mention Nadim Pasha, credits Colonel Safwat Beg with obtaining the shaykh's pardon by successfully pleading his case before the authorities in Istanbul. Nikitine, "Les Kurdes racontés," 152–54. According to al-Brifkani, Colonel Safwat Beg acted on behalf of Nazim Pasha, who appointed him as his representative in Mosul and charged him with establishing order and stability in that region. Al-Brifkani, 8. The British, by urging leniency toward Shaykh 'Ubayd Allah and courtesy toward captured members of his family, seem to have played some part in bringing about the peaceful settlement of this problem. The shaykh, according to Wigram and Wigram, was "pleased to attribute it largely to the friendly offices of the British." However, these authors make it clear that Nadim Pasha's intervention was decisive. See

Wigram and Wigram, 140. It appears that the shaykh found another sympathizer in As'ad Pasha al-Durzi, commander of the Twelfth Army Corps, who briefly served as acting *wali* of Mosul. With a view toward conciliating the shaykh, As'ad Pasha apparently recommended that the shaykh be awarded the Majidi order, third class. See Damaluji, *Imarat Bahdinan*, 98.

58. Nikitine, "Les Kurdes racontés," 152–54. Wigram and Wigram, 140–41, briefly referred to the battle of Bab Sefan and the casualties inflicted on the government troops.

59. Nikitine, "Les Kurdes racontés," 154.

60. Ibid.

61. Safwat Beg himself is reported to have crossed the frontier and joined the Russians shortly thereafter. Ibid.

62. Ibid.

63. For more details on the policies pursued by Sulayman Nadif as *wali* of Mosul, particularly with regard to Shaykh 'Abd al-Salam, see Damaluji, *Imarat Bahdinan*, 98–105.

64. Nikitine, "Les Kurdes racontés," 154.

65. Ibid.

66. A graphic account of the hanging of Shaykh 'Abd al-Salam and his companions is given by Damaluji, who witnessed the bizarre and moving spectacle. Damaluji, an Ottoman official who had incurred the *wali*'s displeasure, was an inmate of the jail in which Shaykh 'Abd al-Salam was being held. According to him, the prisoners were marched into the prison courtyard, where four scaffolds had been erected, and a Kurdish religious dignitary, Amin Effendi Qaradaghi, was waiting to perform the last rites for the condemned men (Talgin al-Shahada). As the shaykh was led to the gallows, he reportedly said: "I want to have a word with the *wali*." When asked what was it that he wished to tell him, he answered: "Life and death are the same to me, but my death in this manner is not in the interest of the government. If my life is spared, I shall offer assistance to the army—one thousand fully laden mules." This we are told was on the eve of Turkey's entry into the war. The shaykh was informed on behalf of the *wali* that the "die was cast." Then came the turn of the shaykh's three companions. They included two personal servants, Mahmud and Musa, and a Rikani tribal chieftain, Muhammad Agha Hayashti. Mahmud, a youth of twenty, walked boldly to the scaffold shouting: "Long live the God of Barzan! I am his scapegoat, I am his offering!" Musa, a sixty-year-old man, said: "Ashes upon the head of the government! The Barzanis will not be annihilated by my death." The Rikani *agha*, Muhammad Hayashti, a seventy-year-old man, kept saying: "I am a Rikani, I am not a Zibari. I am Muhammad Hayashti, do not strangle me. I have not done a thing." When taken to the scaffold, he murmured: "In the name of the Merciful, the Compassionate." See Damaluji, *Imarat Bahdinan*, 103–4. Cf. Nikitine, "Les Kurdes racontés," 155.

67. Damaluji maintains that the *wali*, in order to justify his action, staged an "uprising," which he claimed was carried out by the shaykh's followers with the object of setting the shaykh free by force. After putting down the alleged uprising, the *wali* had the shaykh tried by court martial, found guilty, and sentenced to death. He thus was able to forestall any attempt by the higher authorities in Istanbul to save the shaykh's life. According to Damaluji, Sulayman Nadif buried Shaykh 'Abd al-Salam and his companions in an unknown grave so that his tomb should not become a place of pilgrimage. Damaluji, *Imarat Bahdinan*, 104–5.

68. Ibid., 99, 165–67.

69. Despite the fact that several writers mention this rebellion, the meager information given is often strangely inconsistent with regard to the names and titles of the leaders of the revolt. These names appear variously as: Mullas Selim, Shahab al-Din, and 'Ali, in Zaki, *Khulasat Tarikh al-Kurd*, 272; and as Khalifa Selim and 'Ali Agha, in Nikitine, *Les Kurdes*, 195, where they are de-

scribed as partisans of Shaykh 'Abd al-Qadir of Nehri. Safrastian, however, maintained that the rebellion was inspired and led by Shaykh Sa'id 'Ali of Khizan, a district near Bidlis. See Safrastian, 72–74.

70. Yalman, 209.

71. Chirguh, *La question Kurde,* 19; Zaki, *Khulasat Tarikh al-Kurd,* 272. Cf. Safrastian, 74, where it is stated that Shaykh Sa'id 'Ali occupied the town of Bidlis for one week.

72. The rebellion was suppressed with great severity, according to Nikitine, *Les Kurdes,* 195, and Major E. W. C. Noel, *Note on the Kurdish Situation* (Baghdad: Government Press, 1919), 3.

73. For accounts of this rebellion and of the shaykh's capture and hanging, see Chirguh, *La question Kurde,* 19; Zaki, *Khulasat Tarikh al-Kurd,* 272; and Safrastian, 74. According to Safrastian, the shaykh was captured while attempting to flee to the neighboring mountains with four of his followers, all of whom were hanged with him.

6. Russia's Kurdish Policy

1. In accordance with this treaty, Persia gave up all claims to Transcaucasia, ceding to Russia the khanates of Karabagh, Sheki, Shirwan, Derbend, Kuba, Baku, and Talish. The treaty also confirmed Russia's previous occupation of Ganja (Elizavetpol). Moreover, Persia pledged not to maintain warships in the Caspian Sea. A. Dirr, "Gulistan," in *Encyclopaedia of Islam,* 1st ed., 3:182.

2. As a result of this treaty, Persia ceded Erivan and Nakhichivan, agreed to pay an indemnity of 20 million rubles (5 million tumans), which was later reduced, and, most important of all, concluded an agreement regulating the legal status of Russian subjects. This treaty became the historic origin of Persian capitulations because all subsequent agreements between Persia and other European powers were modeled on it. V. Minorsky, "Turkman-Cai," in *Encyclopaedia of Islam,* 1st ed., 8:896.

3. It seems that one of the chief amusements of the evening consisted of listening to a Kurd who sang songs of the recent Russo-Persian wars. The songs, which were scornful of Persian prowess and told of the Persian crown prince's discomfiture, were greeted with undisguised delight amid peals of laughter by the assembled Kurds. James Baille Fraser, *A Winter's Journey (Tatar) from Constantinople to Teheran, with Travels Through Various Parts of Persia &c* (London: R. Bentley, 1838), 1:308.

4. The other two prerequisites were: ensuring the flow of reinforcements to the Anatolian front and obtaining an absolute guarantee of peace with Persia. W. E. D. Allen and Paul Muratoff, *Caucasian Battlefields: A History of the Wars on the Turco-Caucasian Border, 1828–1921* (Cambridge: Cambridge Univ. Press, 1953), 32.

5. Kurdish resentment was soon to express itself in a series of major uprisings in the Soran, Bahdinan, Bohtan, and Baban principalities and other regions. Ibid., 31.

6. For further details on the Russians' success in enlisting the aid of Kurdish chieftains during the Russo-Turkish War of 1828–1829, see Aleksandr Kleonakovich Ushakoff, *Geschichte der Feldzüge in der Asiatischen Turkei Während der Jahre 1828 und 1829,* vols. 1 and 2 (Leipzig: n.p., 1838), passim; William Monteith, *Kars and Erzeroum with the Campaigns of Prince Paskiewitch in 1828 and 1829* (London: Longman, Brown, Green, and Longmans, 1856), 231 and passim.

7. Monteith, 220–21, 262.

8. Ibid., 264.

9. Ushakoff, 2:18, also 1:318.

10. Allen and Muratoff, 39.

11. Monteith, 263–64.

12. Ibid., 264.

13. Allen and Muratoff, 40.

14. Ibid., 44.

15. The most comprehensive work on the Kurds' role in the Russo-Turkish wars is Averianov's *Kurdi v Voinakh Rossi*. This work, which was published in Tiflis in 1900, is not available in the United States.

16. Minorsky, "Kurds."

17. Ibid.; Nikitine, *Les Kurdes,* 194; Zaki, *Khulasat Tarikh al-Kurd,* 255–56.

18. F. V. Greene, *The Russian Army and Its Campaigns in Turkey in 1877–1878* (New York: D. Appleton, 1879), 384–85.

19. Chirguh, *La question Kurde,* 17–18; Minorsky, "Kurds."

20. Nikitine, *Les Kurdes,* 242. This is probably a reference to 'Ali's miraculous sword, *dhu al-fagar* or *dhu al-fiqar.* This sword is said to have belonged to the Prophet, who obtained it as booty in the battle of Badr and later passed it on to 'Ali. For details concerning this sword, see E. Mittwoch, "Dhu'l-Fakar," in *Encyclopaedia of Islam,* 1st ed., 2:959; also C. Huart, "'Ali b. Abi Talib," in *Encyclopaedia of Islam,* 1st ed., 1:283–85.

21. Lobanov-Rostovsky pointed out in 1933 that Russia pursued this policy in order to placate its own Armenian subjects, who were "nervously reacting to the sufferings of their brethren across the border." Andrei Lobanov-Rostovsky, *Russia and Asia* (New York: Macmillan, 1933), 201.

22. Ibid. In Lobanov-Rostovsky's words, "The championing of their cause by Great Britain would mean the extension of British influence into that most vulnerable zone along the Caucasian frontier at a time when the rivalry between the two powers was at its most acute stage" (201).

23. For a discussion of Bismarck's attitude toward Russia, see Marriott, *The Eastern Question,* 390–92; also J. A. R. Marriott, *The European Commonwealth* (Oxford: Oxford Univ. Press, 1918), 276–77. For a detailed and excellent account of the Berlin Conference and the policies pursued by the various powers participating in the conference, see Medlicott, passim.

24. Bernard Pares, *A History of Russia,* 4th ed. rev. (New York: Alfred A. Knopf, 1946), 383.

25. Ibid., 391, 393.

26. Ibid., 409–14, and 393–94; see also Lobanov-Rostovsky, 202.

27. On Bulgaria's attitude toward Russia and Stephen Stambuloff's role, see Marriott, *The Eastern Question,* 349ff. and 362.

28. Ibid., 398–99.

29. Ibid.

30. For a discussion of Russo-Armenian relations at this time, see Sarkis Atamian, *The Armenian Community: The Historical Development of a Social and Ideological Conflict* (New York: Philosophical Library, 1955), 114–17. On the Armeno-Tatar massacres, see Luigi Villari, *Fire and Sword in the Caucasus* (London: T. F. Unwin, 1906).

31. *Krasny Arkhiv* 26 (1928), 118–19, cited in Walter Kolarz, *Russia and Her Colonies* (London: George Philip and Son, 1952), 215.

32. Sazonov, the Russian foreign minister, maintained that despite Germany's avowed friendship for Turkey and its strong stand in favor of that country during these negotiations, its attitude was influenced by other considerations. According to him, "In the opinion of our Ambassador, Herr Von Gogow's displeasure was due to the fact that the German Government itself

hoped to raise the question of the Armenian reforms, and could not, therefore, be pleased to see itself forestalled in that intention." Sergiei Dmitrievich Sazonov, *The Fateful Years* (London: Jonathan Cape, 1928), 141–46.

33. For a detailed account giving the official Russian version of the negotiations and signature of the Armenian Convention, see Russia, Ministry of Foreign Affairs, *Sbornik deplomaticheskikh dokumentov: Reformy v Armenii: 26 Noiabria 1912 g–10 Maia 1914 g* (Petrograd: Government Press, 1915).

34. M. Phillips Price, "Russia and the Kurds," *Manchester Guardian Weekly* 63, no. 11 (Sept. 14, 1950), 15.

35. Yalman, 209.

36. E. W. Noel, *Note on the Kurdish Situation,* 11.

37. Notable examples are 'Abd al-Razzaq Beg Bedir Khan, Kamil Beg Bedir Khan, Sayyid Taha of Nehri, and others whose activities have already been dealt with.

38. Longrigg, *Iraq, 1900–1950,* 67.

39. Price, "Russia and the Kurds," 15.

40. Longrigg, *Iraq, 1900–1950,* 67.

41. Ibid.

42. Basile Nikitine, letter to the editor, *Manchester Guardian,* Sept. 21, 1950.

43. Ibid.

44. Ibid.

45. E. W. Noel, *Note on the Kurdish Situation,* 11.

46. Ibid.

47. Louis Fischer, *The Soviets in World Affairs: A History of the Relations Between the Soviet Union and the Rest of the World* (New York: Vintage Books, 1960), 1:391–92.

48. Ibid., 394, 412.

49. Edgar Turlington, "The Settlement of Lausanne," *American Journal of International Law* 18, no. 4 (Oct. 1924), 702. Cf. Arnold J. Toynbee and Kenneth P. Kirkwood, *Turkey* (New York: Charles Scribner's Sons, 1927), 111–25.

50. *Izvestia,* Feb. 14, 1923.

51. Fischer, 2:612.

52. Ibid., 2:732.

53. Ibid., 2:732–33.

54. Pierre Rondot, "L'alphabet Kurde en caractères Latins d'Arménie Soviétique," *Revue des Etudes Islamiques,* no. 3 (1933): 411–17. See also Rondot, "L'adoption des caractères Latins et le mouvement culturel chez les Kurdes de l'U.R.S.S.," *Revue de Etudes Islamiques,* no. 1 (1935): 87–96.

55. *Revolyutsiya i Natsionalnosti,* no. 80, Oct. 1936: 55–60; cited by Kolarz, 251.

56. Ibid.

7. The Kurds and World War I

1. On the outbreak of hostilities in Persia and the involvement of Kurds and Persians in the war, see Sir Percy Sykes, *A History of Persia,* 2 vols. (London: Macmillan, 1915), 436ff.; and Gustave Demorgny, *La question persane et la guerre, la rivalité anglo-russe en Perse* (Paris: L. Tenin, 1916), 284ff.

2. For a brief sketch of Zaki's career, see Zaki, *Khulasat Tarikh al-Kurd,* 469–72.

3. Ibid., 274.

4. Ibid. These tribal forces were estimated at about one thousand. Bell, *Review of the Civil Administration*, 4.

5. Zaki, *Khulasat Tarikh al-Kurd*, 274–75.

6. Ibid., 277–78.

7. Ibid., 278.

8. Ibid., 279. According to Soane, the population of Sulaymaniya, which was estimated at about twenty thousand in November 1914, had declined to twenty-five hundred by November 1918, when the British occupied the town. Famine and disease were rapidly killing the survivors. See Iraq (British Administration), Office of the Civil Commissioner, *Administration Report of Sulaimaniyah Division for the Year 1919* (Baghdad: Government Press, 1920).

9. Yalman, 218–19.

10. Jamal Pasha, one of the three strongmen who ruled Turkey during the war, gave a detailed but biased account of these events. See Djemal (Ahmad) Pasha, *Memories of a Turkish Statesman, 1913–1919* (London: Hutchison, 1922), 280ff. He claimed that the Armenians killed 1.5 million Turks and Kurds. Yalman, however, regarded this figure as a gross exaggeration and asserted that it could not have been much higher than forty thousand. Yalman, 221–22.

11. E. W. Noel, *Note on the Kurdish Situation*, 5.

12. Kenneth Mason, "Central Kurdistan," *Geographical Journal* 54, no. 6 (1919): 339.

13. Ibid., 329.

14. Ibid., 330. Mason asserted (331) that the Armenian units attached to the Russian forces under General Chernozoubov killed five thousand men, women, and children at Rawanduz. However, this assertion is refuted by Basile Nikitine, Russian consul at Urmiya, who accompanied the Caucasian army in its trust into the Rawanduz region. Nikitine, "Rawandiz-Ruindiz." For an authoritative description of the Nehri-Rawanduz region and the route taken by the Russian Caucasian army in its invasion of central Kurdistan, see Nikitine, "La systeme routier du Kurdistan," *La Geographie* 63, nos. 5–6 (May-June 1935): 363–85.

15. Mason, 330–31.

16. Bell, *Review of the Civil Administration*, 44–46. For further information on the Russian thrust into the Khanaqin region in 1916, see E. J. R., 2, and G. R. Driver, "The Kurdish Question," *Persia Magazine* (London) 1, no. 3 (Sept. 1921): 107.

17. For a detailed description of the Russian troops' predations in the Khanaqin region, see E. J. R., 3, and Bell, *Review of the Civil Administration*, 44–45.

18. Bell, *Review of the Civil Administration*, 45, and E. J. R., 4.

19. Upon their return to the Khanaqin-Qizil-Robat region, the Turks are said to have executed a number of local notables, including a member of a prominent Sulaymaniya family, for sending their flocks northward to the Lesser Zab. See Bell, *Review of the Civil Administration*, 46.

20. Ibid. For further details on the suffering of this region's population, which seems to have been reduced by flight and disease to one-third of its prewar size, see Iraq (British Administration), *Reports of Administration for 1918 of Divisions and Districts of the Occupied Territories in Mesopotamia: I. Khaniqin District* (Madras: Vasanta Press, 1919), 32–34.

21. Bell, *Review of the Civil Administration*, 47.

22. William T. Ellis, *The Yankee Cadi: Being an Account of the Services Performed in Persia by William A. Shedd during and before the Great War* (privately reprinted from the *Century* [Feb. 1919]), 19. The Russian consul at Urmiya, Basile Nikitine, also requested the American Relief Committee to do what it could to alleviate the Kurds' suffering. Nikitine, *Les Kurdes*, 297–98. The committee provided the Kurds with what food it could, but "they died like flies and though

we tried to help them, our best efforts could hardly touch the surface of their misery." Shedd, 236–37.

23. Chirguh, *La question Kurde,* 23; Sureya Bedir Khan, *The Case of Kurdistan Against Turkey* (Philadelphia: Kurdish Independence League, 1927), 32–33. Also E. W. Noel, *Note on the Kurdish Situation,* where extracts from this law are given.

24. Chirguh, *La question Kurde,* 23; S. Bedir Khan, 32–33.

25. E. J. R., 2; Driver, *Kurdistan and the Kurds,* 77; Bell, *Review of the Civil Administration,* 60; Sir Arnold T. Wilson, *Loyalties: Mesopotamia,* vol. 2: *1917–1920* (Oxford: Oxford Univ. Press, 1936), 130.

26. Nikitine, *Les Kurdes,* 195. According to Nikitine, 'Abd al-Razzaq Bedir Khan was in St. Petersburg in 1909. Nikitine, letter to the editor of the *Manchester Guardian,* Sept. 21, 1950. No doubt 'Abd al-Razzaq Beg's relations with the Russians were strengthened while he was attached to the Turkish embassy in St. Petersburg. [Elphinston], "The Azizan," 250.

27. Nikitine, *Les Kurdes,* 195.

28. E. M. Noel, *Diary,* 54–55.

29. Ibid., 63.

30. Ibid., 55.

31. Driver, *Kurdistan and the Kurds,* 113.

32. Hay, *Two Years in Kurdistan,* 353.

33. According to Nikitine, Sayyid Taha's sojourn in Russia was undertaken as a result of certain charges of disloyalty brought against him before the authorities in Istanbul by his uncle and bitter rival Shaykh 'Abd al-Qadir. Nikitine, "Les Kurdes racontés," 154.

34. Bell, *Review of the Civil Administration,* 65.

35. Driver, *Kurdistan and the Kurds,* 106.

35. Ibid.

37. Bell, *Review of the Civil Administration,* 69.

38. Nikitine, *Les Kurdes,* 195.

39. Driver, *Kurdistan and the Kurds,* 101.

40. According to Bell *(Review of the Civil Administration,* 60), the meeting between Sharif Pasha and Sir Percy Cox took place in Marseilles, but according to Sir Arnold Wilson *(Loyalties,* 2:130), it took place in London.

41. Ibid.

42. E. J. R., 7; Driver, *Kurdistan and the Kurds,* 101–2; A. T. Wilson, *Loyalties,* 2:130.

43. E. J. R., 7; Driver, *Kurdistan and the Kurds,* 102; A. T. Wilson, *Loyalties,* 2:130. These sources attribute Sharif Pasha's concern over southern Kurdistan to the fact that he was himself a southern Kurd by birth. However, it seems to me that Sharif Pasha's preoccupation with southern Kurdistan, besides whatever personal ties he may have had with the region, was influenced primarily by the fact that it lay in the path of British forces advancing northward in the direction of Mosul.

44. E. J. R., 8; Driver, *Kurdistan and the Kurds,* 102.

45. Chirguh, *La question Kurde,* 24. According to Safrastian, this agreement was reached between Sharif Pasha and Boghos Nubar Pasha. Aharonian's name is not mentioned. Safrastian, 77.

46. Chirguh included a photograph and French translation of one of the letters of invitation sent to members of the Kurdish National Committee. The letter is signed by Ibrahim al-Haydari, former Shaykh al-Islam and member of a prominent Kurdish religious family from the Arbil province. Chirguh, *La question Kurde,* 25.

47. Ibid., 24–25.

48. Driver, *Kurdistan and the Kurds,* 99.

49. *The Treaties of Peace, 1919–1923* (New York: Carnegie Endowment for International Peace, 1924), 2:807–8. For a discussion of the portion of the Treaty of Sèvres dealing with Kurdistan, see Chirguh, *La question Kurde,* 25–26; Safrastian, 77–78; K. Bedir Khan, 243–44; Nikitine, *Les Kurdes,* 196–97; Zaki, *Khulasat Tarikh al-Kurd,* 282–83; and Minorsky, "Kurds."

50. *The Treaties of Peace,* 2:807.

51. Ibid.

52. Ibid.

53. Ibid., 2:807–8.

54. Ibid., 2:808.

8. The Situation of the Kurds in Turkey, Persia, and Syria after World War I

1. Driver, *Kurdistan and the Kurds,* 81–82; Bell, *Review of the Civil Administration,* 66; Driver, "The Kurdish Question," 109.

2. Driver, *Kurdistan and the Kurds,* 82.

3. Ibid.; Bell, *Review of the Civil Administration,* 66.

4. Bell, *Review of the Civil Administration,* 66.

5. Ibid., 67; Driver, *Kurdistan and the Kurds,* 86; Driver, "The Kurdish Question," 110.

5. Bell, *Review of the Civil Administration,* 67; cf. Driver, *Kurdistan and the Kurds,* 83.

7. Driver, *Kurdistan and the Kurds,* 82.

8. Ibid., 82–83. Cf. Driver, "The Kurdish Question," 110.

9. Driver, *Kurdistan and the Kurds,* 84. Cf. Bell, *Review of the Civil Administration,* 66.

10. Driver, *Kurdistan and the Kurds,* 84.

11. Ibid., 85.

12. Ibid., 84.

13. Ibid.

14. Ibid., 84–85.

15. Efforts to form a Kurdish club in Urfa were unsuccessful as late as July 1919, owing to the town notables' hesitant attitude.

16. Bell, *Review of the Civil Administration,* 66; Driver, *Kurdistan and the Kurds,* 95.

17. Driver, *Kurdistan and the Kurds,* 85.

18. Ibid.

19. Ibid. 85–86.

20. Noel cited in Bell, *Review of the Civil Administration,* 67; Driver, *Kurdistan and the Kurds,* 95.

21. Bell, *Review of the Civil Administration,* 67–88; Driver, *Kurdistan and the Kurds,* 95–96.

22. E. W. Noel, *Note on the Kurdish Situation,* 18.

23. Minorsky, "Kurds."

24. E. J. R., 7; Driver, *Kurdistan and the Kurds,* 75; A. T. Wilson, *Loyalties,* 2:130.

25. E. J. R., 7; Driver, *Kurdistan and the Kurds,* 75.

26. A. T. Wilson, *Loyalties,* 2:130.

27. Bell, *Review of the Civil Administration,* 69. Cf. E. W. Noel, *Note on the Kurdish Situation,* 18.

28. Bell, *Review of the Civil Administration,* 69.

29. Ibid., 70. Bell, an influential member of the civil commissioner's staff, perhaps best con-

veyed the humorous note struck by this strange missive: "A personal grievance, which was from our point of view a side issue, pre-occupied him. One of the ill-wishers, of whom he has many (on this occasion it was a Persian official), had conceived the idea of sending him a bomb wrapped in a parcel. His indignant description of the episode cannot be better recorded than in his own words: 'I barely had time,' he complained, 'to throw it at my brother when it went off.' "

30. E. J. R., 14; Bell, *Review of the Civil Administration,* 62.

31. E. J. R., 14; Bell, *Review of the Civil Administration,* 62; Driver, *Kurdistan and the Kurds,* 83, 89, 93.

32. E. J. R., 14; Driver, *Kurdistan and the Kurds,* 89.

33. Driver, *Kurdistan and the Kurds,* 93.

34. Ibid.

35. Ibid., 94.

36. It should be pointed out here that under the Kajar dynasty, Azerbayjan was traditionally the seat of the heirs apparent.

37. Driver, *Kurdistan and the Kurds,* 93–94.

38. Sometimes also written as "Semiqo" or "Semitko."

39. Simko appears to have been a rather attractive man of good presence. For a description of his physical appearance, see Edmonds, *Kurds, Turks, and Arabs,* 305.

40. A. C. Wratislaw, British consul in Tabriz at the time, gave a detailed account of the murder of Ja'far Agha, with a photograph showing him and two of his followers hanging by their feet. See Albert Charles Wratislaw, *A Consul in the East* (London: Blackwood, 1924), 207–9. For another account of this murder, accompanied by a number of photographs, see G. Ghilan, "Les Kurdes persans et l'invasion Ottomane," *Revue du Monde Musulman* 5, no. 5 (May 1908), 3–6. See also Nikitine, *Les Kurdes,* 79, 263–64, for a French translation of a *lawij* lamenting the assassination of Ja'far Agha. Cf. Minorsky, "Kurds," 290.

41. Bell, *Review of the Civil Administration,* 69; Minorsky, "Kurds."

42. German victories in the European theater, culminating in Russia's collapse, apparently induced Simko to reconsider his alliance. He asked Mar Sham'un to meet him in conference to discuss the new situation created by these events. Mar Sham'un duly arrived, with a number of his followers, at the appointed meeting place in the village of Koni Shahr near Salmas. As Mar Sham'un and his party left the meeting, which was reported to have been conducted in an atmosphere of cordiality, they were fired upon from all sides. For more details on the background of this alliance and an account of Mar Sham'un's murder, see Wigram and Wigram, 378–81; cf. Shedd, 237–39; Frederick G. Coan, *Yesterdays in Persia and Kurdistan* (Claremont, Calif.: Saunders Studio Press, 1939), 266–67; Longrigg, *Iraq, 1900–1950,* 97.

43. According to Wigram and Wigram, the Assyrian followers of Mar Sham'un, maddened by the murder of their chief, stormed Simko's castle, where they found a letter from the governor of Tabriz, Mukht-i-Shams, suggesting to Simko that he get rid of Mar Sham'un. See Wigram and Wigram, 379.

44. *Oriente Moderno,* 1, no. 9 (Feb. 15, 1922), 548; cf. Arnold J. Toynbee, *Survey of International Affairs, 1925,* vol. 1: *The Islamic World Since the Peace Settlement* (London: Oxford Univ. Press, 1927), 538–39.

45. *Oriente Moderno,* 1, no. 9 (Feb. 15, 1922), 548; cf. Toynbee, 1:539.

46. For a discussion of the state of affairs in Persia at that time, see Toynbee, 1:539ff.

47. Ibid., 1:539.

48. *Oriente Moderno,* 2, no. 2 (July 15, 1922), 115, cited in Toynbee, 1:539.

49. Ibid.

50. *Oriente Moderno,* 1, no. 10 (Mar. 15, 1922).

51. According to Edmonds, Simko had lost his baggage and equipment, his wife had been killed, and his six-year-old son, "the apple of his eye," was missing. Edmonds, *Kurds, Turks, and Arabs,* 305.

52. Ibid.

53. Ibid.

54. Great Britain, Colonial Office, *Report on Iraq Administration, April, 1922 to March, 1923* (London: H.M. Stationery Office, 1924), 34; Longrigg, *Iraq, 1900–1950,* 144.

55. Edmonds, *Kurds, Turks, and Arabs,* 310 and 313.

56. C. J. Edmonds, "A Kurdish Newspaper: 'Rozh-i Kurdistan,' " *Journal of the Central Asian Society* 12, part 1 (Jan. 1925), 89.

57. Great Britain, Colonial Office, *Report on Iraq Administration, April, 1922 to March, 1923,* 37.

58. Great Britain, Colonial Office, *Report by H.B.M's Government to the Council of the League of Nations on the Administration of Iraq for the Year 1926* (London: H.M. Stationery Office, 1927), 26.

59. Great Britain, Colonial Office, *Report by H.B.M's Government to the Council of the League of Nations on the Administration of Iraq for the Year 1927* (London: H.M. Stationery Office, 1928), 61–62.

60. Great Britain, Colonial Office, *Report by H.B.M's Government to the Council of the League of Nations on the Administration of Iraq for the Year 1928* (London: H.M. Stationery Office, 1929), 4.

61. Great Britain, Colonial Office, *Report by H.B.M's Government to the Council of the League of Nations on the Administration of Iraq for the Year 1929* (London: H.M. Stationery Office, 1930), 44.

62. Hamilton, 162–64.

63. In this connection, Elphinston has pointed out that the Kurds of Jazira, "who form the major part of the total 250,000 [Kurds in Syria] are the southern extremities of Kurdish tribes in Turkey which were lopped off by the frontier." Elphinston, "Kurds and the Kurdish Question," 46–47.

64. Driver, *Kurdistan and the Kurds,* 86.

65. Iraq (British Administration), Office of the Civil Commissioner, *Administration Report of the Mosul Division for the Year 1921,* 2.

66. Ibid.

67. A. H. Hourani, *Syria and Lebanon: A Political Essay* (London: Oxford Univ. Press, 1946), 56–57.

68. Eliahu Epstein, "Al-Juzireh," *Journal of the Royal Central Asian Society* 27, part 1 (Jan. 1940): 68–82.

69. Damascus has traditionally been a center of Kurdish émigrés from all over Kurdistan. No doubt many of them have been attracted to Damascus because it is connected in their minds with the greatest Kurd of all times, Salah al-Din, whose tomb is in that city. This tendency was also encouraged by the fact that the great Kurdish mystic, Mawlana Khalid, the founder of the Naqshbandi order in Kurdistan, died in that city and was buried there.

70. Immigrants of Kurdish descent carried on Khoybun activities in the United States. Chirguh, *La question Kurde,* 37; Yusuf Malik, *Kurdistan Aw Bilad al-Akrad* (Kurdistan or the Country of the Kurds) (Beirut: Sadir Press, 1945), 35.

71. Nikitine, *Les Kurdes,* 200; Basile Nikitine, "Badrkhani," in *Encyclopaedia of Islam, New Edition,* 1:871.

72. Hourani, *Syria and Lebanon,* 215.

73. Ibid., 216.

9. Disorder in the Mosul and Arbil Divisions of Iraqi Kurdistan after World War I

1. Bell, *Review of the Civil Administration,* 62.

2. Ibid. Cf. Driver, *Kurdistan and the Kurds,* 89.

3. Bell, *Review of the Civil Administration,* 62.

4. Ibid.; Driver, *Kurdistan and the Kurds,* 89; A. T. Wilson, *Loyalties,* 2:147; Driver, "The Kurdish Question," 111. Despite the recurrence of 'Abd al-Rahman Agha's name in connection with these events, the murder of Captain Pearson was attributed to a Goyan chief, one Hassu Dinu. Iraq (British Administration), Office of the Civil Commissioner, *Administration Report of the Mosul Division for the Year 1921,* 7–8.

5. Bell, *Review of the Civil Administration,* 62.

6. Ibid.

7. Ibid., 62–63.

8. Ibid., 63.

9. According to Bell, the British had decided to extend their administration to 'Amadiya in order to facilitate the repatriation of the Assyrian refugees because the nearest and the most convenient approach to their country lay through that region. Ibid., 71. Wilson maintained that he had not been consulted about this step, which he regarded as premature. He asserted that he had acquiesced only because of the undesirable aftereffects of a withdrawal. A. T. Wilson, *Loyalties,* 2:148.

10. Bell, *Review of the Civil Administration,* 72.

11. A. T. Wilson, *Loyalties,* 2:148; cf. Bell, *Review of the Civil Administration,* 71.

12. This attitude finds strong support in the religious tradition of the Middle East. A number of hadiths attributed to the Prophet Muhammad express the strongest condemnation of the tax collector. According to one such hadith, the Prophet is reported to have said, "The tax collector is [destined to be] in hell fire," and according to another, "The tax collector will not enter paradise." Pious Muslims since the earliest days of Islam have followed the Prophet's example in condemning the tax collector. The abhorrence with which the Jews regarded the publicans is quite evident in the New Testament as well as in rabbinical literature. On the Muslim attitude, see W. Bjorkman, "Maks," in *Encyclopaedia of Islam,* 1st ed., 5:176–77; for a list of pertinent hadiths, see "Ashshar," in *Concordance et indices de la tradition Musulmane,* edited by A. J. Wensinck (1933; reprint, Leiden: E. J. Brill, 1938), 4:172–73. On the Jewish attitude, see W. F. Adeney, "Publican," in *A Dictionary of the Bible,* 8th ed., edited by James Hastings (New York: Charles Scribner's Sons, 1906), 4:172–73; and C. I. Feltoe, "Publican," in *A Dictionary of Christ and the Gospels,* edited by James Hastings (New York: Charles Scribner's Sons, 1906–11), 2:455.

13. Damaluji mentions that in the course of his official duties in the year 1905 he came across some instances of inhuman practices in connection with the collection of taxes in the Nerwa and Rikan *nahiya*s (subdistricts). According to him, the female children of persons incapable of paying their taxes were taken away from their parents and given to government officials in lieu of

salaries that the government had not been able to pay for several months. Damaluji, *Imarat Bahdinan,* 50–51.

14. Throughout the nineteenth century, a state of incipient war existed between the Assyrians and their Kurdish neighbors. According to Rich, the Bahdinan princes of 'Amadiya were compelled to maintain special guards to protect themselves against the sudden incursions of the Assyrians. Rich, 1:156. Likewise, the long-standing feud between the Tiyari Assyrians and the Barwari Kurds continued for many years and claimed many lives on both sides. Wigram and Wigram, 314ff. Cf. Damaluji, *Imarat Bahdinan,* 110–16. During World War I, the Assyrians were assailed from many sides and were finally ejected from their homeland in Hakari as a result of a massive attack from the south. This force, which was organized by the *wali* of Mosul, consisted mainly of Bahdinan Kurds. Wigram and Wigram, 369–70; Damaluji, *Imarat Bahdinan,* 116.

15. A. T. Wilson, *Loyalties,* 2:148; also Bell, *Review of the Civil Administration,* 71.

16. A. T. Wilson, *Loyalties,* 2:149.

17. Ibid.

18. Ibid.

19. Ibid.

20. Bell, *Review of the Civil Administration,* 72.

21. A. T. Wilson, *Loyalties,* 2:149.

22. Ibid., 2:150–51. Cf. Bell, *Review of the Civil Administration,* 7.

23. Bell, *Review of the Civil Administration,* 72; A. T. Wilson, *Loyalties,* 2:151.

24. The Oramari chieftain's name appears also as "Situ" and "Sutu."

25. Bell, *Review of the Civil Administration,* 72; A. T. Wilson, *Loyalties,* 2:151–52.

26. Bell, *Review of the Civil Administration,* 72–73; A. T. Wilson, *Loyalties,* 2:152.

27. Bell, *Review of the Civil Administration,* 73; A. T. Wilson, *Loyalties,* 2:153.

28. Bell, *Review of the Civil Administration,* 73; A. T. Wilson, *Loyalties,* 2:153.

29. Bell, *Review of the Civil Administration,* 73; A. T. Wilson, *Loyalties,* 2:153.

30. The wording of the given quotation is identical in both Bell, *Review of the Civil Administration,* 73, and A. T. Wilson, *Loyalties,* 2:153.

31. A. T. Wilson, *Loyalties,* 2:153.

32. In November 1919, at the time of the outbreak in Zibar, as mentioned earlier, the Turks seem to have regarded Suto Agha as a reliable instrument of their policy. However, less than a year later, in 1920, he was reported to have been writing letters to the British authorities in Mosul protesting his friendship to them. Iraq (British Administration), Office of the Civil Commissioner, *Administration Report of the Mosul Division for the Year 1920* (Baghdad: Government Press, 1921), 12.

33. Iraq, Civil Commissioner, *Civil Administration Mesopotamia: Administration Report (1919), Part I, "Mosul"* (Baghdad: Government Press, 1920), 16. This act of vengeance appears to have been just another episode in the bitter feud between Suto Agha and the *aghas* of Rikan. "The Tale of Suto and Tatu" graphically describes the character of this violent and ruthless man, who had become a legendary figure even during his lifetime. It tells how, on an earlier occasion, Suto exacted terrible vengeance on his enemies, the Rikani *aghas.* Nikitine and Soane, 69–106. For the story of how Suto caused the destruction of four hundred Cossacks, see Wigram and Wigram, 369.

34. The 1919 outbreak in Sulaymaniya is dealt with in chapter 10.

35. Hay, *Two Years in Kurdistan,* 159.

36. Ibid., 184.

37. Ibid., 195.

38. Ibid., 267–68.

39. A. T. Wilson, *Loyalties,* 2:285. Cf. Sir James Aylmer Lowthrop Haldane, *The Insurrection in Mesopotamia 1920* (Edinburgh: William Blackwood and Sons, 1922), 246. For a detailed description of this episode, see Hay, *Two Years in Kurdistan,* 286–94.

40. These anxious times at Arbil are described at some length and in greater detail in A. T. Wilson, *Loyalties,* 2:286–89; and in Hay, *Two Years in Kurdistan,* 281–347.

41. A. T. Wilson, *Loyalties,* 2:290.

42. Iraq (British Administration), Office of the Civil Commissioner, *Administration Report of the Mosul Division for the Year 1920,* 10.

43. Ibid.

44. Ibid.

45. Yusuf Beg, we are informed, was a high-handed feudal chieftain from the neighborhood of Rawanduz. After an attack launched by his men against a minor tribal chief and his followers, reportedly in utter disregard if not in defiance of the British political officer, Captain Hay, he was arrested and brought before that official. In the course of the ensuing altercation, he is said to have called out to his men to come and kill Captain Hay. The latter had him seized and imprisoned and made arrangements for his removal to Kirkuk early the next morning. When the gendarmes came to take Yusuf Beg, he resisted, and they had to tie him onto the mule that was to carry him to his destination. We are informed that his guards, after a few hours on the road, discovered that he had expired. Captain Hay, who described him as "the most dangerous man in the district," said afterward, "I am convinced that his death was not intentionally caused by the gendarmes, though it was a most providential event." For details concerning Yusuf Beg, his arrest, and his death, see W. R. Hay and P. O. Arbil, *Note on Rowanduz* (Baghdad: Government Press, 1920), 1–2; also Hay, *Two Years in Kurdistan,* 204–24.

46. Nuri Bawil Agha appears to have been a person possessed of a remarkable personality. Despite the fact that it was he who tried to assassinate Captain Hay in the Rawanduz gorge, the latter paid warm tribute to Nuri Bawil Agha's qualities as a man and as a leader. On the blood feud between him and Isma'il Beg, see Hay, *Two Years in Kurdistan,* 275–76 and passim.

47. On Hamada Chin and his band of outlaws, see ibid., 233; and Hamilton, 93–103.

48. Iraq (British Administration), Office of the Civil Commissioner, *Administration Report of the Mosul Division for the Year 1920,* 10. For more details, see Hay, *Two Years in Kurdistan,* 311–47.

49. According to Haldane, Surchi losses amounted to 60 killed and 140 drowned. Haldane, 247. Cf. A. T. Wilson, *Loyalties,* 2:291; Iraq (British Administration), Office of the Civil Commissioner, *Administration Report of the Mosul Division for the Year 1920,* 10.

50. A. T. Wilson, *Loyalties,* 2:291.

51. The Zibaris under Faris Agha and the Barzanis under Shaykh Ahmad appear to have combined for the purpose of contesting the Assyrian refugees' passage to their mountain homes in Hakari. However, they failed to achieve their objective. Barzan was occupied and destroyed by the Assyrian force, which was reported to have moved northward in pursuit of Faris Agha, who had fled in the direction of Oramar. Iraq (British Administration), Office of the Civil Commissioner, *Administration Report of Mosul Division for the Year 1920,* 10–11, and 13.

52. Ibid., 11

53. Iraq (British Administration), Office of the Civil Commissioner, *Administration Report of the Mosul Division for the Year 1921,* 9.

10. Shaykh Mahmud and the Rise and Fall of the South Kurdish Confederation in Iraqi Kurdistan after World War I

1. The British apparently were reluctant to intrude into the Khanaqin region for two reasons. First, the British military authorities in Baghdad apparently did not wish to offend the sensibilities of their Russian allies, who seemed unwilling to countenance the presence of a British representative in their zone of occupation. Second, it was feared that if the Russians were ultimately compelled to withdraw from Khanaqin, the association of a British representative with them would be harmful to British prestige. E. J. R., 4; Bell, *Review of the Civil Administration,* 44–45.

2. On the activities of Mustafa Pasha, paramount chieftain of the Bajalan, see E. J. R., 2–4; Bell, *Review of the Civil Administration,* 42–45; Iraq (British Administration), *Reports of Administration for 1918: Khaniqin District,* 34; Driver, "The Kurdish Question," 107.

3. Bell, *Review of the Civil Administration,* 46.

4. Ibid.

5. Kifri was occupied on April 28, Tuz Khurmatu on April 29, and Kirkuk on May 7, 1918. A. T. Wilson, *Loyalties,* 2:8–9.

6. This force, which was raised by Major Soane and organized by Captain R. C. Geard, fought as part of a column led by Colonel Underhill. It is reported to have given a good account of itself in this and other engagements with the Turks. Frederick James Moberly, *The Campaign in Mesopotamia* (London: H.M. Stationery Office, 1927), 4:152 note. Cited in A. T. Wilson, *Loyalties,* 2:84.

7. Iraq (British Administration), *Reports of Administration for 1918: Khaniqin District,* 32–33; also A. T. Wilson, *Loyalties,* 2:84–85.

8. Iraq (British Administration), *Reports of Administration for 1918: Khaniqin District,* 32–33.

9. Ibid.

10. A. T. Wilson, *Loyalties,* 2:86; E. J. R., 5–6; Bell, *Review of the Civil Administration,* 48; Driver, "The Kurdish Question," 108–9.

11. A. T. Wilson, *Loyalties,* 2:86; E. J. R., 6; see also Bell, *Review of the Civil Administration,* 48.

12. A. T. Wilson, *Loyalties,* 2:86–87. An official British report discussed Shaykh Mahmud's appointment and mentioned certain measures that the British intended to take in order to consolidate his position. The report stated: "At the beginning of June a letter was sent from the Civil Commissioner to Shaikh Mahmud appointing him British representative in Sulaimaniyah and district, and at the same time plans were set on foot to enlist Kurdish levies in Khaniqin district to enable British Officers to take up a force of Irregulars to the northern limits of the district, and initiate the recruiting of levies in the neighbourhood of Halabja. It was hoped by this means to establish the position of Shaikh Mahmud, and as long as Kirkuk was held by the British there was every indication that these plans would have been successful." Iraq (British Administration), *Reports of Administration for 1918: Khaniqin District,* 33.

13. A. T. Wilson, *Loyalties,* 2:9.

14. Ibid., 2:87. Cf. Bell, *Review of the Civil Administration,* 48; Driver, "The Kurdish Question," 108; E. J. R., 6.

15. According to Driver, "Turkish retribution was visited upon all who espoused the allied cause, except the Sheikh." Driver, "The Kurdish Question," 108; see also E. J. R., 6.

16. A. T. Wilson, *Loyalties,* 2:87; Bell, *Review of the Civil Administration,* 48.

17. E. J. R., 6; Driver, "The Kurdish Question," 108.

18. Bell, *Review of the Civil Administration*, 48; A. T. Wilson, *Loyalties*, 2:6.

19. A. T. Wilson, *Loyalties*, 2:88.

20. Ibid., 2:87.

21. Ibid., 2:86.

22. The force of Kurdish levies that the British were endeavoring to recruit was intended for the occupation of Halabja and eventually for harassing the Turks in the neighborhood of Sulaymaniya. E. J. R., 6.

23. Bell, *Review of the Civil Administration*, 59.

24. Ibid. Cf. E. J .R., 9; A. T. Wilson, *Loyalties*, 2:127–28.

25. Bell, *Review of the Civil Administration*, 59–60; A. T. Wilson, *Loyalties*, 2:128; E. J. R., 9.

26. E. J. R., 9–10; Bell, *Review of the Civil Administration*, 60; A. T. Wilson, *Loyalties*, 2:128.

27. For a brief and authoritative sketch of the Indian states' position within the British Indian Empire and their relation to the British government, see K. M. Panikkar, *Indian States*, Oxford Pamphlets on Indian Affairs no. 4 (Mysore City, India: Oxford Univ. Press, 1942).

28. The British developed the system of indirect rule over the years. However, since the systematization and successful application of indirect rule by Sir F. D. Lugard (later Lord Lugard) in Nigeria, it came to be largely associated with his name. For a detailed account of this system as he conceived and applied it, see Frederick John Dealtry Lugard, *The Dual Mandate in British Tropical Africa* (London: William Blackwood and Sons, 1923).

29. For a detailed discussion of Sandeman's life and tribal policies, see Thomas Henry Thornton, *Colonel Sir Robert Sandeman: His Life and Work on Our Indian Frontier* (London: J. Murray, 1895); Richard Isaac Bruce, *The Forward Policy and Its Results: Or, Thirty-five Years' Work Amongst the Tribes on Our North-Western Frontier of India* (London: Longmans, Green, 1900); Hittu Ram, *Sandeman in Baluchistan* (Calcutta: Government Printing Office, 1916); and C. Collin Davies, *The Problem of the North-West Frontier, 1890–1908, With a Survey of Policy Since 1849* (Cambridge: Cambridge Univ. Press, 1932).

30. The "forward policy," as opposed to the "closed border policy," was one of the most controversial issues among British administrators in India throughout most of the nineteenth century. See Davies, *The Problem of the North-West Frontier*, 71–98, and Bruce.

31. Davies, *The Problem of the North-West Frontier*, 33; C. Collin Davies, "The North-West Frontier, 1843–1918," in *The Cambridge History of the British Empire*, vol. 5: *The Indian Empire, 1858–1918* (New York: Macmillan, 1929), 448.

32. Bruce was for many years one of Sandeman's closest and most trusted associates in Baluchistan.

33. For details concerning the failure of the Bruce or *maliki* system among the Mahsuds, see Davies, *The Problem of the North-West Frontier*, 34, 124–26; Davies, "The North-West Frontier," 455–56. Cf. William Barton, *India's North-West Frontier* (London: J. Murray, 1939), 214–15.

34. Bruce, 170–71.

35. A. T. Wilson, *Loyalties*, 2:129; see also Bell, *Review of the Civil Administration*, 60–61; E. J. R., 10. The account of this meeting is almost identical in all three of these sources. Although the information given in the text is based primarily on Wilson's version, I have incorporated minor details not given by him from the other two sources.

36. A. T. Wilson, *Loyalties*, 2:129; see also Bell, *Review of the Civil Administration*, 61; E. J. R., 10.

37. A. T. Wilson, *Loyalties*, 2:129; Bell, *Review of the Civil Administration*, 61; E. J. R., 10.

38. E. J. R., 10; Bell, *Review of the Civil Administration*, 61; A. T. Wilson, *Loyalties*, 2:129.

39. E. J. R., 10; Bell, *Review of the Civil Administration*, 60–61; A. T. Wilson, *Loyalties*, 2:130.

40. E. J. R., 10; Bell, *Review of the Civil Administration*, 60–61; A. T. Wilson, *Loyalties*, 2:129.

41. Bell, *Review of the Civil Administration*, 60, 61.

42. Ibid., 61.

43. Iraq (British Administration), Office of the Civil Commissioner, *Administration Report of Sulaimaniyah Division for the Year 1919* (Baghdad: Government Press, 1920), 1.

44. Ibid. Cf. Bell, *Review of the Civil Administration*, 64.

45. Iraq (British Administration), Office of the Civil Commissioner, *Administration Report of Sulaimaniyah Division for 1919*, 2, 9–10.

46. Not only the levies but the civilian officials of the new administration are said to have been under an oath to support Shaykh Mahmud. Lees, "Two Years in South Kurdistan," 254. According to Bell, "The Kurdish levies led by Kurdish officers were ready to support Shaikh Mahmud, to whose influence they owed their appointment." Bell, *Review of the Civil Administration*, 64. Cf. A. T. Wilson, *Loyalties*, 2:135.

47. Bell, *Review of the Civil Administration*, 63; cf. A. T. Wilson, *Loyalties*, 2:135.

48. A. T. Wilson, *Loyalties*, 2:135.

49. Iraq (British Administration), Office of the Civil Commissioner, *Administration Report of Sulaimaniyah Division for 1919*, 2, emphasis in original.

50. Ibid., 3.

51. For a description of Soane's character, his bitter tongue, and his habit of writing reports "sometimes couched in language which verged on the insubordinate," see A. T. Wilson, *Loyalties*, 2:82–83; also Sir Arnold T. Wilson, "E. B. Soane—A Memoir," in *To Mesopotamia and Kurdistan*, by E. B. Soane, ix-xvii (London: John Murray, 1926).

52. Iraq (British Administration), Office of the Civil Commissioner, *Administration Report of Sulaimaniyah Division for 1919*, 3.

53. Ibid.

54. Longrigg cited in ibid., 3–4.

55. Ibid., 4.

56. Iraq (British Administration), Office of the Civil Commissioner, *Administration Report of the Kirkuk Division for the Year 1918* (Baghdad: Government Press, 1919), 432.

57. *Hurriya* is an Arabic word that means "freedom" or "liberty." It was a term some writers applied to the period of constitutional reforms that followed the overthrow of Sultan 'Abdul Hamid by the Young Turks.

58. Iraq (British Administration), Office of the Civil Commissioner, *Administration Report of Kirkuk Division for 1918*, 1, 417.

59. Bell, *Review of the Civil Administration*, 63.

60. Edmonds, *Kurds, Turks, and Arabs*, 30.

61. Bell, *Review of the Civil Administration*, 63. Cf. E. J. R., 13.

62. E. J. R., 12; also Bell, *Review of the Civil Administration*, 63.

63. Lees, "Two Years in South Kurdistan," 253–54.

64. A. T. Wilson, *Loyalties*, 2:134; also Longrigg, *Iraq, 1900–1950*, 104.

65. For a brief biography and a detailed list of the works of Shaykh Ma'ruf, see Muhammad Amin Zaki, *Tarikh al-Sulaymaniya wa-Anha'iha* (The History of Sulaymaniya and Its Outlying Districts), translated from Kurdish into Arabic by al-Mulla Jameel Ahmad al-Rozhbeyani (Baghdad: al-Nashr Wa al-Tiba'a, 1951), 219–24; cf. Edmonds, *Kurds, Turks, and Arabs*, 71.

66. Edmonds's *Kurds, Turks, and Arabs,* 74ff., gives rather detailed information on the miracles achieved by Kak Ahmad. Cf. Zaki, *Tarikh al-Sulaymaniya,* 224.

67. Shaykh Sa'id's activities are dealt with in detail in chapter 12.

68. A. T. Wilson, *Loyalties,* 2:139. It is evidently to this episode as described by Wilson that Soviet writer K. Sarezhin referred in his article "Iraq Today: Geographical Sketch," *New Times,* no. 6 (Mar. 15, 1945), 22.

69. For the effects of the Anglo-French Declaration and President Wilson's Fourteen Points on the people of British-occupied Mesopotamia in general, see A. T. Wilson, *Loyalties,* 2:102–3 and passim. Also Bell, *Review of the Civil Administration,* 126–27.

70. "The Sharif's agents, too, were working in North Kurdistan and were, by playing on the religious feelings of the Moslems, seeking the aggrandisement of their master." E. J. R., 17. See also Driver, *Kurdistan and the Kurds,* 98; Bell, *Review of the Civil Administration,* 59. On Sharifian appeal to the Kurds during the attack on Tal A'far, see Iraq (British Administration), Office of the Civil Commissioner, *Administration Report of Mosul Division for 1920,* 2–3.

71. Kurdish nationalist activity after World War I emerged in Istanbul, Cairo, Paris, Damascus, and several localities in Turkish, Iraqi, and Persian Kurdistan.

72. According to a British report, "And behind the Turks lay Russia in revolt, with Bolshevism ready to lend its aid to all who had a grievance against the existing order of the world and to proclaim (not without reason) that it had proved inadequate for the regulation of human affairs." Bell, *Review of the Civil Administration,* 59. Another official report pointed out: "It may be noted that talk about the Bolshevists had been steadily increasing during the year in Mosul. Mustafa Kemal's alliance with them is taken for granted, and he is popularly supposed to have received large supplies of gold from them." Iraq (British Administration), Office of the Civil Commissioner, *Administration Report of Mosul Division for 1920,* 5.

73. E. J. R., 11; Driver, *Kurdistan and the Kurds,* 81; Bell, *Review of the Civil Administration,* 58–59.

74. Driver, *Kurdistan and the Kurds,* 80; A. T. Wilson, *Loyalties,* 2:131–32.

75. A. T. Wilson, *Loyalties,* 2:152–53.

76. On French propaganda, see Driver, *Kurdistan and the Kurds,* 80–81; E. J. R., 11; A. T. Wilson, *Loyalties,* 2:132.

77. A. T. Wilson, *Loyalties,* 2:285–86, 212, and 92; Longrigg, *Iraq, 1900–1950,* 81–82; Lees, "Two Years in South Kurdistan," 255.

78. According to A. T. Wilson, "Troops were leaving the country in large numbers every month, but there was no corresponding reduction of military duties. . . . Merchants and others returning from Basrah and Baghdad to Sulaimani told of soldiers leaving daily by ship and train; and in the minds of many the belief that we would once more evacuate Kurdistan and leave the inhabitants to their own devices, or to machinations of rival claimants to power, hardened into certainty." A. T. Wilson, *Loyalties,* 2:135, 138, 283; cf. Lees, "Two Years in South Kurdistan," 260–61; Longrigg, *Iraq, 1900–1950,* 118–21.

79. E. J. R., 15; Bell, *Review of the Civil Administration,* 64.

80. A. T. Wilson, *Loyalties,* 2:134.

81. Lees, "Two Years in South Kurdistan," 255. Cf. A. T. Wilson, *Loyalties,* 2:134.

82. A. T. Wilson, *Loyalties,* 2:134–35; cf. Lees, "Two Years in South Kurdistan," 255–56; and Longrigg, *Iraq, 1900–1950,* 104.

83. Soane's dislike for the Barzinja shaykhs developed during his sojourn in disguise in southern Kurdistan twelve years earlier. He no doubt was influenced by the Jaf Begzada of Hal-

abja, in particular Lady 'Adela, with whom he was on very friendly terms. Soane severely criticized Shaykh Mahmud and his family in his book *To Mesopotamia and Kurdistan in Disguise* and in a number of official reports, such as his *Report on the Sulaimania District of Kurdistan* (1918).

84. Bell, *Review of the Civil Administration,* 64.

85. Iraq (British Administration), Office of the Civil Commissioner, *Administration Report of Sulaimaniyah Division for 1919,* 1–2.

86. Lees, "Two Years in South Kurdistan," 256.

87. Iraq (British Administration), Office of the Civil Commissioner, *Administration Report of Sulaimaniyah Division for 1919,* 1–2, 4.

88. Bell, *Review of the Civil Administration,* 64; A. T. Wilson, *Loyalties,* 2:134–35.

89. Iraq (British Administration), Office of the Civil Commissioner, *Administration Report of Sulaimaniyah Division for 1919,* 2.

90. According to A. T. Wilson, he had been informed of the delicate situation at Sulaymaniya and had intended to go there for consultations with Shaykh Mahmud, but the rebellion prevented him from doing so. "I had arranged to fly there," he wrote, "towards the end of May to meet Shaykh Mahmud in person and to endeavour to reach a solution which could make it possible to retain the framework of Kurdish autonomy." A. T. Wilson, *Loyalties,* 2:136.

91. It is strange that a number of British sources (namely, E. J. R., 16; Driver, *Kurdistan and the Kurds,* 90; and Bell, *Review of the Civil Administration,* 66) began their account of the rebellion by saying, "The outbreak was sudden and unexpected." Lees more accurately stated: "The political situation was pregnant with possibilities; could we succeed in our attempt to clip gradually the wings of our own nominee, or would he attempt an independent flight before our plans matured?" Lees, "Two Years in South Kurdistan," 256.

92. On the activities of Mahmud Khan Dizli prior to his attack on Sulaymaniya, see ibid., 258–59. Cf. Driver, *Kurdistan and the Kurds,* 90; E. J. R., 16; Bell, *Review of the Civil Administration,* 64; Edmonds, *Kurds, Turks, and Arabs,* 30.

93. E. J. R., 16; Driver, *Kurdistan and the Kurds,* 90; Bell, *Review of the Civil Administration,* 64; A. T. Wilson, *Loyalties,* 2:136; Edmonds, *Kurds, Turks, and Arabs,* 30.

94. According to one source, the money seized amounted to two hundred thousand rupees—a rather large sum of money in southern Kurdistan at the time. Driver, *Kurdistan and the Kurds,* 90.

95. The flag, according to Edmonds, consisted of a red crescent on a green background. Edmonds, *Kurds, Turks, and Arabs,* 30.

96. A. T. Wilson stated that the shaykh "appointed his own retainers to take control of every district." Wilson, *Loyalties,* 2:136. Other contemporaneous sources mentioned the appointment of "his own *qaimmaqam.*" Driver, *Kurdistan and the Kurds,* 90; E. J. R., 16; Bell, *Review of the Civil Administration,* 64. The *qaimmaqam* in question, according to Edmonds, was Shaykh Muhammad Gharib, Shaykh Mahmud's brother-in-law and close associate in the rebellion; as we shall see, he was captured at the Bazyan Pass and was later tried by a court martial along with the shaykh. Edmonds, *Kurds, Turks, and Arabs,* 102.

97. Lees, "Two Years in South Kurdistan," 15, 259–60; A. T. Wilson, *Loyalties,* 2:136. Cf. Driver, *Kurdistan and the Kurds,* 90; E. J. R., 16; Bell, *Review of the Civil Administration,* 64; Edmonds, *Kurds, Turks, and Arabs,* 30.

98. For details, see Lees, "Two Years in South Kurdistan," 260.

99. Lees relates his trying and at times comical experiences in ibid., 260–64.

100. E. J. R., 16; also Bell, *Review of the Civil Administration,* 65.

101. A. T. Wilson, *Loyalties*, 2:136–37; Edmonds, *Kurds, Turks, and Arabs*, 31.

102. A. T. Wilson, *Loyalties*, 2:137.

103. Ibid. The British appear to have been convinced that the only way to achieve this end was to break Shaykh Mahmud's power once and for all. An authoritative British source made the interesting disclosure that the British were unwilling to negotiate with the shaykh despite his readiness to do so. According to Bell, "By June 11th, in spite of a success gained over a British reconnissance party, he was ready to negotiate; but matters had gone too far." Bell, *Review of the Civil Administration*, 65.

104. A. T. Wilson, *Loyalties*, 2:137; also Edmonds, *Kurds, Turks, and Arabs*, 31.

105. A. T. Wilson, *Loyalties*, 2:137; also Edmonds, *Kurds, Turks, and Arabs*, 46.

106. Viewed from the west, from the flat plain facing the gap of the Bazyan Pass, the Qara Dagh range rises in an almost perpendicular manner like an immense wall shutting off everything beyond it to the east. The absence of foothills magnifies its mass and gives it a forbidding aspect. The two shoulders flanking the V-shaped gap rise abruptly in monolithic grandeur to a height of seventeen hundred feet above the level of the pass. Edmonds, *Kurds, Turks, and Arabs*, 45, and A. T. Wilson, *Loyalties*, 2:137–58.

107. For more details, see A. T. Wilson, *Loyalties*, 2:138; and Edmonds, *Kurds, Turks, and Arabs*, 46.

108. The Bazyan Pass, which is the principal gateway connecting the mountain regions east of the Qara Dagh with the Mesopotamian plain and the outside world, has been of great commercial and strategic importance throughout the ages. It was here that the Hamawand brigades used to waylay caravans and entrap Ottoman forces sent against them. Soane, *To Mesopotamia and Kurdistan*, 328, 329, and passim. In 1805, a little more than a century before Shaykh Mahmud's rebellion, the pass was the scene of a similar conflict between the great Kurdish prince ʿAbd al-Rahman Pasha Baban and the pasha of Baghdad. Having risen against his Ottoman overlords, ʿAbd al-Rahman Pasha decided to make a decisive stand at this easily defensible point. With this object in mind, he blocked the narrow entrance to the pass with a solid wall except for a conveniently small gate, and installed a few pieces of cannon to cover the approaches to the gap. Although his plan was successful at first, it was foiled when Muhammad Beg, a son of Khalid Pasha Baban and a cousin and rival of ʿAbd al-Rahman, led the Ottoman army by a little-known route. The Kurdish leader thus found his position turned and was compelled to withdraw. The pasha of Baghdad then razed the fortifications before advancing to Sulaymaniya. Rich, 1:59. Al-Munshiʾ al-Baghdadi, who accompanied Rich as a secretary during his travels in Kurdistan, gave a similar but more abbreviated account. See Sayyid Muhammad ibn al-Sayyid Ahmad al-Husayni al-Munshiʾ al-Baghdadi, *Rihlat al-Munshiʾ al-Baghdadi* (The Journey of the al-Munshiʾ al-Baghdadi), translated from Persian into Arabic by ʿAbbas al-ʿAzzawi (Baghdad: at-Tijara wa at-Tibaʿa Press, 1948), 58. The Bazyan Pass has been identified with the pass of Babite of the cuneiform inscriptions. Ephraim Avigdor Speiser, "Southern Kurdistan in the Annals of Ashurnasirpal and Today," *Annual of the American School of Oriental Research* (Jerusalem) 8 (1926–27), 3 and 16–17; also C. J. Edmonds, "The Place Names of the Avroman Parchments," *Bulletin of the School of Oriental and African Studies* 14, no. 3 (1952): 478–82. The Babite Pass figures prominently in the annals of the three campaigns launched by Ashurnasirpal III (1047–1027 B.C.) against the people of Zamua, whose country conformed roughly to the present Sulaymaniya province in Iraq. It is interesting to note that the cause of Ashurnasirpal's wars against the Zamuans was not very different from that which impelled the Ottoman army to move against ʿAbd al-Rahman Pasha in 1805 and the British army against Shaykh Mahmud in 1919. According to Speiser, the annals attribute the wars

to the refusal of Nur-Adad, the prince of Dagara, to remain a vassal of Assyria. When the prince raised the standard of revolt, he was joined by all the people of Zamua. When the Assyrian king marched against the Zamuans, he found that "the Pass of Babite is fortified and closed up with a wall." In the ensuing battle for the pass, the rebels lost 1,460 men. For further details, see Speiser, "Southern Kurdistan," 15.

109. For details on these tribes' activities, see Iraq (British Administration), Office of the Civil Commissioner, *Administration Report of the Kirkuk Division for the Year 1920* (Baghdad: Government Press, 1921), 6–12.

110. Edmonds, *Kurds, Turks, and Arabs*, 49.

111. Hafsa Khan, Shaykh Mahmud's cousin and sister-in-law, is credited with having extended her protection to the officers during the period of their imprisonment. According to Edmonds, her husband, Shaykh Qadir, who was the commanding officer of the levies, took the chief British instructor of the levies, Major A. M. Daniels, to their home, where he stayed for several days. While he was there, Hafsa is reported to have slept in the passage across from the doorway of his room to ensure that no harm came to him. Ibid., 83. Cf. Barth, 120–21.

112. Edmonds stated that he learned from two levy officers after the Bazyan battle that Shaykh Mahmud had left word to put the prisoners to death if the day went against him. Edmonds, *Kurds, Turks, and Arabs*, 47.

113. On the freeing of the British prisoners, see Lees, "Two Years in South Kurdistan," 264–65; A. T. Wilson, *Loyalties*, 2:138; Edmonds, *Kurds, Turks, and Arabs*, 47.

114. A. T. Wilson, *Loyalties*, 2:138–39. According to Bell, the shaykh's sentence was ten years' imprisonment, and his brother-in-law, Shaykh Muhammad Gharib, was given five years and a fine of ten thousand rupees. Bell, *Review of the Civil Administration*, 65. According to Lees, the shaykh was sentenced to twenty years of penal servitude in India and that his associates were given less-severe sentences. Lees, "Two Years in South Kurdistan," 265. According to Edmonds, the shaykh's sentence was reduced to ten years' imprisonment and that he was sent to India. Edmonds, *Kurds, Turks, and Arabs*, 52.

115. According to A. T. Wilson, the shaykh was treated leniently because he had not molested the British prisoners and because the policy of the British government in the disputed Mosul *wilayat* was such as not to justify the execution of the rebel leader. A. T. Wilson, *Loyalties*, 2:139.

116. This statement by Lieutenant-General Sir George MacMunn was made on March 14, 1928, at the conclusion of a lecture given by G. M. Lees at the Central Asian Society. Lees, "Two Years in South Kurdistan," 277.

117. Driver, *Kurdistan and the Kurds*, 92. This point perhaps needs some elaboration. This source evidently meant that Shaykh Mahmud did not possess a properly trained cavalry rather than that he had any lack of mounted warriors. Edmonds mentions that prior to the British attack on the Bazyan Pass, some two hundred horsemen were observed scouting. Edmonds, *Kurds, Turks, and Arabs*, 46. Driver mentioned that horses were among the spoils captured by the British after the battle. Driver, "The Kurdish Question," 113.

118. Driver, *Kurdistan and the Kurds*, 92. Cf. Bell, *Review of the Civil Administration*, 65.

119. Driver, *Kurdistan and the Kurds*, 92.

120. Edmonds, *Kurds, Turks, and Arabs*, 46.

121. Driver, *Kurdistan and the Kurds*, 92.

122. The bulk of Shaykh Mahmud's supporters in the Sulaymaniya region appear to have been tenants from his villages in the neighborhood. Lees, "Two Years in South Kurdistan," 254; also Barth, 127.

123. Driver, *Kurdistan and the Kurds,* 90; Lees, "Two Years in South Kurdistan," 273, 275; A. T. Wilson, *Loyalties,* 2:135; Edmonds, *Kurds, Turks, and Arabs,* 30 and passim.

124. Different sources have given various figures for the number of Hawramani (Awramani) and Meriwani tribesmen who joined Shaykh Mahmud's rebellion. An official report (Driver, *Kurdistan and the Kurds,* 90) gave the figure of 150,100 foot soldiers and 50 mounted, for the Hawramanis only; Lees ("Two Years in South Kurdistan," 259) gave the figure as 500, and A. T. Wilson (*Loyalties,* 2:136) put the total number of the warriors from across the Persian frontier at 300. Cf. E. J. R., 16; Bell, *Review of the Civil Administration,* 64.

125. Mahmud Khan Dizli, the chief of the Bahram-Begi family of the Hawraman, was the person who spearheaded the shaykh's rebellion by taking possession of Sulaymaniya. Some time later he was captured at Sinna in Persian Kurdistan at the instigation of a British officer. Both he and his companion, Mahmud Khan of Kanisenan, were handed over to the British authorities in Mesopotamia. Mahmud Khan Dizli was deported to India, but was allowed to return to his country a few months later. After his return, he was reported to have lost no time in resuming his anti-British activities. Lees, "Two Years in South Kurdistan," 258–59, 265; see also Edmonds, *Kurds, Turks, and Arabs,* 122, 180. One official source's assertion that the Persian Kurds returned to their country soon after the fall of Sulaymaniya is only partially true. Both the Hawramanis and the Meriwanis continued to harass the British for a long time afterward from their mountain country, which dominates the Shahrizur plain. E. J. R., 16.

126. One source discounted the importance of the role played by the Meriwanis, stating that their attitude toward the shaykh remained uncertain throughout the rebellion. Driver, *Kurdistan and the Kurds,* 90. This assertion is not borne out by the information contained in the preceding note or by note 127.

127. After the Persian government handed over Mahmud Khan of Kanisenan to the British, they brought him to Baghdad and imprisoned him for a year. He was released in July 1920 and allowed to return to his country in the Meriwan region of Persia. His return appears to have so frightened the Persian governor of Meriwan, one Arfa al-Mulk, that he fled to Sinna. The Persian government is then reported to have offered the governorship to a Meriwani chieftain by the name of Kaikhosru Khan, who is said to have declined the honor. Before long, the whole of the Meriwan region apparently passed under the joint control of the two Meriwani chieftains, Mahmud Khan of Kanisenan and Kaikhosru Khan. However, the two chieftains were soon reported to have fallen out with each other over the Persian governor's property. Iraq (British Administration), Office of the Civil Commissioner, *Administration Report of Sulaimaniyah Division for 1920,* 5.

128. A. T. Wilson, *Loyalties,* 2:135; Driver, *Kurdistan and the Kurds,* 90. On Karim-i Fattah Beg, see Lees, "Two Years in South Kurdistan," 273, 275; Edmonds, *Kurds, Turks, and Arabs,* 245–46 and passim.

129. A. T. Wilson, *Loyalties,* 2:135. Cf. Edmonds, *Kurds, Turks, and Arabs,* 30.

130. Sayyid Muhammad Jabbari, who was the chief of some two dozen villages in the region south of Chamchamal, was and continued to be one of the most devoted supporters of Shaykh Mahmud. Edmonds, *Kurds, Turks, and Arabs,* 37 and 39. Cf. Iraq (British Administration), Office of the Civil Commissioner, *Administration Report of the Sulaimaniyah Division for the Year 1920* (Baghdad: Government Press, 1922), 4. The assertion that Sayyid Muhammad Jabbari and his followers abandoned Shaykh Mahmud on June 5, 1919, as claimed by an official British report, is not true. Driver, *Kurdistan and the Kurds,* 90.

131. Some fifty Shaykh Bizaini tribesmen are said to have joined the shaykh, most of whom are reported to have left him. Driver, *Kurdistan and the Kurds,* 90. Cf. Edmonds, *Kurds, Turks, and*

Arabs, 37. Edmonds identifies Faris Agha as a nephew of Tawfiq Agha of Qasrok, a grandson of Mulla 'Abbas, one of the four brothers from whom the Shaykh Bizaini group claims descent. Ibid., 38–42.

132. According to the official report already referred to, the Isma'il Uzairi tribe participated in the fighting at Tasluja Pass but dispersed to their homes in the Sulaymaniya valley soon after. Driver, *Kurdistan and the Kurds,* 90.

133. The Shuwans under 'Azza-i-Sharif Jalal are said to have numbered 250 and are reported to have fought at Qara Hanjir. Ibid., 90. Cf. Edmonds, *Kurds, Turks, and Arabs,* 276, where 'Azza-i-Sharif Jalal is referred to as a notorious brigand.

134. Shaykh 'Abd-Allah is said to have controlled about a dozen villages and to have been an early partisan of the shaykh. Edmonds, *Kurds, Turks, and Arabs,* 39.

135. E. J. R., 16. It should be pointed out here that not all the Jaf or all the Pizhdar were for the British and against Shaykh Mahmud. Thus, although the Lady 'Adila and most of the Begzada at Halabja were for the British, her stepson Hamid Beg was for the shaykh. Lees, "Two Years in South Kurdistan," passim. Likewise, although Babakir-i-Salim Agha, the paramount chief of the Pizhdar, was for the British, his relative 'Abbas-i Mahmud Agha was against them. Edmonds, *Kurds, Turks, and Arabs,* 229.

136. Bell, *Review of the Civil Administration,* 65.

11. Shaykh Mahmud's Second Rebellion

1. This agreement was reached by an exchange of notes between Sir Edward Grey, the British foreign minister, and M. Paul Cambon, the French ambassador in London, on the mentioned date. See V. Minorsky, "The Mosul Question," *Bulletin of the Reference Service on International Affairs of the American Library in Paris,* nos. 9–10 (Apr. 15, 1926): 8–45.

2. In accordance with the Sykes-Picot Agreement, a wedge of territory comprising the Mosul *wilayat* was made part of the French zone with the obvious intention of separating the Russian and the British zones. Russia appears to have looked with disfavor on the appearance of a new power along its future borders. Its objections were contained in a memorandum submitted by M. Sazonov on February 29, 1916. However, in a new note submitted on April 2, 1916, Russia agreed to the project on condition that the regions south of Van and Bidlis be included in the Russian zone. Ibid.

3. A. T. Wilson, *Loyalties,* 2:21.

4. For the text of the national pact, see H. W. V. Temperley, *A History of the Peace Conference of Paris,* vol. 6 (London: Henry Frowde, Hodder and Stoughton, 1924), 605–6.

5. The Cairo Conference was attended by the high commissioner in Iraq, Sir Percy Cox, a number of British officials, and two Iraqi ministers—the minister of defense, Ja'far Pasha al-Askari, and the minister of finance, Sasun Effendi Hiskayl. Great Britain, Colonial Office, *Report on Iraq Administration, October, 1920 to March, 1922* (London: H.M. Stationery Office, 1923), 10. Cf. Edmonds, *Kurds, Turks, and Arabs,* 117–18.

6. We are informed that this statement was issued in accordance with the policy agreed upon at the Cairo Conference; see Great Britain, Colonial Office, *Report on Iraq Administration, October, 1920 to March, 1922,* 11. For the text of the statement, see p. 126.

7. Ibid., 15. Cf. Edmonds, *Kurds, Turks, and Arabs,* 118.

8. Edmonds, *Kurds, Turks, and Arabs,* 118.

9. Soane appears to have left Kurdistan because he disapproved of the new British policy in that area. Ibid., 122.

10. Great Britain, Colonial Office, *Report on Iraq Administration, April, 1922 to March, 1923,* 32.

11. Ibid., 33.

12. See Ibid. Cf. Edmonds, *Kurds, Turks, and Arabs,* 245.

13. Özdemir was a Circassian of Egyptian origin. He appears to have thrown his lot in with the Kemalists in 1919 and after his advent to Iraqi Kurdistan was to play an important role in the frontier regions. The epithet *özdemir* means "iron shoulders." See Great Britain, Colonial Office, *Report on Iraq Administration April, 1922 to March, 1923,* 33. Cf. Edmonds, *Kurds, Turks, and Arabs,* 245. According to Edmonds (p. 247), Özdemir arrived on June 23, 1922, and was styled "Commander of the National Rising."

14. Great Britain, Colonial Office, *Report on Iraq Administration, April, 1922 to March, 1923,* 34. Cf. Edmonds, *Kurds, Turks, and Arabs,* 245.

15. Edmonds, *Kurds, Turks, and Arabs,* 245–46.

16. Great Britain, Colonial Office, *Report on Iraq Administration, April, 1922 to March, 1923,* 34.

17. Edmonds, *Kurds, Turks, and Arabs,* 248ff.

18. Great Britain, Colonial Office, *Report on Iraq Administration, April, 1922 to March, 1923,* 35. Cf. Edmonds, *Kurds, Turks, and Arabs,* 246, where the pertinent passage from the Colonial Office report is cited. On the long-expected arrival of Karim-i Fattah Beg among the Turks at Rawanduz, see Edmonds, *Kurds, Turks, and Arabs,* 252.

19. The British intercepted a number of letters addressed by the Turkish commander at Jazirat ibn ʿUmar to the notables at Rawanduz. In these letters, the Turkish officer assured the recipients that the Mosul *wilayat* would not be allowed to join Iraq and invited them to respond to the call of a holy war. After emphasizing the religious ties and promising help, the writer ended by saying: "May the curse of the polytheists fall upon those who sold their religion to the English and upon Faisal and upon his followers. Amen." Edmonds, *Kurds, Turks, and Arabs,* 246.

20. Ibid., 250.

21. According to Edmonds, a terrific heat wave and a particularly severe outbreak of virulent malaria that had prostrated four-fifths of Minet's force induced the British commander to make this decision. See Edmonds, *Kurds, Turks, and Arabs,* 252.

22. Ibid.

23. Ibid., 253–55.

24. For more details on this fiasco, see ibid., 255–59.

25. E. B. Soane, "Evacuation of Kurdistan: An Ill-Fated Expedition," *Journal of Central Asian Society* 10, part 1, (1923): 73–75.

26. Great Britian, Colonial Office, *Report on Iraq Administration, April, 1922 to March, 1923,* 35.

27. Ibid. Cf. Soane, "Evacuation of Kurdistan," 73–74; and Edmonds, *Kurds, Turks, and Arabs,* 260.

28. Great Britain, Colonial Office, *Report on Iraq Administration, April, 1922 to March, 1923,* 35; and Edmonds, *Kurds, Turks, and Arabs,* 260. According to Soane, there were 450,000 rupees in the treasury and five hundred rifles in the armory. See Soane, "Evacuation of Kurdistan," 74.

29. Great Britain, Colonial Office, *Report on Iraq Administration, April, 1922 to March, 1923,* 35.

30. Ibid.; Edmonds, *Kurds, Turks, and Arabs,* 296, 298.

31. Edmonds, *Kurds, Turks, and Arabs,* 298.

32. Great Britain, Colonial Office, *Report on Iraq Administration, April, 1922 to March, 1923*, 35; Edmonds, *Kurds, Turks, and Arabs*, 296.

33. Great Britain, Colonial Office, *Report on Iraq Administration, April, 1922 to March, 1923*, 35.

34. Ibid., 33; also Edmonds, *Kurds, Turks, and Arabs*, 122–23.

35. Great Britain, Colonial Office, *Report on Iraq Administration, April, 1922 to March, 1923*, 33.

36. Ibid. Cf. Edmonds, *Kurds, Turks, and Arabs*, 260. According to Edmonds (124), the British seemed to have hesitated a great deal before deciding on Shaykh Mahmud's reinstatement. Major Goldsmith, political officer at Sulaymaniya, favored the idea, but Edmonds was strongly opposed to it and was inclined to sponsor the appointment of Sayyid Taha of Nehri. Major Noel, too, apparently did not favor the reappointment of Shaykh Mahmud. The British at one time considered the appointment of the senior member of the princely Baban family, but he was found to be completely out of touch with the state of affairs in Sulaymaniya.

37. Ibid., 301. Great Britain, Colonial Office, *Report on Iraq Administration, April, 1922 to March, 1923*, 36.

38. Edmonds, *Kurds, Turks, and Arabs*, 301.

39. Ibid. It is interesting to note that according to Edmonds, this decree was "given in Sulaimani, the capital of Kurdistan," and the cabinet whose formation it announced was described as the "Cabinet of Kurdistan."

40. Rambout, 57.

41. For a study of this newspaper, see Edmonds, "A Kurdish Newspaper."

42. Great Britain, Colonial Office, *Report on Iraq Administration, April, 1922 to March, 1923*, 37.

43. The shaykh, however, was not without his saving graces. On more than one occasion, he gave ample proof of being a gallant opponent. When visited by a British journalist at his mountain retreat in the village of Darikali, where he was spending the last years of his life, he displayed neither petulance nor meanness when talking about his old adversaries and showed that he had a soft spot for them in his heart. According to the journalist, Shaykh Mahmud expressed friendly sentiments toward England. Obviously in a jocular mood, he was quoted as having made the following remark: " 'Tell the British government,' he said, 'that I am ready to start a revolution for them at any time,' and his eyes twinkled at the thought." Nancy Jenkins, *Illustrated London News*, Jan. 15, 1949, cited in *Bulletin du Centre d'Etudes Kurdes*, no. 8 (1949), 8.

44. Great Britain, Colonial Office, *Report on Iraq Administration, April, 1922 to March, 1923*, 36; cf. Edmonds, *Kurds, Turks, and Arabs*, 301.

45. Great Britain, Colonial Office, *Report on Iraq Administration, April, 1922 to March, 1923*, 36–37.

46. Ibid., 36. Cf. Edmonds, *Kurds, Turks, and Arabs*, 310, 314.

47. Great Britain, Colonial Office, *Report on Iraq Administration, April, 1922 to March, 1923*, 36.

48. Ibid., 36–37. Cf. Edmonds, *Kurds, Turks, and Arabs*, on the changed attitude of one of Shaykh Mahmud's influential relatives, Shaykh 'Abd al-Karim of Qadir Karam (310), and on the attitude of the Jaf Begzada (311).

49. Great Britain, Colonial Office, *Report on Iraq Administration, April, 1922 to March, 1923*, 37.

50. Ibid., 38.

51. Great Britain, Parliament, *Papers by Command: Lausanne Conference* (1923), Cmd. 1814 (London: H.M. Stationery Office, [1924]); and *Papers by Command: Treaty of Peace Signed with Turkey and Other Instruments Signed at Lausanne, 24 July 1923,* Cmd. 1929 (London: H.M. Stationery Office, [1924]).

52. Great Britain, Colonial Office, *Report on Iraq Administration, April, 1922 to March, 1923,* 38.

53. Ibid.

54. Ibid.

55. Ibid. Cf. Edmonds, *Kurds, Turks, and Arabs,* 312; Rambout, 58–59.

56. Edmonds, *Kurds, Turks, and Arabs,* 312.

57. Ibid., 405–13.

58. Great Britain, Colonial Office, *Report on Iraq Administration, April, 1922 to March, 1923.*

59. Ibid. According to Edmonds, the contingent of Kurdish volunteers amounted to 150 persons; see Edmonds, *Kurds, Turks, and Arabs,* 308.

60. Great Britain, Colonial Office, *Report on Iraq Administration, April, 1922 to March, 1923.*

61. Edmonds, *Kurds, Turks, and Arabs,* 308.

62. According to Edmonds, King Faysal, the prime minister, and the *mutasarrif* of Arbil, supported by Corwallis, Boudillon, and Lyon, wanted to appoint an ordinary civil servant as *qaimmaqam.* The high commissioner, supported by the air officer commanding the RAF in Iraq, insisted on the appointment of Sayyid Taha as the "bullet-proof" official. (The British applied this term to those persons who, as a result of their tribal connections, were almost immune against the assassin's bullet because of the risk of incurring a feud.) The reason for their insistence was that the Turks were expected to send swarms of adventurers across the border with the object of committing various depredations calculated to keep the whole region in turmoil. Ibid., 326.

63. Ibid., 304–5. Cf. Great Britain, Colonial Office, *Report on Iraq Administration, April, 1922 to March, 1923,* 39.

64. Great Britain, Colonial Office, *Report on Iraq Administration, April, 1922 to March, 1923,* 39.

65. Ibid. See also Edmonds, *Kurds, Turks, and Arabs,* 314; Longrigg, *Iraq, 1900 to 1950,* 145–46.

66. Edmonds, *Kurds, Turks, and Arabs,* 318.

67. Great Britain, Colonial Office, *Report on Iraq Administration, April, 1922 to March, 1923,* 39.

68. Edmonds, *Kurds, Turks, and Arabs,* 314–15.

69. Ibid., 315.

70. Great Britain, Colonial Office, *Report on Iraq Administration, April, 1922 to March, 1923,* 39.

71. According to Edmonds, most of the planes sent out to drop the proclamations on February 23 failed, because of a mischance, to reach their destination. Consequently, other planes were sent on the following day. Edmonds, *Kurds, Turks, and Arabs,* 315–16. The high commissioner's report stated that the proclamations were dropped on February 24. Great Britain, Colonial Office, *Report on Iraq Administration, April, 1922 to March, 1923,* 39.

72. Edmonds mentions that Shaykh Mahmud was aided in these negotiations by his brother, Shaykh Qadir, as well as by a number of Sulaymaniya notables. See Edmonds, *Kurds, Turks, and Arabs,* 316.

73. Great Britain, Colonial Office, *Report on Iraq Administration, April, 1922 to March, 1923*, 39.

74. Ibid., 39–40. Cf. Edmonds, *Kurds, Turks, and Arabs*, 316–17.

75. Great Britain, Colonial Office, *Report on Iraq Administration, April, 1922 to March, 1923*, 40.

76. Ibid.

77. Edmonds, *Kurds, Turks, and Arabs*, 319.

78. The meaning popularly ascribed to the Arabic word *haqq* is "truth." However, the more exact meaning of the word, particularly as a theological and Sufi technical expression, is "reality," which, in the language of mystics, is applied to God. Hence, Edmonds states that in the use of this expression there was "a subtle appeal to fanaticism." Ibid.

79. Ibid., 296–97. About Salmond's appointment, Edmonds states: "It is my firm conviction that the appointment of Sir John Salmond came only just in time to save Iraq; we were on the run and, had the wilayat of Mosul been lost, Baghdad and Basra alone could hardly have made a viable state."

80. Ibid., 298–300.

81. Ibid., 318–19.

82. Ibid., 327–28.

83. Ibid., 330–31.

84. Ibid., 336.

85. Edmonds states that while in Sulaymaniya he used the room that had been Shaykh Mahmud's office in which to transact official business. There was a photograph of the shaykh on the wall behind the chair and a Kurdish flag with a tinsel crown, ready to be attached as a distinguishing sign for the royal standard. Ibid., 331–32.

86. Ibid., 337.

87. According to Edmonds, the number of refugees who eventually left the town totaled two thousand. Ibid., 338.

88. Ibid., 345.

89. Ibid., 346.

90. Ibid., 350.

91. See ibid., 365.

92. Ibid.

93. Ibid., 371–72, 377–78.

94. Ibid., 387.

95. Colonel Elphinston, who happened to be serving in Iraq at the time, made the following interesting comment on Shaykh Mahmud's fund-raising activities: "I remember in 1927, when he was a fugitive across the Persian border, we planned to limit his resources by protecting the nomad Kurdish tribes from the depredations of Sheikh Mahmud's tax collectors. We discovered, however, that these same tribesmen who professed by day to be grateful for our protection were sending him by night the full quota demanded of them, so great was the religious awe in which he was held." Elphinston, "Kurds and the Kurdish Question," 45.

96. Edmonds, *Kurds, Turks, and Arabs*, 422 n. 1.

12. The Kurdish Rebellions in Turkey

1. Chirguh, *La question Kurde,* 31; Rambout, 26; S. Bedir Khan, 46a.

2. Toynbee, 507.

3. To most sources the leader of this revolt is known as Shaykh Saʿid of Piran; a few, however, attribute him to other localities. Toynbee, 507, and Rondot, "Les tribus Montagnardes," 48, call him Shaykh Saʿid of Palu. Kral calls him Shaykh Saʿid of Genj. See August Ritter von Kral, *Kamal Attaturk's Land,* translated by Kenneth Benton (Vienna: Wilhelm Braumuller, 1938), 21.

4. Toynbee, 507–8. For a brief history of Shaykh Saʿid's family, see Rondot, "Les tribus Montagnardes," 48.

5. S. Bedir Khan, 46; Chirguh, *La question Kurde,* 32; Rambout, 26; Kurdish League, *Memorandum on the Situation of the Kurds,* 11.

6. The inopportune outbreak of the rebellion is said to have occurred when a detachment of Turkish soldiers clashed with a number of Shaykh Saʿid's followers. S. Bedir Khan, 462; Chirguh, *La question Kurde,* 32; Rambout, 26. Safrastian claims that the premature uprising was deliberately provoked by the Turks: "But, owing to successful espionage the Turks forestalled the event. Sheikh Saʿid was summoned to the Turkish headquarters but, suspecting foul play, he called upon his bodyguard, only a few hundred strong, to rise on March 7th, 1925 instead of March 21st, as planned." Safrastian, 82–83.

7. Chirguh, *La question Kurde,* 32; Rambout, 26; Safrastian, 83.

8. Toynbee, 509. Safrastian maintains that the insurgents succeeded in occupying the southern section of Diyarbakr. Safrastian, 83.

9. Toynbee, 509.

10. This agreement is also known as the Franklin-Bouillon Agreement of 1921. Kurdish and pro-Kurdish sources have emphasized the decisive advantage gained by the Turks through the use of the Syrian section of the Baghdad Railway. See, for example, S. Bedir Khan, 48; Chirguh, *La question Kurde,* 32; Rambout, 26; Safrastian, 83. In 1927, Toynbee, however, pointed out that before these Turkish reinforcements had a chance to influence the military situation, Shaykh Saʿid's abortive attempt to capture Diyarbakr had greatly weakened the rebels. According to Toynbee, this effort, which cost the rebels heavy casualties, marked the turn of the tide. Toynbee, 509.

11. *Times* (London), Mar. 28, 1925; cited in Toynbee, 509.

12. *Times* (London), Apr. 1, 1925; cited in Toynbee, 509–10.

13. Toynbee, 510. Toynbee referred to the Turkish military communiqué that appeared in *Oriente Moderno,* 5:239–40, in *Times* (London), Apr. 13, and in *Le Temps,* Apr. 13.

14. Toynbee, 510.

15. Captain Armstrong, who served as British military attaché in Turkey, gave a grim picture of the retribution meted out to the Kurds after the rebellion. H. C. Armstrong, *Grey Wolf, Mustafa Kemal: An Intimate Study of a Dictator* (London: A. Barker, 1932), 265.

16. A detailed breakdown of these figures is given in Chirguh, *La question Kurde,* 49–52. A résumé of these same figures can be found in Rambout, 28. These figures cover casualties suffered in the years 1925–28.

17. S. Bedir Khan, 52–53. This figure, besides appearing too high, gives no clue as to the number of those who were killed and the number who survived.

18. Chirguh, *La question Kurde,* 33.

19. Ibid., 32–33. Cf. S. Bedir Khan, 48.

20. Kurdish League, *Memorandum on the Situation of the Kurds,* 12; cf. Rambout, 27; and *Bulletin du Centre d'Etudes Kurdes,* no. 2 (1948), 9.

21. S. Bedir Khan, 53. This citation purports to be from the Turkish newspaper *Vakit* of June

28, 1925. Cf. Rambout, 27; Kurdish League, *Memorandum of the Situation of the Kurds,* 12; *Bulletin du Centre d'Etudes Kurdes,* no. 2 (1948), 9; Malik, 18.

22. Toynbee, 510. Cf. S. Bedir Khan, 53; Rambout, 27; Kurdish League, *Memorandum on the Situation of the Kurds,* 12; *Bulletin du Centre d'Etudes Kurdes,* no. 2 (1948), 9.

23. Toynbee, 510. On September 2, 1925, the Grand National Assembly issued a decree closing down all *takiyas, zawiyas,* and *turbas* and suppressing all religious fraternities throughout the republic. Toynbee, 72–73.

24. Ibid., 511.

25. Great Britain, Colonial Office, *Report by H.B.M.'s Government to the Council of the League of Nations on the Administration of Iraq for the Year 1925* (London: H.M. Stationery Office, 1926), 12.

26. Ibid.

27. According to Longrigg, the various elements fleeing before the Turkish armies and seeking refuge in Iraq during the early part of 1926 included the following: an undetermined number of the Miran; ten thousand Goyan; one thousand Christians from the Tur 'Abdin region; and nearly ten thousand Artushi. Longrigg, *Iraq, 1900–1950,* 157. Cf. Toynbee, 511.

28. Toynbee, 510–11.

29. Toynbee, discussing these issues at some length, pointed out that official sources took special pains to emphasize the reactionary and religious aspects of the rebellion. He cited as examples a speech delivered by Ismet Pasha in the Grand National Assembly on April 7, 1925; an article written by Hilmi Beg, the *wali* of Ma'murat al-'Aziz, for the newspaper *Tanin,* Apr. 11, 1925; and the official report of the trial of Shaykh Sa'id. Ibid., 508 n. 3.

30. Toynbee seriously questioned the validity of the charges brought against members of the opposition. He cited the example of Husayn Jahit Beg, the well-known editor of *Tanin,* who was accused of reactionary activities, tried by the Independence Tribunals, and sentenced to perpetual exile. Toynbee pointed out that Husayn Jahit Beg had always been a staunch westernizer. In his opinion, there was no evidence to indicate that either Husayn Jahit or the other members of the opposition were responsible for Shaykh Sa'id's revolt. Ibid.

31. Kral, 21.

32. Sir A. Telford Waugh, *Turkey: Yesterday, Today, and Tomorrow* (London: Chapman and Hall, 1930), 263.

33. P. Gentizon, "L'insurrection Kurde," *Revue de Paris* 32, no. 20 (Oct. 15, 1925): 834–56.

34. Ibid., 841–43.

35. Rambout juxtaposes Gentizon's statement with the statements made by the prosecutor and the president of the court, and inquires sarcastically: "Is M. Gentizon better informed than the judges?" Rambout, 27.

36. Toynbee, 508 fn. 3.

37. Ibid., 508–9.

38. Toynbee and Kirkwood, 264–73.

39. Armstrong, 225.

40. The rebellions of 1925, 1930, and 1937 are said to have been masterminded by imperialist intrigue and directed against Turkish and Soviet interests. See "Kurdy." These charges, however, are not repeated in subsequent editions of *Bolshaia Sovetskaia Entsiklopediia,* which no doubt reflects the change in Soviet policy toward both Turks and Kurds, as discussed in chapter 7.

41. Cf., for example, Karl Krüger, *Kemalist Turkey and the Middle East* (London: G. Allen and Unwin, 1932).

42. Cf. Kurdish League, *Memorandum on the Situation of the Kurds,* 11ff.; Toynbee and Kirkwood, 275–76.

43. For details concerning clashes in the Agri Dagh region, see S. Bedir Khan, 50–51. Cf. Elphinston, "The Kurdish Question," 96.

44. S. Bedir Khan, 54; Chirguh, *La question Kurde,* 34; Kurdish League, *Memorandum on the Situation of the Kurds,* 12.

45. Chirguh, *La question Kurde,* 34–35; S. Bedir Khan, 54–55; Kurdish League, *Memorandum on the Situation of the Kurds,* 2–13; Elphinston, "The Kurdish Question," 96.

46. Elphinston, "The Kurdish Question," 96. According to S. Bedir Khan, the meeting took place outside Kurdistan, and the creation of the Khoybun was proclaimed on October 28, 1927. S. Bedir Khan, 54. According to Rambout, October 5, 1927, was the date of the creation of this organization, but the meeting place is unknown. Rambout, 29.

47. Elphinston, "The Kurdish Question," 96. On Jaladet Bedir Khan, see W. G. Elphinston, "In Memoriam: The Emir Jaladet Aali Bedr Khan," *Journal of the Royal Central Asian Society* 39, part 1 (Jan. 1952), 91–94; and Pierre Rondot, "L'Emire Djeladet Aali Bederkhan, animateur de la renaissance Kurde," in *Zikra al-Amir Djeladet Beder Khan 1893–1951* (In Memory of Emir Jaladet Bedir Khan, 1893–1951), edited by M. Chalita and Y. Malik (Beirut: n.p., 1952).

48. These earlier groups included: Kurdistan Ta'ali, Kurd Tashkilati Ijtima'iya Jam'iyati, and Kurd Millet Firqasi. Chirguh, *La question Kurde,* 35; Rambout, 29.

49. Ihsan Nuri was a native of Bidlis. The title *pasha,* according to Chirguh, was conferred on him by the unanimous agreement of the Kurdish nation. Chirguh, *La question Kurde,* 35.

50. Ibid.; Rambout, 29; Kurdish League, *Memorandum on the Situation of the Kurds,* 13.

51. Chirguh, *La question Kurde,* 36; Rambout, 30; Kurdish League, *Memorandum on the Situation of the Kurds,* 13.

52. This delegation was composed of the following persons: two members of the Turkish Parliament; the *wali* of Kara Kilisse; the commander of the Twenty-ninth Regiment of the Turkish army; the commander of the province gendarmerie; and the *qaimmaqam*s (deputy commissioners) of Diadin and Bayazid. Chirguh, *La question Kurde,* 36.

53. Among the personal benefits offered to Ihsan Nuri Pasha were promotion to the rank of general and appointment as military attaché to any European capital of his choice.

54. Chirguh gives details on the rejection of the Turkish proposals, including excerpts from a letter written by Ihsan Nuri to the Central Committee of the Khoybun. Ibid., pp. 36–38.

55. Elphinston, "The Kurdish Question," 96; Chirguh, *La question Kurde,* 38; Rambout, 30; Kurdish League, *Memorandum on the Situation of the Kurds,* 13.

56. These losses are said to have included 1,700 prisoners taken, 60 machine guns and 24 cannons confiscated, various quantities of war material captured, 12 planes shot down, 2,800 men killed, and more than 4,000 wounded. Kurdish losses are put at 900 killed and 2,400 wounded. Chirguh, *La question Kurde,* 39. Cf. Rambout, 30. According to Elphinston, the Kurds under Ihsan Nuri Pasha fought well, so that there were 2,000 Turkish casualties. Elphinston, "The Kurdish Question," 96.

57. Chirguh, *La question Kurde,* 39; Rambout, 30.

58. Kurdish League, *Memorandum on the Situation of the Kurds,* 13. Cf. Elphinston, "The Kurdish Question," 96.

59. For details of atrocities committed by the Turks, see Chirguh, *La question Kurde,* 39–40.

Cf. Rambout, 30. It should be pointed out that the Turks on their part claimed that the Kurds were guilty of atrocities. According to Sir Telford Waugh, "The Kurdish rebels in the Diarbekr region had invented what they called the 'Kieur Kanuni' (the blind man's code), a sort of drumhead court-martial, by which they tried the Turks who fell into their hands and inflicted on them mutilations and savage punishments." Waugh, 273.

60. Resolution of the Executive of the Internationale Ouvriere Socialiste (IOS, International Workers' Union) passed at Zurich on August 30, 1930 (7, no. 240), cited in Chirguh, *La question Kurde,* 40. The first paragraph of this resolution is given in Rambout, 31, and in Kurdish League, *Memorandum on the Situation of the Kurds,* 13.

61. These articles are given in Chirguh, *La question Kurde,* 40–42.

62. Krüger, 179.

63. For an informative and interesting discussion of the Turco-Persian frontier dispute, see Edmonds, *Kurds, Turks, and Arabs,* 125–39.

64. Krüger, 116 and 179ff.

65. Rambout, 32; Kurdish League, *Memorandum on the Situation of the Kurds,* 14.

66. Rambout, 32–33; Kurdish League, *Memorandum on the Situation of the Kurds,* 13–15.

67. Elphinston, "Kurds and the Kurdish Question," 44.

68. Elphinston, "The Kurdish Question," 96–97.

69. Nuri Dersimi, *Kürdistan Tarihinde Dersim* (Dersim in the History of Kurdistan) (Aleppo: Ani Matbaasi, 1952), 173–88.

70. Elphinston, "Kurds and the Kurdish Question," 44.

71. Ibid.

72. This force was estimated at the time at twenty-five thousand men. *Le Temps,* Aug. 18, 1937. Cf. Irmine Romanette, *Le Kurdisan et la question Kurde* (Paris: Librairie Marceau, 1935), 18; Rambout, 35–37. In Rambout, the article from *Le Temps* is cited but, obviously owing to a typographical error, the year 1934 is given instead of 1937.

73. *Le Temps,* Aug. 18, 1937.

74. Ibid.

75. Elphinston, "The Kurdish Question," 97.

76. Safrastian, 86.

77. Dersimi, 190–203. Cf. *Le Temps,* Aug. 18, 1937; Rambout, 35–37 and 39.

78. Rambout, 39.

79. *Times* (London), Dec. 31, 1946.

80. *Le Temps,* Aug. 18, 1937. This article is cited in Romanette, 18, and in Rambout, 36.

81. Elphinston, "The Kurdish Question," 97.

82. *Le Monde,* Dec. 28, 1945.

83. According to the *Times* (London) of Dec. 31, 1946, the minister of interior announced in the course of the debate that deported families were being permitted to return to their homes. Cf. Elphinston, "Kurds and the Kurdish Question," 45.

84. Elphinston, "Kurds and the Kurdish Question," 45.

85. *Dicle Kaynagi* (Istanbul) no. 21, 1948; cited in *Bulletin du Centre d'Etudes Kurdes,* no. 4 (1949), 1–2.

86. *Bulletin du Centre d'Etudes Kurdes,* no. 5 (1949), 1–2. This source (pp. 7–8) also reproduced another article by Ahmed Emin Yalman concerning a different episode involving injustice to the Kurds, from the February 11, 1949, issue of *Vatan.* It also gave (pp. 1–8) additional material on the changed Turkish attitude toward the inhabitants of the eastern provinces.

87. Ibid., 2.

88. Patrick (Lord Kinross) Balfour, *Within the Taurus: A Journey in Asiatic Turkey* (London: John Murray, 1954), 144–45.

89. Malcolm Burr, "A Note on the Kurds," *Journal of the Royal Central Asian Society* 33, parts 3 and 4 (July-Oct. 1946): 289–92.

13. The Barzani Rebellion of 1931–1932

1. Edmonds, *Kurds, Turks and Arabs,* 63.

2. Damaluji, *Imarat Bahdinan,* 65.

3. W. C. F. Wilson, "Northern Iraq and Its Peoples," *Journal of the Royal Central Asian Society* 24, part 2 (April 1937), 291.

4. Ibid., 291–92.

5. Ibid., 291.

6. Longrigg, *Iraq, 1900–1950,* 294.

7. *Derebey,* literally "lord of the valley," a Turkish expression applied to the various semiautonomous princes and feudal chieftains throughout the Ottoman Empire. Sultan Mahmud II initiated a systematic attempt to break the power of these rulers and bring their territories under direct government control in the first quarter of the nineteenth century. The Ottoman government succeeded in overthrowing most of these princes by the middle of the century.

8. This statement was made by Brooke Popham in the course of a comment on a speech delivered by Captain Philip Mumford at the Royal Central Asian Society meeting on September 26, 1933. See Philip Mumford, "Kurds, Assyrians, and Iraq," *Journal of the Royal Central Asian Society* 20, part 1 (Jan. 1933), 117.

9. Longrigg has stated that the idea of exploiting bad relations between the Kurds and the Assyrians appealed to certain Baghdad politicians. Longrigg, *Iraq, 1900 to 1950,* 198.

10. Jiyawuk, 138–39.

11. Isma'il Ardalan, *Asrar-e Barzan* (The Secrets of Barzan) (Teheran: Mazahiri Press, 1946), 3.

12. Al-Brifkani, 12–13.

13. Jiyawuk, 49–51.

14. Longrigg, *Iraq, 1900 to 1950,* 158.

15. Ibid., 158, 197.

16. Ibid., 197, 199.

17. It should be pointed out here that Ardalan was the first to deal with this matter and that both al-Brifkani and Jiyawuk apparently followed his lead on a number of points. However, insofar as this question is concerned, the most balanced account of the three is that of al-Brifkani, who correctly traces Barzani difficulties to Ottoman times.

18. Longrigg, *Iraq, 1900 to 1950,* 194–95.

19. Ibid., 195.

20. Hamilton, 299.

21. The eating of pork is commonly associated with Christianity, as circumcision is associated with Islam. Wensinck, 739–40. This fact may have led people to regard Shaykh Ahmad as half Christian.

22. Hamilton, 299. Cf. quotation from Longrigg given earlier.

23. Longrigg, *Iraq, 1900 to 1950,* 195. According to Jiyawuk, military operations started in November 1931.

24. Hamilton, 300.

25. Mumford, 112.

26. Ibid., passim.

27. Jiyawuk, 138.

28. Ibid., 138–39.

29. Ibid. Al-Brifkani related a similar story of Shaykh Ahmad but withheld Shaykh Mahmud's name. According to his version, "certain quarters" asked Shaykh Ahmad to carry out an armed demonstration against the government. The shaykh's verbatim refusal, which is said to have been immediate and unequivocal, was: "I have not made [and shall not make] any armed demonstration, clash, or move against the Iraqi state because it is an Arab Muslim state and it is my Islamic duty to obey it. God Almighty has said: 'Obey God and those who are in charge among you.' " Al-Brifkani, 40.

30. Jiyawuk, 139.

31. Ibid., 140.

32. Ibid.

33. Ibid.

34. A number of details concerning the outbreak of hostilities, including the names of the army commanders and units that participated in the fighting, are given in al-Brifkani, 14.

35. Jiyawuk cited this communiqué and took issue with the casualty figures listed therein. According to him, these figures, given as twenty-three killed and wounded for the government forces and sixty for the rebels, are an error arising out of guesswork. As he saw it, the Barzanis suffered only one death casualty. Jiyawuk, 143–43.

36. Longrigg, *Iraq, 1900 to 1950*, 195; cf. Mumford, 112.

37. Longrigg, *Iraq, 1900 to 1950*, 195; cf. Mumford, 112.

38. See comments of Sir A. T. Wilson and Sir Robert Brooke Popham in Mumford, 116–17.

39. Longrigg, *Iraq, 1900 to 1950*, 195; cf. Mumford, 112–13; al-Brifkani, 14–15.

40. Ibid.

41. Cf. Ardalan, 3.

42. Ibid.

43. Longrigg, *Iraq, 1900 to 1950*, 243.

44. Al-Brifkani, 15–16.

14. The Barzani Rebellion of Mulla Mustafa, 1943–1945, and the Growth of Kurdish Political Organizations

1. Rambout, 72. Cf. Nikitine, *Les Kurdes*, 201. According to Jiyawuk, the mulla's escape was arranged by a certain unnamed shaykh, and Mulla Mustafa was accompanied in his flight by three of his *murid*s (adherents). Jiyawuk, 153–54. According to al-Brifkani, Mulla Mustafa fled disguised as a Muslim cleric (*'alim*). Al-Brifkani, 17. On Mulla Mustafa's escape, see also Ardalan, 4; Najafqoli Pesyan, *Marg Bud Bazgasht Ham Bud* (There Was Death and Return), 2d ed. (Tehran: Sherkate Sahami-ye Chap Press, 1948–49), 1:31; and Longrigg, *Iraq, 1900 to 1950*, 324–25.

2. Al-Brifkani, 27.

3. Jiyawuk, 154; cf. Longrigg, *Iraq, 1900 to 1950*, 325. According to al-Brifkani, Shaykh Ahmad, Mulla Mustafa's elder brother and the spiritual leader of the Barzanis, was paid twenty-five Iraqi dinars (at the time equivalent to one hundred U.S. dollars) a month, whereas Mulla Mustafa was paid twelve dinars a month. Repeated requests by the Barzani leaders resulted in increasing their allowance by only two dinars each a month. Al-Brifkani, 1, 21. Cf. Rambout, 72.

4. This reference is to Colonel W. A. Lyon, a veteran British official in Iraq.

5. Jiyawuk, 153. Jiyawuk claims that upon hearing this statement, he told the shaykh that Colonel Lyon's action was motivated by guile, not by love, and was calculated to make the shaykh say the very words he had just uttered. He then pointed out to the shaykh that the real reason for Colonel Lyon's friendliness was Mulla Mustafa's escape and arrival in Barzan. Jiyawuk does not report the shaykh's reactions to his comments.

6. It appears that Mulla Mustafa had been in such desperate need of additional funds that he had been reduced to using the coins or gold pieces *(ghaziyat)* on his wife's skull cap. A few days before his escape he had asked his wife for some more coins, but she without a word had flung her skull cap to him, which was weighted with two horseshoes instead of with coins. Jiyawuk explains that Kurdish women wear skull caps heavily ornamented with gold or silver coins sewn to the cap. They become so accustomed to this weight on their heads that when the coins are removed, they substitute something of equal heaviness. Ibid., 154.

7. According to Shaykh Ahmad, Mulla Mustafa was slapped in a public bath by a local ruffian who, according to rumor, had been instigated by the governor. When Mulla Mustafa reported the incident to the governor, the latter took no action. Ibid.

8. Ardalan, 4.

9. Al-Brifkani, 17–18.

10. Shortly after these events I personally established the truth of these rumors when I was sent to the Barzan region as inspector of supply for the northern provinces to investigate the economic situation in the area. Cf. Elphinston, "The Kurdish Question," 99.

11. According to Longrigg, Mulla Mustafa joined forces with the Turkish-Kurdish outlaw Sa'id Birokhi. The latter appears to have been captured by a Turkish column, whereas Mulla Mustafa continued to gain in strength. Longrigg, *Iraq, 1900 to 1950,* 325.

12. Al-Brifkani, 17–18; "Unrest in Kurdistan," *Times* (London), Apr. 11, 1946.

13. Longrigg, *Iraq, 1900 to 1950,* 325.

14. Ibid.

15. Prior to this, the mulla had appealed to the British ambassador to intervene on his behalf with the government. However, he had been unequivocally informed that he would receive no British support. Ibid. Cf. Jiyawuk, 156; Ardalan, 6; al-Brifkani, 19.

16. "Unrest in Kurdistan"; Longrigg, *Iraq, 1900 to 1950,* 325; Ardalan, 6; Jiyawuk, 157; al-Brifkani, 19.

17. The Kurdish *qada*s of Mosul were to be amalgamated into a single administrative unit to be known as the *liwa* of Dohuk.

18. The first three demands listed are mentioned in Ardalan, 7; Pesyan, 2:32; and Jiyawuk, 157.

19. Ardalan,7; Pesyan, 2:32.

20. Jiyawuk, 157.

21. Ibid.

22. Ibid., 158–59.

23. "Unrest in Kurdistan"; Longrigg, *Iraq, 1900 to 1950,* 325.

24. The following Kurdish army officers were eventually appointed to serve as liaison officers: Amin Rawanduzi at Rawanduz; 'Izzat 'Abd al-'Aziz at Beleh; Mustafa Khoshnaw at Barzan; Mir Haj Ahmad at 'Aqra; Majid 'Ali at 'Amadiya; Sayyid 'Aziz Sayyid 'Abdullah at Margasur and Baradost; and Du'ad 'Arif at Pizhdar. Ardalan, 7. Cf. al-Brifkani, 19; Jiyawuk, 157.

25. Longrigg, *Iraq 1900 to 1950,* 327. Cf. Jiyawuk, 156.

26. The prime minister did not return to Iraq until February 7, 1944. Jiyawuk, 159.

27. The council had before it two reports on this problem, one submitted by Majid Mustafa and the other by a special committee charged with investigating the Barzani rebellion. Ibid., 159. Cf. 'Abd al-Razzaq al-Hasani, *Tarikh al-Wazarat al-'Iraqiya* (The History of Iraqi Cabinets) (Sidon: al-'Irfan Press, 1950), 6:274.

28. Apparently this point refers to the home of the lowland section of the Piran tribe on the Bitwen plain in Iraq, rather than to the home of the highland section of the Piran across the frontier in Iran.

29. Jiyawuk, 160–61.

30. Ibid., 161; al-Hasani, 6:275.

31. For a detailed account of Shaykh Ahmad's trip home, see Jiyawuk, 160–61.

32. Amin 'Abd al-Ilah, a brother of the Iraqi queen Alaya, was appointed regent of Iraq in 1939 after the death of the thirty-seven-year-old King Ghazi in an automobile accident. Al-Ilah served as regent until Faysal, the four-year-old son of Ghazi and Alaya, was old enough to be king.

33. For an interesting but unflattering account of Fattah Agha by a Soviet writer, with references to him as a "feudal potentate" and "an active executer of British directives," see V. Stepanov, "A Visit to the Kurds," *New Times,* no. 25 (June 15, 1949), 23–24. I met Fattah Agha in Arbil in the spring of 1944 and remember him as a pleasant but rather uncommunicative individual.

34. Jiyawuk, 163.

35. According to Jiyawuk, a high British official serving with the Iraq government informed him that the general opinion in Baghdad official circles was that Mulla Mustafa would do well to avoid any untoward developments by returning to his country as soon as possible. Ibid., 165.

36. Al-Hasani, 6:275.

37. Longrigg, *Iraq, 1900 to 1950,* 325.

38. Ibid.

39. Ibid., 325–26.

40. Ibid.

41. "Unrest in Kurdistan," 5; al-Hasani, 6:275; Longrigg, *Iraq, 1900 to 1950,* 326. This amnesty excluded Kurdish army officers and government officials who had participated in the Barzani rebellion, a decision that later was to become a serious source of friction between the government and the Barzani leaders.

42. Longrigg, *Iraq, 1900 to 1950,* 327.

43. "Unrest in Kurdistan," 5.

44. Note 5 in this chapter mentions Jiyawuk's criticism of these demands; cf. al-Brifkani, 21.

45. "Unrest in Kurdistan."

46. Al-Brifkani, 20–21; Jiyawuk, 170; al-Hasani, 275.

47. "Unrest in Kurdistan." Cf. Longrigg, *Iraq, 1900 to 1950,* 327.

48. For more details on the futile contacts maintained between the Barzani leaders and their emissaries, on the one hand, and the Iraqi and British officials, on the other, see Ardalan, 27–31.

49. These assurances were contained in a letter from the British ambassador conveyed to Mulla Mustafa by Captain Stokes on March 25, 1945. The mulla is reported to have replied, "We will either die or obtain our freedom." Ibid., 27.

50. Al-Brifkani, 22; Ardalan, 31.

51. Al-Brifkani, 22.

52. Longrigg, *Iraq, 1900 to 1950,* 327.

53. Ibid.

54. *Times* (London), Sept. 18, 1945.

55. "Unrest in Kurdistan." Longrigg puts their number at two thousand. Longrigg, *Iraq, 1900 to 1950,* 327.

56. Muhammad Shirzad, *Nidal al-Akrad* (The Struggle of the Kurds) (Cairo: n.p., 1946), 24.

57. Ardalan, 11.

58. Ibid.

59. Ibid., 12, where a copy of a letter addressed by the Hiva to Mulla Mustafa on this matter is given.

60. Ibid., 7; see also Jiyawuk, 157.

61. Ardalan, 7.

62. Al-Brifkani, 20–21.

63. Kurdish nationalist publications from Iran, such as *Nishtman* (Native Land), reached Hiva members regularly. Longrigg, *Iraq, 1900 to 1950,* 324, 326.

64. The Iraqi government is reported to have accused 'Izzat 'Abd al-'Aziz, who had gone on an extended tour of Syria and Egypt, of having contacted the Khoybun. Ardalan, 10; also Jiyawuk, 149. Cf. William Linn Westermann, "Kurdish Independence and Russian Expansion," *Foreign Affairs* 24, no. 4 (July 1946), 675–86, where the Khoybun's role in the Kurdish nationalist movements in Iraq and Iran is greatly exaggerated.

65. Walter Z. Laqueur, *Communism and Nationalism in the Middle East,* 2d ed. (New York: Frederick A. Praeger, 1957), 225–27. Cf. Longrigg, *Iraq, 1900 to 1950,* 326.

66. Ardalan, 27–31.

67. Ibid., 22, 28–29.

68. Rambout, 75. It is interesting to note that the Kurdish Iraq army officers who joined the Barzani forces and who formed the nucleus of the Hiva came from all over Iraqi Kurdistan. Thus, 'Izzat 'Abd al-'Aziz came from 'Amadiya, Mustafa Khushnaw from Batwata, 'Abd al-Hamid Baqir from Khanaqin, Muhammad Mahmud from Sulaymaniya, Ahmad Isma'il from Arbil, and Hifd Allah Isma'il from 'Aqra. Ardalan, 10.

69. Ibid., 7.

70. Ibid.

71. Jiyawuk, 157.

72. Ardalan, 8.

73. Shirzad, 24.

74. Ibid., 24–25.

75. The full text of the "Manifesto of the Communist Party of the Kurds of Iraq" is given in ibid., 25–27.

76. Ibid., 27–28.

77. Ibid., 28–29.

78. Laqueur, 226–27.

79. Ibid., 227.

80. Ibid., 342, n. 20.

15. The Kurdish Republic of Mahabad

1. Elphinston, "The Kurdish Question," 97. In addition to the large military stores seized by the Kurds, deserters from the Iranian army are reported to have given their arms to the Kurdish tribesmen. Archie Roosevelt, Jr., "The Kurdish Republic of Mahabad," *Middle East Journal* 1, no. 3

(July 1947), 248. (Roosevelt served as U.S. assistant military attache in Tehran from March 1946 to Feb. 1947.)

2. Ann K. S. Lambton, *Landlord and Peasant in Persia: A Study of Land Tenure and Land Revenue Administration* (London: Oxford Univ. Press, 1953), 285.

3. According to Roosevelt, "The Kurds, like other Iranians forced to abandon their native dress by Reza Shah, kept their clothes hidden in their homes, a symbol of their national pride, until the Allied invasion, when they suddenly blossomed out in them. . . . Reza Shah's restrictions on their dress had served to make him and his regime all the more hated." Roosevelt, 251 n. 1; also Hamilton, 296.

4. As described earlier, Simko Agha of the Shikak and a number of Kurdish tribal chieftains were treacherously murdered near Ushnu; Riza Shah also imprisoned Shaykh Sayyid Taha of Nehri and later reportedly poisoned him. William O. Douglas, *Strange Lands and Friendly People* (New York: Harper and Bros., 1951), 125–26. Douglas gives details on the exile of the Bakhtiari chieftains, the execution of eighty Lur chieftains (104–9), and the death of the paramount chieftain of the Qashqais, who was served poisoned coffee while in prison (139). According to Douglas, Riza Shah resorted so often to poisoned coffee that it came to be known as "Pahlavi coffee."

5. A good example of this practice is provided by the Galbaghi tribe, which was uprooted from its home in Kurdistan and dispersed in such places as Hamadan, Isfahan, and Yazd, and whose villages were given over to a Turkish-speaking population transplanted from other parts of the country. After Riza Shah's abdication, the Galbaghi returned to their former homes. Lambton, 285–86.

6. Elphinston, "The Kurdish Question," 97.

7. Ibid.

8. Lambton, 286.

9. Roosevelt, 248.

10. Elphinston, "The Kurdish Questions," 98; also Elphinston, "Kurds and the Kurdish Question," 46.

11. Roosevelt, 248.

12. Longrigg, who reports this incident, does not say whether these chieftains came from the British zone or from the Kurdish-held regions, nor does he elaborate on the exact nature of their offer. Longrigg, *Iraq, 1900 to 1950*, 324.

13. Elphinston, "The Kurdish Question," 97; Roosevelt, 248; Longrigg, *Iraq, 1900 to 1950*, 324.

14. Elphinston, "The Kurdish Question," 98; Roosevelt, 248; Longrigg, *Iraq, 1900 to 1950*, 324.

15. Roosevelt, 248.

16. Elphinston, "The Kurdish Question," 98. According to Longrigg, Hama Rashid, who was an Iraqi by birth and who had at one time claimed dual nationality, was detained at Kirkuk upon recrossing the Perso-Iraqi frontier. Longrigg, *Iraq, 1900 to 1950*, 324.

17. Roosevelt, 248.

18. Ibid.

19. "Axis Propagandists in Turkey—Incitement of Kurds," *Times* (London), Apr. 29, 1942.

20. Roosevelt, 251.

21. Witold Rajkowski, "Another Danger Spot—Kurdistan," *World Review* (June 1946), 31.

22. Roosevelt, 251.

23. Ibid., 250. Cf. Douglas, 57ff.

24. Roosevelt, 250.

25. Ibid.

26. Ibid., 251.

27. Ibid., 252.

28. Ibid.

29. Ibid., 252–53.

30. Ibid.

31. Pesyan, 2:152. According to Nikitine, Qadi Fattah was the senior member of the family during World War I. Nikitine, *Les Kurdes,* 136 n. 1.

32. Pesyan, 2:153.

33. Roosevelt, 262. It is interesting in this connection to compare the character of Qadi Muhammad with that of Sattar Khan, the famous leader of the "national volunteers" in Azerbayjan during the constitutional disturbances. For details concerning the gradual deterioration of Sattar Khan's character, see Edward Granville Browne, *The Persian Revolution of 1905–1909* (Cambridge: Cambridge University Press, 1910), 570.

34. Pesyan, 1:176.

35. Roosevelt, 261.

36. Ibid.

37. Ibid.

38. Haji Baba Shaykh, who served as prime minister of the Mahabad regime, told of a trip he once made to Baku in the company of other Kurdish leaders. According to him, Atakishov, one of several Soviet generals they met, gave them certain instructions (the nature of which he did not reveal) that he insisted they should follow to the letter, threatening dire punishment for those who refused to do so. Haji Baba claimed that a crisis developed when he voiced opposition to the general's orders and Qadi Muhammad threatened to take poison. He stated that finally, after a stay of fifteen days, they were allowed to return home. It seems that a number of Kurdish leaders visited Baku more than once. According to Haji Baba, Qadi Muhammad went to Baku twice and Sayf Qadi three times. See Pesyan, 2:173–74.

39. Roosevelt, 254; Kurdish League, *Memorandum sur la situation des Kurdes et leurs revendications* (Paris: Imprimerie Louis Jean-Gap, 1948), 38, and *Bulletin du Centre d'Etudes Kurdes* (1948), 17 (also published by the Kurdish League).

40. Quoted in Roosevelt, 255. Cf. Kurdish League, *Memorandum sur la situation des Kurdes,* 39; Kurdish League, *Memorandum on the Situation of the Kurds,* 21–22; *Bulletin du Centre d'Etudes Kurdes* (1948), 17–18.

41. Pesyan, 2:156–60; cf. Nikitine, *Les Kurdes,* 201–2; Rambout, 102–3.

42. *Daily Express* (London), Mar. 16, 1946; also Rambout, 101–2.

43. Rambout, 104.

44. Stepanov, 24.

45. Roosevelt, 262.

46. Both of these publications were called *Kurdistan,* and both served as official organs of the Mahabad regime. Ibid., 262. Cf. Rambout, 103.

47. Roosevelt, 262.

48. Rambout, 104.

49. In a note presented to the Soviet Union, the Iranian government complained that "Kurdish chiefs had imported printing machinery and newsprint from the Soviet Union for the fur-

therance of their activities." *Times* (London), Nov. 28, 1945. According to Roosevelt, the Red Army presented the printing equipment to the Democrat Party of Kurdistan. Roosevelt, 262–63.

50. Ibid., 263.

51. Ibid., 264.

52. Kurdish League, *Memorandum sur la situation des Kurdes,* 40–41; also Rambout, 105.

53. Kurdish League, *Memorandum sur la situation des Kurdes,* 41; "Resumé du memorandum sur la situation des Kurdes," *Bulletin du Centre d'Etudes Kurdes,* no. 2 (1948), 19; *Summary of the Memorandum on the Situation of the Kurds and Their Claims* (Paris: Imprimerie Louis Jean-Gap, 1949), 23. Cf. Rambout, 106.

54. Kurdish League, *Memorandum sur la situation des Kurdes,* 41; Rambout, 106; Kurdish League, *Memorandum on the Situation of the Kurds,* 23.

55. Rambout, 107; Kurdish League, *Memorandum sur la situation des Kurdes,* 41; Kurdish League, *Memorandum on the Situation of the Kurds,* 23.

56. For discussions of this political split among the Kurds, see Maurice Ferro, "La République Autonome Kurd d'Azerbaidjan," *Le Monde,* May 8, 1946; *The Scotsman,* Nov. 26, 1946; Nikitine, letter to editor, *Manchester Guardian,* Sept. 15, 1950.

57. On these tribes' attitudes, see Roosevelt, 252–53, 265–66. I deal with the causes of tribal opposition to the Mahabad regime in a subsequent section of this chapter.

58. Ibid., 252–53, 265.

59. Ibid., 260.

60. Ibid., 260 n. 8.

61. Ibid., 257 n. 3.

62. Ibid., 268.

63. Ibid., 252; Douglas, 82.

64. Ibid., 73–76.

65. Roosevelt, 259, n. 5. Cf. Pesyan, 2:158.

66. Roosevelt, 265.

67. Douglas, 59.

68. Ibid., 73.

69. Pesyan, 2:174.

70. Ibid., 2:92.

71. Roosevelt, 267–68.

72. Pesyan, 2:45–47, passim.

73. Roosevelt, 265.

74. According to Pesyan, these revelations were made by Shaykh Ahmad in the course of an interview after the collapse of the Mahabad regime. Before the Barzani chieftain would grant the interview, he produced a Qur'an and asked his interviewer to solemnly swear that he had nothing but Iran's interests and welfare at heart. Pesyan, 2:25–26.

75. It should be noted that the Mamish, who frowned upon the Mahabad Republic's Russian connection and actively opposed Qadi Muhammad, were among the most pro-Turkish elements in the war of 1914–18. After a fierce battle between Cossack units and Kurdish tribal cavalry, Bayiz (Bayazid) Pasha, paramount chieftain of the Mamish, who lost a son in this battle, is said to have sent the following telegram: "My younger son, who killed many Russians, died of his wounds and has become a sacrifice to the sultan. If it pleases God, my other sons and myself similarly look forward to sacrificing ourselves for our caliph." Nadif, *Battariye Ile Atash,* 62, cited in al-'Azzawi, 2:116 n. 1.

76. As noted earlier, 'Amr Khan Sharifi, paramount chieftain of the Shikak, was an early supporter of the Mahabad regime. According to Douglas, 'Amr Khan spent ten years in Turkish jails, presumably for having fought against the Turks during the war. Douglas, 74.

77. Roosevelt, 265.

78. Ibid., 266.

79. Ibid.

80. Ibid.

81. Ibid.

82. Pesyan 2:169.

83. Ibid., 2:173.

84. Ibid.

85. These events induced a well-known Kurdish nationalist writer to remark that the Lurs had proved on more than one occasion that they were among the most steadfast and faithful of all Kurdish nationalists. [Hilmi], *The Map of Kurdistan,* 8, cited in Rambout, 80.

86. In addition to these four officers, fifteen other persons were executed. Thousands of Kurdish tribesmen are reported to have demonstrated in protest against these executions. *Daily Express* (London), June 23, 1947. Cf. al-Brifkani, 29–30.

87. *Denge Kurdistan,* no. 2 (Aug. 1949), 10.

88. Ibid., 11. Cf. *Bulletin du Centre d'Etudes Kurdes,* no. 4, 10–11.

89. On Pishevari and other Azerbayjani Democrat leaders, see L. P. Elwell-Sutton, "Political Parties in Iran," *Middle East Journal* 3, no. 1 (Jan. 1949): 45–62. On members of the Azerbayjani cabinet as constituted at the time, see George Lenczowski, "The Communist Movement in Iran," *Middle East Journal* 1 (1947), 43n. 37 and passim.

90. According to Roosevelt, the aim of the Azerbayjan Democrat Party was "to stage a revolution, declare the province independent, and possibly request incorporation in the Soviet Union." Roosevelt, 253.

91. Ibid., 264. According to an Iranian source, Asadov appears to have exercized a large measure of control at Mahabad. Pesyan, 1:174.

92. Pesyan, 1:161.

93. Roosevelt, 264–65.

94. Ibid., 267.

95. *New York Times,* Mar. 21, 1946; *Times* (London), Mar. 21, 1946; *Manchester-Guardian,* Mar. 21, 1946; *Daily Telegraph,* Mar. 21, 1946; *Evening Standard,* Mar. 21, 1936.

96. *Times* (London), Mar. 23, 1946.

97. *New York Times,* Apr. 4, 1946; *Times* (London), Apr. 4, 1946. It is interesting to note that these same figures, in addition to being carried by Western newspapers, were given by an American scholar in an article appearing in *Foreign Affairs.* See Westermann, 676.

16. The Kurds and the Kurdish Question after the Fall of Mahabad

1. At the outbreak of World War II, General Weygand reached an agreement with the leaders of the Khoybun whereby the latter undertook not to engage in anti-Turkish activities. After the collapse of the Vichy regime in Syria and the occupation of that country by the British, the British renewed the same agreement with the Kurdish leaders. Elphinston, "In Memoriam," 93.

2. Ibid. During the war, Colonel Elphinston was in charge of Kurdish affairs for British intelligence.

3. Edmonds, "The Kurds of Iraq," 59–60.

4. Rajkowski, "Another Danger Spot," 29.

5. Jacob C. Hurewitz, *Diplomacy in the Near and Middle East: A Documentary Record, 1944–1956,* vol. 2 (Princeton, N.J.: Van Nostrand, 1956), 143–43; *New York Times,* Mar. 20, 1945. This move was followed by unofficial Soviet claims to Kars, Ardahan, and a stretch of the Black Sea coastline in Lazistan. "The Background of Russo-Turkish Relations," *The World Today* 2, no. 2 (Feb. 1946), 57–58.

6. *The Observer* (London), Nov. 11, 1945.

7. *Daily Express,* Mar. 16, 1946. Cf. Rambout, 101–2.

8. The Soviet forces eventually left Iran on May 8, 1946.

9. *The Scotsman,* Mar. 12, 1946.

10. *News of the World,* Mar. 24, 1946.

11. *New York Times,* Mar. 25, 1946.

12. Cited in *New York Times,* June 16, 1946; *Sunday Times* (London), June 16, 1946.

13. For a discussion relating this proposal to the situation in Kurdistan, see *The Observer,* Aug. 18, 1946.

14. *Sunday Times* (London), July 30, 1950; *New York Times,* June 7, 1950.

15. *New York Times,* Aug. 18, 1950; *New York Times,* Sept. 5, 1950; *New York Times,* Sept. 6, 1950; *Manchester Guardian,* Sept. 7, 1950.

16. *New York Times,* Sept. 5, 1950.

17. *New York Times,* Sept. 11, 1950. See also note addressed in the name of the Kurdish delegation on Sept. 13, 1950, to the United Nations secretary-general, the great powers, and other members of the United Nations, in *Bulletin du Centre d'Etudes Kurdes,* no. 13 (1950): 4–6.

18. "Sud'ba Plemeni Jawanrudi," in *Mezhdunarodnaia Zhizn* 4 (Apr. 1956): 122–23.

19. Longrigg, *Iraq, 1900–1950,* 326.

20. Ibid.

21. Ibid., 353.

22. Ibid., 346.

23. Ibid.

24. Ibid., 347.

25. C. J. Edmonds, "The Kurds and the Revolution in Iraq," *Middle East Journal* 13, no. 1 (winter 1959), 2.

26. Ibid.

27. A. N. O., "Nationalism in Iraq," *The World Today* 5, no. 1 (Jan. 1949), 18.

28. *Le Monde,* Dec. 7, 1951.

29. Edmonds, "Middle East Focus on the Kurds."

30. This memorandum was originally presented in September 1942 to General De Gaulle, Wendell Wilkie, and Colonel W. G. Elphinston of the British Intelligence Service. However, owing to international considerations at the time, the text was not made public until 1948. Pierre Rondot, "Les revendications nationales Kurdes (1943–1949)," *Cahiers de l'Orient Contemporain* 18–19 (1949), 65–66; Rambout, 137–38. For the English text of this memorandum, see *Bulletin du Centre d'Etudes Kurdes,* no. 6 (1949): 2–11; French text, 12–18.

31. This memorandum was published under the title *Kurdistan: La question Kurde* (Beirut, 1945) and was also issued in brochure form under the title *Memorandum sur le Kurdistan et annexes,* prepared by the Kurdish League (Paris, 1945). Rondot, "Les revendications," 66.

32. The text of this letter is given in *Bulletin du Centre d'Etudes Kurdes,* no. 5 (1949): 8–10.

33. *Bulletin du Centre d'Etudes Kurdes,* no. 6, 18–19.

34. Ibid., 19–21.

35. Ibid., 21–22.

36. Ibid., 22–23.

37. Ibid., 23–24.

38. Ibid., 24. Cf. Rambout, 141–42.

39. Rambout, 144–45.

40. For the text of this memorandum, see *Palestine Post,* Mar. 28, 1946; also Rondot, "Les revendications," 69; Longrigg, *Iraq, 1900–1950,* 335.

41. *Bulletin du Centre d'Etudes Kurdes,* no. 6 (1949), 24–26.

42. Ibid., 27–28.

43. Ibid., 28–31.

44. Ibid., 31–32.

45. The full text of this memorandum, prepared by the Kurdish League, was published in French under the title *Memorandum sur la situation des Kurdes et leurs revindications.* Summaries of this memorandum were published in French, English, and Italian. The French summary, entitled "Resume du memorandum sur la situation Kurdes et leurs revendications" appeared in *Bulletin du Centre d'Etudes Kurdes,* no. 2 (1948): 1–21. The English summary is entitled *Summary of the Memorandum on the Situation of the Kurds and Their Claims,* and the Italian summary is entitled *Situazione dei Kurdi e loro revendizazioni* (Rome: n.p., 1949).

46. For the text of this letter, see *Bulletin du Centre d'Etudes Kurdes,* no. 2 (1948), 22–23.

47. *Bulletin du Centre d'Etudes Kurdes,* no. 6, 33–34.

48. *Bulletin du Centre d'Etudes Kurdes,* no. 5, 8–10.

49. *Bulletin du Centre d'Etudes Kurdes,* no. 4, 8–10.

50. Rondot, "La nation Kurde," 65.

51. Ibid., 65–66.

52. This letter was one of several written by the Congress of Kurdish Students held in Munich from October 4 to October 8, 1958, under the sponsorship of the Society of Kurdish Students in Europe. Edmonds, "The Kurds and the Revolution," 8.

53. Ibid., 9.

54. Ibid.

55. This delegation, headed by the veteran Kurdish nationalist Sharif Pasha, also included Dr. Emir Kamuran Bedir Khan, Dr. M. W. Zaza, and Dr. Ferzende Shikak. Pierre Rondot, "Où en est la question Kurde?" *L'Afrique et l'Asie* 2, no. 2 (1949), 52–53.

56. Ibid., 53.

57. Quoted in Mumford, 119.

58. Maurice Clair, "An Interview with the Emir Badir Khan," *al-Sha'b,* Dec. 17, 1951.

59. The interview took place in the spring of 1955 in Paris.

60. 'Abd al-Rahman 'Azzam, "al-Wihdah al-'Arabiya" (The Pan-Arab Movement), *al-Hilal* (Cairo) 1, part 4 (Sept.-Oct. 1943), 465.

61. Edmonds, "The Kurds and the Revolution," 8.

62. "An Explanation from the Society of the Kurdish Students in Europe," *Khabat,* no. 83 (Oct. 1959).

63. Ibid.

64. Republic of Iraq, Higher Committee for Communication, *Thawrat 14 Tammuz fi 'Amiha al-Awwal* (The July 14th Revolution in Its First Year) (Baghdad: Dar al-Akhbar Press, 1959), 11.

65. Khalid al-Naqshbandi came from the well-known shaykhly family of Bamerni near

'Amadiya. The other members of the Council of Sovereignty were Muhammad Mahdi Kubba, a Shi'i Arab, and Najib al-Ruba'i, a Sunni Arab, who acted as president of the council. Cf. Edmonds, "The Kurds and the Revolution," 3.

66. Ibid.

67. Ibid.

68. Mimeographed copy of the Interim Constitution distributed by the embassy of the Republic of Iraq, Washington, D.C.

69. An example of the fanciful language 'Arif used in his speeches is his definition of the Iraqi republic as "a democratic, socialist, patriotic, divinely ordained, khaki-clad, soldier's republic." Republic of Iraq, Ministry of Defense, *Mahkamat al-Sha'b: al-Jalsat al-Sirriya* (The People's Court: The Secret Sessions). (Baghdad: Government Press, 1959), 374.

70. In the course of 'Arif's later trial for allegedly attempting to assassinate Qasim, a number of witnesses, some of them his friends who shared his pan-Arab ideology, complained of his provocative references to the United States as an "imperialist power," as well as his vehement attack on Iran on the very day that the Iranian government had officially recognized the new Republic of Iraq. See the statements by Colonel Rif'at Sirri, Colonel Wasfi Tahir, and Major Jasim al-'Azzawi in ibid., 249, 269, and 276. 'Arif's comments on domestic affairs included such statements as: "From now on, no palaces, no fancy homes, no governors, and no governed." See statement of 'Abd al-Rahman al-Bazzaz, former dean of the Iraq Law College and close friend of the defendant (318). According to Brigadier-General Ahmad Salih al-'Abdi, 'Arif's attacks on property, coupled with such slogans as "No fancy homes, no refrigerators," had frightened the majority of the citizens (374–75). Another officer, Major al-'Azzawi, stated that 'Arif's bitter attack against the landlords in a speech at Kut, attended largely by peasants, had led to serious incidents (277).

71. Political leaders with whom 'Arif had clashed included Kamil Chadirchi, leader of the leftist National Democratic Party, and Siddiq Shanshal, one of the leaders of the rightist Independence Party. Ibid., 437, 288–89. The extent to which 'Arif alienated some of his military colleagues is evident from the statements a number of them made about it. See statements of Colonel Maher (461–65); Colonel A. W. Amin (251–65); and Colonel Adil (391–95).

72. Much valuable information may be gleaned from the record of 'Arif's trial, particularly from his own statements and from various witnesses' statements. See the proceedings of the Mahdawi Court in ibid., passim. For a summary of 'Arif's fall, see Majid Khadduri, *Republican Iraq* (Oxford: Oxford University Press, 1969), 92–98.

73. It is evident from the witnesses' statements and from what 'Arif himself repeatedly said that he and Qasim were great friends. 'Arif, in fact, often referred to Qasim as his elder brother and even as his father. Republic of Iraq, Ministry of Defense, *Mahkamat al-Sha'b*, passim.

74. Ibid., 269.

75. Statement of Major Salim al-Fakhri, in ibid., 405–6. However, the witness stated that on discussing the matter with 'Arif, the latter apologized, saying that he had not intended to insult the shaykh. Moreover, 'Arif did not object when the major suggested that he be permitted to go to the shaykh and offer his apologies on behalf of 'Arif. Ibid., 406. In his defense at the end of his trial, 'Arif made a point of refuting the allegation that he had tried to threaten or insult the Barzani leader. Ibid., 437.

76. Munir Razzuq, *Mu'amarat 'Abd al-Nasir* (The Conspiracies of Nasser) (Baghdad: Dar al-Bilad lil-Sihafa wa-al-Nashir, 1959), 26–27. Cf. *Ittihad al-Sha'b* (Baghdad), Apr. 7, 1959.

77. *Ittihad al-Sha'b* (Baghdad), May 18, 19, and 20, 1959.

78. *Washington Evening Star,* June 1, 1959.

79. Shaykh Rashid was an important leader of the Naqshbandi order of dervishes with head-quarters at the village of Lolan in the Rawanduz district. Mahmud Khalifa Samad was one of the chieftains of the Baradost tribe. Shaykh Muhammad Siddiq, widely known by his nickname "Pusho" ("Little Grass" or "Grassling"), was the eldest son of Sayyid Taha and a great grandson of the famous Shaykh 'Ubayd Allah of Nehri. He was educated in Tehran, where his father was exiled, and spoke Persian, Arabic, and English fluently in addition to Kurdish.

80. *Ittihad al-Sha'b,* May 20, 1959.

81. *Washington Evening Star,* June 1, 1959.

82. Dair Yasin is regarded as an Arab *lidice.* For an Arab leader to compare any group to the Zionists and to draw a parallel between their activities and those of the Zionists at Dair Yasin, is to employ the most severe terms of reproach and condemnation.

83. A black-and-white reproduction of the new coat of arms of Iraq, accompanied by a description and explanation, appeared in a bilingual (Arabic and English) pictorial magazine issued by the Iraq Ministry of Guidance. "The Emblem of the Republic of Iraq," *New Iraq* (Baghdad), no. 1 (Nov. 1959): 4–5.

84. Hasan Talabani is a member of the famous Talabani family of shaykhs in the Kirkuk province. 'Awni Yusif, a Kurd of Arbil, is said to be related to the Barzanis.

85. 'Ali Haydar Sulayman: a graduate of the American University of Beirut and a Kurd from Rawanduz. 'Ismat Kattani: reported to be closely related to the Barzani shaykhs. Jalal Jaf: a member of the ruling family of the great Jaf tribe. Dr. Siddiq Atrushi: a graduate of Clark University and a member of a prominent family in Dohuk.

86. Republic of Iraq, Higher Committee for Communication, *Thawrat, 14 Tammuz,* 210–13.

87. Ibid., 216–17.

88. Ibid., 348.

89. Ibid., 300–301.

90. Ibid., 230.

91. Ibid., 339.

92. Ibid., 355.

93. Ibid., 370–71.

94. In this connection, see an interesting interview with Dr. Atrushi in the Baghdad newspaper *at-Taqaddum,* Oct. 30, 1959.

95. Jagerkhwin is the leading Kurdish poet of Syria.

96. Ibid.

97. Republic of Iraq, Higher Committee for Communication, *Thawrat 14, Tammuz,* 257.

98. Edmonds states in this connection: "Although Mukri, the Doric of Southern Kurdish, has retained a certain prestige, it is the lively and elastic idiom of Sulaimani that has now established itself as the standard vehicle of literary expression, not only in Iraq, but on the Persian side of the frontier, also." Edmonds, *Kurds, Turks and Arabs,* 11. Cf. Edmonds, "A Bibliography, 1937–1944," 187; and Edmonds, "A Bibliography, 1920–1936," 488.

99. *The Scotsman,* Jan. 9, 1951.

100. Among the messages received, one was from Shaykh Ahmad of Barzan (*at-Taqaddum,* Oct. 9, 1959), and another from Shaykh Latif, son of Shaykh Mahmud (*Khabat: an-Nizal,* Nov. 4, 1959). Both messages were couched in strong communist terminology.

101. Ibid.

Conclusion

1. William Thomson, "Nationalism and Islam," in *Nationalism in the Middle East* (Washington, D.C.: Middle East Institute, 1952), 58.

2. Burr, 289–92.

3. M. Phillips Price, "On Kurdish Rising in Persia," letter to the editor, *Times* (London), Apr. 24, 1946.

4. H. M. Burton, "The Kurds," *Journal of the Royal Central Asian Society* 31, part 1 (Jan. 1944): 64–73.

5. Elphinston, "Kurds and the Kurdish Question," 47–49.

6. Rondot, "La nation Kurde," 55–69; Pierre Rondot, "Kurdes et communisme dans le Proche-Orient," *La Vie Intellectuel* (Paris) 26 (Jan. 1959): 109–11.

 *Glossary*

Abbreviations: Ar. = Arabic; Kurd. = Kurdish; N.S. = Neo-Syriac; Pers. = Persian; Turk. = Turkish.

agha: (Turk.) Secular Kurdish tribal chieftain, usually an inherited position.

amir: (Ar.) See *emir.*

'ashirat: (Ar.) A tribe or a subdivision of a tribe.

beg: (Turk.) Title often assumed by Kurdish tribal chieftains; also title formerly conferred by the Ottoman government upon military officers and civil servants.

begzada: (Kurd.) Princely house; the leaders of certain tribes and aristocratic families.

caliph: (Ar.) Originally *khalifa* or "successor." Title assumed by the supreme magistrate of an Islamic state. First used by the four orthodox caliphs and later adopted by others, including the Ottoman sultan. See also *khalifa.*

chardaq: (Turk.) Nomadic Kurds' summer dwelling; a sort of open bower made of beams of wood covered with branches.

darband: (Kurd.) A mountain pass or a gorge. Often one made by a river.

dengbej: (Kurd.) Kurdish troubadour or bard. Also *shair.*

derebey: (Turk.) Literally, "lord of the valley," a Turkish expression applied to certain semiautonomous princes and feudal chieftains throughout the Ottoman Empire.

dervishes: (Turk.) Followers of the leader of a mystic religious order. See also *tarika.*

diwana: (Kurd.) Zealot adherents of the Barzani shaykhs, often referred to as the "madmen."

effendi: (Turk.) Turkish official.

emir: (Turk.) Also *amir* (Ar.) and *mir* (Kurd.). Prince.

farman: (Turk.) Also *ferman.* Royal decree; an edict or document issued by the ruler.

fasl: (Ar.) Settlement of a blood feud.

fatwa: (Ar.) Also *fetwa.* A legal opinion rendered by the mufti or canonical lawyer.

guran: (Kurd.) A generic name applied to detribalized agricultural Kurds; also the name of a great tribe in Persia (Guran) speaking one of the various Dimli dialects. See also *kurmanj, miskin,* and *rayat.*

hoz: (Kurd.) A tribal group of the same lineage

hukmdar: (Kurd.) Governor.

hurriya: (Ar.) Freedom or liberty; used by some writers for the period of constitutional reforms after the overthrow of Sultan 'Abdul Hamid by the Young Turks.

jihad: (Arab.) Holy war.

karamat: (Arab.) Miraculous powers believed to be possessed by shaykhs of mystical religious orders.

khalifa: (Arab.) pl. **khulafa.** Successor. A person appointed by a shaykh or head of a religious brotherhood in a given district. His powers are conferred upon him by the shaykh and therefore derived from him. See also *caliph.*

kharaj: (Arab.) Land tax.

khel: (Kurd.) Tribal unit consisting of a number of tents or households, organized for economic purposes; a subdivision of a *tira.* Similar to *oba.*

kiriv: (N.S. from Ar.) A sponsor or godfather at a Yazidi circumcision ceremony.

kurmanj: (Kurd.) Member of the peasant class in the Suran and Bahdinan areas of Kurdistan; also the term for a collection of dialects (Kurmanji). See also *guran, miskin,* and *rayat.*

liwa: (Ar.) The largest unit below that of the *wilayat* in the Ottoman administrative system, sometimes called a *sanjaq.* The term has been retained in post-Ottoman Iraq and now carries the status of a province.

mahr: (Ar.) A gift (usually money) that is given to the bride by the bridegroom when the contract of marriage is made and that becomes the property of the bride. See also *saddq.*

Majlis: (Ar.) Parliament

Mashyakha: (Ar.) Shaykhship.

mir: (Kurd.) Also *amir* (Ar.) or *emir* (Turk.). Prince.

miskin: (Kurd.) Detribalized agricultural Kurds in the neighborhood of the Bazyan Pass. See also *guran, kurmanj,* and *rayat.*

mudir nahiya: (Ar.) Subdivisional officer charged with the administration of a *nahiya* or subdivision or subdistrict.

mufti: (Ar.) Canon lawyer responsible for rendering legal opinion in conformity with the Shari'a or Islamic law. See *fatwa.*

mulla: (Ar., Pers.) Clergyman.

murid: (Ar.) An adherent of any of the Sufi orders; usually attached to the shaykh of that order; a disciple or follower of a shaykh.

mutasarrif: (Ar.) Commissioner charged with the administration of a *liwa* or *sanjaq* during Ottoman times, who was directly responsible to a *wali* or provincial governor. In post-Ottoman Iraq, the office has assumed the role of governor directly accountable to the central government.

mutasarriflik: (Ar.) Generally means the demands placed on one in a responsible position, but during Ottoman times came to denote in particular those placed on a *mutasarrif.*

nahiya: (Ar.) Smallest unit in the Ottoman administrative system; has been retained in post Ottoman Iraq. A subdivision or subdistrict. See also *mudir nahiya.*

oba: (Turk.) Among the Kurds, a temporary association of stock breeders from different villages, formed in the spring to take the herds to pastures for the summer; requires no kinship or tribal relationships. Similar to a *khel.*

pana: (Ar.) Asylum.

pasha: (Turk.) Title or rank held by generals, viziers, *walis,* etc.

pashalik: (Turk.) Territory governed by a pasha, usually a *wilayat.*

qada (Ar.) A district. The next largest unit of administration below that of a *liwa* or *sanjaq* within the Ottoman system of administration; has been retained in post-Ottoman Iraq.

qadi: (Ar.) Also *qaza* (Kurd.). A judge, especially a judge of the Muslim Shari'a. See *qada.*

qaimmaqam: (Ar.) Deputy commissioner in charge of the administration of a *qada* or district.

ra'is: (Turk.) A hereditary chieftain of a *tira;* a head or leader of any kind of group; an honorific title sometimes used popularly for persons of wealth or supposed distinction. See also *agha*.

rayat: (Kurd.) Subject peasant group; see also *guran, kurmanj,* and *miskin*.

sadaq: (Ar.) Bridal gift; see *mahr*.

sanjaq: (Ar.) See *liwa*.

sardar: (Pers.) Commander in chief; the title by which the paramount chieftains or rulers of the Mukri tribe in Persia were known.

sayyid: (Ar.) A descendent of the Prophet; a term equivalent to the title "Mr." introduced in Iraq after the abolition of titles in the mid-1930s and now common throughout the Arabic-speaking world.

shair: (Kurd.) Also *sha'ir* (Ar.). See *dengbej*.

shahid: (Ar.) Martyr; witness.

Shari'a: (Ar.) Muslim canon law.

shaykh: (Ar.) The head of a Sufi brotherhood, usually a descendent of the Prophet. Also, among Arabs in particular, the chief of a tribe.

shurish: (Kurd.) Revolution

takiya: (Ar.) A building usually consisting of a shrine and a Sufi school *(madrasa)* where members of the order live or congregate.

Tanzimat: (Turk.) The body of reforms and new institutions introduced by Sultan 'Abd al-Majid on November 3, 1839.

Tapu: (Turk.) Entitlement to heritable tenancy on state-owned land as provided by the Ottoman Land Code of 1856. Also denotes the title deed to such rights.

tarika: (Ar., Pers.) The path or the way. The term applied to a Sufi brotherhood.

tira: (Pers.) A subdivision of a tribe, divided into many *khel*s. Sometimes denotes a clan, as among the Jaf of southern Iraqi Kurdistan.

tola: (Kurd.) Vengeance

vizier: (Pers.) Cabinet minister or other high executive of the Ottoman Empire.

wali: (Ar.) Also *vali*. Governor of a *wilayat* appointed by and responsible to the Sultan.

wilayat: (Ar.) Also *vilayet*. Largest administrative unit within the Ottoman Empire, governed by a *wali* or *vali*; a province.

zozan: (Kurd.) Kurdish upland summer retreats.

✳ Bibliography

Publications in Western Languages

Adeney, W. F. "Publican." In *A Dictionary of the Bible,* 8th ed., edited by James Hastings, 4:172–73. New York: Scribner's Sons, 1906.

Ainsworth, William. "Notes Taken on a Journey from Constantinople to Mosul, in 1839–1840." *Journal of the Royal Geographical Society* 10 (1841): 498–529.

———. *Travels and Researches in Asia Minor, Mesopotamia, Chaldea, and Armenia.* Vol. 1. London: John W. Parker, 1842.

Allen, W. E. D., and Paul Muratoff. *Caucasian Battlefields: A History of the Wars on the Turco-Caucasian Border, 1828–1921.* Cambridge: Cambridge Univ. Press, 1953.

Amedroz, H. F. "The Marwanid Dynasty at Mayyafariqin in the 10th and 11th Centuries." *Journal of the Royal Asiatic Society* (Jan. 1903): 123–54.

A. N. O. "Nationalism in Iraq." *The World Today* 5, no. 1 (Jan. 1949): 5–18.

Arakélian, H. "Les Kurdes en Perse." In *Verhandlungen des XIII Internationalen Orientalisten Kongresses—Hamburg, September 1902,* 148–50. Leiden: E. J. Brill, 1904.

Armstrong, H. C. *Grey Wolf, Mustafa Kemal: An Intimate Study of a Dictator.* London: A. Barker, 1932.

Arnold, T. W. "Khalifa." In *E. J. Brill's First Encyclopaedia of Islam,* 1st ed., 4:881–85. Leiden: E. J. Brill, 1913–36.

"Ashshar." In *Concordance et indices de la tradition Musulman,* edited by A. J. Wensinck, 4:172–73. 1933. Reprint. Leiden: E. J. Brill, 1938.

Atamian, Sarkis. *The Armenian Community: The Historical Development of a Social and Ideological Conflict.* New York: Philosophical Library, 1955.

Averianov. *Kurdi v Voinakh Russi.* Tiflis: n.p., 1900. [Not available in the United States.]

"Axis Propagandists in Turkey—Incitement of Kurds." *Times* (London), Apr. 29, 1942.

"The Background of Russo-Turkish Relations." *The World Today* 2, no. 2 (Feb. 1946): 57–59.

Badger, George Percy. *The Nestorians and Their Rituals, with the Narrative of a Mission to Mesopotamia and Coordistan in 1842–1844, and of a Late Visit to Those Countries in 1850.* 2 vols. London: J. Masters, 1852.

Balfour, Patrick (Lord Kinross). *Within the Taurus: A Journey in Asiatic Turkey.* London: John Murray, 1954.

Banse, Ewald. *Auf den Spuren der Bagdadbahn* (On the Trail of the Baghdad Railway). Weimar: A. Duncker, 1913.

Bar Hebraeus. *The Chronography of Gregory 'Abu al-Faruj, the Son of Aaron, the Hebrew Physician, Commonly Known as Bar Hebraeus.* Vol. 1. Translated from Syriac by Ernest A. Wallis Budge. London: Oxford Univ. Press, H. Milford, 1932.

Barth, Fredrik. *Principles of Social Organization in Southern Kurdistan.* Universitets Etnografiske Museum Bulletin no. 7. Oslo: Brødrene Jørgensen, 1953.

Barton, Sir William. *India's North-West Frontier.* London: J. Murray, 1939.

Bedir Khan, Kamuran. "The Kurdish Problem." *Journal of the Royal Central Asian Society* 36, parts 3 and 4 (July-Oct. 1949): 237–48.

Bedir Khan, Sureya. *The Case of Kurdistan Against Turkey.* Philadelphia: Kurdish Independence League, 1927.

Bell, Gertrude Lowthian. *Amurath to Amurath.* 2d ed. London: Macmillan, 1924.

Binder, Henry. *Au Kurdistan en Mésopotamie et en Perse, mission scientifique du Ministère de l'Instruction Publique.* Paris: Maison Quantin, 1887.

Birge, John Kingsley. *The Bektashi Order of Dervishes.* London: Luzac, 1937.

Bjorkman, W. "Maks." In *E. J. Brill's First Encyclopaedia of Islam.* 1st ed., 5:176–77. Leiden: E. J. Brill, 1913–36.

Bois, Thomas. *L'ame des Kurdes à la lumière de leur folklore.* Beirut: n.p., 1946.

———. "Coup d'oeil sur la littérature Kurde." *Revue al-Mashriq* (Beirut) 49 (Mar.-Apr. 1955): 201–39.

Brant, J. "Notes of a Journey Through a Part of Kurdistan, in the Summer of 1838." *Journal of the Royal Geographical Society* 10 (1841): 341–434.

Brown, John P. *The Darvishes: Or, Oriental Spiritualism.* London: H. Milford, 1927.

Browne, Edward Granville. *A Literary History of Persia.* New York: Charles Scribner's Sons, 1902.

———. *The Persian Revolution of 1905–1909.* Cambridge: Cambridge Univ. Press, 1910.

———. *A Year Amongst the Persians: Impressions as to the Life, Character, & Thought of the People of Persia.* 3rd ed. London: A. and C. Black, 1950.

Bruce, Richard Isaac. *The Forward Policy and Its Results; or, Thirty-five Years' Work Amongst the Tribes on Our North-Western Frontier of India.* London: Longmans, Green, 1900.

Buhl, Frants. "Miskin." In *E. J. Brill's First Encyclopaedia of Islam,* 1st ed., 5:520. Leiden: E. J. Brill, 1913–36.

Burr, Malcolm. "A Note on the Kurds." *Journal of the Royal Central Asian Society* 33, parts 3 and 4 (July-Oct. 1946): 289–92.

Burton, H. M. "The Kurds." *Journal of the Royal Central Asian Society* 31, part 1 (Jan. 1944): 64–73.

Cahen, Claude. "Ayyubids." In *Encyclopaedia of Islam, New Edition,* 1:796–807. Leiden: E. J. Brill, 1954–2003.

Chirguh, Bletch. *La question Kurde: Ses origines et ses causes.* Cairo: Paul Barbey, 1930.

Clair, Maurice. "An Interview with the Emir Badir Khan." *al-Sha'b,* Dec. 17, 1951.

Clayton, E. "The Mountains of Kurdistan." *Alpine Journal* 22, no. 97 (Aug. 1887): 293–300.

Coan, Frederick G. *Yesterdays in Persia and Kurdistan.* Claremont, Calif.: Saunders Studio Press, 1939.

Cressey, George Babcock. *Asia's Lands and Peoples: A Geography of One-Third the Earth and Two-Thirds Its People.* New York: McGraw-Hill, 1951.

Cuinet, Vital. *La Turqie d'Asie, géographie administrative, statistique, descriptive et raisonnée de chaque province de l'Asie-Mineure.* Vol. 2. Paris: E. Leroux, 1891.

Curzon, George N. *Persia and the Persian Question*. Vol. 1. London: Longmans, Green, 1892.

Davies, C. Collin. "The North-West Frontier, 1843–1918." In *The Cambridge History of the British Empire*, vol. 5: *The Indian Empire, 1858–1918*, 448–75. New York: J. Macmillan, 1929.

———. *The Problem of the North-West Frontier, 1890–1908, With a Survey of Policy Since 1849*. Cambridge: Cambridge Univ. Press, 1932.

Dawes, Rufus R., comp. *A History of the Establishment of Diplomatic Relations with Persia*. Marietta, Ohio: E. R. Alderman and Sons, 1887.

Demorgny, Gustave. *La question persane et la guerre, la rivalité anglo-russe en Perse*. Paris: L. Tenin, 1916.

Dickson, Bertram. "Journeys in Kurdistan." *Geographical Journal* 35, no. 4 (Apr. 1910): 357–78.

Dirr, A. "Gulistan." In *E. J. Brill's First Encyclopaedia of Islam*, 1st ed., 3:182. Leiden: E. J. Brill, 1913–36.

Djemal (Ahmad) Pasha. *Memories of a Turkish Statesman, 1913–1919*. London: Hutchinson, 1922.

Douglas, William O. *Strange Lands and Friendly People*. New York: Harper and Bros., 1951.

Driver, G. R. "The Kurdish Question." *Persia Magazine* (London) 1, no. 3 (Sept. 1921): 107–17.

———. "The Name Kurd and Its Philological Connexions." *Journal of the Royal Asiatic Society* 10 (July 1923): 393–403.

———. "Studies in Kurdish History." *Bulletin of the School of Oriental Studies* 2, no. 3 (1922): 491–511.

———, comp. *Kurdistan and the Kurds*. London: Royal Anthropological Institute, 1919.

Edmonds, C. J. "A Bibliography of Southern Kurdish, 1920–1936." *Journal of the Royal Central Asian Society* 24 (July 1937): 487–97.

———. "A Bibliography of Southern Kurdish, 1937–1944." *Journal of the Royal Central Asian Society* 32 (Apr. 1945): 185–91.

———. "A Kurdish Newspaper: 'Rozh-i Kurdistan.' " *Journal of the Central Asian Society* 12, part 1 (Jan. 1925): 83–90.

———. "The Kurds and the Revolution in Iraq." *Middle East Journal* 13, no. 1 (winter 1959): 1–10.

———. "The Kurds of Iraq." *Middle East Journal* 11, no. 1 (winter 1957): 52–62.

———. *Kurds, Turks, and Arabs: Politics, Travel, and Research in North-Eastern Iraq, 1919–1925*. London: Oxford Univ. Press, 1957.

———. "Middle East Focus on the Kurds." *Daily Telegraph* (London), July 22, 1958.

———. "The Place Names of the Avroman Parchments." *Bulletin of the School of Oriental and African Studies* 14, no. 3 (1952): 478–82.

———. "Soane at Halabja: An Echo." *Journal of the Royal Central Asian Society* 23 (Oct. 1936): 622–25.

Elliot, Sir Henry, and Gertrude Elliot. *Some Revolutions and Other Diplomatic Experiences*. London: J. Murray, 1922.

Ellis, William T. *The Yankee Cadi: Being an Account of the Services Performed in Persia by William A. Shedd during and before the Great War*. Privately reprinted from *The Century* (Feb. 1919).

[Elphinston, W. G.] "The Azizan or the Princes of Bohtan." *Journal of the Royal Central Asian Society* 36, parts 3–4 (July-Oct. 1949): 249–51.

Elphinston, W. G. "In Memoriam: The Emir Jaladet Aali Bedr Khan." *Journal of the Royal Central Asian Society* 39, part 1 (Jan. 1952): 91–94.

————. "The Kurdish Question." *International Affairs* (London) 22, no. 1 (Jan. 1946): 91–103.

————. "Kurds and the Kurdish Question." *Journal of the Royal Central Asian Society* 35, part 1 (Jan. 1948): 38–51.

Elwell-Sutton, L. P. "Political Parties in Iran." *Middle East Journal* 3, no. 1 (Jan. 1949): 45–62.

"The Emblem of the Republic of Iraq." *New Iraq* (Baghdad), no. 1 (Nov. 1959): 4–5.

Epstein, Eliahu. "Al-Jazireh." *Journal of the Royal Central Asian Society* 27, part 1 (Jan. 1940): 68–82.

"Euphrates." In *Encyclopaedia Britannica,* 11th ed. (1910–11), 94–98.

"An Explanation from the Society of the Kurdish Students in Europe," *Khabat,* no. 83 (Oct. 1959): n.p.

Feltoe, C. I. "Publican." In *A Dictionary of Christ and the Gospels,* edited by James Hastings, 2:455. New York: Charles Scribner's Sons, 1917.

Ferro, Maurice. "La République Autonome Kurde d'Azerbaidjan." *Le Monde,* May 8, 1946.

Fesch, Paul. *Constantinople aux derniers jours d'Abdul-Hamid.* Paris: M. Riviere, 1907.

Fischer, Louis. *The Soviets in World Affairs: A History of the Relations Between the Soviet Union and the Rest of the World.* 2 vols. New York: Vintage Books, 1960.

Fisher, William Bayne. *The Middle East: A Physical, Social, and Regional Geography.* London: Methuen, 1950.

Fraser, James Baillie. *Travels in Koordistan, Mesopotamia, &c. Including an Account of Parts of Those Countries Hitherto Unvisited by Europeans: With Sketches of the Character and Manners of the Koordish and Arab Tribes.* Vol. 2. London: Richard Bentley, 1840.

————. *A Winter's Journey (Tatar) from Constantinople to Teheran, with Travels Through Various Parts of Persia &c.* Vol. 1. London: R. Bentley, 1838.

Frodin, John. "La morphologie de la Turquie sud-est." *Geografiska Annaler* (Stockholm) 19 (1937): 1–28.

Fyzee, As'ad 'Ali Asgar. *Outlines of Muhammadan Law.* Calcutta: Oxford Univ. Press, 1949.

Gentizon, P. "L'insurrection Kurde." *Revue de Paris* 32, no. 20 (Oct. 15, 1925): 834–56.

Ghilan, G. "Les Kurdes persans et l'invasion Ottomane." *Revue du Monde Musulman* 5, no. 5 (May 1908): 1–22.

Gibb, H. A. R. "The Armies of Saladin." *Cahiers d'Histoire Egyptienne* (Cairo) 3 (May 1951): 304–20.

————. *Modern Trends in Islam.* Chicago: Univ. of Chicago Press, 1947.

Grant, Ashahel. *The Nestorians: Or, The Lost Tribes: Containing Evidence of Their Identity; An Account of Their Manners, Customs, and Ceremonies; Together with Sketches of Travel in Central Assyria, Armenia, Media, and Mesopotamia; and Illustrations of Scripture Prophecy.* London: J. Murray, 1841.

Greene, F. V. *The Russian Army and Its Campaigns in Turkey in 1877–1878.* New York: D. Appleton, 1879.

H. A. "L'hospitalité Kurde." *Hawar* 1 (Aug. 8, 1932): 7–8.

Haldane, Sir James Aylmer Lowthrop. *The Insurrection in Mesopotamia 1920.* Edinburgh: William Blackwood and Sons, 1922.

Hamilton, A. M. *Road Through Kurdistan: The Narrative of an Engineer in Iraq.* London: Faber and Faber, 1937.

Handbook of Mesopotamia. 4 vols. Prepared for Great Britain National Intelligence Division. London: Naval Staff, Intelligence Department, 1917–18.

Harmatta, Janos. "Studies in the Languages of the Iranian Tribes in South Russia." *Acta Orientalia* (Budapest) 1 (1951): 261–314.

Harris, Walter B. "A Journey in Persian Kurdistan." *Geographical Journal* 6, no. 5 (Nov. 1895): 453–57.

Hartmann, R. "Djazirat B. Omar." In *E. J. Brill's First Encyclopaedia of Islam*, 1st ed., 2:1030–31. Leiden: E. J. Brill, 1913–36.

———. "Al-Furat." In *E. J. Brill's First Encyclopaedia of Islam*, 1st ed., 3:118–20. Leiden: E. J. Brill, 1913–36.

Hay, Major W. R. *Two Years in Kurdistan: Experiences of a Political Officer, 1918–1920*. London: Sidgwick and Jackson, 1921.

Hertslet, Edward. *The Map of Europe by Treaty: Showing the Various Political and Territorial Changes Which Have Taken Place Since the General Peace of 1814*. 4 vols. London: Butterworths, 1875–91.

Hourani, A. H. *Minorities in the Arab World*. London: Oxford Univ. Press, 1946.

———. *Syria and Lebanon: A Political Essay*. London: Oxford Univ. Press, 1946.

Huart, C. "'Ali b. Abi Talib." In *E. J. Brill's First Encyclopaedia of Islam*, 1st ed., 1:283–85. Leiden: E. J. Brill, 1913–36.

Huart, C., and L. Lockhart. "Agha Muhammad Shah." In *Encyclopaedia of Islam, New Edition*, 1:246–47. Leiden: E. J. Brill, 1954–2003.

Huntington, E. "The Valley of the Upper Euphrates River and Its People." *Bulletin of the American Geographical Society* 34, no. 4 (1902): 301–10.

Hurewitz, Jacob C. *Diplomacy in the Near and Middle East: A Documentary Record, 1944–1956*. Vol. 2. Princeton, N.J.: Van Nostrand, 1956.

Ivanov, W. "Notes on the Ethnology of Khurasan." *Geographical Journal* 67 (1926): 143–58.

———, ed. *The Truth-Worshippers of Kurdistan: Ahl-i Haqq Texts*. Isma'ili Society Series A, no. 7. Leiden: E. J. Brill, 1953.

Jaba, Alexandre. *Dictionnaire Kurdo-Français*. St. Petersburg: Commissionaire de l'Academie Impériale des Sciences, 1879.

———. *Recueil de notices et récits Kourdes servant à la connaissance de la langue*. St. Petersburg: Eggers, 1860.

Kazemzadeh, Firuz. *The Struggle for Transcaucasia*. New York: Philosophical Library, 1951.

al-Kazi, Mirza Muhammad Djewad. "Studien aus dem Rechtsleben in Kurdistan." *Zeitschrift fur Vergleichende Rechtiswissenschaft* (Stuttgart) 22, part 3 (1909): 321–47.

Kirk, George. *The Middle East in the War: Survey of International Affairs 1939–1946*. London: Oxford Univ. Press, 1952.

Kohn, Hans. *Nationalism and Imperialism in the Hither East*. Translated by M. H. Green. London: George Routledge and Sons, 1932.

Kolarz, Walter. *Russia and Her Colonies*. London: George Philip and Son, 1952.

Kral, August Ritter von. *Kamal Ataturk's Land*. Translated by Kenneth Benton. Vienna: Wilhelm Braumuller, 1938.

Kramers, J. H. "Sarliyah." In *E. J. Brill's First Encyclopaedia of Islam*, 1st ed., 7:174. Leiden: E. J. Brill, 1913–36.

———. "Selim I." In *E. J. Brill's First Encyclopaedia of Islam*, 1st ed., 7:214–17. Leiden: E. J. Brill, 1913–36.

Krüger, Karl. *Kemalist Turkey and the Middle East*. London: G. Allen and Unwin, 1932.

Kurdish League. *Memorandum on the Situation of the Kurds and Their Claims.* Paris: Imprimerie Louis Jean-Gap, 1949.

———. *Memorandum sur la situation des Kurdes et leurs revendications.* Paris: Imprimerie Louis Jean-Gap, 1948.

"Kurdistan." In *The Encyclopaedia of Missions: Descriptive, Historical, Biographical, Statistical,* 2d ed., edited by Edwin Bliss, Henry Dwight, and H. Allen Tupper, 530–32. New York: Funk and Wagnalls, 1910.

"Kurdy." In *Bol'shaia Sovetskaia Entsiklopedia,* 2d ed. Moscow, 1953.

Labarre, Weston. "The Cultural Basis of Emotions and Gestures." *Journal of Personality* 16, no. 1 (Sept. 1947): 49–63.

Lambton, Ann K. S. *Landlord and Peasant in Persia: A Study of Land Tenure and Land Revenue Administration.* London: Oxford Univ. Press, 1953.

Lane-Poole, Stanley. *Saladin.* New York: G. P. Putnam's Sons, 1901.

Laqueur, Walter Z. *Communism and Nationalism in the Middle East.* 2d ed. New York: Frederick A. Praeger, 1957.

Laurie, Thomas. *Dr. Grant and the Mountain Nestorians.* 3rd ed. Boston: Gould and Lincoln, 1853.

Layard, Sir Austen Henry. *Discoveries in the Ruins of Nineveh and Babylon: With Travels in Armenia, Kurdistan, and the Desert.* 2 vols. New York: Harper and Bros., 1853.

———. *Nineveh and Its Remains.* Vol. 1. New York: G. P. Putnam, 1849.

Leach, E. R. *Social and Economic Organisation of the Rowanduz Kurds.* London School of Economics and Political Science Monographs on Social Anthropology no. 3. London: Percy Lund, Humphries, 1940.

Lees, G. M. "The Middle East." In *World Geography of Petroleum,* edited by Wallace Everett Pratt, 159–202. Princeton, N.J.: Princeton Univ. Press for the American Geographical Society, 1950.

———. "Two Years in South Kurdistan." *Journal of the Royal Central Asian Society* 15, part 3 (1928): 253–77.

Lenczowski, George. "The Communist Movement in Iran." *Middle East Journal* 1 (1947): 29–45.

Lescot, Roger. *Textes Kurdes.* Vol. 2: *Mamé Alan.* Paris: Geunther, 1940.

Lobanov-Rostovsky, Andrei. *Russia and Asia.* New York: Macmillan, 1933.

Lockhart, Laurence. *Nadir Shah: A Critical Study Based Mainly on Contemporary Sources.* London: Luzac, 1938.

Longrigg, Stephen H. *Four Centuries of Modern Iraq.* London: Oxford Univ. Press, 1925.

———. *Iraq, 1900 to 1950: Political, Social, and Economic History.* London: Oxford Univ. Press for the Royal Institute of International Affairs, 1953.

Lugard, Frederick John Dealtry. *The Dual Mandate in British Tropical Africa.* London: William Blackwood and Sons, 1923.

Macdonald, D. B. "Derwish." In *E. J. Brill's First Encyclopaedia of Islam,* 1st ed., 2:949–51. Leiden: E. J. Brill, 1913–36.

———. "Dhikr." In *E. J. Brill's First Encyclopaedia of Islam,* 1st ed., 2:958. Leiden: E. J. Brill, 1913–36.

———. "Fatwa." In *E. J. Brill's First Encyclopaedia of Islam,* 1st ed., 3:92–93. Leiden: E. J. Brill, 1913–36.

———. "Karama." In *E. J. Brill's First Encyclopaedia of Islam,* 1st ed., 4:744. Leiden: E. J. Brill, 1913–36.

———. "Mahdi." In *E. J. Brill's First Encyclopaedia of Islam,* 1st ed., 5:111–15. Leiden: E. J. Brill, 1913–36.

Mandelstam, André. *Le sort de l'Empire Ottoman.* Paris: Librairie Payot et Cie, 1917.

Margoliouth, D. S. "Mahdi." In *Encyclopaedia of Religion and Ethics,* edited by James Hastings, 8:336–40. New York: Charles Scribner's Sons, 1917–30.

Marriott, J. A. R. *The Eastern Question: An Historical Study in European Diplomacy.* Oxford: Oxford Univ. Press, 1924.

———. *The European Commonwealth.* Oxford: Oxford Univ. Press, 1918.

Mason, Kenneth. "Central Kurdistan." *Geographical Journal* 54, no. 6 (1919): 329–47.

Massignon, Louis. "Tarika." In *E. J. Brill's First Encyclopaedia of Islam,* 1st ed., 8:667–72. Leiden: E. J. Brill, 1913–36.

———. "Tasawwuf." In *E. J. Brill's First Encyclopaedia of Islam,* 1st ed., 8:681–85. Leiden: E. J. Brill, 1913–36.

Maunsell, F. R. "Central Kurdistan." *Geographical Journal* 18, no. 2 (Aug. 1901): 121–43.

———. "Kurdistan." *Geographical Journal* 3, no. 2 (Feb. 1894): 81–92.

McCoan, James Carlile. *Our New Protectorate: Turkey in Asia.* London: Chapman and Hall, 1879.

Medlicott, William Newton. *The Congress of Berlin and After.* London: Methuen, 1938.

Meier, F. "Der Name der Yazidis." In *Westöstliche Abhandlungen Rudolf Tschudi,* edited by F. Meier, 244–57. Weisbaden: Harrassowitz, 1954.

Menzel, T. "Yezidi." In *E. J. Brill's First Encyclopaedia of Islam,* 1st ed., 8:1163–70. Leiden: E. J. Brill, 1913–36.

The Middle East: A Political and Economic Survey. 2d ed. London: Oxford Univ. Press for the Royal Institute of International Affairs, 1954.

Miller, William. *The Ottoman Empire and Its Successors, 1801–1927.* Cambridge: Cambridge Univ. Press, 1934.

Millingen, Frederick. *Wild Life among the Koords.* London: Hurst and Blackett, 1870.

Minorsky, V. "Ahl-i Hakk." In *Encyclopaedia of Islam, New Edition,* 1:260–63. Leiden: E. J. Brill, 1954–2003.

———. "Ak Koyunlu." In *Encyclopaedia of Islam, New Edition,* 1:311–12. Leiden: E. J. Brill, 1954–2003.

———. "'Annazids." In *Encyclopaedia of Islam, New Edition,* 1:512–13. Leiden: E. J. Brill, 1954–2003.

———. "The Guran." *Bulletin of the School of Oriental and African Studies* 11, no. 1 (1943): 75–103.

———. "Kurdistan." In *E. J. Brill's First Encyclopaedia of Islam,* 1st ed., 4:1130–32. Leiden: E. J. Brill, 1913–36.

———. "Kurds." In *E. J. Brill's First Encyclopaedia of Islam,* 1st ed., 4:1132–55. Leiden: E. J. Brill, 1913–36.

———. "The Mosul Question." *Bulletin of the Reference Service on International Affairs of the American Library in Paris,* nos. 9–10 (Apr. 15, 1926): 8–45.

———. "Les origines des Kurdes." In *Actes du XXe Congrès International des Orientalistes, Bruxelles, 5–10 Septembre 1938,* 143–52. Louvain: Bureaux du Musson, 1940.

———. "Le plus ancien texte Kurde." *Bulletin Mensuel du Centre d'Etudes Kurdes,* no. 10 (1950): 8–10.

———. "Sawdj Bulak." In *E. J. Brill's First Encyclopaedia of Islam,* 1st ed., 7:186–92. Leiden: E. J. Brill, 1913–36.

———. *Studies in Caucasian History*. Cambridge Oriental Series no. 6. London: Taylor's Foreign Press, 1953.

———. "Turkman-Cai." In *E. J. Brill's First Encyclopaedia of Islam*, 1st ed., 8:896. Leiden: E. J. Brill, 1913–36.

Mittwoch, E. "Dhu'il-Fakar." In *E. J. Brill's First Encyclopaedia of Islam*, 1st ed., 2:959. Leiden: E. J. Brill, 1913–36.

Moberly, Frederick James. *The Campaign in Mesopotamia*. Vol. 4. London: H.M. Stationery Office, 1927.

Molyneux-Seel, L. "A Journey in Dersim." *Geographical Journal* 44, no. 1 (July 1914): 49–68.

Monteith, William. *Kars and Erzeroum with the Campaigns of Prince Paskiewitch in 1828 and 1829*. London: Longman, Brown, Green, and Longmans, 1856.

Mumford, Phillip. "Kurds, Assyrians, and Iraq." *Journal of the Royal Central Asian Society* 20, part 1 (Jan. 1933): 110–19.

Newin, C. "Le nombre des repas chez les Kurdes." *Hawar* 1, no. 13 (Dec. 14, 1932): 8–10.

Nikitine, Basile. "Les Afsars d'Urumiyeh." *Journal Asiatique* 34 (Jan.-Mar. 1929): 67–123.

———. "Badrkhani." In *Encyclopaedia of Islam, New Edition*, 1:871. Leiden: E. J. Brill, 1954–2003.

———. "La féodalité Kurde." *Revue du Monde Musulman* 60 (1925): 1–26.

———. "Kurdes." In *Dictionnaire Diplomatique*, 1:1201. Paris: Académie Diplomatique Internationale, 1933.

———. "Les Kurdes et le Christianisme." *Revue de l'Histoire des Réligions* 85, no. 3 (May-June 1922): 147–56.

———. *Les Kurdes: Etude sociologique et historique*. Paris: Imprimerie Nationale Librairie C. Klincksieck, 1956.

———. "Les Kurdes racontés par eux-mêmes." *L'Asie Française* (1925): 148–57.

———. "Kurdish Stories from My Collection." *Bulletin of the School of Oriental Studies* 4, part 1 (1926): 121–38.

———. Letter to the editor. *Manchester Guardian*, Sept. 21, 1950.

———. "La poésie lyrique Kurde." *L'Ethnographie* (Paris), no. 45 (1947–50): 39–53.

———. "Problème Kurde." *Politique Etrangère* 11, no. 3 (July 1946): 251–62.

———. "Quelques observations sur les Kurdes." *Mercure de France* 145, no. 543 (Feb. 1921): 662–74.

———. "Rawandiz Ruiyndiz." In *E. J. Brill's First Encyclopaedia of Islam*, 1st ed., 6:912–14. Leiden: E. J. Brill, 1913–36.

———. "Shamdinan." In *E. J. Brill's First Encyclopaedia of Islam*, 1st ed., 7:303–6. Leiden: E. J. Brill, 1913–36.

———. "Un sujet de fable: Variantes Kurdes et Persanes." *Revue d'Ethnographie et des Traditions Populaires* 3, no. 10 (1922): 129–40.

———. "Superstitions des Chaldéens du Plateau d'Ourmiah." *Revue d'Ethnographie et des Traditions Populaires* 4, no. 14 (1923): 149–81.

———. "La systeme routier du Kurdistan." *La Geographie* 63, nos. 5–6 (May-June 1935): 363–85.

———. "La vie domestique Kurde." *Revue d'Ethnographie et des Traditions Populaires* 3, no. 12 (1922): 334–44.

Nikitine, Basile, and E. B. Soane. "The Story of Suto and Tato." *Bulletin of the School of Oriental Studies* 3, part 1 (1923): 69–106.

Noel, Major E. W. C. "The Character of the Kurds as Illustrated by Their Proverbs and Popular Sayings." *Bulletin of the School of Oriental Studies* 1, part 4 (1921): 79–90.

Oswald, Felix. *A Treatise on the Geology of Armenia.* London: Felix Oswald, 1906.

Panikkar, K. M. *Indian States.* Oxford Pamphlets on Indian Affairs no. 4. Mysore City, India: Oxford Univ. Press, 1942.

Pares, Bernard. *A History of Russia.* 4th ed. rev. New York: Alfred A. Knopf, 1946.

Pedersen, J. "Kasam." In *E. J. Brill's First Encyclopaedia of Islam,* 1st ed., 4:783–85. Leiden: E. J. Brill, 1913–36.

Perkins, Justin. "Journal of a Tour from Oroomiah to Mosul Through the Koordish Mountains, and a Visit to the Ruins of Nineveh." *Journal of the American Oriental Society* 2 (1851): 69–119.

Price, M. Phillips. "On Kurdistan Rising in Persia," letter to the editor. *Times* (London), Apr. 24, 1946.

———. "Russia and the Kurds." *Manchester Guardian Weekly* 63, no. 11 (Sept. 14, 1950).

———. "Through Iraqi Kurdistan." *Manchester Guardian Weekly* 63, no. 19 (Nov. 9, 1950).

Rajkowski, Witold. "Another Danger Spot—Kurdistan." *World Review* (June 1946): 29–31.

———. "A Visit to Southern Kurdistan." *Geographical Journal* 107, nos. 3–4 (1946): 128–34.

Ram, Hittu. *Sandeman in Baluchistan.* Calcutta: Government Printing Office, 1916.

Rambout, Lucien. *Les Kurdes et le droit: Des textes, des faits.* Paris: Editions du Cerf, 1947.

Ramsaur, Ernest Edmondson, Jr. *The Young Turks: Prelude to the Revolution of 1908.* Princeton Oriental Studies, Social Science no. 2. Princeton, N.J.: Princeton Univ. Press, 1957.

Rawlinson, H. C. "Notes on a Journey from Tabriz, Through Persian Kurdistan, to the Ruins of Takhti-Soleiman." *Journal of the Royal Geographical Society* 10 (1841): 1–158.

Rich, Claudius James. *Narrative of a Residence in Koordistan.* 2 vols. London: James Duncan, 1836.

Ritter, Helmut Werner. *"Picatrix" das Ziel des Weisen von Pseudo-Magriti.* London: Warburg Institute, 1962.

Romanette, Irmine. *Le Kurdistan et la question Kurde.* Paris: Librairie Marceau, 1935.

Rondot, Pierre. "L'adoption des caractères Latins et le mouvement culturel chez les Kurdes de l'U.R.S.S." *Revue des Etudes Islamiques,* no. 1 (1935): 87–96.

———. "L'alphabet Kurde en caractères Latins d'Arménie Soviétique." *Revue des Etudes Islamiques,* no. 3 (1933): 411–17.

———. "L'Emire Djeladet Aali Bederkhan, animateur de la renaissance Kurde." In *Zikra al-Amir Djeladet Beder Khan 1893–1951* (In Memory of Emir Jaladet Bedir Khan, 1893–1951), edited by M. Chalita and Y. Malik. Beirut: n.p., 1952.

———. "Kurdes et communisme dans le Proche-Orient." *La Vie Intellectuel* (Paris) 26 (Jan. 1959): 109–11.

———. "La nation Kurde en face des mouvements Arabes." *Orient* 2, no. 7 (1958): 55–69.

———. "Où en est la question Kurde?" *L'Afrique et l'Asie* 2, no. 2 (1949): 51–55.

———. "La question Kurde dans l'Orient contemporain." *Bulletin Mensuel du Centre d'Etudes Kurdes* no. 12 (1950): 1–15.

———. "Les revendications nationales Kurdes (1943–1949)." *Cahiers de l'Orient Contemporain* 18–19 (1949): 65–66.

———. "Les tribus Montagnardes de l'Asie Anterieure: Quelques aspects sociaux des populations Kurdes et Assyriennes." *Bulletin d'Etudes Orientalis/Institut Français de Damas* 6 (1936): 1–49.

Roosevelt, Archie. "The Kurdish Republic of Mahabad." *Middle East Journal* 1, no. 3 (July 1947): 247–69.

Ross, E. Denison. "Shaddad." In *E. J. Brill's First Encyclopaedia of Islam,* 1st ed., 7:246. Leiden: E. J. Brill, 1913–36.

Safrastian, Arshak. *Kurds and Kurdistan.* London: Harvill Press, 1948.

Sarezhin, K. "Iraq Today: Geographical Sketch." *New Times,* no. 6 (Mar. 15, 1946): 22–26.

Sazonov, Sergiei Dmitrievich. *The Fateful Years.* London: Jonathan Cape, 1928.

Schacht, J. "Nikah." In *E. J. Brill's First Encyclopaedia of Islam,* 1st ed., 6:912–14. Leiden: E. J. Brill, 1913–36.

———. "Talak." In *E. J. Brill's First Encyclopaedia of Islam,* 1st ed., 8:636–40. Leiden: E. J. Brill, 1913–36.

Scher, Addai. "Episodes de l'histoire du Kurdistan." *Journal Asiatique* 15 (Jan.-Feb. 1910): 119–39.

Seligman, Brenda Z. "Studies in Semitic Kinship. II. Cousin Marriage." *Bulletin of the School of Oriental Studies* 3 (1923–25): 263–79.

Shedd, Mary Lewis. *The Measure of a Man: The Life of William Ambrose Shedd, Missionary to Persia.* New York: George H. Doran, 1922.

Shiel, J. "Notes on a Journey from Tabriz Through Kurdistan via Van, Bitlis, Se'ert, and Erbil, to Sulaimaniyah, in July and August, 1836." *Journal of the Royal Geographical Society* 8 (1838): 54–101.

Soane, E. B. "Evacuation of Kurdistan: An Ill-Fated Expedition." *Journal of Central Asian Society* 10, part 1 (1923): 73–75.

———. "The Southern Kurd." *Journal of the Central Asian Society* 9, part 1 (1922): 44–45.

———. *To Mesopotamia and Kurdistan in Disguise. With Historical Notices of the Kurdish Tribes and the Chaldeans of Kurdistan.* 2d ed. London: John Murray, 1926.

Sobernheim, Morton. "Saladin." In *E. J. Brill's First Encyclopaedia of Islam,* 1st ed., 7:84–89. Leiden: E. J. Brill, 1913–36.

Speer, Robert E. *"The Hakim Sahib," the Foreign Doctor: A Biography of Joseph Plumb Cochran, M.D. of Persia.* New York: Fleming H. Revell, 1911.

Speiser, Ephraim Avigdor. *Mesopotamian Origins: The Basic Population of the Near East.* London: H. Milford, 1930.

———. "Southern Kurdistan in the Annals of Ashurnasirpal and Today." *Annual of the American School of Oriental Research* (Jerusalem) 8 (1926–27): 1–33.

Spies, O. "Mahr." In *E. J. Brill's First Encyclopaedia of Islam,* 1st ed., 5:137–38. Leiden: E. J. Brill, 1913–36.

Stack, Edward. *Six Months in Persia.* New York: G. P. Putnam and Sons, 1882.

Stamp, L. Dudley. *Asia: A Regional and Economic History.* London: Methuen, 1959.

Stepanov, V. "A Visit to the Kurds." *New Times,* no. 24 (June 8, 1949): 23–28, and no. 25 (June 15, 1949): 23–26.

Streck, M. "Bohtan." In *E. J. Brill's First Encyclopaedia of Islam,* 1st ed., 2:739–40. Leiden: E. J. Brill, 1913–36.

Süssheim, K. "'Abd Allah Djewdet [Jawdat]." In *E. J. Brill's Encyclopaedia of Islam,* vol. 9: Supplement, 55–60. Leiden and London: E. J. Brill and Luzac, 1935.

Sykes, Mark. *The Caliphs' Last Heritage: A Short History of the Turkish Empire.* London: Macmillan, 1915.

———. *Dar-u al-Islam.* London: Bickers and Son, 1904.

Sykes, Sir Percy. *A History of Persia.* 2 vols. London: Macmillan, 1915.

Taylor, J. G. "Travels in Kurdistan, with Notices of the Sources of the Eastern and Western Tigris and Ancient Ruins in the Neighborhood." *Journal of the Royal Geographical Society* 35 (1865): 21–55.

Temperley, H. W. V. *A History of the Peace Conference of Paris.* Vol. 6. London: Henry Frowde and Hodder and Stoughton, 1924.

Thomson, William. "Nationalism and Islam." In *Nationalism in the Middle East,* 51–60. Washington, D.C.: Middle East Institute, 1952.

Thornton, Thomas Henry. *Colonel Sir Robert Sandeman: His Life and Work on Our Indian Frontier.* London: J. Murray, 1895.

Thurnwald, R. "Blood Vengeance Feud." In *Encyclopaedia of the Social Sciences,* 2:598–99. New York: Macmillian, 1930–35.

Toynbee, Arnold J. *Survey of International Affairs, 1925.* Vol. 1: *The Islamic World Since the Peace Settlement.* London: Oxford Univ. Press, 1927.

Toynbee, Arnold J., and Kenneth P. Kirkwood. *Turkey.* New York: Charles Scribner's Sons, 1927.

The Treaties of Peace, 1919–1923. Vol. 2. New York: Carnegie Endowment for International Peace, 1924.

Turlington, Edgar. "The Settlement of Lausanne." *American Journal of International Law* 18, no. 4 (Oct. 1924): 696–706.

"Unrest in Kurdistan." *Times* (London), Apr. 11, 1946.

Ushakoff, Aleksandr Kleonakovich. *Geschichte der Feldzüge in der Asiatischen Turkei Während der Jahre 1828 und 1829.* Vols. 1 and 2. Leipzig: n.p., 1838.

Villari, Luigi. *Fire and Sword in the Caucasus.* London: T. F. Unwin, 1906.

Waugh, A. Telford. *Turkey: Yesterday, Today, and Tomorrow.* London: Chapman and Hall, 1930.

Weber, Max. *Essays in Economic Sociology.* Edited by Richard Swedeberg. Princeton, N.J.: Princeton Univ. Press, 1999.

——— *The Theory of Social and Economic Organization.* 2d ed. New York: Oxford Univ. Press, 1950.

Wensinck, A. J. "Khitan." In *E. J. Brill's First Encyclopaedia of Islam,* 1st ed., 4:956–60. Leiden: E. J. Brill, 1913–36.

Westermann, William Linn. "Kurdish Independence and Russian Expansion." *Foreign Affairs* 24, no. 4 (July 1946): 674–88.

Wiedemann, M. "Ibrahim Pasha's Gluck und Ende." *Asien* no. 3 (1909): 34–37.

Wigram, W. A., and Sir Edgar T. A. Wigram. *The Cradle of Mankind: Life in Eastern Kurdistan.* 2d ed. London: A. and C. Black, 1922.

Wilson, Sir Arnold T. "E. B. Soane—A Memoir." In *To Mesopotamia and Kurdistan in Disguise,* by E. B. Soane, ix-xvii. London: John Murray, 1926.

———. *Loyalties: Mesopotamia.* Vol. 2: *1917–20.* Oxford: Oxford Univ. Press, 1936.

Wilson, C. W., and H. C. Rawlinson. "Kurdistan." In *Encyclopaedia Britannica,* 11th ed. (1910–11), 5:949–51.

Wilson, S. G. *Persian Life and Customs.* New York: Fleming H. Revell, 1900.

Wilson, W. C. F. "Northern Iraq and Its Peoples." *Journal of the Royal Central Asian Society* 24, part 2 (Apr. 1937): 287–99.

Wratislaw, Albert Charles. *A Consul in the East.* London: Blackwood, 1924.

Wright, Dr. Austin H., and Edward Breath. [Report on their visit to Bedir Khan (as representatives of the American Mission in Persia).] *Missionary Herald* 42, no. 11 (Nov. 1846): 381–82.

Yalman, Ahmad Emin. *Turkey in the World War.* New Haven, Conn.: Yale Univ. Press, 1930.

Zeidner, Robert. "Kurdish Nationalism and the New Iraqi Government." *Middle Eastern Affairs* 10, no. 1 (Jan. 1959): 24–31.

Zettersteen, K. V. "Marwanids." In *E. J. Brill's First Encyclopaedia of Islam,* 1st ed., 5:309–10. Leiden: E. J. Brill, 1913–36.

Publications in Middle Eastern Languages (Arabic, Kurdish, Persian, and Turkish)

Ardalan, Isma'il. *Asrar-e Barzan* (The Secrets of Barzan). Teheran: Mazahiri Press, 1946.

'Azzam, 'Abd al-Rahman. "al-Wihda al-Arabiya" (The Pan-Arab Movement). *al-Hilal* (Cairo) 1, part 4 (Sept.-Oct. 1943): n.p.

al-'Azzawi, 'Abbas. *'Asha'ir al-'Iraq* (The Tribes of Iraq), vol. 1, and *al-Kurdiya* (The Kurdish Tribes), vol. 2. Baghdad: al-Ma'arif Press, 1947.

al-Baghdadi, 'Abd al-Qahir ibn Tahir. *Mukhtasar Kitab al-Farq bayna al-Firaq* (The Abridged Book of Differences among the Sects). Edited by A. S. Hakim. Cairo: Matba'at al-Hilal, 1924.

al-Baghdadi, Sayyid Muhammad ibn al-Sayyid Ahmad al-Husayni al-Munshi'. *Rihlat al-Munshi' al-Baghdadi* (The Journey of the al-Munshi' al-Baghdadi). Translated from Persian into Arabic by 'Abbas al-'Azzawi. Baghdad: at-Tijara wa al-Tiba'a Press, 1948.

Bayur, Yusuf Hikmet. *Türk Inkılâbı Tarihi, Türk Tarikh Kurumu Yayınlarından* (The History of the Turkish Revolution). Vol. 8. Istanbul: Ma'arif Mataba'asi Press for the Turkish Historical
Association, 1940.

al-Bidlisi, Ameer Sharaf Khan. *Sharafnama: Fi Tarikh al-Duwal wa al-Imarat al-Kurdiya* (History of the Kurdish Governments and Princedoms). Translated from Persian into Arabic with commentary by Muhammad Jamil Bendi Rozhbeyani. Baghdad: al-Naja Press, 1953.

al-Brifkani, Muhammad. *Haqa'iq Tarikhiya 'an al-Qadiya al-Barzaniya* (Historical Truths Regarding the Barzani Problem). Baghdad: Matba'at Sharikat al-Tiba'a wa al-Nashr al-'Ahliya Press, 1953.

Chirguh, Bletch. *al-Qadiya al-Kurdiya: Madi al-Kurd wa Hadirihim* (The Kurdish Problem: The Past and the Present of the Kurds). Hoybun Publication no. 5. Cairo: al-Sa'ada Press, 1930.

Damaluji, Siddiq. *Imarat Bahdinan al-Kurdiya Aw Imarat al-'Imadiya* (The Kurdish Princedom of Bahdinan or the Princedoms of 'Amadiya). Mosul, Iraq: al-Ittihad al-Jadida Press, 1952.

———. *al-Yazidiya* (The Yazidis). Mosul, Iraq: al-Ittihad Press, 1948.

Dânişmend, İsma'il Hâmi. *İzahlı Osmanlı Tarihi Kronolojisi* (An Explanation of the Chronology of Ottoman History). Vol. 9. Istanbul: Türkiye Basımevi, 1955.

Dersimi, Nuri. *Kürdistan Tarihinde Dersim* (Dersim in the History of Kurdistan). Aleppo: Ani Matbaasi, 1952.

al-Ghulami, 'Abd al-Mun'im. *Baqaya al-Firaq al-Batiniya fi Liwa al-Mawsul* (Remnants of Batini Sects in Mosul Province). Mosul, Iraq: al-Ittihad Press, 1950.

Gövsa, İbrahim Alâettin. *Türk Meşhurları Ansiklopedisi* (Encyclopedia of Famous Turks). Istanbul: Yedigun Nesriya, n.d.

al-Gurani, 'Ali Sido. *Min 'Amman ila al-'Amadiya* (From 'Amman to 'Amadiya). Cairo: al-Sa'ada Press, 1939.

Hartmann, R. "Dicle, Dicla." In *Islam Ansiklopedisi,* 3:582–85. Istanbul: Milli Egitin Basimevi, 1945.

al-Hasani, 'Abd al-Razzaq. *Tarikh al-Wazarat al-'Iraqiya* (The History of Iraqi Cabinets). Vol. 6. Sidon, Lebanon: al-'Irfan Press, 1950.

Jiyawuk, Ma'ruf. *Ma'sat Barzan al-Mazluma* (The Tragedy of Barzan the Oppressed). Baghdad: al-'Arabiya Press, 1954.

Khaznidar, Ma'ruf. "Malhamat Mem u Zin" (The Epic of Mem u Zin). *Al-Risala al-Jadida* (Cairo) 1 (1971): n.p.

Malik, Yusuf. *Kurdistan Aw Bilad al-Akrad* (Kurdistan, or the Country of the Kurds). Beirut: Sadir Press, 1945.

Mokri, Mohammad. *'Ashayar-e Kord.* Vol. 1: *Il-e Sanjabi Tarikhcheh Joghrafiya, Tireha.* (Kurdish Tribes; vol. 1: The Sinjabi Tribe: Short History, Geography, Branches). Tehran: Danish Bookstore, n.d.

al-Nawawi, Muhyi al-Din 'Abu Zakariya Yahya al-Hizami. *Minhaj Al-Talibin: Manuel de Jurisprudence Musulmane selon le rite de Chafi'i* (Methodology for the Seekers of Knowldege: A Manual of Muslim Jurisprudence According to the Rule of al-Shafi'i). Vol. 2. Arabic text and French translation by Lodewijk Willem Van Den Berg. Batavia: Imp. du Gouvernement, 1883.

Nuri, Ihsan. *Tarikh-e Rishe Nezhadi-ye Kord* (History of the Racial Origin of the Kurd). Tehran: Sepehr Press, 1955.

Pesyan, Najafqoli. *Marg Bud Bazgasht Ham Bud* (There Was Both Death and Return). 2 vols. 2d ed. Tehran: Sherkate Sahami-ye Press, 1948–49.

Razzuq, Munir. *Mu'amarat 'Abd al-Nasir* (The Conspiracies of 'Abd al-Nasir). Baghdad: Dar al-Bilad lil-Sihafa wa-al-Nashr, 1959.

al-Sa'igh, Sulayman. *Tarikh al-Mawsil* (The History of Mosul). Cairo: al-Salafiya Press, 1923.

Sajjadi, 'Ala al-Din. *Mejûy Edebî Kurdî* (History of Kurdish Literature). Baghdad: al-Ma'arif Press, 1952.

Shirzad, Muhammad. *Nidal al-Akrad* (The Struggle of the Kurds). Cairo: n.p., 1946.

"Sud'ba Plemeni Jawanrudi." In *Mezhdunarodnaia Zhizn* 4 (Apr. 1956): 122–23.

Zaki, Muhammad Amin. *Khulasat Tarikh al-Kurd wa Kurdistan Min Aqdam al-'Usur Hatta al-'An* (The Summary of the History of the Kurds and Kurdistan from the Most Ancient Times up to the Present). Translated from Kurdish into Arabic by Muhammad 'Ali 'Awni. Cairo: al-Sa'ada Press, 1939.

———. *Tarikh al-Duwal wa al-'Imarat al-Kurdiya fi al-'Ahd al-Islami* (The History of Kurdish States and Principalities during the Muslim Period). Translated from Kurdish into Arabic by Muhammad 'Ali 'Awni. Cairo: al-Sa'ada Press, 1945.

———. *Tarikh al-Sulaymaniya wa-Anha'iha* (The History of Sulaymaniya and Its Outlying Districts). Translated from Kurdish into Arabic by al-Mulla Jameel Ahmad al-Rozhbeyani. Baghdad: al-Nashir wa al-Tiba'a, 1951.

Government Documents

Bell, Gertrude Lowthian (Great Britain, Office of the Civil Commissioner, Iraq). *Review of the Civil Administration of Mesopotamia, 1914–1920.* London: H.M. Stationery Office, 1920.

E. J. R. (Great Britain, Office of the Civil Commissioner, Iraq). *Precis of Affairs in Southern Kurdistan during the Great War.* Baghdad: Government Press, 1919.

Great Britain. *Correspondence Respecting the Kurdish Invasion of Persia. Turkey No. 5 (1881).* C. 2851. London: H.M. Stationery Office, 1881.

Great Britain. Colonial Office. *Report by H.B.M.'s Government to the Council of the League of Nations on the Administration of Iraq for the Year 1925.* London: H.M. Stationery Office, 1926.

————. *Report by H.B.M.'s Government to the Council of the League of Nations on the Administration of Iraq for the Year 1926*. London: H.M. Stationery Office, 1927.

————. *Report by H.B.M.'s Government to the Council of the League of Nations on the Administration of Iraq for the Year 1927*. London: H.M. Stationery Office, 1928.

————. *Report by H.B.M.'s Government to the Council of the League of Nations on the Administration of Iraq for the Year 1928*. London: H.M. Stationery Office, 1929.

————. *Report by H.B.M.'s Government to the Council of the League of Nations on the Administration of Iraq for the Year 1929*. London: H.M. Stationery Office, 1930.

————. *Report on Iraq Administration, October, 1920 to March, 1922*. London: H.M. Stationery Office, 1923.

————. *Report on Iraq Administration, April, 1922 to March, 1923*. London: H.M. Stationery Office, 1924.

————. *Report on Iraq Administration, April, 1923 to December, 1924*. London: H.M. Stationery Office, 1925.

————. *Report to the Council of the League of Nations on the Administration of Iraq for the Year 1928*. London: H.M. Stationery Office, 1929.

————. *Report to the Council of the League of Nations on the Administration of Iraq for the Year 1929*. London: H.M. Stationery Office, 1930.

————. *Special Report by His Majesty's Government in the United Kingdom of Great Britain and Northern Ireland to the Council of the League of Nations on the Progress of Iraq during the Period 1920–1931*. London: H.M. Stationery Office, 1931.

Great Britain. Foreign Office. *Correspondence Respecting the Condition of the Populations in Asia Minor and Syria. Turkey No. 4 (1880)*. C. 2537. London: H.M. Stationery Office, 1880.

————. *Correspondence Respecting the Condition of the Populations in Asia Minor and Syria. Turkey No. 10 (1879)*. C. 2432. London: H.M. Stationery Office, 1879.

————. *Franco-British Convention of December 23, 1920, on Certain Points Connected with the Mandates for Syria and the Lebanon, Palestine and Mesopotamia*. Presented by the Secretary of State for Foreign Affairs to Parliament. Cmd. 1195. Misc. No. 4 (1921). London: H.M. Stationery Office, 1921.

————. *League of Nations: Decision Relating to the Turco-Irak Frontier Adopted by the Council of the League of Nations, Geneva, December 16, 1925*. Presented by the Secretary of State for Foreign Affairs to Parliament. Cmd. 2562. Misc. No. 17 (1925). London: H.M. Stationery Office, 1925.

————. *Letter from His Majesty's Government to the Secretary-General of the League of Nations and Proceedings of the Council of the League Regarding the Determination of the Turco-Irak Frontier and the Application to Irak of Article 22 of the Covenant of the League*. Presented by the Secretary of State for Foreign Affairs to Parliament. Cmd. 2624. Misc. No. 3 (1926). London: H.M. Stationery Office, 1926.

————. *Report to the Council of the League of Nations by General F. Laidoner on the Situation in the Location of the Provisional Line of the Frontier Between Turkey and Irak Fixed at Brussels on October 29, 1924*. Cmd. 2557. Misc. No. 15 (1925). London: H.M. Stationery Office, 1925.

————. Historical Section. *Turkey in Asia*. London: H.M. Stationery Office, 1920.

Great Britain. Parliament. *Papers by Command: Lausanne Conference (1923)*. Cmd. 1814. London: H.M. Stationery Office, [1924].

————. *Papers by Command: Treaty of Peace with Turkey and Other Instruments Signed at Lausanne on 24 July 1923*. Cmd. 1929. London: H.M. Stationery Office, [1924].

Hay, Major W. R., and P. O. Arbil. (Great Britain, Office of the Civil Commissioner, Iraq). *Note on Rowanduz.* Baghdad: Government Press, 1920.

Iraq. *Reports of Administration for 1918 of Divisions and Districts of the Occupied Territories in Mesopotamia: I. Khaniqin District.* Madras: Vasanta Press, 1919.

Iraq (British Administration), Office of the Civil Commissioner. *Administration Report of the Kirkuk Division for the Year 1918.* Baghdad: Government Press, 1919.

———. *Administration Report of the Kirkuk Division for the Year 1920.* Baghdad: Government Press, 1921.

———. *Administration Report of the Mosul Division for the Year 1920.* Baghdad: Government Press, 1921.

———. *Administration Report of the Mosul Division for the Year 1921.* Baghdad: Government Press, 1922.

———. *Administration Report of the Sulaimaniyah Division for the Year 1919.* Baghdad: Government Press, 1920.

———. *Administration Report of the Sulaimaniyah Division for the Year 1920.* Baghdad: Government Press, 1922.

Iraq. Civil Commissioner. *Civil Administration Mesopotamia: Administration Report (1919), Part I, "Mosul."* Baghdad: Government Press, 1920.

League of Nations. Council. *Question of the Frontier Between Turkey and Iraq: Report Submitted to the Council of the League of Nations by the Commission Instituted by the Council Resolution of September 30th, 1924.* C. 400. M. 147 (1925), vii. Lausanne: League of Nations, 1925.

Noel, E. M. *Diary of Major E. M. Noel, C.I.E., D.S.O., on Special Duty in Kurdistan, from June 14th to September 21st, 1919.* Basra, Iraq: Government Press, 1920.

Noel, Major E. W. C. (Great Britain, Office of the Civil Commissioner, Iraq). *Note on the Kurdish Situation.* Baghdad: Government Press, 1919.

Republic of Iraq. Higher Committee for Communication. *Thawrat 14 Tammuz fi 'Amiha al-Awwal* (The July 14th Revolution in Its First Year). Baghdad: Dar al-Akhbar Press, 1959.

Republic of Iraq. Ministry of Defense. *Mahkamat al-Sha'b: al-Jalsat al-Sirriya* (The People's Court: The Secret Sessions). Baghdad: Government Press, 1959.

Russia. Ministry of Foreign Affairs. *Sbornik diplomaticheskikh dokumentov: Reformy v Armenii: 26 Noiabria 1912 g–10 Maia 1914 g.* Petrograd: Government Press, 1915.

Soane, Major E. B. (Great Britain, Office of the Civil Commissioner). *Notes on the Tribes of Southern Kurdistan.* Baghdad: Government Press, 1918.

———. *Report on the Sulaimania District of Kurdistan. With Some Notice of the Frontier Tribes of Turkey and Persia, and History of the Frontier Question of the Two Countries.* Calcutta: Superintendent of Government Printing, 1918.

United Nations. *Demographic Yearbook, 1952.* New York: United Nations, Department of Economic Affairs, 1952.

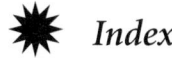 *Index*

Italic page number denotes illustration.